THE SOCIAL ORGANIZATION OF LAW

Introductory Readings

Austin Sarat
Amherst College

Foreword by
Sally Engle Merry

Roxbury Publishing Company
Los Angeles, California

Library of Congress Cataloging-in-Publication Data
the social organization of law: introductory readings/ edited by Austin Sarat.
p. cm.
ISBN 1-931719-20-9
1. Sociological jurisprudence. 2. Culture and Law. 3. Violence (Law). 4. Law—United States—Cases. I. Sarat, Austin.
K370.S643 2004
340'.115—dc22
2003066729 CIP

THE SOCIAL ORGANIZATION OF LAW: Introductory Readings

Publisher: Claude Teweles
Managing Editor: Dawn VanDercreek
Production Editor: Renee Burkhammer Ergazos
Copy Editor: Ann West
Cover Design: Marnie Kenney
Typography: SDS Design info@sds-design.com

Printed on acid-free paper in the United States of America.

This book meets the standards of recycling of the Environmental Protection Agency.

ISBN 1-931719-20-9

ROXBURY PUBLISHING COMPANY
P. O. Box 491044
Los Angeles, California 90049-9044
Voice: (310) 473-3312 • Fax:(310) 473-4490
Email: roxbury@roxbury.net
Website: www.roxbury.net

To my son Benjamin

Contents

Part III: Access to Justice: The Demand for Law and Law's Demands

Preface

The study of law is an exciting area for undergraduates who are interested in the complex and gripping issues with which it deals every day. However, these dramatic, headline-grabbing issues may lead students to think that they already know the law and how it operates when they arrive in our classes. This is both a pedagogical problem and a pedagogical opportunity.

The problem is that students often enter classes with fixed views. For some, law is simply a matter of rules. "Tell me the rules," they seem to say, "so I can know the law." For these students, a healthy dose of rule skepticism, an introduction to the way power is exercised in and through law, and some familiarity with the social organization of law may be most necessary. Other students see no difference between law and power. For them, legal decisions are simply rationalizations of preferences and positions "determined" by one's place in the social hierarchy. Exploring the complexities of legal interpretation, whether by judges reading legal cases or by administrators trying to figure out a social problem, may be what is most needed. In either case, teachers of law in the liberal arts have the great advantage of starting with interested students. As teachers, we can begin with the familiar and move to add complexity and novelty to the subject.

This book seeks to provide the materials and framework within which to cultivate the interests students bring to classes and the beginning point for this journey from the familiar to the strange. It is organized around a distinctive and perhaps controversial perspective, which highlights the relationship of law and violence and the social factors that explain how law works in the world. Instructors who do not wish to use that framework will find, in the readings selected and commentary provided, a platform on which they can build their own framework. Whether you choose to follow my framework or to impose your own, my purpose in putting this book together is to treat legal study as a vital part of the liberal arts, in which students learn the law that they need to know in their lives as citizens and in which they learn the skills of moral argument, close reading, and the analysis of complex social phenomena. The materials chosen provide not only an understanding of law, but also a way of teaching skills through law.

Among the distinctive features of this book is its combination of classics in the field with more topical material. Juxtaposing the two shows students the continuing meaning of the former and adds depth to the latter. My introductions and notes and questions open up issues and enable students to link the material from one to another. They provide a continuing stimulus to further inquiry, helping students both to understand what they have read and to frame ways of bringing that reading into their world. I hope that these features serve to remind students of the challenge and excitement of understanding law's efforts to work in everyday life.

Let me end with a note of gratitude to the many people without whom this book would never have come into being. First, I want to thank Claude Teweles and his terrific colleagues at Roxbury Publishing. Claude's patience and interest were indispensable throughout. I also want to acknowledge the continuing intellectual companionship of my colleagues and students in Amherst College's Department of Law, Jurisprudence, and Social Thought and Amherst's Dean of the Faculty, Greg Call, for his support. Thanks also to the reviewers whose criticism, suggestions, and encouragement were very helpful. I am particularly grateful to Penelope Van Tuyl, Amherst College class of 2003, research assistant extraordinaire. Finally, thanks to my family, Stephanie, Lauren, Emily, and Ben for their love and support. ◆

About the Editor

Austin Sarat is William Nelson Cromwell Professor of Jurisprudence & Political Science at Amherst College. He is a former President of the Law & Society Association and past President of the Association for the Study of Law, Culture, and the Humanities. He holds a Ph. D. in Political Science from the University of Wisconsin and a J.D. from Yale Law School.

He is the author of more than one hundred scholarly articles and the author or editor of more than forty books, including *Law's Violence; The Killing State; Pain, Death, and the Law; Divorce Lawyers and Their Clients;* and *When the State Kills: Capital Punishment and the American Condition.* His public writing has appeared on the op-ed pages of such newspapers as *The Los Angeles Times* and in magazines like the *American Prospect.* In 1997, he received The Harry Kalven Award given by the Law & Society Association for "distinguished research on law and society." At Amherst College, he was a cofounder of the College's newest academic department, Law, Jurisprudence, & Social Thought and is chair of the Colloquium on the Constitution and the Imagining of America. He teaches Secrets and Lies; The Social Organization of Law; Punishment, Politics, and Culture; Murder; and Myth, Film, and the Law. He has appeared on *The O'Reilly Factor* and provided commentary on National Public Radio's *The Connection,* on MSNBC News, and Fox News among others. His teaching has been featured in the *New York Times,* the *Boston Globe,* on National Public Radio, and on *The Today Show.* ✦

Foreword

Law is all around us, shaping our society and even our lives in ways we fail to recognize. Some of law's influence is obvious to us. Newspapers are full of legal decisions with often dramatic consequences: George W. Bush becomes president instead of Al Gore, affirmative action is upheld at a major law school, another murderer is executed. Law affects public life, but it also shapes and circumscribes everyday life in families and neighborhoods in ways that are less obvious. In order to feel safer, a young woman who is frightened of her angry, violent boyfriend can take out a restraining order against him. Copyright laws influence the materials that are available to students in college courses. Regulations on food and drugs determine what we eat and what pills we can take. Welfare regulations differentiate between the deserving poor and those who are deemed undeserving. Like the water fish swim in, law is always there but goes unnoticed, except when it fails to act.

This collection explores how courts, police, judges, prosecutors, and lawyers work within the myriad social organizations that make up the legal system. What these organizations do is not always the same as what the laws say, although there are some connections. Nor does the law work the same way for everyone. People who are rich and white experience a different type of law than those who are poor and brown, and women sometimes encounter a different justice than men. The articles in this book provide an eye-opening look at what law is by examining what law does—when it acts, when it fails to act, and why it works the way it does. The book is full of stories about the people who work inside the law and those who feel its effects or absences when outside its reach.

Understanding how this system works and how it is shaped by differences in wealth, color, and gender is critically important to good citizenship.

As the selections in this book show, the law is full of contradictions. In theory, law protects society from violence, but law itself is violent, using force to prevent and punish violence. This is one of the deep conundrums of law. Only its controlled and regulated use of violence makes society safer, but this safety comes at the price of allowing the law to use violence. There is always the risk that the law will abuse its exclusive power to impose violence on citizens. Many people feel that this is an unacceptable risk inherent in the use of the death penalty.

As readers explore the stories and arguments in this book, they will repeatedly confront this puzzle about law. Through these engaging and provocative articles, the reader will gain a deeper and richer understanding of the legal system, not as a set of rules or a guarantor of social order, but as a dynamic, messy, and very human mechanism trying to sort out the complex dilemmas of everyday life. Despite law's flaws, it is nevertheless guided by an abstract vision of justice. This book reveals law as a social phenomenon and as an institution that shapes society, while it clearly demonstrates that the study of law lies at the heart of a good liberal arts education. ✦

—Sally Engle Merry
Marion Butler McLean Professor in
the History of Ideas
Professor of Anthropology,
Wellesley College

Introduction

Law seeks to work in the world. It seeks to order, change, and give meaning to the society of which it is a part. It deploys various tools—rules and regulations, rewards and incentives, threats and promises—to accomplish these meaning-giving, ordering, changing tasks. But what gives law its special character is the fact that when all is said and done, it can, and does, deploy violence.

It will come as no surprise to say that violence of all kinds is done every day with the explicit authorization of legal institutions and officials or with their tacit acquiescence. Some of this violence is done directly by legal officials, some by citizens acting under a dispensation granted by law, and some by persons whose violent acts subsequently will be deemed acceptable.

As the legal scholar Robert Cover once observed, despite its significance, law's violence has played a small role, and occupied little space, in legal theory and jurisprudence.[1] This book is designed to help remedy this omission. Although some scholars now attend to the literary dimensions of legal life and some to the normative or philosophical ideas with which law is engaged, law, unlike literature or philosophy, orders the social world in a direct way. This book starts with this simple premise—law seeks to work in the world—and describes law and legal processes as socially organized, thereby connecting legal study to the study of society in two different senses.

First, the readings in this book highlight law's responsiveness to various dimensions of social stratification. They draw attention to the question of when, why, and how legal decisions respond to the social characteristics (e.g., race, class, gender) of those making the decisions as well as those who are subject to them and when, why, and how they should do so. These questions inevitably raise issues of justice and fairness. In so doing, they highlight the moral dimensions of legal life.

Second, the book treats law itself as a social organization, emphasizing the complex relations among its various component parts (e.g., judges and jurors, police and prosecutors, appellate and trial courts). In this regard, the book examines the traditional subjects of professional legal study—namely, appellate court opinions—and describes some of the most pressing controversies concerning the nature of legal interpretation while asking how those opinions take on meaning in social life. It also asks whether, and how, judicial decisions are translated into practice. Can those at the top of law's own bureaucratic structure effectively control the behavior of others in the legal system's chain of command? This question directs attention to the putative gap between law on the books and law in action.

Questions about law's social organization are venerable questions in the social scientific study of law. They allow teachers in a variety of disciplines to come to the study of law in a coherent and engaging way. Other texts and readers provide materials with which teachers might construct these arguments about the social organization of law. This reader provides a thematically integrated treatment of these arguments, putting the question of how the law is socially organized at the center of its concerns. It integrates treatment of law's various institutions and actors into a broader framework, which highlights the challenges that law faces as it seeks to work in the world.

The book offers students a perspective on legal life that treats law as a set of institutions and practices combining moral argument, distinctive interpretive traditions, and the social organization of violence. It is based on the belief that the systematic study of law advances the goals of a liberal education. This

1

conclusion rests on two general observations: one concerns the importance of law in culture and society and the other, the capacity of legal study to engage and enhance the intellectual, analytic, and imaginative capacities of undergraduates.

First, law pervades much of our lives and provides a forum in which the distinctive temper of a culture may find expression. In this country and abroad, it plays a major, though variable, role in articulating values and dealing with conflict. Although the role of law has never been more substantial or controversial in the United States, in countries from Argentina and Brazil to South Africa and those of Eastern Europe, people are seeking to develop their own versions of the rule of law as a means of ordering their societies.

The pervasiveness of law reflects human tendencies to engage in normative argument as a regular part of social interaction and to interpret social action in the language of right and wrong. Law, however, is more than a branch of applied ethics; in many cultures, the concept of legal legitimacy is associated not only with the adequacy or normative appeal of legal commands, but also with elaborate rhetorical practices and traditions of reading and interpreting. Finally, law finds its most vivid expression when moral argument and interpretation issue in force. Although law depends on persuasion, inducements, and voluntary compliance, force (or its possible application) remains the critical tool for legal enforcement.

The study of law invites examination of a wide range of critical questions about persons and the ways they live together, raising issues traditionally linked to liberal inquiry. Legal study of the kind that this book is designed to promote provides a useful and engaging way to sharpen students' skills as readers, as interpreters of culture, and as citizens schooled in what Aristotle would have regarded as a kind of practical wisdom, a knowledge that extends beyond theoretical understanding to civic and moral action. To understand legal materials, students are required to develop habits of close reading and hone their interpretive, imaginative, and analytic abilities. Understanding those materials requires great attentiveness, the ability to see how arguments are constructed, and the willingness to imagine alternative possibilities. Because law is concerned with resolving disputes, the student of law is invited to test his or her ethical arguments and textual understandings in a context where decisions must be made and force often must be deployed. In each of these respects, legal study complements the general education objectives of the liberal arts.

As the late A. Bartlett Giamatti wrote when he was President of Yale,

> The law is not simply a set of forensic or procedural skills. It is a vast body of knowledge, compounded of historical material, modes of textual analysis and various philosophical concerns. It is a formal inquiry into our behavior and ideals that proceeds essentially through language. It is a humanistic study—both as a body of material wrought of words and a set of analytic skills and procedural claims involving linguistic mastery. . . . To argue, therefore, for courses in the parts, principles and purposes of law is not to argue for "professional" training in college in the techniques, accumulated lore and diverse iterations of method that training for the profession also entails. It is rather to argue for philosophic, textual and historical concerns, as one would argue for the teaching of any humanistic or . . . scientific inquiry meant to educate the nonprofessionally inclined student. It is to argue that the medium of cohesion and conflict, ligature and litigation, that is the law, must be part of the educated person's perspective in order to appreciate one of the grandest, systematic ways of thinking human beings have developed for their survival.[2]

Traditionally, texts about law and society have been organized around major actors and

institutions with chapters on police, defense lawyers, prosecutors, judges, and so forth. This book takes a different approach. Because law seeks to work in the world, legal institutions are preoccupied with issues of social organization, with the question of how they can respond effectively to social demands and to social problems. At the same time, they face the dilemma of responding to inconsistent and contradictory demands. People want law to be impartial and evenhanded, yet they also want legal institutions and officials to be sympathetic and responsive. They want law to be accessible, but worry about a so-called litigation explosion. They want law to be an effective deterrent and hence want adequate severity, but also demand equity and lenient treatment. Finally, law needs to both dispense and control violence, to allow and yet control discretion. Exploring these paradoxes provides the organizational frame for this book.

Notes

1. "Violence and the Word," 95 *Yale Law Journal* (1986), 1601.

2. "The Law and the Public," address to the Second Circuit Judicial Conference, September, 1982, pp. 36–37. Judge Richard Posner, also an Adjunct Professor of Law at the University of Chicago, echoes Giamatti's sentiment. "Law," Posner argues, is now "an interesting subject of intellectual contemplation, a very important social system . . . studied for its own sake quite apart from any training in the legal profession." *National Law Journal, January 9, 1989.* ✦

Part I

When Law Fails

It is very hard to imagine society without law. This challenge arises because law does many things without which organized social life would be very difficult. Law sets down rules for the conduct of citizens. Here you might think of the criminal law, the laws prohibiting robbery, assault, and murder. Where a society is committed to the "rule of law," it establishes rules for those who make the law, e.g., the procedures that legislatures must follow if they are to enact valid law. In addition, ordinary citizens may look to law to establish mechanisms and procedures through which they can resolve disputes. If neighbors, for example, cannot agree on the precise location of their property line, they may bring their disagreement to a court for resolution. In each of these areas, law also contains visions of justice, of what a society must do or refrain from doing if it is to respect the rights and dignity of its citizens. Thus, for example, when the Eighth Amendment to the Constitution forbids the infliction of "cruel and unusual punishment" on those found guilty of crimes, it recognizes that even criminals have rights.

Each of these things helps to establish society's minimum normative content, its basic framework of shared values. Perhaps most important, law also seeks to bring order and security into the world. Its rules tell us what we can and cannot do. Law establishes agencies, such as the police, whose job it is to translate those rules into action and, in so doing, provide a framework of safety within which citizens can go about their daily lives.

The readings in the first section of this book present several examples of instances in which that framework of the police did not protect citizens. They each describe violence outside the law and thus remind us of the dangers of a world beyond law. We confront violence arising unexpectedly in a recreational setting, in the family, on the streets of our cities, and in a terrorist attack on the United States. If law seeks to work in the world, what can we learn about its nature and limits by examining examples of the dangerous world that law seeks to order?

As you read the selections in Section I, ask yourself whether each, or any, should be counted as a failure of the law. Or, are they tragedies that no legal order, no matter how diligent and effective, could reasonably be expected to prevent? Your answer to these questions might change as a result of reading the selections in Section II, each of which presents a different argument about how law is supposed to serve the society of which it is a part. ✦

Section I

The Limits of Legal Protection

Chapter 1

Hockey Dad's Death Probed as Homicide

Edward Hayward and David Talbot, the Boston Herald

A *father takes his son to an informal hockey practice in a safe, suburban community and ends up dead. An otherwise "respectable" man loses his temper and ends up a killer.*

The following newspaper article reports the death of Michael Costin. Costin, father of four, died at the hands of another father, Thomas Junta, after a fight at an ice-skating rink. These men had minimal contact with each other before this incident, and there is no evidence that Junta went to the rink intending to harm Costin. Instead, as the article suggests, Costin's death resulted from the escalation of an argument between the two fathers over what Junta believed to be inappropriately rough play during a pick-up hockey game in which their sons were participating.

The article variously describes the attack as an assault and a homicide. An assault is an attempt to inflict injury on another person combined with the ability to do so. No striking or bodily harm is necessary for a threat to constitute an assault, though in the case of Michael Costin and Thomas Junta, force was used. Homicide refers to the killing of one human being by another. A person is guilty of a criminal homicide if they purposely, knowingly, recklessly, or negligently causes the death of another person.

The homicide in this case is typical of the extralegal violence that some legal theorists believe law is designed to guard against. It was circumstantial and emotional rather than planned and cold-blooded, and it occurred in a setting that few would have thought of as a place of real danger.

As you read this article, you might ask if this is the kind of incident that the law could or should have prevented. Does the death of Michael Costin represent a failure of law?

Investigators launched a homicide probe yesterday into the death of a Lynnfield father who took his three sons to play a game of pick-up hockey only to receive a vicious beating, allegedly at the hands of a fellow hockey dad during a Reading ice-rink altercation.

Michael A. Costin, 40, died at Lahey Clinic Medical Center Thursday night following removal of life-support systems.

He was found by his sons following the assault Wednesday afternoon that allegedly erupted from a shouting match over rough game play.

The Middlesex District Attorney's office and state and Reading police expect results of an autopsy slated for today as they investigate the role of Thomas Junta, 42, of Reading, who allegedly argued then attacked or fought with Costin at the Burbank Ice Arena. "Authorities are treating [Costin's] death as a possible homicide pending an autopsy," DA Martha Coakley's office said. "No determination has yet been made regarding the manner or cause of Mr. Costin's death."

A clerk magistrate's hearing is scheduled for Friday in Woburn District Court to determine whether criminal complaints should be issued against Junta.

Relatives and friends of both men remained stunned that an informal game could end with Costin unconscious in front of a soda machine and bleeding profusely from his mouth and head.

Costin's mother, Joan, a registered nurse at AtlantiCare Medical Center in Lynn, said she learned of her son's assault when she received a frantic phone call from one of her grandsons while another cradled their wounded father's head.

"The kids called and said, 'Daddy's on the ground. He's not breathing. He's not waking up.' They couldn't wake him up," she tearfully recalled yesterday.

"I've never even heard of something like this," she said. "All it was was a stick practice."

Police and the parents of children with Costin at the rink said the informal pick-up game got a little rough, with one of Costin's sons getting into a shoving match with a Reading boy, allegedly Junta's son.

Junta and the elder Costin, who was playing goalie in the game, allegedly traded verbal jabs before play resumed. Junta, who was in the stands, wanted Costin to stop the fighting quickly, according to witnesses.

"Once ice time ended at about 4 p.m., Junta was waiting for Costin at the only gate used to enter or exit the ice," said Kris Pike, whose son went to the rink with Costin that day.

A few steps away, near the entrance to the locker room, Junta allegedly put Costin in a headlock and began to pummel him with his fists and kick him with his knee, Pike said. Costin fought back before the rink managers broke up the fight and told Junta to leave the facility, Reading Police Chief Edward Marchand said.

"He left—he could have kept going," Marchand said. Once in the locker room, a bleeding Costin told the boys, "I can't believe this guy," Pike said. Costin took off his skates and then left the locker room.

Pike and another mother said he typically went to the snack machines to get the boys' sports drinks or sodas.

"The next thing the kids know, they heard some kind of banging and they left the locker room half-dressed," said Pike. "They found Mr. Costin lying there on the ground on his back with blood coming out of his mouth."

Pike listened to her son tell police investigators Costin was outside the locker room "10 seconds, maybe" before they heard the banging.

Marchand said witnesses described the 6-foot-1, 275-pound Junta allegedly slugging away at the 6-foot, 150-pound Costin, who was pinned to the floor.

"He was kneeling on his chest and hitting him," Marchand said. "The victim was knocked to the ground. He was down and he was struck when he was down."

Junta could not be reached for comment. A check of recent records found no criminal convictions for Junta.

The rink was closed yesterday.

Several friends of Costin said he would not go looking for a fight, especially in the presence of any of his four children, of whom he was the sole caretaker.

But Costin had a lengthy criminal record, with 36 arraignments between 1979 and 1995 on charges ranging from assault and battery on a police officer, to illegal gun possession, to violation of restraining orders.

That history was at odds with his reputation among Lynnfield parents, who trusted him to give kids rides to hockey or baseball practice. "He was just a nice father who took the boys to hockey practice," said Pike. "He loved watching his children and playing sports with his kids."

Just as Costin was described throwing batting practice in the park or hauling a hockey net to a frozen pond, neighbors described Junta as a doting father.

"Tom was in the yard with his kids all the time playing basketball," said Grace Riley, 83, who lives two doors down from the Junta home on Hancock Street. "He was with his kids all the time."

Neighbor Barry Vargus, 16, said Junta often held cook-outs.

"He's a cool guy. He's completely normal to me, like a second father," he said. "He'd tie my skates for me, buy me a drink. He was always joking around."

NOTES AND QUESTIONS

1. Legal officials were not present during the assault described in the newspaper. As they tried to find out what happened they had to reconstruct the facts, sorting through different versions of events, evaluating the credibility of the witnesses to the assault and homicide, and putting together evidence to determine whether a crime was committed and whether Thomas Junta should be charged with a violating a criminal law. The process of investigating a crime, even one committed in public, is always a bit like solving a mystery, piecing together bits of information, separating facts from opinion, and keeping in mind what the law requires if someone is to be charged and ultimately convicted of a crime. In all of this, not all facts are "legally relevant."

2. Among the facts that the newspaper thought were relevant to it readers were the size differences between the two men. Thomas Junta weighed 275 pounds; Michael Costin weighed 150 pounds. As you try to imagine what happened at the Reading ice-rink, how important is this fact to you?

3. How about the report that the victim of the assault had "a lengthy criminal record?" Is that useful in your reconstruction of the events? If you were a defense lawyer in a case like the one described in the newspaper article, how would you use the fact of the victim's "lengthy criminal record"?

4. According to the National Crime Victimization Survey, there were more than two million violent crimes in the United States in 2001. Does this number seem large or not so large? How would you try to figure out whether there is an acceptable level of violent crime? What else would you want to know? Does the total number of violent crimes influence the way you think about the Costin case?

Chapter 2

Dad Sentenced to 6 to 10 Years for Rink Death

Geraldine Baum, the Los Angeles Times

After an extensive investigation, Thomas Junta *was arrested and charged with a criminal homicide in the death of Michael Costin. Eventually his case went to trial, where he claimed that Michael Costin had initiated the confrontation and that in the course of defending himself from that attack, Costin was killed. The jury did not believe Junta's version of what happened in the Reading ice-hockey rink and convicted him of involuntary manslaughter.*

Involuntary manslaughter is less serious than murder. Criminal homicide is manslaughter when it is committed without malice and deliberation. It is involuntary manslaughter when a death occurs in the commission of some (other) unlawful act.

As the next selection tells us, in such cases state sentencing guidelines suggest a three- to five-year prison sentence for first time offenders. However, the judge in Junta's case sentenced him to a prison term somewhat longer than the term in the guidelines: six to ten years.

Does the punishment given to Junta seem right?

Crime: Thomas Junta fatally beat Michael Costin, another father, in July 2000 after their children finished a pickup game of hockey.

Hockey dad Thomas Junta was sentenced Friday to 6 to 10 years in prison for beating another father, Michael Costin, to death at a suburban Boston ice rink while their children watched. Although Junta faced as much as 20 years in jail for his involuntary manslaughter conviction, the sentence was harsher than many expected because state guidelines call for a three- to five-year prison term for first offenses. Junta's attorney Thomas Orlandi Jr. said Friday that he would appeal the decision.

However, Middlesex Superior Court Judge Charles Grabau, in explaining his sentence, noted that Junta had a record of violence and that the crime during the summer of 2000 was made that much more heinous because so many children, including Junta's own son and the victim's three sons, witnessed the brutality. The judge also noted that Junta continued the beating after many people tried to stop him. Junta, 44, began sobbing in the Cambridge, Mass., courtroom before the sentencing as Orlandi read letters he had written to his two children.

"Remember, hockey is supposed to be fun, but it's just a game," Junta wrote to 12-year-old Quinlan, who was among those pleading with his father to stop the beating. The boy had testified that Junta acted in self-defense.

But in a moving statement about Costin, who had led a troubled life, the dead man's middle son, Michael, implored the judge to be tough on Junta:

> My dad isn't there in the morning to wake me up. My dad isn't there when I play sports. My dad doesn't cook us dinner anymore. . . . Please teach Thomas Junta a lesson.

. . .During the sentencing, Junta, wearing handcuffs, said little. He hung his head for most of the time and cried intermittently. He spoke once, quietly. "I'd just like to apologize to both families and thank my family for all their support of me," he said. The defense called no witnesses.

Before being led away. Junta raised his shackled hands to blow a kiss and wave to his family seated behind him.

Later, chief prosecutor Martha Coakley issued a statement saying she was satisfied with the sentence, but she also conceded that nothing good had come of this case.

"One and a half years ago, the Costin family lost a father, the full impact of which they continue to feel to this day," she said. "Today, a second father is sentenced to a substantial prison term. Clearly, there are no winners in this case."

Notes and Questions

1. The facts relevant in deciding whether someone should be arrested, charged, and convicted of a crime and those relevant to the question of punishment are often not the same. When it comes to sentencing, law traditionally has taken a broad view of relevance, considering the background of the offender, his prior criminal record, the effect of the punishment on his family, the impact of the crime on the victim or victim's family, and whether a punishment would help to prevent similar crimes in the future. Today, sentencing guidelines tend to focus on the seriousness of the crime and the offender's prior record.

2. The judge cited Junta's prior criminal record, the fact that the crime was witnessed by several children, and that Junta continued to beat Costin after several people tried to stop him. Would you have focused on these things in deciding Junta's sentence? Are there other things that you think are equally important?

3. The newspaper article describes Costin's son's appeal to the judge to be "tough on Junta." Such victim impact statements are now quite common in criminal cases, though they remain controversial. They are controversial because the criminal law has traditionally been regarded as public, not private, law. The state displaces the private victim in prosecuting the case. Doing so is thought to be important in making sure that criminal cases are not vehicles of private vengeance. Do you think that Costin's son should have been allowed to testify about the sentencing of Junta?

4. How significant was Junta's apology? Should it have influenced the sentence?

5. After the sentencing, the prosecutor was quoted as saying that "there are no winners in this case." Do you agree with her assessment? Do you think that Junta's sentence will help to protect others from assaults and criminal homicides in the future?

Reprinted from: Geraldine Baum, "Dad Sentenced to 6 to 10 Years for Rink Death" in the *Los Angeles Times*, January 26, 2002. Copyright © 2002. Reprinted with permission of the *Los Angeles Times*. ✦

Chapter 3

DeShaney v. Winnebago

Does the government have a duty to protect citizens from the kind of attack that took the life of Michael Costin? As first glance, the answer to this question would seem to be "yes." One of the fundamental purposes of law is to provide protection and security, and when citizens are left unprotected from violence, the law would seem to have failed.

But, as the next reading indicates, things are not that simple. There is a difference between what we might want *the government to do* and what the government is legally *obligated to do*. There is also a difference between what the government must *try* to do for everyone and what the government *ought* to do for any particular citizen.

In DeShaney v. Winnebago, the United States Supreme Court was asked to decide whether the failure of Wisconsin's Department of Social Services to prevent the tragic abuse of Joshua DeShaney by his father, Randy, violated his rights under the Fourteenth Amendment's due process clause. That clause states that "no person shall be deprived of life, liberty, or property without due process of law." It seems to guarantee that before a government acts to take away life, liberty, or property, it must follow certain procedures. But under the tradition of "substantive due process," the word *liberty* in the Fourteenth Amendment has been used to recognize substantive rights not specified elsewhere in the Constitution or Bill of Rights.

In this case, Joshua DeShaney's mother argued that liberty included the right to be protected from private violence of the kind inflicted by his father. She sought money damages by filing under 42 United States Code Section 1983. This law, passed to protect newly freed slaves in the aftermath of the Civil War in 1871, states that

> *Every person who, under color of any statute, ordinance, regulation, custom, or usage, of any State or Territory or the District of Columbia, subjects, or causes to be subjected, any citizen of the United States or other person with the jurisdiction thereof to the deprivation of any rights, privileges, or immunities secured by the Constitution and laws, shall be liable to the party injured in an action at law, suit in equity, or other proper proceeding for redress, except that in any action brought against a judicial officer for an act or omission taken in such officer's judicial capacity, injunctive relief shall not be granted unless a declaratory decree was violated or declaratory relief was unavailable. For the purposes of this section, any Act of Congress applicable exclusively to the District of Columbia shall be considered to be a statute of the District of Columbia.*

Mrs. DeShaney argued that the Department of Social Services, acting under "color" of the law, had caused her son to be subject to a deprivation of his due process rights and, therefore, was liable under Section 1983. As you will see, the Supreme Court was unpersuaded.

Chief Justice Rehnquist delivered the opinion of the Court.

Petitioner is a boy who was beaten and permanently injured by his father, with whom he lived. Respondents are social workers and other local officials who received complaints that petitioner was being abused by his father and had reason to believe that this was the case, but nonetheless did not act to remove petitioner from his father's custody. Petitioner sued respondents claiming that their failure to act deprived him of his liberty in violation of the Due Process Clause of the Fourteenth Amendment to the United States Constitution. We hold that it did not. . . .

I

The facts of this case are undeniably tragic. Petitioner Joshua DeShaney was born in 1979. In 1980, a Wyoming court granted his parents a divorce and awarded custody of Joshua to his father, Randy DeShaney. The father shortly thereafter moved to Neenah, a city located in Winnebago County, Wisconsin, taking the infant Joshua with him. There he entered into a second marriage, which also ended in divorce.

The Winnebago County authorities first learned that Joshua DeShaney might be a victim of child abuse in January 1982, when his father's second wife complained to the police, at the time of their divorce, that he had previously "hit the boy causing marks and [was] a prime case for child abuse." App. 152–153. The Winnebago County Department of Social Services (DSS) interviewed the father, but he denied the accusations, and DSS did not pursue them further. In January 1983, Joshua was admitted to a local hospital with multiple bruises and abrasions. The examining physician suspected child abuse and notified DSS, which immediately obtained an order from a Wisconsin juvenile court placing Joshua in the temporary custody of the hospital. Three days later, the county convened an ad hoc "Child Protection Team"—consisting of a pediatrician, a psychologist, a police detective, the county's lawyer, several DSS caseworkers, and various hospital personnel—to consider Joshua's situation. At this meeting, the Team decided that there was insufficient evidence of child abuse to retain Joshua in the custody of the court. The Team did, however, decide to recommend several measures to protect Joshua, including enrolling him in a preschool program, providing his father with certain counseling services, and encouraging

his father's girlfriend to move out of the home. Randy DeShaney entered into a voluntary agreement with DSS in which he promised to cooperate with them in accomplishing these goals.

Based on the recommendation of the Child Protection Team, the juvenile court dismissed the child protection case and returned Joshua to the custody of his father. A month later, emergency room personnel called the DSS caseworker handling Joshua's case to report that he had once again been treated for suspicious injuries. The caseworker concluded that there was no basis for action. For the next six months, the caseworker made monthly visits to the DeShaney home, during which she observed a number of suspicious injuries on Joshua's head; she also noticed that he had not been enrolled in school, and that the girlfriend had not moved out. The caseworker dutifully recorded these incidents in her files, along with her continuing suspicions that someone in the DeShaney household was physically abusing Joshua, but she did nothing more. In November 1983, the emergency room notified DSS that Joshua had been treated once again for injuries that they believed to be caused by child abuse. On the caseworker's next two visits to the DeShaney home, she was told that Joshua was too ill to see her. Still DSS took no action.

In March 1984, Randy DeShaney beat 4-year-old Joshua so severely that he fell into a life-threatening coma. Emergency brain surgery revealed a series of hemorrhages caused by traumatic injuries to the head inflicted over a long period of time. Joshua did not die, but he suffered brain damage so severe that he is expected to spend the rest of his life confined to an institution for the profoundly retarded. Randy DeShaney was subsequently tried and convicted of child abuse.

Joshua and his mother brought this action under 42 U. S. C. § 1983 in the United States District Court for the Eastern District of Wisconsin against respondents Winnebago County, DSS, and various individual employees of DSS. The complaint alleged that respondents had deprived Joshua of his liberty without due process of law, in violation of his rights under the Fourteenth Amendment, by failing to intervene to protect him against a risk of violence at his father's hands of which they knew or should have known.

II

The Due Process Clause of the Fourteenth Amendment provides that "[n]o State shall . . .deprive any person of life, liberty, or property, without due process of law." Petitioners contend that the State deprived Joshua of his liberty interest in "free[dom] from . . .unjustified intrusions on personal security," see *Ingraham v. Wright*, 430 U.S. 651, 673 (1977), by failing to provide him with adequate protection against his father's violence. The claim is one invoking the substantive rather than the procedural component of the Due Process Clause; petitioners do not claim that the State denied Joshua protection without according him appropriate procedural safeguards, see *Morrissey v. Brewer*, 408 U.S. 471, 481 (1972), but that it was categorically obligated to protect him in these circumstances, see *Youngberg v. Romeo*, 457 U.S. 307, 309 (1982).

But nothing in the language of the Due Process Clause itself requires the State to protect the life, liberty, and property of its citizens against invasion by private actors. The Clause is phrased as a limitation on the State's power to act, not as a guarantee of certain minimal levels of safety and security. It forbids the State itself to deprive individuals of life, liberty, or property without "due process of law," but its language cannot fairly be extended to impose an affirmative obligation on the State to ensure that those interests do not come to harm through other means. Nor does history support such an expansive reading of the constitutional text. Like its counterpart in the Fifth Amendment, the Due Process Clause of the Fourteenth Amendment was intended to prevent government "from abusing [its]

power, or employing it as an instrument of oppression," *Davidson v. Cannon, supra*, at 348; see also *Daniels v. Williams, supra*, at 331 ("to secure the individual from the arbitrary exercise of the powers of government," and "to prevent governmental power from being 'used for purposes of oppression'") (internal citations omitted); *Parratt v. Taylor*, 451 U.S. 527, 549 (1981) (Powell, J., concurring in result) (to prevent the "affirmative abuse of power"). Its purpose was to protect the people from the State, not to ensure that the State protected them from each other. The Framers were content to leave the extent of governmental obligation in the latter area to the democratic political processes.

Consistent with these principles, our cases have recognized that the Due Process Clauses generally confer no affirmative right to governmental aid, even where such aid may be necessary to secure life, liberty, or property interests of which the government itself may not deprive the individual. See, e.g., *Harris v. McRae*, 448 U.S. 297, 317–318 (1980). . . . If the Due Process Clause does not require the State to provide its citizens with particular protective services, it follows that the State cannot be held liable under the Clause for injuries that could have been averted had it chosen to provide them.[1] As a general matter, then, we conclude that a State's failure to protect an individual against private violence simply does not constitute a violation of the Due Process Clause.

Petitioners contend, however, that even if the Due Process Clause imposes no affirmative obligation on the State to provide the general public with adequate protective services, such a duty may arise out of certain "special relationships" created or assumed by the State with respect to particular individuals. Brief for Petitioners 13–18. Petitioners argue that such a "special relationship" existed here because the State knew that Joshua faced a special danger of abuse at his father's hands, and specifically proclaimed, by word and by deed, its intention to protect him against that danger. *Id.*, at 18–20. Having actually undertaken to protect Joshua from this danger—which petitioners concede the State played no part in creating—the State acquired an affirmative "duty," enforceable through the Due Process Clause, to do so in a reasonably competent fashion. Its failure to discharge that duty, so the argument goes, was an abuse of governmental power that so "shocks the conscience," *Rochin v. California,* 342 U.S. 165, 172 (1952), as to constitute a substantive due process violation.

We reject this argument. It is true that in certain limited circumstances the Constitution imposes upon the State affirmative duties of care and protection with respect to particular individuals.

. . . [W]hen the State takes a person into its custody and holds him there against his will, the Constitution imposes upon it a corresponding duty to assume some responsibility for his safety and general well-being. See *Youngberg v. Romeo, supra,* at 317 ("When a person is institutionalized—and wholly dependent on the State[,] . . . a duty to provide certain services and care does exist").[2] The rationale for this principle is simple enough: when the State by the affirmative exercise of its power so restrains an individual's liberty that it renders him unable to care for himself, and at the same time fails to provide for his basic human needs—e.g., food, clothing, shelter, medical care, and reasonable safety—it transgresses the substantive limits on state action set by the Eighth Amendment and the Due Process Clause. See *Estelle v. Gamble, supra,* at 103–104; *Youngberg v. Romeo, supra,* at 315–316. The affirmative duty to protect arises not from the State's knowledge of the individual's predicament or from its expressions of intent to help him, but from the limitation which it has imposed on his freedom to act on his own behalf. See *Estelle v. Gamble, supra,* at 103 ("An inmate must rely on prison authorities to treat his medical needs; if the authorities fail to do so, those needs will not be met"). In the substantive due process analysis, it is the State's affirmative act of restraining the individual's freedom to act on his own behalf—through incarceration, institutionalization, or other similar restraint of personal liberty—which is the "deprivation of liberty" triggering the protections of the Due Process Clause, not its failure to act to protect his liberty interests against harms inflicted by other means.[3]

. . . While the State may have been aware of the dangers that Joshua faced in the free world, it played no part in their creation, nor did it do anything to render him any more vulnerable to them. That the State once took temporary custody of Joshua does not alter the analysis, for when it returned him to his father's custody, it placed him in no worse position than that in which he would have been had it not acted at all; the State does not become the permanent guarantor of an individual's safety by having once offered him shelter. Under these circumstances, the State had no constitutional duty to protect Joshua.

. . . Judges and lawyers, like other humans, are moved by natural sympathy in a case like this to find a way for Joshua and his mother to receive adequate compensation for the grievous harm inflicted upon them. But before yielding to that impulse, it is well to remember once again that the harm was inflicted not by the State of Wisconsin, but by Joshua's father. The most that can be said of the state functionaries in this case is that they stood by and did nothing when suspicious circumstances dictated a more active role for them. In defense of them it must also be said that had they moved too soon to take custody of the son away from the father, they would likely have been met with charges of improperly intruding into the parent-child relationship, charges based on the same Due Process Clause that forms the basis for the present charge of failure to provide adequate protection.

The people of Wisconsin may well prefer a system of liability which would place upon the State and its officials the responsibility for failure to act in situations such as the present one. They may create such a system, if they do not have it already, by changing the tort law of the State in accordance with the regular law-making process. But they should not have it thrust upon them by this Court's expansion of the Due Process Clause of the Fourteenth Amendment.

Affirmed.

JUSTICE BLACKMUN, DISSENTING

... Today, the Court purports to be the dispassionate oracle of the law, unmoved by "natural sympathy." *Ante,* at 202. But, in this pretense, the Court itself retreats into a sterile formalism which prevents it from recognizing either the facts of the case before it or the legal norms that should apply to those facts. ... [T]he facts here involve not mere passivity, but active state intervention in the life of Joshua DeShaney—intervention that triggered a fundamental duty to aid the boy once the State learned of the severe danger to which he was exposed.

The Court fails to recognize this duty because it attempts to draw a sharp and rigid line between action and inaction. But such formalistic reasoning has no place in the interpretation of the broad and stirring Clauses of the Fourteenth Amendment. Indeed, I submit that these Clauses were designed, at least in part, to undo the formalistic legal reasoning that infected antebellum jurisprudence, which the late Professor Robert Cover analyzed so effectively in his significant work entitled *Justice Accused* (1975).

Like the antebellum judges who denied relief to fugitive slaves, see *id.,* at 119–121, the Court today claims that its decision, however harsh, is compelled by existing legal doctrine. On the contrary, the question presented by this case is an open one, and our Fourteenth Amendment precedents may be read more broadly or narrowly depending upon how one chooses to read them. Faced with the choice, I would adopt a "sympathetic" reading, one which comports with dictates of fundamental justice and recognizes that compas-

sion need not be exiled from the province of judging. Cf. A. Stone, *Law, Psychiatry, and Morality* 262 (1984) ("We will make mistakes if we go forward, but doing nothing can be the worst mistake. What is required of us is moral ambition. Until our composite sketch becomes a true portrait of humanity we must live with our uncertainty; we will grope, we will struggle, and our compassion may be our only guide and comfort").

Poor Joshua! Victim of repeated attacks by an irresponsible, bullying, cowardly, and intemperate father, and abandoned by respondents who placed him in a dangerous predicament and who knew or learned what was going on, and yet did essentially nothing except, as the Court revealingly observes, *ante,* at 193, "dutifully recorded these incidents in [their] files." It is a sad commentary upon American life, and constitutional principles—so full of late of patriotic fervor and proud proclamations about "liberty and justice for all"—that this child, Joshua DeShaney, now is assigned to live out the remainder of his life profoundly retarded. Joshua and his mother, as petitioners here, deserve—but now are denied by this Court—the opportunity to have the facts of their case considered in the light of the constitutional protection that 42 U. S. C. § 1983 is meant to provide.

Notes

1. The State may not, of course, selectively deny its protective services in certain disfavored minorities without violating the Equal Protection Clause. See *Yick Wo v. Hopkins,* 118 U.S. 356 (1886). But no such argument has been made here.

2. Even in this situation, we have recognized that the State "has considerable discretion in determining the nature and scope of its responsibilities." *Youngberg v. Romeo,* 457 U.S., at 317.

3. Of course, the protections of the Due Process Clause, both substantive and procedural, may be triggered when the State, by the affirmative acts of its agents, subjects an involuntarily

confined individual to deprivations of liberty which are not among those generally authorized by his confinement. See, e.g., *Whitley v. Albers,* (shooting inmate); *Youngberg v. Romeo,* (shackling involuntarily committed mental patient); *Hughes v. Rowe,* 449 U.S. 5, 11 (1980) (removing inmate from general prison population and confining him to administrative segregation); *Vitek v. Jones,* 445 U.S. 480, 491–494 (1980) (transferring inmate to mental health facility).

NOTES AND QUESTIONS

1. In the majority opinion, Justice Rehnquist expresses sympathy for Joshua, but decides against him. Why does he express such sympathy?

2. Rehnquist finds that the Fourteenth Amendment "is phrased as a limitation on the State's power to act, not as a guarantee of certain minimal levels of safety and security." Even if state officials behave badly, negligently, by failing to protect someone from an injury that they could have reasonably foreseen and prevented, Rehnquist finds that they have violated no constitutional right. In other cases, citizens have brought suit alleging violations of rights founded in the common law of negligence and seeking money damages arising from the failure of local police to protect them from assaults. Negligence law imposes on everyone a duty to avoid conduct that would result in reasonably foreseeable injuries to others. Yet generally, courts have been reluctant to impose such a duty on the police and thus have refused to hold them liable for such failures. This reluctance arises because government officials have greater immunity and protection from lawsuits than do ordinary citizens unless that immunity is specifically removed from them by statutes like Section 1983.

3. Despite this immunity, courts have found that government officials have a duty to citizens when they have a "special relationship" with them. As Rehnquist puts it, "a duty may arise out of certain, 'special relationships' created or assumed by the State with respect to particular individuals." What examples does Rehnquist provide of such special relationships?

4. In his dissent in *DeShaney,* Justice Blackmun accuses the majority of relying on what he calls "formalistic reasoning." Formalism is the view that judges can and should decide cases by reference to the language of the law even when the literal application of that language has bad consequences. Blackmun thinks that formalistic reasoning is especially misplaced in this case. Why? Do you agree with him?

5. Blackmun states that the law can and should be read "more broadly or more narrowly" depending on the judge's own preference and that judicial decisions should be made with a view toward insuring that the law "comports with the dictates of fundamental justice and recognizes that compassion need not be exiled from the province of judging." This approach to judging is called judicial activism. What are the advantages and disadvantages of judicial activism?

6. *DeShaney* exemplifies a problem in the social organization of law, namely, the failure of the State's bureaucratic apparatus to function efficiently and effectively. What kinds of incentives or penalties should be used to encourage bureaucrats to avoid the kinds of mistakes that occurred in the DeShaney case?

Reprinted from: *Deshaney v. Winnebago County of Social Services,* 489 U.S. 189 (1989) ✦

Chapter 4

A Crime of Self-Defense

Bernhard Goetz and the Law on Trial

George P. Fletcher

The next reading describes a situation that is quite different from the tragedies that befell Michael Costin or Joshua DeShaney. This situation involved a New Yorker named Bernhard Goetz. It occurred during the early 1980s, a time when crime rates in American cities were high and when the fear of crime was even higher. At that time, cities in general, and New York in particular, seemed to be very dangerous places where the law was unable to adequately protect their residents.

In 1981, Goetz was mugged by three youths in a subway station. He was very upset with the way the police and prosecutor handled that incident, believing that they were more concerned with legal technicalities than with responding effectively to a serious crime. As a result, he started carrying a gun.

Three years later, in the winter of 1984, Goetz shot four young African-American males who approached him on the subway and asked for a match, the correct time, and five dollars. As a result of this notorious incident, Goetz was labeled the "subway vigilante" and portrayed as a hero who had to defend himself because the legal system was unable or unwilling to do what was necessary to insure public safety. Subsequently, Goetz was charged with assault with a deadly weapon and attempted murder, among other things. However, he claimed that his was an act of justifiable self-defense.

The law allows citizens to use violence, if it is necessary for them to do so, when faced with an imminent threat of death or serious bodily injury. In making this allowance, the legal system recognizes its own inability to prevent private violence and to protect citizens from it. Although the legal requirements of self-defense are quite strict, the law recognizes that mistakes will happen because people may sometimes believe that they are in imminent danger when they are not. It treats cases of mistaken belief as self-defense cases provided that the mistaken belief is one of a "reasonable person" similarly situated.

Following a seven-week trial in mid-1987, a jury of ten whites and two blacks found Goetz guilty of unlawful possession of a weapon, but found him not guilty on 17 counts of attempted murder and assault. The courtroom audience erupted into applause after the verdict was announced. In deciding whether Goetz had acted criminally, the jury believed that Goetz had acted reasonably, especially because he had been mugged before. The subway vigilante remained a hero to many; after delivering the verdict, the jurors took turns asking for his autograph.

However, before the criminal case was over, Darrell Cabey, who had been paralyzed and partially brain damaged in the shooting, filed a civil suit against Goetz. Cabey's case depended largely on Goetz's own comments during the December 22, 1984, incident; after shooting Cabey, Goetz said, "You don't look too bad; here's another," and then shot him a second time. On April 24, 1996, a jury found that Goetz had acted recklessly and deliberately inflicted emotional distress on Cabey and awarded him $43,000,000 in damages.

The selection from George P. Fletcher's A Crime of Self-Defense raises questions about the doctrine of self-defense. What is it, and under what conditions should private citizens be allowed to use lethal force on their own? This reading also calls attention to the significance of racial difference in structuring perceptions of danger, reminding us of the significance of race in the social organization of law. Would Goetz *have acted in the same way if he had been approached on a New York subway by four Caucasian males?*

A SHOOTING IN THE SUBWAY

December 22, 1984, the Saturday before Christmas, about 1:00 P.M., Bernhard Goetz leaves his apartment at 55 West 14th Street and walks to the subway station at the corner of Seventh Avenue and 14th Street. He enters a car on the number 2 line, the IRT express running downtown, and sits down close to four black youths. The youths, seeming drifters on the landscape of the city, are noisy and boisterous, and the 15 to 20 other passengers have moved to the other end of the car. Goetz is white, 37 years old, slightly built, and dressed in dungarees and a windbreaker. Something about his appearance beckons. One of the four, Troy Canty, lying nearly prone on the long bench next to the door, asks Goetz as he enters, "How are ya?" Canty and possibly a second youth, Barry Alien, then approach Goetz, and Canty asks him for five dollars. Goetz asks him what he wants. Canty repeats: "Give me five dollars."

Suddenly, the moving car resounds with gunshots, one aimed at each of the young blacks.

At this point the story becomes uncertain. According to Goetz's subsequent confession, he pauses, goes over to a youth sitting in the two-seater by the conductor's cab at the end of the car, looks at him, and says, "You seem to be [doing] all right; here's another," and fires a fifth shot that empties his five-shot Smith & Wesson .38 revolver. The bullet enters Darrell Cabey's body on his left side, traverses the back, and severs his spinal cord. There are other interpretations of these events, particularly an argument that Goetz hit Cabey on the fourth rather than the fifth shot, but in the early days after the shooting these alternative accounts are not widely disseminated.

Someone pulls the emergency brake and the train screeches to a halt. The passengers flee the car, but two women remain, immobilized by fear. Goetz says some soothing words to the fearful women, and then a conductor approaches and asks him whether he is a cop. The gunman replies, "They tried to rip me off." He refuses to hand over his gun and quietly walks to the front of the car, enters the platform between cars, patiently unfastens the safety chain, jumps to the tracks below, and disappears into the dark of the subway tunnel. Three young black kids lie bleeding on the floor of the train; Darrell Cabey sits wounded and paralyzed in the end seat.

A mythical figure is born—an unlikely avenger for the fear that both unites and levels all urban dwellers in the United States. If the four kids had mugged a passenger, newspaper reporters would have sighed in boredom. There are, on the average, 38 crimes a day on the New York subways. If a police officer had intervened and shot four kids who were hassling a rider for money, protests of racism and police brutality would have been the call of the day. This was different. A common man had emerged from the shadows of fear. He shot back when others only fantasize their responses to shakedowns on the New York subways.

Like the Lone Ranger, the mysterious gunman subdues the criminals and disappears into the night. If he had been apprehended immediately, the scars and flaws of his own personality might have checked the public's tendency to romanticize him. The analogy to Charles Bronson's avenging crime in *Death Wish* is on everyone's lips. The *Times* remains cautious, but the *Post,* from the beginning, dubs the unknown gunman the "subway vigilante." The police participate in this posturing of the case by setting up an "avenger hotline." They expect to receive tips leading to an arrest and eventually they get one, but at first they are swamped with calls supporting the "avenger." Though Mayor Ed Koch condemns the violence, he too inflates the incident by describing it as the act of a vigilante. No common criminal, this one. An everyman had come out of the crowd and etched his actions, right or wrong, in the public imagination.

With no offender to bear down on, the press has only the four black kids to portray in the news; the picture they present is not attractive. Uneducated, with criminal records, on the prowl for a few dollars, they exemplify the underclass of teenage criminals feared by both blacks and whites. In October of the same year, Darrell Cabey, age 19, had been arrested in the Bronx on charges of armed robbery. In 1983, James Ramseur, age 18, and Troy Canty, age 19, had both served short sentences for petty thievery. Barry Allen, age 18, had twice pled guilty to charges of disorderly conduct. James Ramseur and Darrell Cabey are found with a total of three screwdrivers in their pockets—the tools of their petty thievery. The few witnesses who come forward describe the behavior of the four youths before Goetz entered the car as "boisterous."

The emerging information supports the picture that frustrated New Yorkers want to believe in. Four stereotypical muggers who harass and hound a frail-looking middle-class "whitey." That he should turn out, against all odds, to be armed confirms the extraordinary nature of true, spontaneous justice. It is not often that things turn out right, and here in the season of religious miracles comes an event in which good triumphs over evil. . . .

From the very beginning, the Goetz proceedings are caught in a political dialectic between the rush of popular support for the "subway vigilante" and the official attitude of outrage that anyone would dare usurp the state's task of keeping law and order. While the public calls into the newly established police hotline to express support for the wanted man, public officials, ranging from President Reagan to black leaders to Mayor Koch, come out strongly against "vigilantism" on the streets. The general public might applaud a little man's striking back against uncontrolled

violence, but the President speaks of the "breakdown of civilization" when people like Bernhard Goetz "take the law into their own hands." Hazel Dukes of the NAACP calls Goetz a 21st-century version of a Ku Klux Klan "nightrider."

These pitted, hostile forces eventually find their way into well-prepared channels of legal argument and customary patterns of legal maneuvering. The legal system converts our ill-understood rage into a stylized mode of debate about broader issues of criminal responsibility and fair procedure. The "breakdown of civilization" never comes to pass, precisely because the issue of defending oneself against a threat in the subway can be formulated as a question beyond passion and instinctual conflict. . . .

The man at the center of attention, Bernhard Goetz, remained an enigma to trial observers. Born of a Jewish mother and a German father, Lutheran by practice but regarded as Jewish by his childhood friends, reared in the small upstate New York town of Rhinebeck but living in the dense urban mosaic of 14th Street in Manhattan, Goetz eludes conventional categories. He has always sought in fact to be his own person, speaking out against authority when others would be silent. As a nuclear engineer working on submarines, he would point out design and manufacturing defects to the Navy that his bosses in private industry allegedly preferred to suppress. As an individualist who could not readily surrender to corporate authority, Goetz eventually gravitated to running his own electronic repair service out of his 14th Street apartment.

If we were looking for a psychological account of Goetz's shooting, we might focus on his tumultuous relationship with his father. That he bought a heavy-duty gun, a 9-mm semiautomatic pistol, on September 4, 1984, during the week of his father's funeral, should be enough to rivet our attention on that relationship. That Goetz's father was known for his authoritarian tendencies and that Goetz displays a clear resistance to authority might invite further inquiry, and so might the elder Goetz's being accused and tried for allegedly abusing two young boys when Bernie was 13 years old. In view of the family's persistent faith in the elder Goetz's innocence, the torment of witnessing his father's prosecution may have contributed to the younger Goetz's later contempt for the legal system. These intriguing facts are critical to understanding Bernhard Goetz as a human being.

Goetz resists interviews that probe the foundation of his actions on December 22, 1984, but his four hours of taped confession provide a strikingly revealing glimpse into the way he, nine days after the event, explained the events to himself. As his own rambling free associations teach us, Goetz came to think of street mugging in New York as a game with fixed rules and reciprocal expectations. As he says, "they know the rules of the game and they're serious about the rules." Among the most basic are these: "you can't carry a gun and you can't kill somebody." Before the ritual collapsed into a spasm of violence, Ramseur tried to call Goetz's attention to a bulge in his pocket. Goetz had no doubt that Ramseur was bluffing. Undoubtedly, some muggers carry guns, but in this case Goetz's insouciant confidence that the bulge was "bullshit" turned out to be well founded.

Goetz's judgment of Canty's opener "How are ya?" also reveals his sense for the ritual of mugging. This was an ambiguous move by Canty. It obviously did not have the crisp, hard edge of "Okay, motherfucker, give it up." That was the standard opening line of an ex-mugger, one of Goetz's acquaintances who, as he says, "taught me a little about taking care of myself." Canty did not use this code language, and therefore Goetz did not take his opener to be a "threat," though "in certain circumstances that [line] can be a real threat."

The innocent-sounding "How are you doing?" rings with associations for Goetz: "And a question like that, 'how are you doing,' it normally means nothing. But in a certain frame

of reference, there's an implication." And his mind turns to the brutal mugging of Al, his doorman at Courtney House on West 14th Street, whose travail began with an innocent-sounding "How are you doing?" On the videotape he describes a potential mugger's opening with "How are you?" or "How are you doing?" as "legally . . . a nothing statement and . . . an everyday statement." The curious use of "legally" in this context reflects Goetz's understanding of the rules of the game: for an opening line to count "legally," it had to be an unequivocal declaration that the game was on.

At the point that Canty was standing next to him asking for money, and Goetz saw him smiling—"his eyes were shiny, and he was enjoying himself . . . he had a big smile on his face"—fear took over and Goetz prepared himself quickly for action. He laid down his pattern of fire from left to right. But still in the mode of move and countermove, he needed "verification" that the game had reached the point of no return. Thus he asked Canty again, "What did you say?" When Canty responded with another demand for money, Goetz seized the initiative and the game dissolved into pools of blood.

In Goetz's thinking about what he did, the game metaphor is critical to his sense of rectitude. He was attacked, he waited for verification, and then he gained the upper hand. Those are the critical facts. As he states the "correct" rule of law, a rule he incorrectly attributes to English law of several decades ago, "if a person is attacked and then gains the upper hand, he should not be answerable in law."

Goetz played by the rules as he understood them, but he did not expect the New York system of criminal justice to understand and sympathize with him. His two previous encounters with the criminal justice system left him bruised and cynical. He was mugged in 1981 when three youths jumped him as he was carrying electronic equipment in the subway. They threw him to the ground and injured his knees; he collided with a glass door and the handle went into his chest. An off-duty sanitation officer helped Goetz subdue Fred Clark, the leader of the group. It seemed to Goetz fundamentally unjust that he was kept in the station under interrogation for over six hours and that the police let Clark go, Goetz thinks, in less than half that time. Worse than that, the female prosecutor handling the case did not charge the assailants with robbery, but only with what Goetz called "mischievous mischief." Apparently, there was no evidence that they were after his money or his property, without which an assault does not amount to the more serious crime of robbery. According to Goetz, the significant fact in the minds of the officials was that the muggers had ripped his jacket (and thus a charge of criminal mischief). It is not clear why the police and prosecutor chose this charge instead of assault, but in any event, Goetz found unbearable the legalistic concern about the details of what seemed to him an obviously serious crime.

He adjusted quickly to what he perceived to be another game. He was so frustrated that the police would not file charges of attempted robbery that, in what seems to be a follow-up telephone interview with the Manhattan police, he said:

> Look, whatever you want me to say, I'll say, if you want me to lie, I'll lie. . . . I'll say whatever it takes to, you know to arrest these guys, or to get these guys, or whatever it is.

He was surprised that the police rebuked him for his willingness to falsify evidence.

His second encounter with the police followed immediately thereafter. Though he admits that he started carrying a gun right after the mugging, he tried to follow the rules for obtaining a pistol permit. He claims to have spent $2,000 on preparing the papers and filing an application for a license. The license division of the city police turned him down with a flippant explanation to the effect that they could not give a license to everyone who

applied for one. These two experiences with the NYPD left Goetz with a constant irritation that the city was concerned only about "technicalities."

Goetz's fears of being beaten and maimed come repeatedly to the surface of his confession. In the audiotape, he is almost reluctant to admit that he was afraid. He rationalizes away his fear as one of the necessities of "combat." Fear "makes you think and analyze . . . and speeds up your mind . . . it builds up your adrenalin. . . ." Anticipating the testimony of a defense expert, Dr. Bernard Yudwitz, on his behalf, he says that when the fear takes over, "the upper level of your mind . . . just turn[s] off . . . and you react." On the videotape, visibly more agitated by the probing of Assistant District Attorney Susan Braver, he concedes terror without linking it to its combat utility: he felt that he "was about to be beaten into a pulp." And he elaborates an extended metaphor of himself as akin to a cornered "rat":

> . . . you start poking it with . . . red hot needles and . . . you wind up doing it again . . . [and if the] rat turns viciously on you and just becomes a vicious killer, which is . . . really what I was, then don't go passing statements of morality. . . .

Legal argument is rooted in a shared faith in reason. The law moves forward by comparing one case with another, judging whether they are alike or different, whether the solution for one applies as well to the next. None of these judgments would be possible without the guidance of reason. Our passions divide us, but reason unites us in the quest for answers that all can accept. The clearest manifestation of reason in legal argument is the fact of argument itself. We know that appealing to another's reason differs from appealing to his or her prejudice or self-interest. An appeal to reason testifies to respect for the person to be persuaded. An appeal to prejudice or passion expresses contempt; it denigrates the other from a person to be persuaded by argument to an object to be manipulated by playing on emotional forces.

As Maimonides said about God, however, it is easier to postulate what reason is not than to conclude what it is. Reason is not passion, not prejudice, not the drive for pleasure. As God transcends the material world, reason transcends these impulses of the human condition. The analogy with the divine dignifies human reason, but as we can never be sure that we know whether God exists and in what form, we can readily slip into skepticism about both the existence and the dictates of our reason. . . .

The agony of Bernhard Goetz illustrates in one tangled life both the promise and the despair of the legal system. Unlike modern skeptics, Goetz has a strong vision of right and wrong. In his four-hour taped confession in New Hampshire, he repeatedly says that it is up to others to decide whether he was right or wrong. He does not want to be let off on grounds of mental illness. As he says:

> You decide. I became a vicious animal and if you think that is so terrible, I just wish anyone could have been there in my place. Anyone who is going to judge me, fine, I was vicious. My intent was to kill 'em, and, and you just decide what's right and wrong.

In his own moral vision, he had rightfully done everything possible to comply with the law, but it was clear that the law was wrongfully unresponsive to his fears of a repeat mugging. His contempt for the legal system generated a sense of justified self-reliance in carrying a loaded gun in public, whether he had bureaucratic approval or not. Yet his rebellion against the system went further than satisfying his immediate needs. Though never charged with gunrunning, he admits in his confession that he frequently bought guns and sold them to friends at cost.

Goetz's rage at the legal system, of course, does not control our judgment of what he did. His conception of right and wrong cannot displace the necessity of a community judgment about the rights and wrongs of carrying unlicensed weapons and shooting four youths on the subway. The problem of our judging Goetz is most acute in the tangle of passionate and reasoned arguments that run through the law of self-defense. If he is guilty of a crime of self-defense, it would be by virtue of our judgment that his beliefs do not prevail over the rule of reason in the law. Yet to have confidence in our judgment about whether Goetz acted criminally, though in perceived self-defense, we need to understand the complicated moral sentiments triggered by an argument of self-defense.

PASSION AND REASON IN SELF-DEFENSE

Self-defense was always the central issue in the Goetz case—from the decision of the first grand jury not to indict on the shooting charges to the final verdict in June 1987. A legal system is possible only if the state enjoys a monopoly of force. When private individuals appeal to force and decide who shall enjoy the right to "life, liberty and the pursuit of happiness," there can be no pretense of the rule of law. Yet the state's monopoly also entails an obligation to secure its citizens against violence. When individuals are threatened with immediate aggression, when the police cannot protect them, the monopoly of the state gives way. The individual right of survival reasserts itself. No inquiry could be more important than probing this boundary between the state's obligation to protect us and the individual's right to use force, even deadly force, to repel and disarm an aggressor. There is no simple rule that traces this boundary between the authority of the state and the right of individuals to protect themselves. The inquiry itself generates an ongoing debate about the values that lie at the foundation of the legal system.

As the Goetz case wound its way through the courts, the lawyers and judges proceeded on a general set of assumptions about the contours of self-defense. Merely examining these general points of law, however, will not be sufficient to understand the fierce, continuing debate about the legitimacy of Goetz's shooting Troy Canty, Barry Alien, James Ramseur, and Darrell Cabey. Behind the general principles of self-defense swirl conflicting moral and ideological theories about when and why self-defense is legitimate. Some of these theories appeal to our passions; others, to our reason. Our passions pull us in the direction of seeing the act of defense as punitive, as the vengeful response of a private citizen against those who deserve to suffer. The passionate response is captured in the refrain heard throughout the Goetz trial: "These kids got what they deserved." Our reason pulls toward understanding self-defense not as an act of punitive justice, but as a necessary means for vindicating a stable social order. By examining these conflicting theories, we can begin to understand why, from the outset, blacks and whites, liberals and conservatives, have disagreed so vehemently about the Goetz case.

The New York Penal Law (NYPL), under which Goetz was tried, identifies self-defense as one of several justifications for crimes of violence. Other examples of justification are the provisions on necessity (choosing the lesser evil under the circumstances), and the use of force in law enforcement. Consent is also a justification for physical intrusions and taking the property of another, even though the New York statute does not discuss consent as a distinct defense. The point of a *justification* is that it renders a nominal violation lawful—in conformity with the *jus,* or higher, unwritten law of legitimate conduct.

Claims of justification are distinguishable from other claims that bar conviction for crime, such as the claims of duress ("Someone forced me to do it") and insanity ("My disease forced me to do it"). These claims do not render conduct lawful and proper. No one would say that an insane man has a right to kill, or that his killing conforms with higher principles of rightful conduct. These other claims of defense, often called excuses, merely negate the actor's personal responsibility for the violation. It is unquestionably wrong for an insane man to kill, but his mental condition undercuts his responsibility for his wicked deed.

The struggle between passion and reason in the law of self-defense is played out against a background of shared, albeit vague, assumptions about the contours of the defense. First, in order to be properly resisted, an attack must be *imminent.* Further, the defender's response must be both *necessary* and *proportional* to the feared attack. And finally, the defender must act with the *intention* not of hurting the victim per se, but of thwarting the attack. There is no statute or authoritative legal source that expresses this consensus, but lawyers all over the world would readily concur that these are the basic, structural elements of a valid claim of self-defense.

The requirement of *imminence* means that the time for defense is now! The defender cannot wait any longer. This requirement distinguishes self-defense from the illegal use of force in two temporally related ways. A preemptive strike against a feared aggressor is illegal force used too soon; and retaliation against a successful aggressor is illegal force used too late. Legitimate self-defense must be neither too soon nor too late.

In the case of a preemptive strike, the defender calculates that the enemy is planning an attack or surely is likely to attack in the future, and therefore it is wiser to strike first than to wait until the actual aggression. Preemptive strikes are illegal in international law as they are illegal internally in every legal system of the world. They are illegal because they are not based on a visible manifestation of aggression; they are grounded in a prediction of how the feared enemy is likely to behave in the future. . . .

If we assume that the requirement of an imminent attack is satisfied, the question remains whether the other elements of justifiable self-defense are present in his subway shooting. Goetz's firing each of the five shots must have been *necessary* under the circumstances. Was there an effective response less drastic than firing the gun at the four feared assailants? Was it necessary to shoot? Would it not have been enough merely to show the gun in its holster? Or to draw and point the weapon without firing? Goetz had twice scared off muggers on the street merely by drawing the gun.

But the uneven grind of the accelerating train made Goetz's footing uncertain. During his initial exchange with Canty he rose to his feet and was standing in close quarters with his feared assailants. Showing the gun in the holster or drawing it would have risked one of the four young men's taking the gun away and shooting him. Gauging necessity under the circumstances turns, in the end, on an elusive prediction of what would have happened if Goetz had tried this or that maneuver short of shooting. There is no objective way of knowing for sure what indeed was necessary under the circumstances.

The requirement of *proportionality* adds a problem beyond the necessity of the defensive response. To understand the distinction between proportionality and necessity, think about the ratio between the means of resistance and the gravity of the attack. Necessity speaks to the question whether some less costly means of defense, such as merely showing the gun or firing a warning shot into the air, might be sufficient to ward off the attack. The requirement of proportionality addresses the ratio of harms emanating from both the attack and the defense. The harm done in disabling the aggressor must not be excessive or disproportionate relative to the harm threatened and likely to result from the attack.

The preceding three characteristics of self-defense—imminence, necessity, and proportionality—speak to the objective characteristics of the attack and the defense in response. In order to establish that these requirements are satisfied, we need not ask any questions about what Goetz himself knew and thought as he shot the four youths. But suppose that while being attacked without knowing it, he started shooting with the aim of inflicting harm on the four black youths. In this hypothetical situation, could he invoke self-defense on the ground that his act in fact frustrated the attack? It would be a de facto act of self-defense, even though Goetz had his own reasons for shooting.

The consensus among Western legal systems is that in order to invoke a sound claim of self-defense, the defender must know about the attack and act with the *intention* of repelling it. Why should Goetz receive the benefit of a justification if he acted maliciously, without fear of attack? Surprisingly, some leading scholars think that in a case of criminal homicide, the accused should be able to invoke self-defense even if he does not know about the attack. Their argument is that if you cannot be guilty of homicide by killing someone who is already dead (no matter what your intent), you should not be guilty of homicide by killing an aggressor (no matter what your intent). No harm, no crime. And there is arguably no harm in killing an aggressor. . . .

These four elements, then—imminence, necessity, proportionality, and intention—provide the general framework for the law of self-defense. The first three elements bear on the objective reality of the circumstances of using force; the fourth element of intention speaks to what the actor knows and his reasons for acting. The actor's subjective perceptions of reality introduce an additional element in the analysis that goes beyond his intention to repel the attack. If Goetz was mistaken about whether an attack was imminent and whether his defensive response was necessary and proportional, he might well be excused for acting under circumstances that do not meet the objective requirements of self-defense. In most legal systems of the world, the case of mistaken or putative self-defense is clearly distinguished, in terminology and legal consequences, from real self-defense based upon the criteria of imminence, necessity, and proportionality. The essential difference is that real self-defense justifies the use of force, while putative self-defense merely excuses it.

Under American law, and in particular New York law, there is no distinction between mistaken and real self-defense. Indeed the law is geared to the case of mistaken self-defense, the assumption being that whatever is true about the case of a subjective but mistaken perception of reality would be true about a correct perception of imminence, necessity, and proportionality. The New York statute applies, therefore, whenever the defendant "reasonably believes" that the conditions of self-defense are present. Of this phrase and its problematic meaning, there will be more to say later.

The requirements of imminence, necessity, and proportionality, expressed in different terms in different languages, are found in virtually every legal system in the world. Yet these basic structural elements account only for the surface language of the law. Beneath the surface there surge conflicting moral and ideological forces that drive the interpretation of the law in particular directions. We may all be united in the terms in which we discuss self-defense, but we are divided in our loyalties to unarticulated theories that account for our willingness now to stretch the law broadly, now to interpret it narrowly. These deeper forces shaping our interpretation reflect the confrontation between passion and reason in the law. . . .

NOTES AND QUESTIONS

1. Should the law of self-defense allow for mistake? Would it be better to abandon the reasonable belief standard and say that persons cannot qualify for self-defense unless they can show that, at the time they used lethal force, their life was actually in danger?

2. The Goetz case highlights the role of race in organizing perceptions of difference and of danger. Should law pay attention to race? If so, when and why? If not, why not?

3. One place in which race might enter the legal system is through the reasonable belief standard. It may be that the perception of danger is heightened where racial difference is in play. Should the law ever recognize that racism, an irrational fear based on racial stereotypes, might be the basis of a reasonable belief in an imminent threat?

4. Some argue that, to be fair, the law should pay attention to the special circumstances of battered wives who kill their abusers and then claim self-defense. Sometimes those killings occur in situations that would not ordinarily support a claim that the killer had a reasonable belief in imminent danger or that the killing was necessary. Thus, for example, if a battered woman kills her abuser while he is asleep rather than waiting for him to awaken and begin an attack on her, it may be difficult for her to claim that her fear was that of a reasonable person similarly situated. Should courts recognize a special test for battered women—e.g., the reasonably prudent battered woman standard—in judging their self-defense claims? What would be the difference, if any, between a reasonable battered woman standard and a reasonable racist standard?

5. Fletcher states, "Legal argument is rooted in a shared faith in reason." He says that law seeks to replace passion and emotion with "the guidance of reason." How does this insight apply to the arguments in *DeShaney*? What would Fletcher likely say about the place of reason in the opinions of Justice Rehnquist and Justice Blackmun?

Chapter 5

In the Nation's Capital, It's the Season of Insecurity

Jon Schmitz, the Pittsburgh Post-Gazzette

Personal tragedies of the kind described in the previous readings remind all of us of the violence of the world beyond law. Since September 11, 2001, however, citizens of the United States have lived with a new and troubling reality, a global terrorist network able to strike within the borders of this nation. Terrorism is not only an illegal act, it is also an attack on law itself. The terrorist refuses to honor the legal prohibition on murder or the injunction of the laws of war to avoid attacks on civilian populations. Terrorism attacks the fabric of order, rationality, and security that legal orders seek to provide. It consciously and directly seeks to instill fear and uncertainty and to undermine confidence in legal and governmental institutions.

Whether or not you believe that September 11 changed everything, one thing seems certain; for the foreseeable future there will be a greater awareness of danger, a greater sensitivity to potential threats. New procedures designed to provide greater protection from terrorism have been put in place—at the nation's borders, in our airports, and in our dealings with other countries. Critics allege that America's response to terrorism has gone too far and that, in the name of security, Congress and the executive branch have unnecessarily abridged our freedoms.

The following reading describes responses to the threat of terrorism that were implemented in Washington, D.C. The second reading is by law professor Harold Koh, who argues that whatever we might do to respond to terrorism, we must not sacrifice our essential commitments as a nation. We must not do anything that would violate the "spirit of the laws." What does he mean by this phrase? Who determines what the spirit of the laws requires or forbids? Is Koh too committed to an idealistic vision of law? Is this idealism out-of-date in the post-September 11 world?

The bad news came from the armed guard with the walkie-talkie who was standing at the barricade not far from the phalanx of concrete barriers.

On this sunny, pleasant Friday afternoon, citizens of the United States of America were not welcome in their United States Capitol. Security reasons. Only those with "official business" and valid credentials were allowed. Kind of like the Pentagon and the FBI and CIA headquarters. The sentinel patiently informed us, and other disappointed visitors, about what it takes to gain entry to the seat of our government these days: Arrive at 7 a.m., get in line, hope to snag one of the scarce tour passes and hope the House or Senate remains in session, because when the gavels come down, the building goes off limits.

Check back later this summer, the guard suggested. The choking security regulations are gradually being eased, he said. The threat of terrorism may not be subsiding, but some of the anxiety evidently is.

This is a city with a serious case of the willies.

Virtually every public structure of consequence is rimmed with concrete jersey barriers or sewer piping, intended to prevent truck bomb attacks. Roads are blocked off and travel restricted for those who aren't "authorized personnel."

The concrete barriers are scattered about in crooked, haphazard patterns, as if they were put down in a panic.

Visitors quickly learn the drill of emptying pockets of car keys and change and placing camera bags and purses on the conveyor belts of X-ray machines—even when entering a museum.

One public asset outside the security perimeter, the city's soft underbelly, is the subway. Metal detectors wouldn't work there. People may wait hours to get on an airplane, but not to ride from L'Enfant Plaza to Metro Center.

I wondered whether to be troubled by the lack of security there, or disheartened by the abundance of it everywhere else.

The heightened state of alert isn't confined to Washington, of course. We see it at government buildings in Pittsburgh, where metal detectors are de rigueur, and especially at the ballpark, where some of the security measures rival those of a penitentiary.

Take backpacks. Or, more accurately, don't take them. The Pirates and Major League Baseball won't let you into the stadium with them. Purses are OK. There appears to be nothing to stop a baseball fan from sauntering in with a .44 tucked in his belt. But a rucksack—which conceivably could be used to conceal anything from a small nuclear device to the far more dangerous contraband hoagie—is banned.

Water bottles are permitted, unless you opened yours to take a swig on the way to the ballpark. If the seal is broken, it's verboten. It's OK, however, to wet your whistle with a half-dozen beers in the parking lot before advancing to the secure environs of PNC Park.

Water bottles, even open ones, seemed to be OK everywhere we went in Washington.

Our traveling party had three grown-ups and four young folks, all in town for a family wedding. Two of the grown-ups were natives of the D.C. area and remembered school field trips to the Capitol, the Bureau of Engraving and Printing (publishing house for our paper money) and FBI headquarters.

The FBI currently is closed to tourists. The money factory, like the Capitol, hands out a limited number of tour tickets early in the morning. Sleep in and you lose some of the privileges of citizenship.

The restrictions caught us unprepared.

Jackie, the aspiring political scientist—or as she puts it, "future mudslinging campaign manager"—had her heart set on seeing the U.S. Senate in action, or even its typical inaction. Cousin Chris from San Diego wanted to visit the FBI, but settled instead for an FBI sweat shirt.

Kelly and Lauren posed for photos in a congressman's office (strangely, the congressional office buildings, targets of anthrax attacks, are not off limits like the Capitol). We detoured to the Supreme Court, Union Station and the Air and Space Museum, and strolled the Mall—seemingly the only other place in the city that doesn't have metal detectors.

Despite the obstacles, daughter Jackie was enthralled with the city and declared her intention to work there someday. Her father, who harbored similar intentions long ago, before the city took on its siege mentality, cringed.

The Capitol has withstood two centuries of adversity. The British burned it in 1814. Puerto Rican terrorists opened fire in the House chamber in 1954, wounding four members, and there were bombings in 1971 and 1983.

Through it all, the building has remained open to the people. Until now.

Atop the Capitol, at Washington's apex, the bronze Statue of Freedom peers down on a labyrinth of fencing and concrete, and on a city whose *insecurities* are in full view.

Reprinted from: Jon Schmitz, "Saturday Diary: In the Nation's Capital, It's the Season of Insecurity" in the *Pittsburgh Post-Gazette*. May 25, 2002. Copyright © 2003. Reprinted with the permission of the *Pittsburgh Post-Gazette*.✦

Chapter 6
The Spirit of the Laws

Harold Hongju Koh

On September 11, 2001, members of Osama bin Laden's Al Qaeda terrorist network apparently hijacked four civilian passenger airplanes and flew them into the World Trade Center and the Pentagon, killing approximately 3,000 innocent civilians from more than 80 different countries. In the days since, I have been struck by how many Americans—and how many lawyers—seem to have concluded that, somehow, the destruction of four planes and three buildings has taken us back to a state of nature in which there are no laws or rules. In fact, over the years, we have developed an elaborate system of domestic and international laws, institutions, regimes, and decision-making procedures precisely so that they will be consulted and obeyed, not ignored, at a time like this.

In thinking about our response, we need to ask not just what the letter of the law permits and forbids, but which course of action most closely comports with the spirit of the laws. If such a "law-friendly" course exists, we should follow it; doing so will keep the law on our side, will keep us on the moral high ground, and will preserve the vital support of our allies, international institutions, and the watching public as the crisis proceeds. In seeking such a course, the best single benchmark will be the number of innocent civilians—of whatever nationality—who are killed, injured, or whose human rights are violated by

acts committed on all sides of this crisis. In the months ahead, our success at minimizing civilian casualties will act as the proverbial miner's canary: a telling gauge of whether our response remains faithful to the law, and an ominous warning of when it starts to veer in the wrong direction.

At the same time, we must acknowledge that September 11 is a tragedy potentially momentous enough to reshape the very architecture of the domestic and international legal system developed in the wake of World War II. Internationally, the "Bush Doctrine" of declaring "war" on all terrorist networks of global reach and those states who "harbor" them has challenged the positivistic, state-centric, U.N. Charter-based understanding of the use of force that dominated the post-Cold War era.[1] Domestically, the event has already triggered a troubling wave of antiterrorism legislation and executive orders—linking domestic law enforcement and foreign intelligence functions, restricting civil liberties (especially of aliens), and authorizing the use of military courts—that challenge the core understandings of what I have elsewhere called "The National Security Constitution."[2] At this writing, it remains to be seen whether our response to September 11 will unwisely undermine norms developed and internalized over the decades or prudently refurbish them to meet a twenty-first century reality. Ultimately, the legal legacy of September 11 will depend upon the fidelity of America's actions to the spirit of the laws that undergird its post-war charter of global freedom and cooperation.

THE INTERNATIONAL REALM

To paraphrase Justice Arthur Goldberg, international law is "not a suicide pact."[3] Under international law, no one should be able to kill thousands of innocent civilians simply for going to work in the morning, then threaten to do so again with impunity.

International law thus appropriately grants the United States considerable freedom to pursue precisely the kind of broad-based response that it has undertaken in the aftermath of September 11: an approach that includes forceful and targeted military action, as part of a much larger strategy of diplomatic coalition-building, economic sanctions and assets-tracing, counterintelligence, law enforcement, public diplomacy, and democratization. . . .

However, a narrow, legalistic focus should not obscure the bigger picture: September 11 was an attack, not just on innocent civilians, but on the very spirit of international law. As U.N. Secretary-General Kofi Annan put it, September 11 "struck at everything [the United Nations] stands for: peace, freedom, tolerance, human rights, . . .the very idea of a united human family[,] . . . all our efforts to create a true international society, based on the rule of law." The terrorists sought to jeopardize not just American security but the entire postwar system of free global transport, communications, markets, and self-government that the United Nations and the Bretton Woods international economic organizations have sought to build. At stake is the "positive face of globalization": the ability, which we had come to take for granted, to fly across borders at a moment's notice, to invest money in 24-hour worldwide markets, and to communicate with others around the world at any moment, all without fear or impediment.

September 11 thus challenges the international community to mobilize this constructive face of globalization to overcome its most destructive face. In so doing, the greatest task will be building and mobilizing a durable coalition of countries that share respect for the universal values of human rights and the rule of law. In particular, as the world's leading democracy, the United States must enlist the world's other democracies, which numbered only 25 three decades ago but which have grown to some 120 today. These countries should join the coalition not solely out of a fear that they too might be attacked, but from an affirmative recognition that they too have

enormous stakes in maintaining the postwar agenda of global freedom and cooperation that the terrorists have put in jeopardy. . . .

The newly announced Bush Doctrine of declaring "war" on global terrorist networks and the states who harbor them fits awkwardly with the positivistic, state-centric, U.N. Charter-focused understanding of the use of force that dominates international law. Under that understanding, as one commentator puts it, "absent actions in self-defense under U.N. Charter Article 51, uses of force against the territorial integrity or political independence of another state must be [affirmatively] authorized by [the Security Council] under Chapter VII." If not, the positivist vision declares, they must be illegal, even if—like the NATO military actions in Kosovo—they are in some sense morally justified by the need to prevent or minimize gross human rights violations. In this case, the September 11 strikes constituted not just armed attacks, but "crimes against humanity," namely, murder and other inhumane acts committed as part of a widespread or systematic attack directed against any civilian population.[4] Further, if, as President Bush declared, these acts are treated not as isolated attacks, but as "acts of war," the September 11 attacks plainly constitute war crimes as well.[5]

In this case, the direct perpetrators of the human rights violations are non-state actors operating in many countries with varying degrees of passive or active governmental support. Within the U.N. Charter framework, forceful actions against states within whose territory such actors may be found can only be justified on the grounds of vicarious state responsibility. As in the Kosovo situation, the textual restrictions on state-to-state uses of force embodied in the U.N. Charter fail to address or remedy adequately the human rights violations that such terrorists and their state supporters may inflict. In the months ahead, international lawyers need to reexamine the presumption that the need to respect Article 2(4) automatically trumps our global duty to prevent genocide or to forestall terrorist acts upon civilians that strike at the very spirit of the U.N. Charter.

In short, human rights and the spirit of the U.N. Charter require a forceful response to September 11. But if the United States invokes human rights to justify forceful action, it must necessarily accept human rights as a binding constraint on its own use of force. If the United States chooses to treat this as a "war," it is strictly bound to observe the international laws of war, which terrorists scorn, but responsible democracies must obey. That means American and British military exercises must scrupulously avoid targeting civilians, using indiscriminate weapons, or carelessly striking civilian targets or humanitarian aid centers. As this conflict unfolds, the United States and its coalition partners can only rebut a claim of double standards by demonstrating that they have genuinely internalized international legal commitments to respect human rights. . . .

. . . Any tally of the human rights injuries inflicted upon innocent civilians during this crisis must include those Americans and aliens within its borders who are arbitrarily detained; who are discriminated against based on racial profiling; whose privacy is abused; whose right to travel, speak, or associate is unconstitutionally restricted; and whose victimization by hate crimes goes unaddressed, all in the name of rooting out terrorists.

For all the talk of "war," as a legal matter, the United States is neither formally in a state of war, nor even in a congressionally declared national emergency. In authorizing the President to respond, Congress did not declare war. Had it done so, it would have triggered a series of extraordinary statutory powers that authorize the President in times of declared war to seize property, businesses, and manufacturing facilities; to restrict otherwise lawful political activities; and to obtain wiretaps without a court order. Instead, Congress passed, and the President signed, a Use of Force resolution, which declared that the September 11 attacks "posed an unusual and extraordinary threat to the national security and foreign policy of the United States" and gave the President very broad discretion without time limit to use "all necessary and appropriate force against all entities"—whether foreign or domestic—"so long as he determines that they planned, authorized, committed, or aided the September 11 attacks," and so long as such force is used "in order to prevent future attacks."

But under our National Security Constitution, the President is our commander-in-chief, not the king. As I suggested some years ago:

> In foreign as well as domestic affairs, the Constitution requires that we be governed by separated institutions *sharing* foreign policy powers. . . . [With regard to most issues,] governmental decisions regarding foreign affairs must transpire within a sphere of concurrent authority, under presidential management, but bounded by the checks provided by congressional consultation and judicial review.[6]

The War Powers Resolution, which Congress passed over presidential veto in 1973, is one such sphere. It is a framework statute, which imposes consultation, reporting, and durational limits on presidential war-making. Significantly, Congress's Use of Force Resolution does not repeal or supersede the War Powers Resolution, but rather explicitly invokes that law. Therefore, as this conflict escalates, the American people, through their elected representatives in Congress, have a legal right to receive reports and to be consulted by the President with respect to troop commitments abroad, and to authorize the long-term maintenance of U.S. Armed Forces in hostile or imminently hostile situations. What is critical, once again, is the spirit of the law: the War Powers Resolution rests on the commonsense notion that before the President takes us into an extended and escalating undeclared war, he should both regularly consult with and genuinely listen to elected officials who do not owe their jobs to him. . . .

In the same way as September 11 has begun to distort the shape of international law, it has already begun to warp the balance between domestic national security and civil liberties law that has prevailed for more than half a century. The National Security Act of 1947, enacted just after World War II, formalized several guiding principles of United States national security law. The first was a division of management: overt wars would be managed by military officials subject to civilians under presidential control; covert intelligence-gathering would be carried out by agencies directed by the President with the advice of the National Security Council; and the CIA would be expressly denied police, subpoena, law-enforcement and internal security functions to ensure that it would act as a national security agency, not as a domestic law enforcement unit. Second, the Supreme Court has long recognized aliens lawfully admitted to our shores as "persons" entitled to the equal protection of the laws, who—with the exception of the right to vote—enjoy a range of civil and political rights while residing in the United States roughly comparable to that of United States citizens. Third, executive action, even in the name of national security, has been subject both to congressional oversight and regular, albeit usually deferential, judicial review. Indeed, as recently as three months before September 11, the Supreme Court held that a law allowing indefinite detention of immigrants who could not be deported would pose a "serious constitutional problem."

In just the few months since, each of these three principles has been placed under tremendous strain. In the days following the attack, the President obscured the distinction between foreign intelligence and domestic law enforcement by creating an Office of Homeland Security virtually overnight. Under the direction of a Cabinet-level official not subject to congressional confirmation, the Office has been vested with sweeping but vague powers to coordinate domestic efforts against *terrorism*, including collection and analysis of information regarding activities of terrorists and terrorist groups within the United States.

Second, in response to intense White House pressure, and after radically truncated deliberation, Congress passed sweeping antiterrorism legislation—the so-called "USA PATRIOT Act" ("Uniting and Strengthening America by Providing Appropriate Tools Required to Intercept and Obstruct Terror")— with potentially devastating impact on the civil liberties of aliens living in the United States.[7] The USA PATRIOT Act allows the Attorney General to detain non-citizens at length as suspected "terrorists" with minimal procedural safeguards.[8] Even without the new statute, by early November, more than 1,100 aliens and citizens had been detained on offenses unrelated to terrorism, some apparently based on associational activity. This detention authority, already broad, was then greatly expanded by the new antiterrorism law.

The law allows information obtained during criminal investigations—with respect to U.S. citizens as well as aliens—to be distributed to U.S. intelligence agencies without meaningful limitation on how those agencies can use the obtained information; grants the government "sneak and peek authority" to conduct covert searches of homes and private places in furtherance of criminal investigations; authorizes law enforcement officials to access and disseminate highly personal student records of U.S. and foreign students; and grants officials expanded wiretap authority to circumvent the probable cause requirement of the Fourth Amendment, allowing for potentially chilling invasions of privacy.

In early November, Attorney General John Ashcroft alarmed lawyers and civil libertarians further by approving an order that would permit federal prison authorities to monitor communications between lawyers and their clients in federal custody, even if they have not been charged with any crime, whenever surveillance would be deemed necessary to prevent violence or *terrorism*. A string of commentators have begun to discuss the necessity of relaxing our constitutional prohibition against torture in the name of fighting the war against *terrorism*. Finally, at about the same time, President Bush declared an "extraordinary emergency," and signed an order placing any non-citizen he designates (potentially including nonresidents in the United States) as an accused terrorist under the control of the Secretary of Defense, who would then offer that person a "full and fair" trial before an ad hoc special military tribunal without guarantee of due process, appeal, or judicial review. Although Justice Department officials defended the fairness of these military tribunals by reference to *Ex parte Quirin*,[9] a World War II case upholding the constitutionality of a secret military tribunal that executed German saboteurs, they nowhere mentioned the history of that case, which one legal historian has called "a fascinating tale of . . . a prosecution designed to obtain the death penalty; questions of judicial disqualification; a rush to judgment; an agonizing effort to justify a *fait accompli*; negotiation, compromise, and even an appeal to patriotism in an effort to achieve a unanimous opinion." Not surprisingly, these intemperate actions have triggered a firestorm of protest, not just from the political left, but from across the American political spectrum.

The constitutionality of these laws will no doubt be challenged in court. Nevertheless, the troubling message is that in just the first weeks after September 11, U.S. officials rushed to impose precisely the kind of extreme crisis restrictions that led to the *Pentagon Papers* case[10] and the Alien and Sedition Acts. Thus, as with international law, we can evaluate the course ahead by applying the following domestic rule of thumb: *the more the President chooses to respond to the unfolding crisis by acting secretly, unilaterally, or by sacrificing the Bill of Rights or core principles of our National Security Constitution, the more likely it will be for him to violate*

'*the spirit of the laws' in the months—and crises—to come.*

I do not deny the need for vigorous law enforcement in the face of an unprecedented terrorist threat. But neither can I escape the feeling that by creating such laws, we are helping the terrorists to take our freedoms. When the media calls this the "second Pearl Harbor," as an Asian American, I cannot forget that the first Pearl Harbor triggered the internment of tens of thousands of loyal Americans based solely on their Asian ethnicity. What too few recall is that this was the only time that the Supreme Court applied the test of strict scrutiny to a racial classification, but nevertheless upheld the restrictive law. Many forget that some of America's most heralded civil libertarians—President Franklin Delano Roosevelt, who signed the executive order; Earl Warren, then-Attorney General of California; Supreme Court Justices Hugo Black and William O. Douglas—not only failed to challenge the internment, but affirmatively ratified it. Nor can I forget Justice Jackson's haunting words in his Korematsu dissent: that that precedent "lies about like a loaded weapon ready for the hand of any authority that can bring forward a plausible claim to an urgent need." Unfortunately, there seems to be no shortage of domestic authorities now prepared to make that claim.

At this writing, it remains uncertain whether the response to September 11 will undermine domestic civil liberties norms that have been developed and internalized over the centuries. As the U.N. Special Rapporteur for the Independence of the Judiciary noted in his recent appeal, President Bush's military tribunals order is regrettable for "the wrong signals it sent, not only in the United States, but around the world" about the uncertain commitment the United States has to the rule of law. Such extreme measures not only signal the U.S. government's imprudent willingness to sacrifice fundamental human rights as a rule of law, but also send the troubling message that the destruction of four planes and three buildings is cause enough to sacrifice the spirit of the laws that is fundamental to this country's self-conception as the Land of the Free.

CONCLUSION

The post-Cold War era, my colleague John Lewis Gaddis has said, began with the collapse of one structure—the Berlin Wall—and ended with the collapse of another—the World Trade Center. After September 11, as Justice Harry Blackmun liked to say, "Freedom is not free." What he meant is that we love our freedoms. We took them for granted. Now we have to fight for them. We have to defend them. But most of all we have to use them.

In the months ahead, it will not be enough to defend our freedoms, *we must use those freedoms.* We need to speak out forthrightly about human rights violations, whether they are committed by terrorists or our allies, or even our own government officials. We need to reaffirm, loudly and publicly, that it is never unpatriotic to question what our government chooses to do in our name, especially in time of war.

We must respond to the September 11 tragedy in the spirit of the laws: seeking justice, not vengeance; applying principle, not merely power. We must respond according to the values embodied in our domestic and international commitments to human rights and the rule of law. If we are at war, that war will affect our children's future, and that future—I submit—is far too important for us, as lawyers, to leave to the politicians and the generals.

Notes

1. See President George W. Bush, *Address to a Joint Session of Congress and the American People,* Washington, D.C. (Sept. 20, 2001), http://www.whitehouse.gov/news/releases/2001/09/20010920-8.html ("Americans should not expect one battle, but a lengthy campaign, unlike any other we have ever seen. . . . We will starve terrorists of funding, turn them one against another, drive them from place to place, until there is no refuge or no rest [*sic*]. And we will pursue nations that provide aid or safe haven to *terrorism*. Every nation, in every region, now has a decision to make. Either you are with us, or you are with the terrorists. From this day forward, any nation that continues to harbor or support *terrorism* will be regarded by the United States as a hostile regime.").

2. Harold Hongju Koh, *The National Security Constitution: Sharing Power After the Iran-Contra Affair (1990).*

3. *Kennedy v. Mendoza-Martinez,* 372 U.S. 144, 160 (1963) (Goldberg, J.) (noting that "the Constitution is not a suicide pact").

4. Crimes against humanity are crimes under customary international law, prohibited by all persons irrespective of nationality or national laws. For a list of the acts that rise to the level of crimes against humanity, see *Rome Statute of the International Criminal Court,* July 17, 1998, art. 7, U.N. Doc. A/CONF.183/9 (1998) [hereinafter ICC Statute].

5. War crimes include such acts undertaken in international armed conflict as "intentionally directing attacks against the civilian population as such or against individual civilians not taking direct part in hostilities." For a range of the acts that rise to the level of war crimes, see ICC Statute, supra note 17, art. 8(2)(b).

6. Koh, supra note 2, at 69. ("In short, the structural principle that animates our National Security Constitution is *balanced institutional participation.*").

7. *Uniting and Strengthening America by Providing Appropriate Tools Required to Intercept and Obstruct Terror,* H.R. 3162, 107th Cong. (2001) (enacted and signed into law October 26, 2001, as Pub. L. No. 107-56) [hereinafter USA PATRIOT Act]. For critical analyses of the provisions of the USA PATRIOT Act, see ACLU, *Fact Sheets on the USA PATRIOT Act,* http://www.aclu.org/safeandfree. The clear import of the statute's patriotic title is that it would have been unpatriotic to vote against it, something that only one member of both Houses—Senator Russell D. Feingold of Wisconsin—was courageous enough to do. Had the bill been called the "Round Up the Usual Suspects Act," a title perhaps better suited to its

substantive provisions, it might have received less unanimous support and more careful legislative scrutiny.

8. Immigrants certified by the Attorney General must be charged within seven days with a criminal offense or an immigration violation, but could potentially face indefinite detention, if their country of origin refuses to accept them, upon the Attorney General's finding of "reasonable grounds to believe" that they are involved in *terrorism* or other activity that poses a danger to national security. USA PATRIOT Act, supra note 42, § 412.

9. 17 U.S. 1 (1942).

10. *New York Times Co. v. United States,* 403 U.S. 713 (1971). For a discussion of this case, see Koh, supra note 3, at 137.

Excerpt from the U.S.A. PATRIOT Act

SEC. 412. MANDATORY DETENTION OF SUSPECTED TERRORISTS; HABEAS CORPUS; JUDICIAL REVIEW.

(a) IN GENERAL—The Immigration and Nationality Act (8 U.S.C. 1101 et seq.) is amended by inserting after section 236 the following:

MANDATORY DETENTION OF SUSPECTED TERRORISTS; HABEAS CORPUS; JUDICIAL REVIEW

SEC. 236A. (a) DETENTION OF TERRORIST ALIENS—

(1) CUSTODY—The Attorney General shall take into custody any alien who is certified under paragraph (3).

(2) RELEASE—Except as provided in paragraphs (5) and (6), the Attorney General shall maintain custody of such an alien until the alien is removed from the United States. Except as provided in paragraph (6), such custody shall be maintained irrespective of any relief from removal for which the alien may be eligible, or any relief from removal granted the alien, until the Attorney General determines that the alien is no longer an alien who may be certified under paragraph (3). If the alien is finally determined not to be removable, detention pursuant to this subsection shall terminate.

(3) CERTIFICATION—The Attorney General may certify an alien under this paragraph if the Attorney General has reasonable grounds to believe that the alien—

(A) is described in section 212(a)(3)(A)(i), 212(a)(3)(A)(iii), 212(a)(3)(B), 237(a)(4)(A)(i), 237(a)(4)(A)(iii), or 237(a)(4)(B); or

(B) is engaged in any other activity that endangers the national security of the United States.

(4) NONDELEGATION—The Attorney General may delegate the authority provided under paragraph (3) only to the Deputy Attorney General. The Deputy Attorney General may not delegate such authority.

(5) COMMENCEMENT OF PROCEEDINGS—The Attorney General shall place an alien detained under paragraph (1) in removal proceedings, or shall charge the alien with a criminal offense, not later than 7 days after the commencement of such detention. If the requirement of the preceding sentence is not satisfied, the Attorney General shall release the alien.

(6) LIMITATION ON INDEFINITE DETENTION—An alien detained solely under paragraph (1) who has not been removed under section 241(a)(1)(A), and whose removal is unlikely in the reasonably foreseeable future, may be detained for additional periods of up to six months only if the release of the alien will threaten the national security of the United States or the safety of the community or any person.

(7) REVIEW OF CERTIFICATION—The Attorney General shall review the certification made under paragraph (3) every 6 months. If the Attorney General determines, in the Attorney General's discretion, that the certification should be revoked, the alien may be released on such conditions as

the Attorney General deems appropriate, unless such release is otherwise prohibited by law. The alien may request each 6 months in writing that the Attorney General reconsider the certification and may submit documents or other evidence in support of that request.

(b) HABEAS CORPUS AND JUDICIAL REVIEW

(1) IN GENERAL—Judicial review of any action or decision relating to this section (including judicial review of the merits of a determination made under subsection (a)(3) or (a)(6)) is available exclusively in habeas corpus proceedings consistent with this subsection. Except as provided in the preceding sentence, no court shall have jurisdiction to review, by habeas corpus petition or otherwise, any such action or decision.

(2) APPLICATION—

(A) IN GENERAL—Notwithstanding any other provision of law, including section 2241 (a) of title 28, United States Code, habeas corpus proceedings described in paragraph (1) may be initiated only by an application filed with—

(i) the Supreme Court;

(ii) any justice of the Supreme Court;

(iii) any circuit judge of the United States Court of Appeals for the District of Columbia Circuit; or

(iv) any district court otherwise having jurisdiction to entertain it.

(B) APPLICATION TRANSFER—Section 2241(b) of title 28, United States Code, shall apply to an application for a writ of habeas corpus Described in subparagraph (A).

(3) APPEALS—Notwithstanding any other provision of law, including section 2253 of title 28, in habeas corpus proceedings described in paragraph (1) before a circuit or district judge, the final order shall be subject to review, on appeal, by the United States Court of Appeals for the District of

Columbia Circuit. There shall be no right of appeal in such proceedings to any other circuit court of appeals.

(4) RULE OF DECISION—The law applied by the Supreme Court and the United States Court of Appeals for the District of Columbia Circuit shall be regarded as the rule of decision in habeas corpus proceedings described in paragraph (1).

(c) STATUTORY CONSTRUCTION—The provisions of this section shall not be applicable to any other provision of this Act.'.

(b) CLERICAL AMENDMENT—The table of contents of the Immigration and Nationality Act is amended by inserting after the item relating to section 236 the following:

Sec. 236A. Mandatory detention of suspected terrorist; habeas corpus; judicial review.

(c) REPORTS—Not later than 6 months after the date of the enactment of this Act, and every 6 months thereafter, the Attorney General shall submit a report to the Committee on the Judiciary of the House of Representatives and the Committee on the Judiciary of the Senate, with respect to the reporting period, on—

(1) the number of aliens certified under section 236A(a)(3) of the Immigration and Nationality Act, as added by subsection (a);

(2) the grounds for such certifications;

(3) the nationalities of the aliens so certified;

(4) the length of the detention for each alien so certified; and

(5) the number of aliens so certified who—

(A) were granted any form of relief from removal;

(B) were removed;

(C) the Attorney General has determined are no longer aliens who may be so certified; or

(D) were released from detention ✦

NOTES AND QUESTIONS

1. The newspaper article "In the Nation's Capital, It's the Season of Insecurity" describes a variety of security regulations that were initiated in the aftermath of September 11, including blocked off roads, travel restrictions, and searches at the entrances of buildings. Do any of these things strike you as unreasonable or unnecessarily intrusive?

2. The article highlights inconsistency in these security measures. What do you think is responsible for such inconsistency?

3. Harold Koh argues that the attacks of September 11 posed and continue to pose a stark challenge to both domestic and international law. He worries that in our war on terror, one of the casualties will be the spirit of the laws. In the international arena, he seems especially concerned that America will act in ways that weaken the framework of multilateral institutions epitomized by the United Nations. Writing in the winter of 2002, he says, "At this writing, it remains to be seen whether our response to September 11 will unwisely undermine norms developed and internalized over the decades or prudently refurbish them to meet a twenty-first century reality." Among the most controversial post-September 11th events was the development of the doctrine of "preventive war" and the invasion of Iraq. Why is preventive war so worrisome? From your knowledge of the circumstances leading up to the war in Iraq, is that war an exam-

ple of an action that undermined international law?

4. Koh is particularly critical of the "USA PATRIOT Act," which was passed by Congress on October 26, 2001. He thinks that it tilts the delicate balance of security and respect for civil liberties too far in the direction of the former and away from the latter. One section of the Act, Section 412 (reproduced above), grants the Attorney General of the United States new powers to detain noncitizens as suspected terrorists without following the usual procedures of due process. Do you agree with Koh that this section goes too far and in so doing threatens the spirit of the law?

5. From attacks on individuals like Michael Costin(Chapters 1 and 2) and Joshua DeShaney (Chapter 3) to the events of September 11 we are constantly reminded of the limits of law, of its limited ability to prevent harm and protect us from danger. But, as the reading by Koh suggests, we value other things in law, e.g., civil liberties and respect for privacy. Those things may make it harder for legal officials to keep us safe. The limits of legal protection may arise from a set of commitments in a legal order in which physical safety is but one value among many, one among the many purposes that law serves.

Reprinted from: Harold Hongju Koh, "The Spirit of Laws" in *43 Harvard International Law Journal*, Winter 2002, 23. Reprinted with the permission of Harvard International Law.✦

Section II

What Law Is For

Chapter 7
Leviathan

Thomas Hobbes

Why do we have law? What is law for? What can or should citizens expect from the legal system? Can law do more than provide a framework for security? Can it maximize human freedom or promote community? These are long debated and contentious questions. But they are more than mere philosophical abstractions. Because law is a practical enterprise, the answers to these questions have "real world" consequences.

One way of trying to answer them is to imagine what life would be like in the absence of a functioning legal order. This strategy is typical of many so-called social contract theorists. They describe a hypothetical time before law, a "state of nature." Most suggest that people could not long endure life in such a condition. It would be, by definition, anarchic, chaotic, and unproductive. People would have the semblance of human freedom, but their ability to act freely, and to realize their purposes and projects, would be severely curtailed by the unchecked actions of others. To quote Thomas Hobbes, life would be "solitary, poor, nasty, brutish, and short." In this condition it is rational, so the argument goes, for persons to will a limit on their own freedom, to trade a little freedom for security. Governments and laws are then created through a common agreement or a contract, what Hobbes calls a covenant, for the purpose of guaranteeing that security.

As you read Hobbes, consider how accurate his description of the state of nature is. Does his neglect of what some would see as the "good qualities" of persons—e.g., kindness and compassion—undermine your confidence in the picture he presents?

...**N**ature hath made men so equall, in the faculties of body, and mind; as that though there bee found one man sometimes manifestly stronger in body, or of quicker mind then another; yet when all is reckoned together, the difference between man, and man, is not so considerable, as that one man can thereupon claim to himselfe any benefit, to which another may not pretend, as well as he. For as to the strength of body, the weakest has strength enough to kill the strongest, either by secret machination, or by confederacy with others, that are in the same danger with himselfe.

And as to the faculties of the mind, (setting aside the arts grounded upon words, and especially that skill of proceeding upon generall, and infallible rules, called Science; which very few have, and but in few things; as being not a native faculty, born with us; nor attained, (as Prudence,) while we look after somewhat else,) I find yet a greater equality amongst men, than that of strength. For Prudence, is but Experience; which equall time, equally bestowes on all men, in those things they equally apply themselves unto. That which may perhaps make such equality incredible, is but a vain conceipt of ones owne wisdome, which almost all men think they have in a greater degree, than the Vulgar; that is, than all men but themselves, and a few others, whom by Fame, or for concurring with themselves, they approve. For such is the nature of men, that howsoever they may acknowledge many others to be more witty, or more eloquent, or more learned; Yet they will hardly believe there be many so wise as themselves: For they see their own wit at hand, and other mens at a distance. But this proveth rather that men are in that point equall, than unequall. For there is not ordinarily a greater signe of the equall distribution of any thing, than that every man is contented with his share.

From Equality Proceeds Diffidence

From this equality of ability, ariseth equality of hope in the attaining of our Ends. And therefore if any two men desire the same thing, which neverthelesse they cannot both enjoy, they become enemies; and in the way to their End, (which is principally their owne conservation, and sometimes their delectation only,) endeavour to destroy or subdue one an other. And from hence it comes to passe, that where an Invader hath no more to feare, than an other mans single power; if one plant sow, build, or possesse a convenient Seat, others may probably be expected to come prepared with forces united, to dispossesse, and deprive him, not only of the fruit of his labour, but also of his life, or liberty. And the Invader again is in the like danger of another.

From Diffidence Warre

And from this diffidence of one another, there is no way for any man to secure himselfe, so reason able, as Anticipation; that is, by force, or wiles, to master the persons of all men he can, so long, till he see no other power great enough to endanger him: And this is no more than his own conservation requireth, and is generally allowed. Also because there be some, that taking pleasure in contemplating their own power in me acts of conquest, which they pursue farther than their security requires; if others, that otherwise would be glad to be at ease within modest bounds, should not by invasion increase their power, they would not be able, long time, by standing only on their defence, to subsist. And by consequence, such augmentation of dominion over men, being necessary to a mans conservation, it ought to be allowed him.

Againe, men have no pleasure, (but on the contrary a great deale of griefe) in keeping company, where there is no power able to over-awe them all. For every man looketh that his companion should value him, at the same rate he sets upon himselfe: And upon all signes of contempt, or undervaluing, naturally endeavours, as far as he dares (which amongst them that have no common power, to keep them in quiet, is far enough to make them destroy each other,) to extort a greater value from his contemners, by dommage; and from others, by the example.

So that in the nature of man, we find three principall causes of quarrell. First, Competition; Secondly, Diffidence; Thirdly, Glory.

The first, maketh men invade for Gain; the second, for Safety; and the third, for Reputation. The first use Violence, to make themselves Masters of other mens persons, wives, children, and cattell; the second, to defend them; the third, for trifles, as a word, a smile, a different opinion, and any other signe of undervalue, either direct in their Persons, or by reflexion in their Kindred, their Friends, their Nation, their Profession, or their Name.

Out of Civil States, There Is Always Warre of Every Against Every One

Hereby it is manifest, that during the time men live without a common Power to keep them all in awe, they are in that condition which is called Warre of every Warre; and such a warre, as is of every man, against every man. For WARRE, consisteth not in Battell onely, or the act of fighting; but in a tract of time, wherein the Will to contend by Battell is sufficiently known: and therefore the notion of *Time,* is to be considered in the nature of Warre; as it is in the nature of Weather. For as the nature of Foule weather, lyeth not in a showre or two of rain; but in an inclination thereto of many dayes together: So the nature of War, consisteth not in actuall fighting; but in the known disposition thereto, during all the time there is no assurance to the contrary. All other time is PEACE.

The Incommodities of Such a War

Whatsoever therefore is consequent to a time of Warre, where every man is Enemy to every man; the same is consequent to the time, wherein men live without other security, than what their own strength, and their own invention shall furnish them withall. In such condition, there is no place for Industry; because the fruit thereof is uncertain: and consequently no Culture of the Earth; no Navigation, nor use of the commodities that may be imported by Sea; no commodious Building; no Instruments of moving, and removing such things as require much force; no Knowledge of the face of the Earth; no account of Time; no Arts; no Letters; no Society; and which is worst of all, continuall feare, and danger of violent death; And the life of man, solitary, poore, nasty, brutish, and short. . . .

OF THE CAUSES, GENERATION, AND DEFINITION OF A COMMON-WEALTH

THE END OF COMMON-WEALTH, PARTICULAR SECURITY

. . . The finall Cause, End, or Designe of men, (who naturally love Liberty, and Dominion over others,) in the introduction of that restraint upon themselves, (in which wee see them live in Common-wealths,) is the foresight of their own preservation, and of a more contented life thereby; that is to say, of getting themselves out from that miserable condition of Warre, which is necessarily consequent (as hath been shewn) to the naturall Passions of men, when there is no visible Power to keep them in awe, and tye them by feare of punishment to the performance of their Covenants, and observation of those Lawes of Nature. . . .

WHICH IS NOT TO BE HAD FROM THE LAW OF NATURE

For the Lawes of Nature (as *Justice, Equity, Modesty, Mercy,* and (in summe) *doing to others, as wee would be done to,*) of themselves, without the terrour of some Power, to cause them to be observed, are contrary to our naturall Passions, that carry us to Partiality, Pride, Revenge, and the like.

And Covenants, without the Sword, are but Words, and of no strength to secure a man at all. Therefore notwithstanding the Lawes of Nature, (which every one hath then kept, when he has the will to keep them, when he can do it safely,) if there be no Power erected, or not great enough for our security; every man will and may lawfully rely on his own strength and art, for caution against all other men. And in all places, where men have lived by small Families, to robbe and spoyle one another, has been a Trade, and so farre from being reputed against the Law of Nature, that the greater spoyles they gained, the greater was their honour; and men observed no other Lawes therein, but the Lawes of Honour; that is, to abstain from cruelty, leaving to men their lives, and instruments of husbandry. And as small Familyes did then; so now do Cities and Kingdomes which are but greater Families (for their own security) enlarge their Dominions, upon all pretences of danger, and fear of Invasion, or assistance that may be given to Invaders, endeavour as much as they can, to subdue, or weaken their neighbours, by open force, and secret arts, for want of other Caution, justly; and are remembred for it in after ages with honour. . . .

. . .[T]he agreement of these creature Naturall; that of men, is by Covenant only, which is Artificiall!: and therefore it is no wonder if there be somewhat else required (besides Covenant) make their Agreement constant and lasting; which is a Common Power, to keep them in awe, and to direct their actions to the Common Benefit. . . .

NOTES AND QUESTIONS

1. Should we take Hobbes literally when he writes, "Nature hath made men so equal, in the faculties of body and mind?" By what logic does this equality lead to what he deems a state of war?

2. How does Hobbes characterize the "Laws of Nature"? Do you agree with his characterization, or is he too pessimistic? How would you revise it, if at all?

3. Why does Hobbes assert that "Men have no pleasure . . . where there is no power

able to over-awe them all"? Does this contradict the concept of liberty? Can there be liberty without security?

4. How ought we to interpret Hobbes' reasoning that "Covenants without the sword, are but words, and of no strength to secure man at all"? If the power to "secure man" lies wholly in the use of force (the sword), what is the importance of law (the Covenant)?

5. What, according to Hobbes, is the relationship between law and government? Do you agree with his interpretation? What does the Leviathan represent?

6. What is the purpose of the Commonwealth? Do you share Hobbes' professed faith in such a social organization? What about the structure of the Commonwealth inspires confidence, and what about it leaves you skeptical?

7. Hobbes describes the Commonwealth as being "made by Covenant of every man with every man." Are governments truly founded on such broad agreements among citizens? Are some citizens more enfranchised than others? What about later generations of citizens? Do they have the right to amend or reject the original Covenant?

Chapter 8

Law as a Weapon in Social Conflict

Austin T. Turk

F*or Hobbes, law is a tool of the Leviathan, used to control and order society. In this conception, everyone has a shared, if not equal, stake in law. It performs a crucial function for society. There is, however, little attention to how particular laws emerge and why they take the form they do, whose interests they serve, and who might oppose them. But surely, law is an important part of the dynamism of social and political life. It is an important resource in the struggle for advantage, which marks almost every society and political order. Who makes the law and what the law condones or prohibits are crucial markers of power and status.*

The next reading argues that analysis of law should focus particularly on the role of law in, and as a tool of, social conflict. Law, Austin T. Turk argues, "is a set of resources for which people contend and with which they are better able to promote their own ideas and interests against others. . . ." As you read the Turk selection, consider how he defines power. What are the historical and political processes through which the role of law in social conflict changes?

Despite persistent challenges by proponents of a wide range of alternative theoretical and ideological perspectives, the most prevalent conception of law explicit or implicit in recent research on law and society is that articulated most notably in the works of Fuller (1964, 1971) and Selznick (1961, 1968, 1969) and prominent in such influential sourcebooks as Aubert (1969), Nader (1969), and Schwartz and Skolnick (1970). Law is characterized as essentially a means for settling or precluding disputes by (a) articulating the requirements of an idea of justice (expressed as prerequisites for sustained interaction and the viable organization of social life), and (b) restraining those whose actions are incompatible with such requirements. Accordingly, the presumptive aims of socio-legal research are to determine how legal concepts, institutions, and processes function in preventing, minimizing, or resolving conflicts; how such legal mechanisms emerge or are created; how they relate to complementary non-legal mechanisism; and how they can be made more effective.

Not to deny either that law often does contribute to conflict management or that the quest for a just and secure social order is honorable and necessary, the objectives in this paper are (1) to note certain fundamental limitations of what may be termed the moral functionalist conception of law; (2) to marshal arguments for a conception of law free of those limitations—i.e., the conception of law as a form or dimension of social power (as empirically more a partisan weapon in than a transcendent resolver of social conflicts); and (3) to formulate a set of basic empirical propositions about law and social conflict to which the power conception of law directs socio-legal research.

LAW AS CONFLICT MANAGEMENT

To *define* law as a means of conflict management is to leave theory and research on law and society without an analytical framework independent of particular ethical and theoretical preferences and aversions. While it may facilitate critiques of totalitarian or bureaupathic decisions and actions taken "in the name of law," such a definition appears at the same time to impede the development of an understanding of law in which evidence of its regulatory functions is integrated with evidence of its disruptive and exploitive uses and effects. Merely condemning the seamier side of law as perversions or departures from "the rule of law," and attributing them to human fallibility or wickedness, encourages neglect of the possibly systemic linkages between the "good" and "bad" features of law as it is empirically observed. Moreover, insofar as the moral functionalist conception of law has directly or by default encouraged such neglect, it has left socio-legal research vulnerable to charges of bias favoring certain culture-specific ideas and institutions, and helped to provoke the radical counter-assertion that exploitation and disruption constitute the defining reality of law while regulation is only illusion and suppression (see Lefcourt, 1971; Zinn, 1971; Quinney 1974).

A related difficulty with the moral functionalist conception of law is that *legal* means of conflict management tend to be equated with *peaceful* ones; and there is a strong inclination to assume that consensual, non-coercive methods are the only really effective ways of preventing or managing conflicts. . . .

LAW AS POWER

Given that law is intimately linked with social diversity and conflict, the most parsimonious explanation of the linkage seems to be that people find they cannot trust strangers. As the scale and complexity of social relatedness increase, so does the diversity of human experiences. The more diverse the experiences people have had, the more diverse their perceptions and evaluations of behavioral and relational alternatives may be. The greater the diversity of perceptions and evaluations, the greater may be the variability in what is perceived as justice in the specific terms of everyday life. (The implied distinction is between "norms in action" versus whatever similarities might be found in terms either of a general belief in justice as an ab-

stract value, or of verbal responses to hypothetical questioning regarding the substantive meanings and relative importance of various normative statements or labels.) Aware that others' ideas of justice may vary from their own, people try—in accord with their own ideas and interests as they understand them—to maintain or gain control of, or to contest or evade, the processes by which normative expectations come to be formally articulated and enforced across, rather than only within, the boundaries of culturally homogeneous groups (whether the salient boundaries be those of families, clans, tribes, nations, or other groupings).

The empirical reality of law—apparently well understood in practice if not in theory—seems, then, to be that it is a set of resources for which people contend and with which they are better able to promote their own ideas and interests against others, given the necessity of working out and preserving accommodative relationships with strangers. To say that people seek to gain and use resources to secure their own ideas and interests is, of course, to say that they seek to have and exercise *power*. While the meaning of power is far from set, a convenient starting point is to view power as the control of resources, and the exercise of power as their mobilization in an effort to increase the probability of acceptable resolutions of actual or potential conflicts. Although it helps to recognize that "law is power," a more specific conceptualization of what *kinds* of resource control are possible is necessary if we are to arrive at a useful understanding of what the general proposition means. I see five kinds of resource control, all represented in the cultural and social structural reality of law. These are (1) control of the means of direct physical violence, i.e., *war* or *police* power; (2) control of the production, allocation, and/or use of material resources, i.e., *economic* power; (3) control of decision-making processes, i.e., *political* power; (4) control of definitions of and access to knowledge, beliefs, values, i.e., *ideological* power;

and (5) control of human attention and living-time, i.e., *diversionary* power.

1. Having the law on one's side in a conflict implies that one can rightfully use or call upon others (allies, champions, or the authorities claiming jurisdiction over the area, people, or matters involved) to use violence to support one's claims against others. Modern polities are characterized by the presence and availability of control agencies specializing in the accretion, organization, and use of the means of violence, and asserting the principle that violence is—excepting more and more narrowly defined emergency situations—a resource reserved for official use only. Decisions by authorities, including decisions regarding the respective claims of disputing parties, are accompanied by the implied threat of physical coercion should any of the affected parties refuse to act in accord with such decisions.

2. People's life chances are affected just as decisively by how much their economic power is enhanced or eroded by law. The invention and elaboration of property and tax laws, in particular, reflect and help implement decisions on (1) what kinds of activities, products, and people should be rewarded more and what kinds less, and (2) how great should be the range between maximum and minimum rewards. "Radicals" seek modifications of law so as to change the criteria for reward, and very often also to reduce the range of rewards; "liberals" seek modifications so as to insure at least a "decent" minimum in the range of rewards, and may accept—if they do not seek—some reduction in the range; "conservatives" resist modification, but may accept some "decent minimum." Though orderly (usually meaning limited and gradual) economic changes can be facilitated by law, economic decisions

once articulated in and supported by law become postulates which further elaborations and even modifications of the law must satisfy. Radical economic changes, therefore, become increasingly difficult to effect by legal means because they require not legal reasoning to satisfy the postulates of a body of law, but rather a new set of postulates and thus a new body of law.

3. The formulae and procedures of legal decision-making are integral to the workings of politically organized societies. Organizational decisions are in significant ways influenced by and expressed through legal decisions. Most important, the law as culture and as social structure provides the rubric for articulating, interpreting, and implementing organizational norms and decisions. As a substantive and procedural model and as an ultimate support for institutional normative structures, the law contributes—as Seiznick (1969) and many others have demonstrated—to private as well as public social ordering, and provides some of the weightiest criteria for assessing proposed changes and resolving internal as well as inter-organizational conflicts. While non-legal factors clearly affect political struggle in general and organizational decision-making in particular, the law—as the most authoritative record of events and as the definitive model, criterion, and arbiter of rightness—is itself a political resource of major importance.

4. Legal concepts and thought-ways develop in the course of pragmatic efforts by men to comprehend problems of social interaction so as to manage them—including the problematics of dominating the lives of other people. Though not in this regard different from other products of such efforts, law as culture has an especially strong impact upon the

frames of reference people use to give meaning to their situations. Those definitions of the real, the true, and the worthy given legal expression or approval are thereby given the support of what is not only one of the most prestigious of cultural structures, but also that structure most directly supported by the apparatus of political control. The reality or value of alternative conceptions can be denied either by simply denying recognition in law, or else more forcefully by explicitly rejecting them in ways ranging from the most extreme forms of suppression to the most subtle forms of rejection in practice conjoined with verbal acceptance or toleration. Censorship by omission or commission is nonetheless censorship. Yet, the greatest importance of law as an ideological resource probably lies not in the facts of deliberate or inadvertent intervention on behalf of some perceptual alternatives versus others, but in the fact that legalism is the cultural bedrock of political order. The very concept of legality is designed to promote adherence to the ground rules of conventional politics (Turk, 1972:15–16), which amount to agreement among contending parties on the supreme value of their common membership in a polity which must be preserved.

5. Human attention and living-time are finite resources—a trite but profoundly consequential observation. Insofar as the rhetoric and the real workings of law occupy men's attention and time to the exclusion of other phenomena—perhaps of greater import for the probability and quality of life—the law exerts diversionary power. As entrepreneurs of the news, publishing, advertising, and entertainment industries have long known, at least the more reassuring, titillating, or lurid aspects of law can in the name of "human interest" and "information" be presented to capture and hold the public's attention. Nor have the obviously close links between diversionary and ideological power been neglected. Preoccupation with the law, especially in its more attractive and innocuous aspects, not only diverts attention from potentially more dangerous concerns (from the perspective of authorities, *de facto* including loyal oppositions) but also reinforces the sense of law as an overwhelming, scarcely challengeable reality and criterion of reality.

The conception of law as a set of resources, as power, is methodologically superior to the conception of law as conflict regulator in that the relationship between law and conflict is not assumed, but left open for investigation, and the distinction between legal and non-legal phenomena is grounded in empirical observations rather than normative assumptions. Instead of asking *how* law regulates conflict, the investigator is encouraged to ask *whether* law regulates or generates conflict, or in what ways and in what degree the use of legal power does both. Instead of assuming that legal and non-legal actions and relations are somehow differentiated by criteria of moral legitimacy or functional necessity, the investigator asks whether and how the invocation of such criteria and the introduction of the distinction itself exemplify the control and mobilization of ideological and diversionary resources. Freed from arbitrary ideological and theoretical constraints, the investigator directly confronts the empirical realities that legal power can be used in ways inconsistent as well as consistent with normative criteria of legality, that the empirical relevance of such criteria is decided by the actions rather than the claims of those who wield legal power, and that the law—since it is necessarily promulgated, interpreted, implemented, or enforced by people with specific social and cultural involvements—can never really be neutral vis-à-vis social conflicts. . . .

References

Baxi, Upendra 1974 "Comment-Durkheim and legal evolution: some problems of disproof. *Law and Society Review* 8(Summer):645–651.

Black, Donald J. 1972 "The boundaries of legal sociology." *Yale Law Journal* 81(May):1086–1100.

—— 1973 "The mobilization of law," *Journal of Legal Studies* 2(January):125–149.

Chambliss, William J. and Robert B. Seidman 1971 *Law, Order, and Power.* Reading, Mass: Addison-Wesley.

Diamond, Stanley 1971 "The rule of law versus the order of custom," pp. 115–144 in Robert P. Wolff (ed.), *The Rule of Law.* New York: Simon and Schuster.

Etzioni, Amitai 1968 *The Active Society.* New York: The Free Press.

Fuller, Lon L. 1964 *The Morality of Law.* New Haven: Yale University.

—— 1971 "Human interaction and the law," pp. 171–217 in Robert P. Wolff (ed.), *The Rule of Law.* New York: Simon and Schuster.

Gamson, William A. 1968 *Power and Discontent.* Homewood, IL: Dorsey.

Gibbs, Jack P. 1968 "Definitions of law and empirical questions," *Law and Society Review* 2(May):429–446.

Hall, Jerome 1963 *Comparative Law and Social Theory.* Baton Rouge: Louisiana State University.

Lefcourt, Robert (ed.) 1971 *Law Against the People.* New York: Vintage Books.

Quinney, Richard 1974 *Critique of Legal Order.* Boston: Little, Brown.

Russell, Bertrand 1938 *Power: A New Social Analysis.* London: Allen and Unwin.

Schermerhorn, Richard A. 1961 *Society and Power.* New York: Random House.

Schwartz, Richard D. 1974 "Legal evolution and the Durkheim hypothesis: a reply to Professor Baxi." *Law and Society Review* 8(Summer):653–668.

Schwartz, Richard D. and James C. Miller 1964 "Legal evolution and societal complexity." *American Journal of Sociology* (September):159–169.

Schwartz, Richard D. and Jerome H. Skolnick (eds.) 1970 *Society and the Legal Order.* New York: Basic Books.

Selznick, Philip 1961 "Sociology and natural law." *Natural Law Forum* 6:84–108.

—— 1968 "The sociology of law," pp. 50–59 in David L. Sills (ed.), *International Encyclopedia of the Social Sciences,* vol. 9. New York: Macmillan and The Free Press.

—— 1969 *Law, Society, and Industrial Justice.* New York: Russell Sage Foundation.

Turk, Austin T. 1969 *Criminality and Legal Order.* Chicago: Rand McNally.

—— 1972 *Legal Sanctioning and Social Control.* Washington D. C.: Supt. of Docs., U. S. Government Printing Office, DHEW Pub. No. (HSM) 72-9130.

Wimberley, Howard 1973 "Legal evolution: One further step," *American Journal of Sociology* 79(July):78–83.

Wolff, Robert P. (ed.) 1971 *The Rule of Law.* New York: Simon and Schuster.

Zinn, Howard 1971 "The conspiracy of law," pp. 15–36 in Robert P. Wolff (ed.), *The Rule of Law.* New York: Simon and Schuster.

Notes and Questions

1. What is the "moral functionalist" conception of law? What is it about law as conflict management that Turk objects to? What does he argue is the purpose of law?

2. How, according to Turk, does social diversity shape the "empirical reality of law"? Is law likely to play a bigger role in certain social conflicts than in others? What examples come to mind? How might this change over time?

3. What five types of "resource control" does Turk deem central to understanding law as power? How useful do you find these categories of power? What, if anything, would you revise?

4. Turk concludes that law "can never really be neutral vis-à-vis social conflicts." Do you agree? If so, is law's bias at all problematic? Can there be justice without legal neutrality?

5. Compare and contrast Turk's understanding of law with that of Hobbes. Do you tend to see law more in terms of Hobbsian consent or Turk's picture of power struggle and coercion? How do you suppose your social position (your race, class, gender) affects how you perceive the law?

Reprinted from: Austin T. Turk, "The Law as a Weapon in Social Conflict" in *Society for the Study of Social Problems,* eds. Charles Reasons and Robert Rich, pp. 276–291. Copyright © 1976. Reprinted with the permission of Austin T. Turk. ✦

Chapter 9
On Liberty

John Stuart Mill

If security is the overriding purpose of law, or if law is a resource in social conflict, it makes sense that law would have extensive powers, and that, in Hobbes' (Chapter 7) vivid image, government would be a "Leviathan." But perhaps there is, or ought to be, more to law than that. Many theorists believe that law should not be primarily a tool of state power, as it is for Hobbes, or simply an instrument through which some advance their interests at the expense of others. Instead, it should be a check on power. For some theorists, what is crucial is "the rule of law," namely, the proposition that government power should be exercised according to rules and that government must respect rules. Others believe that law, rightly designed and rightly understood, can advance crucial human purposes.

The next reading provides examples of the latter argument. John Stuart Mill was a great theorist of human freedom. He thought that law was often used inappropriately to control domains of conduct that ought to be free from outside interference. Somewhat surprisingly, he believed that this was a particular issue in democracies. Mill worried that democracies had a monstrous appetite for the constriction of freedom. Democracies suffer all too frequently from the "tyranny of the majority," controlling their citizens from the inside out, pressuring them in subtle and not so subtle ways to do what everyone else is doing or think what everyone else is thinking.

Unlike Hobbes, who wrote about the establishment of civil society and government, Mill began with already constituted societies. In such societies, the great and continuing problem is to delineate the limits of legitimate interference with individual freedom, to identify when and in regard to what things legal regulations should be enacted. In the selection that follows, Mill argues that the only basis on which law should interfere with a person's action would be to prevent harm to someone else. In other spheres, personal choice should be respected and individuals should be free to pursue their own good in their own way.

Should the highest goal of law be to maximize the sphere of individual freedom, or are there more important values that ought to be pursued?

. . . **L**ike other tyrannies, the tyranny of the majority was at first, and is still vulgarly, held in dread, chiefly as operating through the acts of the public authorities. But reflecting persons perceived that when society is itself the tyrant—society collectively over the separate individuals who compose it—its means of tyrannising are not restricted to the acts which it may do by the hands of its political functionaries. Society can and does execute its own mandates; and if it issues wrong mandates instead of right, or any mandates at all in things with which it ought not to meddle, it practises a social tyranny more formidable than many kinds of political oppression, since, though not usually upheld by such extreme penalties, it leaves fewer means of escape, penetrating much more deeply into the details of life, and enslaving the soul itself. Protection, therefore, against the tyranny of the magistrate is not enough: there needs protection also against the tyranny of the prevailing opinion and feeling; against the tendency of society to impose, by other means than civil penalties, its own ideas and practices as rules of conduct on those who dissent from them; to fetter the development, and, if possible, prevent the formation, of any individuality not in harmony with its ways, and compels all characters to fashion themselves upon the model of its own. There is a limit to the legitimate interference of collective opinion with individual independence: and to find that limit, and maintain it against encroachment, is as indispensable to a good condition of human affairs, as protection against political despotism.

But though this proposition is not likely to be contested in general terms, the practical question, where to place the limit—how to make the fitting adjustment between individual independence and social control—is a subject on which nearly everything remains to be done. All that makes existence valuable to any one, depends on the enforcement of restraints upon the actions of other people. Some rules of conduct, therefore, must be imposed, by law in the first place, and by opinion on many things which are not fit subjects for the operation of law. What these rules should be is the principal question in human affairs; but if we except a few of the most obvious cases, it is one of those which least progress has been made in resolving. No two ages, and scarcely any two countries, have decided it alike; and the decision of one age or country is a wonder to another. Yet the people of any given age and country no more suspect any difficulty in it, than if it were a subject on which mankind had always been agreed. The rules which obtain among themselves appear to them self-evident and self-justifying. This all but universal illusion is one of the examples of the magical influence of custom, which is not only, as the proverb says, a second nature, but is continually mistaken for the first. The effect of custom, in preventing any misgiving respecting the rules of conduct which mankind impose on one another, is all the more complete because the subject is one on which if is not generally considered necessary that reasons should be given, either by one person to others or by each to himself. People are accustomed to believe, and have been encouraged in the belief by some who aspire to the character of philosophers, that their feelings, on subjects of this nature, are

better than reasons, and render reasons unnecessary. The practical principle which guides them to their opinions on the regulation of human conduct, is the feeling in each person's mind that everybody should be required to act as he, and those with whom he sympathises, would like them to act. No one, indeed, acknowledges to himself that his standard of judgment is his own liking; but an opinion on a point of conduct, not supported by reasons, can only count as one person's preference; and if the reasons, when given, are a mere appeal to a similar preference felt by other people, it is still only many people's liking instead of one. To an ordinary man, however, his own preference, thus supported, is not only a perfectly satisfactory reason, but the only one he generally has for any of his notions of morality, taste, or propriety, which are not expressly written in his religious creed; and his chief guide in the interpretation even of that.

Men's opinions, accordingly, on what is laudable or blamable, are affected by all the multifarious causes which influence their wishes in regard to the conduct of others, and which are as numerous as those which determine their wishes on any other subject. Sometimes their reason—at other times their prejudices or superstitions: often their social affections, not seldom their antisocial ones, their envy or jealousy, their arrogance or contemptuousness: but most commonly their desires or fears for themselves—their legitimate or illegitimate self-interest. Wherever there is an ascendant class, a large portion of the morality of the country emanates from its class interests, and its feelings of class superiority. The morality between Spartans and Helots,[1] between planters and negroes, between princes and subjects, between nobles and roturiers,[2] between men and women, has been for the most part the creation of these class interests and feelings: and the sentiments thus generated react in turn upon the moral feelings of the members of the ascendant class, in their relations among themselves. Where, on the other hand, a class, formerly ascendant, has lost its ascendancy, or where its ascendancy is unpopular, the prevailing moral sentiments frequently bear the impress of an impatient dislike of superiority.[3] Another grand determining principle of the rules of conduct, both in act and forbearance, which have been enforced by law or opinion, has been the servility of mankind towards the supposed preferences or aversions of their temporal master or of their gods. This servility, though essentially selfish, in not hypocrisy; it gives rise to perfectly genuine sentiments of abhorrence; it made men burn magicians and heretics. Among so many baser influences, the general and obvious interests of society have of course had a share, and a large one, in the direction of the moral sentiments: less, however, as a matter of reason, and on their own account, than as a consequence of the sympathies and antipathies which had little or nothing to do with the interests of society, have made themselves felt in the establishment of moralities with quite as great force. . . .

The object of this Essay is to assert one very simple principle, as entitled to govern absolutely the dealings of society with the individual in the way of compulsion and control, whether the means used be physical force in the form of legal penalties, or the moral coercion of public opinion. That principle is, that the sole end for which mankind are warranted, individually or collectively, in interfering with the liberty of action of any of their number, is self protection. That the only purpose for which power can be rightfully exercised over any member of a civilised community, against his will, is to prevent harm to others. His own good, either physical or moral, is not a sufficient warrant. He cannot rightfully be compelled to do or forbear because it will be better for him to do so, because it will make him happier, because, in the opinions of others, to do so would be wise, or even right. These are good reasons for remonstrating with him, or reasoning with him, or persuading him, or entreating him, but not for compelling him, or visiting him with any evil in case he do otherwise. To justify that, the conduct from which it is desired to deter him must be calculated to produce evil to some one else. The only part of the conduct of any one, for which he is amenable to society, is that which concerns others. In the part which merely concerns himself, his independence is, of right, absolute. Over himself, over his own body and mind, the individual is sovereign. . . .

. . . [T]here is a sphere of action in which society, as distinguished from the individual, has, if any, only an indirect interest; comprehending all that portion of a person's life and conduct which affects only himself, or if it also affects others, only with their free, voluntary, and undeceived consent and participation. When I say only himself, I mean directly, and in the first instance; for whatever affects himself, may affect others *through* himself; and the objection which may be grounded on this contingency, will receive consideration in the sequel. This, then, is the appropriate region of human liberty. It comprises, first, the inward domain of consciousness; demanding liberty of conscience in the most comprehensive sense; liberty of thought and feeling; absolute freedom of opinion and sentiment on all subjects, practical or speculative, scientific, moral, or theological. The liberty of expressing and publishing opinions may seem to fall under a different principle, since it belongs to that part of the conduct of an individual which concerns other people; but, being almost of as much importance as the liberty of thought itself, and resting in great part on the same reasons, is practically inseparable from it. Secondly, the principle requires liberty of tastes and pursuits; of framing the plan of our life to suit our own character; of doing as we like, subject to such consequences as may follow: without impediment from our fellow-creatures, so long as what we do does not harm them, even though they should think our conduct foolish, perverse, or wrong.

Thirdly, from this liberty of each individual, follows the liberty, within the same limits, of combination among individuals; freedom to unite, for any purpose not involving harm to others: the persons combining being supposed to be of full age, and not forced or deceived.

No society in which these liberties are not, on the whole, respected, is free, whatever may be its form of government; and none is completely free in which they do not exist absolute and unqualified. The only freedom which deserves the name, is that of pursuing our own good in our own way, so long as we do not attempt to deprive others of theirs, or impede their efforts to obtain it. Each is the proper guardian of his own health, whether bodily, or mental and spiritual. Mankind are greater gainers by suffering each other to live as seems good to themselves, than by compelling each to live as seems good to the rest.

Though this doctrine is anything but new, and, to some persons may have the air of a truism, there is no doctrine which stands more directly opposed to the general tendency of existing opinion and practice. Society has expended fully as much effort in the attempt (according to its lights) to compel people to conform to its notions of personal as of social excellence. . . .

Notes

1. The Helots in the Greek city-state of Sparta were state slaves under allotment to landowners.

2. Persons of low rank; commoners; plebeians.

3. As in the slogan "Liberté, Egalité, Fraternité," at the time of the French Revolution.

Notes and Questions

1. According to Mill, it is imperative that people resist the tendency of society to impose its own ideas and practices as rules of conduct on those who dissent from them. Does Mill equate law with tyranny? Explain.

2. Where is the line that separates the will of the majority from a tyranny of the majority? Why does Mill believe that finding this line is indispensable to a good condition of human affairs in the protection against political despotism?

3. As Mill points out, no two ages or two countries have produced the same set of laws. How does he account for this? What does it suggest about the nature of law and about the relationship between law and society?

4. Is Mill's conception of law and of its practical application similar to that of Turk? On what grounds do the two men differ?

5. What is the harm principle? What rationale does Mill offer? Do you consider it reasonable? Why or why not?

6. Practically speaking, how easy is the harm principle to follow? What guidance, if any, does Mill offer for how we should define harms? What would you include in this category? What would you exclude? How much gray area is there between the two categories (consider, for example, laws governing hate speech)?

7. How should we interpret Mill's harm principle when debating laws governing reproduction? Does this theory help us understand the situation of pregnant women? May the government, on the basis of Mill's harm principle, legitimately compel a woman to carry a fetus to term?

Chapter 10

Lawrence v. Texas

in so doing protecting the private sphere from the tyranny of the majority.

OPINION

JUSTICE KENNEDY DELIVERED THE OPINION OF THE COURT

"Over himself," Mill wrote, *"over his own body and mind, the individual is sovereign." Good law should respect, insofar as possible, the sovereignty of the individual over himself. Many read Mill (Chapter 9) as cautioning against legislating morality, that is, legislating one set of values or preferences as if they, and only they, were acceptable. Yet, the United States has had a long history of legislating morality, of imposing legal regulations of so-called victimless crimes. This has been especially the case with regard to sexuality and sexual practices.*

In the summer of 2003, the United States Supreme Court—in Lawrence v. Texas—*put legislating morality in the domain of sexuality on trial. In that case, two gay men, who had been prosecuted under a Texas statute criminalizing homosexual sodomy, challenged the law, alleging that it violated their constitutionally protected rights, in particular their right to privacy. Seventeen years earlier, the Court upheld a challenge to a similar law in the state of Georgia, citing a long history of disapproval of, and restrictions on, homosexuality as the basis of refusing to recognize a right of privacy for consensual homosexual sodomy.*

In Lawrence, *the Court changed course. Justice Kennedy, sounding like John Stuart Mill, said, "The issue is whether the majority may use the power of the State to enforce [its] views on the whole society through the operation of the criminal law." In the domain of homosexual sodomy, he said that it may not. The Court's decision treated the law, in particular the United States Constitution, as a barrier between citizen and state, limiting the powers of the latter, and*

...Liberty protects the person from unwarranted government intrusions into a dwelling or other private places. In our tradition the State is not omnipresent in the home. And there are other spheres of our lives and existence, outside the home, where the State should not be a dominant presence. Freedom extends beyond spatial bounds. Liberty presumes an autonomy of self that includes freedom of thought, belief, expression, and certain intimate conduct. The instant case involves liberty of the person both in its spatial and more transcendent dimensions.

I

The question before the Court is the validity of a Texas statute making it a crime for two persons of the same sex to engage in certain intimate sexual conduct.

In Houston, Texas, officers of the Harris County Police Department were dispatched to a private residence in response to a reported weapons disturbance. They entered an apartment where one of the petitioners, John Geddes Lawrence, resided. The right of the police to enter does not seem to have been questioned. The officers observed Lawrence and another man, Tyron Garner, engaging in a sexual act. The two petitioners were arrested, held in custody over night, and charged and convicted before a Justice of the Peace.

The complaints described their crime as "deviate sexual intercourse, namely anal sex, with a member of the same sex (man)." App. to Pet. for Cert. 127a, 139a. The applicable state law is Tex. Penal Code Ann. § 21.06(a) (2003). It provides: "A person commits an offense if he engages in deviate sexual intercourse with another individual of the same sex." The statute defines "deviate sexual intercourse" as follows:

(A) any contact between any part of the genitals of one person and the mouth or anus of another person; or

(B) the penetration of the genitals or the anus of another person with an object. § 21.01(1).

The petitioners exercised their right to a trial *de novo* in Harris County Criminal Court. They challenged the statute as a violation of the Equal Protection Clause of the Fourteenth Amendment and of a like provision of the Texas Constitution. Tex. Const., Art. 1, § 3a. Those contentions were rejected. The petitioners, having entered a plea of *nolo contendere*, were each fined $200 and assessed court costs of $141.25. App. to Pet. for Cert. 107a–110a.

The Court of Appeals for the Texas Fourteenth District considered the petitioners' federal constitutional arguments under both the Equal Protection and Due Process Clauses of the Fourteenth Amendment. After hearing the case *en banc* the court, in a divided opinion, rejected the constitutional arguments and affirmed the convictions. 41 S. W. 3d 349 (Tex. App. 2001). The majority opinion indicates that the Court of Appeals considered our decision in *Bowers v. Hardwick,* 478 U.S. 186, 92 L. Ed. 2d 140, 106 S. Ct. 2841 (1986), to be controlling on the federal due process aspect of the case. Bowers then being authoritative, this was proper.

We granted certiorari, 537 U.S. 1044, 154 L. Ed. 2d 514, 123 S. Ct. 661 (2002), to consider three questions:

1.   "Whether Petitioners' criminal convictions under the Texas "Homosexual Conduct" law—which criminalizes sexual intimacy by same-sex couples, but not identical behavior by different-sex couples—violate the Fourteenth Amendment guarantee of equal protection of laws?

2.   "Whether Petitioners' criminal convictions for adult consensual sexual intimacy in the home violate their vital interests in liberty and privacy protected by the Due Process Clause of the Fourteenth Amendment?

3.   "Whether *Bowers v. Hardwick,* 478 U.S. 186, 92 L. Ed. 2d 140, 106 S. Ct. 2841 (1986), should be overruled?" Pet. for Cert. i.

The petitioners were adults at the time of the alleged offense. Their conduct was in private and consensual.

II

We conclude the case should be resolved by determining whether the petitioners were free as adults to engage in the private conduct in the exercise of their liberty under the Due Process Clause of the Fourteenth Amendment to the Constitution. For this inquiry we deem it necessary to reconsider the Court's holding in *Bowers.* . . .

The facts in *Bowers* had some similarities to the instant case. A police officer, whose right to enter seems not to have been in question, observed Hardwick, in his own bedroom, engaging in intimate sexual conduct with another adult male. The conduct was in violation of a Georgia statute making it a criminal offense to engage in sodomy. One difference between the two cases is that the Georgia statute prohibited the conduct whether or not the participants were of the same sex, while the Texas statute, as we have seen, applies only to participants of the same sex. Hardwick was not prosecuted, but he brought an action in federal court to declare the state statute invalid. He alleged he was a practicing homosexual and that the criminal prohibition violated rights guaranteed to him by the Constitution. The Court, in an opinion by Justice White, sustained the Georgia law. Chief Justice Burger and Justice Powell joined the opinion of the Court and filed separate, concurring opinions. Four Justices dissented. 478 U.S., at 199 (opinion of Blackmun, J., joined by Brennan, Marshall, and STEVENS, JJ.); id., at 214 (opinion of STEVENS, J., joined by Brennan and Marshall, JJ.).

The Court began its substantive discussion in *Bowers* as follows: "The issue presented is whether the Federal Constitution confers a fundamental right upon homosexuals to engage in sodomy and hence invalidates the laws of the many States that still make such conduct illegal and have done so for a very long time." Id., at 190. That statement, we now conclude, discloses the Court's own failure to appreciate the extent of the liberty at stake. To say that the issue in *Bowers* was simply the right to engage in certain sexual conduct demeans the claim the individual put forward, just as it would demean a married couple were it to be said marriage is simply about the right to have sexual intercourse. The laws involved in *Bowers* and here are, to be sure, statutes that purport to do no more than prohibit a particular sexual act. Their penalties and purposes, though, have more far-reaching consequences, touching upon the most private human conduct, sexual behavior, and in the most private of places, the home. The statutes do seek to control a personal relationship that, whether or not entitled to formal recognition in the law, is within the liberty of persons to choose without being punished as criminals.

This, as a general rule, should counsel against attempts by the State, or a court, to define the meaning of the relationship or to set its boundaries absent injury to a person or abuse of an institution the law protects. It suffices for us to acknowledge that adults may choose to enter upon this relationship in the confines of their homes and their own private lives and still retain their dignity as free persons. When sexuality finds overt expression in intimate conduct with another person, the conduct can be but one element in a personal bond that is more enduring. The liberty protected by the Constitution allows homosexual persons the right to make this choice.

Having misapprehended the claim of liberty there presented to it, and thus stating the claim to be whether there is a fundamental right to engage in consensual sodomy, the *Bowers* Court said: "Proscriptions against that conduct have ancient roots." Id., at 192. In academic writings, and in many of the scholarly *amicus* briefs filed to assist the Court in this case, there are fundamental criticisms of the historical premises relied upon by the majority and concurring opinions in *Bowers*. Brief for Cato Institute as *Amicus Curiae* 16–17; Brief for American Civil Liberties Union et al. as *Amici Curiae* 15–21; Brief for Professors of History et al. as *Amici Curiae* 3–10. We need not enter this debate in the attempt to reach a definitive historical judgment, but the following considerations counsel against adopting the definitive conclusions upon which *Bowers* placed such reliance.

At the outset it should be noted that there is no longstanding history in this country of laws directed at homosexual conduct as a distinct matter. Beginning in colonial times there were prohibitions of sodomy derived from the English criminal laws passed in the first instance by the Reformation Parliament of 1533. The English prohibition was understood to include relations between men and women as well as relations between men and men. See, e.g., *King v. Wiseman*, 92 Eng. Rep. 774, 775 (K. B. 1718) (interpreting "mankind" in Act of 1533 as including women and girls). Nineteenth-century commentators similarly read American sodomy, buggery, and crime-against-nature statutes as criminalizing certain relations between men and women and between men and men. See, e.g., 2 J. Bishop, Criminal Law § 1028 (1858); 2 J. Chitty, Criminal Law 47–50 (5th Am. ed. 1847); R. Desty, A Compendium of American

Criminal Law 143 (1882); J. May, The Law of Crimes § 203 (2d ed. 1893). The absence of legal prohibitions focusing on homosexual conduct may be explained in part by noting that according to some scholars the concept of the homosexual as a distinct category of person did not emerge until the late 19th century. See, e.g., J. Katz, The Invention of Heterosexuality 10 (1995); J. D'Emilio & E. Freedman, Intimate Matters: A History of Sexuality in America 121 (2d ed. 1997) ("The modern terms *homosexuality* and *heterosexuality* do not apply to an era that had not yet articulated these distinctions"). Thus early American sodomy laws were not directed at homosexuals as such but instead sought to prohibit nonprocreative sexual activity more generally. This does not suggest approval of homosexual conduct. It does tend to show that this particular form of conduct was not thought of as a separate category from like conduct between heterosexual persons.

Laws prohibiting sodomy do not seem to have been enforced against consenting adults acting in private. A substantial number of sodomy prosecutions and convictions for which there are surviving records were for predatory acts against those who could not or did not consent, as in the case of a minor or the victim of an assault. As to these, one purpose for the prohibitions was to ensure there would be no lack of coverage if a predator committed a sexual assault that did not constitute rape as defined by the criminal law. Thus the model sodomy indictments presented in a 19th-century treatise addressed the predatory acts of an adult man against a minor girl or minor boy. Instead of targeting relations between consenting adults in private, 19th-century sodomy prosecutions typically involved relations between men and minor girls or minor boys, relations between adults involving force, relations between adults implicating disparity in status, or relations between men and animals.

To the extent that there were any prosecutions for the acts in question, 19th-century evidence rules imposed a burden that would make a conviction more difficult to obtain even taking into account the problems always inherent in prosecuting consensual acts committed in private. Under then-prevailing standards, a man could not be convicted of sodomy based upon testimony of a consenting partner, because the partner was considered an accomplice. A partner's testimony, however, was admissible if he or she had not consented to the act or was a minor, and therefore incapable of consent. See, e.g., F. Wharton, Criminal Law 443 (2d ed. 1852); 1 F. Wharton, Criminal Law 512 (8th ed. 1880). The rule may explain in part the infrequency of these prosecutions. In all events, that infrequency makes it difficult to say that society approved of a rigorous and systematic punishment of the consensual acts committed in private and by adults. The longstanding criminal prohibition of homosexual sodomy upon which the *Bowers* decision placed such reliance is as consistent with a general condemnation of nonprocreative sex as it is with an established tradition of prosecuting acts because of their homosexual character.

The policy of punishing consenting adults for private acts was not much discussed in the early legal literature. We can infer that one reason for this was the very private nature of the conduct. Despite the absence of prosecutions, there may have been periods in which there was public criticism of homosexuals as such and an insistence that the criminal laws be enforced to discourage their practices. But far from possessing "ancient roots," *Bowers*, 478 U.S., at 192, American laws targeting same-sex couples did not develop until the last third of the 20th century. The reported decisions concerning the prosecution of consensual, homosexual sodomy between adults for the years 1880–1995 are not always clear in the details, but a significant number involved conduct in a public place. See Brief for American Civil Liberties Union et al. as *Amici Curiae* 14–15, and n. 18.

It was not until the 1970's that any State singled out same-sex relations for criminal prosecution, and only nine States have done so. See 1977 Ark. Gen. Acts no. 828; 1983 Kan. Sess. Laws p. 652; 1974 Ky. Acts p. 847; 1977 Mo. Laws p. 687; 1973 Mont. Laws p. 1339; 1977 Nev. Stats. p. 1632; 1989 Tenn. Pub. Acts ch. 591; 1973 Tex. Gen. Laws ch. 399; see also *Post v. State,* 1986 OK CR 30, 715 P.2d 1105 (Okla. Crim. App. 1986) (sodomy law invalidated as applied to different-sex couples). Post-*Bowers* even some of these States did not adhere to the policy of suppressing homosexual conduct. Over the course of the last decades, States with same-sex prohibitions have moved toward abolishing them. See, e.g., *Jegley v. Picado,* 349 Ark. 600, 80 S. W. 3d 332 (2002); *Gryczan v. State,* 283 Mont. 433, 942 P.2d 112 (1997); *Campbell v. Sundquist,* 926 S.W.2d 250 (Tenn. App. 1996); *Commonwealth v. Wasson,* 842 S.W.2d 487 (Ky. 1992); see also 1993 Nev. Stats. p. 518 (repealing Nev. Rev. Stat. § 201.193).

In summary, the historical grounds relied upon in *Bowers* are more complex than the majority opinion and the concurring opinion by Chief Justice Burger indicate. Their historical premises are not without doubt and, at the very least, are overstated.

It must be acknowledged, of course, that the Court in *Bowers* was making the broader point that for centuries there have been powerful voices to condemn homosexual conduct as immoral. The condemnation has been shaped by religious beliefs, conceptions of right and acceptable behavior, and respect for the traditional family. For many persons these are not trivial concerns but profound and deep convictions accepted as ethical and moral principles to which they aspire and which thus determine the course of their lives. These considerations do not answer the question before us, however. The issue is whether the majority may use the power of the State to enforce these views on the whole society through operation of the criminal law. "Our obligation is to define the liberty of all, not to mandate our own moral code." *Planned Parenthood of Southeastern Pa. v. Casey,* 505 U.S. 833, 850, 120 L. Ed. 2d 674, 112 S. Ct. 2791 (1992). . . .

Of even more importance, almost five years before *Bowers* was decided, the European Court of Human Rights considered a case with parallels to *Bowers* and to today's case. An adult male resident in Northern Ireland alleged he was a practicing homosexual who desired to engage in consensual homosexual conduct. The laws of Northern Ireland forbade him that right. He alleged that he had been questioned, his home had been searched, and he feared criminal prosecution. The court held that the laws proscribing the conduct were invalid under the European Convention on Human Rights. *Dudgeon v. United Kingdom,* 45 Eur. Ct. H. R. (1981) P52. Authoritative in all countries that are members of the Council of Europe (21 nations then, 45 nations now), the decision is at odds with the premise in *Bowers* that the claim put forward was insubstantial in our Western civilization.

In our own constitutional system the deficiencies in *Bowers* became even more apparent in the years following its announcement. The 25 States with laws prohibiting the relevant conduct referenced in the *Bowers* decision are reduced now to 13, of which 4 enforce their laws only against homosexual conduct. In those States where sodomy is still proscribed, whether for same-sex or heterosexual conduct, there is a pattern of nonenforcement with respect to consenting adults acting in private. The State of Texas admitted in 1994 that as of that date it had not prosecuted anyone under those circumstances. *State v. Morales,* 869 S.W.2d 941, 943, 37 Tex. Sup. Ct. J. 390.

Two principal cases decided after *Bowers* cast its holding into even more doubt. In *Planned Parenthood of Southeastern Pa. v. Casey,* 505 U.S. 833, 120 L. Ed. 2d 674, 112 S. Ct. 2791 (1992), the Court reaffirmed the substantive force of the liberty protected by the Due Process Clause. The *Casey* decision again confirmed that our laws and tradition afford constitutional protection to personal decisions relating to marriage, procreation, contraception, family relationships, child rearing, and education. Id., at 851. In explaining the respect the Constitution demands for the autonomy of the person in making these choices, we stated as follows:

> These matters, involving the most intimate and personal choices a person may make in a lifetime, choices central to personal dignity and autonomy, are central to the liberty protected by the Fourteenth Amendment. At the heart of liberty is the right to define one's own concept of existence, of leaning, of the universe, and of the mystery of human life. Beliefs about these matters could not define the attributes of personhood were they formed under compulsion of the State. *Ibid.*

Persons in a homosexual relationship may seek autonomy for these purposes, just as heterosexual persons do. The decision in *Bowers* would deny them this right.

The second post-*Bowers* case of principal relevance is *Romer v. Evans,* 517 U.S. 620, 134 L. Ed. 2d 855, 116 S. Ct. 1620 (1996). There the Court struck down class-based legislation directed at homosexuals as a violation of the Equal Protection Clause. *Romer* invalidated an amendment to Colorado's constitution which named as a solitary class persons who were homosexuals, lesbians, or bisexual either by "orientation, conduct, practices or relationships," id., at 624 (internal quotation marks omitted), and deprived them of protection under state antidiscrimination laws. We concluded that the provision was "born of animosity toward the class of persons affected" and further that it had no rational relation to a legitimate governmental purpose. Id., at 634.

As an alternative argument in this case, counsel for the petitioners and some *amici* contend that *Romer* provides the basis for declaring the Texas statute invalid under the Equal Protection Clause. That is a tenable argument, but we conclude the instant case requires us to address whether *Bowers* itself has continuing validity. Were we to hold the statute invalid under the Equal Protection Clause some might question whether a prohibition would be valid if drawn differently, say, to prohibit the conduct both between same-sex and different-sex participants.

Equality of treatment and the due process right to demand respect for conduct protected by the substantive guarantee of liberty are linked in important respects, and a decision on the latter point advances both interests. If protected conduct is made criminal and the law which does so remains unexamined for its substantive validity, its stigma might remain even if it were not enforceable as drawn for equal protection reasons. When homosexual conduct is made criminal by the law of the State, that declaration in and of itself is an invitation to subject homosexual persons to discrimination both in the public and in the private spheres. The central holding of *Bowers* has been brought in question by this case, and it should be addressed. Its continuance as precedent demeans the lives of homosexual persons.

The stigma this criminal statute imposes, moreover, is not trivial. The offense, to be sure, is but a class C misdemeanor, a minor offense in the Texas legal system. Still, it remains a criminal offense with all that imports for the dignity of the persons charged. The petitioners will bear on their record the history of their criminal convictions. Just this Term we rejected various challenges to state laws requiring the registration of sex offenders. *Smith v. Doe,* 538 U.S., 155 L. Ed. 2d 164, 123 S. Ct. 1140 (2003); *Connecticut Dept. of Public Safety v. Doe,* 538 U.S. 1, 155 L. Ed. 2d 98, 123 S. Ct. 1160 (2003). We are advised that if Texas convicted an adult for private, consensual homosexual conduct under the statute here in question the convicted person would come within the registration laws of a least four States were he or she to be subject to their jurisdiction. Pet. for Cert. 13, and n. 12 (citing Idaho Code §§ 18-8301 to 18-8326 (Cum. Supp. 2002); La. Code Crim. Proc. Ann., §§ 15:540-15:549 (West 2003); Miss. Code Ann. §§ 45-33-21 to 45-33-57 (Lexis 2003); S. C. Code Ann. §§ 23-3-400 to 23-3-490 (West 2002)). This underscores the consequential nature of the punishment and the state-sponsored condemnation attendant to the criminal prohibition. Furthermore, the Texas criminal conviction carries with it the other collateral consequences always following a conviction, such as notations on job application forms, to mention but one example.

The foundations of *Bowers* have sustained serious erosion from our recent decisions in *Casey* and *Romer*. When our precedent has been thus weakened, criticism from other sources is of greater significance. In the United States criticism of *Bowers* has been substantial and continuing, disapproving of its reasoning in all respects, not just as to its historical assumptions. See, e.g., C. Fried, Order and Law: Arguing the Reagan Revolution—A Firsthand Account 81–84 (1991); R. Posner, Sex and Reason 341–350 (1992). The courts of five different States have declined to follow it in interpreting provisions in their own state constitutions parallel to the Due Process Clause of the Fourteenth Amendment, see *Jegley v. Picado*, 349 Ark. 600, 80 S. W. 3d 332 (2002); *Powell v. State*, 270 Ga. 327, 510 S. E. 2d 18, 24 (1998); *Gryczan v. State*, 283 Mont. 433, 942 P.2d 112 (1997); *Campbell v. Sundquist*, 926 S.W.2d 250 (Tenn. App. 1996); *Commonwealth v. Wasson*, 842 S.W.2d 487 (Ky. 1992).

To the extent *Bowers* relied on values we share with a wider civilization, it should be noted that the reasoning and holding in *Bowers* have been rejected elsewhere. The European Court of Human Rights has followed not *Bowers* but its own decision in *Dudgeon v. United Kingdom*. See *P. G. & J. H. v. United Kingdom*, App. No. 00044787/98, P56 (Eur. Ct. H. R., Sept. 25, 2001); *Modinos v. Cyprus*, 259 Eur. Ct. H. R. (1993); *Norris v. Ireland*, 142 Eur. Ct. H. R. (1988). Other nations, too, have taken action consistent with an affirmation of the protected right of homosexual adults to engage in intimate, consensual conduct. See Brief for Mary Robinson et al. as *Amici Curiae* 11–12. The right the petitioners seek in this case has been accepted as an integral part of human freedom in many other countries. There has been no showing that in this country the governmental interest in circumscribing personal choice is somehow more legitimate or urgent.

The doctrine of *stare decisis* is essential to the respect accorded to the judgments of the Court and to the stability of the law. It is not, however, an inexorable command. *Payne v. Tennessee*, 501 U.S. 808, 828, 115 L. Ed. 2d 720, 111 S. Ct. 2597 (1991) ("*Stare decisis* is not an inexorable command; rather, it 'is a principle of policy and not a mechanical formula of adherence to the latest decision'") (quoting *Helvering v. Hallock*, 309 U.S. 106, 119, 84 L. Ed. 604, 60 S. Ct. 444 (1940). In Casey we noted that when a Court is asked to overrule a precedent recognizing a constitutional liberty interest, individual or societal reliance on the existence of that liberty cautions with particular strength against reversing course. 505 U.S., at 855–856; see also id., at 844 ("Liberty finds no refuge in a jurisprudence of doubt "). The holding in *Bowers*, however, has not induced detrimental reliance comparable to some instances where recognized individual rights are involved. Indeed, there has been no individual or societal reliance on *Bowers* of the sort that could counsel against overturning its holding once there are compelling reasons to do so. *Bowers* itself causes uncertainty, for the precedents before and after its issuance contradict its central holding.

The rationale of *Bowers* does not withstand careful analysis. . . .

Bowers was not correct when it was decided, and it is not correct today. It ought not to remain binding precedent. *Bowers v. Hardwick* should be and now is overruled.

The present case does not involve minors. It does not involve persons who might be injured or coerced or who are situated in relationships where consent might not easily be refused. It does not involve public conduct or prostitution. It does not involve whether the government must give formal recognition to any relationship that homosexual persons seek to enter. The case does involve two adults who, with full and mutual consent from each other, engaged in sexual practices common to a homosexual lifestyle. The petitioners are entitled to respect for their private lives. The State cannot demean their existence or control their destiny by making their private sexual conduct a crime. Their right to liberty under the Due Process Clause gives them the full right to engage in their conduct without intervention of the government. "It is a promise of the Constitution that there is a realm of personal liberty which the government may not enter." *Casey, supra,* at 847. The Texas statute furthers no legitimate state interest which can justify its intrusion into the personal and private life of the individual.

Had those who drew and ratified the Due Process Clauses of the Fifth Amendment or the Fourteenth Amendment known the components of liberty in its manifold possibilities, they might have been more specific. They did not presume to have this insight. They knew times can blind us to certain truths and later generations can see that laws once thought necessary and proper in fact serve only to oppress. As the Constitution endures, persons in every generation can invoke its principles in their own search for greater freedom.

The judgment of the Court of Appeals for the Texas Fourteenth District is reversed, and the case is remanded for further proceedings not inconsistent with this opinion.

It is so ordered.

NOTES AND QUESTIONS

1. What three questions did the Supreme Court agree to consider in *Lawrence v. Texas?*

2. Justice Kennedy writes for the majority that the Court previously misapprehended the claim of liberty presented to it in *Bowers v. Hardwick.* What are the key differences between the previous Court's interpretations of liberty and the interpretation of the current Court?

3. The Supreme Court upheld the criminalization of consensual sodomy in *Bowers,* citing the fact that proscriptions against that conduct have ancient roots. On what grounds does Kennedy dismiss this historical consideration in the ruling for *Lawrence?* Do you agree with his analysis?

4. Justice Sandra Day O'Connor concurred in the judgment in *Lawrence,* but dissented from the part of the majority opinion that overturned *Bowers.* Writing separately, O'Connor explained that she found the Texas antisodomy statute unconstitutional on the grounds that it violated the equal protection clause of the Fourteenth Amendment. The Georgia statute considered in *Bowers* had criminalized all sodomy for heterosexual *and* homosexual adults alike. This was not the case in Texas. By O'Connor's logic, the Texas statute was unconstitutional only because heterosexual couples were afforded greater liberty in their sexual conduct. Do you find this argument compelling? Does the government have the right to legislate morality so long as all citizens are held to the same standards?

5. If we apply Mill's harm principle (in Chapter 9) to the facts of *Lawrence,* is the Court ruling just? Some argue that the decriminalization of homosexual sodomy imperils the sanctity of marriage. Should this be considered a harm in the eyes of the law? Others argue that the ruling in *Lawrence* creates a legal slippery slope, undermining criminal stat-

utes that outlaw pedophilia, incest, and bigamy. Do you agree?

6. In his dissent, Justice Antonin Scalia's accusation that six of his colleagues had taken sides in the culture war was widely quoted in media coverage of this case.

Was *Lawrence* a radical decision by the court? Why or why not?

Reprinted from: Lawrence and Garner, *Petitioners v. Texas,* 156 L. Ed. 3d 508 (2003). ✦

Chapter 11

Law as Rhetoric, Rhetoric as Law

The Arts of Cultural and Communal Life

James Boyd White

Unlike the instrumentalism of Hobbes (Chapter 7) and Turk (Chapter 8) and the individualism of Mill (Chapter 9) and the Supreme Court's decision in Lawrence v. Texas *(Chapter 10), the reading by James Boyd White takes a different perspective. Law, he insists, ought not to be thought of or treated as if it were a machine for accomplishing any particular purpose. Instead, law should be treated as "an activity, and in particular as a rhetorical activity." As he sees it, the law is "the particular set of resources made available by a culture for speech and argument on those occasions, and by those speakers, we think of as legal."*

The law is a means of persuasion used by members of a community in their pursuit of the good. Law, for White, is an arena for the articulation and discussion of shared values. It provides a vehicle for a conversation about what kind of community we wish to be. Through legal argument we create, as well as discover, answers to questions of justice and ethics. Note that White is quite hopeful about the work that lawyers do in making legal arguments. He sees lawyers as pursuing a noble profession, one which is valuable in the creation of human character and indispensable in shaping a decent way of living. Law, White argues, helps us "to attend to the spiritual or meaningful side of our collective life."

In this paper I shall suggest that law is most usefully seen not, as it usually is by academics and philosophers, as a system of rules, but as a branch of rhetoric; and that the kind of rhetoric of which law is a species is most usefully seen not, as rhetoric usually is, either as a failed science or as the ignoble art of persuasion, but as the central art by which community and culture are established, maintained, and transformed. So regarded, rhetoric is continuous with law, and like it, has justice as its ultimate subject.

I do not mean to say that these are the only ways to understand law or rhetoric. There is a place in the world for institutional and policy studies, for taxonomies of persuasive devices, and for analyses of statistical patterns and distributive effects. But I think that all these activities will themselves be performed and criticized more intelligently if it is recognized that they too are rhetorical. As for law and rhetoric themselves, I think that to see them in the way I suggest is to make sense of them in a more nearly complete way, especially from the point of view of the individual speaker, the individual hearer, and the individual judge. . . .

[T]he law is at present usually spoken of (by academics at least) as if it were a body of more or less determinate rules, or rules and principles, that are more or less perfectly intelligible to the trained reader. Law is in this sense objectified and made a structure. The question "What is law?" is answered by defining what its rules are, or by analyzing the kinds of rules that characterize it. The law is thus abstracted and conceptualized: H.L.A. Hart's major book on jurisprudence was appropriately entitled *The Concept of Law*.[1] Sophisticated analysis of law from this point of view distinguishes among various kinds of legal rules and among different sets or subsets of legal rules: substantive rules are distinguished from procedural or remedial rules, or primary rules from secondary rules, or legal rules from more general principles.

This idea of law and legal science fits with, and is perhaps derived from, the contemporary conception of our public political world as a set of bureaucratic entities, which can be defined in Weberian terms as nationalized institutions functioning according to ends-means rationality. These institutions have goals, purposes, or aims, which they achieve more or less perfectly as they are structured and managed more or less well.

In this way, the government (of which the law is a part) and in fact the entire bureaucratic system, private as well as public, tends to be regarded, especially by lawyers, managers, and other policy-makers, as a machine acting on the rest of the world. This naturally reduces the rest of the world to the object upon which the machine acts. Human actors outside the governmental world are made the objects of manipulation through a series of incentives or disincentives. Actors within the legal-bureaucratic structure either are "will-servers" (whose obligation is to obey the will of a political superior) or are "choice-makers" (who are in a position of political superiority charged with the responsibility of making choices, usually thought of as "policy choices," that affect the lives of others). The choices themselves are likewise objectified: the items of choice are broken out of the flux of experience and the context of life so that they can be talked about in the bureaucratic-legal mode. This commits the system to what is thought to be measurable (especially to what is measurable in material ways) to short-term goals, and to a process of thought by calculation. The premises of cost-benefit analysis are thus integral to the bureaucracy as we normally imagine it. Whatever cannot be talked about in these bureaucratic ways is simply not talked about. Of course all systems of discourse have domains and boundaries, principles of exclusion and inclusion, but this kind of bureaucratic talk is largely unself-conscious about what it excludes. The world it sees is its whole world.

Law then becomes reducible to two features: policy choices and techniques of their implementation. Our questions are "What do we want?" and "How do we get it?" In this way the conception of law as a set of rules merges with the conception of law as a set of institutions and processes. The overriding metaphor is that of the machine; the overriding value is that of efficiency, conceived of as the attainment of certain ends with the smallest possible costs.

I

I shall sketch out a somewhat different way of conceiving of law, and indeed of governmental processes generally: not as a bureaucratic but as a rhetorical process. In doing this, I shall also be suggesting a way to think about rhetoric, especially that kind of rhetoric—I call it "constitutive rhetoric"—of which law can I think be seen as a species.

I want to start by thinking of law not as an objective reality in an imagined social world, not as a part of a constructed cosmology, but from the point of view of those who actually engage in its processes, as something we do and something we teach. This is a way of looking at law as an activity, and in particular as a rhetorical activity.

I want to direct attention to three related aspects of the lawyer's work. The first is the fact that the lawyer, like any rhetorician, must always start by speaking the language of his or her audience, whatever it may be. This is just a version of the general truth that to persuade anybody you must in the first instance speak a language that he or she regards as valid and intelligible. If you are a lawyer, this means that you must speak either the technical language of the law—the rules, cases, statutes, maxims, and so forth, that constitute the domain of your professional talk—or, if you are speaking to jurors or clients or the public at large, some version of the ordinary English of your time and place. Law is in this sense always culture-specific. It always starts with an external, empirically discoverable set of cultural resources into which it is an intervention.

This suggests that one (somewhat circular) definition of the law might be the particular set of resources made available by a culture for speech and argument on those occasions, and by those speakers, we think of as legal. These resources include rules, statutes, and judicial opinions, of course, but much more as well: maxims, general understandings, conventional wisdom, and all the other resources, technical and nontechnical, that a lawyer might use in defining his or her position and urging another to accept it.[2] To define "the law" in this way, as a set of resources for thought and argument, is an application of Aristotle's traditional definition of rhetoric, for the law in this sense is one set of those "means of persuasion" that he said it is the art of rhetoric to discover.

This suggests that the lawyer's work has a second essential element, the creative process to which I have just alluded. For in speaking the language of the law, the lawyer must always be ready to try to change it: to add or to drop a distinction, to admit a new voice, to claim a new source of authority, and so on. One's performance is in this sense always argumentative, not only about the result one seeks to obtain but also about the version of the legal discourse that one uses—that one creates—in one's speech and writing. That is, the lawyer is always saying not only, "Here is how this case should be decided," but also, "Here—in this language—is the way this case and similar cases should be talked about. The language I am speaking is the proper language of justice in our culture." The legal speaker always acts upon the language that he or she uses, to modify or rearrange it; in this sense legal rhetoric is always argumentatively constitutive of the language it employs.

The third aspect of legal rhetoric is what might be called its ethical or communal character, or its socially constitutive nature. Every time one speaks as a lawyer, one establishes for the moment a character—an ethical identity, or what the Greeks called an *ethos*—for oneself, for one's audience, and for those one talks about, and in addition one proposes a relation among the characters one defines. One cre-

ates, or proposes to create, a community of people, talking to and about each other. The lawyer's speech is thus always implicitly argumentative not only about the result—how should the case be decided?—and about the language—in what terms should it be defined and talked about?—but also about the rhetorical community of which one is at that moment a part. The lawyer is always establishing in performance a response to the questions, "What kind of community should we, who are talking the language of the law, establish with each other, with our clients, and with the rest of the world? What kind of conversation should the law constitute, should constitute the law?"

. . . [T]he fact that the law can be understood as a comprehensibly organized method of argument, or what I call a rhetoric, means that it is at once a social activity—a way of acting with others—and a cultural activity—a way of acting with a certain set of materials found in the culture. It is always communal, both in the sense that it always takes place in a social context and in the sense that it is always constitutive of the community by which it works. Both the lawyer and the lawyer's audience live in a world in which their language and community are not fixed and certain but fluid, constantly remade, as their possibilities and limits are tested. The law is an art of persuasion that creates the objects of its persuasion, for it constitutes both the community and the culture it commends.

This means that the process of law is at once creative and educative. Those who use this language are perpetually learning what can and cannot be done with it as they try—and fail or succeed—to reach new formulations of their positions. It also means that both the identity of the speakers and their wants are in perpetual transformation. If this is right, the law cannot be a technique, as the bureaucratic model assumes, by which "we" get what we "want," for both "we" and our "wants" are constantly remade in the rhetorical process. The idea of the legal actor as one who is either making policy choices himself (or herself) or obeying the choices made by others is inadequate, for he is a participant in the perpetual remaking of the language and culture that determines who he is and who we are. The law is not merely a bureaucracy or a set of rules, but a community of speakers of a certain kind: a culture of argument, perpetually remade by its participants.

All three of these aspects of the lawyer's work flow from the fact that the law is what I have called culture-specific, that is, that it always takes place in a cultural context into which it is always an intervention. But it is in a similar way socially specific: it always takes place in a particular social context, into which it is also an intervention. By this I mean nothing grand but simply that the lawyer responds to the felt needs of others, who come to him or her for assistance with an actual difficulty or problem. (These felt needs may of course be partly the product of the law itself, and the very "intervention" of the law can create new possibilities for meaning, for motive, and for aspiration.) From this point of view, the law can be seen, as it is experienced, not as a wholly independent system of meaning, but as a way of talking about real events and actual people in the world. It is a way of telling a story about what has happened in the world and claiming a meaning for it by writing an ending to it. The lawyer is repeatedly saying, or imagining himself or herself saying: "Here is 'what happened,' here is 'what it means,' and here is 'why it means what I claim.'" The process is at heart a narrative one because there cannot be a legal case without a real story about real people actually located in time and space and culture. Some actual person must go to a lawyer with an account of the experience upon which he or she wants the law to act, and that account will always be a narrative. The client's narrative is not simply accepted by the lawyer but subjected to questioning and elaboration, as the lawyer sees first one set of legal relevances, then another. In the formal legal process, that story is then

retold, over and over, by the lawyer and by the client and by others, in developing and competing versions, until by judgment or agreement an authoritative version is achieved. This story will in the first instance be told in the language of its actors. That is where the law begins; in a sense that is also where it ends, for its object is to provide an ending to that story that will work in the world. And since the story both begins and ends in ordinary language and experience, the heart of the law is the process of translation by which it must work, from ordinary language to legal language and back again.

The language that the lawyer uses and remakes is a language of meaning in the fullest sense. It is a language in which our perceptions of the natural universe are constructed and related, in which our values and motives are defined, and in which our methods of reasoning are elaborated and enacted. By defining roles and actors, and by establishing expectations as to the propriety of speech and conduct, it gives us the terms for constructing a social universe. Law always operates through speakers located in particular times and places speaking to actual audiences about real people; its language is continuous with ordinary language; it always operates by narrative; it is not conceptual in its structure; it is perpetually reaffirmed or rejected in a social process; and it contains a system of internal translation by which it can reach a range of hearers. All these things mark it as a rhetorical system.

II

What I have said means something, I think, about what we can mean by "rhetoric" as well as what we mean by "law." What I have been describing is not merely an art of estimating probabilities or an art of persuasion, but an art of constituting culture and community. It is of this kind of rhetoric that I think the law is a branch. . . .

What kind of community shall it be? How will it work? In what language shall it be formed? These are the great questions of rhetorical analysis. It thus always has justice and ethics—and politics, in the best sense of that term—as its ultimate subjects.

The domain of constitutive rhetoric, as I think of it, thus includes all language activity that goes into the constitution of actual human cultures and communities. Even the kind of persuasion Plato called dialectic, in which the speaker is himself willing, even eager, to be refuted, is in this sense a form of rhetoric, for it is the establishment of community and culture in language.

III

Like law, rhetoric invents; and, like law, it invents out of something rather than out of nothing. It always starts in a particular culture and among particular people. There is always one speaker addressing others in a particular situation, about concerns that are real and important to somebody, and speaking a particular language. Rhetoric always takes place with given materials. One cannot idealize rhetoric and say, "Here is how it should go on in general." As Aristotle saw—for his *Rhetoric* is, for the most part, a map of claims that are persuasive in his Greek world—rhetoric is always specific to its material. There is no Archimedean point from which rhetoric can be viewed or practiced.

This means that the rhetorician—that is, each of us when we speak to persuade or to establish community in other ways—must accept the double fact that there are real and important differences among cultures and that each person is to a substantial degree the product of his or her own culture. The rhetorician, like the lawyer, is engaged in a process of meaning-making and community-building of which he or she is in part the subject. To do this requires him or her to face and to accept the condition of radical uncertainty in which we live: uncertainty as to the meaning of words, uncertainty as to their effect on others, uncertainty as to our own character and motivations. The knowledge out of which the

rhetorician ultimately functions will not be scientific or theoretical but practical, experiential—the sense that one knows how to do things with language and with others. This is, in fact, our earliest social and intellectual knowledge, the knowledge we acquire as we first begin to move and act in our social universe and learn to speak and understand. It is the knowledge by which language and social relations are made.

The rhetorician thus begins not with the imagined individual in imagined isolation (as Hobbes or Locke does), and not with the self, isolated from all of its experience except that of cogitation (as Descartes does), but where Wittgenstein tells us to begin, with our abilities of language, gesture, and meaning. This knowledge is itself not reducible to rules or subject to expression in rules, though many analysts wish that it were; rather it is the knowledge by which we learn to manage, evade, disappoint, surprise, and please each other, as we understand the expectations that others bring to what we say. This knowledge is not provable in the scientific sense, nor is it logically rigorous. For these reasons, it is unsettling to the modern scientific and academic mind. But we cannot go beyond it, and it is a mistake to try. In this fluid world without turf or ground, we cannot walk but we can swim. And we need not be afraid to do this—to engage in the rhetorical process of life—for all of us, despite our radical uncertainties, already know how to do it. By attending to our own experience, and that of others, we can learn to do it better if we try.

IV

...This means that one question constantly before us as lawyers is what kind of culture we shall have, as well as what kind of community we shall be. What will be our language of approval and disapproval, praise and blame, admiration and contempt? What shall be the terms by which we identify and refine—by which we create—our motives and combine them into coherent wholes? This way of conceiving of law invites us to include in our zone of attention and field of discourse what others, operating under present suppositions, cut out, including both the radical uncertainty of most forms of knowledge and the fact that we, and our resources, are constantly remade by our own collective activities. The pressure of bureaucratic discourse is always to think in terms of ends and means; but in practice ends-means rationality is likely to undergo a reversal by which only those things can count as ends for which means of a certain kind exist. This often results in a reduction of the human to the material and the measurable, as though a good or just society were a function of the rate of individual consumption, not a set of shared relations, attitudes, and meanings. To view law as rhetoric might help us to attend to the spiritual or meaningful side of our collective life. . . .

Notes

1. H. L. A. Hart, *The Concept of Law* (1961).

2. In light of the current view of law as a set of rules, it is worth stressing that while much legal argument naturally takes the form of interpreting rules, or redefining them, and while some rules are obviously of greater authority than others, the material as a whole is not structured as a set of rules with a hierarchical or other order, nor is it reducible to a set of rules. The rule is often the subject as well as the source of argument, with respect to its form, its content, and its relation to other rules. Perhaps the best way to understand what a rule is, as it works in the legal world, is to think of it not as a command that is obeyed or disobeyed but as the topic of thought and argument—as one of many resources brought to bear by the lawyer and others both to define a question and to establish a way to approach it.

NOTES AND QUESTIONS

1. How does White describe those who understand law as a bureaucratic process, "as if it were a body of more or less determinate rules"? Does this remind you of arguments made by Hobbes, Turk, or Mill? What is it about this concept of law that dissatisfies White?

2. What does White mean when he describes law as a "rhetorical process"? How is this different from understanding law as a bureaucratic process? What is "constitutive rhetoric"?

3. What is the dual role of the lawyer in White's conception of law? How does culture affect the practice of law? At the same time, how does law as a rhetorical practice shape culture and community?

4. White argues, "Law is an art of persuasion that creates the objects of its persuasion, for it constitutes both the community and the culture it commends." How does White explain this idea? What about his argument do you find compelling or useful?

5. How useful is White's characterization of law for explaining the transformation of Supreme Court opinions from *Bowers v. Hardwick* to *Lawrence v. Texas?*

6. Is there any room for objective truth in White's conception of law? What about Mill's "harm principle"?

Conclusion to Part I

This Part described some of the limits of law as well as some of the grandest of its aspirations. The world in which law works is filled with challenges, and no legal system can succeed in meeting them all. From the tragic loss of life that occurs daily throughout America to the failures of our institutions to protect our most vulnerable citizens, from the issues that racial difference and racism pose for law to the new and dramatic threat of terrorism, legal institutions must make choices. They choose how to allocate resources; how to deploy police, social workers, and other legal officials; how to respond to requests for help; how to react when citizens are injured; and how to balance our competing desires for freedom and security in the face of new dangers.

As you think about the challenges that law faces, I hope you will put the need to make choices at the center of your attention. In-deed, perhaps nothing is more important than to think about law as a framework within which choices must be made. These choices are informed by the workings of institutions, the values and backgrounds of the people working in them, and the values of the various groups contending for, or seeking to avoid, the attention of legal officials.

The readings in Part I also remind us that law is an arena within which people play out hopes and aspirations for themselves, their communities, and the societies of which they are a part. Law responds to the world as it is, but also helps to make and remake that world. Law deals with cruelties and pain, but also provides a framework for realizing visions of the good. As you think about law, I invite you to think about the world that you would like to help bring into being and about the role that legal rules, institutions, and officials need to have in that enterprise. ✦

Suggested Additional Readings for Part I

THE LIMITS OF LEGAL PROTECTION

Albert Alschuler, "Mediation With a Mugger," 99 *Harvard Law Review* (1986).

David Cole and James X. Dempsey, *Terrorism and the Constitution: Sacrificing Civil Liberties in the Name of National Security.* New York: New Press, 2002.

Darnell Hawkins, ed., *Violent Crime: Assessing Race and Ethnic Differences.* New York: Cambridge University Press, 2003.

Kim Holmes and Edwin Meese, "The Administration's Anti-Terrorism Package: Balancing Security and Liberty," *The Heritage Foundation Backgrounder* (October 3, 2001).

Cynthia Lee, *Murder and the Reasonable Man: Passion and Fear in the Criminal Courtroom.* New York: New York University Press, 2003.

Michael Rand, *Violent Crime by Strangers.* Washington, D. C.: U. S. Department of Justice, Bureau of Justice Statistics, 1982.

Stephen Schulhofer, "At War With Liberty: Post-9-11, Due Process and Security Have Taken a Beating," *American Prospect* (Spring 2003), A5.

Robert Weisberg, "Private Violence as Moral Action: The Law as Inspiration and Example," in *Law's Violence,* Austin Sarat and Thomas R. Kearns, eds. Ann Arbor: University of Michigan Press, 1993, 175.

Riss v. City of New York, 240 N.E.2d 860 (1968).

Sorichetti v. City of New York, 492 N.Y.S.2d 591 (1985).

WHAT LAW IS FOR

Harold Berman and William Greiner, *The Nature and Functions of Law.* Mineola, NY: Foundation Press, 1966.

Patricia Bolling, *Privacy and the Politics of Intimate Life.* Ithaca, NY: Cornell University Press, 1996.

Lon Fuller, *The Morality of Law.* New Haven, CT: Yale University Press, 1964.

Jean Hampton, *Hobbes and the Social Contract Tradition.* New York: Cambridge University Press, 1986.

James Boyd White, *Justice as Translation: An Essay in Cultural and Legal Criticism.* Chicago: University of Chicago Press, 1990. ✦

Part II

The Search for Law

As law seeks to work in the world and to accomplish its varied purposes, it confronts several different problems of social organization. The next part of the book—The Search for Law—introduces three different dilemmas that characterize the social organization of law. In Section III, it lays out the framework around which the rest of the book is organized.

The first problem of social organization involves the question of accessibility. How accessible is law? Is it, as critics of the litigation explosion would suggest, too accessible or is it not accessible enough? Is it equally accessible to all regardless of their social characteristics?

Second is the question of severity and leniency. Is law too severe or not severe enough? What is the right balance of severity and leniency? Is the law more severe with some people than it is with others? How does this balancing of severity and leniency work to legitimate law?

The third dilemma involves the image of law as a top-down, hierarchically controlled bureaucracy in which appellate judges sit at the top issuing commands, which others routinely follow. Juxtaposed to this image is the call for low-level discretion and the desire that law responds equitably to individual differences. ✦

Section III

Three Dilemmas of Social Organization

Chapter 12
Before the Law

Franz Kafka

How accessible should law be? If law is too accessible, it may be flooded with demands and unable to respond effectively to any of them. If it is not accessible enough, citizens, even those with legitimate needs, may be unable to get help.

To ask about the accessibility of law it is, of course, necessary to say what law is. Is it a set of institutions and the officials who work in them? Is it a set of words on the page, law on the books? Is it a set of aspirations, ideals that are only partially captured in what law says or what it does? Is it all of these things in different combinations?

And, what does getting access entail? Does it mean having an opportunity to present your case to a legal official? Does it mean having sufficient knowledge to understand how law works? All of these aspects are in play in Kafka's famous parable, "Before the Law."

In this tale "a man from the country" seeks admittance to the "Law." As you read this, ask: What is the law to which he seeks admission? Does his belief that law should be equally accessible to everyone express and embody a contemporary idea?

Before the Law stands a doorkeeper. To this doorkeeper there comes a man from the country and prays for admittance to the Law. But the doorkeeper says that he cannot grant admittance at the moment. The man thinks it over and then asks if he will be allowed in later. "It is possible," says the doorkeeper, "but not at the moment." Since the gate stands open, as usual, and the doorkeeper steps to one side, the man stoops to peer through the gateway into the interior. Observing that, the doorkeeper laughs and says: "If you are so drawn to it just try to go in despite my veto. But take note: I am powerful. And I am only the least of the doorkeepers. From hall to hall there is one doorkeeper after another, each more powerful than the last. The third doorkeeper is already so terrible that even I cannot bear to look at him." These are difficulties the man from the country has not expected; the Law, he thinks, should surely be accessible at all times and to everyone, but as he now takes a closer look at the doorkeeper in his fur coat, with his big sharp nose and long, thin, black Tartar beard, he decides that it is better to wait until he gets permission to enter. The doorkeeper gives him a stool and lets him sit down at one side of the door. There he sits for days and years. He makes many attempts to be admitted, and wearies the doorkeeper by his importunity. The doorkeeper frequently has little interviews with him, asking him questions about his home and many other things, but the questions are put indifferently, as great lords put them, and always finish with the statement that he cannot be let in yet. The man, who has furnished himself with many things for his journey, sacrifices all he has, however valuable, to bribe the doorkeeper. The doorkeeper accepts everything, but always with the remark: "I am only taking it to keep you from thinking you have omitted anything." During these many years the man fixes his attention almost continuously on the doorkeeper. He forgets the other doorkeepers, and this first one seems to him the sole obstacle preventing access to the Law. He curses his bad luck, in his early years boldly and loudly; later, as he grows old, he only grumbles to himself. He becomes childish, and since in his yearlong contemplation of the doorkeeper he has come to know even the fleas in his fur collar, he begs the fleas as well to help him and to change the doorkeeper's mind. At length his eyesight begins to fail, and he does not know whether the world is really darker or whether his eyes are only deceiving him. Yet in his darkness he is now aware of a radiance that streams inextinguishably from the gateway of the Law. Now he has not very long to live. Before he dies, all his experiences in these long years gather themselves in his head to one point, a question he has not yet asked the doorkeeper. He waves him nearer, since he can no longer raise his stiffening body. The doorkeeper has to bend low toward him, for the difference in height between them has altered much to the man's disadvantage. "What do you want to know now?" asks the doorkeeper; "you are insatiable." "Everyone strives to reach the Law," says the man, "so how does it happen that for all these many years no one but myself has ever begged for admittance?" The doorkeeper recognizes that the man has reached his end, and, to let his failing senses catch the words, roars in his ear: "No one else could ever be admitted here, since this gate was made only for you. I am now going to shut it."

Notes and Questions

1. What is the nature of law as represented in this parable? How universal is Kafka's representation of law?

2. Who is the doorkeeper? Does he belong to the realm of the law, or is he also on the outside? From whom or from what does he derive his power?

3. Though the door to the law "stands open as usual and the doorkeeper steps to one side," the man from the country spends his entire life waiting outside the door. Why, if he feels so adamant that "the law should be accessible to every man at all times," does he choose to wait for the doorkeeper's permission to pass through?

4. How should we understand the relationship between the doorkeeper and the man from the country? What does the area outside the door represent?

5. What does it mean that the doorkeeper accepts bribes from the country man? Why does the doorkeeper always refuse admittance to the man from the country? How should we interpret the gatekeeper's comment, "I take this only to keep you from feeling that you have left something undone?"

6. Why can the man from the country not perceive the "radiance that streams immortally from the door of the law" until he is nearing the end of his life? What does the radiance represent?

7. Why does the doorkeeper shut the door at the end? What does it mean that the man from the country is never admitted to the law?

Chapter 13

Property, Authority and the Criminal Law

Douglas Hay

Law structures and guides human behavior in a variety of ways: through the content of the rules that it makes, the way its officials behave, and/or the severity of the penalties it imposes on those who do not conform to its requirements. Those penalties must be severe enough to deter potential offenders, but not so severe as to be, or appear to be, unjust. How a legal order balances severity and leniency is an important component of its social organization and plays a role in determining whether people regard the legal system as fair and legitimate.

Every legal system develops and declares a set of rules and penalties for violations of the rules that it promulgates. This is "the law on the books." But the law on the books is not always an accurate guide to the law in action. What the law actually does may have little to do with what it says. The pronouncements of legislatures and courts are but one part of the calculus that determines how legal officials actually behave.

Law may be, and often is, severe in the penalties that are formally prescribed for violations of rules. Yet the penalties actually imposed may not match those prescriptions. This difference results from the discretionary power that officials have to interpret, apply, and implement the written law. It opens up the question of how discretionary decisions are made and whether they are made in a way that favors some while disadvantaging others.

In the next reading, Douglas Hay presents a historical account of the criminal law in eighteenth-century England. Hay's article is a classic in the social study of law. It develops a perspective that emerges from the tradition of seeing law as a tool in social conflict, especially in class conflict. Hay's interest is in the ways legal ideology serves to maintain social inequality, to manufacture the consent of those who are socially disadvantaged.

One crucial aspect of legal ideology involves the interplay of severity and leniency in the criminal law. Thus, Hay tells his readers that in English law, death penalties were prescribed for a wide range of crimes, including offenses against property. Yet, in practice, few persons were executed. This gap, this paradox of severity and leniency, was essential to the legitimation of a deeply unequal social system. It set the stage for displays of majesty, justice, and mercy that reinforced the authority of the existing distribution of property.

The rulers of eighteenth-century England cherished the death sentence. The oratory we remember now is the parliamentary speech, the Roman periods of Fox or Burke, that stirred the gentry and the merchants. But outside Parliament were the labouring poor, and twice a year, in most counties in England, the scarlet-robed judge of assize put the black cap of death on top of his full-bottomed wig to expound the law of the propertied, and to execute their will. "Methinks I see him," wrote Martin Madan in 1785, with a countenance of solemn sorrow, adjusting the cap of judgement on his head. . . . His Lordship then, deeply affected by the melancholy part of his office, which he is now about to fulfill, embraces this golden opportunity to do most exemplary good—He addresses, in the most pathetic terms, the consciences of the trembling criminals . . .shows them how just and necessary it is, that there should be laws to remove out of society those, who instead of contributing their honest industry to the public good and welfare, have exerted every art, that the blackest villainy can suggest, to destroy both. . . . He then vindicates the *mercy,* as well as the *severity* of the law, in making such examples, as shall not only protect the innocent from outrage and violence, but also deter others from bringing themselves to the same fatal and ignominious end. . . . He acquaints them with the certainty of speedy death, and consequently with the necessity of speedy repentance—and on this theme he may so deliver himself, as not only to melt the wretches at the bar into contrition, but the whole auditory into the deepest concern—Tears express their feelings—and many of the most thoughtless among them may, for the rest of their lives, be preserved from thinking lightly of the first steps to vice, which they now see will lead them to destruction. The dreadful sentence is now pronounced—every heart shakes with terror—the almost fainting criminals are taken from the bar—the crowd retires—each to his several home, and carries the mournful story to his friends and neighbours;—the day of execution arrives—the wretches are led forth to suffer, and exhibit a spectacle to the beholders, too awful and solemn for description.[1]

This was the climactic moment in a system of criminal law based on *terror*: 'if we diminish the terror of house-breakers,' wrote Justice Christian of Ely in 1819, 'the terror of the innocent inhabitants must be increased, and the comforts of domestic life must be greatly destroyed.' He himself had dogs, firearms, lights and bells at his own country home, and took a brace of double-barrelled pistols to bed with him every night.[2] But his peace of mind mostly rested on the knowledge that the death sentence hung over anyone who broke in to steal his silver plate. A regular police force did not exist, and the gentry would not tolerate even the idea of one. They remembered the pretensions of the Stuarts and the days of the Commonwealth, and they saw close at hand how the French monarchy controlled its subjects with spies and informers. In place of police, however, propertied Englishmen had a fat and swelling sheaf of laws which threatened thieves with death. The most recent account suggests that the number of capital statutes grew from about 50 to over 200 between the years 1688 and 1820.[3] Almost all of them concerned offences against property. . . .

Once property had been officially deified, it became the measure of all things. Even human life was weighed in the scales of wealth and status: 'the execution of a needy decrepit assassin,' wrote Blackstone, 'is a poor satisfaction for the murder of a nobleman in the bloom of his youth, and full enjoyment of his friends, his honours, and his fortune.'[4] Again and again the voices of money and power declared the sacredness of property in terms hitherto reserved for human life. Banks were credited with souls and the circulation of gold likened to that of blood. Forgers, for example, were almost invariably hanged, and gentlemen knew why: 'Forgery is a stab to commerce, and only to be tolerated in a commercial nation when the foul crime of murder is pardoned.'[5] In a mood of unrivalled assurance and complacency, Parliament over the century created one of the bloodiest criminal codes in Europe. Few of the new penalties were the product of hysteria, or ferocious reaction; they were part of the conventional wisdom of England's governors. . . .

But if most of the law and the lawyers were concerned with the civil dealings which propertied men had with one another, most men, the unpropertied labouring poor, met the law as criminal sanction: the threat or the reality of whipping, transportation and hanging. Death had long been a punishment for theft in England, and several of the most important statutes were passed in Tudor times. But the gentry and merchants and peers who sat in Parliament in the eighteenth century set new standards of legislative industry, as they passed act after act to keep the capital sanction up to date, to protect every conceivable kind of property from theft or malicious damage.[6]

Yet two great questions hang over this remarkable code. The first concerns the actual number of executions. The available evidence suggests that, compared to some earlier periods, the eighteenth-century criminal law claimed few lives. At the beginning of the seventeenth century, for example, it appears that London and Middlesex saw four times as many executions as 150 years later.[7] Equally interesting is the fact that in spite of the growth in trade and population, the increasing number of convictions for theft, and the continual creation of new capital statutes throughout the eighteenth century, the number of executions for offences against property remained relatively stable, especially after 1750. . . .

Most historians and many contemporaries argued that the policy of terror was not working. More of those sentenced to death were pardoned than were hanged; thieves often escaped punishment through the absence of a police force, the leniency of prosecutors and juries, and the technicalities of the law; transported convicts were so little afraid that they often returned to England to pick pockets on hanging days; riot was endemic. The critics of the law argued that the gibbets and corpses paradoxically weakened the enforcement of the law: rather than terrifying criminals, the death penalty terrified prosecutors and juries, who feared committing judicial murder on the capital statutes. Sir Samuel Romilly and other reformers led a long and intelligent campaign for the repeal of some laws, arguing

from statistics that convictions would become more numerous once that fear was removed. The reformers also used the arguments of Beccaria, who suggested in 1764 that gross and capricious terror should be replaced by a fixed and graduated scale of more lenient but more certain punishments. His ideas were widely canvassed in England, as well as on the continent. Even Blackstone, the high priest of the English legal system, looked forward to changes on these lines. Yet Parliament resisted all reform. Not one capital statute was repealed until 1808, and real progress, had to wait until the 1820s and 1830s.

Why the contradiction? If property was so important, and reform of the criminal law would help to protect it, why did gentlemen not embrace reform? Given the apparently fierce intentions of the legislature, why was the law not changed to make enforcement more certain? Historians searching for the roots of the modern criminal law and the modern police usually devote most of their attention to the triumph of reform in the nineteenth century. But the victors in the eighteenth century were the conservatives, the hangers and gibbeters, and they resolutely ignored over fifty years of cogent criticism. . . .

. . .[T]he criminal law is as much concerned with authority as it is with property. For wealth does not exist outside a social context, theft is given definition only within a set of social relations, and the connections between property, power and authority are close and crucial. The criminal law was critically important in maintaining bonds of obedience and deference, in legitimizing the status quo, in constantly recreating the structure of authority which arose from property and in turn protected its interests.

But terror alone could never have accomplished those ends. It was the raw material of authority, but class interest and the structure of the law itself shaped it into a much more effective instrument of power. . . .

. . .[T]he criminal law was extremely important in ensuring, in his words, that 'opinion' prevailed over 'physical strength.' The opinion was that of the ruling class; the law was one of their chief ideological instruments.[8] It combined the terror worshipped by Nourse with the discretion stressed by Paley, and used both to mould the consciousness by which the many submitted to the few. Moreover, its effectiveness in doing so depended in large part on the very weaknesses and inconsistencies condemned by reformers and liberal historians. In considering the criminal law as an ideological system, we must look at how it combined imagery and force, ideals and practice, and try to see how it manifested itself to the mass of unpropertied Englishmen. We can distinguish three aspects of the law as ideology: majesty, justice and mercy. Understanding them will help us to explain the divergence between bloody legislation and declining executions, and the resistance to reform of any kind.

II

MAJESTY

. . .In the court room the judges' every action was governed by the importance of spectacle. Blackstone asserted that 'the novelty and very parade of . . .[their] appearance have no small influence upon the multitude':[9] scarlet robes lined with ermine and full-bottomed wigs in the seventeenth-century style, which evoked scorn from Hogarth but awe from ordinary men. The powers of light and darkness were summoned into the court with the black cap which was donned to pronounce sentence of death, and the spotless white gloves worn at the end of a 'maiden assize' when no prisoners were to be left for execution.

Within this elaborate ritual of the irrational, judge and counsel displayed their learning with an eloquence that often rivalled that of leading statesmen. There was an acute consciousness that the courts were platforms for addressing 'the multitude'. . . .

In its ritual, its judgements and its channelling of emotion the criminal law echoed many of the most powerful psychic components of religion. The judge might, as at Chelmsford, emulate the priest in his role of human agent, helpless but submissive before the demands of his deity. But the judge could play the role of deity as well, both the god of wrath and the merciful arbiter of men's fates. For the righteous accents of the death sentence were made even more impressive by the contrast with the treatment of the accused up to the moment of conviction. The judges' paternal concern for their prisoners was remarked upon by foreign visitors and deepened the analogy with the Christian God of justice and mercy. . . .

JUSTICE

'Justice' was an evocative word in the eighteenth century, and with good reason. The constitutional struggles of the seventeenth had helped to establish the principles of the rule of law: that offences should be fixed, not indeterminate; that rules of evidence should be carefully observed; that the law should be administered by a bench that was both learned and honest. These achievements were essential for the protection of the gentry from royal greed and royal tyranny, and for the regulation, in the civil side of the courts, of the details of conveyancing, entailing, contracting, devising, suing and releasing. Since the same judges administered the criminal law at its highest levels, on the same principles, even the poorest man was guaranteed justice in the high courts. Visitors remarked on the extreme solicitude of judges for the rights of the accused, a sharp distinction from the usual practice of continental benches. . . .

Equally important were the strict procedural rules which were enforced in the high courts and at assizes, especially in capital cases. Moreover, most penal statutes were interpreted by the judges in an extremely narrow and formalistic fashion. In part this was based on seventeenth-century practice, but as more capital statutes were passed in the eighteenth century the bench reacted with an increasingly narrow interpretation. Many prosecutions founded on excellent evidence and conducted at considerable expense failed on minor errors of form in the indictment, the written charge. If a name or date was incorrect, or if the accused was described as a 'farmer' rather than the approved term 'yeoman,' the prosecution could fail. The courts held that such defects were conclusive, and gentlemen attending trials as spectators sometimes stood up in court and brought errors to the attention of the judge. These formalisms in the criminal law seemed ridiculous to contemporary critics, and to many later historians. Their argument was (and is) that the criminal law, to be effective, must be known and determinate, instead of capricious and obscure. Prosecutors resented the waste of their time and money lost on a technicality; thieves were said to mock courts which allowed them to escape through so many verbal loopholes. But it seems likely that the mass of Englishmen drew other conclusions from the practice. The punctilious attention to forms, the dispassionate and legalistic exchanges between counsel and the judge, argued that those administering and using the laws submitted to its rules. The law thereby became something more than the creature of a ruling class—it became a power with its own claims, higher than those of prosecutor, lawyers, and even the great scarlet-robed assize judge himself. To them, too, of course, the law was The Law. The fact that they reined it, that they shut their eyes to its daily enactment in Parliament by men of their own class, heightened the illusion. When the ruling class acquitted men on technicalities they helped instill a belief in the disembodied justice of the law in the minds of all who watched. In short, its very inefficiency, its absurd formalism, was part of its strength as ideology.

'Equality before the law' also implied that no man was exempt from it. It was part of the lore of politics that in England social class did not preserve a man even from the extreme sanction of death. This was not, of course, true. But the impression made by the execution of a man of property or position was very deep. As executions for forgery became increasingly common throughout the century, more such respectable villains went to the gallows. . . .

Yet the idea of justice was always dangerous, straining the narrow definitions of the lawyers and the judges. It was easy to claim equal justice for murderers of all classes, where a universal moral sanction was more likely to be found, or in political cases, the necessary price of a constitution ruled by law. The trick was to extend that communal sanction to a criminal law that was nine-tenths concerned with upholding a radical division of property. Though Justice seemed impartial in crimes against the person, wrote Mandeville,

> Yet, it was thought, the sword she bore
> Check'd but the Desp'rate and the Poor;
> That, urged by mere Necessity,
> Were tied up to the wretched Tree
> For Crimes, which not deserv'd that Fate
> But to secure the Rich, and Great.[10]

In times of dearth, when the rulers of England were faced with food riots by men desperate with hunger and convinced of the rights of their case the contradiction could become acute. At such times two conceptions of justice stood in sharp opposition: an older, Christian version of natural rights, which guaranteed even the poorest man at least life; and the justice of the law of property, sanctioned by the settlements of the seventeenth century. . . .

The justice of English law was thus a powerful ideological weapon in the arsenal of conservatives during the French Revolution. Wicked Lord Ferrers, juries and *habeas corpus* were leading themes in anti-Jacobin popular literature. They were usually contrasted with tyrannical French aristocrats, the inquisitorial system of law and *lettres de cachet*. In countering the influence of Tom Paine, the conservatives repeatedly emphasized the central place of law in the English constitution. . . .

Eighteenth-century 'justice' was not, however, a nonsense. It remained a powerful and evocative word, even if it bore a much more limited meaning than a twentieth-century (or seventeenth-century) egalitarian would give it. In a society radically divided between rich and poor, the powerful and the powerless, the occasional victory of a cottager in the courts or the rare spectacle of a titled villain on the gallows made a sharp impression. Moreover, it would be wrong to suggest that the law had to be wholly consistent to persuade men of its legitimacy. 'Justice,' in the sense of rational, bureaucratic decisions made in the common interest, is a peculiarly modern conception. It was gaining ground in the eighteenth century. Most reformers worked to bring about such law, and of all schemes Jeremy Bentham's was the logical conclusion. Yet his plan for a criminal code that was precise, consistent and wholly enforced was alien to the thought of most eighteenth-century Englishmen. They tended to think of Justice in personal terms, and were more struck by understanding of individual cases than by the delights of abstract schemes. Where authority is embodied in direct personal relationships, men will often accept power even enormous, despotic power, when it comes from the 'good King,' the-father of his people, who tempers justice with mercy. A form of this powerful psychic configuration was one of the most distinctive aspects of the unreformed criminal law. Bentham could not understand it, but it was the law's greatest strength as an ideological system, especially among the poor, and in the countryside.

MERCY

The prerogative of mercy ran throughout the administration of the criminal law, from the lowest to the highest level. At the top sat the high court judges, and their free use of the royal pardon became a crucial argument in the arsenal of conservatives opposing reform. At the lowest Jurisdiction, that of the Justice of the Peace, the same discretion allowed the magistrate to make decisions that sometimes escaped legal categories altogether. Although he frequently made obeisance to the rules when convicting, as we have seen, he could dispense with them when pardoning, and the absence of a jury made it even easier for him to do so. Latitude in the direction of mercy caused some critics to complain that many justices, partly from laziness or carelessness 'but frequently from benevolent views improperly indulged,' judged cases 'partly or entirely by their own unauthorized ideas of equity.' This element of discretion impressed Weber when he examined the office of JP. He compared it to Arabic 'khadi justice'—a formalistic administration of law that was nevertheless based on ethical or practical judgements rather than on a fixed, 'rational' set of rules. It could combine rigid tradition with 'a sphere of free discretion and grace of the ruler.'[11] Thus it allowed the paternalist JP to compose quarrels, intervene with prosecutors on behalf of culprits, and in the final instance to dismiss a case entirely. The right of the pardon was not limited, however, to high court judges and Justices of the Peace. The mode of prosecution, the manner of trial and the treatment of condemned convicts gave some of the same power to all men of property. 'Irrationality,' in the sense used by Weber, and the 'grace of the ruler' which grew from it pervaded the entire administration of the law. . . .

. . .There is a danger, which perhaps this essay has not avoided, of giving the impression that a system of authority is *something* rather than the actions of living men. The invisible hand of Adam Smith's political economy was metaphor, shorthand for an effect rather than a cause; it was a description of recurrent patterns of useful behaviour forged out of the energy, conflicts and greed of thousands of individuals in a capitalist market. In a somewhat similar way, much of the ideological structure surrounding the criminal law was the product of countless short-term decisions. It was often a question of intuition, and of trial and error. In handling a mob it was useful to appeal to ideals of English justice: but that was a lesson that was slowly learned over many generations, and rarely raised to the level of theory. The necessity of gauging reactions to executions was an immediate problem of public order, not a plot worked out by eighteenth-century experts in public relations for a fee. The difficulty for the historian of the law is twofold. He must make explicit convictions that were often unspoken, for if left unspoken we cannot understand the actions of the men who held them.[12] Yet in describing how convictions and actions moulded the administration of justice, he must never forget that history is made by men, not by the Cunning of Reason or the Cunning of System. The course of history is the result of a complex of human actions—purposive, accidental, sometimes determined—and it cannot be reduced to one transcendent purpose. The cunning of a ruling class is a more substantial concept, however, for such a group of men is agreed on ultimate ends. However much they believed in justice (and they did); however sacred they held property (and they worshipped it); however merciful they were to the poor (and many were); the gentlemen of England knew that their duty was, above all, to rule. On that depended everything. They acted accordingly. . . .

Many historians, confronted with the hegemony of the eighteenth-century ruling class, have described it in terms of absolute control and paternal benevolence. Max Beloff argued that after the Restoration they enjoyed an unparalleled sense of security which explained 'the leniency with which isolated disturbances were on the whole treated, when compared with the ferocity shown by the same class towards their social inferiors in the times of the Tudors and early Stuarts.'[13] It seems more likely that the relative insecurity of England's governors, their crucial dependence on the deference of the governed, compelled them to moderate that ferocity. More recent writing has stressed the importance of patronage[.] . . .

Yet it is difficult to understand how those loyalties endured when patronage was uneven, interrupted, often capricious. Many contemporaries testified to the fickleness of wealth: disappointed office-seekers, unemployed labourers or weavers, paupers dumped over parish boundaries. Riot was a commonplace; so too were hangings. Benevolence, in short, was not a simple positive act: it contained within it the ever-present threat of malice. In economic relations a landlord keeping his rents low was benevolent because he could, with impunity, raise them. A justice giving charity to a wandering beggar was benevolent because he could whip him instead. Benevolence, all patronage, was given meaning by its contingency. It was the obverse of coercion, terror's conspiracy of silence. When patronage failed, force could be invoked; but when coercion inflamed men's minds, at the crucial moment mercy could calm them.

A ruling class organizes its power in the state. The sanction of the state is force, but it is force that is legitimized, however imperfectly, and therefore the state deals also in ideologies. Loyalties do not grow simply in complex societies: they are twisted, invoked and often consciously created. Eighteenth-century England was not a free market of patronage relations. It was a society with a bloody penal code, an astute ruling class who manipulated it to their advantage, and a people schooled in the lessons of Justice, Terror and Mercy. The benevolence of rich men to poor, and all the ramifications of patronage, were upheld by the sanction of the gallows and the rhetoric of the death sentence.

Notes

1. Martin Madan, *Thoughts on Executive Justice with Respect to Our Criminal Laws, Particularly on the Circuit*, 1785, pp. 26–30.

2. Edward Christian, *Charges Delivered to Grand Juries in the Isle of Ely*, 1819, pp. 259.

3. Sir Leon Radzinowicz, *A History of English Criminal Law and Its Administration From 1750*, 4 vols., 1948–68, vol. I, p. 4.

4. William Blackstone, *Commentaries on the Laws of England* (12th ed. by Edward Christian), 1793–1795, vol. II, p. 2.

5. John Holliday, *The Life of Lord Mansfield*, 1797, p. 149.

6. The extension of benefit of clergy (the right to a lesser sentence of transportation on first conviction for the capital crime of grand larceny) made it increasingly possible to avoid the gallows. The development of clergy since the sixteenth century was countered in the eighteenth by many statutes removing it from particular kinds of larceny. Other capital statutes at the same time extended the death penalty to offences never punished so severely before.

7. The figures are inexact and inconsistent but it appears that the average number of executions per year was 140 in London and Middlesex in the years 1607–1616 and 33 per year for the period 1749–1809. The eighteenth-century figures vary from a low decadal average of 21 (1790–1799) to a maximum of 53 (1790–1889); Radzinowicz, vol. I, pp. 141, 147, citing Jeaffreson and the *Report* from the Select Committee on Criminal Laws, 1819. The numbers of executions in Devon between 1598 and 1639 were also as high as 74 a year; J. S. Cockburn, *A History of English Assizes, 1598–1714,* Cambridge, 1972, PP. 94–96.

8. By ideology I mean 'a specific set of ideas designed to vindicate or disguise class interest . . ., A. Gerschenkron, *Continuity in History and Other Essays,* Cambridge, Mass., 1968, p. 65.

9. Blackstone, *Commentaries,* vol. III, p. 356.

10. *The Fable of the Bees,* 1705.

11. *From Max Weber,* ed. H. H. Gerth and C. Wright Mills, 1970, pp. 216–221. Brougham anticipated Weber in 1828, declaring 'there is not a worse-constituted tribunal on the face of the earth, not even that of the Turkish Cadi, than that at which summary convictions on the Game Laws constantly take place; I mean a bench or a brace of sporting justices': see J. L. and Barbara Hammond, *The Village Labourer* (1911), 1966, p. 188.

12. Those who describe beliefs that are widely held but seldom expressed are often unrepresentative figures. Nourse was an Anglican cleric who converted to Roman Catholicism and literature, Madan another eccentric clergyman whose call for more hangings was repudiated by the judges. The Evangelicals (More, Gisborne) were often embarrassingly direct in their social prescriptions, Cottu was a foreigner, and Christian was a long-winded, egotistical bore. For these reasons they sometimes raised in arguent points that more conventional men thought banal or indiscreet, or did not think consciously of at all.

13. Max Beloff, *Public Order and Popular Disturbances 1660–1714,* 1938, p. 154.

Notes and Questions

1. What was the relationship between authority and property in eighteenth-century England? How did this social relationship affect the structure and implementation of the law?

2. What does Hay mean when he describes "law as ideology" in eighteenth-century England? What were the three most important tools for executing this type of law? How did each of the three tools contribute to what Hay describes as the "divergence between bloody legislation and declining executions"?

3. Hay points out, "When the ruling class acquitted men on technicalities they helped instill a belief in the disembodied justice of the law in the minds of all who watched." How did judicial procedure build and perpetuate these illusions in the minds of citizens? Were these illusions a good thing for the propertyless classes? For the society as a whole? What did justice mean to members of different classes?

4. In what way does Hay's account of class conflict in eighteenth-century England reflect Hobbes' and Turk's (Chapters 7, 8) ideas about law's purpose? How did the British legal system enable and perpetuate an extremely unequal distribution of wealth? Was this just? In your

opinion, does Hay's account lend more support to Hobbes' ideas of law based on consent or to Turk's picture of law's coercion?

5. The property-owning class in eighteenth-century England defied critics, relying more upon the harsh threats of a voluminous criminal code than it did upon the consistent application of the appropriate statutory punishment. Does this undermine Hobbes' warning that "Covenants without the sword are but words, and of no strength to secure man at all"? Why or why not?

6. What parallels, if any, do you see between contemporary American legal practices and Hay's depiction of eigh-

teenth-century legal practice? Explain. How effectively are leniency and severe punishment used in contemporary American law to serve the purposes of justice and order?

7. In your opinion, how much discretion should agents of the law (e.g., judges, police) have in enforcing criminal statutes? When left to their own discretion, what criteria should they use to choose between severe punishment and leniency?

Reprinted from: Douglas Hay, "Property, Authority and the Criminal Law" from *Albion's Fatal Tree*, pp. 17–18, 19, 22, 23, 26, 27, 29, 32–33, 35, 37, 39–40, 52–53, 61–63. Copyright © 1975 by Douglas Hay. Reprinted with the permission of Douglas Hay. ✦

Chapter 14

Violence and the Word

Robert M. Cover

Robert M. Cover's "Violence and the Word" lays out a framework for understanding the social organization of law's violence. Cover argues that law should operate as a top-down, hierarchically controlled machinery for the deployment of violence. Judges sit on the top of that machinery, interpreting rules, and determining when and against whom violence should be applied. Others (e.g., police, prosecutors, wardens) should, in Cover's view, respond to judicial decisions and rulings as if they were commands, following them to the letter.

As the readings by Thomas Hobbes (Chapter 7) and Douglas Hay (Chapter 13) make clear, law seeks to work in the world by organizing and deploying coercive force and violence. Law is socially organized in the sense that it is itself a complex bureaucracy designed to authorize and implement violence. Law's violence is different and preferable to extralegal violence, in part because it is more orderly, more organized, and because the violence that law deploys is governed by common, normative standards.

To understand law, we must understand its complex bureaucratic structure. We must attend to the capacity of judges and other officials to control the violence that is done in law's name: violence deployed by the police against citizens, violence that constitutes the system of criminal punishment. Those who authorize law's violence are not typically those who impose it. In every legal system there is the need to develop mechanisms of coordination and control such that authorization and action proceed harmoniously. But this sets up another dilemma for law. If these mechanisms of coordination and control are too rigidly hierarchical, law will be inflexible and unable to proceed in a responsive manner. On the other hand, if they are not hierarchical enough, law's violence will be undisciplined and unresponsive to the rules and standards that govern it.

INTRODUCTION: THE VIOLENCE OF LEGAL ACTS

Legal interpretation[1] takes place in a field of pain and death. This is true in several senses. Legal interpretive acts signal and occasion the imposition of violence upon others: A judge articulates her understanding of a text, and as a result, somebody loses his freedom, his property, his children, even his life. Interpretations in law also constitute justifications for violence which has already occurred or which is about to occur. When interpreters have finished their work, they frequently leave behind victims whose lives have been torn apart by these organized, social practices of violence. Neither legal interpretation nor the violence it occasions may be properly understood apart from one another. This much is obvious, though the growing literature that argues for the centrality of interpretive practices in law blithely ignores it.[2] . . .

There are societies in which contrition or shame control defendants' behavior to a greater extent than does violence. Such societies require and have received their own distinctive form of analysis.[3] But I think it is unquestionably the case in the United States that most prisoners walk into prison because they know they will be dragged or beaten into prison if they do not walk. They do not organize force against being dragged because they know that if they wage this kind of battle they will lose—very possibly lose their lives.

If I have exhibited some sense of sympathy for the victims of this violence, it is misleading. Very often the balance of terror in this regard is just as I would want it. But I do not wish us to pretend that we talk our prisoners into jail. The "interpretations" or "conversations" that are the reconditions for violent incarceration are themselves implements of violence. To obscure this fact is precisely analogous to ignoring the background screams or visible instruments of torture in an inquisitor's interrogation. The experience of the prisoner is, from the outset, an experience of being violently dominated, and it is colored from the beginning by the fear of being violently treated.[4]

The violence of the act of sentencing is most obvious when observed from the defendant's perspective. Therefore, any account which seeks to downplay the violence or elevate the interpretive character or meaning of the event within a community of shared values will tend to ignore the prisoner or defendant and focus upon the judge and the judicial interpretive act. Beginning with broad interpretive categories such as "blame" or "punishment," meaning is created for the event which justifies the judge to herself and to others with respect to her role in the acts of violence. I do not wish to downplay the significance of such ideological functions of law. But the function of ideology is much more significant in justifying an order to those who principally benefit from it and who must defend it than it is in hiding the nature of the order from those who are its victims. . . .

There is, however, a fundamental difference between the way in which "punishment" operates as an ideology in popular or professional literature, in political debate, or in general discourse, and the way in which it operates in the context of the legal acts of trial,

imposition of sentence, and execution. For as the judge interprets, using the concept of punishment, she also acts—through others—to restrain, hurt, render helpless, even kill the prisoner. Thus, any commonality of interpretation that may or may not be achieved is one that has its common meaning destroyed by the divergent experiences that constitute it. Just as the torturer and victim achieve a "shared" world only by virtue of their diametrically opposed experiences, so the judge and prisoner understand "punishment" through their diametrically opposed experiences of the punishing act. It is ultimately irrelevant whether the torturer and his victim share a common theoretical view on the justifications for torture—outside the torture room. They still have come to the confession through destroying in the one case and through having been destroyed in the other. Similarly, whether or not the judge and prisoner share the same philosophy of punishment, they arrive at the particular act of punishment having dominated and having been dominated with violence, respectively.

THE ACTS OF JUDGES: INTERPRETATIONS, DEEDS AND ROLES

We begin, then, not with what the judges say, but with what they do.

> The judges deal pain and death. That is not all that they do. Perhaps that is not what they usually do. But they *do* deal death, and pain. From John Winthrop through Warren Burger they have sat atop a pyramid of violence, dealing. . . .

In this they are different from poets, from critics, from artists. It will not do to insist on the violence of strong poetry, and strong poets. Even the violence of weak judges is utterly real—a naive but immediate reality, in need of no interpretation, no critic to reveal it. Every prisoner displays its mark. Whether or not the violence of judges is justified is not now the point—only that it exists in fact and differs from the violence that exists in literature or in the metaphoric characterizations of literary critics and philosophers. I have written elsewhere that judges of the state are jurispathic—that they kill the diverse legal traditions that compete with the State.[5] Here, however, I am not writing of the jurispathic quality of the office, but of its homicidal potential.[6]

The dual emphasis on the acts of judges and on the violence of these acts leads to consideration of three characteristics of the interpretive dimension of judicial behavior. Legal interpretation is (1) a practical activity, (2) designed to generate credible threats and actual deeds of violence, (3) in an effective way. In order to explore the unseverable connection between legal interpretation and violence, each of these three elements must be examined in turn.

LEGAL INTERPRETATION AS A PRACTICAL ACTIVITY

Legal interpretation is a form of practical wisdom. . . .

Legal interpretation is practical activity in quite another sense, however. The judicial word is a mandate for the deeds of others. Were that not the case, the practical objectives of the deliberative process could be achieved, if at all, only through more indirect and risky means. The context of a judicial utterance is institutional behavior in which others, occupying preexisting roles, can be expected to act, to implement, or otherwise to respond in a specified way to the judge's interpretation. Thus, the institutional context ties the language act of practical understanding to the physical acts of others in a predictable, though not logically necessary, way. These interpretations, then, are not only "practical," they are, themselves, practices.

INTERPRETATION WITHIN A SYSTEM DESIGNED TO GENERATE VIOLENCE

Because legal interpretation is as a practice incomplete without violence—because it de-

pends upon the social practice of violence for its efficacy—it must be related in a strong way to the cues that operate to bypass or suppress the psycho-social mechanisms that usually inhibit people's actions causing pain and death. Interpretations which occasion violence are distinct from the violent acts they occasion. When judges interpret the law in an official context, we expect a close relationship to be revealed or established between their words and the acts that they mandate. That is, we expect the judge's words to serve as virtual triggers for action. We would not, for example, expect contemplations or deliberations on the part of jailers and wardens to interfere with the action authorized by judicial words. But such a routinization of violent behavior requires a form of organization that operates simultaneously in the domains of action and interpretation. In order to understand the violence of a judge's interpretive act, we must also understand the way in which it is transformed into a violent deed despite general resistance to such deeds; in order to comprehend the meaning of this violent deed, we must also understand in what way the judge's interpretive act authorizes and legitimates it. . . .

INTERPRETATION AND THE EFFECTIVE ORGANIZATION OF VIOLENCE

A third factor separates the authorization of violence as a deliberative, interpretive exercise from the deed. Deeds of violence are rarely suffered by the victim apart from a setting of domination.[7] That setting may be manifestly coercive and violent or it may be the product of a history of violence which conditions the expectations of the actors. The imposition of violence depends upon the satisfaction of the social preconditions for its effectiveness. Few of us are courageous or foolhardy enough to act violently in an uncompromisingly principled fashion without attention to the likely responses from those upon whom we would impose our wills.[8]

If legal interpretation entails action in a field of pain and death, we must expect, therefore, to find in the act of interpretation attention to the *conditions of effective domination*. To the extent that effective domination is not present, either our understanding of the law will be adjusted so that it will require only that which can reasonably be expected from people in conditions of reprisal, resistance and revenge,[9] or there will be a crisis of credibility. The law may come over time to bear only an uncertain relation to the institutionally implemented deeds it authorizes. Some systems, especially religious ones, can perpetuate and even profit from a dichotomy between an ideal law and a realizable one.[10] But such a dichotomy has immense implications *if built into* the law. In our own secular legal system, one must assume this to be an undesirable development.

LEGAL INTERPRETATION AS BONDED INTERPRETATION

Legal interpretation, therefore, can never be "free;" it can never be the function of an understanding of the text or word alone. Nor can it be a simple function of what the interpreter conceives to be merely a reading of the "social text," a reading of all relevant social data. Legal interpretation must be capable of transforming itself into action; it must be capable of overcoming inhibitions against violence in order to generate its requisite deeds; it must be capable of massing a sufficient degree of violence to deter reprisal and revenge.

In order to maintain these critical links to effective violent behavior, legal interpretation must reflexively consider its own social organization. In so reflecting, the interpreter thereby surrenders something of his independence of mind and autonomy of judgment, since the legal meaning that some hypothetical Hercules (Hyporcules) might construct out of the sea of our legal and social texts is only one element in the institutional practice we call law. Coherent legal meaning is an element in legal interpretation. But it is an element potentially in tension with the need to generate effective action in a violent context. And neither effective action nor coherent meaning can be maintained, separately or together, without an entire structure of social cooperation. Thus, legal interpretation is a form of bonded interpretation, bound at once to practical application (to the deeds it implies) and to the ecology of jurisdictional roles (the conditions of effective domination). The bonds are reciprocal. For the deeds of social violence as we know them also require that they be rendered intelligible—that they be both subject to interpretation and to the specialized and constrained forms of behavior that are "roles." And the behavior within roles that we expect can neither exist without the interpretations which explain the otherwise meaningless patterns of strong action and inaction, nor be intelligible without understanding the deeds they are designed to effectuate.

Legal interpretation may be the act of judges or citizens, legislators or presidents, draft resisters or right-to-life protesters. Each kind of interpreter speaks from a distinct institutional location. Each has a differing perspective on factual and moral implications of any given understanding of the Constitution. The understanding of each will vary as roles and moral commitments vary. But considerations of word, deed, and role will always be present in some degree. The relationships among these three considerations are created by the practical, violent context of the practice of legal interpretation, and therefore constitute the most significant aspect of the legal interpretive process. . . .

Such a well-coordinated form of violence is an achievement. The careful social understandings designed to accomplish the violence that is capital punishment, or to refrain from that act, are not fortuitous or casual products of circumstance. Rather, they are the products of design, tied closely to the secondary rules and principles which provide clear criteria for the recognition of these and other interpretive acts as, first and foremost, *judicial* acts. Their "meaning" is always secondary to their provenance. No wardens, guards or executioners wait for a telephone call from the latest constitutional law scholar, jurisprude or critic before executing prisoners, no matter how compelling the interpretations of these others may be. And, indeed, they await the word of judges only insofar as that word carries with it the formal indicia of having been spoken in the judicial capacity. The social cooperation critical to the constitutional form of cooperation in violence is, therefore, also predicated upon the recognition of the judicial role and the recognition of the one whose utterance performs it.

There are, of course, some situations in which the judicial role is not well-defined but is contested. Nonetheless, social cooperation in constitutional violence as we know it requires at least that it be very clear who speaks as a judge and when. The hierarchical ordering among judicial voices must also be clear or subject to clarification. We have established, then, the necessity for rules and principles that locate authoritative interpreters and prescribe action on the basis of what they say. The rules and principles that locate authoritative voices for the purposes of action point to the defect in a model of judicial interpretation that centers around a single coherent and consistent mind at work. For here in the United States there is no set of secondary rules and principles more fundamental than those which make it impossible for any single judge, however Herculean her understanding of the law, ever to have the last word on legal meaning as it affects real cases. In the United States—with only trivial exceptions—no judge sitting alone on a significant legal issue is immune from appellate review. Conversely, whenever any judge sits on the court of last resort on a significant legal issue, that judge does not sit alone. A complex of secondary rules determines this situation. These rules range from the statutes which generally give a right to at least one appeal from final judgments of trial courts, to special statutes which

require that there be appellate review of death sentences, to the constitutional guarantee that the writ of habeas corpus not be suspended.[11] Final appellate courts in the United States have always had at least three judges. Some state constitutions specify the number. No explicit provision in the United States Constitution defines the Supreme Court in such a way that requires that it be made up of more than a single judge. But both invariant practice and basic understandings since 1789 have made the idea of a single-Justive Supreme Court a practical absurdity. Given the clarity of the expectation that Supreme judicial bodies be plural, it seems doubtful to me whether such an imaginary Court should be held to satisfy the constitutional requirement that there be a Supreme Court.[12]

If some hypothetical Herculean judge should achieve an understanding of constitutional and social texts—an interpretation—such that she felt the death penalty to be a permissible and appropriate punishment in a particular case, she would be confronted at once with the problem of translating that conviction into a deed. Her very understanding of the constitutionality of the death penalty and the appropriateness of its imposition would carry with it—as part of the understanding—the knowledge that she could not carry out the sentence herself. The most elementary understanding of our social practice of violence ensures that a judge know that she herself cannot actually pull the switch. This is not a trivial convention. For it means that someone else will have the duty and opportunity to pass upon what the judge has done. Were the judge a trial judge, and should she hand down an order to execute, there would be another judge to whom application could be made to stay or reverse her decision. The fact that someone else has to carry out the execution means that this someone else may be confronted with two pieces of paper: let us say a warrant for execution of the sentence of death at a specified time and place and a stay of execution from an appellate tribunal. The someone else—the warden, for simplicity's sake—is expected to determine which of these two pieces of paper to act upon according to some highly arbitrary, hierarchical principles which have nothing to do with the relative merits or demerits of the arguments which justify the respective substantive positions.

It is crucial to note here that if the warden should cease paying relatively automatic heed to the pieces of paper which flow in from the judges according to these arbitrary and sometimes rigid hierarchical rules and principles, the judges would lose their capacity to do violence. They would be left with only the opportunity to persuade the warden and his men to do violence. Conversely, the warden and his men would lose their capacity to shift to the judge primary moral responsibility for the violence which they themselves carry out. They would have to pass upon the justifications for violence in every case themselves, thereby turning the trial into a sort of preliminary hearing. There are, indeed, many prisons in this world that bear some resemblance to this hypothetical situation. There are systems in which the most significant punishment decisions are made by those who either perform or have direct supervisory authority over the performance of the violence itself.

We have done something strange in our system. We have rigidly separated the act of interpretation—of understanding what ought to be done—from the carrying out of this "ought to be done" through violence. At the same time we have, at least in the criminal law, rigidly linked the carrying out of judicial orders to the act of judicial interpretation by relatively inflexible hierarchies of judicial utterances and firm obligations on the part of penal officials to heed them. Judges are both separated from, and inextricably linked to, the acts they authorize. . . .

So let us be explicit. If it seems a nasty thought that death and pain are at the center of legal interpretation, so be it. It would not be better were there only a community of argu-

ment, of readers and writers of texts, of interpreters. As long as death and pain are part of our political world, it is essential that they be at the center of the law. The alternative is truly unacceptable—that they be within our polity but outside the discipline of the *collective* decision rules and the individual efforts to achieve outcomes through those rules. The fact that we require many voices is not, then, an accident or peculiarity of our jurisdictional rules. It is intrinsic to whatever achievement is possible in the domesticating of violence.

CONCLUSION

There is a worthy tradition that would have us hear the judge as a voice of reason; see her as the embodiment of principle. The current academic interest in interpretation, the attention to community of meaning and commitment, is apologetic neither in its intent or effect. The trend is, by and large, an attempt to hold a worthy ideal before what all would agree is an unredeemed reality. I would not quarrel with the impulse that leads us to this form of criticism.

There is, however, danger in forgetting the limits which are intrinsic to this activity of legal interpretation; in exaggerating the extent to which any interpretation rendered as part of the act of state violence can ever constitute a common and coherent meaning. I have emphasized two rather different kinds of limits to the commonality and coherence of meaning that can be achieved. One kind of limit is a practical one which follows from the social organization of legal violence. We have seen that in order to do that violence safely and effectively, responsibility for the violence must be shared; law must operate as a system of cues and signals to many actors who would otherwise be unwilling, incapable or irresponsible in their violent acts. This social organization of violence manifests itself in the secondary rules and principles which generally ensure that no single mind and no single will can generate the violent outcomes that follow from interpretive commitments. No single individual can render any interpretation operative as law—as authority for the violent act. While a convergence of understandings on the part of all relevant legal actors is not necessarily impossible, it is, in fact, very unlikely. And, of course, we cannot flee from the multiplicity of minds and voices that the social organization of law-as-violence requires to some hypothetical decision process that would aggregate the many voices into one. We know that—aside from dictatorship—there is no aggregation rule that will necessarily meet elementary conditions for rationality in the relationships among the social choices made.

While our social decision rules cannot guarantee coherence and rationality of meaning, they can and do generate violent action which may well have a distinct coherent meaning for at least one of the relevant actors. We are left, then, in this actual world of the organization of law-as-violence with decisions whose meaning is not likely to be coherent if it is common, and not likely to be common if it is coherent.

This practical, contingent limit upon legal interpretation is, however, the less important and less profound of the two kinds of limits I have presented. For if we truly attend to legal interpretation as it is practiced on the field of fear, pain, and death, we find that the principal impediment to the achievement of common and coherent meaning is a necessary limit, intrinsic to the activity. Judges, officials, resisters, martyrs, wardens, convicts, may or may not share common texts; they may or may not share a common vocabulary, a common cultural store of gestures and rituals; they may or may not share a common philosophical framework. There will be in the immense human panorama a continuum of degrees of commonality in all of the above. But as long as legal interpretation is constitutive of violent behavior as well as meaning, as long as people are committed to using or resisting the social organizations of violence in making

their interpretations real, there will always be a tragic limit to the common meaning that can be achieved.

The perpetrator and victim of organized violence will undergo achingly disparate significant experiences. For the perpetrator, the pain and fear are remote, unreal, and largely unshared. They are, therefore, almost never made a part of the interpretive artifact, such as the judicial opinion. On the other hand, for those who impose the violence the justification is important, real and carefully cultivated. Conversely, for the victim, the justification for the violence recedes in reality and significance in proportion to the overwhelming reality of the pain and fear that is suffered.

Between the idea and the reality of common meaning falls the shadow of the violence of law, itself.

Notes

1. I have used the term "legal interpretation" throughout this essay, though my argument is directed principally to the interpretive acts of judges. To this specifically *judicial* interpretation my analysis of institutional action applies with special force. Nonetheless, I believe the more general term "legal interpretation" is warranted, for it is my position that the violence which judges deploy as instruments of a modern nation-state necessarily engages anyone who interprets the law in a course of conduct that entails either the perpetration or the suffering of this violence.

2. There has been a recent explosion of legal scholarship placing interpretation at the crux of the enterprise of law. A fair sampling of that work may be seen in the various articles that have appeared in two symposia. *Symposium: Law and Literature,* 60 TEX. L. REV. 373 (1982); *Interpretation Symposium,* 58 S. CALIF. L. REV. 1 (1985) (published in two issues). The intense interest in "interpretation" or "hermeneutics" in recent legal scholarship is quite a different phenomenon from the traditional set of questions about how a particular word, phrase, or instrument should be given effect in some particular context. It is, rather, the study of what I have called "a nor-

mative universe . . . held together by . . . interpretive commitments . . ." Cover, *The Supreme Court, 1982 Term—Foreword: Nomos and Narrative*, 97 HARV. L. REV. 4, 7 (1983). Or, in Ronald Dworkin's words, it is the study of the effort "to impose meaning on the institution . . . and then to restructure it in the light of that meaning." R. DWORKIN, LAW'S EMPIRE 47 (1986) [emphasis in original]. Dworkin, in *Law's Empire,* has written the most elaborate and sophisticated jurisprudence which places the meaning-giving, constructive dimension of interpretation at the heart of law. James Boyd White has been another eloquent voice claiming primacy for what he has called the "culture of argument." White has raised rhetoric to the pinnacle of jurisprudence. See J. B. WHITE, WHEN WORDS LOSE THEIR MEANING (1984); J. B. WHITE, HERACLES' BOW (1985).

The violent side of law and its connection to interpretation and rhetoric is systematically ignored or underplayed in the work of both Dworkin and White. White, in chapter nine of *Heracles' Bow,* comes closest to the concerns of this essay. He launches a critique of the practice of criminal law in terms of its unintelligibility as a "system of meaning" in the absence of significant reforms. White does not see violence as central to the breakdown of the system of meaning. But he does contrast what the judge says with what he does in the saying of it. Still, White reiterates in this book his central claim that "law . . . is best regarded not as a machine for social control, but as what I call a system of constitutive rhetoric: a set of resources for claiming, resisting, and declaring significance." Id. at 205. I do not deny that law is all those things that White claims, but I insist that it is those things in the context of the organized social practice of violence. And the "significance" or meaning that is achieved must be experienced or understood in vastly different ways depending upon whether one suffers that violence or not. In *Nomos and Narrative,* I also emphasized the world-building character of interpretive commitments in law. However, the thrust of *Nomos* was that the creation of legal meaning is an essentially cultural activity which takes place (or *best* takes place) among smallish groups. Such meaning-creating activity is not

naturally coextensive with the range of effective violence used to achieve social control. Thus, because law is the attempt to build future worlds, the essential tension in law is between the elaboration of legal meaning and the exercise of or resistance to the violence of social control. Cover, supra, at 18: "[T]here is a radical dichotomy between the social organization of law as power and the organization of law as meaning." This essay elaborates the senses in which the traditional forms of legal decision cannot be easily captured by the idea of interpretation understood as interpretation normally is in literature, the arts, or the humanities.

3. On the distinction between "shame cultures" and "guilt cultures," see generally E. DODDS, THE GREEKS AND THE IRRATIONAL (1951), and J. REDFIELD, NATURE AND CULTURE IN THE ILIAD (1975). For an analysis of a modern "shame culture," see R. BENEDICT, THE CHRYSANTHEMUM AND THE SWORD: PATTERNS OF JAPANESE CULTURE (1946).

4. This point and others very similar to it are made routinely in the literature that comes out of prisons. See, e.g., E. CLEAVER, SOUL ON ICE 128–130 (1968); J. WASHINGTON, A BRIGHT SPOT IN THE YARD: NOTES & STORIES FROM A PRISON JOURNAL 5 (1981).

5. Cover, supra note 2, at 40–44.

6. The violence of judges and officials of a posited constitutional order is generally understood to be implicit in the practice of law and government. Violence is so intrinsic to this activity, so taken for granted, that it need not be mentioned. For instance, read the Constitution. Nowhere does it state, as a general principle, the obvious—that the government thereby ordained and established has the power to practice violence over its people. That, as a general proposition, need not be stated, for it is understood in the very idea of government. It is, of course, also directly implicit in many of the specific powers granted to the general government or to some specified branch or official of it. E.g., U.S. CONST. art. I, § 8, cl. 1 ("Power To lay and collect Taxes . . . and provide for the common Defence"); id., cl. 6 ("To provide for the Punish-

ment of counterfeiting"); id., cl. 10 ("To define and punish Piracies"); id., cl. 11 ("To declare War"); id., cl. 15 ("To provide for calling forth the Militia to execute the Laws of the Union, suppress Insurrections and repel Invasions"); id., art. IV, § 2, cls. 2–3 (providing for rendition of fugitives from justice and service).

7. My colleague, Harlon Dalton, reports a view among some people who have clerked for judges on the Second Circuit Court of Appeals that the judges seem reluctant to affirm convictions from the bench when they believe the defendant to be in the courtroom. Dalton suggests two reasons for the tendency to reserve decision in such cases. First, the judges desire to give the appearance of deliberation in order to minimize, to the extent possible, the loser's dissatisfaction with the outcome; second, and more important, the judges desire to avoid having a disgruntled defendant (whose inhibitions against perpetrating violence are not what they might be) decide to "approach the bench," as it were. Dalton relates the scene he witnessed when clerking for a then-quite-new district judge who made the mistake of pronouncing sentence in the small robing room behind the courtroom. (The courtroom was temporarily unavailable for one reason or another.) The defendant's request that his family be present during sentencing was of course granted. As a result, the judge had to confront a weeping wife, dejected children, a lawyer who was now able to emote on an intimate stage, and a defendant who was able to give his allocution eye-to-eye with the judge from a distance of, at most, ten feet. It was impossible, therefore, for the judge to hide or insulate himself from the violence that would flow from the words he was about to utter, and he was visibly shaken as he pronounced sentence. Even so, neither he nor Dalton was prepared for what followed. The defendant began alternately shouting and begging the judge to change his mind; his wife began sobbing loudly; the defendant lurched forward with no apparent purpose in mind except, literally, to get to the judge who was doing this awful thing to him. Because the seating in the robing room was not designed with security in mind, it took the marshall a

moment or two—a long moment or two—to restrain the defendant. Then, because the room's only exit was behind where the defendant and his family had been seated, the judge had to wait until they were, respectively, forced and importuned to leave before he could make his exit, thus witnessing first hand how his words were translated into deeds. I am grateful to Harlon Dalton for these accounts.

8. It is the fantasy of so acting which accounts for the attraction of so many violent heroes. Where systems of deterrence and justice do in fact depend, or have depended, upon his risk acts of violence, there have been great temptations to avoid too high principles. In many feuding societies the principle social problem appears not to have been how to stop feuds, but how to get reluctant protagonists to act in such a manner as to protect vulnerable members or avenge them. W. Miller, *Choosing the Avenger: Some Aspects of the Bloodfeud in Medieval Iceland and England*, 1 LAW AND HIST. REV. 159, 160–162, 175 (1983).

9. See the corpus of Miller's work on the Icelandic feuds. Id. at 175–194. See also W. Miller, *Gift, Sale, Payment, Raid: Case Studies in the Negotiation and Classification of Exchange in Medieval Iceland*, 61 SPECULUM 18–50 (1986); cf. E. AYERS, VENGEANCE AND JUSTICE: CRIME AND PUNISHMENT IN THE 19TH CENTURY AMERICAN SOUTH 18 (1984) ("Honor and legalism . . . are incompatible. . . .").

10. For example, the account of the dispute within Shi'ite legal theory as to whether it was permissible to set up an avowedly Shiah government before the advent of the Twelfth Imam reflects this dichotomy in a religious context. See R. MOTTAHEDEH, THE MANTLE OF THE PROPHET: RELIGION AND POLITICS IN IRAN 172–173 (1985). According to Shi'ite belief, only the advent of this "Imam of the age" would bring the possibility of a perfect Islamic political community. Id. At 92–93.

11. See, e.g., 28 U.S.C. § 1291 (1982) (providing for appeals as of right from final decisions of district courts); id. §§ 46(b), 46(c) (providing for hearing of cases by U.S. Courts of Appeals in panels of three judges unless rehearing en

banc is ordered); U.S. CONST. art. I, § 9, cl. 2 (protecting writ of habeus corpus).

12. 28 U.S.C. § 1 (1982) (providing for Supreme Court of nine Justices, of whom six constitute a quorum). The one rather significant historical exception to the generalization in the text gives me some pause with respect to the conclusion about the constitutionality of a single-justice Supreme Court. It is true, of course, that the Chancellor was, in form, a single-justice high court. And, while it has not been the rule, some American court systems have preserved a chancery, though often with multi-judge appellate courts in equity.

NOTES AND QUESTIONS

1. Why must law employ violence to be effective? What does Cover argue are the practical limitations to understanding law as ideology? Do you agree? Is the law enforceable without violence?

2. Why does Cover draw an analogy between the judge-prisoner relationship and that of torturers and the tortured? Is he likening a judge to a torturer? How does Cover characterize the job of judges within the American legal system?

3. How is law's violence any different from random violence? Should there be any sort of limit to law's violence (e.g., the death penalty)? Why or why not?

4. According to Cover, what are the three primary characteristics of judicial interpretation? In this model, how does judicial interpretation shape the overall social organization of law?

5. What does Cover mean when he says that legal interpretation "can never be free . . . can never be an understanding of the text word alone"? How, according to Cover, are judges "both separated from and inextricably linked to, the acts [of violence] they authorize?" What does he mean by the term "bonded interpretation"?

6. Cover paints a picture of the American legal system as particularly hierarchical. How, according to Cover, does the hierarchy facilitate the smooth functioning of the legal system? Are there any drawbacks to this rigid hierarchy?

7. How compatible is Cover's concept of law with White's depiction of law (Chapter 11) as a rhetorical process?

Conclusion to Part II

The three readings in Part II illustrate great diversity in the kinds of scholarship that inform the study of law in the liberal arts. As students of law, we draw on, and are the fortunate beneficiaries of, rich and varied scholarly traditions, from the intricate and complex literary allusions of Kafka, to Hay's neo-Marxist history, to Cover's law professor precision in the analysis of law's violence. Although this may be small comfort for readers for whom literary work or history or more straightforward legal scholarship is not obviously compelling, it provides different avenues through which each of us may traverse law's complex social organization.

Attention to bureaucratic complexity, and the maneuvers of officials, is highlighted in all of the three readings despite their differences. The guard in Kafka's parable stands in as a figure of law. The elaborate staging and drama of criminal trials that Hay describes do not happen by accident. Examples of the more mundane division of labor between judges and wardens that Cover analyzes remind us that law acts through persons, groups, and institutions, and that those people, groups, and institutions do not inevitably and automatically work in coordinated and cooperative ways. Getting them all on the same page takes considerable effort and often extended negotiation.

As you read more about each of the three images of law's social organization that this section introduces, you will encounter descriptions of the efforts and negotiations that occur in different arenas of the legal system, that involve different actors, and that focus on different substantive problems. In some of these arenas, the descriptions will be as opaque as Kafka's parable; in others, they will be as dramatic as Hay's description; in still others, as mundane as the world that Cover discusses. The opaque, the dramatic, the mundane, each of these is a crucial component of law's social organization. ✦

Suggested Additional Readings for Part II

Kafka

Ronald Gray, ed., *Kafka: A Collection of Critical Essays.* Englewood Cliffs, NJ: Prentice Hall, 1962.

Ronald Hayman, *Kafka: A Biography.* New York: Oxford University Press, 1982.

Franz Kafka, *The Trial.* Willa and Edwin Muir, trans. New York: Alfred A. Knopf, 1937.

Law and Ideology

Patricia Ewick, "Ideology and Consciousness," in *The Blackwell Companion to Law and Society,* Austin Sarat, ed. New York: Blackwell Publishing, 2004.

Alan Hunt, "The Ideology of Law: Advances and Problems in Recent Applications of the Concept of Ideology to the Analysis of Law," 19 *Law & Society Review* (1985), 11.

"Special Issue: Law and Ideology," 22 *Law & Society Review* (1988), 623.

Susan Silbey, "Ideology, Power, and Justice," in *Justice and Power in Sociolegal Studies,* Bryant Garth and Austin Sarat, eds. Evanston, IL: Northwestern University Press, 1998.

E. P. Thompson, *Whigs and Hunters: The Origins of the Black Act.* New York: Pantheon Books, 1975.

Robert Cover

Martha Minow, Michel Ryan, and Austin Sarat, *Narrative, Violence, and the Law: The Essays of Robert Cover.* Ann Arbor: University of Michigan Press, 1992. ✦

Part III

Access to Justice: The Demand for Law and Law's Demands

Legal systems have contingent, not fixed, relationships to the social world. They can be organized to be more or less responsive, more or less accessible. How much they are involved in dealing with the mess and trouble of social life, as well as what law recognizes as a problem serious enough to warrant a legal response or remedy, are political questions rather than matters of logic. Whose problems get attention is, as Austin T. Turk (Chapter 8) suggested, a function of the resources parties are able to bring to bear and is a mark of their social and political standing.

The readings in this part examine the accessibility of the American legal system from two perspectives, one quantitative, the other qualitative. Along the first dimension, Sections IV and V discuss the issue of litigation, that is, the use of courts to deal with disputes. They examine how much litigation occurs in the United States and whether courts and lawyers are well equipped to handle the volume of litigation.

Along the qualitative dimension, Sections VI and VII describe the accessibility of law to women and to poor people. These are two dimensions of the question of how law responds to social stratification and social difference. Do gender and class differences matter? And if so, how do they matter? ✦

Section IV

*Lining-Up at the
Door of Law*

Chapter 15

The Emergence and Transformation of Disputes

Naming, Blaming, Claiming

William L. F. Felstiner
Richard L. Abel
Austin Sarat

litigation. The reading by Felstiner, Abel, and Sarat points to a different starting place. Instead of taking a top-down view, they advocate a bottom-up view, one that begins not from official legal institutions (a court), but from the social world itself, and from the perspective of people who experience problems. Felstiner, Abel, and Sarat suggest that we should attend to the social life of troubles and the way those troubles develop. They ask us to analyze the psychological and social factors that influence what people do when they have grievances, and they provide a vocabulary for examining what they call "the emergence and transformation of disputes."

In their view, the first step in the translation of what they call "unperceived" injurious events into perceived injurious events involves naming a grievance. Subsequently someone must be "blamed," and ultimately a claim for redress must be made and resisted. Only at this point is access to law likely to be sought.

What do people do when they have a problem, a grievance, or a dispute? What role does law play in dealing with problems, responding to grievances, and resolving disputes? The political theorist Judith Shklar once observed that the world is full of misfortune and injustice, but the former is not the same as the latter. A misfortune is an event for which no one can be held accountable (e.g., it rains on the day we have planned a picnic); an injustice has some human agent who can reasonably be blamed (e.g., someone turns on the sprinkler system during our picnic). Seeking a legal remedy for a misfortune never seems appropriate; seeking a legal remedy for an injustice may sometimes seem like the right thing to do.

Yet, the difference between a misfortune and an injustice does not exist as a fact of nature. It is instead socially constructed. What one person regards as a misfortune, another will regard as an injustice and vice versa.

Scholars studying these issues have often begun by examining cases that come to court. They seek to understand the world of disputing behavior by studying disputes that eventuate in

...Our purpose in this paper is to provide a framework within which the emergence and transformation of disputes can be described. The history of the sociological study of disputing displays a backward movement, starting with those legal institutions most remote from society—appellate courts—and gradually moving through trial courts, legislatures, administrative agencies, prosecutors, and the police to a focus on disputes and disputing in society and the role of the citizenry in making law. The transformation perspective places disputants at the center of the sociological study of law; it directs our attention to individuals as the creators of opportunities for law and legal activity: people make their own law, but they do not make it just as they please.

WHERE DISPUTES COME FROM AND HOW THEY DEVELOP

We come to the study of transformations with the belief that the antecedents of disputing are as problematic and as interesting as the disputes that may ultimately emerge. We begin by setting forth the stages in the development of disputes and the activities connecting one stage to the next. Trouble, problems, personal and social dislocation are everyday occurrences. Yet, social scientists have rarely studied the capacity of people to tolerate substantial distress and injustice. . . . We do, however, know that such "tolerance" may represent a failure to perceive that one has been injured; such failures may be self-induced or externally manipulated. Assume a population living downwind from a nuclear test site. Some portion of that population has developed cancer as a result of the exposure and some has not. Some of those stricken know that they are sick and some do not. In order for disputes to emerge and remedial action to be taken, an unperceived injurious experience (unPIE, for short) must be transformed into a perceived injurious experience (PIE). The uninformed cancer victims must learn that they are sick. The transformation perspective directs our attention to the differential transformation of unPIEs into PIEs. It urges us to examine, in this case, differences in class, education, work situation, social networks, etc. between those who become aware of their cancer and those who do not, as well as attend to the possible manipulation of information by those responsible for the radiation.

There are conceptual and methodological difficulties in studying this transformation. The conceptual problem derives from the fact that unPIE is inchoate, PIE in the sky so to speak. It can only be bounded by choosing someone's definition of what is injurious. Frequently this will not be a problem. An injurious experience is any experience that is disvalued by the person to whom it occurs. For the most part, people agree on what is disvalued. But such feelings are never universal. Where people do differ, these differences, in fact, generate some of the most important research questions: why do people who perceive experience similarly *value* it differently, why

do they *perceive* similarly valued experience differently, and what is the relation between valuation and perception? From a practical perspective, the lack of consensus about the meaning of experiences does not interfere with any of these tasks, since their purpose is to map covariation among interpretation, perception, and external factors. But if, on the other hand, the research objective is to provide a census of injurious experiences, then the lack of an agreed-upon definition is more serious. In a census, the researcher must either impose a definition upon subjects and run the risk that the definition will fail to capture all injurious experience or permit subjects to define injurious experience as they wish and run the risk that different subjects will define the same experience differently and may include experiences the researcher does not find injurious. . . .

The next step is the transformation of a perceived injurious experience into a grievance. This occurs when a person attributes an injury to the fault of another individual or social entity. By including fault within the definition of grievance, we limit the concept to injuries viewed both as violations of norms and as remediable. The definition takes the grievant's perspective: the injured person must feel wronged and believe that something might be done in response to the injury, however politically or sociologically improbable such a response might be. A grievance must be distinguished from a complaint against no one in particular (about the weather, or perhaps inflation) and from a mere wish unaccompanied by a sense of injury for which another is held responsible (I might like to be more attractive). We call the transformation from perceived injurious experience to grievance *blaming*: our diseased shipyard worker makes this transformation when he holds his employer or the manufacturer of asbestos insulation responsible for his asbestosis.

The third transformation occurs when someone with a grievance voices it to the person or entity believed to be responsible and asks for some remedy. We call this communication *claiming*. A claim is transformed into a dispute when it is ejected in whole or in part. Rejection need not be expressed by words. Delay that the claimant construes as resistance is just as much a rejection as is a compromise offer (partial rejection) or an outright refusal.

The sociology of law should pay more attention to the early stages of disputes and to the factors that determine whether naming, blaming, and claiming will occur. Learning more about the existence, absence, or reversal of these basic transformations will increase our understanding of the disputing process and our ability to evaluate dispute processing institutions. We know that only a small fraction of injurious experiences ever mature into disputes. . . . Furthermore, we know that most of the attrition occurs at the early stages: experiences are not perceived as injurious; perceptions do not ripen into grievances; grievances are voiced to intimates but not to the person deemed responsible. A theory of disputing that looked only at institutions mobilized by disputants and the strategies pursued within them would be seriously deficient. It would be like constructing a theory of politics entirely on the basis of voting patterns when we know that most people do not vote in most elections. Recognizing the bias that would result, political scientists have devoted considerable effort to describing and explaining political apathy. . . . Sociologists of law need to explore the analogous phenomenon—grievance apathy.

The early stages of naming, blaming, and claiming are significant, not only because of the high attrition they reflect, but also because the range of behavior they encompass is greater than that involved in the later stages of disputes, where institutional patterns restrict the options open to disputants. Examination of this behavior will help us identify the social structure of disputing. Transformations reflect social structural variables, as well as personality traits. People do—or do not—perceive an experience as an injury, blame someone else, claim redress, or get their claims accepted because of their *social position* as well as their individual characteristics. The transformation perspective points as much to the study of social stratification as to the exploration of social psychology.

Finally, attention to naming, blaming, and claiming permits a more critical look at recent efforts to improve "access to justice." The public commitment to formal legal equality, by the prevailing ideology of liberal legalism has resulted in substantial efforts to equalize access at the later stages of disputing, where inequality becomes more visible and implicates official institutions; examples include the waiver of court costs, the creation of small claims courts, the movement toward informalism, and the provision of legal services. . . . Access to justice is supposed to reduce the unequal distribution of advantages in society; paradoxically it may amplify these inequalities. The ostensible goal of these reforms is to eliminate bias in the ultimate transformation: disputes into lawsuits. If, however, as we suspect, these very unequal distributions have skewed the earlier stages by which injurious experiences become disputes, then current access to justice efforts will only give additional advantages to those who have already transformed their experiences into disputes. That is, these efforts may accentuate the effects of inequality at the earlier, less visible stages, where it is harder to detect, diagnose, and correct. . . .

THE CHARACTERISTICS OF TRANSFORMATION

PIEs, grievances, and disputes have the following characteristics: they are subjective, unstable, reactive, complicated, and incomplete. They are *subjective* in the sense that transformations need not be accompanied by any observable behavior. A disputant discusses his problem with a lawyer and consequently reappraises the behavior of the opposing party. The disputant now believes that his opponent was not just mistaken but acted in bad faith. The content of the dispute has been transformed in the mind of the disputant, although neither the lawyer nor the opposing party necessarily knows about the shift.

Since transformations may be nothing more than changes in feelings, and feelings may change repeatedly, the process is *unstable.* This characteristic is notable only because it differs so markedly from the conventional understanding of legal controversies. In the conventional view of disputes, the sources of claims and rejections are objective events that happened in the past. It is accepted that it may be difficult to get the facts straight, but there is rarely an awareness that the events themselves may be transformed as they are processed. This view is psychologically naive: it is insensitive to the effect of feelings on the attribution of motive and to the consequences of such attributions for the subject's understanding of behavior. . . .

Even in ordinary understanding, disputing is a *complicated* process involving ambiguous behavior, faulty recall, uncertain norms, conflicting objectives, inconsistent values, and complex institutions. It is complicated still further by attention to changes in disputant feelings and objectives over time. Take the stereotypical case of personal injury arising out of an automobile accident. A conventional analysis (e.g., the one often borrowed from economics) assumes that the goals of the defendant driver are to minimize his responsibility and limit the complainant's recovery. A transformation view, on the other hand, suggests that the defendant's objectives may be both less clear and less stable. Depending on his insurance position, his own experience, his empathy for, relationship to and interaction with the injured person, and the tenor of discussions he may have with others about the accident and its aftermath, the defendant may at various times wish to maximize rather than minimize both his own fault and the com-

plainant's recovery or to take some intermediate position. A transformation approach would seek to identify these active and their effects in order to account for such shifts in objective. . . .

The Importance of Studying Transformations

. . .[T]ransformation studies render problematic one of the most fundamental political judgments about disputing—that there is too much of it, that Americans are an over-contentious people, far too ready to litigate. . . . The transformation perspective suggests that there may be too *little* conflict in our society. Many studies are "court-centered." They assess conflict from the point of view of courts which perceive their resources to be limited. . . . From this viewpoint, any level of conflict that exceeds the court's capacities is "too much." Things look very different, however, if we start with the *individual* who has suffered an injurious experience. That is what the transformation's point of view makes us do. It encourages inquiry into why so few such individuals even get some redress. So the transformation perspective naturally prompts questions that have been largely ignored thus far: why are Americans so slow to perceive injury, so reluctant to make claims, and so fearful of disputing—especially of litigating? One hypothesis tentatively advanced in some early research is that the cult of competence, the individualism celebrated by American culture, inhibits people from acknowledging—to themselves, to others, and particularly to authority—that they have been injured, that they have been bettered by an adversary. . . .

Transformation studies should also enable us to be more specific about the "culture" of different dispute processing agents and institutions. For instance, the conventional wisdom maintains that divorce lawyers exacerbate conflict, mistrust, and stress. The current interest in custody mediation is more a reflection of skepticism about the usefulness of lawyers (and the adversary process that is their stock in trade) than a failure of confidence in the wisdom of family court judges. Yet *all* lawyers do not mismanage custody cases. Transformation studies that observe lawyer-client interactions over time could tell us which values, experiences, techniques, contexts, or personalities differentiate constructive lawyers from those who tend to complicate an already difficult problem They could also tell us when clients (and not their lawyers) use litigation for purposes of perpetuating family conflict rather than resolving it.

Conclusion

The importance of studying the emergence and transformation of disputes should not blind us to its difficulties. Since the study of transformations must focus on the minds of respondents, their attitudes, feelings, objectives, and motives (as these change over time), it must be longitudinal and based upon a high level of rapport between researcher and informant. The difficulties in such research are considerable: the most obvious problems arise in devising techniques that minimize reactivity to researcher suggestion while providing researchers with adequate signals about the timeliness of a new wave of interviews.

In order to identify the salient influences on transformations, it is necessary to select for research substantive areas of disputing where high levels of variance can be expected. But different substantive fields are likely to exhibit variation at different stages. For instance, there is probably a low level of PIEs in the relationship between lay persons and professionals but a high level in landlord-tenant interactions; a low level of fellow-through on consumer disputes but a high level in claims concerning serious personal injuries. As a result, the development of an empirical understanding of transformations will require many studies with limited objectives rather than a few large-scale projects. . . .

Although the emergence and transformation of disputes is personal and individualized, it has an important political dimension. Ultimately what we are concerned with is the capacity of people to respond to trouble, problems, and injustice. We believe that the study of dispute processing has been too removed from the actual difficulties and choices that accompany the recognition that one's life is troubled and that relief from trouble is uncertain, contingent, and costly. Recognition and action may not be appropriate or desirable in every instance. We do believe, however, that a healthy social order is one that minimizes barriers inhibiting the emergence of grievances and disputes and preventing their translation into claims for redress.

Notes and Questions

1. How have disputes traditionally been studied by sociologists? How is Felstiner, Abel, and Sarat's perspective different?

2. According to Felstiner, Abel, and Sarat, what role do "value" and "perception" play in identifying an injurious experience? Are some kinds of problems more likely to be recognized or labeled as grievances?

3. What differentiates unPIEs, PIEs, grievances, and disputes? How might such social factors as race, class, and gender influence an individual's process of transformation through various levels of dispute? What social attributes do you believe are most favorable to an individual obtaining redress for an injury?

4. Are Felstiner, Abel, and Sarat making the case that every perceived injury ought to be litigated? Would such a scenario create a more just society? Is such a scenario feasible?

5. What do Felstiner, Abel, and Sarat suggest about the question of whether law is too accessible or not accessible enough? What are the merits of studying conflict

from a more "court-centered" point of view? Is the right of the individual to legal redress important for a "healthy social order?"

6. If you were to design a study of the emergence and transformation of disputes, what type of conflict might you study (e.g., Felstiner, Abel, and Sarat suggest analyzing landlord/tenant relationships)? What do you suppose would be the most significant social factors contributing either to successful litigation or to the abandonment of a legal claim? Now consider how the situation of two disputants might change if one were a different race or gender from the other. What new challenges or questions does such a scenario raise for you?

Reprinted from: William L.F Felstiner, Richard L. Abel, and Austin Sarat, "The Emergence and Transformation of Disputes: Naming, Blaming, Claiming" in the *Law and Society Review*, 15:3-4 (1980-1981), pp. 631–654. Copyright © 1980, 1981. Reprinted with the permission of the Law and Society Association. ✦

Chapter 16

Liability

The Legal Revolution and Its Consequences

Peter W. Huber

As many Americans know, there is an ongoing debate about the so-called litigation explosion in the United States and the consequences of using the courts to contest our economic, political, and social lives. Since 1986, 45 states and the District of Columbia have enacted tort reforms into law. Thirty states have modified the law of punitive damages, the law that allows juries to award extra damages to punish wrongdoers. Twenty-nine states penalize parties who bring frivolous lawsuits and seven states have enacted comprehensive product liability reforms.

Medical liability reforms have also been enacted in most states. President George W. Bush has sought to discourage litigation in the area of medical malpractice by proposing federal limitations on jury awards in malpractice cases. The President's proposal would limit awards for pain and suffering to $250,000. Proponents of such a cap point to skyrocketing medical insurance premiums. They contend that such premiums are driving some doctors from the practice of medicine. Opponents say that limitations on jury awards would deprive victims of their day in court without solving the insurance problem.

Public opinion polls report that 83 percent of Americans think there are too many lawsuits filed in the United States and that greedy personal injury lawyers are to blame. But how many lawsuits are too many lawsuits? How do we know when there is "too much" litigation?

This is not as easy a question as it might at first appear to be. "Too much" is very much a subjective judgment. Perhaps we can say whether there is too much litigation by establishing a baseline of what would be an acceptable level of litigation. That baseline might derive from history or from a comparison of the litigation rate in the United States with other countries. Or, as Felstiner, Abel, and Sarat suggest in Chapter 15, judging whether we have too many lawsuits requires some assessment about the number of potential lawsuits that exist at any one time.

Whatever the baseline, Peter W. Huber thinks that there is too much litigation in the United States and, as a consequence, our society is both less free than it should be and less innovative than it might be. He is particularly interested in developments in the law governing accidents, commonly known as the law of torts. As he describes these developments, the law has moved away from encouraging people to act freely and take responsibility for things that go wrong in their lives. With the development of so-called strict liability, manufacturers of products can be held legally liable even if they have acted in a reasonable fashion. The result has been to encourage people to file suit in situations of misfortune or in situations when they could have avoided a problem by taking simple precautions.

In Chapter 17, Richard L. Abel takes issue with Huber. Abel argues that we have too little rather than too much litigation. He calls the problem that we face "an epidemic of injuries" caused by manufacturers of products and providers of services. According to Abel, injuries should not be left uncompensated. People should be encouraged to seek access to law. As he sees it, Huber's argument is part of a broad-based conservative effort to erode the social safety net.

As you read Huber and Abel, consider who has the better argument? What baseline does each of them use in judging whether we have too much litigation?

It is one of the most ubiquitous taxes we pay, now levied on virtually everything we buy, sell, and use. The tax accounts for 30 percent of the price of a stepladder and over 95 percent of the price of childhood vaccine. It is responsible for one-quarter of the price of a ride on a Long Island tour bus and one-third of the price of a small airplane. It will soon cost large municipalities as much as they spend on fire or sanitation services.

Some call it a safety tax, but its exact relationship to safety is mysterious. It is paid on many items that are risky to use, like ski lifts and hedge trimmers, but it weighs even more heavily on other items whose whole purpose is to make life safer. It adds only a few cents to a pack of cigarettes, but it adds more to the price of a football helmet than the cost of making it. The tax falls especially hard on prescription drugs, doctors, surgeons, and all things medical. Because of the tax, you cannot deliver a baby with medical assistance in Monroe County, Alabama. You cannot buy several contraceptives certified to be safe and effective by the Food and Drug Administration (PDA), even though available substitutes are more dangerous or less effective. If you have the stomach upset known as hyperemesis, you cannot buy the pill that is certified as safe and effective against it. The tax has orphaned various drugs that are invaluable for treating rare but serious diseases. It is assessed against every family that has a baby, in the amount of about $300 per birth, with an obstetrician in New York City paying $85,000 a year.

Because of the tax, you cannot use a sled in Denver city parks or a diving board in New York City schools. You cannot buy an American Motors "CJ" Jeep or a set of construction plans for novel airplanes from Burt Rutan, the pioneering designer of the *Voyager*. You can no longer buy many American-made brands of sporting goods, especially equipment for amateur contact sports such as hockey and lacrosse. For a while, you could not use public transportation in the city of St. Joseph, Missouri, nor could you go to jail in Lafayette County in the same state. Miami canceled

plans for an experimental railbus because of the tax. The tax has curtailed Little League and fireworks displays, evening concerts, sailboard races, and the use of public beaches and ice-skating rinks. It temporarily shut down the famed Cyclone at the Astroland amusement park on Coney Island.

The tax directly costs American individuals, businesses, municipalities, and other government bodies at least $80 billion a year, a figure that equals the total profits of the country's top 200 corporations. But many of the tax's costs are indirect and unmeasurable, reflected only in the tremendous effort, inconvenience, and sacrifice Americans now go through to avoid its collection. The extent of these indirect costs can only be guessed at. One study concluded that doctors spend $3.50 in efforts to avoid additional charges for each $1 of direct tax they pay. If similar multipliers operate in other areas, the tax's hidden impact on the way we live and do business may amount to a $300 billion dollar annual levy on the American economy.

The tax goes by the name of *tort liability*. It is collected and disbursed through litigation. The courts alone decide just who will pay, how much, and on what timetable. Unlike better-known taxes, this one was never put to a legislature or a public referendum, debated at any length in the usual public arenas, or approved by the president or by any state governor. And although the tax ostensibly is collected for the public benefit, lawyers and other middlemen pocket more than half the take.

The tort tax is a recent invention. Tort law has existed here and abroad for centuries, of course. But until quite recently it was a backwater of the legal system, of little importance in the wider scheme of things. For all practical purposes, the omnipresent tort tax we pay today was conceived in the 1950s and set in place in the 1960s and 1970s by a new generation of lawyers and judges. In the space of twenty years they transformed the legal landscape, proclaiming sweeping new rights to sue. Some grew famous and more grew rich selling their services to enforce the rights that they themselves invented. But the revolution they made could never have taken place had it not had a component of idealism as well. Tort law, it is widely and passionately believed, is a public-spirited undertaking designed for the protection of the ordinary consumer and worker, the hapless accident victim, the "little guy." Tort law as we know it is a peculiarly American institution. No other country in the world administers anything remotely like it.

From Consent to Coercion

Tort law is the law of accidents and personal injury. The example that usually comes to mind is a two-car collision at an intersection. The drivers are utter strangers. They have no advance understanding between them as to how they should drive, except perhaps an implicit agreement to follow the rules of the road. Nor do they have any advance arrangement specifying who will pay for the damage. Human nature being what it is, the two sides often have different views on both these interesting questions. Somebody else has to step in to work out rights and responsibilities. This has traditionally been a job for the courts. They resolve these cases under the law of *torts* or civil wrongs.

But the car accident between strangers is comparatively rare in the larger universe of accidents and injuries. Just as most intentional assaults involve assailants and victims who already know each other well, most unintended injuries occur in the context of commercial acquaintance—at work, on the hospital operating table, following the purchase of an airplane ticket or a home appliance. And while homicide is seldom a subject of advance understanding between victim and assailant, unintentional accidents often are. More often than not, both parties to a transaction recognize there is some chance of misadventure, and prudently take steps to address it beforehand.

Until quite recently, the law permitted and indeed promoted advance agreement of that character. It searched for understandings between the parties and respected them where found. Most accidents were handled under the broad heading of *contract*—the realm of human cooperation—and comparatively few relegated to the dismal annex of tort, the realm of unchosen relationship and collision. The old law treated contract and tort cases under entirely different rules, which reflected this fairly intuitive line between choice and coercion.

Then, in the 1950s and after, a visionary group of legal theorists came along. Their leaders were thoughtful, well-intentioned legal academics at some of the most prestigious law schools, and judges on the most respected state benches. They were the likes of the late William Prosser, who taught law at Hastings College, John Wade, Professor of Law at Vanderbilt University, and California Supreme Court Justice Roger Traynor. They are hardly household names, but considering the impact they had on American life they should be. Their ideas, eloquence, and persistence changed the common law as profoundly as it had ever been changed before. For short, and in the absence of a better term, we will refer to them as the founders of modern tort law, or just the *Founders*. If the name is lighthearted, their accomplishments were anything but.

The Founders were to be followed a decade or two later by a much more sophisticated group of legal economists, most notably Guido Calabresi, now Dean of the Yale Law School, and Richard Posner of the University of Chicago Law School and now a federal judge on the Seventh Circuit Court of Appeals. There were many others, for economists seem to be almost as numerous as lawyers, and the application of economic theory to tort law has enjoyed mounting popularity in recent years as tort law has itself become an industry. An economist, it has been said, is someone who observes what is happening in practice and goes off to study whether it is possible in theory. The new tort economists were entirely true to that great tradition. Indeed, they carried it a step forward, concluding that the legal revolution that had already occurred was not only possible but justified and necessary. Mustering all the dense prose, arcane jargon, and elaborate methodology that only the very best academic economists muster, they set about proving on paper that the whole new tort structure was an efficient and inevitable reaction to failures in the marketplace. Arriving on the scene of the great tort battle late in the day, they courageously congratulated the victors, shot the wounded, and pronounced the day's outcome satisfactory and good.

Like all revolutionaries, the Founders and their followers, in the economics profession and elsewhere, had their own reasons for believing and behaving as they did. Most consumers, they assumed, pay little attention to accident risks before the fact. Ignoring or underestimating risk as they do, consumers fail to demand, and producers fail to supply, as much safety as would be best. As a result, manufacturers, doctors, employers, municipalities, and other producers get away with undue carelessness, and costly accidents are all too frequent. To make matters worse, consumers buy less accident insurance than they really need, so injuries lead to unneeded misery and privation and some victims become public charges.

With these assumptions as their starting point, the new tort theorists concluded that the overriding question that the old law asked—how did the parties agree to allocate the costs of the accident?—was irrelevant or worse. The real question to ask was: How can society best allocate the cost of accidents to minimize those costs (and the cost of guarding against them), and to provide potential victims with the accident insurance that not all of them currently buy or can afford? The answer, by and large, was to make producers of goods and services pay the costs of accidents. A broad rule to this effect, it was argued, can accomplish both objectives. It forces providers to be careful. It also forces

consumers to take accident costs into account, not consciously but by paying a safety-adjusted price for everything they buy or do. And it compels the improvident to buy accident insurance, again not directly but through the safety tax. It has a moral dimension too: People should be required to take care before the accident and to help each other afterward, for no other reason than that it is just, right, and proper to insist that they do so.

The expansive new accident tax is firmly in place today. In a remarkably short time, the Founders completely recast a centuries-old body of law in an entirely new mold of their own design. They started sketching out their intentions only in the late 1950s; within two short decades they had achieved virtually every legal change that they originally planned. There were setbacks along the way, of course; the common law always develops in fits and starts, with some states bolder and others more timid, and the transformation of tort law was no exception. But compared with the cautious incrementalism with which the common law had changed in centuries past, an utter transformation over a twenty-year span can fairly be described as a revolution, and a violent one at that. . . .

What brought us this liability tax, in short, was a wholesale shift from consent to coercion in the law of accidents. Yesterday we relied primarily on agreement before the fact to settle responsibility for most accidents. Today we emphasize litigation after the fact. Yesterday we deferred to private choice. Today it is only public choice that counts, more specifically the public choices of judges and juries. For all practical purposes, contracts are dead, at least insofar as they attempt to allocate responsibility for accidents ahead of time. Safety obligations are now decided through liability prescription, worked out case by case after the accident. The center of the accident insurance world has likewise shifted, from *first-party* insurance chosen by the expected beneficiary, to *third-party* coverage driven by legal compulsion.

Paralleling this shift from consent to coercion has been a shift from individual to group responsibility. The old contract-centered law placed enormous confidence in individuals to manage the risks of their personal environments. The new, tort-dominated jurisprudence prefers universal rules with no opt-out provisions. Tort law now defines acceptable safety in lawn mower design, vaccine manufacture, heart surgery, and ski slope grooming, without regard to the preferences of any individual consumer or provider. If the courts declare there is to be a safety tax on a vaccine at such and such a level, the tax will surely be paid, whatever other arrangements the buyer or user of the vaccine or the FDA, let alone the manufacturer, may prefer or can afford. In a similar spirit, the old law relied on the political branches of government to make those safety choices that only a community as a whole can responsibly oversee. The new again prefers control through the instrument of the lawsuit. Safety standards have been entirely socialized, but in a peculiar sort of way that freezes out not only private choice but also public prescription through all government authority other than the courts. The new accident insurance is likewise furnished on a universal and standardized plan, whether or not one or another of us might prefer a different set of policy terms or a different insurance carrier.

Though we have gone a great distance, there is no reason to believe that the journey is over. In the first place, the momentum of accumulated logic is likely to keep the system moving for the indefinite future, as newly established legal principles are deployed to open up fresh areas of litigation. There is also great financial momentum in the system. The tens of thousands of plaintiffs' lawyers who advertise for clients, dig up the cases, marshal the evidence, and take the claims to court, now have considerable economic muscle on their side. In 1988, asbestos lawyers were beginning to collect fees that will total about $1 billion, and were looking, so to speak, for new places to invest this money. Among the candidate targets were fiberglass and other insulators, tobacco, and various chemicals. The early claims against the Dalkon Shield intrauterine contraceptive device funded second- and third-generation lawsuits against other IUDs, spermicides and morning sickness drugs. The lawyers who started careers as small-town traffic accident litigators were later to take on automakers, municipalities, taverns, and distilleries. As the Founding generals won their victories, the ranks of their followers swelled. And as the armies grew, the perimeters of the tort empire were pushed out further still. Despite occasional initiatives in state legislatures, and interminable hand wringing in Congress, no armistice seems imminent.

The statistics confirm this picture of restless, ceaseless expansion. The number of tort suits filed has increased steadily for over two decades. So has the probability that any given suit will conclude in an award. And the average size of awards has grown more rapidly still. Multiplied together these three trends produce the universal tort tax so pervasive in our world today.

Begin with the number of cases. Traffic accident claims, which account for about 40 percent of all tort cases today, have held steady or even declined as states have passed no-fault laws. But other cases have been on a steep rise. Cases where appliances, factory machinery, chemicals, automobiles, and other products are blamed for injuries increased fourfold between 1976 and 1986. More medical malpractice suits were filed in the decade ending in 1987 than in the entire previous history of American tort law. One survey found that damage claims against cities doubled between 1982 and 1986. In the space of a single year, between 1984 and 1985, claims filed against the federal government grew from 41,000 to 54,000, and the amount demanded from $112 billion to $149 billion, an increase of over 30 percent by either measure.

The plaintiff's probability of winning has also risen steadily. The likelihood of success rose from 20 to 30 percent in a product case in the 1960s to more than 50 percent in the 1980s, with similar increases in other classes of lawsuit, again excluding traffic cases.

Finally, there has been sharp growth in the size of awards. The average judgment in all tort cases rose from an inflation-adjusted $50,000 in the early 1960s to more than $250,000 in the early 1980s—a fivefold increase. The inflation-adjusted median award—the amount exceeded in half of all judgments—has been rising steadily too, by more than 80 percent in the same period. Average verdicts against cities rose almost tenfold, to $2 million. The first jury verdict exceeding $1 million came in 1962; in 1975 there were fewer than twenty; today there are over 400 a year, an increase that could not possibly be ascribed to inflation alone. Inflation-adjusted awards in medical malpractice cases have doubled about every seven years.

Tort law, once a remote and sleepy province of the law's empire, has become one of its most bustling and dynamic centers of activity. . . .

BACKFIRE

If you pay a steep, unsettling, and broad-based tax, you expect something in return. The Founders promised the world that their tax would bring measurable progress toward two deeply held social goals: protecting life and limb, and helping the injured when accidents do happen nevertheless. How well has the tort tax achieved these goals? The record is a mountain of pretentious failure.

High taxes drive up some prices, and the new tort system has certainly done that. Taxes drive other things off the market altogether, and that too has happened. The immediate impact of the new legal rules has been a marked increase in price and a decline in the availability of a wide range of goods and ser-

vices. That much was expected, indeed welcomed, by the Founders. Hazardous goods should cost more, they felt, to reflect the risk; too-hazardous goods should not be sold at all.

What was unexpected was the propensity of the tort tax to fall where it is least needed and most difficult to bear. Contrary to all original expectations, the first major casualties of the new legal regime have been many of the methods by which society pursues safety itself. Hospital emergency-room services are perilous in liability terms because emergency room patients are in trouble to begin with. Vaccines are hazardous (again, from the legal perspective) because the children who receive them are susceptible to a host of diseases and reactions often indistinguishable from vaccine side effects. Running a municipal police department, ambulance service, town dump, or waste cleanup service invites litigation because these activities are aimed at situations that are risky from the beginning. Selling an antimiscarriage drug, contraceptive, abortion, or obstetrical service is legally dangerous because pregnancy itself is risky for both mother and child. And modern tort law has written an altogether new conclusion to the parable of the Good Samaritan, making it unwise to stop at the roadside accident without first checking in with your local insurance agent and lawyer. In its search for witches, the modern tort system has undoubtedly found a few and reduced them to ashes. But too many wonder drugs have also been gathered into the flames.

The larger fallacy in the Founders' grand scheme was the idea that the most attractive defendants would stick around to be sued, in case after case, after it became clear what was happening. As our right to sue the butcher, brewer, and baker after the sale has grown, our freedom to make the purchase in the first place has declined. The purveyors of meat, beer, and such withdraw only partially, by demanding a higher price; the purveyors of rare drugs, Yellowstone hiking, and rural obstetrical services have often been driven from the market altogether. An unbounded and im-possible-to-waive right to sue necessarily overtakes and destroys the right to make deals with people who place a high premium on staying in business and out of court. While the consumer has indeed acquired a new and sometimes valuable right to sue, he has done so only by surrendering an older right, the right to contract, which in the long run is worth far more.

What about the aim of providing more and better insurance against accidents? It has fared no better than the goal of improving safety, and for much the same reason. How much insurance we get depends not only on how much we want to buy but on how much others are willing to sell. The Founders sought to increase the demand for liability insurance, and they undoubtedly did just that. But at the same time they decimated the supply. The net effect was less insurance all around.

Across the board, modern tort law weighs heavily on the spirit of innovation and enter-prise. The Founders confidently expected that their reforms would provide a constant spur to innovate. The actual effect has been quite the opposite. The old tort rules focused on the human actors, inquiring whether the technol-ogist was careful, prudently trained, and properly supervised. The new rules place technology itself in the liability dock. But ju-rors, who generally can reach sensible judg-ments about people, perform much less well when they sit in judgment on technology.

Under jury pressure, the new touchstones of technological legitimacy have become age, fa-miliarity, and ubiquity. It is the innovative and unfamiliar that is most likely to be condemned. One feature after another of the new system presses in the same direction. Consider the gilt-edged safety warnings that the new tort rules demand. Honing a warning to a fine point of perfection requires years of market and litigation experience, which means that es-tablished products now do comparatively well in tort suits based on warnings, while innova-tive challengers are vulnerable. The new rules

also force providers to sell not only a product or service but also an accident insurance con-tract with it. But the availability of reasonably priced insurance depends on the accumula-tion of actuarial experience—something that all established technologies have but no truly innovative one ever does.

As a result of these and other similar forces, it is far safer, in liability terms, to sell an old, outdated oral contraceptive than a new IUD or sponge. It is more prudent, at least from the le-gal perspective, to stick with the tried-and-true technologies for car frame design, or aircraft engines, or vaccine formulation than to exper-iment boldly with something new. Does a pes-ticide manufacturer wish to steer clear of the courts? Any lawyer knows that the best legal bet is an old, familiar chemical, which has been used for years by every farmer in the commu-nity, rather than the latest exotic breakthrough in genetic engineering. Is the electric power company seeking at all costs to avoid liability? It will find coal to be the safest possible fuel in those terms, and uranium the most dangerous, though the ranking of actual risks may be the reverse.

The result is to ingrain a bias against inno-vation at all levels of the economy—for which we pay a heavy price, not just in money and in our nation's competitive position in the world, but in safety once again. The lay mind is accus-tomed to equate familiarity with safety, but newer, more often than not, is in fact safer than older. Life expectancy in this country has in-creased at the astonishing rate of three months per year throughout the twentieth century, not because of the proliferation of litigation but because of the constant press of technological innovation—innovation that is now being slowed and sometimes even reversed by the ongoing legal assault.

The Founders can hardly be faulted for their intentions, which were honorable, or their dis-positions, which were kindly. But they were re-markably naive and optimistic about the legal system in particular and the world in general, and much further from omniscience than they so earnestly believed. Theirs was a tidy, linear world where simple stimuli in the courts would produce simple responses among producers and insurers. They thought they were dealing with a mule, which if prodded judiciously in the rear would proceed forward. But the beast was really an octopus, with no discernible rear to speak of, and capable of the most unpredictable reactions from the most unexpected directions.

Chapter 17

The Crisis Is Injuries, Not Liability

Richard L. Abel

Most commentators who invoke the shibboleth "tort crisis" maintain that the problem is too much liability and that this is a recent and temporay phenomenon. They blame trigger-happy litigants, greedy lawyers, irresponsible juries, and bleeding-heart judges. They deplore the increased cost of insurance, its unavailability to some, the willingness of others to "go bare," and the impact of all this on the production of vital goods and services. Like all effective propaganda, this account contains a kernel of truth. Victims obtain more favorable outcomes in the tort system today than they did in the past—although re-

covery is still based on fault. Juries occasionally award large verdicts, but many are reduced by judges, and most verdicts are small (for example, half were less than $8,000 in Cook County, Illinois, between 1960 and 1979). Indeed, if the largest verdicts are excluded, the median has actually been declining.[1]

Propaganda does not mislead through lies, however, but through partial truths. The jeremiads about the "tort crisis" ignore the fact that fluctuations in insurance premiums, which affect everyone, are at least as much a function of interest-rate cycles as of changes in liability rules or jury awards. And they greatly exaggerate the extent to which inflation in the price of goods and services is attributable to higher insurance premiums, which normally constitute an insignificant fraction of total costs.

I see the problem very differently—as an epidemic of injuries with deep historical roots and structural causes. Successful tort claims do not create accident cost: they merely shift them from victims to tortfeasors. It is tortfeasors who inflict costs on society by injuring victims. Liability costs are high because injuries are frequent and serious. Several independent surveys reveal that a majority of people suffer at least one serious injury during their lives.[2] Far too few of them recover damages from a tortfeasor. The present tort system is largely responsible for this failure, which leaves victims uncompensated, allows entrepreneurs to continue creating unreasonable risks and causing injuries, and permits moral dereliction to go unpunished.

MANY INJURY VICTIMS FAIL TO CLAIM

The few studies that attempt to determine what proportion of those legally entitled to tort damages actually recover amply support the conclusion that many eligible victims fail to claim. A joint study by the American Bar Association and the American Bar Foundation ascertained that only 16 percent of those who reported tort problems consulted lawyers about them.[3] Another investigation, comparing expert judgments about injuries caused by medical malpractice with subsequent claims, found that only 10 percent of victims claimed, and only 4 percent recovered damages. Even among those who suffered a significant permanent partial disability, less than 15 percent claimed damages, and only 6.5 percent recovered.[4] A third study of hospital records found that only 6.7 percent of significant injuries caused by medical malpractice led to claims and noted that even this figure was inflated, since the cause of many injuries could not be identified from the records.[5] And a fourth inquiry found that 40 percent of the incidents that physicians reported to their own insurers as malpractice never resulted in claims.[6]

Medical patients may fail to claim because they do not recognize they have suffered a compensable injury or are (perhaps justifiably) pessimistic about the speed and likelihood of recovery. Injured workers fail to claim for a different reason: fear of employer retaliation for the liability costs, increased insurance premiums, or intensified scrutiny by agencies charged with protecting worker safety. Although the National Safety Council estimated that there were 11,600 workplace deaths in 1985, employers reported only 3,750 to the U.S. Bureau of Labor Statistics. Chrysler recently paid over $300,000 in fines to settle charges that it willfully failed to report worker injuries, and the U.S. Department of Labor has filed similar charges against other major corporations, including Union Carbide, Monsanto, Shell Oil, Fina, and USX Corporation.[7] The California Supreme Court has allowed employees to sue the Johns-Manville Corporation in tort (rather than claiming workers' compensation, usually the exclusive remedy), because for decades the company concealed health records showing that those workers were suffering from asbestos exposure.[8] And a study whose methodol-

ogy resembled that of the medical malpractice research cited above found that only about 37 percent of work-accident victims claim workers' compensation, which is available by law regardless of employer or employee fault.[9]

Even road-accident victims often fail to claim, although police generally record the event, most tortfeasors and victims are strangers to each other, and liability insurance is widespread. In New York City in the late 1950s, 64 percent of those suffering slight shock or contusion recovered some compensation within two years; but it seems likely that recovery was less frequent among that half of the victims who could not be located by the researchers.[10] In Michigan in the 1960s, only 14 percent of automobile-accident victims even retained a lawyer, although half of those suffering more serious injury did so.[11]

The most comprehensive study of claims by the injured was conducted in England in the late 1970s.[12] Among those who suffered at least two weeks of incapacity, 47 percent of road-accident victims considered claiming, as did 46 percent of work-accident victims and 9 percent of victims in other accidents. A third of road-accident victims consulted lawyers, along with a quarter of work-accident victims and 3 percent of other accident victims. Victims obtained some recover from tortfeasors in 29 percent of road accidents, 19 percent of work accidents; and 2 percent of other accidents. Because 86 percent of all accidents fell within this last category, only 12 percent of those who suffered two weeks of incapacity from injuries recovered any damages. Although this study did not attempt to ascertain which accident victims were legally entitled to damages, the proportion must have been far greater than 12 percent. . . .

TORT VICTIMS SHOULD CLAIM DAMAGES

. . . Most scholars agree that tort law has three principal objectives: redressing the violation of important norms, compensating victims, and discouraging unsafe behavior.

All torts are normative violations. The tortfeasor has behaved unreasonably and caused injury to another. To preserve and strengthen the violated norm is imperative to publicize the violation and punish the wrongdoer. Émile Durkheim argued that transgressions offer society an opportunity to punish thereby reasserting its commitment to the broken norm.[13] Repeated failure to punish violations invites nullification. There is also evidence that expectations about the availability of compensation strongly influence the victim's attribution of moral blarney. Increasing victim confidence in the possibility of recovery, therefore, would have the salutary effect of reinforcing moral censure.

Normative violations must also be redressed for the sake of the victim's psychological well-being. Some societies require tortfeasors to apologize to victims as part of the remedial process. In others, honor compels victims or their kin to seek revenge. American social structure and culture may preclude these responses, but the victim's hurt and anger still demand legal redress in *every* case. Unredressed wrongs allow resentment to fester, breeding feelings of pervasive injustice and persecution and sometimes leading to acts of violence. This is one reason why the American criminal justice system has recently sought to reinvolve victims in the prosecution of criminals.

Nineteenth-century American law made the defendant's (and sometimes the plaintiff's) *moral* fault a central element of all tort claims. Contemporary tort law tends to emphasize compensation instead. Some advocates of compensation are motivated by compassion for the victim; others are more concerned with restoring victims to productive life so that they do not become dependent on public or private welfare. But both perspectives deem it essential that every needy victim have the greatest possible opportunity to claim tort damages. Disagreements about

the quantum of damages—pain and suffering, punitive damages, collateral sources, and ceilings—do not diminish the importance of increasing the frequency of claims. . . .

Although there is disagreement about whether tort liability should be fault-based (negligence) or strict (predicated on mere causation), no one would deny the importance of discouraging dangerous behavior. Indeed, scholars who differ in most other respects agree that this is its most important function. Even if we were willing to allow victims to choose whether to seek an apology or compensation, we could not be equally indifferent about whether they mobilized the deterrent sanction of tort liability. Dangerous behavior is a continuing threat to people other than its immediate victim. The importance of tort liability as an incentive for safety is magnified by the conservative attack on government regulation (most devastating during the Reagan administration), complemented by the perennial suspicions of liberals about the capacity of industry to capture its regulators. We have no choice, therefore, but to make tort law the most effective regulatory instrument possible.

Research has repeatedly confirmed that the likelihood of suffering punishment is at least as important in influencing behavior as the severity of the penalty, and probably more important. . . .

It is in the residual category of accidents—those suffered by consumers and bystanders as a result of the production and sale of goods and services for profit—that tort liability is most likely to reduce risk. Here, damage awards not only encourage potential tortfeasors to be safer but also inform consumers about dangerous goods and services. Lawsuits responding to toxic shock syndrome, injuries caused by ILJDs, and airplane crashes undoubtedly shape consumer choice. Free market advocates who deplore government regulation should welcome the role of tort claims in reducing market imperfections by increasing consumer information. The data strongly suggest, however, that the very claims that could do the most to reduce injury are rarely made. The definitive English study found that 86 percent of the injuries that incapacitated their victims for at least two weeks occurred in environments other than the road or the workplace. Yet only 3 percent of those victims claimed, and only 2 percent recovered damages. Although some of this difference reflects the fact that no one was legally liable rather than the failure of victims to claim damages to which they are legally entitled, and profit-seeking entrepreneur operating within a competitive market would have to discount the threat of tort liability very heavily in deciding how much to spend on safety. This indifference to safety is not a matter of personal callousness, because it does not reflect individual choice; an entrepreneur who fails to cut safety costs whenever the tort system permits it will be put out of business by a competitor who does.

Increasing the frequency of claims is imperative, therefore, if tort law is to perform its undisputed functions. The failure of victims to claim erodes the norm against injuring others, allows anger and resentment to fester, leaves the most disadvantaged victims uncompensated and often impoverished, and tolerates—indeed encourages—dangerous behavior. A higher claims rate could improve the functioning of the tort system more dramatically than *any* other politically feasible change. If all injury victims claimed, the English study suggests, the impact of tort law could triple in road accidents, quadruple in work accidents, and increase thirtyfold in the residual category, which represents 86 percent of all accidental injuries (the actual effect, of course, would depend on how many of these claims prevailed). . . .

Conclusion

For at least a decade, insurance companies, the medical profession, and corporate defendants have been deploring the "litigiousness" of Americans, who allegedly file unjustified claims for trivial or imaginary injuries. The media have disseminated this view, and many members of the public have uncritically accepted it. But the myth is false.[14] The real problem with the tort system is the *failure* of accident victims to claim.

The most significant reform of the system—far more consequential than incremental changes in substantive or procedural law—would be an increase in the rate of claiming. This would strengthen the norm against endangering and injuring others, relieve the anger of victims, ameliorate their financial plight, and encourage safety. Collective solicitation of victims would be an important step in this direction. All lawyers, but especially those who represent the injured, have a strong interest in launching such a program. It is inexpensive and requires no governmental action. Opponents of such a reform will have great difficulty explaining why lawyers should not advise injured victims of their legal rights. Lawyers, who long have been on the defensive, will be visibly engaged in helping victims. They will be increasing access to the legal system and reducing the bias against those disadvantaged by race, gender, age, and class. And they will be curtailing the risks to which all of us are exposed. Asserting tort claims and helping others to do so is a vital civic duty.

Notes

1. Mark Peterson and George Priest, *The Civil Jury: Trends in Trials and Verdicts* (Santa Monica, Calif.: Rand Corporation, 1981).

2. Barbara Curran, *The Legal Needs of the Public* (Chicago: American Bar Foundation, 1977), 117; Donald Harris et al., *Compensation and Support for Illness and Injury* (Oxford: Clarendon Press, 1984), 31; "Census Study Reports 1 in 5 Suffering From a Disability," *New York Times,* 23 Dec. 1986.

3. Curran, 145.

4. Patricia Danzon, *Medical Malpractice: Theory, Evidence, and Public Policy* (Cambridge, Mass: Harvard University Press, 1985), 19–20, 23.

5. L. Pocincki, S. Dagger, and B. Schwartz, "The Incidence of Latrogenic Injuries," *Appendix to Report of the Secretary's Commission on Medical Malpractice* (Washington, D.C.: U.S. Department of Health, Education and Welfare, 1973), 50–70.

6. Office of the Secretary, U.S. Department of Health, Education and Welfare, *Study of Medical Malpractice Claims Closed in 1970* (Washington, DC: U.S. Department of Health, Education and Welfare, 1973).

7. Holcomb Noble, "Certain Numbers Can Kill," *New York Times,* 28 November 1986; idem, "Chrysler Will Pay $295,000 Fine for Violations in Injury Records," *New York Times,* 31 Jan. 1987.

8. *Johns-Manville Products Corp. v. Superior Court,* 27 Cal.3d 465. 612 P.2d 948 165 Cal Rptr 858 (1980).

9. Lois Sincere, "Processing Workers' Compensation Claims in Illinois," *American Bar Foundation Research Journal* (1982), 1073, 1105.

10. Robert Hunting and Gloria Neuwirth, *Who Sues in New York City: A Study of Automobile Accident Claims* (New York: Columbia University Press, 1962), 4–8, 36–39.

11. Alfred Conard, "The Economic Treatment of Automobile Injuries," *Michigan Law Review* 63 (1964): 279, 285.

12. Harris et al.

13. Émile Durkheim, *The Division of Labor in Society* (Glencoe, IL: Free Press, 1933), chap. 2; Kai Erikson, *Wayward Puritans* (New Haven, CT: Yale University Press, 1968).

14. Marc Galanter, "Reading the Landscape of Disputes: What We Know and Don't Know (And Think We Know) About Our Allegedly Contentious and Litigious Society," *UCLA Law Review* 31 (1983): 4.

Notes and Questions

1. What is "tort liability"? Why does Huber refer to it as a tax? How does tort liability differ from contract liability?

2. What is the economic rationale behind the development of modern tort law? Do you find the Founders' concerns compelling? Why or why not?

3. In Chapter 16, Huber argues that the current freedom of the consumer to sue has been achieved "only by surrendering an older right, the right to contract, which in the long run is worth far more." Do you agree with Huber on the relative value of the right to sue versus the right to contract? Why or why not?

4. Huber points out that "contract-centered law placed enormous confidence in individuals to manage the risks of their personal environments." Is such enormous confidence reasonable? How might people's race, class, and/or gender affect their ability (for better or for worse) to "manage the risks of their personal environment"?

5. According to Abel in Chapter 17, what are the three principal objectives of the tort system? In your opinion, are the courts the best arena to pursue any or all of these objectives? Why or why not? Why does Abel insist that "increasing the frequency of claims is imperative"?

6. What do Huber and Abel each say about the most desirable allocation of the costs of an accident?

7. How does Huber weigh the rights of the individual against the "common good"? What about Felstiner, Abel, and Sarat? Are their concerns different or the same as Huber's? How does Abel's perspective compare? Is any position more just than another?

8. Abel argues that tort liability is an important means of discouraging dangerous behavior. However, what Abel deems dangerous, Huber argues is just the reasonable risk associated with technological advancement. Whose argument do you find more compelling?

9. What criteria would you use if you had to decide what constituted "reasonable" levels of risk for a person to assume when

purchasing a product or service? Would your criteria vary at all if the product were more of a "high stakes" product (e.g., medical care)? What if a consumer is unable to afford the most reputable brand? Does this make a difference?

10. Is there a reasonable balance between the "litigation explosion" that Huber la-

ments and the "epidemic of injuries" that Abel decries? How would you propose to reconcile the two?

Reprinted from: Richard L. Abel, "The Crisis Is Injuries, Not Liability" from *Proceedings of the Academy of Political Science*, 37:1(1988), pp. 31–41. Copyright © 1988. Reprinted with the permission from *Proceedings of the Academy of Political Science.* ✦

Chapter 18

How the Jury Decided How Much the Coffee Spill Was Worth

Andrea Gerling, the Wall Street Journal

Much of the recent argument about the litigation explosion is fueled by "horror stories," stories of unusual suits with large, seemingly unwarranted judgments. These stories are the product of sensationalized media reporting, which presents this outcome in a rather straightforward manner as resulting from greedy lawyers all too eager to take unworthy cases and juries that are hostile to corporate defendants.

The next reading examines one of the most celebrated of such stories, the so-called McDonald's hot coffee case. In this case, Stella Liebeck, 79 years old, was sitting in the passenger seat of her grandson's car, having purchased a cup of McDonald's coffee at the drive-up window. After the car stopped, she tried to hold the cup securely between her knees while removing the lid. However, the cup tipped over, pouring scalding hot coffee onto her. She received third-degree burns over 16 percent of her body, necessitating hospitalization for eight days, whirlpool treatment for her wounds, skin grafting, and disability for more than two years. Despite these extensive injuries, she offered to settle with

McDonald's for $20,000. However, McDonald's refused. The case eventually went to trial.

Accounts of the trial indicate that the jury heard the following evidence:

> By corporate specifications, McDonald's sells its coffee at 180 to 190 degrees Fahrenheit; Coffee at that temperature, if spilled, causes third-degree burns (the skin is burned away down to the muscle/fatty-tissue layer) in two to seven seconds; Third-degree burns do not heal without skin grafting and treatments that cost tens of thousands of dollars and result in permanent disfigurement, extreme pain and disability of the victim for many months, and in some cases, years; The chairman of the department of mechanical engineering and bio-mechanical engineering at the University of Texas testified that this risk of harm is unacceptable, as did a widely recognized expert on burns, the editor in chief of the leading scholarly publication in the specialty, The Journal of Burn Care and Rehabilitation.

McDonald's admitted that it knew about the risk of serious burns from its scalding hot coffee for more than 10 years—the risk was brought to its attention through numerous other claims and suits; From 1982 to 1992, McDonald's coffee burned more than 700 people, many receiving severe burns to the genital area, inner thighs, and buttocks; Not only men and women, but also children and infants have been burned by McDonald's scalding hot coffee, in some instances due to inadvertent spillage by McDonald's employees; At least one woman had coffee dropped in her lap through the service window, causing third-degree burns to her inner thighs and other sensitive areas, which resulted in disability for years; Witnesses for McDonald's admitted in court that consumers are unaware of the extent of the risk of serious burns from spilled coffee served at McDonald's required temperature; McDonald's admitted that it did not warn customers of the nature and extent of this risk and could offer no explanation as to why it did not; McDonald's witnesses testified that it did not intend to turn down the heat. As one witness put it, 'No, there is no current plan to change the procedure that we're using in that regard right now;' McDonald's admitted that its coffee is 'not fit for consumption' when sold because it causes severe scalds if spilled or drunk; Liebeck's physician testified that her injury was one of the worst scald burns he had ever seen."

The jury awarded Liebeck $200,000 in compensatory damages, reduced to $160,000 because the jury found her 20 percent at fault, and $2.7 million in punitive damages for McDonald's callous conduct. However, the trial judge lowered the punitive damages to $480,000. Subsequently, the parties entered a post-verdict settlement.

As you read the article, consider the following: Why didn't McDonald's agree to settle this case before trial? What does the fact that the judge reduced their award suggest about whether the jury's award was reasonable?

When a law firm here found itself defending McDonald's Corp. in a suit last year that claimed the company served dangerously hot coffee, it hired a law student to take temperatures at other local restaurants for comparison.

After dutifully slipping a thermometer into steaming cups and mugs all over the city, Danny Jarrett found that none came closer than about 20 degrees to the temperature at which McDonald's coffee is poured, about 180 degrees.

It should have been a warning.

But McDonald's lawyers went on to dismiss several opportunities to settle out of court, apparently convinced that no jury would punish a company for serving coffee the way customers like it. After all, its coffee's temperature helps explain why McDonald's sells a billion cups a year. But now—days after a jury here

awarded $2.9 million to an 81-year-old woman scalded by McDonald's coffee—some observers say the defense was naive.

"I drink McDonald's coffee because it's hot, the hottest coffee around," says Robert Gregg, a Dallas defense attorney who consumes it during morning drives to the office. "But I've predicted for years that someone's going to win a suit, because I've spilled it on myself. And unlike the coffee I make at home, it's really hot. I mean, man, it hurts."

McDonald's, known for its fastidious control over franchisees, requires that its coffee be prepared at very high temperatures, based on recommendations of coffee consultants and industry groups that say hot temperatures are necessary to fully extract the flavor during brewing. Before trial, McDonald's gave the opposing lawyer its operations and training manual, which says its coffee must be brewed at 195 to 205 degrees and held at 180 to 190 degrees for optimal taste. Since the verdict, McDonald's has declined to offer any comment, as have its attorneys. It's unclear if the company, whose coffee cups warn drinkers that the contents are hot, plans to change its preparation procedures. . . .

Public opinion is squarely on the side of McDonald's. Polls have shown a large majority of Americans—including many who typically support the little guy—to be outraged at the verdict. And radio talk show hosts around the country have lambasted the plaintiff, her attorneys and the jurors on air. Declining to be interviewed for this story, one juror explained that he already had received angry calls from citizens around the country.

It's a reaction that many of the jurors could have understood—before they heard the evidence. At the beginning of the trial, jury foreman Jerry Goens says he "wasn't convinced as to why I needed to be there to settle a coffee spill."

At that point, Goens and the other jurors knew only the basic facts: that two years earlier, Stella Liebeck had bought a 49-cent cup of coffee at the drive-in window of an Albuquerque McDonald's, and while removing the lid to add cream and sugar had spilled it, causing third-degree burns of the groin inner thighs and buttocks. Her suit filed in state court in Albuquerque, claimed the coffee was "defective" because it was so hot.

What the jury didn't realize initially was the severity of her burns. Told during the trial of Liebeck's seven days in the hospital and of her skin grafts, and shown gruesome photographs, jurors began taking the matter more seriously. "It made me come home and tell my wife and daughters don't drink coffee in the car, at least not hot," says juror Jack Elliott.

Even more eye-opening was the revelation that McDonald's had seen such injuries many times before. Company documents showed that in the past decade McDonald's had received at least 700 reports of coffee burns ranging from mild to third degree, and had settled claims arising from scalding injuries for more than $500,000.

Some observers wonder why McDonald's, after years of settling coffee-burn cases, chose to take this one to trial. After all, the plaintiff was a sympathetic figure—an articulate, 81-year-old former department store clerk who said under oath that she had never filed suit before. In fact, she said, she never would have filed this one if McDonald's hadn't dismissed her request, for compensation for pain and medical bills, with an offer of $800. . . .

As the trial date approached, McDonald's declined to settle. At one point, Morgan says he offered to drop the case for $300,000, and was willing to accept half that amount. But McDonald's didn't bite.

Only days before the trial, Judge Scott ordered both sides to attend a mediation session. The mediator, a retired judge, recommended that McDonald's settle for $225,000, saying a jury would be likely to award that amount. The company didn't follow his recommendation.

Instead, McDonald's continued denying any liability for Liebeck's burns. The com-

pany suggested that she may have contributed to her injuries by holding the cup between her legs and not removing her clothing immediately. And it also argued that "Mrs. Liebeck's age may have caused her injuries to have been worse than they might have been to a younger individual," since older skin is thinner and more vulnerable to injury.

The trial lasted seven sometimes mind-numbing days. Experts dueled over the temperature at which coffee causes burns. A scientist testifying for McDonald's argued that any coffee hotter than 130 degrees could produce third-degree burns, so it didn't matter whether McDonald's coffee was hotter. But a doctor testifying on behalf of Liebeck argued that lowering the serving temperature to about 160 degrees could make a big difference, because it takes less than three seconds to produce a third-degree burn at 190 degrees, about 12 to 15 seconds at 180 degrees and about 20 seconds at 160 degrees.

The testimony of Appleton, the McDonald's executive, didn't help the company, jurors said later. He testified that McDonald's knew its coffee sometimes caused serious burns, but hadn't consulted burn experts about it. He also testified that McDonald's had decided not to warn customers about the possibility of severe burns, even though most people didn't think it possible. Finally, he testified that McDonald's didn't intend to change any of its coffee policies or procedures, saying, "There are more serious dangers in restaurants."

Elliott, the juror, says he began to realize that the case was about "callous disregard for the safety of the people."

Next for the defense came P. Robert Knaff, a human-factors engineer who earned $15,000 in fees from the case and who, several jurors said later, didn't help McDonald's either. Knaff told the jury that hot-coffee burns were statistically insignificant when compared to the billion cups of coffee McDonald's sells annually.

To jurors, Knaff seemed to be saying that the graphic photos they had seen of Liebeck's burns didn't matter because they were rare. "There was a person behind every number, and I don't think the corporation was attaching enough importance, to that," says juror Betty Farnham.

When the panel reached the jury room, it swiftly arrived at the conclusion that McDonald's was liable. "The facts were so overwhelmingly against the company," says Farnham. "They were not taking care of their consumers."

Then the six men and six women decided on compensatory damages of $200,000, which they reduced to $160,000 after determining that 20 percent of the fault belonged with Liebeck for spilling the coffee.

The jury then found that McDonald's had engaged in willful, reckless, malicious or wanton conduct, the basis for punitive damages. Morgan had suggested penalizing McDonald's the equivalent of one to two days of companywide coffee sales, he estimated at $1.35 million a day. During the four-hour deliberation, a few jurors unsuccessfully argued for as much as $9.6 million in punitive damages. But in the end, the jury settled on $2.7 million. McDonald's asked the judge for a new trial. Judge Scott has asked both sides to meet with a mediator to discuss settling the case before he rules on McDonald's request. The judge also has the authority to disregard the jury's finding or decrease the amount of damages.

One day after the verdict, a local reporter tested the coffee at the McDonald's that had served Liebeck and found it to be a comparatively cool 158 degrees. But industry officials say they doubt that this signals any companywide change. After all, in a series of focus groups last year, customers who buy McDonald's coffee at least weekly say that "morning coffee has minimal taste requirement, but must be hot," to the point of steaming.

Notes and Questions

1. Does this case better illustrate the problem of a "litigation explosion" or the gravity of an "epidemic of injuries?"

2. In the context of Felstiner, Abel, and Sarat's (Chapter 15) "Emergence and Transformation of Disputes," consider the path Ms. Liebeck took from the moment of the spill to the verdict in the court case. Would Felstiner, Abel, and Sarat agree that her injury ought to have been litigated? Why or why not? What about Huber (Chapter 16)?

3. Was the verdict in this case reasonable? Why or why not? How well does the verdict address the three principal objectives of tort law that Abel (Chapter 17) outlines (redressing the violation of important norms, compensating victims, and discouraging unsafe behavior)?

4. Suppose for a moment that the facts of the case were different, and the plaintiff were, say, a wealthy, young male with a state-of-the-art cup holder in his car that he had failed to use at the time of the coffee spill. Would that change how you would assign fault or negligence in the case? Should such assignment of responsibility be contingent upon social factors (race, class, gender)?

5. McDonald's argued at trial that Ms. Liebeck's coffee spill was statistically insignificant relative to all the unspilled coffee sold in McDonald's franchises every year. The jury did not agree. Which argument do you find more compelling? How would Huber and Abel each respond to the argument over statistical significance versus individual human suffering? What about Felstiner, Abel, and Sarat?

6. How might the outcome of this widely publicized case change the general atti-

tude of restaurant proprietors toward customer safety in the future? In your opinion, would such a change be positive or negative? Why?

Chapter 19

Jurors' Judgments of Business Liability in Tort Cases

Implications of the Litigation Explosion Debate

Valerie P. Hans
William S. Lofquist

How responsible are juries like the one in the McDonald's coffee case described in the previous reading? Juries that make large damage awards in questionable cases are one of the factors that scholars, like Huber (Chapter 16), believe encourages frivolous lawsuits. Yet most disputes never get to court, and of those that do most are settled between the parties without trial. The 1992 Civil Justice Survey of State Courts estimated that only 3 percent of 762,000 tort, contract, and property disputes disposed of by the courts were resolved by a jury or a judge's decision after a trial.

What this means is that jury verdicts are rare. It may be, however, that the verdicts are very consequential in terms of their influence on how people perceive the legal system and on whether citizens seek access to the courts.

The next reading reports on a study of jurors in cases brought by individuals against businesses. Contrary to popular belief, jurors are typically skeptical of the claims made by indi-viduals in these cases. In the course of their deliberations, they are more likely to focus on the actions and motivations of those who bring the cases than on the responsibilities of business. Finally, jurors speak about the litigation explosion and the importance of limiting awards in even meritorious cases.

This article reports and analyzes findings from a study with tort jurors in business cases. The project, which uses interview methods, provides twin opportunities. First, the interviews allow us to make a unique contribution to a lively debate in scholarly and policy circles about the jury's role in an alleged litigation explosion.... Second, jurors' accounts of decisionmaking in business trials provide a window for observing how laypersons approach and decide issues of business responsibility. Studying jurors' accounts permits us to examine whether and how lay conceptualizations of business responsibility are distinct from other liability and responsibility judgments.

CONTROVERSY OVER THE JURY IN PERSONAL INJURY LAWSUITS

The civil jury has come under strong attack for its performance in cases involving business and corporate parties. Although the criticisms vary somewhat, most critics assert that juries perform poorly in business cases and recommend that the role of the civil jury in business litigation be subject to greater regulation or even eliminated. Some critics and courts question the jury's competence to decide complex issues related to business wrongdoing. . . . These critics argue that although the jury has an important place in the criminal justice system, its ability to understand and decide complicated business and economic disputes is limited. Scholars point to the unpredictability and wide variability in civil jury verdicts and awards as evidence of the weakness of the jury as a civil dispute resolution mechanism (e.g., Huber 1990; Olson 1991; Priest 1990).

A second line of attack asserts that juries are biased against corporate defendants in personal injury cases (Huber 1988; Olson 1991). According to this argument, which enjoys substantial business and political support, the populist character of the jury predisposes it to sympathize with the injured individual rather than with the large, impersonal corporation. In this view, jurors bend the evidence or the law so that they may compensate the injured plaintiff and satisfy their own feelings of equity. Closely related to this argument is the assertion that the jury is furthering a litigation explosion by granting large awards in meritless lawsuits against "deep-pockets" defendants such as big businesses (Daniels 1989; Huber 1988). . . .

RESULTS

In general, our research findings are consistent with the view that the contributions of the civil jury to the litigation explosion are exaggerated. Rather than revealing jurors willing or eager to impose on business the costs of plaintiffs' injuries, our findings show that jurors were suspicious of the legitimacy of plaintiffs' claims and concerned about the personal and social costs of large jury awards. Despite insistence on product safety and high expectations of business, jurors were generally favorable toward business, skeptical more about the profit motives of individual plaintiffs than of business defendants, and committed to holding down awards. Below we provide evidence for our conclusions from the tort jurors' interviews and questionnaire data.

TORT JURORS' ATTITUDES TOWARD CIVIL LITIGATION

Jurors' responses to questionnaire items about the legitimacy of civil lawsuits revealed considerable skepticism toward plaintiffs and civil litigation. . . . [T]ort jurors had strong neg-

ative views about the frequency and legitimacy of civil lawsuits. About four of every five jurors believed that "People are too quick to sue, rather than trying to solve disputes in some way," and asserted: "There are far too many frivolous lawsuits today." Just a third of the jurors agreed that "Most people who sue others in court have legitimate grievances." Jurors rejected the statement that "By making it easier to sue, the courts have made this a safer society" by a ten-to-one margin. However, just one-third went so far as to assert that "The large number of lawsuits show that our society is breaking down." . . .

TORT JURORS' SKEPTICISM TOWARD PLAINTIFFS

As their general responses to questions about civil litigation imply, the tort jurors approached their own cases with considerable suspicion about the plaintiff. Indeed, in these personal injury lawsuits, jurors focused most on the plaintiffs in the case, rather than on the businesses that were sued. Consistent with other research (e.g., Pennington & Hastie 1986) showing that criminal jurors develop a story of the incident leading to the trial and make motivational inferences about the parties in the cases, the civil jurors in our study actively developed stories about the accidents that injured the plaintiffs and about the paths the plaintiffs traveled to arrive at the courthouse. The stories usually revolved around the motivations of the plaintiffs and their attorneys rather than the responsibilities or characteristics of businesses. . . .

Jurors' dubiousness about plaintiff claims led them to scrutinize the personal behavior of plaintiffs, trying to understand their motives and to assess the reasonableness of their claims. Seemingly no aspect of the plaintiffs' behavior was beyond question. Jurors often penalized plaintiffs who did not meet high standards of credibility and behavior, including those who did not act or appear as injured as they claimed, those who did not appear deserving due to their already high standard of living, those with preexisting medical conditions, and those who did not do enough to help themselves recover from their injuries. . . .

Although the majority of jurors were suspicious of plaintiff claims, jurors were not uniformly critical. In a number of cases a minority of jurors spoke up for the legitimacy of plaintiff claims. For example, in workplace accidents . . . , jurors who favored the plaintiff tried to explain away his failure to use safety equipment by arguing that his supervisor should not have told him to undertake the risky action, and pointed out that because the worker was new to the job, it would have been hard to refuse. In an asbestos case in which other jurors had derided the plaintiffs ("I figured that they were comfortable and they were just out to get a large sum of money to take trips and buy bigger boats"), one juror in the minority used the plaintiffs' comfortable lifestyle to maintain in their favor: "It wasn't like they were just trying to sue 'cause they had money or they wouldn't be taking all these vacations and having all these boats. . . . It wasn't just all about money. . . . They gave me an impression they just wanted to get what was rightfully theirs." On the whole, however, plaintiffs were subjected to a surprising degree of suspicion regarding motivation and deservingness that, as we detail below, was not typically imposed on defendants.

In addition, and probably contributing to the scrutiny shown plaintiffs, there was the widespread impression among jurors that the civil litigation system is overburdened by claimants seeking awards in meritless cases. As one juror put it: "People are too quick to sue nowadays. They're looking for the deep pockets." Comments about excessive and meritless litigation were accompanied by expressions of concern about higher insurance premiums and businesses passing on costs to customers.

These negative comments about plaintiffs might seem to be at odds with the fact that plaintiffs won 14 out of the 18 trials. Yet many of these comments occurred in cases in which the plaintiff prevailed on the verdict. Some jurors used anti-plaintiff remarks to argue against liability, while others employed them to argue against high awards. Jurors who were doubtful about liability often compromised with the other jurors on liability in exchange for a reduced award. . . .

TORT JURORS' ATTITUDES TOWARD BUSINESS

Comparing the reactions of jurors to personal injury plaintiffs and business defendants produced some surprising results. Contrary to the skepticism shown plaintiffs, corporate defendants were typically not subjected to such vigorous scrutiny. Even when jurors concluded, as they did in most cases, that the legal requirements for liability had been met and that a plaintiff award was in order, the majority of jurors expressed neutral or positive views of the business litigants. Findings of liability thus were not typically associated with conclusions that businesses had intended to harm workers or consumers or with condemnations of the business community. . . .

THE CORPORATION AS GHOST

The questionnaire responses suggest that jurors might be quite demanding of corporate defendants, particularly in instances in which the safety of the public is at issue. Yet we found little evidence of tough standards and punitiveness toward the corporation in the specific cases decided by the tort jurors. An unexpected finding was that the ways in which jurors talked about businesses were much less concrete than the way in which they evaluated plaintiffs. Part of the reason for this difference may be traced to the fact that in many cases no individual from the corporation presented trial testimony. There's an adage that it is hard to punish corporations because they have "no body to kick, no soul to damn." Continuing the metaphor, the corporation is often a "ghost" in the courtroom. In our study, the attorney was often the only representative of the business in court. In most of the cases in the sample, the CEOs stayed away. Jurors often wondered where they were. Yet the business executives' absence seemed to work to their advantage, in that jurors had few grounds on which to make the kinds of detailed evaluations and inferences about their behavior that characterized their judgments of the plaintiffs.

When asked how they were affected by the presence of a corporation in their case, many jurors replied that they were not influenced by the presence of a corporation. As one juror stated, "It didn't really affect me. I try to be fair with people." Another replied, "It didn't matter whether it was an individual or a corporation. I was more interested in the exact testimony that was presented." When we asked jurors to take the next step, and comment as to whether they viewed corporations differently from individuals, a commonly expressed view was that "businesses and corporations are made up of individuals. They don't act as a body that has no mind or anything. They are individuals and it's kind of a fallacy for me to think that a business [is different from] the people who make up the business." . . .

Thus, in many personal injury cases, the jurors' attention was captured by the individual-level drama and concrete specifics of the case. Though some jurors expressed disdain for the profit motives of corporations, most paid particular attention to the actions and motivations of particular actors, especially the plaintiff. The plaintiffs were more likely to be in the courtroom and easily identifiable. As jurors developed accounts of what happened in the accident, the absence of the corporation or the difficulty of finding a way to conceptualize it as an actor seemed to minimize its consideration by jurors. Tort jurors held high standards for business in the abstract, as we saw in their questionnaire responses, yet these standards became more diffused or difficult to apply as jurors approached the concrete task of assess-

ing responsibility and compensation in individual cases. . . .

In a few cases in which multiple parties potentially caused a workplace accident, some jurors thought that the corporate setting made it difficult to figure out what had happened. They imagined that simpler scenarios would occur in cases with individual parties. One juror said, "I guess it would be different if it was just a person in a home. . . . Hopefully you would have more explicit information and would know what the heck was going on rather than everybody hinting at this is what happened or that is what happened and nobody having an accident report." Another juror from the same case agreed, saying, "I think if it was at home, someone would know exactly what happened. But this was sort of a mystery." These remarks are consistent with scholarly research that diffusion of responsibility can limit the culpability attributed to actors within hierarchical groups such as corporations (Kelman & Hamilton 1989; Hans 1990).

Finally, there was some scattered concern about the profit motive causing business to cut corners. During one of the asbestos jury deliberations, two automobile workers talked about their own experiences within a corporate environment. One of them recounted a statement the other made during jury deliberation: "You people in here have probably never worked for the type of production company that these companies were. We have. We know what goes on. If it's anything that cuts the bottom line, boy, forget it. It's out. . . . All big corporations, look, the bottom line is profit. If it's not profitable, or anything that cuts into the profit, forget it, we don't do it." However, contrary to our initial expectations, such comments derogating business were rare compared to the more frequent negative evaluations of the plaintiffs and their mercenary motives. . . .

DEEP POCKETS

Because critics routinely assert that the deep pockets of the corporation influence jury awards, it was of great interest to examine how jurors treated the business defendant's financial resources. In the interviews, the feature of a corporate party most often mentioned by jurors was its financial resources. However, jurors were sharply divided in their views of the appropriateness of considering financial resources. A clear minority of the sample took the position succinctly summarized by a juror about the companies in an asbestos case: "Well, we figured they could afford to pay."

A much more common position was that the organization's assets should not be and were not relevant to the liability and award decisions. In advancing this view, a number of jurors brought up the fact that *other* members of their jury mentioned the deep pockets of the corporation but that *they personally* disagreed that a company's ability to pay should be considered in arriving at an award. In a workplace accident case:

> There were a few individuals on the jury that felt the fact that there's a corporation involved, the corporation can afford to put up the money for this situation. . . . [T]hey felt like, well, we're just dealing with big business and no person is really going to be hurt. So we'll award some money to these people and we'll take care of poor [George] who fell off the beam. That bothered me. I didn't see that there was any reason that the fact that a corporation was involved had anything to do with it at all. And in fact I was very adamant in deliberation that we should not be deciding this case on the fact that we feel sorry for [George]. . . .

DISCUSSION

JUROR DECISIONMAKING AND THE LITIGATION EXPLOSION

. . . Media stories, insurance industry advertisements, and popular wisdom often portray the American civil jury as generous to plaintiffs who sue corporations (Daniels 1989; Hans 1989; Huber 1988; Olson 1991). In the critics' eyes, jurors fail to discriminate between meritorious and frivolous lawsuits,

and reward plaintiffs excessively from the deep pockets of corporate defendants.

This article furnishes some contrary evidence from the subjective perspectives of the jurors. The interviews revealed that civil jurors expressed skepticism of plaintiff claims, described a conservative approach to determining awards, and reported expending effort to treat corporations the same as individuals. By their own accounts, jurors were strongly committed to the responsibilities they had not only to the parties but also to the community. Their recognition of the greater financial and other resources of the business corporation was tempered by their concern about the negative societal consequences of high awards. Most asserted that corporations and individuals should be judged by the same standard of responsibility. . . .

A second important contribution of our study to the growing critical commentary on the litigation explosion debate is its elaboration of the role of juror conceptualizations of business responsibility. Despite evidence of concern about business wrongdoing and high expectations of business, at least in the abstract, at the level of the case, jurors rarely demonstrated the scrutiny or expressed the negativity toward corporations that they showed toward individual plaintiffs, and sometimes had trouble concluding that business entities should be responsible. This was due in part to the absence in many cases of an identifiable corporate presence in the courtroom. Our research suggests two additional factors. First, consistent with the difficulties identified by sociolegal scholars of attaching legal responsibility to corporate entities, jurors showed a decided preference for discussing responsibility in terms of individual actors rather than organizational actors. Second, jurors found it difficult to accept the implications of some legal rules for business liability. When asked to hold contractors liable for injuries to workers hired by a subcontractor, for example, jurors faced a conflict with lay notions of responsibility. Holding the contractor liable extended the line of responsibility too far; imposing liability on the immediate employer or on the workers themselves was more congruent with jurors' causal schemas. Although jurors reported complying with the law, their awards were probably reduced, as jurors with differing views of the appropriateness of liability compromised with one another to arrive at a collective award. . . .

References

Appel, Andrea (1991) "Do Judicial Instructions Bridge the Deep Pockets Gap?" Honors thesis, University of Delaware, Newark.

Austin, Arthur D. (1984) *Complex Litigation Confronts the Jury System: A Case Study.* Frederick, MD: University Publications of America.

Daniels, Stephen (1989) "The Question of Jury Competence and the Politics of Civil Justice Reform: Symbols, Rhetoric, and Agenda-Building," 52 *Law & Contemporary Problems* 269.

——. (1990) "Tracing the Shadow of the Law: Jury Verdicts in Medical Malpractice Cases," *Justice System Journal* 4.

Daniels, Stephen, & Joanne Martin (1986) "Jury Verdicts and the 'Crisis' in Civil Justice," 11 *Justice System Journal* 321.

Drazen, Dan (1989) "The Case for Special Juries in Toxic Tort Litigation," *Judicature* 292.

Galanter, Marc (1983) "Reading the Landscape of Disputes: What We Know and Don't Know (and Think We Know) about Our Allegedly Contentious and Litigious Society," 31 *UCLA Law Rev.* 4.

——. (1986) "The Day after the Litigation Explosion," 46 *Maryland Law Rev.* 3.

Hans, Valerie P. (1990) "Attitudes Toward Corporate Responsibility: A Psycholegal Perspective," 69 *Nebraska Law Rev.* 158.

Huber, Peter (1988) *Liability: The Legal Revolution and Its Consequences.* New York: Basic Books.

——. (1990) "Junk Science and the Jury," *Univ. of Chicago Legal Forum* 273.

Kelman, Herbert, & Virginia L. Hamilton (1989) *Crimes of Obedience.* Cambridge, MA: Harvard Univ. Press.

Olson, Walter K. (1991) *The Litigation Explosion: What Happened When America Unleashed the Lawsuit.* New York: Dutton.

Priest, George L. (1985) "The Invention of Enterprise Liability: A Critical History of the Intellectual Foundations of Modern Tort Law," 14 *Journal of Legal Studies* 461.

——. (1990) "The Role of the Civil Jury in a System of Private Litigation," *Univ. of Chicago Legal Forum* 161.

Case Cited

In re Japanese Electronics Antitrust Litigation, 631 F.2d 1069 (3rd Cir. 1980).

Notes and Questions

1. On what grounds do critics attack the competence of civil juries to rule in personal injury lawsuits? Do you agree? Why or why not?

2. Contrary to popular belief, Hans and Lofquist reveal a tendency of jurors toward rather than against pro-business attitudes. How do you explain this tendency? What personal stake do jurors feel they have in civil litigation verdicts? In your opinion, do jurors display a greater reverence for the rights of the individual or for the common good?

3. Do juror responses to Hans and Lofquist's questionnaire corroborate or challenge Felstiner, Abel, and Sarat's characterization (Chapter 15) of the emergence and transformation of disputes in the United States today? According to Hans and Lofquist's study, how was "the path the plaintiffs traveled to arrive at the courthouse" important to jurors? In your estimation, should this path be important?

4. According to Hans and Lofquist, what is the significance of the corporate defendant's financial resources (deep pockets) for the verdict and jury award in a case?

Should there to be any connection between corporate assets and civil liability?

5. Hans and Lofquist report that "Jurors often penalized plaintiff . . . [such as] those who did not appear deserving due to their already high standards of living, those with preexisting medical conditions, and those who did not do enough to help themselves recover from their injuries." How does this finding reflect on Huber's account of the state of civil litigation?

6. Do Hans and Lofquist's findings change the way you read either Huber or Abel? If so, how?

Reprinted from: Valerie P. Hans and William S. Lofquist, "Jurors' Judgments of Business Liability in Tort Cases: Implications for the Litigation Explosion Debate" in *Law and Society Review*, 26:1, 1992, pp. 85–115. Copyright © 1992. Reprinted with the permission of the Law and Society Association. ✦

Section V

Lawyers in Civil Cases

Chapter 20

Lawyers and Consumer Protection Laws

Stewart Macaulay

The accessibility of law is to some extent determined by the accessibility of lawyers and legal services. Lawyers hold the key to the law for ordinary Americans. What they tell people about rights and duties goes a long way in determining whether people will make claims and pursue legal redress. In addition, lawyers can facilitate access by employing "contingent fee" arrangements. Under these arrangements, clients pay nothing for the services the lawyer provides unless, and until, they win their case. Critics allege that such fee arrangements contribute to the litigation explosion. But the fee structure is not the only factor determining the accessibility of lawyers. A variety of other things—e.g., social distance between client and lawyer, a sense of appropriateness, the relative ease of finding someone who specializes in a particular area of law—are also important.

The next three readings examine what lawyers do in civil cases, the services they provide, and the difference they make in terms of the results that people get when they bring their problems to law. The first, by Stewart Macaulay, describes the role of lawyers in one particular field, consumer protection. He argues that lawyers know little about the details of consumer protection law. Instead they rely on common sense and ideas about fairness to decide whose complaint is meritorious and whose is not. In so doing,

they screen out many claims for redress. They do not act merely as a tool for their clients.

As you read this essay, ask yourself if there is something about consumer problems that might account for what Macaulay describes. If lawyers do not know what the law is, what influences on legal outcomes are efforts to extend legal rights in new areas likely to have?

TOWARDS A NEW MODEL OF THE PRACTICE OF LAW

In Western culture the lawyer has been regarded with both admiration and suspicion for centuries. Both judgments seem to rest on a widely held image of what it is that lawyers do or ought to do. On one hand, the profession paints a picture of itself defending individual liberties by advocacy and facilitating progress by creative social engineering (see, e.g., Bloomfield, 1976; Nash, 1965). Novels, plays, motion pictures, and television programs have reinforced this view. On the other hand, a debunking tradition ... shows lawyers as people who profit from the misfortunes of others, as manipulators who produce results for a price without regard to justice, and as word magicians who mislead people into accepting what is wrong. Fiction supports this view too. Yet much of this writing may cost us understanding because the debunkers accept the classic stereotype of good lawyering as a yardstick, measured against which actual practice falls short.

In this classical model of practice, *lawyers apply the law.* They try cases and argue appeals guided by their command of legal norms. They negotiate settlements and advise clients largely in light of what they believe would happen if matters were brought before legal agencies. Of course, it is this mastery of a special body of knowledge, certified by success in law school and passing a bar examination, which gives one the status of being a lawyer and justifies the privileges which come with being a member of the profession (see Abel, 1979a). In the common law version of the model, *lawyers represent clients in an adversary system.* They take stock of a client's situation and desires and seek to further the client's interests as far as is possible legally. The lawyer is a "hired gun" who does not judge the client but vigorously asserts all of the client's claims of right, limited only by legal ethics. Lawyers place the interests of clients ahead of their own. A high place in the legends of the profession, for example, is awarded to the heroic and lonely advocate for an unpopular client, who battles for justice in the face of threats to person and pocketbook. However, even these aggressive lawyers cannot go too far because of the operation of the adversary system. An aggressive lawyer on one side will be matched on the other, and from this kind of advocacy a proper outcome will emerge. As a result, lawyers need not, and should not, be influenced by their own ethical judgment of the client's cause. (For a recent criticism of this positivist theory of practice, see Simon, 1978.)

Only the most innocent could think that this classical model describes professional practice. The model may reflect some of what goes on, but it is, at best, a distortion. Both Wall Street and Main Street lawyers often operate in situations where they do not know much about the relevant legal norms or where those norms play an insignificant part in influencing what is done. Lawyers regularly engage in the politics of bargaining, seeking to work out solutions to problems which are acceptable to the various interests. Rather than playing hired gun for one side, lawyers often mediate between their client and those not represented by lawyers. They seek to educate, persuade and coerce *both* sides to adopt the best available compromise rather than to engage in legal warfare. Moreover, in playing all of their roles, ranging from arguing a case before the Supreme Court of the United States to listening to an angry client, lawyers are influenced by their own values and self-interest. They will be more eager to do things which

they find satisfying and not distasteful and which will contribute to their income both today and in the future.

The legal profession may find the classical model valuable in justifying its activities and status (see Abel, 1979a). The public may benefit too insofar as this conventional view of practice is a normative indicator of what a lawyer ought to do and what influences behavior. Nonetheless, the classical model has costs: it may serve to mislead clients about what lawyers can, should, or will do. It may obstruct serious thought about the techniques and ethics of counseling, mediation and negotiation. And it may undermine effective efforts at reforms through law. Over the past twenty years when reformers have won victories in such areas as civil rights, sex and racial discrimination, and consumer protection, their successes have come in the form of cases, statutes, and regulations which, along with other things, have granted rights to individuals or groups (see, e.g., Flink, 1978; Cohen, 1975; Field, 1978; Frenzel, 1977; Scheingold, 1974). But the actual nature of law practice may leave these rights as little more than symbolic words on paper with only marginal life as resources in the process of negotiation.

This case study will develop some ideas about an expanded picture of the practice of law. I will consider the roles played by lawyers in connection with a number of consumer protection laws which create individual rights. This will not be a report of the full impact of these laws. That would require an examination of such things as the effects of the consumer movement and publicity given to consumer issues, the activity of governmental agencies at both the state and federal level, and the threat of more drastic laws which might be passed in the future. Instead, the subject of the present study is lawyers, and the focus on consumer laws serves as a way of looking at the behavior of various types of attorneys....

LAWYERS FOR CONSUMERS

Lawyers see but a small percentage of all of the situations where someone might assert a claim under the many consumer protection laws (see Mayhew and Reiss, 1969). Some claims are never asserted because consumers fail to recognize that the product they receive is defective, that the forms used in financing the transaction fail to make the required disclosures, or that the debt collection tactics used by a creditor are prohibited (Best and Andreasen, 1977). Other claims are recognized but resolved in ways not involving lawyers.

Some consumers see the cost of any attempt to resolve a minor consumer problem as not worth the effort. Resolving never to buy from the offending merchant or manufacturer again, they just "lump it" (Best and Andreason, 1977; Haefner and Leckenby, 1975; Mason and Himes, 1973; Warland, Herrmann and Willits, 1975). Some fix a defective item themselves, while others complain to the seller or the creditor and receive an adjustment which satisfies them. It is likely that most potential claims under consumer protection statutes are resolved in one of these ways (Curran, 1977: 109–10, 140, 196).

Some consumers go directly to remedy agents without consulting lawyers. For example, they may turn to the Better Business Bureau in Milwaukee or to one or more of several state agencies which mediate consumer complaints (cf. Steele, 1975; Thompson, 1979). A few may go directly to a small claims court. Others contact the local district attorney who, at least in the smaller counties in Wisconsin, often offers a great deal of legal advice or even a rather coercive mediation service to consumers who are potential supporters in the next election.

Many lawyers in private practice reported to us that they never saw a case involving an individual consumer. Those who represented businesses and practice in the larger firms were likely to say this, but some business lawyers reported that they answered questions about consumer matters from clients and friends. Other lawyers talked about encountering consumer cases only now and then. Lawyers did see what they called "products liability" cases where a defective item had caused personal injury. However, these cases typically do not fall under consumer protection statutes, and the fact of personal injury opens the door to the chance of a substantial recovery. A specialized group of attorneys is expert in the techniques of asserting or defending products liability cases. Most lawyers knew these specialists and many referred cases to them. No similar network of access to specialists in consumer protection law seemed to exist. Several attorneys mentioned one lawyer whom they thought was an expert in consumer protection, but when I interviewed him, he said that he now tried to avoid such cases.

Those few dissatisfied consumers who survive the screening process and come to lawyers may have special characteristics or kinds of problems. First, some people will bring cases to lawyers that others would see as trivial but which they see as a matter of principle. Second, when regular clients appear with minor consumer problems, a lawyer may attempt to handle them in order to keep a client's good will; one lawyer called this a kind of "loss-leader" service. For example, a lawyer in a small county had drafted a wealthy farmer's estate plan and set up a corporation to handle some of his dealings in land development. The farmer, dissatisfied with a Chevrolet dealer's attempts to make a new car run satisfactorily, called his lawyer and told him to straighten out matters. The lawyer successfully negotiated with the dealer and sent the farmer a bill for only a nominal amount. Third, debtors who cannot pay are sometimes pushed into a lawyer's office by the actions of a creditor. The debtor or the lawyer may see consumer protection law as offering a way to lift some or all of the burden of indebtedness for an expensive item such as a car, a recreational vehicle, or a mobile home. Problems which the consumer might have been willing to overlook may now become the basis for a legal attempt to rescind the sale (cf. Landers, 1977).

Consumer cases also are brought to the attention of lawyers through informal social channels. Officers of a corporation which has retained a lawyer to deal with business problems may also ask for personal advice about how to deal with an expensive purchase about which they are dissatisfied. Many lawyers pointed out that they had friends, relatives, and neighbors who asked for advice informally. People who might not make a visit to a lawyer's office about a consumer matter will raise their problem with a lawyer they see at a church supper, a PTA meeting, or a cocktail party. One lawyer noted that it was hard to have a drink at a bar in Madison on a football weekend without being called on for free legal advice. Few of these problems ever become cases, but occasionally lawyers find one that demands more than a few minutes of talk.

Decisions about whether or not to contact a lawyer are affected by personal factors. One lawyer remarked that many people seem to need reassurance that it is legitimate to complain and make trouble for others (cf. Sniderman and Brody, 1977). Many people are hesitant about admitting that they were cheated by a retailer or manufacturer when they think they should have known better. Some lawyers said that most of their clients—both those who come to their office and those who ask for advice during informal contacts—come to them through friendship networks. A former client may talk with a friend at work or at a bar and end up sending the friend to see the lawyer (see Curran, 1977: 202, 203). Some people seem to need the encouragement of friends before they can take the plunge (Ladinsky, 1976; Lochner, 1975). There seems to be a "folk culture" that defines, among other things, which kinds of cases one should take to a lawyer, which call for solutions not involving lawyers, and which should be just forgotten. Those facing aggressive debt

collection procedures are likely to be told to see lawyers; those with complaints about the quality of products are usually advised just to forget it.

Many lawyers seek to avoid taking clients with consumer protection problems (Curran, 1977: 204). Firms that specialize in representing businesses discourage individuals from bringing their personal problems to the firm by the expensive elegance of their offices and often by the location of those offices. Everything about these firms tends to tell potential clients that these are expensive professionals who deal only with important people on important matters. One who is not to the manor born would hesitate to waste the time of this professional establishment with a mere personal matter.

Even lawyers who look more approachable have techniques for avoiding cases they do not want to take. Receptionists try to screen cases so that minor personal matters will not waste their bosses' time (cf. Hosticka, 1979). Lawyers engage in techniques of conversion or transformation of attitudes. Some try to brush off individuals by talking to them briefly on the telephone in order to keep them from coming to the office. Some listen to people who come to the office for only a few minutes and then interrupt to spell out the cost of legal services. These attorneys see their role as that of educating would-be clients to see that they cannot afford to pursue the matter. The lawyer serves as a gatekeeper, keeping people from burdening the legal system.

If the potential client with a consumer matter is not rejected out of hand, lawyers may still limit their response to nonadversary roles. One part played fairly often might be that of the therapist or knowledgeable friend. The client is allowed to blow off steam and vent anger to a competent-seeming professional sitting in an office surrounded by law books and the other stage props of the profession. By body language and discussion, the lawyer can lead the client to redefine the situation so that he or she can accept it. What appeared to the client to be a clear case of fraud or bad faith comes on close examination to be seen as no more than a misunderstanding.

The lawyer may then "help" the client consider the practical options open in the situation. It may be against the client's interests to pursue the matter: legal action may cost more than it is worth, either directly or indirectly in terms of the client's long-run interests. The client may also have adopted too narrow—perhaps too legalistic—a view of the case.

The client's grievance may be one which the lawyer could translate into a perfectly legitimate—indeed compelling—legal argument, but the "law" may not be the only standard by which the merits of each party will be judged. Such arguments, needless to say, may anger the potential client; or they may make the client feel foolish for being upset and bothering a lawyer. On the other hand, by helping the client see the case in a new light, the lawyer may be indulging in a kind of therapy.

Perhaps the lawyer will take a further step and combine the therapist role with that of an information broker or a coach, hearing the complaint and then referring the client elsewhere for a remedy. This gets the would-be client out of the office less unhappy than had the lawyer just rejected the case and offered nothing. People can be sent to state agencies which mediate consumer claims or to private organizations such as the Better Business Bureau. Some lawyers go further and try to coach clients on how to complain effectively to a seller or creditor or how to handle a case in a small claims court without a lawyer. Sometimes this information and coaching may be of more help than formal legal advice. Consumers may need to be reassured that they have a legitimate complaint, to be given the courage to complain, to learn where to go and whom to see, and to be given a few good rhetorical ploys to use in the process of solving their problems. Sometimes the coaching does not help the client. The referral only prompts the client to give up. Few lawyers

know what happens when they tell a client to complain to the seller or go to a state agency. Clients rarely report back to the lawyer unless they are friends or neighbors. On the other hand, such referrals may serve to help lawyers see themselves as helpful people.

Attorneys who become more involved in a case may find themselves playing the part of go-between or informal mediator. They may telephone or write the seller or creditor to state the consumer's complaint. The very restatement of that complaint by a professional is likely to make it a complex communication. On one level, the attorney is reporting a version of the situation which may be unknown to the seller or creditor even in cases where consumers have complained before seeing a lawyer. The lawyer may be able to organize a presentation so that the basis of the complaint is more understandable, and transform it so that it is more persuasive. The fact that the report comes from a lawyer is likely to give the complaint at least some minimal legitimacy. The lawyer is saying that he or she has reviewed the buyer or debtor's story, that the assertions of fact are at least plausible, and that the buyer or debtor has reason to complain if these are the facts.

The lawyer is more likely than the consumer to get to talk to someone who has authority to do something about a problem. For example, the consumer may have gotten no farther than the sales person, while the lawyer may gain access to the manager or owner of the business. The lawyer is likely to speak as a social equal of the representative of the seller or debtor, though such may not be the case for the consumer. This may be important. A retailer, for example, may care little about the opinions of a factory worker complainant, but wish to avoid having a professional judge him or her as foolish or unreasonable. Finally, the attorney's professional identification conveys a tacit threat that an unsatisfactory response could be followed by something the seller or creditor might find unpleasant. Indeed the unstated and vague threat of further action may be coercive precisely because it is vague. If sellers and creditors were aware of the cost barriers to litigation, and if they knew, or appreciated, just how much of a paper tiger most attorneys are in consumer matters, they would be less easily intimidated.

At this point, a seller or creditor may assert that the client has just misunderstood the situation or has told the lawyer only part of the story. At this stage lawyers often discover that a client's case is not as clear-cut as the client claimed. However, sellers and creditors still are more likely to make conciliatory responses to lawyers than to buyers or debtors, as long as the lawyers do not ask for too much. And it is part of a lawyer's stock in trade to know how much is too much (cf. Ross, 1970). One lawyer told us:

> I enjoy negotiation. Of course, what happens is not determined by the merits. . . . One has a discussion about what is best for everyone. You do not make an adversary matter out of it. It is a game, and it is funny or sad, depending on how you look at it. You call the other side and tell him that you understand that he has a problem satisfying customers but that you have a client who is really hot and wants to sue for the principle of the thing. Then you say, "Maybe I can help you and talk my client into accepting something that is reasonable." The other side knows what you are doing. It is a game. You never want to get to the merits of the case.

The seller or creditor is likely to make some kind of gesture so that the lawyer will not have to return to the client empty-handed. The simplest gesture the seller or creditor can make is a letter of apology, explaining how the problem occurred and accepting some or all of the blame. A supervisor may attempt to blame an employee with whom the consumer dealt, perhaps remarking that it is difficult to find good sales people or mechanics. Manufacturers often blame dealers, and dealers, in turn, seem eager to pass the blame on to manufacturers. In addition to an apology, the merchant may

also offer token reparations such as minor repairs or free samples of its products.

More rarely, the lawyer may be able to persuade a seller or manufacturer to offer the consumer a refund or replacement for a defective product. Sometimes a lawyer can gain a refund or replacement even where the flaw in the thing purchased was not so material as to warrant "revocation of acceptance" under Section 2-608 of the Uniform Commercial Code. New car dealers or fly-by-night merchants are unlikely to do this; new car dealers are tightly controlled by manufacturers, who seem to value cost control more than consumer goodwill (see Whitford, 1968); fly-by-night operators seldom worry about repeat business. But Sears, Montgomery Ward, J. C. Penney, and many other large department stores, have an announced policy of consumer satisfaction. One can get his or her money back without having to establish that there is something materially wrong with the product (see Ross and Littlefield, 1978). Other retailers and manufacturers do not announce this as their policy, but will grant refunds or replacements selectively when their officials think that the customer has reason to complain or if repeat business is valued. In such cases, a telephone call from a lawyer may be enough to swing the balance in favor of the complainant—it probably seems easier to make a refund than to argue with a lawyer. Occasionally, a lawyer may be able to persuade a new car dealer who has sold a client a used car to pay some percentage of the cost of repairs of a major item such as a transmission, provided the work is done in the dealer's shop. A lawyer may be able to persuade a creditor to give a client more time in which to pay rather than repossessing the item in dispute. But lawyers are seldom able to persuade a seller or creditor to pay a large sum as damages to an aggrieved buyer or debtor.

The lawyer's view of the adequacy of the remedy offered by the merchant or lender will necessarily turn on a reappraisal of the client's case in light of the other side's story, the ease of taking further action, the likelihood of success of such action, and the client's probable reaction to what has been offered. The lawyer may have to persuade the client to see the situation in a new light. The response of the merchant or lender must also be considered. The axiom that "there are two sides to every story" now becomes a reality for the client. An important part of the lawyer's task now is to persuade the client to see the problem as an adjustment between competing claims and interests, rather than as one warranting a fight for principle. From the lawyer's perspective, the client must now be guided to the view that what the merchant or lender has offered is probably the best that could be expected. Anything more may require legal services more costly than the client can afford or is prepared to pay. . . .

Only in rare instances will lawyers go further than conciliatory negotiation in a consumer matter. If the antagonist fails to offer a satisfactory settlement, the lawyer may counter with more explicit threats of unpleasant consequences. But some lawyers report that once overt threats are made, one is likely to have to draft and file a complaint before any offer of settlement will be made by the other side. One reason is that serious threats from a lawyer are likely to prompt sellers or creditors to send the matter to their lawyers. But even at this point, the lawyers for both sides have every reason to settle rather than litigate. Some consumer cases do go to trial—we can find appellate opinions to put in law school casebooks—but they are unusual and atypical of the mass of consumer complaints. . . .

Lawyers for Business

In contrast to lawyers for individuals, attorneys for business play fairly traditional lawyer's roles when they deal with consumer law: they lobby, draft documents, plan procedures, and respond to particular disputes by negotiating and litigating. Indeed, our idea of what is a traditional lawyer's job may flow largely from what this part of the bar does for clients who can afford to pay for these services. As Hazard (1978: 152) puts it, "One of

the chief reasons why competent lawyers go into corporate work is precisely that business clients are willing to invest enough in their lawyers to permit them to develop the highest possible levels of professional skill. Indeed, it is not far wrong to say that lawyers for big corporations are the only practitioners regularly afforded latitude to give their technical best to the problems they work on." But even when we turn to business practice, the classical model of lawyering is only a rough approximation of what happens. This suggests that the amount of the potential fee is not the only factor prompting problems with the classical view. I will consider each of these traditional kinds of lawyer's work in the business setting, looking at what is done for clients, which lawyers do what kinds of work, and the degree of independent control exercised by lawyers in each instance.

Lawyers working for manufacturers, distributors, retailers and financial institutions are likely to be present at the creation of any law that purports to aid the consumer. For example, the decision of the Supreme Court of Wisconsin (1970) that found the revolving charge account plan of the J. C. Penney Company to run afoul of the state's usury statute was a major chapter in the story of consumer protection in Wisconsin (see Davis, 1973). Lawyers from several of the state's largest and most prestigious law firms were involved in defending revolving charge accounts in the challenge before the courts and in the complex negotiation which led to legislation reversing the Supreme Court's decision in exchange for support of what became the Wisconsin Consumer Act. Perhaps less dramatically, lawyers representing both state and national businesses have been involved in the process of administrative rulemaking that has produced such consumer protection regulations as those governing warranties on mobile homes, procedures for authorizing repairs on automobiles, and door-to-door sales. . . .

After consumer laws and regulations are passed, business lawyers help their clients cope with them. Much of the work involves drafting documents and setting up procedures for using these forms. For example, both the federal Truth-in-Lending Law and the Wisconsin Consumer Act required a complete reworking of most of the form contracts used to lend money and sell on credit. The Magnuson-Moss Warranty Act demanded that almost every manufacturer, distributor and retailer selling consumer products rewrite any warranty given with the product and create new procedures to make information about these warranties available to consumers. (See Fayne and Smith, 1977; Wisdom, 1979, for a description of how national manufacturers' lawyers have coped with this statute.) This is traditional lawyers' work, requiring a command of the needs of the business, a detailed understanding of the law, and drafting skills. Moreover, the uncertainties and complexities of many consumer protection laws call for talented lawyering if the job is to be done right.

Counseling business clients about consumer protection laws and drafting the required contracts and forms is the stock-in-trade of the largest firms in the state and a small group of lawyers with a predominantly business practice; some of this work is also done by the inside legal staff of some large corporations (McConnell and Lillis, 1976). Some of this work can be mass-produced by lawyers for trade associations. Many lenders, retailers, and suppliers of services in smaller cities rely on standard forms supplied by these trade associations. Small manufacturers and financial institutions may send problems concerning consumer protection laws to lawyers in Milwaukee or Madison, either directly or through a referral by their local attorney. There is also a "trickle-down" effect: lawyers who are not expert in consumer law often collect copies of the work product of the more expert, receiving them from clients who get them from trade associations or through friends who work for the larger law firms. They may simply copy these forms or they

may produce variations on them but with little or no independent research. . . .

Finally, business lawyers do become directly involved in the process of settling particular disputes when attempts to avoid or otherwise deal with them have failed; lawyers in the largest firms seldom have to help ward off individual consumers, but some lawyers for business regularly are involved in particular cases. For example, lawyers represent banks and other creditors in collections work. At one time this was a routine procedure that yielded a default judgment and made clear the creditor's right to any property involved. However, many of the traditional tactics of debt collection have been ruled out of bounds or are now closely regulated by state and federal laws. Lawyers who do collections work describe what seems to them to be a new legal ritual to be followed whenever a debtor who is armed with legal advice resists a collection effort. The lender first attempts to collect by its own efforts, and then it files suit, often in a small claims court. The debtor responds, asserting that something was wrong with the credit transaction under the Truth-in-Lending Act or the Wisconsin Consumer Act, or by asserting that the creditor engaged in "conduct which can reasonably be expected to threaten or harass the customer . . ." or used "threatening language in communication with the customer . . ." as is prohibited and sanctioned by the Wisconsin Consumer Act (Wis. Stat. §§427.104 [g], [h] [1975]). The lender then has to respond, either by offering to settle or by claiming to be ready to litigate the legal issues. Then the lawyers on both sides negotiate and, occasionally, battle before a judge.

Large retailers who sell relatively expensive products or services face a regular flow of consumer complaints. Almost all of them are resolved without the participation of lawyers, but an attorney may have to enter the picture occasionally. This may not happen until the consumer files a complaint in court. Often the business lawyer will be facing an unrepresented consumer in a small claims court. Several of these lawyers commented that the consumer was only formally unrepresented since the judge often seemed to serve both as judge and attorney for the plaintiff, particularly in pre-trial settlement negotiations. These are expensive cases for a business to defend if the consumer gets a chance to present the merits of the claim to the court. One law firm in Madison represents one of the largest automobile manufacturers in such matters, but it sees only three of four such cases a year. Interestingly, these cases almost never involve an application of the many consumer protection laws or even the Uniform Commercial Code; the real issue is almost always one of fact concerning whether the product or service was defective. The law firm's recommendation about whether to settle is almost always final. Their recommendation will be rejected only where the manufacturer wants to defend a particular model of its automobiles against a series of charges that the model has a particular defect; the manufacturer may be far more worried about a government order to recall that model than a particular buyer's claim....

. . .[S]ome business lawyers concede that occasionally they must persuade their clients to change practices or to respond to a particular dispute in what the lawyers see as a reasonable manner. For example, these lawyers may tell their clients that they must appear to be fair when they are before an agency in order to have any chance of winning in this era of consumer protection. In this way, they may be able to legitimate sitting in judgment on the behavior of their clients and occasionally manipulating the situation to influence clients' choices.

A few of the lawyers we interviewed reported having to act to protect their own self-interest when dealing with a business client. One prominent lawyer, for example, described a case where he represented an out-of-state book club in a proceeding before one of the state regulatory agencies; he took the case only as a favor to a friend who had some indirect connection with the club's officers. As the case unfolded, the lawyer discovered that the book club had failed to send books to many people who had paid for them. It was not clear whether the situation involved fraud or merely bad business practices. The lawyer insisted that the book club immediately get books or refunds to all of its Wisconsin customers and sign a settlement agreement with the agency which bound the club to strict requirements for future behavior. The attorney explained that the business had been trading on his reputation as a lawyer when it got him to enter the case on its behalf. Once it became clear that the administrative agency had a good case against the client involving conduct at least on the borders of fraud, the lawyer felt that the client was obligated to help him maintain his reputation as an attorney who represented only the most ethical businesses.

In conclusion, there is evidence of the continuing truth of Willard Hurst's (1950: 344–345) observations about the historical role of the bar:

> The lawyer's office served in all periods as what amounted to a magistrate's court; what was done in lawyers' offices in effect finally disposed of countless trouble cases, whether preventively, or by discouraging wasteful lawsuits, or by settling claims over the bargaining table. After the 1870's, as the lawyer assumed a broader responsibility in his client's business decisions, a corollary result was to extend the occasions and degree to which the lawyer was called on to judge the rights and duties of his client, with a decisive effect on future action. . . . Elihu Root remarked, " . . .about half the practice of a decent lawyer consists in telling would-be clients that they are damned fools and should stop."

About the only amendment of Root's statement needed to bring it up to date is that it is not necessary for a business lawyer to tell a client anything in order to bring much damned fool behavior to an end. The lawyer often has the power to channel the behavior of clients without their awareness of what is being done. Of course, the business lawyer is likely to share the views of his or her clients that consumer protection statutes, rather than customary business practices, call for damned fool behavior.

DISCUSSION

In this section I will try to integrate the findings of this study into a broader picture of the practice of law, with some special attention to a question central to other recent research on the legal profession: are lawyers agents of social control or are they so tied to their clients as to lack the professional autonomy so often ascribed to them?

A descriptive model of practice would accept much of the classical view as a starting point. Traditionally, we have emphasized lawyers being involved in certain transformations: clients bring problems to lawyers who, in Cain's terms (1979: 343), "translate [issues] into a meta-language in terms of which a binding solution can be found." For example, lawyers translate client desires to transfer property to others into such legal forms as declarations of trust, deeds, and wills. Lawyers try to convert some of the many factors involved in an automobile accident into a winning cause of action for negligence (cf. Hosticka, 1979). Indeed, as Abel (1979a) points out, it is the lawyer's authority over this meta-language which gives the profession much of its status and market control; one goes to law school to master it in order to enter the profession, and entry usually is gained by passing a bar examination where that mastery can be displayed.

However, even when clients come to lawyers for relatively defined services such as drafting a will or a contract, the lawyers' work may involve often overlooked interactions whereby lawyers influence the outcome, and these interactions also must be part of our sketch of practice. For example, some may hesitate to ask for certain provisions in their

will if they fear even implicit disapproval by a lawyer who, with his grey hair, three-piece suit, and symbols of membership in the legal profession, may be seen to represent conventional morality. The lawyer, also, may ask questions necessary for counseling or drafting which force the client to consider possible consequences and make choices that he or she has not foreseen or has avoided thinking about. The lawyer may tell a client that the law blocks taking certain action, but sometimes an attorney can suggest other ways of achieving at least some of the client's purposes. Just by explaining the requirement for a cause of action in negligence, the lawyer can affect the client's memory, or willingness to lie, and thus affect the outcome (cf. Fair and Moskowitz, 1975).

If our model is to have a wider focus, we will have to recognize other translations and transformations which only indirectly involve legal rules but which often take place in interactions between attorneys, clients, opponents, and legal officials. As I have pointed out in this article, lawyers play many roles in these interactions, including the gatekeeper who teaches clients about the costs of using the legal system, the knowledgeable friend or therapist, the broker of information or coach, the go-between or informal mediator, the legal technician, and the adversary bargainer-litigator. In playing these roles, lawyers often have to transform their clients' perception of the problem and their goals. Sometimes clients do come to lawyers seeking fairly specific services—a client may want to make a will, to convey property, or gain a license to run a television station. However, the lawyer is often involved in transforming both the client's perception of the problem and the goals. Sometimes the lawyer will turn away a client, saying that (1) the client has no case legally, (2) it is against the client's best interest to pursue the matter as the costs will exceed the likely benefits, (3) the client is unreasonable to complain or seek certain ends as judged by standards other than the law, or (4) some mixture of these arguments. On the other hand, the lawyer may seek, in Aubert's terms (1963), to redefine a conflict of value into a conflict of interest which can be settled by payment of a reasonable amount of money rather than by a public declaration of right and wrong.

And the lawyer may be involved in transforming the views of the opponent about both the client and the situation so that an acceptable settlement will be forthcoming. Sometimes lawyers use their status as experts in the law, legal arguments, and express or implied threats of legal action in this process of persuasion. Often, however, a legal style of argument fades into the background. The attorney may not be too sure about the precise legal situation or may worry about seeming to coerce the other party. In such situations lawyers are likely to appeal to some mixture of the interest of the opponent and to standards of reasonableness apart from claims of legal right. Then, as I have stressed, if there is a settlement offer, the lawyer must sell it to the client, and here again appeals are likely to be made primarily in terms of reasonableness or interest rather than right.

The research reported here shows lawyers for individuals playing these nonadversary roles without great knowledge of the contours of consumer law, while the lawyers for corporations act more traditional parts—lobbying, counseling, drafting documents, and defending cases after complaints are filed. However, lawyers for corporations are at least occasionally pushed out of the character of legal technician. For example, a lawyer for one of the nation's largest law firms, who has an extensive corporate practice, sees himself as engaged in "the lay practice of psychiatry." He explains that a manager of a large corporation often is worried about making a decision, but he or she has few people with whom to talk openly. Others in the corporation tend to be rivals; psychiatric help is unthinkable as it would indicate weakness. However, it is legitimate to see an attorney seeking legal advice.

Often this lawyer finds himself asking questions which lead the manager to see the options and their likely costs and benefits. The questions are justified as necessary in the process of giving legal advice; their actual function, the lawyer says, is a very directive short-term therapy. Sometimes he does not need to ask many questions, because it is enough to serve as an audience while the manager thinks aloud. Another lawyer engaged in corporate commercial litigation sees lawyers as curbing the influence of ego and pride on the part of business executives in dispute resolution. Frequently, the lawyer is the one raising cost-benefit considerations which point towards settlement to engineers who refuse to admit that they have ever made a mistake or to managers who want to teach the other side a lesson. Of course, this is but anecdotal evidence, but it suggests that if we are to make our model of practice more true to reality, we need to investigate corporate as well as individual lawyers' nontraditional roles. . . .

. . .[M]any of the nonadversary roles played by lawyers also seem to have some social value—experts in coping with the claims of other individuals, corporations or the government by using all available tools including, but not limited to, legal rules can offer useful help to citizens. Perhaps the classical position does serve as a golden lie (Plato, *The Republic*, Book III), misleading both lawyers and the public for a good purpose. Yet it has costs, particularly as more and more people discover that lawyers' behavior so often fails to conform to the model. There seems, moreover, no reason to assume—without even making an attempt—that we cannot rationalize when a lawyer can be expected to refuse a case, to mediate and play counsel for the situation and when to vindicate rights. Perhaps no ideological statement ever can be without flaw (cf. Unger, 1976), but the classical picture of the practice seems to fit the legal profession of the 1980s so poorly as to be embarrassing.

References

ABEL, Richard L. (1979) "Socializing the Legal Profession: Can Redistributing Lawyers' Services Achieve Social Justice?" 1 *Law & Policy Quarterly* 5.

BEST, Arthur and Alan R. ANDREASEN (1977) "Consumer Response to Unsatisfactory Purchases: A Survey of Perceiving Defects, Voicing Complaints, and Obtaining Redress," 11 *Law & Society Review* 701.

BLOOMFIELD, Maxwell H. (1976) *American Lawyers in a Changing Society, 1776–1876.* Cambridge: Harvard University Press.

DAVIS, Jeffrey (1973) "Legislative Restriction of Creditor Powers and Remedies: A Case Study of the Negotiation and Drafting of the Wisconsin Consumer Act," 72 *Michigan Law Review* 1.

FAIR, Daryl R. and David H. MOSKOWITZ (1975) "The Lawyer's Role: Watergate as Regularity Rather than Aberration," 2 *Journal of Contemporary Law* 75.

FIELD, Thomas G., Jr. (1978) "Appraising Private and Public Roles in Returning Small Economic Losses to Consumers: A Comparative Inquiry," 29 *Mercer Law Review* 773 (1978).

FLINK, Marc D. (1978) "Note: Private Enforcement Under the Fair Debt Collection Practices Act." 28 *Case Western Law Review* 710.

HAEFNER, James and John LECKENBY (1975) "Consumers' Use and Awareness of Consumer Protection Agencies," 9 *Journal of Consumer Affairs* 205.

HAZARD, Geoffrey C., Jr. (1978) *Ethics in the Practice of Law.* New Haven: Yale University Press.

HOSTICKA, Carl J. (1979) "We Don't Care About What Happened, We Only Care About What Is Going to Happen: Lawyer-Client Negotiations of Reality," 26 *Social Problems* 599.

HURST, James Willard (1950) *The Growth of American Law: The Law Makers.* Boston: Little, Brown.

LADINSKY, Jack (1976) "The Traffic in Legal Services: Lawyer-Seeking Behavior and the Channeling of Clients," 11 *Law & Society Review* 207.

LANDERS, Jonathan M. (1977) "Some Reflections on Truth in Lending," 1977 *University of Illinois Law Forum* 669.

McCONNELL, Jon P. and Charles M. LILLIS (1976) "A Comment on the Role Structure, and Function of Corporate Legal Departments," 14 *American Business Law Journal* 227.

MASON, Joseph and Samuel HIMES (1973) "An Exploratory Behavioral and Socio-Economic Profile of Consumer Action About Dissatisfaction with Selected Household Appliances," 7 *Journal of Consumer Affairs* 121.

MAYHEW, Leon and Albert J. REISS, Jr. (1969) "The Social Organization of Legal Contacts," 34 *American Sociological Review* 309.

NASH, Gary B. (1965) "The Philadelphia Bench and Bar, 1800–1861," 7 *Comparative Studies in Society & History* 203 (1965).

ROSS, H. Laurence (1970) *Settled Out of Court: The Social Process of Insurance Claims Adjustments.* Chicago: Aldine.

ROSS, H. Laurence and Neil O. LITTLEFIELD (1978) "Complaint as a Problem-Solving Mechanism," 12 *Law & Society Review* 199.

SCHEINGOLD, Stuart A. (1974) *The Politics of Rights: Lawyers, Public Policy, and Political Change.* New Haven: Yale University Press.

SIMON, William H. (1978) "The Ideology of Advocacy: Procedural Justice and Professional Ethics," 1978 *Wisconsin Law Review* 29.

SNIDERMAN, Paul M. and Richard A. BRODY (1977) "Coping: The Ethic of Self-Reliance," 21 *American Journal of Political Science* 501.

STEELE, Eric H. (1975) "Fraud, Disputes, and the Consumer: Responding to Consumer Complaints," 123 *University of Pennsylvania Law Review* 1107.

THOMPSON, Frank (1979) "U.W. Researchers 'Mapping' Consumer Complaints," *The Public I* (July, 1979) 6.

WARLAND, Rex H., Robert O. HERMANN, and Jane WILLITS (1975) "Dissatisfied Consumers: Who Gets Upset and Who Takes Action," 9 *Journal of Consumer Affairs* 148.

WHITFORD, William C. (1968) "Strict Products Liability and the Automobile Industry: Much Ado About Nothing," 1968 *Wisconsin Law Review* 83.

———. (1973) "The Functions of Disclosure Regulation in Consumer Transactions," 1973 *Wisconsin Law Review* 400.

WHITFORD, William C. and Spencer KIMBALL (1974) "Why Process Consumer Complaints? A Case Study of the Office of the Commissioner of Insurance of Wisconsin," 1974 *Wisconsin Law Review* 639.

WISDOM, Michael T. (1979) "An Empirical Study of the Magnuson-Moss Warranty Act," 31 *Stanford Law Review* 1117.

Case Cited

State v. J. C. Penney Co., 48 W12d 125, 179 NW2d 641 (1970).

Notes and Questions

1. What role do lawyers play in the classical model of the practice of law? How should the adversary system work in theory?

2. According to Macaulay, how is the actual behavior of lawyers different from what theory prescribes? What is problematic in his review about thinking in terms of the classical model of the practice of law? Do you agree with his assessment?

3. Macaulay points out that many of the reforms achieved since 1960 in consumer protection law may ultimately end up "as little more than symbolic words on paper, with only marginal life as resources in the process of negotiation." Why is this? Is scant knowledge of consumer protection law and the general aversion to seeking legal redress primarily the fault of consumers or of their lawyers? Why are lawyers for business often more informed about consumer protection laws than are lawyers for individuals?

4. How well does Macaulay's depiction of consumer protection law fit into Felstiner, Abel, and Sarat's framework (Chapter 15) of "naming, blaming, and claiming?" What factors, as described by Macaulay, affect which plaintiffs make it through naming, blaming, or claiming in consumer protection suits?

5. What parallels would you draw between Kafka's parable (Chapter 12) and Macaulay's account of consumer protection law? If disgruntled consumers are compensated via mediation rather than litigation, were they or were they not allowed to pass thorough the door?

6. Lawyers can be very effective as mediators in consumer protection cases. The disgruntled consumer is often appeased with a letter of apology, replacement merchandise, and/or a special discount offer. If both the consumer and the business are satisfied with the terms of such compromises, is justice served? In terms of law and deterrence, does it make any difference if a lawyer handles a consumer protection case as a mediator between consumer and business or as an adversary of the business? Is the lawyer's obligation limited to the immediate interests of the client or should the legal rights of future consumers matter?

Chapter 21

The Justice Broker

Lawyers and Ordinary Litigation

Herbert M. Kritzer

Assuming that lawyers are available and willing to pursue claims for their clients, what services do they typically provide? From some of the previous readings, one might conclude that they typically act as zealous advocates for their clients, pushing adversarial solutions to every problem. Yet as Macaulay notes in Chapter 20, lawyers dealing with consumer protection problems often try to work out compromises rather then pursue all-or-nothing solutions.

The reading by Herbert M. Kritzer generalizes beyond the consumer protection area and offers what he labels a "brokerage perspective" on the work of lawyers in civil cases. In contrast to what one might expect if one were to think about lawyers only as professionals, brokers act as intermediaries for their clients, not as hired guns. They try to work out arrangements to transfer "information, money, property" between two parties. Instead of looking for the kind of win-lose resolution that trials provide (i.e., large monetary awards of the kind obtained in the McDonald's coffee case), they serve as brokers who pursue settlements in which each party gets less than its preferred result.

Are certain kinds of lawyers more or less likely to play a brokerage role? Are they more or less likely to play that role in particular matters or when dealing with particular clients?

The work of lawyers in ordinary litigation has many of the characteristics of what is commonly called *brokerage*. I define a broker as "a person hired to act as an intermediary." This suggests a distinction between the idea of acting as an alter ego, which is the notion typically used when talking about the professional, and the idea of acting as an *intermediary*. The former carries with it the expectation that persons acting as alter egos work solely in the interests of their clients, with no concerns or interests of their own (the "pure service" image). In its most general sense, the term intermediary carries no connotation whatever regarding the intermediary's own interests. Defining the broker as a *hired* intermediary indicates that the broker acts on behalf of the client but has a set of interests that intervenes on, or even conflicts with, the goal of pure service.

While the broker and the professional differ regarding the business dimension of relationships with clients, the two images do not represent a fully contrasting dichotomy. Instead, they are alternative conceptions that combine contrasting and complementary elements; used jointly, they provide a better vehicle for understanding the work of lawyers in ordinary litigation than either one does in isolation. The two perspectives taken together reflect the tensions and contradictions that underlie the daily work of lawyers in the American civil justice system. They capture the reality of an occupation whose members have been socialized to a professional ideal but who must cope with a set of working realities that often conflict with that ideal.

CONCEPTUALIZING THE BROKER

The concept of the broker is not well developed in the social science literature. It has been most extensively used by anthropologists, and the best conceptual treatment is to be found in the work of Boissevan (1969; 1974: 147–169). His development of the concept starts by distinguishing between two types of resources to which people need access in social, political, and economic life: first-order resources, such as land, jobs, education, and money, and second-order resources consisting of "strategic contacts with . . . people who control resources directly or have access to such persons (1974, 147)." A person who specializes in dispensing second-order resources for personal profit or gain is a broker. Central to this role is the interactional nature of the work within a stable context that extends beyond any single transaction; in Boissevan's terms these contexts involve networks, action-sets, and cliques. Thus, a broker is someone who serves as an intermediary between persons seeking and dispensing first-order resources within a set context and who engages in this activity for personal gain. . . .

This discussion highlights two of the characteristics that distinguish brokers from other kinds of actors. First, brokers serve as intermediaries; . . .they bring together distributors and recipients of first-order resources. More generally, brokers aid in transfers of information, money, property, and the like between two parties; those parties can be individuals and/or organizations (including governmental institutions such as the court system). Second, in aiding these transfers, brokers extract a "tax" of some sort (whether that be a fee, a percentage, or some sort of future obligation); "in other words, brokers are motivated by their own interests, either long term, short term, or both, rather than by altruism or some other "moral" base.

With this as background, let me briefly point out the other ways in which the broker image sheds useful light on the work of lawyers in ordinary litigation. First, the image of the broker combines the expectation of specialized, expert knowledge (e.g., in the case of the real estate broker, different methods of financing) with what can be described as "insider" knowledge (the current selling prices of houses in a neighborhood, to continue the real estate broker example). One can easily identify the kinds of insider knowledge that are important to lawyering in litigation: going

rates for particular injuries (or, in criminal cases, for particular offenses), recent trends in jury verdicts for particular kinds of cases, the attitudes of trial judges as related to the situations of a lawyer's clients, and the style and experience of the opposing party's lawyer.

Second, central to the image of the broker is a process of regularized interaction with other "players" (other brokers, specialists, organizations, etc.) as a necessary basis for delivering the service required by the client; the image of a professional does not preclude such interaction, but nothing in that image explicitly recognizes the importance of the interaction process. Interaction of the type associated with brokering is a major part of the work of the lawyer, particularly litigation work. The lawyer must interact with other lawyers and with court personnel, including judges, magistrates, commissioners, and clerks; as I will discuss shortly, research on the criminal justice system has shown that this regularized interaction results in the creation of a "courtroom workgroup" that defines the day-to-day operation of the system (Eisenstein and Jacob, 1977).

Third, while the image of the professional is grounded in the assumption that the client plays a secondary role in the decision-making process, usually following the advice and/or instructions of the professional (this is clearest in the doctor-patient relationship), the broker image portrays the broker as being specifically instructed by the client and then carrying out those instructions in the best way possible. Much of what both corporate services lawyers (see Kagan and Rosen, 1985: 411) and personal services lawyers (see Cain, 1979) do falls in the category of carrying out the instructions of the client, whether that be reviewing the papers for a $100 million securities offering or preparing a simple will. Expert knowledge may be required to construct the documents so that they meet legal requirements, but the goal is usually defined fairly explicitly by the client. Lawyers involved in litigation, particularly where the lawyer is being paid on a percentage basis, may in fact be less bound by explicit instructions from a client than are lawyers carrying out other kinds of work.

Table 21.1 provides a capsule contrast of the two images along four dimensions: (1) the centrality of the fee-paying aspects of the relationship with the client; (2) the relative importance of expertise based on insider (what I will later refer to as "informal legal") versus technical (what I will term "formal legal") knowledge; (3) the positioning of the professional/broker as an intermediary between the client and other actors in the process; and (4) the autonomy of the professional/broker vis-à-vis the client. . . .

LAWYERING IN CIVIL LITIGATION AS A BROKERAGE FUNCTION

In the previous discussion, I identified four dimensions that distinguish between the activities of the professional and those of the broker. . . . [T]his section briefly discusses what the brokerage image would lead one to expect with regard to lawyering in ordinary civil litigation. I will draw on prior research concerned with ordinary civil litigation.

Concerning the nature of the expertise required for day-to-day civil litigation I have already noted Carlin's findings that solo practitioners handling injury cases devote relatively little of their time to activities that draw on their formal legal knowledge (i.e., the technical use of the law and the skills learned in law school). Carlin's report of how lawyers handle

personal injury cases is consistent with Ross's analysis of the claims adjusters on the other side of the relationship (1980), where the emphasis is again on the kind of knowledge that insiders have (necessary documents, "building up specials," etc.) and not on expertise based on formal training. Ross, in summarizing Carlin's analysis of the work of the solo practitioner, characterizes much of that work as brokerage (1980: 75) and, in reference to negligence work, says that it "may be easily regarded as brokerage rather than the profession of law" (Ross, 1980: 77). Ross implicitly draws a distinction between the professional and the broker, but never really develops that distinction beyond the simple statement of its existence.

A second concern [is] the role of the fee-paying relationship between the lawyer and the client and how that impinges on the lawyer's work. I already noted the argument that the interests of lawyer and client frequently clash, and how, in the case of the contingent fee lawyer, this may lead to a less than zealous advocacy. More than half of Carlin's account of the personal injury work of lawyers revolve around the nature of referrals and the question of payment for such referrals (1962: 80F), one very common feature was the dependence on recommendations from past clients. Much of the rest of Carlin's discussion concerns the dependence of the clients on their lawyers; for example, the lawyer is often in a position to make loans to clients to tide them over until a settlement is reached, or to insure

---

Table 21.1
The Professional and the Broker

Dimension	Professional	Broker
Centrality of fee-paying relationship	Low	High
Nature of expertise	Technical/formal	Insider/informal
Position occupied by professional/broker vis-à-vis other actors	[unspecified]	Intermediary between client and other actors
Autonomy/client control	Professional controls	Client instructs/broker responds

that bills incurred by the client (e.g.. for medical expenses) are paid, either promptly or eventually (Carlin 1962: 79–80). This dependence is institutionalized in the norm that the settlement payment is made in the form of a check payable jointly to the lawyer and client and sent directly to the lawyer; the lawyer then deducts the fee expenses, and any "loans," paying the balance to the client (Carlin, 1962: 74). The fee-paying relationship is most evident when the lawyer is paid on a contingency basis, but it may also be evident for hourly fee lawyers who take cases from regular clients on a routine basis with little regard for the particulars of the individual case.

The issue of control is central in Rosenthal's analysis of the underlying conflicts in relations between contingent fee lawyers and their clients (1974). The problem for clients, in Rosenthal's view, is to insure that their interests dominate the work of the lawyers; for the client with a contingent fee lawyer, this means insuring that the lawyer does not shortchange the client's case. As Wessel points out (1976; see also Johnson, 1980–1981: 569–584), the exact opposite may be true for the hourly fee lawyer, where the short-term incentives may provide a motivation to overwork the case in order to build up the amount of time billed to the client. The answer to these problems is for the client to control at least the quantity, if not the specific content, of what the lawyer does on the client's behalf. On the other hand, the common assumption among those directly involved in the litigation process is that lawyers should control the clients so that the lawyers may exercise their professional judgment in an autonomous fashion. Where the client is financially dependent on the attorney such as when the fee is to be paid on a percentage (contingency) basis, this dimension may be problematic for the brokerage argument. It will be interesting to see what differences, if any, emerge in the domain of client control/autonomy between lawyers paid on hourly versus contingent fees.

The discussion of the intermediary role of the criminal defense lawyer can be easily extended to the lawyer in civil litigation. In both contexts, the lawyer serves as the intermediary between client and justice system, broadly defined. Where the criminal defense lawyer stands between the client and prosecutors, judges, and other court personnel, the lawyer in civil litigation stands between the client and representatives of the opposing party (lawyers, claims adjusters, etc.), and between the client and other litigation participants, such as experts (e.g., doctors and engineers), judges, and other court personnel. As with the criminal lawyer, it is the ongoing involvement with a broadly defined workgroup that shapes the day-to-day activities of litigation. In his study of lawyers in nonurban Missouri, Landon (1985: 95) reported that one lawyer told prospective clients at their first meeting that "You can hire me to fight your case, but you can't hire me to hate the opposing attorney!" The need to maintain cordial relationships among actors who frequently interact is not limited to rural settings; it arises from the natural desire to have a relatively pleasant and harmonious work environment. Maintaining such an environment often can work to the benefit of the client, at least in terms of convenience and time (e.g., scheduling or minimizing court sessions), if not in terms of eventual outcomes.

Ross points out important workgroup components in the relationship between personal injury plaintiffs' lawyers and insurance adjusters. First, he notes that these two actors share a common interest in the quick disposal of cases and that they share the insider knowledge of the going rates associated with various kinds of injuries (1980: 86). Second, in his discussion of the pressures that might come to bear on an attorney to agree to a lower settlement for a particular case than might be achievable by holding out, Ross notes the difficulties that a refusal by the lawyer to accept such a settlement might create for obtaining desirable settlements in future cases (1980: 82).

SUMMARY

. . . [I]n some ways the broker image is better for explaining the work of lawyers in ordinary litigation, while in other ways the professional image is better. The tensions inherent in the two images suffuse the working context of lawyers handling ordinary litigation, and one of the dilemmas that lawyers must cope with is how to deal with these tensions. The distinction also suggests important questions about the monopoly lawyers possess for handling certain kinds of disputes in the United States. . . .

References

Boissevain, Jeremy. 1969. "Patrons as Brokers." 16 *Sociologische Gids* 379–386.

———. 1974. *Friends of Friends: Networks, Manipulators and Coalitions.* Oxford: Basil Blackwell.

Cain, Maureen. 1979. "The General Practice Lawyer and the Client: Towards a Radical Conception." 7 *International Journal of the Sociology of Law* 331–354.

Carlin, Jerome E. 1962. *Lawyers on Their Own: A Study of Individual Practitioners in Chicago.* New Brunswick, N.J.: Rutgers University Press.

Eisenstein, James and Herbert Jacob. 1977. *Felony Justice: An Organizational Analysis of Criminal Courts.* Boston: Little, Brown.

Johnson, Earl, Jr. 1980–1981. "Lawyers' Choice: A Theoretical Appraisal of Litigation Investment Decisions." 15 *Law & Society Review* 567–610.

Johnson, Terence J. 1972. *Professions and Power.* London: Macmillan.

Kagan, Robert A. and Robert Eli Rosen. 1985. "On the Social Significance of Large Law Firm Practice." 37 *Stanford Law Review* 399–443.

Landon, Donald D. 1985. "Clients, Colleagues, and Community: The Shaping of Zealous Advocacy in Country Law Practice." 1985 *American Bar Foundation Research Journal* 81–111.

Rosenthal, Douglas. 1974. *Lawyer and Client: Who's in Charge?* New York: Russell Sage.

Ross, H. Laurence. 1980. *Settled Out of Court: The Social Process of Insurance Claims Adjustment* (Rev. 2nd Ed.). New York: Aldine.

Wessel, Milton R. 1976. *The Rule of Reason: A New Approach to Corporate Litigation.* New York: Addison-Wesley.

NOTES AND QUESTIONS

1. What is the role of a broker in business? What is the difference between a broker and a professional "acting as an alter ego?"

2. What are "first order" and "second order" resources? What do they have to do with brokerage?

3. In your opinion, how well does Kritzer's "brokerage perspective" translate a business concept into legal terms? Is it an apt comparison? What does this analogy suggest about the role that lawyers play, and the motivations that drive them in the civil litigation process?

4. How does the "brokerage perspective" echo Macaulay's account (Chapter 20) of the role lawyers often play as mediators for consumer grievances? In what ways are the two legal roles different? What accounts for this difference (consider, for example, the types of clients in each case and what suits they typically bring)?

5. Kritzer argues that brokers are "motivated by their own interests . . . rather than by altruism or some other 'moral' base." What effect would you expect lawyers' profit motives to have on the overall accessibility of law?

6. How does accessibility differ between a contingent-fee lawyer and an hourly-fee lawyer? What, according to Kritzer, are the benefits and drawbacks of each payment scheme? In your opinion, is one superior to the other?

Reprinted from: Herbert M. Kritzer, *The Justice Broker: Lawyers and Ordinary Litigation*, pp. 12–19. Copyright © 1990. Reprinted with the permission of Oxford University Press, Inc. ✦

Chapter 22

The Impact of Legal Counsel on Outcomes for Poor Tenants in New York City's Housing Court

Results of a Randomized Experiment

Carroll Seron
Martin Frankel
Gregg Van Ryzin
Jean Kovath

The next reading assesses what difference it makes if a person is represented by a lawyer. Using an unusual randomized experiment, Seron et. al. argue that the presence of counsel makes a substantial difference in the outcome regardless of the substantive merits of a legal case. Tenants in New York City's Housing Court who have lawyers are much less likely to have judgments entered against them than are those who were not represented by a lawyer. They are also much less likely to be subject to an eviction for failure to pay rent. In this study, having a lawyer turns out to be an important resource for those defending themselves against the claims of others.

As you read this selection consider if lawyers play a more important role when clients are relatively poor and disadvantaged? Do Seron and her coauthors make a persuasive case for the importance of providing legal services to poor people?

This article reports findings from a randomized experiment to test the effects of a program that provided legal representation to low-income tenants in New York City's Housing Court. While almost all landlords in Housing Court have the benefit of legal representation, the vast majority of tenants do not (Task Force 1986; Community & Training Resource Center 1993). Legal advocates for the poor have thus argued for a right to legal counsel in Housing Court, similar to the right that exists in Criminal Court, on grounds that it would ensure due process of law and procedural safeguards in an area of vital interest to tenants, their families, and society (*Gideon v. Wainwright* 1963). Aside from the question of cost, arguments against a right to counsel in Housing Court center primarily on the administrative burden on the Court that such an expansion of legal assistance might entail (Heydebrand & Seron 1990). Briefly, the findings from the experiment show that low-income tenants with legal representation experience significantly more beneficial outcomes than their counterparts who do not have legal representation, independent of the merits of the case. Furthermore, the findings from this experiment suggest that the presence of legal representation may impose only modest time delays or other indicators of administrative burden on the court system and may even be more efficient for the courts in certain respects. . . .

BACKGROUND

In the early 1970s, the State of New York created a specialized Housing Court Part under the jurisdiction of the Civil Court of the

City of New York (hereafter referred to as Housing Court) to enforce state and local laws regulating housing conditions and to adjudicate landlord-tenant disputes. A number of other large cities established specialized housing courts as well during this time (Golowitz 1999). While New York's Housing Court hears disputes between landlords and tenants over a range of issues, by far the most common case is a claim filed by a landlord to evict tenants for nonpayment of rent. Annually, New York's Housing Court handles about 300,000 cases and issues nearly 100,000 warrants of eviction (Galowitz 1999). Although the vast majority of tenants in Housing Court appear in court *pro se* (that is, they represent themselves without an attorney), most landlords have lawyers. For example, one study found that 21 percent of tenants in Housing Court were represented by a lawyer, whereas 78 percent of landlords were represented by a lawyer (Citywide Task Force on Housing Court [Task Force] 1986). A more recent study estimated that only 12 percent of tenants have legal representation, compared to 98 percent of landlords (Community Training and Resource Center 1993).

New York's Housing Court plays a crucial role in the city, particularly as it affects the housing conditions and welfare of the city's poor. Seventy percent of New York City's 2.8 million households are renters, 500,000 of which have incomes below the federal poverty line (Schill & Scafidi 1999). The housing stock of the city is very old and in comparatively poor condition, with low-income households much more likely to live in the most dilapidated and neglected buildings. Still, rents in New York remain unaffordable to many: 19 percent of the city's renters and 95 percent of low-income renters pay half or more of their income in rent (Schill & Scafidi 1999). The city has long had a chronically low rental-housing vacancy rate, particularly at lower rent levels, and homelessness continues to be a major social problem that many believe is linked to the city's housing woes. It is impor-

tant to note that New York's housing market is characterized by extensive rental controls and other housing regulations that, although designed to protect tenants and maintain housing standards, further complicate Housing Court adjudication.

The lack of legal representation for most tenants, the severe housing problems of the city, and the complex regulatory system in New York have led legal advocates for the poor to argue for a right to counsel in Housing Court (Scherer 1988). This argument rests in large part on the principle of due process of law, a key element of which is protection against procedural error. It is often argued, however, that legal representation slows down the wheels of adjudication. Lawyers may be effective, but they engender inefficiencies by filing multiple motions, or they may demand changes in scheduling to stall resolution of the dispute (Heydebrand & Seron 1990). Such tactics and delays may in turn encourage tenants to hold out without paying rent and deprive landlords of vital rental income to maintain and operate their buildings.

In 1993, the Interest on Lawyer Accounts Fund (IOLA) of New York provided funds to support The Pro Bono Project against Homelessness. The funds were jointly granted to the Legal Aid Society Community Law Offices in the Society's Volunteer Division (hereafter referred to as CLO) and to the Association of the Bar of the City of New York (ABCNY), and CLO was designated as project coordinator. The goal of the project was to enlist the services of volunteer (i.e., pro bono) attorneys, many from the largest law firms in the city, to represent low-income tenants in Housing Court. Because of the enormous need for attorneys, a related goal of the program was to "concentrate on cases that meet two principal requirements: a) they could lead to eviction and b) they give reason to believe that a lawyer could have a significant impact on the outcome" (Housing Court Litigation Project 1992–1993:4). Also, in focusing on eviction cases, a goal of the study was to protect families against breakup, a common side effect of homelessness.

CLO established an in-take office in the Manhattan Housing Court, with support from the Administrative Judge of the Civil Court. Staff from CLO managed the program, including screening of cases and assignment and supervision of pro bono attorneys. Attorneys from 17 firms were recruited and received basic training by CLO attorneys in the housing code and related matters of litigating in Housing Court. Because the volunteer attorneys in the program were not specialists or even necessarily experienced in Housing Court litigation prior to the program, CLO staff assisted the volunteer attorneys in developing a plan of action for each case. The staff paralegal worked on the welfare aspects of the case with the volunteer attorney, while the staff attorney assisted the volunteer attorney in preparing papers and thinking through case strategies. In other words, CLO attorneys worked closely with volunteer attorneys on all phases of the case, including negotiating, drafting stipulations of settlements, and trying cases before the Court.

An independent evaluation of the program was requested as a condition of funding. The evaluation was intended to answer two primary empirical questions:

1. Does the provision of legal counsel affect outcomes for low-income tenants in Housing Court, including final judgments, warrants of eviction, and stipulations requiring rent abatement or repairs to the property?

2. Does the provision of legal counsel for low-income tenants produce delays and other inefficiencies for the Court, including a lengthening of the average time required by the Court to dispose of a case and an increase in the number of motions filed? . . .

METHOD

The evaluation was designed as a randomized experiment involving a treatment group of legal aid-eligible tenants that was targeted to receive legal counsel through the Pro Bono Project and a control group that was not. In the terminology of research designs, the evaluation is a simple randomized experiment with a post-test only (Cook & Campbell 1979). . . .

FINDINGS

The data in Table [22.1] report the comparison of outcomes for treatment and control cases for the first hypothesis, i.e., the pro-

---

Table 22.1
Comparison of Outcomes for Treatment and Control Groups

Outcome	Treatment	Control	Test Statistic, *p*-Value (two-tailed test)
Default or failure of tenant to appear	15.8% (*n* = 133)	28.2% (*n* = 124)	$X^2 = 5.82$, $p = 0.016$
Judgment against tenant	31.8% (*n* = 132)	52.0% (*n* = 123)	$X^2 = 10.71$, $p = 0.001$
Warrant of eviction issued	24.1% (*n* = 133)	43.5% (*n* = 124)	$X^2 = 10.95$, $p = 0.001$
Stipulation requiring rent abatement	18.8% (*n* = 133)	3.2% (*n* = 124)	$X^2 = 15.54$, $p\,0.001$
Stipulation requiring repairs	45.9% (*n* = 133)	28.2% (*n* = 124)	$X^2 = 8.53$, $p = 0.003$

gram has a beneficial effect on the outcomes experienced by tenants. These results represent a conservative estimate of the treatment effect because, as mentioned, a substantial minority of tenants in the treatment group was never provided with an attorney. Still, on all five measures, tenants in the treatment group experienced significantly more beneficial outcomes in Housing Court than controls. Not only are the effects highly significant statistically, but the magnitude of the differences are also large in substantive terms. Notably, while approximately 28 percent of the control cases show defaults or failure to appear in Housing Court, only about 16 percent of treatments do so. And although judgments were issued against 52 percent of control cases, only approximately 32 percent of the treatment cases had judgments against them. Similar differences in favor of the treatment group can be seen in the percentage of warrants for eviction and the percentage of stipulations for rent abatements and repairs.

The findings reported in Table [22.2] address the issue of delays or burdens on the Court, again looking only at the effect of initial assignment. Overall, the findings reported in Table [22.2] do not provide much evidence in support of the hypothesis that lawyers create inefficiencies for the court system. Though treatment cases sit on the docket for significantly more time (about 111 days) than

control cases (approximately 82 days), treatment cases do not generate significantly more court appearances or motions than control cases. In fact, the findings actually suggest that lawyers may create some efficiencies for the Court. Treatment cases are significantly less likely to have post-judgment motions filed (approximately 13 percent) than control cases (29 percent). Post-judgment motions may take one of three forms: (1) motions seeking a stay on eviction and extensions of time to pay arrears; (2) motions seeking to set aside the stipulation entered into, as it was unduly harsh or improvidently entered into; and (3) motions seeking to be restored to an apartment after eviction. Post-judgment motions are especially burdensome for the Court because they require a case to be reviewed and reopened after what was supposed to have been a final resolution of the dispute. These results suggest that counsel are effective in obtaining stipulations and compliance, and this in turn may produce significantly fewer of these motions when clients are represented. ...

DISCUSSION AND CONCLUSION

The findings from this experiment clearly show that when low-income tenants in New York City's Housing Court are provided with legal counsel, they experience significantly more beneficial procedural outcomes than

Table 22.2
Comparison of Court Process Indicators for Treatment and Control Groups

Court Process Indicator	Treatment	Control	Test Statistic, *p*-Value (two-tailed test)
Mean number of court appearances	4.15 (*n* = 119)	3.61 (*n* = 108)	*t* = 2.22, *p* = 0.138
Mean number of days from answer to final judgment	111.48 (*n* = 124)	82.32 (*n* = 120)	*t* = 5.05, *p* = 0.026
Mean number of motions filed	0.95 (*n* = 133)	1.12 (*n* = 124)	*t* = 0.89, *p* = 0.347
One or more post-judgment motions filed	12.8% (*n* = 133)	29.0% (*n* = 124)	X^2 = 10.35, *p* = 0.001

their *pro se* counterparts. Represented tenants are much less likely to have a final judgment and order of eviction against them and more likely to benefit from a stipulation requiring a rent abatement or repair to their apartment. Because this evaluation is based on a true randomized experiment, these differences in outcomes can be attributed solely to the presence of legal counsel and are independent of the merits of the case. Moreover, these outcomes do not appear to come at much expense in terms of the efficiency of the Court; in fact, the presence of an attorney at the tenant's side may actually enhance efficiency by reducing the number of motions, particularly post-judgment motions. . . .

References

Citywide Task Force on Housing Court (1986) "5 Minute Justice: 'Ain't Nothing Going on But the Rent!'" A Report of the Monitoring Subcommittee of the Citywide Task Force on Housing Court. New York: Citywide Task Force.

Community Training and Resource Center and Citywide Task Force on Housing Court, Inc. (1993) "Housing Court, Evictions, and Homelessness: The Costs and Benefits of Establishing a Right to Counsel." New York: Community Training and Resource Center and Citywide Task Force on Housing Court, Inc.

Cook, Thomas D., & Donald T. Campbell (1979) *Quasi-Experimentation: Design and Analysis Issues for Field Settings.* Boston: Houghton Mifflin.

Golowitz, Paula (1999) "The Housing Court's Role in Maintaining Affordable Housing," in M. Schill, ed., *Housing and Community Development in New York City.* Albany: State Univ. of New York Press.

Heydebrand, Wolf, & Carroll Seron (1990) *Rationalizing Justice: The Political Economy of the Federal District Courts.* Albany: State Univ. of New York Press.

Housing Court Pro Bono Project of the Legal Aid Society and the Association of the Bar of the City of New York (1992–1993). *The Pro Bono Project Against Homelessness.*

Scherer, Andrew (1988) "Gideon's Shelter: The Need to Recognize a Right to Counsel for Indigent Defendants in Eviction Proceedings," 23 *Harvard Civil Rights-Civil Liberties Law Rev.* 557–588.

Schill, Michael H., & Benjamin P. Scafidi (1999) "Housing Conditions and Problems in New York City," in M. Schill, ed., *Housing and Community Development in New York City,* Albany: State Univ. of New York Press.

Case Cited

Gideon v. Wainwright, 372 U.S. 336; Sup. Ct. 792 (1963)

Notes and Questions

1. What two empirical questions did Seron and colleagues' study set out to answer? How are these questions linked with the constitutional right to due process of law?

2. According to this study, how did the increase in legal representation of tenants affect verdicts in the New York City Housing Court?

3. What does it mean, in this context, to have "access" to the law? Is the very existence of New York City's Housing Court sufficient? To what extent has a tenant who appears before the court without professional legal counsel been "admitted to the law"?

4. What do you suppose would happen to the overall volume of litigation if civil courts guaranteed the same right to counsel that currently exists in criminal courts? Ought we to be more concerned with the potential abuse of such a guarantee or with the inequities of legal access that currently exist between landlords and tenants?

5. What do Seron and colleagues suggest about the likelihood of a litigation explosion? How convincing is this argument? Are manageable court dockets

and readily available legal services for the poor mutually exclusive goals, or not?

6. What is the nature of the relationship between lawyers and their clients, as depicted in Seron et. al.'s study? How does this compare with Macaulay's (Chapter 20) and Kritzer's (Chapter 21) accounts of the role lawyers play vis-à-vis their cli-

ents in the civil litigation process? How do you explain the difference?

Reprinted from: Carroll Seron, Gregg Van Ryzin, Martin Frankel, and Jean Kovath, "The Impact of Legal Counsel on Outcomes for Poor Tenants in New York City's Housing Court: Results of a Randomized Experiment" in *Law and Society Review*, 35:2, 2001, pp. 419–434. Copyright © 2001. Reprinted with the permission of the Law and Society Association. ✦

Section VI

Whose Law Is It Anyway?

Chapter 23

Rusk v. Maryland

As we have already seen, social differences matter to law. Legal officials notice and respond to gender, class, race, and other markers of social identity and group membership. As a result, the aspiration to blind justice, to a legal system in which social inequality is not translated into legal inequality, is often unrealized. Who we are plays a key role in our ability to get access to law and obtain legal decisions that reflect our values and respond to our needs.

The readings in this chapter take up one example of the ways legal rules and legal proceedings reflect social differences by examining the treatment of violence against women and sexual harassment. So profound is the impact of social difference in and on law that some theorists claim that law itself has a "gender," that it is male because it embodies perspectives and values that have historically reflected the view, norms, and values of men. The readings in this section provide case studies and careful examinations of gender's impact on legal rules and legal institutions and the responses of women to what Felstiner, Abel, and Sarat call "perceived injurious events" in Chapter 15.

Rape is a crime of violence and an abuse of power rather than simply being about sex. Yet traditionally, instead of focusing on the alleged offender, his acts, and his intention, what the criminal law refers to as his mens rea, it focused instead on the behavior of the victim. Crucial to the inquiry has been the question of consent. Simply put, rape was treated as sex without consent. Because the law was so preoccupied with insuring that the man had notice of the victim's nonconsent, it required that victims physically resist.

Rusk v. Maryland *exemplifies this traditional view. In this case, a man met a woman at a bar, got her to give him a ride home, and insisted that she go inside with him. Once inside, they had sex. The woman charged that the sex was nonconsensual even though she did not physically resist. Her failure to resist, she said, arose from her fear that the man would harm her if she did not comply with his demands. The defendant was charged with, and convicted of, rape and appealed his conviction, claiming that their sexual encounter was consensual and that his words and actions could not have created in the mind of his victim a "reasonable" fear of harm. Agreeing with his argument about the unreasonableness of her fear, the appellate court reversed his rape conviction.*

In the selection presented here, the dissenting judge in the appeal, whose views ultimately were vindicated when the case was appealed to a yet higher court, describes the problems with the traditional understanding of rape, including, in particular, its basis in "the taboos and myths of a Victorian age" and its tendency to favor the male perspective. He urges the law to adopt a more realistic view of the problem of violence against women.

Judge Wilner Dissenting

With the deepest respect for the generally superior wisdom of my colleagues who authored or endorsed the majority opinion, but with the equally profound conviction that, in this case, they have made a serious mistake, I record this dissent.

The majority's error, in my judgment, is not in their exposition of the underlying principles of law that must govern this case, but rather in the manner that they have applied those principles. The majority have trampled upon the first principle of appellate restraint. Under the guise of judging the sufficiency of the evidence presented against appellant, they have tacitly—perhaps unwittingly, but none-theless effectively—substituted their own view of the evidence (and the inferences that may fairly be drawn from it) for that of the judge and jury. In so doing, they have not only improperly invaded the province allotted to those tribunals, but, at the same time, have perpetuated and given new life to myths about the crime of rape that have no place in our law today. . . .

Md. Annot. Code art. 27, § 463(a) considers three types of conduct as constituting second degree rape. We are concerned only with the first: a person is guilty of rape in the second degree if he (1) engages in vaginal intercourse with another person, (2) by force or threat of force, (3) against the will, and (4) without the consent of the other person. There is no real question here as to the first, third, or fourth elements of the crime. The evidence was certainly sufficient to show that appellant had vaginal intercourse with the victim, and that such act was against her will and without her consent. The point at issue is whether it was accomplished by force or threat of force; and I think that in viewing the evidence, that point should remain ever clear. *Consent is not the issue here, only whether there was sufficient evidence of force or the threat of force.*

Unfortunately, courts, including in the present case a majority of this one, often tend to confuse these two elements—force and lack of consent—and to think of them as one. They are not. They mean, and require, different things. See *State v. Studham,* 572 P.2d 700 (Utah, 1977). What seems to pause the confusion—what, indeed, has become a common denominator of both elements—is the notion that the victim must actively resist the attack upon her. If she fails to offer sufficient resistance (sufficient to the satisfaction of the judge), a court is entitled, or at least presumes the entitlement, to find that there was no force or threat of force, or that the act was not against her will, or that she actually consented to it, or some unarticulated combination or

synthesis of these elements that leads to the ultimate conclusion that the victim was not raped. Thus it is that the focus is almost entirely on the extent of resistance—*the victim's acts, rather than those of her assailant.* Attention is directed not to the wrongful stimulus, but to the victim's reactions to it. Right or wrong, that seems to be the current state of the Maryland law; and, notwithstanding its uniqueness in the criminal law, and its illogic, until changed by statute or the Court of Appeals, I accept it as binding.

But what is required of a woman being attacked or in danger of attack? How much resistance must she offer? Where is that line to be drawn between requiring that she either risk serious physical harm, perhaps death, on the one hand, or be termed a willing partner on the other? Some answers were given in *Hazel v. State,* 221 Md. 464 (1960). . . .

. . .But what I do accept is what the Court of Appeals said in *Hazel:* (1) if the acts and threats of the defendant were reasonably calculated to create in the mind of the victim—having regard to the circumstances in which she was placed—a real apprehension, due to fear, of imminent bodily harm, serious enough to impair or overcome her will to resist, then such acts and threats are the equivalent of force; (2) submission is not the equivalent of consent; and (3) the real test is whether the assault was committed without the consent and against the will of the prosecuting witness.[1]

Upon this basis, the evidence against appellant must be considered. Judge Thompson recounts most, but not quite all, of the victim's story. The victim—I'll call her Pat—attended a high school reunion. She had arranged to meet her girlfriend Terry there. The reunion was over at 9:00, and Terry asked Pat to accompany her to Fell's Point.[2] Pat had gone to Fell's Point with Terry on a few prior occasions, explaining in court: "I've never met anybody [there] I've gone out with. I met people in general, talking in conversation, most of the time people that Terry knew, not that I have gone down there, and met people as dates." She agreed to go, but first called her mother, who was babysitting with Pat's two-year-old son, to tell her that she was going with Terry to Fell's Point, and that she would not be home late. It was just after 9:00 when Pat and Terry, in their separate cars, left for Fell's Point, alone.[3]

They went to a place called Helen's and had one drink. They stayed an hour or so and then walked down to another place (where they had another drink), stayed about a half hour there, and went to a third place. Up to this point, Pat conversed only with Terry, and did not strike up any other acquaintanceships. Pat and Terry were standing against a wall when appellant came over and said hello to Terry, who was conversing with someone else at the time. Appellant then began to talk with Pat. They were both separated, they both had young children; and they spoke about those things. Pat said that she had been ready to leave when appellant came on the scene, and that she only talked with him for five or ten minutes. It was then about midnight. Pat had to get up with her baby in the morning and did not want to stay out late.

Terry wasn't ready to leave. As Pat was preparing to go, appellant asked if she would drop him off on her way home.[4] She agreed because she thought he was a friend of Terry's. She told him, however, as they walked to her car, "I'm just giving a ride home, you know, as a friend, not anything to be, you now, thought of other than a ride." He agreed to that condition.

Pat was completely unfamiliar with appellant's neighborhood. She had no idea where she was. When she pulled up to where appellant said he lived, she put the car in park, but left the engine running. She said to appellant "Well, here, you know, you are home." Appellant then asked Pat to come up with him and she refused. He persisted in his request, as did she in her refusal. She told him that even if she wanted to come up, she dared not do so. She was separated and it might cause marital

problems for her. Finally, he reached over, turned off the ignition, took her keys, got out of the car, came around to her side, opened the door, and said to her, "Now, will you come up?"

It was at this point that Pat followed appellant to his apartment, and it is at this point that the majority of this Court begins to substitute its judgment for that of the trial court and jury. We know nothing about Pat and appellant. We don't know how big they are, what they look like, what their life experiences have been. We don't know if appellant is larger or smaller than she, stronger or weaker. We don't know what the inflection was in his voice as he dangled her car keys in front of her. We can't tell whether this was in a jocular vein or a truly threatening one. We have no idea what his mannerisms were. The trial judge and the jury could discern some of these things, of course, because they could observe the two people in court and could listen to what they said and how they said it. But all we know is that, between midnight and 1:00 a.m., in a neighborhood that was strange to Pat, appellant took her car keys, demanded that she accompany him, and most assuredly implied that unless she did so, at the very least, she might be stranded.

Now, let us interrupt the tale for a minute and consider the situation. Pat did not honk the horn; she did not scream; she did not try to run away. Why, she was asked. "I was scared. I didn't think at the time what to do." Later, on cross-examination: "At that point, because I was scared, because he had my car keys. I didn't know what to do. I was someplace I didn't even know where I was. It was in the city. I didn't know whether to run. I really didn't think, at that point, what to do. Now, I know that I should have blown the horn. I should have run. There were a million things I could have done. I was scared, at that point, and I didn't do any of them." What, counsel asked, was she afraid of? "Him," she replied. What was she scared that he was going to do? "Rape me, but I didn't say that. It was the way he looked at me, and said, 'Come on up, come on up;' and when he took the keys, I knew that was wrong. I just didn't say, are you going to rape me."

So Pat accompanied appellant to his apartment. As Judge Thompson points out, appellant left her in his apartment for a few minutes.[5] Although there was evidence of a telephone in the room, Pat said that, at the time, she didn't notice one. When appellant returned, he turned off the light and sat on the bed. Pat was in a chair. She testified: "I asked him if I could leave, that I wanted to go home, and I didn't want to come up. I said, 'Now, I came up. Can I go?'" Appellant, who, of course, still had her keys, said that he wanted her to stay. He told her to get on the bed with him, and, in fact, took her arms and pulled her on to the bed. He then started to undress her; he removed her blouse and bra and unzipped her pants. *At his direction,* she removed his clothes. She then said:

"I was still begging him to please let, you know, let me leave. I said, 'you can get a lot of other girls down there, for what you want,' and he just kept saying, 'no;' and then I was really scared, because I can't describe, you know, what was said. It was more the look in his eyes; and I said, at that point—I didn't know what to say; and I said, 'If I do what you want, will you let me go without killing me?' Because I didn't know, at that point, what he was going to do; and I started to cry; and when I did, he put his hands on my throat, and started lightly to choke me; and I said, 'If I do what you want, will you let me go?' And he said, yes, and at that time, I proceeded to do what he wanted me to."

He "made me perform oral sex, and then sexual intercourse." Following that:

"I asked him if I could leave now, and he said, 'Yes;' and I got up and got dressed; and he got up and got dressed; and he walked me to my car, and asked if he could see me again; and I said, 'Yes;' and he asked me for my telephone number; and I said,

'No, I'll see you down at Fell's Point sometime,' just so I could leave."[6]

At this point, appellant returned her car keys and escorted her to her car. She then drove off:

"I stopped at a gas station, that I believe was Amoco or Exon (sic), and went to the ladies' room. From there I drove home. I don't know—I don't know if I rode around for a while or not; but I know I went home, pretty much straight home and pulled up and parked the car.

"I was just going to go home, and not say anything.

"Q Why?

"A *Because I didn't want to go through what I'm going through now.*

"Q What, in fact did you do then?

"A I sat in the car, thinking about it a while, and I thought I wondered what would happen if I hadn't of done what he wanted me to do. So I thought the right thing to do was to go report it, and I went from there to Hillendale to find a police car." (Emphasis supplied.)

How does the majority opinion view these events? It starts by noting that Pat was a 21-year-old mother who was separated from her husband but not yet divorced, as though that had some significance. To me, it has none, except perhaps (when coupled with the further characterization that Pat and Terry had gone "bar hopping") to indicate an underlying suspicion, for which there is absolutely no support in the record, that Pat was somehow "on the make." Even more alarming, and unwarranted, however, is the majority's analysis of Pat's initial reflections on whether to report what had happened. Ignoring completely her statement that she "didn't want to go through what I'm going through now," the majority, in footnote 1, cavalierly and without any foundation whatever, says:

"If, in quiet contemplation after the act, she had to wonder what would have happened, her submission on the side of prudence seems hardly justified. Indeed, if *she* had to wonder afterward, how can a fact finder reasonably conclude that she was justifiably in fear sufficient to overcome her will to resist, at the time." (Emphasis in the original.)

It is this type of reasoning—if indeed "reasoning" is the right word for it—that is particularly distressing. The concern expressed by Pat, made even more real by the majority Opinion of this Court, is one that is common among rape victims, and largely accounts for the fact that most incidents of forcible rape go unreported by the victim. See *F.B.I. Uniform Crime Reports* (1978), p. 14; *Report of Task Force on Rape Control, Baltimore County* (1975); *The Treatment of Rape Victims in the Metropolitan Washington Area,* Metropolitan Washington Council of Governments (1976), p. 4. See also *Rape And Its Victims: A Report for Citizens, Health Facilities, and Criminal Justice Agencies,* LEAA (1975). If appellant had desired, and Pat had given, her wallet instead of her body, there would be no question about appellant's guilt of robbery. Taking the car keys under those circumstances would certainly have supplied the requisite threat of force or violence and negated the element of consent. No one would seriously contend that because she failed to raise a hue and cry she had consented to the theft of her money. Why then is such life-threatening action necessary when it is her personal dignity that is being stolen?

Rape has always been considered a most serious crime, one that traditionally carried the heaviest penalty. But until recently, it remained shrouded in the taboos and myths of a Victorian age, and little real attention was given to how rapes occur, how they may be prevented, and how a victim can best protect herself from injury when an attack appears inevitable. The courts are as responsible for this ignorance and the misunderstandings emanating from it as any other institution in society, and it is high time that they recognize reality.

Rape is on the increase in the United States. The Uniform Crime Reports compiled by the F.B.I show more than a doubling in both the absolute number of forcible rapes and in the rate per 100,000 population between 1965 and 1974. Between 1973 and 1977, forcible rape has increased 19 percent.[7] As the result of the Battelle Study,[8] we now know some things about this crime that we could only guess at before. Nearly half of the rapes occur when this one did, between 8:00 p.m. and 2:00 a.m., and, as in this case, approximately one-third of rape victims had come into contact with their assailants voluntarily, under circumstances other than hitchhiking.[9] *Physical force is absent in over half of reported cases and, in a third of the cases, no weapon is involved.* In rapes occurring in large cities (over 500,000 population), the statistics showed:[10]

Use of physical force   47.4%

Use of weapon:

   none   34.6%

   firearms   21.1%

   sharp instrument   24.6%

   blunt instrument   7.3%

   other   11.6%

Of particular significance is what was learned about *resistance.* The most common type of resistance offered by victims is verbal. Note: verbal resistance is resistance! In cases arising in the large cities, only 12.7 percent of the victims attempted flight, and only 12 percent offered physical resistance.[11] The reason for this is apparent from the next thing learned: that "*[rape] victims who resisted were more likely to be injured than ones who did not.*"[12] The statistics showed, for rapes in large cities, that, where physical resistance was offered, over 71 percent of the victims were physically injured in some way, 40 percent requiring medical treatment or hospitalization.[13]

Said the Report: "*These results indicate one possible danger of the popular notion (and some statutory requirements) that a victim of an attack should resist to her utmost.*" (Emphasis supplied.)

In a second volume of the Report, intended for prosecutors, some of the social attitudes about rape were discussed. With respect to resistance, it was noted (p. 4):

"Perhaps because most women's experience and expertise with violence tends to be minimal, they are unlikely to engage in physical combat or succeed when they do. Many women employ what is referred to as 'passive resistance.' This can include crying, being slow to respond, feigning an inability to understand instructions or telling the rapist they are pregnant, diseased or injured. *While these techniques may not always be successful, their use does suggest that the victim is surely not a willing partner.*" (Emphasis supplied.)

In contrast to some of the inferences sought to be drawn by the majority from Pat's reactions, the Report further points out (Prosecutor's Volume I, p. 5):

"Rather than expressing their emotions, some victims respond to a rape with a calm, composed demeanor or 'controlled reaction.' [Footnote omitted.] These victims do not wish to exhibit emotions, especially in front of a stranger or authority figure like the prosecutor. Psychologically it is important for these victims to demonstrate that they can handle stress in a mature and adult manner. *The appearance of casualness hides and may avoid true and often intense emotions.* This 'control' may result in victim responses which are considered inappropriate such as giggling, smiling or even laughing. *Unfortunately this type of response can cause others to doubt the victim's account of the rape.*" (Emphasis supplied.)

Finally, perhaps in response to the oft-quoted comment of Matthew Hale that still pervades societal thinking about rape ("[Rape] is an accusation easily to be made and hard to be proved, and harder to be defended by the party accused, tho never so innocent"),[14] the Report observes (Vol. II, p. 4):

"*On a national average, 15 percent of all forcible rapes reported to the police were 'determined by investigation' to be unfounded. Given the inherent skepticism of many criminal justice personnel to rape victims and the harassment and invasion of privacy that a reporting victim is likely to confront, it is doubtful that many false accusations proceed past the initial report.* Curtis (1974) asserts that 'contrary to widespread opinion, there is in fact little hard empirical evidence that victims in rape lie more than, say victims in robbery.' Undoubtedly, there are false reports. However, the danger posed by the myth that women 'cry rape' is that police officers and prosecutors will believe it and then place the burden on the victims to prove the contrary." (Emphasis supplied.)

Law enforcement agencies throughout the country warn women not to resist an attack haphazardly, not to antagonize a potential attacker, but to protect themselves from more serious injury. The United States Department of Justice, for example, has published a pamphlet warning, among other things:[15]

"If you are confronted by a rapist, stay calm and maximize your chances for escape. *Think* through what you will do. You should not *immediately* try to fight back. Chances are, your attacker has the advantage. Try to stay calm and take stock of the situation."

Where does this leave us but where we started? A judge and a jury, observing the witnesses and hearing their testimony, concluded without dissent that there was sufficient evidence to find beyond a reasonable doubt that appellant had sexual intercourse with Pat by force or threat of force against her will and without her consent; in other words, that the extent of her resistance and the reasons for her failure to resist further were reasonable. No claim is made here that the jury was misinstructed on the law of rape. Yet a majority of this Court, without the ability to see and hear the witnesses, has simply concluded that, in their judgment, Pat's fear was not a reasonable one, or that there was no fear at all (a point that appellant conceded at oral argument before the Court *en banc*). In so doing, they have ignored the fact of a young woman alone in a strange neighborhood at 1:00 in the morning with a man who had taken her keys and was standing at her open car door demanding that she come with him; they have ignored that she offered the very type of verbal resistance that is prudent, common, and recommended by law enforcement agencies; they have ignored that the reasonableness of Pat's apprehension is inherently a question of fact for the jury to determine, *Tryon v. State*, 567 P.2d 290 (Wyo. 1977); *State v. Baldwin*, 571 S.W.2d 236 (Mo. 1978); *People v. Merritt*, 381 N.E.2d 407 (Ill. App. 1978); *People v. Vicaretti*, 388 N.Y.S.2d 410 (1976); *People v. Coleman*, 89 Cal. App. 3d 312 (1979).[16] Brushing all of this aside, they have countermanded the judgment of the trial court and jury and declared Pat to have been, in effect, an adulteress.[17]

Notes

1. Other courts have stated the rule this way: A rape victim is not required to do more than her age, strength, surrounding facts and all attending circumstances make it reasonable for her to do to manifest her opposition. See *Dinkens v. State*, 546 P.2d 228 (Nev. 1976); *State v. Studham*, 572 P.2d 700 Utah 1977). See also *Schrum v. Com.*, 246 S.E.2d 893 (Va. 1978).

2. Fell's Point is an old section of Baltimore City adjacent to the harbor. It has been extensively renovated as part of urban renewal and, among refurbished homes and shops, hosts a number of cafes and discotheques. It is part of the City's night scene.

3. Pat said that Terry and she lived at opposite ends of town and that Fell's Point was sort of midway between their respective homes.

4. Her testimony about this, on cross-examination, was: "I said I was leaving. I said, excuse me. It's nice meeting you; but I'm getting ready to leave; and he said, 'which way are you going;' and I told him; at that time, he said, 'Would you mind giving me a lift?'"

5. On direct examination, she twice said that he left the room "for a minute" after telling her to sit down. On cross-examination, she said she couldn't remember how long he was gone, but, at counsel's suggestion, said that it was not longer than five minutes.

6. Pat explained this last comment further: "I didn't know what else to say. I had no intention of meeting him again."

7. *See* FBI Uniform Crime Reports (1978), p. 14. *See also* Battelle Study, *infra*, note 8, Prosecutors' Volume 1 (1977), p. 7.

8. This was a study conducted by the Battelle Memorial Institute Law and Justice Study Center under grant from the LEAA (National Institute of Law Enforcement and Criminal Justice). The Report of the study was published during 1977 and 1978. I shall refer to it hereafter as "Battelle Study."

9. Battelle Study, Police Volume 1, p. 20.

10. *Id.*, p. 21. These figures, of course, are not cumulative. Weapons may accompany physical force, or there may be an absence of both.

11. *Id.*, p. 21.

12. *Id.*, p. 22.

13. *Id.*, p. 22.

14. Hale, *The History of the Pleas of the Crown* 635 (1847).

15. *Be on the safe side*, LEAA, U.S. Department of Justice. The pamphlet also advises: "Be selective about new acquaintances; don't *invite* a forcible sexual encounter." *See also, Let Prevention Be Your Guide*, a pamphlet published by the (Baltimore City) Mayor's Coordinating Council on Criminal Justice; *Rape Prevention*, a pamphlet distributed by the Prince George's County Police Department. That pamphlet specifically warns: "Extensive research into thousands of rape cases indicates that attempts at self-defense, such as scream-

ing, kicking, scratching and use of tear gas devices and other weapons, usually have provoked the rapist into inflicting severe bodily harm on the victim. Since it is unlikely you will be able to overcome the rapist by force, you must think about what he will do after you try and fail. Before you do anything, remember . . .IF WHATEVER YOU DO DOES NOT HELP YOU, MAKE SURE THAT IT WILL NOT HARM YOU."

16. The majority opinion cites and reviews at some length *Gonzales v. State*, 516 P.2d 592 (Wyo. 1973). It is worthy of note that the conviction in *Gonzales* was reversed not because of an insufficiency of evidence, but because of an erroneous jury instruction. The Wyoming court made this clear in *Tryon*, 567 P.2d at 292. Indeed, the *Gonzales* court held that the question of whether the victim's apprehension was reasonable was for the jury to determine. See 516 P.2d at 594.

17. Interestingly, appellant was convicted of assault arising out of the same incident, but did not contest the sufficiency of the evidence supporting that conviction. It would seem that if there was not enough evidence of force, or lack of consent, to permit the rape conviction, there was an equal insufficiency to support the assault conviction. The majority is spared, *in this case*, the need to deal with that thorny dilemma.

NOTES AND QUESTIONS

1. Under what definition of rape was *Rusk v. State* decided? Is this a clear and complete definition? Would you change anything about it?

2. How important is context to the facts of this case? Does the size of the alleged assailant relative to the woman matter? What about her age, her demeanor, or the way she was dressed? Does either party's tone of voice make a difference in determining if the sexual encounter was consensual or forced?

3. Two questions treated as overlapping (if not synonymous) by the judges in the majority were the use of force by the assailant and lack of consent on the part of the victim. In the dissent, how does Justice Wilner propose to separate these questions? Why, according to him, is it so important to separate them?

4. Justice Wilner writes in the dissent that, "rape has always been considered a most serious crime, one that traditionally carried the highest penalty." In the United States, about 100,000 rapes of females are reported each year; estimates of unreported rape range from 2 to 10 times that number. What does the incidence of unreported rape suggest about gender and the accessibility of the law?

5. When the victim in *Rusk* is asked why she seriously considered not reporting the crime, she responds, "Because I didn't want to go through what I'm going through now." Is there something extraordinary about the way victims of sexual violence are treated (as compared with other victims in the criminal justice system) that creates a particular barrier between them and the law?

6. Laws in 49 states limit the evidentiary use of a victim's prior sexual history as part of an effort to undermine the credibility of the victim's testimony. Where the prior sexual history is relevant, however, most states' laws authorize the judge to permit cross-examination on this topic at the court's discretion. Only Arizona does not have a rape-shield law.

7. Judge Wilner argues that the majority should have shown more deference to the jury's verdict in *Rusk*. What about the nature of a rape trial makes a jury more adept than the judges of a higher court at delivering a just verdict? Do you agree with Judge Wilner?

Reprinted from: *Rusk v. State of Maryland*, 406 A. 2d 624 (1979). ✦

Chapter 24

Rape

Susan Estrich

Mill (Chapter 9) reminds us that preventing harm is central to our understanding of law. As a result, the criminal law generally focuses on two things: action and intent. Did someone commit a prohibited act, and was this act intentional? In a criminal trial the government has the burden of proving that the accused committed such an act and possessed what in law is called a "guilty mind."

The traditional law of rape has been controversial for many reasons, not the least of which is its tendency to put the victim on trial. In the last several decades, legislatures, reacting to a push from women's groups, have reformed rape law in various ways, in particular by enacting rape shield laws, which limit or prohibit the admission of the victim's prior sexual history to prove consent. One of the most important of the scholarly contributions to the reform effort was the article by Susan Estrich.

This article begins with the excruciating story of Estrich's own rape and uses this account to think through what she calls "the restrictive and sexist views of our society." She illustrates this claim by comparing the way the criminal law treats rape with its treatment of other crimes. This comparison reveals stark differences. Most importantly, Estrich suggests that instead of focusing on what the victim did or said and whether her conduct or words were sufficient to establish nonconsent, the focus should be on the defendant, his acts, and his intent. In her view, rape law asks more of women than it does of victims of other crimes. She concludes by arguing for reform in the law of rape that would, among other things, bring it more into line with the rest of the criminal law.

INTRODUCTION

Eleven years ago, a man held an ice pick to my throat and said: "Push over, shut up, or I'll kill you." I did what he said, but I couldn't stop crying. A hundred years later, I jumped out of my car as he drove away.

I ended up in the back seat of a police car. I told the two officers I had been raped by a man who came up to the car door as I was getting out in my own parking lot (and trying to balance two bags of groceries and kick the car door open). He took the car, too.

They asked me if he was a crow. That was their first question. A crow, I learned that day, meant to them someone who is black.

They asked me if I knew him. That was their second question. They believed me when I said I didn't. Because, as one of them put it, how would a nice (white) girl like me know a crow? Now they were on my side. They asked me if he took any money. He did; but while I remember virtually every detail of that day and night, I can't remember how much. But I remember their answer. He did take money; that made it an armed robbery. Much better than a rape. They got right on the radio with that.

We went to the police station first, not the hospital, so I could repeat my story (and then what did he do?) to four more policemen. When we got there, I borrowed a dime to call my father. They all liked that.

By the time we went to the hospital, they were really on my team. I could've been one of their kids. Now there was something they'd better tell me. Did I realize what prosecuting a rape complaint was all about? They tried to tell me that the "law" was against me. But they didn't explain exactly how. And I didn't understand why. I believed in "the law," not knowing what it was.

Late that night, I sat in the Police Headquarters looking at mug shots. I was the one who insisted on going back that night. My memory was fresh. I was ready. They had four

165

or five to "really show" me; being "really shown" a mugshot means exactly what defense attorneys are afraid it means. But it wasn't anyone of them. After that, they couldn't help me very much. One shot looked close until my father realized that the man had been the right age ten years before. It was late. I didn't have a great description of identifying marks, or the like: No one had ever told me that if you are raped, you should not shut your eyes and cry for fear that this is really happening. You should keep your eyes open focusing on this man who is raping you so you can identify him when you survive. After an hour of looking, I left the police station. They told me they'd be back in touch. They weren't.

A clerk called me one day to tell me that my car had been found minus tires and I should come sign a release and have it towed—no small matter if you don't have a car to get there and are slightly afraid of your shadow. The women from the rape crisis center called me every day, then every other day, then every other week. The police detectives never called at all.

I learned, much later, that I had "really" been raped. Unlike, say, the woman who claimed she'd been raped by a man she actually knew, and was with voluntarily. Unlike, say, women who are "asking for it," and get what they deserve. I would listen as seemingly intelligent people explained these distinctions to me, and marvel; later I read about them in books, court opinions, and empirical studies. It is bad enough to be a "real" rape victim. How terrible to be—what to call it—a "not real" rape victim.

Even the real rape victim must bear the heavy weight of the silence that surrounds this crime. At first, it is something you simply don't talk about. Then it occurs to you that people whose houses are broken into or who are mugged in Central Park talk about it all the time. Rape is a much more serious crime. If it isn't my fault, why am I supposed to be ashamed? If I shouldn't be ashamed, if it was-

n't "personal," why look askance when I mention it?

As this introduction makes clear, I talk about it. I do so very consciously. Sometimes, I have been harassed as a result. More often, it leads women I know to tell me that they too are victims, and I try to help them. I cannot imagine anyone writing an article on prosecutorial discretion without disclosing that he or she had been a prosecutor. I cannot imagine writing on rape without disclosing how I learned my first lessons or why I care so much.

This Article examines rape within the criminal law tradition in order to expose and understand that tradition's attitude toward women. It is, first and foremost, a study of rape law as an illustration of sexism in the criminal law. A second purpose is to examine the connections between the law as written by legislators, as understood by courts, as acted upon by victims, and as enforced by prosecutors. Finally, this Article is an argument for an expanded understanding of rape in the law.

To examine rape within the criminal law tradition is to expose fully the sexism of the law. Much that is striking about the crime of rape—and revealing of the sexism of the system—emerges only when rape is examined relative to other crimes, which the feminist literature by and large does not do. For example, rape is most assuredly not the only crime in which consent is a defense; but it is the only crime that has required the victim to resist physically in order to establish nonconsent. Nor is rape the only crime where prior relationship is taken into account by prosecutors in screening cases; yet we have not asked whether considering prior relationship in rape cases is different, and less justifiable, than considering it in cases of assault.

Sexism in the law of rape is no matter of mere historical interest; it endures, even where some of the most blatant testaments to that sexism have disappeared. Corroboration requirements unique to rape may have been repealed, but they continue to be enforced as a matter of practice in many jurisdictions. The victim of rape may not be required to resist to the utmost as a matter of statutory law in any jurisdiction, but the definitions accorded to force and consent may render "reasonable" resistance both a practical and a legal necessity. In the law of rape, supposedly dead horses continue to run.

The study of rape as an illustration of sexism in the criminal law also raises broader questions about the way conceptions of gender and the different backgrounds and perspectives of men and women should be encompassed within the criminal law.[1] In one of his most celebrated essays, Oliver Wendell Holmes explained that the law does not exist to tell the good man what to do, but to tell the bad man what not to do.[2] Holmes was interested in the distinction between the good and bad man; I cannot help noticing that both are men. Most of the time, a criminal law that reflects male views and male standards imposes its judgment on men who have injured other men. It is "boys' rules" applied to a boys' fight.[3] In rape, the male standard defines a crime committed against women, and male standards are used not only to judge men, but also to judge the conduct of women victims. Moreover, because the crime involves sex itself, the law of rape inevitably treads on the explosive ground of sex roles, of male aggression and female passivity, of our understandings of sexuality—areas where differences between a male and a female perspective may be most pronounced. . . .

. . . [M]y questions are . . . How have the limits on the crime of rape been formulated? What do those limits signify? What makes it rape, as opposed to sex? In what ways is rape defined differently from other crimes? What do those differences tell us about the law's attitudes towards women, men, sex, and sexuality?

The answers I have found are strikingly consistent in each area of the "law." At one end of the spectrum is the "real" rape, what I will call the traditional rape: A stranger puts a gun to the head of his victim, threatens to kill her or beats her, and then engages in intercourse. In

that case, the law—judges, statutes, prosecutors and all—generally acknowledge that a serious crime has been committed. But most cases deviate in one or many respects from his clear picture, making interpretation far more complex. Where less force is used or no other physical injury is inflicted, where threats are inarticulate, where the two know each other, where the setting is not an alley but a bedroom, where the initial contact was not a kidnapping but a date, where the woman says no but does not fight, the understanding is different. In such cases, the law, as reflected in the opinions of the courts, the interpretation, if not the words, of the statutes, and the decisions of those within the criminal justice system, often tell us that no crime has taken place that fault, if any is to be recognized, belongs with the woman. In concluding that such acts—what I call, for lack of a better title, "nontraditional" rapes—are not criminal, and worse, that the woman must bear any guilt, the law has reflected, legitimized, and enforced a view of sex and women which celebrates male aggressiveness and punishes female passivity. And that vision, while under attack in recent years, continues to be a dominant force in our society and in the law of rape.

Finally, this Article is an argument that the law can make a difference—and that it should. But the answer is not to write the perfect statute. While some statutes invite a more restrictive application than others, there is no "model statute" solution to rape law, because the problem has never been the words of the statutes as much as our interpretation of them. A typical statute of the 1890's—punishing a man who engages in sexual intercourse "by force" and "against the will and without the consent" of the woman—may not be all that different from the "model" statute we will enforce in the 1990's.[4] The difference must come in our understanding of "consent" and "will" and "force."

Some of those who have written about rape from a feminist perspective intimate that nothing short of political revolution can redress the failings of the traditional approach to rape, that most of what passes for "sex" in our capitalist society is coerced, and that no lines can or should be drawn between rape and what happens in tens of millions of bedrooms across America.

So understood, this particular feminist vision of rape shares one thing with the most traditional sexist vision: the view that nontraditional rape is not fundamentally different from what happens in tens of millions of bedrooms across America. According to the radical feminist, all of it is rape; according to the traditionalist, it is all permissible sex and seduction. In policy terms, neither is willing to draw lines between rape and permissible sex. As a result, the two visions, contradictory in every other respect, point to the same practical policy implications.

My own view is different from both of these. I recognize that both men and women in our society have long accepted norms of male aggressiveness and female passivity which lead to a restricted understanding of rape. And I do not propose, nor do I think it feasible, to punish all of the acts of sexual intercourse that could be termed coerced. But lines can be drawn between these two alternatives. The law should be understood to prohibit claims and threats to secure sex that would be prohibited by extortion law and fraud or false pretenses law as a means to secure money. The law should evaluate the conduct of "reasonable" men, not according to a *Playboy*-macho philosophy that says "no means yes," but by according respect to a woman's words. If in 1986 silence does not negate consent, at least crying and saying "no" should. . . .

THE DEFINITION OF RAPE: THE COMMON LAW TRADITION

The traditional way of defining a crime is by describing the prohibited act (*actus reus*) committed by the defendant and the prohibited mental state (*mens rea*) with which he must have done it. We ask: What did the defendant do? What did he know or intend when he did it?

The definition of rape stands in striking contrast to this tradition, because courts, in defining the crime, have focused almost incidentally on the defendant—and almost entirely on the victim. It has often been noted that, traditionally at least, the rules associated with the proof of a rape charge —the corroboration requirement, the requirement of cautionary instructions, and the fresh complaint rule—as well as the evidentiary rules relating to prior sexual conduct by the victim,[5] placed the victim as much on trial as the defendant.[6] Such a reversal also occurs in the course of defining the elements of the crime. *mens rea*, where it might matter, is all but eliminated; prohibited force tends to be defined according to the response of the victim; and nonconsent—the *sine qua non* of the offense—turns entirely on the victim's response.

But while the focus is on the female victim, the judgment of her actions is entirely male. If the issue were what the defendant knew, thought, or intended as to key elements of the offense, this perspective might be understandable; yet the issue has instead been the appropriateness of the woman's behavior, according to male standards of appropriate female behavior.

To some extent, this evaluation is but a modern response to the longstanding suspicion of rape victims. As Matthew Hale put it three centuries ago: "Rape is . . .an accusation easily to be made and hard to be proved, and harder to be defended by the party accused, tho never so innocent."[7]

But the problem is more fundamental than that. Apart from the woman's conduct, the law provides no clear, working definition of rape. This rather conspicuous gap in the law of rape presents substantial questions of fair warning for men, which the law not so handily resolves by imposing the burden of warning them on women.

At its simplest, the dilemma lies in this: If nonconsent is essential to rape (and no amount of force or physical struggle is inherently inconsistent with lawful sex), and if no sometimes means yes, and if men are supposed to be aggressive in any event, how is a man to know when he has crossed the line? And how are we to avoid unjust convictions?

This dilemma is hardly inevitable. Partly, it is a product of the way society (or at least a powerful part of it) views sex. Partly, it is a product of the lengths to which the law has gone to enforce and legitimize those views. We could prohibit the use of force and threats and coercion in sex, regardless of "consent." We could define consent in a way that respected the autonomy of women. Having chosen neither course, however, we have created a problem of fair warning, and force and consent have been defined in an effort to resolve this problem.

Usually, any discussion of rape begins (and ends) with consent. I begin instead with *mens rea,* because if unjust punishment of the blameless man is our fear (as it was Hale's), then *mens rea* would seem an appropriate place to start addressing it. At least a requirement of *mens rea* would avoid unjust convictions without adjudicating the "guilt" of the victim. It could also be the first step in expanding liability beyond the most traditional rape.

Without *mens rea,* the fair warning problem turns solely on the understanding of force and consent. To the extent that force is defined apart from a woman's reaction, it has been defined narrowly, in the most schoolboyish terms. But most of the time, force has been defined according to the woman's will to resist, judged as if she could and should fight like a man. Thus defined, force serves to limit our understanding of rape even in cases where a court might be willing to say that this woman did not consent.

Rape is not a unique crime in requiring nonconsent. But it is unique in the definition given to nonconsent. As it has been understood, the consent standard denies female autonomy; indeed, it even denies that women are capable of making decisions about sex, let alone articulating them. Yet consent, properly understood, has the potential to give women greater power in sexual relations and to expand our understanding of the crime of rape. That is, perhaps, why so many efforts have been made to cabin the concept.

MENS REA

It is difficult to imagine any man engaging in intercourse accidentally or mistakenly. It is just as difficult to imagine an accidental or mistaken use of force, at least as force is conventionally defined. But it is not at all difficult to imagine cases in which a man might claim that he did not realize that the woman was not consenting to sex. He may have been mistaken in assuming that no meant yes. He may not have bothered to inquire. He may have ignored signs that would have told him that the woman did not welcome his forceful penetration.

In doctrinal terms, such a man could argue that his mistake of fact should exculpate him because he lacked the requisite intent or *mens rea* as to the woman's required nonconsent.[8] American courts have altogether eschewed the *mens rea* or mistake inquiry as to consent, opting instead for a definition of the crime of rape that is so limited that it leaves little room for men to be mistaken, reasonably or unreasonably, as to consent. The House of Lords, by contrast, has confronted the question explicitly and, in its leading case, has formally restricted the crime of rape to men who act recklessly, a state of mind defined to allow even the unreasonably mistaken man to avoid conviction.

This Section argues that the American courts' refusal to confront the *mens rea* problem works to the detriment of the victim. In order to protect men from unfair convictions, American courts end up defining rape with undue restrictiveness. The English approach, while doctrinally clearer, also tends toward an unduly restricted definition of the crime of rape.

While the defendant's attitude toward consent may be considered either an issue of *mens rea* or a mistake of fact, the key question remains the same. In *mens rea* terms, the question is whether negligence suffices, that is, whether the defendant should be convicted who claims that he thought the woman was consenting, or didn't think about it, in situations where a "reasonable man" would have known that there was not consent. In mistake of fact terms, the question is whether a mistake as to consent must be reasonable in order to exculpate the defendant.[9]

In defining the crime of rape, most American courts have omitted *mens rea* altogether. In Maine, for example, the Supreme Judicial Court has held that there is no *mens rea* requirement at all for rape.[10] In Pennsylvania, the Superior Court held in 1982 that even a reasonable belief as to the victim's consent would not exculpate a defendant charged with rape.[11] In 1982 the Supreme Judicial Court of Massachusetts left open the question whether it would recognize a defense of reasonable mistake of fact as to consent, but it rejected the defendant's suggestion that any mistake, reasonable or unreasonable, would be sufficient to negate the required intent to rape; such a claim was created by the court as bordering on the ridiculous.[12] The following year the court went on to hold that a specific intent that intercourse be without consent was not an element of the crime of rape;[13] this decision has since been construed to mean that there is no intent requirement at all as to consent in rape cases.[14]

To treat what the defendant intended or knew or even should have known about the victim's consent as irrelevant to his liability sounds like a result favorable to both prosecution and women as victims. But experience makes all too clear that it is not. To refuse to inquire into *mens rea* leaves two possibilities: turning rape into a strict liability offense where, in the absence of consent, the man is guilty of rape regardless of whether he (or anyone) would have recognized nonconsent in the circumstances; or defining the crime of rape in a fashion that is so limited that it would be virtually impossible for any man to be convicted where he was truly unaware or mistaken as to nonconsent. In fact, it is the latter approach which has characterized all of the older, and many of the newer, American cases. In practice, abandoning *mens rea* produces the worst of all possible worlds: The trial emerges not as an inquiry into the guilt of the defendant (is he a rapist?) but of the victim (was she really raped? did she consent?). The perspective that governs is therefore not that of the woman, nor even of the particular man, but of a judicial system intent upon protecting against unjust conviction, regardless of the dangers of injustice to the woman in the particular case.

The requirement that sexual intercourse be accompanied by force or threat of force to constitute rape provides a man with some protection against mistakes as to consent. A man who uses a gun or knife against his victim is not likely to be in serious doubt as to her lack of consent, and the more narrowly force is defined, the more implausible the claim that he was unaware of nonconsent.

But the law's protection of men is not limited to a requirement of force. Rather than inquire whether the man believed (reasonably or unreasonably) that his victim was consenting, the courts have demanded that the victim demonstrate her nonconsent by engaging in resistance that will leave no doubt as to nonconsent. The definition of nonconsent as resistance—in the older cases, as utmost resistance,[15] while in some more recent ones, as "reasonable" physical resistance[16]—functions as a substitute for *mens rea* to ensure that the man has notice of the woman's nonconsent.

The choice between focusing on the man's intent or focusing on the woman's is not simply a doctrinal flip of the coin.

First, the inquiry into the victim's nonconsent puts the woman, not the man, on trial.

Her intent, not his, is disputed; and because her state of mind is key, her sexual history may be considered relevant (even though utterly unknown to the man).[17] Considering consent from *his* perspective, by contrast, substantially undermines the relevance of the woman's sexual history where it was unknown to the man.[18]

Second, the issue for determination shifts from whether the man is a rapist to whether the woman was raped. A verdict of acquittal thus does more than signal that the prosecution has failed to prove the defendant guilty beyond a reasonable doubt; it signals that the prosecution has failed to prove the woman's sexual violation—her innocence—beyond a reasonable doubt. Thus, as one dissenter put it in disagreeing with the affirmance of a conviction of rape: "The majority today . . . declares the innocence of an at best distraught young woman."[19] Presumably, the dissenter thought the young woman guilty.

Third, the resistance requirement is not only ill-conceived as a definition of nonconsent,[20] but is an overbroad substitute for *mens rea* in any event. Both the resistance requirement and the *mens rea* requirement can be used to enforce a male perspective on the crime, but while *mens rea* might be justified as protecting the individual defendant who has not made a blameworthy choice, the resistance standard requires women to risk injury to themselves in cases where there may be no doubt as to the man's intent or blameworthiness. The application of the resistance requirement has not been limited to cases in which there was uncertainty as to what the man thought, knew or intended; it has been fully applied in cases where there can be no question that the man knew that intercourse was without consent.[21] Indeed, most of the cases that have dismissed claims that *mens rea* ought to be required have been cases where both force and resistance were present, and where there was no danger of any unfairness.

Finally, by ignoring *mens rea*, American courts and legislators have imposed limits on the fair expansion of our understanding of rape. As long as the law holds that *mens rea* is not required, and that no instructions on intent need be given, pressure will exist to retain some form of resistance requirement and to insist on force as conventionally defined in order to protect men against conviction for "sex." Using resistance as a substitute for *mens rea* unnecessarily and unfairly immunizes those men whose victims are afraid enough, or intimidated enough, or, frankly, smart enough, not to take the risk of resisting physically. In doing so, the resistance test may declare the blameworthy man innocent and the raped woman guilty. . . .

FORCE AND THREATS

This Section examines two views of force in human relations. The first understands force as most schoolboys do on the playground: Force is when he hits me; resistance is when I hit back. That is the definition of force traditionally enforced in rape cases. A second understanding of force, not acknowledged in the law of rape, recognizes that bodily integrity means more than freedom from the force of fists, that power can be exercised without violence, and that coercion is not limited to what boys do in schoolyards.

Virtually every jurisdiction has traditionally made "force" or "threat of force" an element of the crime of rape.[22] Where a defendant threatens his victim with a deadly weapon, beats her, or threatens to hurt her, and then proceeds immediately to have sex, few courts have difficulty finding that force is present. These facts fit the schoolboy definition of force. But when some time elapses between the force and intercourse, when the force is more of the variety considered "incidental" to sex, or when the situation is threatening but no explicit threat of harm is communicated, "force" as defined and required by the criminal law may not be present at all. In such cases, the law fails to recognize, let alone protect, a woman's interest in bodily integrity.

In *Mills v. United States*,[23] in 1897, the defendant seized his victim at gunpoint, told her he was a notorious train robber named "Henry Starr," threatened to kill her, and proceeded to have intercourse with her twice. The trial court instructed the jury:

> The fact is that all the force that need be exercised, if there is no consent, is the force incident to the commission of the act. If there is nonconsent of the woman, the force, I say, incident to the commission of the crime is all the force that is required to make out this element of the crime.[24]

The jury convicted, and the defendant appealed on the ground that this instruction was in error as to the amount of force necessary to constitute rape. The Supreme Court agreed, and reversed the conviction:

> In this charge we think the court did not explain fully enough so as to be understood by the jury what constitutes in law nonconsent on the part of the woman, and what is the force, necessary in all cases of nonconsent, to constitute the crime. . . . But the charge in question . . . covered the case where no threats were made; where no active resistance was overcome; where the woman was not unconscious, but where there was simply nonconsent on her part and no real resistance whatever. . . . More force is necessary when that is the character of nonconsent than was stated by the court to be necessary to make out that element of the crime. That kind of nonconsent is not enough, nor is the force spoken of then sufficient, which is only incidental to the act itself.[25]

The requirement of force is not unique to the law of rape. But rape is different in two critical respects. First, unlike theft, if "force" is not inherent in noncriminal sex, at least physical contact is. Certainly, if a person stripped his victim, flattened that victim on the floor, lay down on top, and took the other person's wallet or jewelry, few would pause before the conclusion of a forcible robbery. Second, rape does not involve "one person" and "another person." It involves, in practice if not in every-

where by definition, a male person using "force" against a female person. The question of whose definition of "force" should apply, whose understanding should govern, is therefore critical.

The distinction between the "force" incidental to the act of intercourse and the "force" required to convict a man of rape is one commonly drawn by courts. Once drawn, however, the distinction would seem to require the courts to define what additional acts are needed to constitute prohibited rather than incidental force. This is where the problems arise. For many courts and jurisdictions, "force" triggers an inquiry identical to that which informs the understanding of consent. Both serve as substitutes for a *mens rea* requirement. Force is required to constitute rape, but force—even force that goes far beyond the physical contact necessary to accomplish penetration—is not itself prohibited. Rather, what is required, and prohibited, is force used to overcome female nonconsent. The prohibition is defined in terms of a woman's resistance. Thus, "forcible compulsion" becomes the force necessary to overcome reasonable resistance.[26] When the woman does not physically resist, the question becomes then whether the force was sufficient to overcome a reasonable woman's will to resist. Prohibited force turns on the judge's evaluation of a reasonable woman's response.

In *State v. Alston*,[27] Mr. Alston and the victim had been involved in a "consensual" relationship for six months. That relationship admittedly involved "some violence" by the defendant and some passivity by the victim. The defendant would strike the victim when she refused to give him money or refused to do what he wanted. As for sex, the court noted that "she often had sex with the defendant just to accommodate him. On those occasions, she would stand still and remain entirely passive while the defendant undressed her and had intercourse with her."[28] This was their "consensual" relationship. It ended when, after being struck by the defendant, the victim left him and moved in with her mother.

A month later, the defendant came to the school which the victim attended, blocked her path, demanded to know where she was living and, when she refused to tell him, grabbed her arm and stated that she was coming with him. The victim told the defendant she would walk with him if he released her arm. They then walked around the school and talked about their relationship. At one point, the defendant told the victim he was going to "fix" her face; when told that their relationship was over, the defendant stated that he had a "right" to have sex with her again. The two went to the house of a friend. The defendant asked her if she was "ready," and the victim told him she did not want to have sexual relations. The defendant pulled her up from the chair, undressed her, pushed her legs apart, and penetrated her. She cried.[29]

The defendant was convicted of rape, and his conviction was affirmed by the intermediate court of appeals.[30] On appeal, the North Carolina Supreme Court agreed that the victim was not required to resist physically to establish nonconsent: The victim's testimony that she did not consent was "unequivocal" and her testimony provided substantial evidence that the act of sexual intercourse was against her will.[31]

But the North Carolina Supreme Court nonetheless reversed on the ground that, even viewing the evidence in the light most favorable to the state, the element of force had not been established by substantial evidence. The victim did not "resist"—physically, at least. And her failure to resist, in the court's evaluation, was not a result of what the defendant did before penetration. Therefore, there was no "force."[32]

The force used outside the school, and the threats made on the walk, "although they may have induced fear," were considered to be "unrelated to the act of sexual intercourse."[33] Indeed, the court emphasized that the victim testified that it was not what the defendant said that day, but her experience with him in the past, that made her afraid. Such past experience was deemed irrelevant.

> Although [the victim's] general fear of the defendant may have been justified by his conduct on prior occasions, absent evidence that the defendant used force or threats to overcome the will of the victim to resist the sexual intercourse alleged to have been rape, such general fear was not sufficient to show that the defendant used the force required to support a conviction of rape.[34]

The undressing and the pushing of her legs apart—presumably the "incidental" force—were not even mentioned as factors to be considered.

State v. Alston is not a unique case, but it is an unusual one. Rape cases between individuals who have had what passes in the law for a "consensual" sexual relationship are rare in the system. In some sense, the supreme court here simply did what is usually done by the women (who don't press charges), by the police (who unfound them), or by the prosecutors (who dismiss them). But it did so to greater legal effect.

Later in 1984, the North Carolina Court of Appeals applied *Alston* to another case where the defendant and the victim knew each other and had had previous sexual relations. In this case, however, the parties were not "boyfriend" and "girlfriend." They were a father and his 15-year-old daughter.

The defendant in *State v. Lester*[35] was the father of three daughters and a son. Prior to the parents' divorce, the defendant frequently beat the children's mother in their presence. He also beat his girlfriend and his son. He had a gun and on one occasion pointed it at his children. He engaged in sexual activity with all three of his daughters. He first had sexual relations with the daughter whose rape was at issue when she was 11 years old. Her mother found out and confronted the defendant. He swore never to touch her again, and then threatened to kill both mother and daughter if they told anyone of his actions. On both of the occasions in question, the victim initially refused her father's demand to take her clothes off and "do it." In both cases, she complied when the demand was repeated and she sensed that her father was becoming angry. The court held that the defendant could be convicted of incest, but not of rape:

> In the instant case there is evidence that the acts of sexual intercourse between defendant and his fifteen-year-old daughter...were against her will. There is no evidence, however, that defendant used either actual or constructive force to accomplish the acts with which he is charged. As *Alston* makes clear, the victim's fear of defendant, however justified by his previous conduct, is insufficient to show that defendant *forcibly* raped his daughter on 25 November and 18 December.[36] ...

That the law prohibiting forced sex understands force in such narrow terms is frustrating enough for its women victims. Worse, however, is the fact that the conclusion that no force is present may emerge as a judgment not that the man did not act unreasonably, but as a judgment that the woman victim did.

Pat met Rusk at a bar. They talked briefly. She announced she was leaving, and he asked for a ride. She drove him home. He invited her up. She declined. He asked again. She declined again. He reached over and took the car keys. She followed him to his room. He went to the bathroom. She didn't move. He told her to remove her slacks and his clothing. She did. After they undressed:

> I said, 'you can get a lot of other girls down there, for what you want,' and he just kept saying, 'no' and then I was really scared, because I can't describe, you know, what was said. It was more the look in his eyes; and I said, at that point—I didn't know what to say; and I said, 'If I do what you want, will you let me go without killing me?' Because I didn't know, at that point, what he was going to do; and I started to cry; and when I did, he put his hands on my throat, and started lightly to choke me;

> and I said, "If I do what you want, will you let me go?' And he said, yes, and at that time, I proceeded to do what he wanted me to.[37]

After sex, the defendant walked her to her car, and asked if he could see her again.

How does a court respond to facts like this? Is "force" established by the "look in his eyes," by light choking (her description)/heavy caresses (his description),[38] or by taking the car keys of an adult woman? Is the latter force, or motor vehicle larceny? If we accept Pat's testimony, as the jury did, then it is established that she was overcome. Is that enough?

Rusk's case was heard *en banc* by both the Maryland Court of Special Appeals and the Maryland Court of Appeals. The Court of Special Appeals reversed the conviction, 8-5.[39] The Maryland Court of Appeals reinstated it, 4-3.[40] All told, twenty-one judges, including the trial judge, considered the sufficiency of the evidence. Ten concluded that Rusk was a rapist. Eleven concluded that he was not.[41]

Those who considered the evidence insufficient focused nearly all their attention not on what Mr. Rusk did or did not do, but on how the woman victim should have responded. Prohibited force was defined according to a hypothetical victim's resistance: The defendant's words or actions must create in the mind of a victim a reasonable fear that if she resisted, he would have harmed her, or that faced with such resistance, he would have used force to overcome her. The intermediate court majority found unpersuasive the argument that an honest fear was sufficient where there is nothing whatsoever to indicate that the victim was "anything but a normal, intelligent, twenty-one-year old, vigorous female."[42] Of course, the question remains as to what is "reasonably" expected of such a female faced with a man who frightens her, in an unfamiliar neighborhood, without her car keys. To the Maryland Court of Appeals dissenters, the answer was clear:

> While courts no longer require a female to resist to the utmost or to resist where re-

sistance would be foolhardy, they do require her acquiescence in the act of intercourse to stem from fear generated by something of substance. She may not simply say, "I was really scared," and thereby transform consent or mere unwillingness into submission by force. These words do not transform a seducer into a rapist. She must follow the natural instinct of every proud female to resist, by more than mere words, the violation of her person by a stranger or an unwelcomed friend. She must make it plain that she regards such sexual acts as abhorrent and repugnant to her natural sense of pride. She must resist unless the defendant has objectively manifested his intent to use physical force to accomplish his purpose.[43]

In the dissenters' view, Pat was not a "reasonable" victim, or even a victim at all. Instead of fighting, she cried. Instead of protecting her virtue, she acquiesced. Far from having any claim that her bodily integrity had been violated, she was adjudged complicit in the intercourse of which she complained. She was "in effect, an adulteress."[44]

In a very real sense, the "reasonable" woman under the view of the eleven judges who would reverse Mr. Rusk's conviction is not a woman at all. Their version of a reasonable person is one who does not scare easily, one who does not feel vulnerability, one who is not passive, one who fights back, not cries. The reasonable woman, it seems, is not a schoolboy "sissy." She is a real man.

The court of appeals majority ultimately affirmed the conviction on the narrowest possible ground. The court stated that "generally, . . .the correct standard" is that the victim's fear must "be reasonably grounded in order to obviate the need for either proof of actual force on the part of the assailant or physical resistance on the part of the victim."[45] Was this victim's fear reasonable? The court strove to avoid the question. The fundamental error of the intermediate court was its violation of the principle of appellate restraint; the question of reasonableness was a question of fact to be left to the jury. Still, the court of appeals could not avoid entirely the obligation to review the sufficiency of the evidence. Thus, "[c]onsidering all of the evidence in the case, *with particular focus upon the actual force applied by Rusk to Pat's neck,* we conclude that the jury could rationally find that the essential elements of second degree rape had been established."[46]

The emphasis on the light choking/heavy caresses is, perhaps, understandable: It is the only "objective" (as the supreme court dissent put it) force in the victim's testimony; it is certainly the only "force" that a schoolboy might recognize. As it happens, however, that force was not applied until the two were already undressed and in bed. Whatever it was—choking or caressing—was a response to the woman's crying as the moment of intercourse approached. It was not, it seems fairly clear, the only force that produced that moment.

Unable to understand force as the power one need not use (at least physically), courts are left either to emphasize the "light choking" or to look for threats of force. Technically, these threats of force may be implicit as well as explicit.[47] But implicit to whom? That a woman feels genuinely afraid, that a man has created the situation that she finds frightening, even that he has done it intentionally in order to secure sexual satisfaction, may not be enough to constitute the necessary force or even implicit threat of force which earns bodily integrity any protection under the law of rape.[48]

In *Goldberg v. State,*[49] a high-school senior working as a sales clerk was "sold a story" by the defendant that he was a free-lance agent and thought she was an excellent prospect to become a successful model. She accompanied him to his "temporary studio" where she testified that she engaged in intercourse because she was afraid. Her reasons for being afraid, according to the appellate court which reversed the conviction, were: "1) she was alone with the appellant in a house with no buildings close by and no one to help her if she resisted, and 2) the appellant was much larger than she was."[50] According to the appellate court, "[i]n the complete absence of any threatening words or actions by the appellant, these two factors, as a matter of law, are simply not enough to have created a reasonable fear of harm so as to preclude resistance and be 'the equivalent of force.'"[51]

The New York Supreme Court, sitting as the trier of fact in a rape case, reached a similar conclusion with respect to the threatening situation facing an "incredibly gullible, trusting, and naive" college sophomore. In *People v. Evans,*[52] the defendant posed as a psychologist conducting a sociological experiment, took the woman to a dating bar to "observe" her, and then induced her to come to an apartment he used as an "office." When she rejected his advances, he said to her: "'Look where you are. You are in the apartment of a strange man. How do you know that I am really who I say I am? How do you know that I am really a psychologist? . . . I could kill you. I could rape you. I could hurt you physically.'"[53] The trial court found his conduct "reprehensible," describing it as "conquest by con job." But it was not criminal; the words were ambiguous, capable of communicating either a threat to use ultimate force or the chiding of a "foolish girl."[54] While acknowledging that the victim might be terrified, the court was not persuaded beyond a reasonable doubt that the guilt of the defendant had been established.[55]

In both *Goldberg* and *Evans,* a woman finds herself alone and potentially stranded in a strange place with a man who is bigger than she. One need not be "incredibly gullible" to find oneself in this situation; one need only, as did the woman in *Rusk,* agree to give an average man (who is bigger than an average woman) a ride home.[56] There are at least four possible doctrinal approaches to these threatening situations, even accepting the courts' understanding that "force" can only be understood in relation to a woman's resistance.[57] It is noteworthy that all the decisions discussed above adopt the approach that not only makes conviction most difficult, but also operates to place guilt most squarely on the victim.

The simplest approach would be to ask whether this woman's will to resist was in fact overcome by this defendant's actions. Is she lying, or did she submit because she was truly frightened? If she is not lying—and none of the courts suggested that any of the women in these cases were actually lying—then affirm the conviction. But what about the poor man who didn't realize that the woman was overcome by fear of him, rather than desire for him? Properly regarded, such a man lacks *mens rea* as to force or consent.[58]

A second approach resolves that problem without relying explicitly on *mens rea.* It asks instead: Were the defendant's acts and behavior intended to overcome this woman's will to resist? Under such a standard, at least Mr. Lester, Mr. Alston, Mr. Goldberg, and Mr. Evans—if not Mr. Rusk as well—will have a hard time claiming that they didn't mean to succeed, and that success was not defined as creating a situation that would frighten the woman into submission.[59]

A third approach probes whether the defendant's acts and statements were calculated to overcome the will of a reasonable woman. This standard, very close to the "reasonable calculation" standard actually used in earlier decisions in Maryland and elsewhere,[60] obviously allows men greater freedom than the second approach. It tolerates their exploitation of naive and gullible women by claiming that, in their "reasonableness calculation," the tactics should not have been threatening enough. Even at its best, the "reasonably calculated" standard creates something of a paradox: If most women have a different understanding of force than most men, then the reasonable calculation standard is one that asks how a reasonable man understands the mind of a reasonable woman. But at least it focuses primarily on the defendant's actions and thoughts and makes his guilt or innocence the center of the trial. . . .

Most striking about these cases is the fact that had these men been seeking money instead of sex, their actions would plainly violate traditional state criminal prohibitions.[61] Had Mr. Goldberg used his modeling agency story to secure money rather than sex, his would be a case of theft by deception or false pretenses. As for Mr. Evans, had he sought money rather than sex as part of his "sociological test," he too could have been found guilty of theft.[62] Neither Goldberg nor Evans could have escaped liability on the ground that a "reasonable person" would not have been deceived, any more than a victim's leaving his front door unlocked or his keys in the automobile ignition serves as a defense to burglary or larceny.[63] Had Mr. Rusk simply taken the woman's car keys, he would have been guilty of larceny or theft.[64] And had Mr. Lester threatened to expose the nude pictures were he not paid, he might well have been guilty of state law extortion.[65]

Lying to secure money is unlawful theft by deception or false pretenses, a lesser crime than robbery, but a crime nonetheless. Yet lying to secure sex is old-fashioned seduction—not first-degree rape, not even third-degree rape. A threat to expose sexual information has long been considered a classic case of extortion, if not robbery itself.[66] But securing sex itself by means of a threat short of force has, in many jurisdictions, been considered no crime at all.

To the argument that it is either impossible or unwise for the law to regulate sexual "bargains" short of physical force, the law of extortion stands as a sharp rebuke: It has long listed prohibited threats in fairly inclusive terms.[67] While extortion may be a lesser offense than robbery, it is nonetheless prohibited. . . .

Consent

This Section will examine what has long been viewed as the most important concept in rape law—the notion of female consent. Nonconsent has traditionally been a required element in the definition of a number of crimes, including theft, assault and battery.[68]

Thus rape may be the most serious crime to encompass a consent defense,[69] but it is certainly not the only one.[70]

Rape is unique, however, in the definition which has been accorded to consent. That definition makes all too plain that the purpose of the consent rule is not to protect female autonomy and freedom of choice, but to assure men the broadest sexual access to women. In matters of sex, the common law tradition views women ambivalently at best: Even when not intentionally dishonest, they simply cannot be trusted to know what they want or to mean what they say. While the cases that engendered this tradition date from the 1870's and 1880's, the law reviews of the 1950's and 1960's, and the appellate cases of the 1970's and 1980's, have perpetuated it.

The justification for the central role of consent in the law of rape is that it protects women's choice and women's autonomy in sexual relations. Or, as one leading commentator put it: "In all cases the law of rape protects the woman's discretion by proscribing coitus contrary to her wishes."[71] Not exactly. As discussed in the preceding Section, the law does not protect the woman from "coitus contrary to her wishes" when there is no "force." Secondly, the definition of nonconsent requires victims of rape, unlike victims of any other crime, to demonstrate their "wishes" through physical resistance. . . .

No similar effort is required of victims of other crimes for which consent is a defense. In trespass, for example, the posting of a sign or the offering of verbal warnings generally suffices to meet the victim's burden of nonconsent; indeed, under the Model Penal Code, the offense of trespass is aggravated where a defendant is verbally warned to desist and fails to do so.[72] A defendant's claim that the signs and the warnings were not meant to exclude him normally goes to his *mens rea* in committing the act, not to the existence of consent.[73]

In robbery, claims that the victim cooperated with the taking of the money or eased the way, and thus consented, have generally been unsuccessful.[74] Only where the owner of the property actively participates in planning and committing the theft will consent be found. Mere "passive submission"[75] or "passive assent"[76] does not amount to consent[77]—except in the law of rape.

That the law puts a special burden on the rape victim to prove through her actions her nonconsent (or at least to account for why her actions did not demonstrate "nonconsent"), while imposing no similar burden on the victim of trespass, battery, or robbery, cannot be explained by the oftobserved fact that consensual sex is part of everyday life. Visiting (trespass with consent) is equally everyday, as is philanthropy (robbery with consent), and surgery (battery with consent). Instinctively, we may think it is easier in those cases to tell the difference between consent and nonconsent. But if so, it is only because we are willing to presume that men are entitled to access to women's bodies (as opposed to their houses or their wallets), at least if they know them,[78] and to accept male force in potentially "consensual" sexual relations. . . .

TOWARD A BROADER UNDERSTANDING

The conduct that one might think of as "rape" ranges from the armed stranger who breaks into a woman's home to the date she invites in who takes silence for assent. In between are literally hundreds of variations: the man may be a stranger, but he may not be armed; he may be armed, but he may not be a stranger; he may be an almost, rather than a perfect, stranger—a man who gave her a ride or introduced himself through a ruse; she may say yes, but only because he threatens to expose her to the police or the welfare authorities; she may say no, but he may ignore her words.

In 1985, the woman raped at gunpoint by the intruding stranger should find most of the legal obstacles to her complaint removed.

That was not always so: As recently as ten years ago, she might well have faced a corroboration requirement, a cautionary instruction, a fresh complaint rule, and a searing cross-examination about her sexual past to determine whether she had nonetheless consented to sex. In practice, she may still encounter some of these obstacles; but to the extent that the law communicates any clear message, it is likely to be that she was raped.

But most rapes do not as purely fit the traditional model, and most victims do not fare as well. Cases involving men met in bars (*Rusk*) or at work (*Goldberg*) or at airports (*Evans*), let alone cases involving ex-boyfriends (*Alston*), still lead some appellate courts to enforce the most traditional views of women in the context of the less traditional rape. And in they system, considerations of prior relationship and the circumstances of the initial encounter, as well as force and resistance and corroboration, seem to reflect a similarly grounded if not so clearly stated view of the limits of rape law.

In thinking about rape, it is not as difficult to decide which rapes are more serious or which rapists deserving of more punishment: Weapons, injury, and intent—the traditional grading criteria of the criminal law—are all justifiable answers to these questions. Most jurisdictions that have reformed their rape laws in the last ten years have focused on creating degrees of rape—aggravated and unaggravated—based on some combination of the presence of weapons and injury. While *mens rea* or mistake needs to be addressed more clearly in some rape laws, and bodily injury more carefully defined in others, these are essentially problems of draftsmanship which are hardly insurmountable.

The more difficult problem comes in understanding and defining the threshold for liability—where we draw the line between criminal sex and seduction. Every statute still uses some combination of "force," "threats" and "consent" to define the crime. But in giving meaning to those terms at the threshold of liability, the law of rape must confront the powerful norms of male aggressiveness and female passivity which continue to be adhered to by many men and women in our society.

The law did not invent the "no means yes" philosophy. Women as well as men have viewed male aggressiveness as desirable and forced sex as an expression of love; women as well as men have been taught and have come to believe that when a woman "encourages" a man, he is entitled to sexual satisfaction. From the sociological surveys to prime time television, one can find ample support in society and culture for even the most oppressive views of women, and the most expansive notions of seduction enforced by the most traditional judges.

But the evidence is not entirely one-sided. For every prime time series celebrating forced sex, there seems to be another true confession story in a popular magazine detailing the facts of a date rape and calling it "rape." College men and women may think that the typical male is forward and primarily interested in sex, but they no longer conclude that he is the desirable man. The old sex manuals may have lauded male sexual responses as automatic and uncontrollable, but some of the newer ones no longer see men as machines and even advocate sensitivity as seductive.

We live, in short, in a time of changing sexual mores—and we are likely to for some time to come. In such times, the law can cling to the past or help move us into the future. We can continue to enforce the most traditional views of male aggressiveness and female passivity, continue to adhere to the "no means yes" philosophy and to the broadest understanding of seduction, until and unless change overwhelms us. That is not a neutral course, however; in taking it, the law (judges, legislators, or prosecutors) not only reflects (a part of) society, but legitimates and reinforces those views.

Or we can use the law to move forward. It may be impossible—and even unwise—to try to use the criminal law to change the way people think, to push progress to the ideal. But recognition of the limits of the criminal sanction need not be taken as a justification for the status quo. Faced with a choice between reinforcing the old and fueling the new in a world of changing norms, it is not necessarily more legitimate or neutral to choose the old. There are lines to be drawn short of the ideal: The challenge we face in thinking about rape is to use the power and legitimacy of law to reinforce what is best, not what is worst, in our changing sexual mores. . . .

In short, I am arguing that "consent" should be defined so that "no means no." And the "force" or "coercion" that negates consent ought be defined to include extortionate threats and deceptions of material fact. As for *mens rea,* unreasonableness as to consent, understood to mean ignoring a woman's words, should be sufficient for liability: Reasonable men should be held to know that no means no, and unreasonable mistakes, no matter how honestly claimed, should not exculpate. Thus, the threshold of liability—whether phrased in terms of "consent," "force" or "coercion," or some combination of the three, should be understood to include at least those nontraditional rapes where the woman says no or submits only in response to lies or threats which would be prohibited were money sought instead.[79] The crime I have described would be a lesser offense than the aggravated rape in which life is threatened or bodily injury inflicted, but it is, in my judgment, "rape." One could, I suppose, claim that as we move from such violent rapes to "just" coerced or nonconsensual sex, we are moving away from a crime of violence toward something else. But what makes the violent rape different—and more serious—than an aggravated assault is the injury to personal integrity involved in forced sex. That same injury is the reason that forced sex should be a crime even when there is no weapon or no beating. In a very real sense, what does make rape different from other crimes, at every level of the offense, is that rape is about sex and sexual violation. Were the essence of the crime the use of the gun or the knife or the threat, we wouldn't need—and wouldn't have—a separate crime.

Conduct is labeled as criminal "to announce to society that these actions are not to be done and to secure that fewer of them are done." As a matter of principle, we should be ready to announce to society our condemnation of coerced and nonconsensual sex and to secure that we have less of it. The message of the substantive law to men, and to women, should be made clear.

That does not mean that this crime will, or should, be easy to prove. The constitutional requirement of proof beyond a reasonable doubt may well be difficult to meet in case where guilt turns on whose account is credited as to what was said. If the jury is in doubt, it should acquit. If the judge is uncertain, he should dismiss.

The message of the substantive law must be distinguished from the constitutional standards of proof. In this as in every criminal case, a jury must be told to acquit if it is in doubt. The requirement of proof beyond a reasonable doubt rests on the premise that it is better that ten guilty should go free than that one innocent man should be punished. But if we should acquit ten, let us be clear that the we are acquitting them not because they have an entitlement to ignore a woman's words, not because what they allegedly did was right or macho or manly, but because we live in a system that errs on the side of freeing the guilty.

Notes

1. Similar questions may be raised, for example, when a woman is prosecuted for killing the husband who battered her, see, e.g., Ibn-Tamas v. United States, 407 A.2d 626 (D.C. 1979), or a man suspected of sexually molesting her children, see, e.g., State v. Wanrow, 88 Wash. 2d 221, 559 P.2d 548 (1977). The law must define the standard of "reasonableness" against which the woman's conduct must be judged for purposes of self-defense or provocation. Is the question what a "reasonable

person" would have done in such a situation, or what a "reasonable woman" would have done? Is there such a thing, in life or in law, as reasonable people, or only men and women, with all their differences?

2. Holmes, *The Path of the Law,* 10 HARV. L. REV. 457, 459 (1897).

3. In referring to "male" standards and "boys' rules," I do not mean to suggest that *every* man adheres to them. A "male view" is nonetheless distinct from a "female view" not only by the gender of most of those who adhere to it, but also by the character of the life experiences and socialization which tend to produce it.

4. The Statutes of the 1990's will no doubt include degrees of rape based on weapons, injuries, or intent, but unless there are dramatic changes in the next ten years, they will continue to rely on some combination of "force" and "consent" in defining the offense.

5. The corroboration, cautionary instruction, and fresh complaint rules will be discussed in Part III, infra, in connection with the Model Penal Code, which retains and defends them all. A full analysis of the application and constitutionality of the various forms of evidentiary shield statutes which have been enacted in recent years is beyond the scope of this Article and the subject of extensive review by others. See, e.g., Berger, supra note 5; Tanford & Bocchino, *Rape Victim Shield Laws and the Sixth Amendment,* 128 U. PA. L. REV. 544 (1980). My attention to the evidentiary questions is limited to certain points of intersection with the substantive criminal law, e.g., how we define the issue as to which prior sexual conduct might be relevant, and whether that is the proper way to frame the question, see infra Section II(A) (*mens rea*), and the distinction drawn in the application of the nonconsent/resistance requirement between chaste and sexually experienced victims, see infra Section II(C) (consent).

6. See, e.g., Berger, supra note 5, at 6-11; S. KATZ & M. MAZUR, UNDERSTANDING THE RAPE VICTIM 199 (1979); Note, *The Victim in a Forcible Rape Case: A Feminist View,* 11 AM. CRIM. L. REV. 335 (1973).

7. M. HALE, THE HISTORY OF THE PLEAS OF THE CROWN 635 (1778). This statement

is the usual basis for the "cautionary" instructions traditionally given in rape cases.

8. Mistakes of fact which are unrelated to elements of the offense are irrelevant to guilt or innocence; those which exculpate do so precisely because they negate the required *mens rea* as to an element of the offense. Thus, it matters not at all if the defendant believed—reasonably or unreasonably —that his victim was a professional model (the example is suggested by one case in which the defendant's stated intent was to have intercourse with a model; the victim was a clerical employee of a modeling agency); it should matter if he believes she is consenting, however, because nonconsent is an element of the crime. In order for the prohibited act to be criminal, it should not be significant, for these purposes, whether nonconsent is considered to be part of the definition of the *actus reus* prohibited by rape law, or a required "circumstance." In either case, the prosecution should be held to prove that the defendant in fact had the requisite mental state, whether it is, in Model Penal Code terms, purpose, knowledge, recklessness or even negligence, as to nonconsent. See G. WILLIAMS, CRIMINAL LAW 137 (1953) ("It is impossible to assert that a crime requiring intention or recklessness can be committed although the accused labored under a mistake that negatived the requisite intention or recklessness. Such an assertion carries its own refutation.") The Model Penal Code has a separate provision as to mistakes of fact, but one which seeks to make clear that mistakes exculpate because, and only because, they negative the required mental state as one or more elements of the offense. Section 2.04(1)(a) provides a mistake of fact defense if "the ignorance or mistake negatives the purpose, knowledge, belief, recklessness or negligence required to establish a material element of the offense." MODEL PENAL CODE § 2.04(1)(a) (1985).

9. Arguably, viewing such situations as cases of a mistake "defense" rather than as cases where the required *mens rea* cannot be established invites a court or legislature to impose the burden of coming forward and of proving the defense on the defendant. But as long as nonconsent is spelled out as an affirmative element of the crime, such a shift at least in the burden of persuasion would raise serious constitutional questions. See Patterson v. New York, 432 U.S. 197 (1977) (New York law requiring defendant to prove affirmative defense not violative of due process clause because defense bears no direct relationship to elements of crime). Still, some states have managed to destroy the symmetry: Pennsylvania, for example, follows the Model Penal Code approach to the point of providing a mistake of fact defense when it negatives the "intent, knowledge, belief, recklessness, or negligence required," but only if the mistake is one "for which there is a reasonable explanation or excuse." 18 PA. CONS. STAT. ANN. tit. 18, § 304 (Purdon 1983). In other words, for some crimes requiring at least recklessness, negligence as to some elements (those conceived of in mistake terms) is sufficient to convict.

10. "The legislature, by carefully defining the sex offenses in the criminal code, and by making no reference to a culpable state of mind for rape, clearly indicated that rape compelled by force or threat requires no culpable state of mind." State v. Reed, 479 A.2d 1291, 1296 (Me. 1984).

11. [D]efendant contends that the court should have instructed the jury that if the defendant reasonably believed that the prosecutrix had consented to his sexual advances that this would constitute a defense to the rape and involuntary deviate sexual intercourse charge. . . The charge requested by the defendant is not now and has never been the law of Pennsylvania. . . If the element of the defendant's belief as to the victim's state of mind is to be established as a defense to the crime of rape then it should be done by our legislature which has the power to define crimes and offenses. We refuse to create such a defense.

Commonwealth v. Williams, 294 Pa. Super. 93, 99-100, 439 A.2d 765, 769 (1982).

12. Commonwealth v. Sherry, 437 N.E.2d 224, 386 Mass, 682 (1982).

13. Commonwealth v. Grant, 391 Mass. 645, 464 N.E.2d 33 (1984).

14. In Commonwealth v. Lefkowitz, 20 Mass. App. Ct. 513, 481 N.E.2d 227, 230, *review de-*

nied, 396 Mass. 1103, 485 N.E.2d 224 (1985), the Massachusetts Appeals Court termed an argument that some intent requirement ought to apply to every element of the offense, including consent, a request for an instruction on specific intent and rejected it out of hand. The trial judge in that case thought the defendants' attitudes toward consent to be irrelevant: In rejecting their proffered instruction, he explained that the jury should "not look at [the case] from the point of view of the defendant's perceptions...I don't think that's the law." *Id.* At 518–519, 481 N.E.2d at 230. His decision was upheld by the Appeals Court on the ground that "specific intent"—a term they never defined—was not required. It seems quite clear that, as used by the Massachusetts court, "specific intent" does not mean a *mens rea* of "purpose" as it has been traditionally understood; rather, it means any *mens rea* at all. Cf. MODEL PENAL CODE § 2.02(1) (1985) (*mens rea* required as to each element of offense); S. KADISH, S. SCHULHOFER & M. PAULSEN, CRIMINAL LAW 277 (1983) ("The term *specific intent* has been productive of untold confusion, partly because courts have not been consistent in their use of it and partly for the more fundamental reason that it is often quite difficult to determine whether a statute should be interpreted to require specific intent—that is, the [Model Penal] Code concept of a true 'purpose.'") (emphasis in original).

And in South Dakota, the state supreme court has held that "evidence of other alleged rapes cannot be deemed to be admissible because it shows intent for the reason that intent is simply not one of the elements of the crime charged." State v. Houghton, 272 N.W.2d 788, 791 (S.D. 1978). See also State v. Cantrell, 234 Kan. 426, 434, 673 P.2d 1147, 1153-54 (1983), *cert. denied,* 105 S. Ct. 84 (1984); People v. Hammack, 63 Mich. App. 87, 91, 234 N.W.2d 415, 417 (1975); Brown v. State, 59 Wis. 2d 200, 213–214, 207 N.W.2d 602, 609 (1973). Two notable exceptions to this pattern among American courts are Alaska and California. See Reynolds v. State, 664 P.2d 621 (Alaska Ct. App. 1983); People v. Mayberry, 15 Cal. 3d 143, 542 P.2d 1337, 125 Cal. Rptr. 745 (1975). In *Mayberry,* the California court held that

the state must prove that a defendant intentionally engaged in intercourse and was at least negligent regarding consent. In *Reynolds,* the Alaska court held that the state must prove that the defendant knowingly engaged in sexual intercourse and recklessly disregarded his victim's lack of consent.

15. See, e.g., King v. State, 210 Tenn. 150, 158, 357 S.W.2d 42, 45 (1962); Moss v. State, 208 Miss. 531, 536, 45 So. 2d 125, 126 (1950); Brown v. State, 127 Wis. 193, 199, 106 N.W. 536, 538 (1906); People v. Dohring, 59 N.Y. 374, 386 (1874). Recent Statutory Developments, at 15031507 (1975).

16. See, e.g., Satterwhite v. Commonwealth, 201 Va. 478, 482, 111 S.E.2d 820, 823 (1960); Goldberg v. State, 41 Md. App. 58, 68, 395 A.2d 1213, 1218–1219 (1979); State v. Lima, 64 Hawaii 470, 476–477, 643 P.2d 536, 540 (1982).

17. See e.g., Government of the Virgin Islands v. John, 447 F.2d 69 (3d Cir. 1971) (holding victim's reputation for chastity relevant to consent); Packineau v. United States, 202 F.2d 681, 687 (8th Cir. 1953); Wynne v. Commonwealth, 216 Va. 355, 356, 218 S.E.2d 445, 446 (1975). Even if such evidence is viewed, as I think it should be, as irrelevant to a woman's credibility as a witness, it may be of some minimal "relevance" to the disputed issue of her state of mind. Prior "similar" acts are generally considered relevant in determining a party's state of mind. While the fact that a woman has sometime previously consented to sex does not mean she is consenting here, if it makes consent any more likely, then it does have some relevance. That it may be not only painful for the woman victim to discuss, but prejudicial to the prosecution's case, is clear; studies have found a woman's prior sexual history to be critical in respondents' evaluations of the seriousness of a claim of rape. See L'Armand & Pepitone, *Judgments of Rape: A Study of Victim-Rapist Relationship and Victim Sexual History,* 8 PERSONALITY AND SOC. PSYCHOLOGY BULL. 134, 136 (1982); Borgida & White, *Social Perceptions of Rape Victims,* 2 LAW & HUM. BEHAV. 339 (1978). The unfairness can go both ways; while sexual history has often been used against sexually experienced women, it can also be used

against men with the misfortune to have had sex with a virgin. One might still conclude that such evidence should be excluded on public policy grounds, but when that is done to a defendant's disadvantage, it at least arguably raises constitutional questions as to the denial of his right to a fair trial and to produce exculpatory evidence. See generally Berger, supra note 5; Tanford & Bocchino, supra note 13. Most statutes grant the judge discretion to decide whether the circumstances of the particular case demand that evidence of prior conduct or reputation be admitted. See Bienen, *Rape III—National Developments in Rape Reform Legislation,* 6 WOMEN'S RTS. L. REP. 171, 201 (1980).

18. A defendant enjoys no constitutional right to present irrelevant evidence; to the extent that the legal issue is framed in terms of his intent, rather than hers, facts about her reputation and history which were unknown to him are far less probative and far more prejudicial, especially in view of the strong public policy grounds favoring exclusion of such evidence. Cf. Berger, supra note 5 (model statute includes distinction based on defendant's knowledge).

    Explicitly recognizing the *mens rea* issue would, of course, allow defendants in states with shield laws to argue that their inability to present evidence of sexual history which they claim was known to them denied them their constitutional right to present exculpatory evidence. Certainly it would be reasonable to require such defendants to present persuasive evidence of the fact of their knowledge in the hearing provided for by most shield statutes. It is not clear why framing the issue in terms of the fact of consent—rather than the defendant's knowledge or intent with respect to consent—could constitutionally provide a woman victim with any more protection of her sexual history; to the extent that the key issue is her intent, a defendant would have an equally strong Sixth Amendment claim as to his right to present *all* evidence (whether known to him or not) that might be relevant to the fact of consent.

19. State v. Rusk, 289 Md. 230, 256, 424 A.2d 720, 733 (1981) (Cole, J., dissenting).

20. See infra text accompanying notes 100–133.

21. See, e.g., Goldberg v. State, 41 Md. App. 58, 68, 395 A.2d 1213 (1979); see also State v. Lima, 64 Hawaii 470, 643 P.2d 536 (1982).

22. Traditional rape statutes typically required both that the intercourse be accomplished "by force" and that it be "against her will." In Wisconsin, for example, the carnal knowledge statute enacted in 1895 and applicable until 1955 provided:

    > Any person who shall ravish and carnally know any female of the age of fourteen years or more, by force and against her will, shall be punished by imprisonment in the state prison not more than thirty years nor less than ten years. . . .

    Law of May 2, 1895, ch. 370, § 2, 1895 WIS. LAWS 753. In 1955, "sexual intercourse" replaced "carnal knowledge" in the statute, but the requirements of "force" and "against her will" remained unchanged. See Note, *Recent Statutory Developments,* supra note 5, at 1504. While force technically appears in the traditional statutes—and in most of the reform statutes as well—in practice it tends to be defined not so much by what the defendant does as by the reaction of the victim. Indeed, one commentator has gone so far as to argue that "'force' is not truly speaking an element of the crime itself, but if great force was not needed to accomplish the act the necessary lack of consent has been disproved in other than exceptional situations." R. PERKINS & R. BOYCE, CRIMINAL LAW 211 (3d ed. 1982).

23. 164 U.S. 644 (1897).

24. *Id.* at 647.

25. *Id.* at 647–648. The reader may be puzzled as to why I am devoting any attention to a decision, even a decision of the United States Supreme Court, which dates from the 1890's. Were *Mills* simply a historical curiosity, the reader would surely be right to question my priorities; it is far too easy to attack 100-year-old cases. But when cases from the 1890's reflect an understanding of force which survives into cases from the 1980's—and *Mills* does—it is no longer a matter of slaying straw men. *Mills* is a living dragon.

26. Kentucky, for example, requires "forcible compulsion" as an element of the rape of a

competent, adult woman. "Forcible compulsion" means:

> physical force that overcomes earnest resistance or a threat, express or implied, that overcomes earnest resistance by placing a person in fear of immediate death or physical injury to himself or another person or in fear that he or another person will be immediately kidnapped.

KY. REV. STAT. § 510.010(2) (1985). As stated, forcible compulsion is defined to require earnest resistance; the prohibition may be formally applicable to the defendant, but the focus and judgment is on the victim. Washington and Hawaii have modified this definition to the extent of not requiring that the resistance be "earnest." WASH. REV. CODE § 9.79.140(5) (1977); HAWAII REV. STAT. § 707–700(11) (Supp. 1980). In Utah, sexual intercourse is prohibited where "the actor compels the victim to submit or participate by force that overcomes such earnest resistance as might reasonably be expected under the circumstances." UTAH CODE ANN. § 76-5-406(1) (1985). In other states, where "force" is included in the statute but not specifically defined, courts have relied on the "judicially determined meaning" of those elements of the common law crime of rape to the same effect. See, e.g., Goldberg v. State, 41 Md. App. 58, 395 A.2d 1213 (1979) (relying on Hazel v. State, 221 Md. 464, 157 A.2d 922 (1960)); see also ILL. REV. STAT. ch. 38, § 11.1 (1982) (requiring "force" and, in comments, stating that definition should be taken from certain common law cases); Note, *Recent Statutory Developments,* supra note 5, at 1512–1514.

27. 310 N.C. 399, 312 S.E.2d 470 (1984).

28. *Id.* at 401, 312 S.E.2d at 471.

29. *Id.* at 401–403, 312 S.E.2d at 471–473.

30. State v. Alston, 61 N.C. App. 454, 300 S.E.2d 857 (1983), *rev'd,* 310 N.C. 399, 312 S.E.2d 470 (1984).

31. 310 N.C. at 408, 312 S.E. 2d at 475.

32. *Id.* at 408, 312 S.E.2d at 476.

33. *Id.*

34. *Id.* at 409, 312 S.E.2d at 476 (emphasis omitted).

35. State v. Lester, 70 N.C. App. 757, 321 S.E.2d 166 (1984), *aff'd,* 313 N.C. 595, 330 S.E.2d 205 (1985).

36. *Id.* at 761, 321 S.E.2d at 168 (emphasis in original).

37. Rusk v. State, 43 Md. App. 476, 478–479, 406 A.2d 624, 626 (1979) (en banc), *rev'd,* 289 Md. 230, 424 A.2d 720 (1981).

38. The difference in their characterizations is noteworthy. It may be that one of them was lying. But it may also be true that neither was lying: that "light choking" to her was nothing more than a "heavy caress" to him; that this is simply one example that happened to survive into an appellate opinion of the differences in how men and women perceive force.

39. Rusk v. State, 43 Md. App. 476, 406 A.2d 624 (1979) (en banc), rev'd, 289 Md. 230, 424 A.2d 720 (1981).

40. State v. Rusk, 289 Md. 230, 424 A.2d 720 (1981).

41. Rusk had been convicted of second degree rape in violation of MD. CODE ANN. art. 27, § 463(a)(1) (1982), which provides in part: "A person is guilty of rape in the second degree if the person engages in vaginal intercourse with another person . . . [b]y force or threat of force against the will and without the consent of the other person."

    Of the 21 judges who reviewed Rusk's conviction, one was a woman. She voted to convict. See 289 Md. at V, 230, 424 A.2d at VII, 720.

42. 43 Md. App. at 482, 406 A.2d at 627.

43. 289 Md. at 255, 424 A.2d at 733 (Cole, J., dissenting).

44. This is exactly how Judge Wilner, the dissenting judge in the Court of Special Appeals, characterizes the majority's decision to reverse Rusk's conviction. 43 Md. App. at 498, 406 A.2d at 636. The Court of Appeals dissenters, for their part, attacked that majority for declaring her to be innocent:

    > The law regards rape as a crime of violence. The majority today attenuates this proposition. It declares the innocence of an at best distraught young woman. It does not demonstrate the defendant's guilt of the crime of rape. 289 Md. at 255–256, 424 A.2d at 733. The debate, quite clearly, is focused not

on whether Rusk is a rapist but on whether Pat is a real victim.

45. 289 Md. at 244, 424 A.2d at 727 (footnote omitted).

46. *Id.* at 246–247, 424 A.2d at 728 (emphasis added). On facts substantially similar to those in *Rusk,* the Wyoming Supreme Court in 1973 reversed a conviction entered by a trial judge sitting without a jury on the ground that the judge had failed to consider the reasonableness of the victim's fear. In Gonzales v. State, 516 P.2d 592 (Wyo. 1973), as in *Rusk,* the victim and the defendant met in a bar, and he requested a ride home. The victim refused, but the defendant got into the car anyway. After unsuccessfully refusing him again, she started driving; he asked her to turn down a road and, according to the Supreme Court:

> He asked her to stop "to go to the bathroom" and took the keys out of the ignition, telling her she would not drive off and leave him. She stayed in the car when he "went to the bathroom" and made no attempt to leave. When he returned he told her he was going to rape her and she kept trying to talk him out of it. He told her he was getting mad at her and then put his fist against her face and said, "I'm going to do it. You can have it one way or the other."

Id. at 593. The trial judge, in finding Mr. Gonzalez guilty of rape, reasoned that a victim "does not have to subject herself to a beating, knifing, or anything of that nature. As long as she is convinced something of a more serious nature will happen, she is then given by law the right to submit." *Id.* at 594 (quoting unreported trial court opinion). Not, however, according to the Wyoming Supreme Court, which found the trial judge's standard to be in error "because it would place the determination solely in the judgment of the prosecutrix and omit the necessary element of a reasonable apprehension and reasonable ground for such fear; and the reasonableness must rest with the fact finder." *Id.*

What is stunning about *Gonzales* is not so much the Wyoming court's statement of the proper standard—it very much resembles that of the other courts noted here—as the fact that the court thought application of that standard to these facts could conceivably lead to a different verdict. The error, in the court's view, was far from harmless: "[T]he evidence of the nature and sufficiency of the threat to justify nonresistance is far from overwhelming in this case." *Id.* The reasonable woman in Wyoming, apparently, is not simply a man, but Superman.

47. See, e.g., People v. Flores, 62 Cal. App. 2d 700, 703, 145 P.2d 318, 320 (Dist. Ct. App. 1944) ("A threat may be expressed by acts and conduct as well as by words."); Hazel v. State, 221 Md. 464, 469, 157 A.2d 922, 925 (1960) ("Acts and threats" may create in victim's mind real apprehension of imminent bodily harm.); State v. Lewis, 96 Idaho 743, 760, 536 P.2d 738, 745 (1975) ("Threats or force can come in forms other than verbalized threats or displays of weaponry.").

48. Cases recognizing threats short of force as sufficient for rape convictions are virtually nonexistent. The closest, perhaps, is the oft-cited People v. Cassandras, 83 Cal. App. 2d 272, 188 P.2d 546 (Dist. Ct. App. 1948), where the defendant used an elaborate ploy to lure the complainant into a hotel, and then threatened to have the hotel clerk report her to the police as a prostitute and to have her children taken away from her. The court, in affirming the defendant's conviction, found that there was sufficient evidence of threats of physical harm, but also implied that mental coercion might be enough to overcome the woman's will.

49. 41 Md. App. 58, 395 A.2d 1213 (Ct. Spec. App. 1979).

50. *Id.* at 69, 395 A.2d at 1219.

51. *Id.*

52. 85 Misc. 2d 1088, 379 N.Y.S.2d 912 (Sup. Ct. 1975), *aff'd,* 55 A.D. 2d 858, 390 N.Y.S.2d 768 (1976).

53. 85 Misc. 2d at 1093, 379 N.Y.S.2d at 917.

54. *Id.* at 1095, 379 N.Y.S.2d at 920.

55. *Id.* at 1096, 379 N.Y.S.2d at 921. Since the *Evans* decision, New York has amended its statute. Historically, New York had strictly enforced a standard of utmost resistance, which required a victim to resist "until exhausted or overpowered." People v. Dohring, 59 N.Y. 374, 386 (1874). By the time of *Evans,* the words of

the law had changed to require earnest resistance; following *Evans,* the New York legislature amended the statute to make clear that the earnest resistance standard was not to be equated with the utmost resistance requirement. 1977 N.Y. LAWS ch. 692. The 1977 version, however, still required "reasonable" earnest resistance. *Id.* § 2.

In 1982, the New York legislature again amended the law. 1982 N.Y. LAWS ch. 560. The new law prohibits the use of actual physical force or "a threat, express or implied, which places a person in fear of immediate death or physical injury to himself, herself or another person, or in fear that he, she or another person will immediately be kidnapped." N.Y. PENAL LAW § 130.00(8) (Consol. 1984). See generally Note, *Elimination of the Resistance Requirement and Other Rape Law Reforms: The New York Experience,* 47 ALBANY L. REV. 871, 872–874 (1983). New York law also includes a misdemeanor provision entitled "sexual misconduct," which occurs when a male "engages in sexual intercourse with a female without her consent." N.Y. PENAL LAW § 130.20(1) (Consol. 1984).

Many states continue to follow New York's earlier definition of "forcible compulsion," and the requirement of "actual physical force" or a threat *which the court* understands to place the victim in fear may continue to protect con-men like Mr. Evans, although it need not.

56. Had there been two or more men involved, rather than one, it seems likely that the defendants in *Goldberg* and *Evans* would have fared far less well in the courts. It is in such cases— and almost only in such cases—that courts consider the situations sufficiently threatening to not require that threats be verbally explicit. In California, four men have long been presumed dangerous: "If one were met in a lonely place by four big men and told to hold up his hands or to do anything else, he would be doing the reasonable thing if he obeyed, even if they did not say what they would do to him if he refused.... We think similar considerations are applicable here [in a rape case]." People v. Flores, 62 Cal. App. 2d 700, 703, 145 P.2d 318, 320 (Cal. Dist. Ct. App. 1944). However two may be enough:

The victim was in the company of two men whom she had met for the first time that evening. On a winter night, she was driven to a remote area, tried to escape, was caught and was thrust back to the car. ...

[S]he submitted in the back seat to the act of intercourse with the defendant while his companion was nearby in the front seat, obviously ready to help defendant restrain and do bodily harm to the victim if she resisted. ...

Jones v. Commonwealth, 219 Va. 982, 986-87, 252 S.E.2d 370, 372 (1979). See also State v. Lewis, 96 Idaho 743, 750, 536 P.2d 738, 745 (1975) (fearing for her life, woman engaged in intercourse with three men). But where only one man is involved, even if he intentionally created the situation which the woman finds threatening, it is rather difficult to find appellate cases; most such complaints are not prosecuted in the first instance. See infra Section IV(B). Where they are, however, courts intent on protecting an individual man's right to "seduce" often reverse rape convictions.

57. To abandon that understanding would suggest either that force itself is unlawful, regardless of whether it is used to coerce submission, or that consent is inconsistent with force. It would, in short, call into question the almost universal common law understanding that regardless of what the man does ("force"), consent remains a defense. See infra Section C.

58. In Model Penal Code terms, if the man recognized but disregarded a substantial risk of nonconsent, he would be reckless; even if he did not recognize the risk, he would be guilty of negligent rape if a reasonable man would have recognized this risk.

59. This is precisely the standard applied to men who engage in theft by false pretenses; gullibility is no defense if the defendant's acts were intended to prey on that gullibility. See W. LaFAVE & A. SCOTT, CRIMINAL LAW 669 (1972); Clarke v. People, 64 Colo. 164, 171 P. 69 (1918); State v. Foot, 100 Mont. 33, 48 P.2d 1113 (1935).

60. See Hazel v. State, 221 Md. 464, 469, 157 A.2d 922, 925 (1960) (citing State v. Thompson,

227 N.C. 19, 40 S.E.2d 620 (1946); State v. Dill, 42 Del. 533, 40 A.2d 443 (1944)):

> [F]orce may exist without violence. If the acts and threats of the defendant were reasonably calculated to create in the mind of the victim . . . a real apprehension, due to fear, of imminent bodily harm, serious enough to impair or overcome her will to resist, then such acts and threats are the equivalent of force.

61. State v. Witherspoon, 648 S.W.2d 279 (Tenn. Crim. App. 1983), is a worthy comparison in this regard. In *Witherspoon,* the defendant, who had been convicted of robbery, claimed on appeal that the government failed to established the causal connection between his conduct and the victim's fear (required to make his taking of money robbery). According to the victim, the defendant came over to her car door so that she was unable to close it; he stood there for a few minutes; then, as he was asking for directions, he grabbed the money bag. The victim testified that she was afraid—not of robbery, but of rape: "Well, at that point I forgot I had the money and the only thing that I could think that he wanted was rape." *Id.* at 280. The court upheld the robbery conviction, reasoning that "the standard for determining whether the victim was put 'in fear' is largely subjective;" that the victim's testimony was credible and not apparently unreasonable; and concluding that "the record tends to indicate not only that the defendant's intention was to 'intimidate and frighten the victim into docile nonresistance and meek compliance,' . . .but also that he succeeded in his purpose, whether or not the victim realized it and whether or not she was able to articulate it at trial." *Id.* at 280, 281. The difference between this standard and its application and the approaches in *Goldberg* and *Evans* could not be greater, particularly since the defendants in the latter two cases pursued far more elaborate schemes to frighten their victims. Notably, all three women feared rape; that fear was enough to sustain a conviction of robbery, but not of the crime feared.

    Moreover, even courts adopting a narrow definition of "physical force" for purposes of robbery statutes have recognized that where defendants manage to avoid physical force or its threatened use through a ruse—i.e., by portraying a police officer—the felonies of larceny by trick or by false pretenses plainly could be charged, in addition to petit larceny. The absence of "physical force" as conventionally defined did not render the taking of money a lawful gift. See People v. Flynn, 123 Misc. 2d 1021, 475 N.Y.S.2d 334 (Sup. Ct. 1984).

62. While defined slightly differently in different jurisdictions, conviction for false pretenses generally requires a false representation of a material fact which causes the victim to pass title or property to the defendant, who knows his representation to be false and intends to use such representation to defraud the victim. See W. LaFAVE & A. SCOTT, supra note 87, at 655; MODEL PENAL CODE § 223.3 comment at 180–181 (1980).

63. In false pretenses statutes, "the almost universal modern rule" is that gullibility or carelessness is no defense, because "the criminal law aims to protect those who cannot protect themselves." W. LaFAVE & A. SCOTT, supra note 87, at 669. See, e.g., State v. Nash, 110 Kan. 550, 204 P. 736 (1922); Clarke v. People, 64 Colo. 164, 171 P. 69 (1981); Lefler v. State, 153 Ind. 82, 54 N.E. 439 (1899); State v. Foot, 100 Mont. 33, 48 P.2d 1113 (1935).

64. See, e.g., MODEL PENAL CODE § 223.2 (1980) ("A person is guilty of theft if he unlawfully takes, or exercises unlawful control over, movable property of another with purpose to deprive him thereof."). Under the Model Penal Code, theft of an automobile is a third degree felony. *Id.* at § 223.1(2)(a).

65. See, e.g., MODEL PENAL CODE § 223.4 (1980); W. LaFAVE & A. SCOTT, supra note 87, at 705; Comment, *Criminal Law—A Study of Statutory Blackmail and Extortion in the Several States,* 44 MICH. L. REV. 461 (1945); Comment, *A Rationale of the Law of Aggravated Theft,* 54 COLUM. L. REV. 84 (1954).

66. W. LaFAVE & A. SCOTT, supra note 87, at 705 (threat to accuse victim of sodomy constitutes robbery).

67. Traditionally, robbery has been limited to threats of immediate bodily harms, threats to destroy the victim's home, or threats to accuse

him of sodomy. Securing property through the use of other threats—threats to accuse an individual of a crime, to impair his credit or business repute, to take to withhold action as an official or cause an official to take or with-hold action, to expose any secret tending to subject the person to contempt or ridicule — have been prohibited as the lesser offense of extortion or blackmail. Notably, extortion encompasses threats to do what is legal and even desirable—to report a crime, for instance. It also encompasses threats to make public information which is true and accurate. Nonetheless, when those threats are used to secure money, in the absence of an honest claim of restitution or indemnification, they are prohibited as criminal. See generally W. LaFAVE & A. SCOTT, supra note 87, at 704–707; MODEL PENAL CODE § 223.4 comments at 201–203 (1980); Lindgren, *Unraveling the Paradox of Blackmail,* 84 COLUM. L. REV. 670 (1984).

68. See Hughes, Consent in Sexual Offences, 25 MOD. L. REV. 672, 673–676 (1962); Williams, *Consent and Public Policy,* 9 CRIM. L. REV. 74, 154 (1962) (pts. 1 & 2); Puttkammer, supra note 6.

By contrast, sexual offenses are a classic and deservedly criticized example of a "morals" offense for which consent is no defense. See Kadish, *The Crisis of Overcriminalization,* 374 ANNALS 157, 159–160 (1967) (criticizing use of criminal law to enforce moral code prohibiting extramarital and abnormal sexual intercourse). "Deviant" sex punishable by law has included homosexual sex, sex with children, oral sex, sex for money, sex outside of marriage, and adultery. But in the long list of prohibited sexual relations, the absence of a separate category of "consensual," violent heterosexual sex is noteworthy; to the extent that such sex has traditionally been prohibited, it is because it has also been fornication or adultery, not because it is violent; in such cases, both man and woman are considered equally guilty.

69. Technically, nonconsent is an element of the offense or a required attendant circumstance. The difference between a defense and the absence of a required element or circumstance is not entirely technical, although it probably

should be; the United States Supreme Court, in determining the constitutionality of requiring defendants to bear the burden of proof of "defenses," has drawn just such a line. *Compare* Patterson v. New York, 432 U.S. 197 (1977) (state may require defendant to prove defense of extreme emotional disturbance) with Mullaney v. Wilbur, 421 U.S. 684 (1975) (state's requirement that defendant prove actions occurred in "heat of passion" to reduce crime from homicide to manslaughter violates due process clause because requisite level of intent must be established by state), *overruled,* Patterson v. New York, 432 U.S. 197 (1977).

70. Virtually the only exception to the rule requiring nonconsent in cases of rape or sexual assault is one oft-cited (and criticized) English case. In The King v. Donovan, [1934] 2 K.B. 498 (C.A.), the accused was charged with caning a girl of seventeen "in circumstances of indecency" for purposes of sexual gratification. His defense was consent, and he appealed his conviction on the ground that the trial judge had failed to instruct the jury that the burden was on the prosecution to establish lack of consent as an element of the offense of indecent assault. The court quashed his conviction on the ground of misdirection of the jury, but in doing so held that where the blows were likely or intended to do bodily harm, consent was no defense. It treated as an exception those cases of "cudgels, foils, or wrestling" which are "manly diversions, they intend to give strength, skill and activity, and may fit people for defence," as well as cases of "rough and undisciplined sport or play, where there is no anger and no intention to cause bodily harm." *Id.* at 508 (quoting M. FOSTER, CROWN LAW 259 (1756)). According to the court, "[n]othing could be more absurd or more repellent to the ordinary intelligence than to regard his conduct as comparable with that of a participant in one of those 'manly diversions'.... Nor is his act to be compared with the rough but innocent horseplay." *Id.* at 509. For criticism of Donovan's "breadth," see, e.g., G. WILLIAMS, supra note 16, at 155.

71. Note, *Forcible and Statutory Rape,* supra note 6, at 71; see also MODEL PENAL CODE §

213.1 comment 4, at 301 (1980) ("The law of rape protects the female's freedom of choice and punishes unwanted and coerced intimacy.").

72. See MODEL PENAL CODE § 221.2(2) (1985) (defiant trespasser).

73. The Model Penal Code requires that the person enter the place "knowing that he is not licensed or privileged to do so." *Id.* at § 221.2(1). It also provides an affirmative defense if the "actor reasonably believed that the owner of the premises, or other person empowered to license access thereto, would have licensed him to enter or remain." *Id.* at § 212.2(3)(c).

74. In Smith v. United States, 291 F.2d 220 (9th Cir. 1961), *cert. denied*, 368 U.S. 834 (1961), for example, a bank teller was approached by the defendant with plans for a bank robbery; the teller pretended to agree, but told the manager, who instructed the teller to hand the defendant a bag when he was "held up." On appeal, the defendant argued that the bank had consented to giving him the money, and thus there was no robbery. The court of appeals rejected the argument and affirmed the conviction, concluding that the bank had not consented but had merely "smoothed the way" for the crime's commission. *Id.* at 221.

75. State v. Neely, 90 Mont. 199, 209, 300 P. 561, 565 (1931) (entrapment of cattle thief).

76. State v. Natalle, 172 La. 709, 716, 135 So. 34, 36 (1931) (entrapment of warehouse thieves).

77. See also Carnes v. State, 134 Tex. Crim. 8, 10, 113 S.W.2d 542, 544 (Tex. Crim. App. 1938); Alford v. Commonwealth, 240 Ky. 513, 42 S.W.2d 711, 712–713 (Ct. App. 1931) People v. Teicher, 52 N.Y.2d 638, 649, 439 N.Y.S.2d 846, 851, 422 N.E.2d 506, 511 (1981).

Similarly, suspects in custody and patients approaching surgery are afforded respect and autonomy that rape victims are not. Under *Miranda v. Arizona*, 384 U.S. 436 (1966), a suspect's "no" must mean no, and questioning must be terminated. *Id.* at 473–474. In the hospital, a doctor may be liable for both criminal and civil penalties unless he secures not simply a "yes" to surgery, but an informed yes. Expansive requirements of informed consent for abortions have been much litigated, see,

e.g., Akron v. Akron Center for Reproductive Health, 462 U.S. 416 (1983), and typical modern statutes establish detailed consent rules which must be followed to negate criminal liability for nonnegligent performance of a therapeutic sterilization, see Comment, *Towards a Consent Standard,* supra note 5, at 639 n.124.

78. That no such presumption is applied to property is evidence in cases holding, for example, that leaving keys in the ignition does not exculpate a thief from prosecution for motor vehicle larceny, nor does leaving a front door unlocked eliminate the trespass. See State v. Plaspohl, 239 Ind. 324, 157 N.E.2d 579 (1959); State v. Moore, 129 Iowa 514, 106 N.W. 16 (1906); W. LaFAVE & A. SCOTT, supra note 87, at 410. In effect, conflicting presumptions are applied to bodily integrity (where a male right of access is presumed) and financial integrity (where a right to privacy and control is protected). Notwithstanding norms of charity, it is presumed that money is something which every individual is entitled to exclusive possession of until and unless he decides to share it. And notwithstanding the law's celebration of chastity and monogamy, a woman's body is presumed to be offered at least to any man whom she knows, drives home, or drinks coffee with, if not every man who desires it.

79. That the problem is more one of understanding than of draftsmanship is amply demonstrated by the statute in the state of Washington. In Washington, rape in the third degree, a felony punishable by up to five years imprisonment, occurs where persons engage in sexual intercourse:

> (a) Where the victim did not consent . . . to sexual intercourse with the perpetrator and such lack of consent was clearly expressed by the victim's words or conduct, or (b) Where there is a threat of substantial unlawful harm to property rights of the victim.

WASH. REV. CODE ANN. § 9A.44.060 (West. Supp. 1986). The provision as to threats, limited as it is to unlawful action and to property rights, is potentially narrower than the Model Penal Code's crime of gross sexual imposition, and certainly narrower than traditional prohibitions of extortion. The provision as to consent, on the other hand, is potentially quite broad; it could be read to criminalize all those cases where force is difficult to prove in traditional terms but the woman said no. That is how I would read it. Others read it differently. Professor Loh of the University of Washington, perhaps the key commentator on the Washington rape statute, and certainly the expert on its practical impact, see supra Section III(C), reads this provision as adding absolutely nothing to a statute which, in the first two degrees of the offense, explicitly requires force and does not mention consent: "The definitions of the first two degrees preempt the content of rape 3 and render its prosecution difficult." Loh, supra note 200, at 552.

NOTES AND QUESTIONS

1. What does Estrich mean by the terms "real rape" and "nontraditional rape"? Would she call sexual coercion (or seduction) a nontraditional form of rape? Would you?

2. In what sense has the American legal system traditionally "put the victim on trial" in rape cases? What is the source of law's preoccupation with the question of consent in rape cases? What is problematic about defining rape in terms of force and consent? How does shifting the focus to *mens rea* change things? Do you find Estrich's argument compelling? Why or why not?

3. Estrich writes, "To examine rape within the criminal-law tradition is to expose fully the sexism of the law." Do you agree? Can the inconsistencies between rape laws and other criminal statutes primarily be attributed to issues of gender and power in the social organization of law, or are there other explanations?

4. Is there anything about the nature of this particular crime that precludes a straightforward definition based upon *actus reus* and *mens rea?* How do cultural factors (attitudes toward sex, gender stereotypes, etc.) affect how the law treats rape? Does this justify the apparent double standard in criminal law?

5. As Estrich describes it, what is the difference between "prohibited force" and "incidental force"? Is the distinction reasonable, or do you concur with Estrich that it creates undesirable and problematic legal complications?

6. How, if at all, would Estrich's focus on *mens rea* have changed the fundamental questions debated in *Rusk v. Maryland?* Could this have assuaged Judge Wilner's concerns about the capacity of an appellate court (as opposed to a jury) to decide the case?

Chapter 25

Risking Relationships

Understanding the Litigation Choices of Sexually Harassed Women

Phoebe A. Morgan

The substance of the law does not, in itself, determine law's accessibility and responsiveness. Even where the law is not biased against women, there still may be substantial barriers to access. They are rooted in the lives women lead or the values they embrace. Among the most important are the barriers arising from marital and family responsibilities, but because women are so different from one another these barriers affect some women but not others. If seeking legal remedy threatens or jeopardizes their responsibilities, women may not take advantage of legal redress even when it is readily available to them.

The next reading focuses on factors that shape women's responses to incidents of sexual harassment. The law prohibiting sexual harassment was established to provide women remedies for acts in the workplace and elsewhere that undermined gender equality. Phoebe A. Morgan's article describes how women who perceive themselves to be the victims of sexual harassment think about using the law to deal with their victimization. Morgan reports that, regardless of the severity of the harassment, relatively few women take legal action. Of all of the reasons why women do not seek legal redress, marital responsibilities and the approval of their family seem most important. For both

those who did sue as well as those who did not, the crucial factor was "the impact that the litigation might have on their families."

Are the familial and relational barriers to litigation described in Morgan's article problems for which law itself can and should be held accountable? Is there anything that the law could do to address these barriers to access?

For most people litigation is a high-risk endeavor. Regardless of the principles at stake, or the amount invested, winning is never guaranteed and losing is always an option (Cornell 1990). Although the rewards can be exceptional for those who win, losing can be demoralizing and financially devastating. What compels ordinary people to assume the risks of litigation and file suit?

Certainly the need for monetary reimbursement for the loss of profits, employment, and even health propel many to sue. Noting increases in the number of such claims, tort reformists have argued that the promise of substantial pecuniary gain encourages the use of civil litigation for personal profit (see, for example, Huber 1988 and also Lieberman 1981). But in addition to financial recoupment and profit, litigation studies have shown that plaintiffs are as often motivated by more intrinsic desires, such as the assertion of self-worth (Bumiller 1988), the expression of personal dignity (McCann 1994), the acknowledgment of cherished principles (Conley & O'Barr 1990), atonement for the loss of a life deemed dear (May & Stengel 1990), and even for revenge (Sloan & Hsieh 1995).

Until recently, men have dominated the civil litigation arena. But, as women's legal status has increased and the social situation of many women has improved, their opportunities for civil litigation have expanded (Hoyman & Stallworth 1986). The introduction of the Violence against Women Act and the broadening of civil rights claims that can be made under Titles VII and IX, have substantially increased the number and type of legal remedies for which women can now file suit. In addition, government agencies like the Equal Employment Opportunity Commission (EEOC) and the Office of Civil Rights (OCR) now offer women the opportunity to litigate their gender discrimination claims with a minimum amount of financial risk.

Perhaps one of the more provocative litigation opportunities extended to women has been the reconceptualization of sexual harassment as a form of civil rights violation (MacKinnon 1979 & 1987). The availability of substantial remedies along with the possibility of punitive awards under Titles VII and IX promises not only to transform the policies and practices of those who employ women, but to revolutionize women's litigation patterns as well (MacKinnon 1993). From 1980 until 1994, for example, the rate of sexual harassment claims filed with the EEOC steadily increased by about 12 percent per year (Bureau of National Affairs 1994). Since 1980, the Supreme Court has ruled on at least seven sexual harassment claims, and the media is now replete with stories of women who have "hit the jackpot" and earned millions through sexual harassment litigation.

Critics worry that increasing the number and type of legal remedies that women can sue for and expanding their access to government litigation aid has done more to raise the number of frivolous litigations than to elevate the legal or social status of women (Lieberman 1981). As one lawyer recently put it, " . . .making it easier for women to sue for sexual harassment will not eliminate the problem of sexual harassment, it will only increase the amount of litigation regarding it" (*NBC Nightly News Report*, 27 June 1998).

Yet, despite the apparent financial lucrativeness of sexual harassment claims making, it remains underreported. Random surveys of federal employees consistently report that though 42–44 percent of working women experience behaviors deemed legally actionable,

only 7 percent actually file formal charges (U.S. Merit Systems Protection Board 1981, 1995, 1988). In addition, Fitzgerald, Swan, & Fisher (1995) estimate that less than 1 percent of those claims are ever heard in a court of law.

While researchers have probed significant amounts of data to discover the various psychological and social factors affecting the reporting choices that sexually harassed women make (see, for example, Gruber 1989; Gwartney-Gibbs & Lach 1992; Fitzgerald et al. 1995; Riger 1991), the social and psychological processes that move women beyond the "naming and claiming" stages (Felstiner, Abel, & Sarat 1980–1981) to actually assigning legal blame have not been closely examined. Given current trends and debates regarding women's responses to sexual harassment, as well as the expansion of opportunity women have for litigation, this seems to be an especially important and perhaps crucial time to theorize in greater depth about the process by which women arrive at the decision to litigate their sexual harassment complaints.

Taking a narrative approach (Ewick & Silbey 1995; Riessman 1993), this article focuses on this one particular choice in the lives of 31 sexually harassed women. It draws upon their actual words to discover how they perceived their risks of litigation, the options they considered, and then to document how they arrived at the decisions they eventually made. . . .

THE RESPONDENTS AND THEIR CHOICES

When viewed as a whole, perhaps one of the more defining characteristics of this group of women was their general dearth of financial and social resources for sustaining successful litigations. Those who shared information about their earnings drew no more than $25,000 per year and few mentioned having any savings or financial holdings. Data measuring their household income were not gathered, but most appeared to be, and many described themselves as being members of either the middle or working classes. At the time of their harassments, most held jobs in either the service or the industrial sectors, and with the exception of Faith and Tina, who were professionals, the rest were semiskilled or unskilled laborers. Only two women had completed graduate programs, five held college degrees, and the rest had high school diplomas or equivalents.

Galanter (1974) argues that legal knowledge and direct experience using it are litigation assets. His work suggests that possession of these assets is likely to affect how potential litigants perceive their options and the choices they are likely to make. More recently, May & Stengel (1990) theorize that, at least among medical malpractice complainants, those with more legal knowledge are *less* likely to sue, while those with more legal experience are *more* likely to sue.

Other than uncontested divorce proceedings and routine child custody filings, only Gail had first-hand experience with high-stakes litigation. Two years prior she had prevailed in a wage discrimination claim against a previous employer. Working as a legal secretary, Alicia had second-hand knowledge of how large corporations sue, and as a lay magistrate, Cecilia's legal knowledge was limited to traffic law.

In addition to a general lack of financial resources and litigation expertise, another dominant characteristic of this group was an abundance of relationships. About one-half of the women were married, and with the exception of Stella and Beth, the other half were engaged in romantic relationships. One-half of the participants had children under the age of 12 and five had teenagers. Three women supported husbands who were either disabled or unemployed. Faith and Gail provided financial support and health care to terminally ill parents. Alicia was pregnant with her first child.

Only three of the 31 women—Stella, Beth, and Tina—did not have the responsibility to care for or support family dependents. None of those who were divorced received any alimony, and a majority of them were single parents raising children with little or no assistance from their ex-husbands. In sum, this particular group had not only an abundance of intimate or familial relationships, but also a significant amount of responsibility to provide and care for the loved ones.

All 31 of the women considered filing a lawsuit, but only four of them—Eve, Beth, Cecilia and Gail—actually did so. At the time of their interview, Beth and Eve had already settled their claims out of court, for the equivalent of one year's wages or $20,000 and $25,000, respectively. Cecilia and Gail's attorneys had filed their suits and each was engaged in the deposition phase of the pretrial process.

At the time they were being interviewed, 10 of the 31 interviewees stated they had definitely arrived at the decision *not* to file a lawsuit. Thus, about 16 women were still weighing their options during the time their narratives were recorded.

While a variety of paths to formal action were considered, 67 percent (21 out of 31) began by filing complaints with government agencies. In only two of those cases (Beth's and June's) did the investigations find sufficient cause for government intervention. Both were cleared through mediation rather than litigation. Complaints without causal findings were disposed of with the issuance of "right-to-sue-letters."[1] Seven women consulted with private attorneys. Zoie and Eve obtained representation upon complete contingency. Cecilia's attorney took her case for a $1,500 deposit and Gail received representation that was billed at a half-price rate of $75 per hour.

FINDINGS

Among these 31 women, job loss, or fear of it, was the primary trigger for a serious consideration of litigation. After careful thought, many of the unemployed eventually chose not to litigate, and some of those who did not lose their jobs decided to seek legal representation. Despite the strict criteria used by government agencies and private attorneys to take cases upon contingency, most believed that, despite these restrictions, there were still choices to be made. The lucky two whose complaints were found to have sufficient cause for government agency intervention, for example, had to decide whether to accept government mediation, or to reject it and pursue litigation on their own. Those who consulted with private attorneys had to decide whether they had the financial resources or emotional fortitude to prevail.

In talking about how they weighed their options, all 31 women referred to familial relationships they deemed to be especially important or precious. Carefully considered were maternal responsibilities, marital commitments, parental approval, and the impact that litigation might have on their families. At times familial ties were counted as assets for successful litigation; at other times they were listed as liabilities.

For most the decision to sue rested upon assessments of their abilities to do so while also being good mothers, wives, and daughters. If the filing of a suit threatened the well-being of family members or to strain familial ties, then potential plaintiffs were reluctant to embrace such a choice. In contrast, if litigation held promise for making life better for their families, or for restoring familial harmony, then it was given serious consideration. In many instances the love of family and their willingness to help out were counted as essential for surviving the rigors of litigation.

MATERNAL RESPONSIBILITIES

For mothers, a key factor affecting their decisionmaking was the impact that legal action might have on the well-being of their children. Some worried that taking legal action might bring harm to their children, others felt they had a responsibility to protect

their children from the aftermath of harassment. Regardless of the choice that was eventually made, mothers commonly evoked maternal responsibility as the final arbiter in their decisionmaking.

Gail, for example, decided to consider litigation seriously when the harassments she had been enduring at her place of work spilled over into her home life and touched the life of her eight-year-old son. As the only woman foreman [sic] working in a large military supply manufacturing plant, for nearly three years Gail had tolerated without complaint a regular stream of sexualized epithets and sexist pranks. Each time she reported the offensive gags to her direct supervisor, he responded by "blowing off" her concerns with assertions that such antics were common among line workers, and that it was her responsibility as a foreman to rise above them. Gail struggled to take his advice, and endured the pranks until the day her son intercepted an obscene telephone call that was meant for her:

> They called up and when my son answered the phone, one of them said, "Hey, did you know that your Momma sucks my dick." It scared him to death! So, I said, "That's it. They can do all kinds of stuff at work but they have to be told that my family is off limits!"

So, as Gail explained in her interview, though she was willing to "take an awful lot on the chin" at work, she had a lot less tolerance for harassment that touched the life of her son. It was concern about his well-being that motivated Gail to go against her supervisor's advice and formally complain. So, in Gail's case, outrage over her son's victimization as well as a sense of responsibility for his safety outweighed the potential risks that formal action might present.

In some cases maternal responsibility deterred rather than facilitated the decision to file suit. While Gail used litigation to meet her obligations as a protector, others worried that taking legal action would make it more difficult for them to meet their children's needs. Unlike many of the women in this study, Alicia had the financial means to pursue litigation. But her interview was filled with talk of her pregnancy and worries about the effect that the stress of such contentious action might have on it.

Alicia's harassment took place in a private law firm where she worked as a legal secretary. When one of the partners in her firm began to make sexualized remarks and off-color jokes about her pregnant body, she knew he was violating a law and that she had a legal right to file charges. Alicia carefully documented each incident and in her seventh month of pregnancy consulted with an attorney who agreed to draft a letter of demand.

Yet, shortly afterward Alicia decided against sending the letter and quit her job instead. When asked why, she explained that a recent obstetrics checkup revealed that her blood pressure was too high, and therefore was putting her pregnancy at risk. In light of this new development, her doctor ordered her to avoid stressful situations and to take better care of herself.

Alicia firmly believed it was the stress of having to cope with her supervisor's remarks that had raised her blood pressure, but through her work inside a legal firm she had also observed how stressful litigation can be. Putting her pregnancy first, she followed the doctor's orders and eliminated both the stress of harassment and the potential stress of litigation by quitting her job entirely. Thus, Alicia decided to take her chances with the risks that came with unemployment rather than put her unborn child through the rigor of contentious action. . . .

These . . . accounts illustrate the hard choices that sexually harassed women with children must make. The need to meet one's maternal responsibilities is pitted against one's own personal desires for retribution and justice. But each woman found her own resolution to the conflict between personal desire and familial responsibility. Those with

"mouths to feed" were much more likely to use litigation as a means for fulfilling their obligations as providers. Others resisted the desire to litigate when doing so appeared to threaten their ability to protect and nurture their young.

Marital Commitment

In deciding whether to pursue litigation, those who were married weighed heavily the effect that litigation might have on their ability to maintain marital harmony and keep commitments they had made to spouses. Among the married, a particularly salient topic of conversation was the emergence of marital discord. All reported that the stress of being harassed—and in some cases of being unemployed as a consequence of harassment—had placed significant strain on marital relations.

As a result, those who were married claimed they were fighting with their spouses more often and the bones of contention involved differing assessments of the seriousness of the situation, as well as conflicting judgements about what should be done.

Jealous and overly protective husbands fumed about what other men were being allowed to do and say to their wives at work. Others fretted over the impact that their wives' unemployment had on their families' economics. While most tried to be sympathetic to their wives' plights, many were also critical of their wives' passive tolerance.

For the women experiencing this type of marital conflict the degree to which they believed that litigation would ease marital tensions or exacerbate them determined the choices they made. In addition, the amount of authority their husbands had in the home, and the desires these men expressed, played crucial roles in the final choices the married women made. . . .

Love as a Litigation Asset

As part of their intake interviews or the initial consultation routines, EEOC officers and private attorneys lectured potential plaintiffs on the difficulties of litigation and the necessity of sufficient emotional and moral resolve. Many of those seeking help from government agents and private attorneys were "lectured" on the "evils" of civil litigation and warned that the process takes a particularly high toll on a plaintiff's health and well-being. Potential plaintiffs were informed that litigation was "ugly," "mean," and consumptive. Implicit in these types of lectures is the notion that successful litigation of sexual harassment complaints demands the effective mobilization of intrinsic resources for maintaining self-esteem, personal fortitude, and high energy (Freeman 1977).

In deciding whether they should sue, the women (sometimes in consultation with their attorneys) inventoried their resources for maintaining resolve and self-esteem. As a means to reduce stress and shore up her self-esteem, Beth enrolled in a college course. Joan's attorney referred her to a clinical psychologist for help in handling the insults of litigation. Yet, because she was unemployed, she felt the counselor's reduced rate of $65 per hour was a luxury she could ill afford. So, like most of the women in this study, Joan turned to family for emotional and moral support. Pledges of unconditional love and expressions of moral support made it easier to accept the risks that accompany legal action and then to survive the emotional rigors that the process of suing can impose.

To add insult to injury, shortly after the city council voted not to renew Celia's contract, the man she had accused filed a multimillion dollar lawsuit against both Cecilia and their former employer. Unemployed and a single mother of two children, Cecilia's spirit was crushed by the news. Interestingly, talk of her mother's love and wise counsel filled her account of these events. In fact, Cecilia credited the unconditional love of her mother more than her attorney's ferocious advocacy for her ability not only to pursue her own lawsuit but also to survive the anxiety and humiliation of countersuit:

. . . .Mom and I don't always agree. She's not a women's libber and to tell you the truth, she doesn't think much of my decision to file a lawsuit. She's always saying, "Leave it to God. Leave it to God." But, even though we disagree, I know she loves me and she's always there for me. She just sits and listens while I go on and on.

So, although Cecilia's mother did not think highly of litigation and did not approve of Cecilia's decision to contest her dismissal, Cecilia counted her mother's love as one of her most precious litigation assets. . . .

LITIGATION AS AN ASSERTION OF AUTONOMY

Most of the women in this study treasured familial relations and either used litigation or avoided it as a means to protect them. The well-being of children as well as the desires of partners were commonly used to justify not only the decision to sue, but also the decision not to sue. Responsibilities to provide and care for family were weighed heavily, while pledges of unconditional love, moral support, and even financial aid facilitated a willingness to enter into the legal unknown. Yet, not all the choices these women described were based solely upon the needs and desires of others, and for some relationality did have its limits. Certainly the more connected these women were, the more relationality played an important role in the choices they made. But in addition to quantity, the quality of familial ties—the degree to which they tethered or liberated the individuals who experienced them—was important as well.

Regardless of their closeness to family and the value placed upon family bonds, common among these narratives were women's valuation of autonomy. Many expressed the desire and even an obligation to fight for what was rightfully or legally theirs. For women unencumbered by the responsibilities and commitments that accompany familial connection, the decision to litigate one's individual rights was certainly easier than it was for those with young children to support or marriages to maintain.

Childless and single, Beth was free to take on the challenge of becoming the first woman to perform construction work inside a large utility company. A survivor of poverty with strong working-class values, she took exceptional pride in her financial independence. She could not contain her outrage when the very same grievance board that had dismissed her sexual harassment complaint also voted to suspend her without pay for grazing the side of a cement mixer truck. Without a second thought, Beth took her grievance to the Human Rights Commission and with their help, she eventually negotiated an out-of-court settlement for $20,000. For Beth, her decision to litigate, as well as her survival of it, was a source of personal pride. A large portion of her narrative involved the day she cashed her settlement check:

> ...it was the first time in my entire life that I did something for me—just for *me*. The first time I ever stood up for myself and said, "Hey, what about me?" So, I felt pretty good about it.

In Beth's case, it was her autonomy and the lack of familial connection that afforded her the opportunity to litigate and find success in it. Without maternal responsibilities or marital commitments, she felt free to seek justice without having to consider the ramifications of such actions for others. Beth's account reveals that in addition to fulfilling the practical need for compensation, the litigation also served to validate the value of individuality and personal independence....

DISCUSSION

When research participants are given the opportunity to control the structure and content of their narratives, we get a rare glimpse of more than *what* they prefer to talk about, we also learn *how* they choose to talk about it (Graham 1984; Riessman 1993). Without prompting, these 31 women chose to talk about how they arrived at the litigation choices they made and they did so by privileging concerns about their familial relationships. The preponderance of references to children, husbands and parents suggests that they believed that relationships—especially those with family—are important topics for research conversation. The strong relational threads inside these narratives also indicate that relationality played an important, and often pivotal, role in the choices these women made.

Previous studies have shown that the nature and strength of relations with attorneys (Miethe 1995), government agents (Gwartney-Gibbs & Lach 1992), employers (McCann 1994) and even opponents (Felstiner et al. 1980–1981) greatly affect how disputants think and feel about litigation. The stories these women told indicate that relationships with their children, marital partners and even their parents may play an equally important role in the litigation decisions these sexually harassed women made. Their motivations to sue, as well as not to sue, included feelings of maternal duty and loyalty to spouses, as well as the unconditional love and support of parents and siblings. Their accounts breathe life into the assertions of relational theorists that, at least among women who are highly connected to others, the integrity of relationships matters a great deal in the legal choices that women make (Ferraro & Pope 1992; West 1987, 1988). Furthermore, my analysis of these stories shows that they matter in a number of complex ways.

A primary consideration for those deciding whether or not to seek legal action was how litigation might affect those to whom they were closely tied. Those with maternal and marital responsibilities gave careful consideration to those options that would enable them to meet their family's financial and emotional needs. When filing suit promised to make life better for loved ones, then the risks and rigors that litigation imposes were worth assuming. Yet, when the stress and demands of legal action threatened to put the well-being of family members at risk, complainants looked for extralegal means to solve their sexual harassment problems. In making the decision to sue, many inventoried the amount of love, care and help upon which they could depend. Litigation became a less daunting proposition in those cases where pledges of support exceeded their families' demand for it.

The relational decisionmaking that characterizes these narratives contrasts, and therefore confronts, a number of taken-for-granted assumptions about the motivations of sexual harassment victims and women litigants. First, both substance and procedure for civil law are premised on a liberal view of human nature that assumes that all legal actors are (or at least should be) autonomous beings and that the choices they make reflect the true nature of their own personal desires (West 1987). Second, the liberal view of litigation often assumes a cost-benefit model of decisionmaking. There is the premise that the litigants are motivated by a desire to maximize personal benefits and minimize personal harms (Cornell 1990; Gleason 1981; Hoyman & Stallworth 1986). Third, behind the legislation of civil rights laws lies the premise that if sufficient options for legal protection and remedy are made available, then those who need them will use them.

But, as these narratives so vividly illustrate, the lives of many women are not completely autonomous and are often profoundly relational. The vast majority of the women in this study were mothers and by definition mothers are not autonomous, but are highly connected to and depended upon by their children (West 1987, 1988). Responsibility to provide for their children forces many mothers into economic dependence upon spouses and employers. For such women, litigation pits the need to meet familial responsibilities against personal longings for formal justice. . . .

Notes

1. Government agencies investigate complaints to determine whether legal action by that agency is warranted. If sufficient cause is found, the agency either files suit or mediates a resolution. If cause for action is deemed insufficient, the complainant is issued the right to pursue his/her claims through private litigation. By law, sexual harassment complainants are precluded from filing a claim without having first obtained the right to do so from the appropriate government agency.

References

Bumiller, Kristen (1988) *The Civil Rights Society: The Social Construction of Victims.* Baltimore: John Hopkins Univ. Press.

Bureau of National Affairs (1994) "New Charges, Backlog Rising," 3 *Current Developments* 616–617.

Conley, John, & William O'Barr (1990) *Rules versus Relationships: The Ethnography of Legal Discourse.* Chicago: Univ. of Chicago Press.

Cornell, Bradford (1990) "The Incentive to Sue: An Option Pricing Approach," 29 *J. of Legal Studies* 173–191.

Ewick, Patricia, & Susan Silbey (1995) "Subversive Stories and Hegemonic Tales: Toward a Sociology of Narrative," 29 *Law & Society Rev.* 197–226.

Felstiner, William, L. F., Richard L. Abel, & Austin Sarat (1980–1981) "Emergence and Transformation of Disputes: Naming, Blaming, Claiming . . .," 15 *Law & Society Rev.* 631–654.

Ferraro, Kathleen J., & Lucille Pope (1993) "Irreconcilable Differences: Battered Women, Police and the Law," in N. Z. Hilton, ed., *Legal Responses to Wife Assault: Current Trends and Evaluation.* Newbury Park, CA: Sage Publications.

Fitzgerald, Louise, Suzanne Swan, & Karla Fisher (1995) "Why Didn't She Just Report Him? The Psychological and Legal Implications of Women's Responses to Sexual Harassment," 51 *J. of Social Issues* 117–138.

Freeman, Jo (1977) "Resource Mobilization and Strategy: A Model for Analyzing Social Movement Actions," in M. N. Zald & J. D. McCarthy, eds., *The Dynamics of Social Movements.* Cambridge: Winthrop Publishers.

Galanter, Marc (1974) "Why the 'Haves' Come Out Ahead: Speculations on the Limits of Legal Change," 9 *Law & Society Rev.* 95–160.

Gleason, Sandra (1981) "The Probability of Redress," in B. Florisha & B. Goldman, eds., *Outsiders on the Inside: Women and Organizations.* Englewood Cliffs, NJ: Prentice Hall.

Graham, Hilary (1984) "Surveying through Stories," in C. Bell & H. Roberts, eds., *Social Researching Politics, Problems, Practice.* London: Routledge & Kegan Paul.

Gruber, James (1989) "How Women Handle Sexual Harassment: A Literature Review," 74 *Social Science Research* 3–7.

Gwartney-Gibbs, Patricia, & Denise Lach (1992) "Sociological Explanations for Failure to Seek Sexual Harassment Remedies," 9 *Mediation Q.* 365–373.

Hoyman, Michele, & Lamont Stallworth (1986) "Suit Filing by Women: An Empirical Analysis," 64 *Notre Dame Law Rev.* 61–82.

Huber, Peter (1988) *Liability: The Legal Revolution and Its Consequences.* New York: Basic Books.

Lach, Denise, & Patricia Gwartney-Gibbs (1993) "Sociological Perspectives on Sexual Harassment and Workplace Dispute Resolution," 42 *J. of Vocational Behavior* 102–115.

Lieberman, Jethro (1981) *The Litigious Society.* New York: Basic Books.

MacKinnon, Catharine (1979) *The Sexual Harassment of Working Women: A Case of Sex Discrimination.* New Haven, CT: Yale Univ. Press.

—— (1987) *Feminism Unmodified: Discourses on Life and Law.* Cambridge: Harvard Univ. Press.

—— (1993) "Reflections on Law in the Everyday Life of Women," in A. Sarat & T. R. Kearns, eds., *Law in Everyday Life.* Ann Arbor: Univ. of Michigan Press.

May, Marlynn L., & Daniel B. Stengel (1990) "Who Sues Their Doctors? How Patients Handle Medical Grievances," 24 *Law & Society Rev.* 106–120.

McCann, Michael (1994) *Rights at Work: Pay Equity Reform and the Politics of Mobilization.* Chicago: Univ. of Chicago Press.

Miethe, Terance (1995) "Predicting Future Litigiousness," 12 *Justice Q.* 563–576.

Riessman, Catherine Kohler (1993) *Narrative Analysis.* Newbury Park, CA: Sage Publications.

Riger, Stephanie (1991) "Gender Dilemmas in Sexual Harassment Policies and Procedures," 46 *American Psychologist* 497–505.

Sloan, Frank A., & Chee Ruey Hsieh (1995) "Injury, Liability and Decision to File a Medical Malpractice Claim," 29 *Law & Society Rev.* 413–429.

U.S. Merit Systems Protection Board (1981) *Sexual Harassment of Federal Workers.* Washington: GPO.

—— (1988) *Sexual Harassment in the Federal Government: An Update.* Washington: GPO.

—— (1994) *Sexual Harassment in the Federal Workplace: Trends, Progress, Continuing Challenges: A Report to the President and the Congress of the United States.* Washington: GPO.

West, Robin (1987) "The Differences in Women's Hedonic Lives: A Phenomenological Critique of Feminist Legal Theory," 3 *Wisconsin Women's Law J.* 81–146.

—— (1988) "Jurisprudence and Gender," 55 *Univ. of Chicago Law Rev.* 1–71.

Notes and Questions

1. Why does Morgan call litigation a "high-risk endeavor"? What is generally at stake when a person decides whether or not to sue? How might sexual harassment litigation be considered particularly high-risk?

2. Morgan reports that though "42–44 percent of working women experience behaviors deemed legal actionable, only 7 percent actually file formal charges." Of the 31 women she interviewed, only 4 filed charges. How should we interpret this fact? Why do most women choose nonlegal means to cope with sexual harassment? To use Felstiner, Abel, and Sarat's terms (Chapter 15), is this an issue of naming, of blaming, or of claiming?

3. According to Morgan, what role do financial resources play in determining

whether a woman brings suit under sexual harassment law? How are gender and social class linked in this context?

4. In your opinion, are sexual harassment statutes examples of the law overstepping its bounds? Is it just to legally regulate unsolicited sexual advances? By Mill's standards (Chapter 9), can sexual harassment be considered a "harm"? Why or why not?

5. Do you think that sexual harassment statutes have helped to reduce overall harassment or not? Some would argue that such statutes unnecessarily treat women as defenseless creatures, incapable of asserting themselves. By this logic, sexual harassment laws actually contribute to women's suffering in the workplace. By advancing an image of frail women in a hostile, sexually charged, macho environment, they perpetuate a myth that women cannot defend themselves except with litigation (which most cannot afford). What do you think of this argument? What would Morgan think?

Reprinted from: Phoebe A. Morgan, "Risking Relationships: Understanding the Litigation Choices of Sexually Harassed Women" in *Law and Society Review*, 33:1, 1999, pp. 67–92. Copyright © 1999. Reprinted with the permission of the Law and Society Association. ✦

Chapter 26

Rights Talk and the Experience of Law

Implementing Women's Human Rights to Protection from Violence

Sally Engle Merry

Some students of law and well-intentioned legal reformers tend to concentrate their energy and efforts on changing the substance of the law. Thus the struggle for greater equality and to overcome barriers and disadvantages faced by persons of color, women, gays and lesbians, and others has often been waged through efforts to enact new laws or alter the way courts interpret existing laws. Sometimes dramatic victories are won (for example *see* Lawrence v. Texas *in Chapter 10); more often change is gradual, piecemeal, and, as a result, hard to see. With regard to rape, sexual harassment, and violence against women, the substance of the law has slowly changed providing greater legal recognition of, and responses to, the injuries women suffer.*

But as the previous reading by Morgan indicates, taking advantage of new recognition and protection encoded in the written law is neither automatic nor easy. The next article discusses the difficulty women encounter in taking advantage of new legal rights, this time in the context of domestic violence. Its author, Sally Engle Merry, discusses the effectiveness of human rights norms in protecting women. In this legal arena, many forces are important in determining how women respond to the available legal rights and remedies. Merry labels them "consciousness, experience, and institutional receptivity."

Asserting rights (e.g., the right not to be battered) requires women to change their views of themselves and adopt a new consciousness. Whether they do so depends on the responses of legal officials to their claims. Turning to law is a learning experience. How police, prosecutors, judges, and other legal officials react when women bring complaints about battering are crucial factors in determining whether formal legal rights get acted on. When legal officials take gender violence seriously, women are more likely to take on the kind of rights-based identity necessary to pursue legal remedies.

Merry also calls our attention to intersections of race, class, and gender. She notes that for working class, poor, and minority women, effective legal redress is even more important than it is for their more privileged peers. This is because battered women who live in poverty may not be able to escape their batterers by moving to a new home or by mobilizing counselors and therapists to intervene. Yet, it is precisely these women who are least likely to be treated with respect and to have their claims taken seriously by legal officials. The Merry article thus provides a vivid illustration of the importance of social and organizational factors in determining the accessibility of law.

INTRODUCTION

From civil rights to human rights, rights talk remains a dominant framework for contemporary social justice movements. But seeing oneself as a rights-bearing subject whose problems are violations of these rights is far from universal. How does a person come to understand his or her problems in terms of rights? It is the contention of this article that the adoption of a rights consciousness requires experiences with the legal system that reinforce this subjectivity. Adoption of rights-defined selves depends on encounters with police, prosecutors, judges, and probation officers that reflect back this identity. Indications that the problem is trivial, that the victim does not really have these rights, or that the offender does not deserve punishment undermine this subjectivity. How to persuade victims to take on a rights-defined self is a critical problem for the battered women's movement, which relies heavily on rights talk to encourage abused women to seek help from the law.[1] It is also fundamental to a range of other rights-based social reform movements that depend on victim activism and rights claiming in order to promote change such as disability rights and employment rights. The human rights movement depends both on government compliance with international treaties and victim advocacy for these rights. Thus, examining how vulnerable populations come to see their difficulties as human rights violations is a fundamental question for human rights activists. This empirical study shows how victims of violence against women come to take on rights consciousness. It describes an interaction between consciousness, experience, and institutional receptivity that is critical to human rights practice.

The battered women's movement has always relied on a criminal justice component to its activism, which encourages victims to see their violation as a crime and to turn to the legal system for help.[2] As the global movement expands in the wake of the Vienna conference in 1993 and Beijing in 1995, a rights approach is increasingly important. The 1993 conference in Vienna focused on human rights and articulated the principle of women's rights as human rights, while the Beijing Fourth World Conference on Women in 1995 emphasized women's rights and reinforced the idea that women's rights are human rights. Yet, despite considerable emphasis on rights by shelter staff and court advocates, battered women are often slow to take on rights. Even after calling the police for

help and filing for temporary restraining orders, battered women are likely to refuse to testify or to drop the restraining order. They clearly fear retaliation by the batterer, but they also resist the shift in subjectivity required by the law. This resistance often stems from a sense of self that is deeply at odds with other senses that are rooted in family, religion, and community. Taking on a rights-defined self in relation to a partner requires a substantial identity change both for the woman and for the man she is accusing. Instead of seeing herself defined by family, kin, and work relationships, she takes on a more autonomous self protected by the state. At the same time, her actions allow the law to define her husband/partner as a criminal under the surveillance and control of the state. A battered woman may be pressured by kin to feel she is a bad wife, while her partner may claim she is taking away his masculinity. The only way she can rescue him from this loss is to deflect the very legal sanctions she has called down upon him. It is hardly surprising that abused women will ask for help from the law, back away, and then ask again. Such women appear to be difficult or "bad" victims since they typically file charges then try to drop them or fail to appear for restraining order hearings. Yet, these women are tacking back and forth across a significant line of identity transformation....

In this article, I argue that the adoption of a rights-defined identity under identity-shifting circumstances such as battering depends on the individual's experience with the law. One of the powerful consequences of gender violence cases to the attention of the legal system is the victim's and perpetrator's encounters with the new subjectivity defined within the discourses and practices of the law. Interactions with police officers, prosecutors, probation officers, judges, shelter workers, feminist advocates and even bailiffs affect the extent to which an individual victim is willing to take on this new identity. Do the police make an arrest or tell him to take a walk? Does the prosecutor press charges or *nolle prosequi* the case? Does the judge impose prison time or dismiss the case? Does she offer a stern lecture or mumble the charge and penalty? These are all indications of how seriously the legal system takes her rights. If the police are friendly to the man and fail to arrest him, if the judge suggests that battering is not a serious offense, and if the court imposes no prison sentence, this experience undermines the woman's rights subjectivity. If police act as if battered women do not have the right to complain about the violence of their husbands, then these women are discouraged from seeing themselves as having such a right. If their partners, relatives, friends, and neighbors tell battered women that a "good wife" does not take her husband to court and that she provoked him, she may also be deterred. Thus, an individual's willingness to take on rights depends on her experience trying to assert them. The more this experience reflects a serious belief that she is a person with a right not to be battered, the more willing she will be to take on this identity. On the other hand, if these rights are treated as insignificant, she may chose to give up and no longer think about her grievances in terms of rights.

To explore subjectivities produced by the encounter with the legal system, my research assistants and I interviewed thirty women and twenty-one men about their experiences with the legal system, and their reactions to the experience. This research was conducted in a small town in Hawai'i, a place typical of rural agricultural regions of the US, but different in its colonial and plantation past and contemporary diversity of ethnicity.[3] All of those interviewed had experiences with the family court and/or the district court, as well as participating in a court-mandated batterer intervention program or women's support group. The interviews were supplemented by an analysis of the discussions within women's support groups and men's batterers groups.[4]...

SHIFTING SUBJECTIVITIES

The post-structuralist concept of the self as the location of multiple and potentially contradictory subjectivities, each established within discourses and discursive practices, provides a helpful way to conceptualize the complex positioning of women who turn to the law in crises of violence. In Henrietta Moore's description of the post-structuralist gendered subject, each individual takes up multiple subject positions within a range of discourses and social practices, so that a single subject is not the same as a single individual.[5] What holds these multiple subjectivities together are the experience of identity, the physical grounding of the subject in a body, and the historical continuity of the subject.[6]

"If subjectivity is seen as singular, fixed, and coherent, it becomes very difficult to explain how it is that individuals constitute their sense of self—their self-representations as subjects—through several, often mutually contradictory subject positions, rather than through one singular subject position."[7] Instead of seeing gender as a single gender system, anthropology has moved toward an understanding of gender by examining how "individuals come to take up gendered subject positions through engagement with multiple discourses on gender."[8] Although this framework appears to emphasize choice, Moore emphasizes that there are dominant and subdominant discourses that are both reproduced and in some ways resisted.[9] This model opens up the possibility of multiple femininities and masculinities within the same context, onto which gender differences are again inscribed, so that some masculinities appear more feminine and others more masculine, with the hierarchical relationship between the genders reinscribed on these variations within a gender in a particular social context.[10] Moore notes that this theory of gender as consisting of multiple, possibly contradictory competing discourses enables the question, how do people take up a position in one discourse rather than another?[11]

This framework provides a way of thinking about battered women's experience with the law. In going to the law, a woman takes on a new subject position, defined in the discourses and social practices of the law. She tries it on, not abandoning her other subject positions as partner or wife, member of a kinship network that usually includes her partner's family as well as her own, along with other subject positions such as "local," Christian, and poor. She is, in a sense, seeing how it goes. The experimental subject position includes assertiveness, claims to autonomy, and mobilization of the power of the law. The encounter with the courts is an exploration of the dimensions of this position, the experience of taking it on, of seeing how it conforms with or contradicts other subject positions she occupies. There are risks: going to court typically precipitates an angry and hostile response from the partner. Indeed, her assumption of this new legally constituted subject position may be interpreted as a direct challenge to his masculinity. Insofar as women are required to confirm a man's masculinity by their adoption of a feminine subject position, "[t]he inability to maintain the fantasy of power triggers a crisis in the fantasy of identity, and violence is a means of resolving this crisis because it acts to reconfirm the nature of a masculinity otherwise denied."[12] Violence is then a sign of the struggle for the maintenance of certain fantasies of identity and power. Violence emerges, in this analysis, as deeply gendered and sexualized and as a consequence of her turning to the law for help.

The woman calling the police and pressing charges is thwarting the fantasy of power and identity of masculinity in dominant discourses. As her partner struggles to reassert his masculinity through reestablishing his control over her, she may find the new subject position within the law an alienating and empty one. It may disrupt her relations with her kin and her partner as she receives pressures to leave him and turn to a new source of support in social services and legal officials. This is a subject position shaped by the discourses of autonomy, choice, and reasonable behavior, not by love, anger, hurt, and ambivalence. The move into this subject position initiates a period of tension, a continual questioning if it is worth it. Those who press on, who continue to take on this subjectivity, are people for whom this new position has something to offer. Perhaps they have less to lose from others who oppose them.

Although there has clearly been a substantial increase in the number of women willing to turn to the courts, many try this position and discard it, returning to a subjectivity less challenging to their partners and perhaps to their kin. Such discarding can be temporary or permanent; individuals frequently proceed through a long sequence of putting on and taking off this subject position, perhaps holding it a little longer each time, depending on what the discursively constituted position of battered woman has to offer and the extent of contradiction with other subject positions. Indeed, women are choosing between two incompatible subject positions, one the rightsbearing subject, the other the good wife. Each represents a vision of the self that produces self-esteem, but the battered woman cannot simultaneously enact both. Choosing either one represents a failure of the other. The practices of the legal system are thus of critical significance to the woman's decision as she ambivalently moves in and out of this subjectivity. Fragmentary evidence around the country of an explosion of cases in the late 1980s followed by a leveling off in the mid-1990s suggests some deep and enduring ambivalence about the legally defined subject position for situations of battering. . . .

Gendered subjectivity is redefined by doing legal activities: through acting as a legally entitled subject in the context of these injuries. As women victimized by violence call the police, walk into courtrooms, fill out forms requesting restraining orders, tell their stories of violence and victimization in forms and in response to official queries, they enact a different self. Such performances reshape the way these women think about themselves and the relationship between their intimate social worlds and the law. Turning to the courts for help in incidents of violence by partners represents a disembedding of the individual in the structure of kin, neighbors, friends, and churches in favor of a new relationship to the state. That one is a subject of the state in paying taxes may be a recognized aspect of the way the law defines the self; the state's obligation to protect a wife from her husband's violence in the home, or even his overbearing and critical manner in the absence of physical violence, has until recently not been a recognized aspect of selves even in the legally constituted American society. Categories such as the private domain of the family, insulated from state supervision by the patriarchal authority of the husband, although at the same time fully constituted by the state in its capacity to marry and divorce, may exist at the level of the unrecognized, the taken for granted, the hegemonic. It is these categories that are challenged by contemporary feminist movements about violence against women. . . .

. . .[T]urning to the legal system for help is a difficult decision, in which the practices of the legal system itself are critically important. Even when a new law specifically criminalizing gender violence was passed in 1973 in Hawai'i, very few women filed cases. It was only after substantial changes in police practice, the elimination of the requirement to use an attorney to get a TRO, and greater attention to these cases by prosecutors and judges, that women began to turn to the law in larger numbers. The impact of an active feminist movement in the town, as well as increasing media attention, clearly affected women's willingness to complain. The law has constituted women as legal subjects no longer mediated by their embeddedness in family relationships, but now standing alone in relation to the state. At the same time, it has reduced the patriarchal privileges of males within the domain of the family. For poor families, such an opening to state surveillance was already well established by regulations governing welfare, child abuse, and housing allowances, and in earlier periods, vagrancy and alcoholism.

Thus, the new terrain is ambiguous, both offering a new legal self protected from violence by men, but providing in practice a far more limited and nuanced legal self whose protection is never fully guaranteed nor experienced. It is through experience, through encounters with the multiple responses of the police, prosecutors, courts, and probation officers, that a new legal subjectivity about gender violence is made, along with a new sense of marriage, family, community, and the place of the law. The law claims for itself the definition of gendered relationships within the family as well as outside the family, but ambivalently and uncertainly, creating areas of leniency and inaction that characterize this sphere of the law. Even as the law restricts men from using violence to control their partners, it does so in a contingent and variable fashion, incorporating the possibility of unmaking, as well as making, this change. There is a tension between the construction of new discourses of rights and the practices through which these promises are disclosed, which mediate the reconstitution of both male and female subjectivity.

One of the tensions is produced by the insistence of the legal system that the women it helps are "good victims."[13] Social movements that advocate the expansion of law into new domains represent the problem as requiring legal sanctions. Stories of innocent victims injured by malicious offenders are clearly the most powerful. These are the stories that have encouraged the law to engage in protecting women from intimate violence. The battered women's movement has always insisted on a broader and more complex analysis of the dynamics of battering,[14] but the law looks for innocent victims, labeling those who fight back as trouble and their problems as garbage cases.[15] The good victim in the law is not a woman who fights back, drinks or takes drugs along with the men, or abuses her children. When women act in violent and provocative ways or refuse to press charges or testify, legal officials are often frustrated. Women who do not fit the image of the good victim become redefined as troublesome and difficult and are likely to receive less assistance. Good victims are also those who follow through with their cases. To begin a legal case, then to drop it, then to go back for another TRO or to call the police again but not to testify in court, earns a woman the label of difficult and "bad" victim. Thus, the very hesitancy and ambivalence about making this identity change that women experience, as well as their desire to defend themselves, conspire to define them as "bad" victims. Obviously, representatives of the legal system and even some feminist shelter workers, are likely to be less supportive of the rights of those who are not "good" victims. And they are less likely to take on rights.

A new "good victim" is being constructed at this point, the battered child.[16] The child preserves an innocence that women seem not always to have. But this frame sometimes reveals the mother as abuser. Abusive mothers are sent to anger management programs as well as their partners, and those who refuse to leave their batterers face having their children removed by the state. Women now experience the expanded surveillance of the law, the demand to produce and analyze experiences with violence in order to have their children returned. And they must choose between staying with a violent man and giving up their children or keeping the children and giving up the man. Thus, the changing cultural construction of the good victim defines the privileged subject of legal assistance and excludes others as unworthy of help.

GENDERING THE TURN TO THE LAW

The interviews that my research assistants and I conducted, which are described in the introduction section of this article, indicate that the encounter with the law affects the way these people think about themselves in fundamental ways, but that there are enormous differences in its impact on men and women. While women respond by trying on and sometimes discarding what they usually see as a more powerful self, but also one whose adoption is scary, men resist and reject a diminished self that is not heard, is sometimes humiliated and ignored, and is subject to penalties both restrictive and expensive. The women talk about gaining courage and appreciating the help of the law, while the men talk about shock, anger, surprise, and a sense of betrayal by the women who have accused them. In an excruciating turn, the women typically feel some concern and even love for the men they have helped to humiliate while the men find solace in moments when the women drop charges or switch from a no-contact to a contact TRO. A woman's willingness to join with her partner in opposing or subverting the law recuperates some of his damaged identity as a man and allows him to confront the legal system, not as a diminished man whose wife no longer submits, but as a stronger man who still controls his wife and can count on her support. Thus, the woman assaults his masculinity by turning to the law, adopting its definition of her autonomous personhood and protection from violence, while gaining for herself greater control over his violence and domination in her relationship with him.

Insofar as gender hierarchies are mapped onto these new subjectivities, the woman could be said to become masculinized and the man feminized in this encounter. Concepts of masculinity and femininity are of course cultural products, culturally variable and the product of particular histories, but within a social space there is some level of shared understandings. I am referring to these concepts as they are located within the dominant American framework of masculinity and femininity, recognizing that there are regional, ethnic, class, and other variations within this general pattern. In the shape that gender takes within this community, the woman who gives in and withdraws from the legal process returns to a more feminized self and allows her male partner to recuperate his masculinity. Because gender is produced by such performances, the way that women and men chart courses through the tensions of violence and its legal regulation shapes their gendered selves. As they do law, they also do gender.

It is not surprising that women would adopt a tentative stance toward this transformation—trying it on, dropping it, trying it again—given the significance of the change and the mutually constitutive nature of gender. The way she plays gender affects the way the man with whom she is in a relationship can play gender. The move back to the more familiar femininity in which the man can oppositionally be a man is undeniably seductive, while the stance of refusing femininity opens her to his sense of betrayal, to the extent to which he is diminished both by the performances of the court and by her very rejection of feminine submissiveness. It is hardly surprising that this position seems scary to women and that they enter and leave it many times before finally seizing it more or less permanently as a new identity. Those women who have taken on this subject position, however, no longer express a sense of scariness and anxiety about court hearings and instead eagerly pursue their assailants in court. Such women may no longer be those most seriously victimized, leading some critics to argue that trivial incidents are coming under the scrutiny of the court. They are, however, the women who have moved through a series of experiments and reinforcements from others into a new subjectivity within the law. This probably accounts for what Judith Wittner finds is the court's central problem and "most baffling contradiction": women with the genuine and serious complaints of the type the court was designed to help frequently drop

out, while women with the most minor and trivial complaints were often those who were most energetic about prosecuting, eager to see the perpetrator punished, and willing to return to court many times.[17] As Ferraro and Pope observe, at the point of arrest there is a dramatic and irreconcilable clash between the culture of power embodied in the law and the relational culture within which battered women live.[18]

Women's ability and willingness to move into this subjectivity depends, of course, on how the law treats them. As the interviews indicate, the police play a critical role in either taking them seriously or telling them the bruises are insignificant or the assault minor. Women notice if the police chat and joke with the batterer. Both men and women attend closely to the demeanor of the judge, the things she says, and the extent to which penalties are actually imposed. As they move into this subjectivity, the support or opposition of kin and friends, including the man's kin, friends, and other women in the support group, are extremely important. One woman said that when she consulted with her friends, for example, they discovered that they were all in the same boat with her. Yet when they talked about their problems and hers, they did not urge her to leave the man. The staff of the feminist advocacy program, Alternatives to Violence (ATV) and the Shelter staff play critical roles in fostering this transformation of self. One woman, for example, said that the support of the ATV advocates in court was very helpful. "They really changed my life around." With the support of others in the women's support group, this woman said she was able to "tell off" her batterer, letting him know that he was "playing with her mind" and that she wanted him to leave her alone. She said in an interview that in the group she learned that despite her boyfriend's constant insults, she had nothing to be ashamed of. She was proud of the certificate she received from attending the support group, and commented that she and others framed them and put them on the wall. Taking on this new identity requires a social shift of some magnitude. For many abused women, their most important relationship is with the man. Taking on this subjectivity inevitably excludes him from her life unless he is willing to adopt the new identity the law offers him. Her ability to make this change depends on the social support she receives for the new identity offered to her by the law.

Difficult as the change is for women, the transformation for men into a new subjectivity that seems less masculine within dominant cultural frameworks is far more challenging. This new subjectivity represents the masculinity of a different social class, one to which few of these men have the education, income, or job skills to aspire. In effect, through the ATV program, the men are offered a masculinity developed by men of wealth and education in which authority over women depends on resources and allows some negotiation of power, an authority constructed by dominant whites, in place of that grounded in strength, physical competence, sexual prowess, and control over women favored by the working-class men in Hilo. As a Native Hawaiian man in the program said, "ATV teaches the haole way of handling conflicts." As Connell's work indicates, masculinities are multiple and developed within particular class and cultural contexts[19]. . . .

Within these general patterns, there is an important difference between those who are new to the law and those who have previous experience as the subjects of legal concern. Two of the men who were interviewed had long histories of court involvement for crimes dating back to their juvenile years. These men expressed none of the sense of outrage or humiliation of the other men; instead they appreciated the contributions of the program to their understanding of how to keep their partners. Some women, on the other hand, who have histories of involvement with the child protective services and thus have been in the position of receiving legal and social service scrutiny and control in order to get their children back, felt little of the sense of awe and scariness inherent in their new subjectivity in the law. They took a far more instrumental view toward what the law could do for them. Similarly, women who had toyed with this new subjectivity for some time and developed a more enduring commitment to it were more deliberate, strategic, and committed to legal remedies and more willing to press forward even when the law let them down.

The adoption or rejection of new subjectivities is not only about the discursive construction of the self in relationship to others, however. Identities cannot be simply assumed and discarded like clothes, although like clothes they are subject to constraint in choice and in the resources available to acquire them. These identities are linked to institutional systems that locate individuals within productive relationships that allow them to acquire skills and secure jobs or deny them these opportunities. For example, batterers' economic marginality means that they cannot adopt the proffered resource-rich expression of masculinity in which power depends on economic providing rather than on violence. Gendered identities are also located within historically created and regionally specific class and ethnic structures. In Hilo, this includes colonialism and the plantation system. The cultural meanings of masculinity and femininity are pulled out of the matrix of opportunities and disabilities provided by these class and ethnic structures, including Native Hawaiian warrior symbolism, sexual prowess among groups which immigrated largely as single males, such as Filipinos, and hard drinking and risk-taking, often sources of masculine pride among whites. These are historically produced subject positions, shaped by larger institutional structures and adopted or discarded only within the constraints of wealth, color, and class. They provide repertoires of gendered subjectivities, and the law does as well. . . .

Conclusions

. . .Women's greater willingness to use the law to deal with gender violence is a response to a powerful feminist movement to redefine the meaning of battering from an inevitable feature of everyday life—an inescapable risk—to a domain of behavior subject to prevention and change. But it is also a response to the law's greater willingness to treat complainants with respect and to take their problems seriously. A more complex set of penalties for batterers has developed both within and outside the law. Of particular importance is the development of new forms of governance that focus on self-management and a redefinition of masculinity. These interventions represent a dramatic shift away from earlier ideas of deterrence through punishment. Instead of changing behavior by imposing punishment, the law now channels offenders into group environments in which their use of violence in work as well as family settings and their ideas about gender relationships come under scrutiny and critique. New images of egalitarian gender relations based on negotiation and responsibility for naming and knowing feelings are taught to men named as batterers. Batterers meet in quasi-therapeutic settings in which they are encouraged to share their experiences and their feelings and learn to name and understand those feelings. At the same time, women are advised that they have rights and encouraged to use the courts to assert these rights. Contemporary systems of governance focus on providing safety for the woman and on retraining batterers, helping them to name and anticipate their feelings, to see new dimensions of choice for their actions, to value themselves, and to change their beliefs about masculinity and marriage.

The new regime affects men differently from women. It has emancipated women from the governance of their husbands and partners and provided them a more autonomous subjectivity defined by a feminist interpretation of the law as providing them the right not to be battered, no matter what they have done. At the same time, it has reduced men's rights to discipline and control their wives. Men sometimes report surprise, dismay, and anger that things that they could do in the past with impunity now earn them prison sentences and the requirement to attend batterers intervention programs. There is no increase in autonomy or freedom experienced by these men; instead they feel more strongly the effect of new forms of governance, directed not only at punishing them but reforming them, training them in new practices of masculinity and performing gender roles in the family. For many of the women, the entitlement to rights from the law is a new experience, as is the support for their autonomy offered by shelter and program staff and the judiciary. For some of the men, state supervision and control is a familiar experience. Almost a third of the men interviewed had previous arrests and some have long histories with the juvenile and adult courts. Almost half the men in the feminist batterer program have been arrested for something in addition to battering according to intake interviews. Thus, the men brought into the court and the violence control program have experienced the criminal justice system in other areas.

These changes do not fall equally on all social classes or races. Working class and poor women are more likely to use the law for help because they lack expensive alternatives such as private counseling or moving to a new house. Poor men are more likely to end up in the courts and treatment programs. Men with race and class privilege have typically escaped the criminalization of their violence in the home, while psychological and economic violence have not been defined as crimes. Men of higher social classes often escape the feminist training program. In the earlier years, a few were sent to the treatment program and protested loudly about the infringement on their rights. More recently, men with greater means are buying their way out of the violence control program through recourse to private counseling services, counseling through their churches, or perhaps changing their patterns of battering from physical to more emotional and verbal strategies. They are more likely to hire an attorney. It is not that only poor men batter, but only poor batterers end up in court and ATV. It is impossible to know how much battering remains hidden behind window shades and unreported to the police. There has been a strong challenge to patriarchal authority in this movement, but it is, in effect, predominantly lower class men who feel this challenge.

The right not to be battered and the capacity to make choices are important extensions of the definition of the autonomous self to a relatively poor and marginalized group of women. Those who arrive in court accused of battering are those whose partners or neighbors were willing to complain. Yet, the right of women to complain about violence has come at a cost: women are encouraged or forced to testify against their partners in court, a dangerous and often undesirable form of participation. As the battered women's movement has come to depend on the legal system for support and for funding, it has had to compromise its support for women, to tone down its rhetoric of patriarchy, and to move toward a service delivery system in which its emancipatory potential is compromised by the need to service cases and to get women to testify. In order for women to adopt this new sense of rights, however, their initial forays into the legal arena require experiences of support from participants in that arena as they struggle to redefine a self between the obligations of the good wife and the entitlements of the autonomous self not to be hit. This is a difficult journey that inevitably means hesitation and vacillation.

This analysis suggests that the adoption of a rights consciousness about a particular form of behavior requires a shift in subjectivity, one that depends on wider cultural understandings and individual experience. It is in the particular interactions and encounters of an individual that this subjectivity shift takes place. That the adoption of rights depends on individual experiences in the social world has significance for a range of rights-based social movements from pay equity and mental health rights to human rights. Such adoptions depend not only on educating people about the availability of rights, but also putting into place practices within legal systems that will reinforce the experience of these rights. This reinforcement depends on social encounters in which those endeavoring to exercise rights, and thus redefining their previous relationships, find positive reinforcement for this change. Human rights are difficult for individuals to adopt as a self-definition in the absence of institutions that will take these rights seriously when they are claimed by individuals. Rights cannot precede concerns about implementation. This analysis suggests that implementation is fundamental to establishing human rights consciousness.

Notes

1. *See* Elizabeth M. Schneider, *Battered Women and Feminist Lawmaking* (2000).

2. *See id.* In her recent comprehensive discussion of law and the battered women's movement, Schneider asks about the implications of using a rights approach for this problem. As she points out, early activists saw the problem as the product of larger structural forces but also relied on the law as a way to define the problem and to intervene in it. The structural analysis of gender violence has persisted in the global human rights movement but is increasingly missing from the US movement. *Id. See also* Susan Schechter, *Women and Male Violence: The Visions and Struggles of the Battered Women's Movement* (1982).

3. Sally Engle Merry, *Colonizing, Hawai'i: The Cultural Power of Law* (2000).

4. Each of these interviews was done in person and lasted between one and two and a half hours. I did twelve of the interviews and my research assistants did the rest. Fourteen of the women's interviews were conducted by Leilani Miller, six by Marilyn Brown, seven by

Madelaine Adelman, and three by me. Leilani Miller's method was to read to the person interviewed what she had written to verify that she had written it in their words while Madelaine taped the interviews. I interviewed nine men, Leilani Miller interviewed six, Linda Andres talked to three, Marilyn Brown two, and Joy Adapon one, all of whom were research assistants on the project. These interviews were conducted between 1991 and 1994, the years of the greatest expansion of gender violence cases in the courts. The interviews included both partners in six couples, although each member was interviewed separately. Interviews were solicited by researchers who attended the men's and women's groups and invited participants to volunteer in exchange for a small stipend. Although interviewees were told that the research was an independent project, it is very likely that they saw the project as closely connected to the ATV program itself.

5. Henrietta Moore, *The Problem of Explaining Violence in the Social Sciences,* in Sex and Violence: Issues in Representation and Experience 141 (Penelope Harvey & Peter Gow eds., 1994).

6. *See id.*

7. *Id.* at 141.

8. *Id.* at 142.

9. *Id.*

10. *Id.* at 146–147.

11. *Id.* at 149.

12. *Id.* at 154.

13. The idea of a "good victim" emerged from my ethnographic research with individuals working with battered women in the courts and women's centers.

14. *See* Schechter, supra note 2.

15. *See* Sally Engle Merry, *Getting Justice and Getting Even: Legal Consciousness Among Working Class Americans* (1990).

16. *See* Barbara J. Nelson, *Making an Issue of Child Abuse* (1984).

17. Judith Wittner, *Reconceptualizing Agency in Domestic Violence Court,* in Community Activism and Feminist Politics: Organizing Across Race, Class, and Gender 88–89 (Nancy A. Naples ed., 1998).

18. Kathleen J. Ferraro & Lucille Pope, *Irreconcilable Differences: Battered Women, Police, and the Law,* in Legal Response to Wife Assault 96–127 (N. Zoe Hilton ed., 1993).

19. R. W. Connell, *Masculinities* (1995); see also Matthew C. Gutmann, *The Meaning of Macho: Being a Man in Mexico City* (1996); Matthew C. Gutmann, *The Ethnographic Gambit: Women and the Negotiation of Masculinity in Mexico City,* 24 American Ethnologist 833–855 (1997); Matthew C. Gutmann, *Trafficking in Men: The Anthropology of Masculinity,* 26 Annual Rev. Anthropology 385–409 (1997); David Gilmore, *Manhood in the Making: Cultural Concepts of Masculinity (1990).*

NOTES AND QUESTIONS

1. What does Merry mean by "multiple subjectivities"? How does this idea help us to think about a battered woman's experience with the law? Can you relate this notion to Morgan's discussion in Chapter 25 of why women do or do not take advantage of statutory protections against sexual harassment?

2. What is a "rights-defined identity?" How does this concept help an individual distinguish between a rights violation and a less serious personal problem? How do you differentiate between the two in your own life? How strong is your rights-defined identity?

3. Why is external affirmation so important to what Merry calls a "rights-defined self"? What type of people are most or least likely to get this kind of external affirmation (consider race, class, gender, etc.)? In the other readings in this chapter are there examples in which the practice of the law has either affirmed or undermined a woman's rights-defined identity?

4. According to Merry, what factors are most important in "the adoption or rejection of new subjectivities"? How similar is her analysis to Felstiner, Abel, and

Sarat's discussion (Chapter 15) of the emergence and transformation of disputes?

5. What is a "good victim"? Compare Merry's discussion of this idea to Estrich's (Chapter 24). How does the legal system's treatment of "good victims" undermine the concept that *all* women have the right to protection from gender violence?

6. For Merry, a criminal statute against gender violence cannot by itself offer women access justice—it does not open law's door wide *enough* for many victimized woman to pass through. Merry argues that the law must, in practice and in attitude, vindicate the woman's funda-mental right to be protected from gender violence (e.g. rape, sexual harassment, domestic abuse). She points to gendered hierarchies of power in our society and demands that the law actively empower women to seek broader rights. How compelling is her argument? What, if anything, does it add to the debate between Abel (Chapter 17) and Huber (Chapter 16) (i.e., "crisis of injuries" vs. "litigation explosion")?

Section VII

Who Speaks and Who Is Heard: The Continuing Significance of Class

Chapter 27

Goldberg v. Kelly

Can and do poor people receive fair and equal legal treatment? Or is the law, as Hay (Chapter 13) suggests, inevitably tied to existing structures of social inequality? Do available mechanisms make it possible for the poor to make their voices heard in the legal system? What assumptions do legal officials make about persons living on state assistance?

These questions have been perennial sources of concern for legal scholars. As we saw in the last chapter, the law is not neutral in regard to our social attributes. The law is socially organized. Yet it remains committed to the principle of formal equality. This principle "guarantees" that people will be treated equally regardless of their material or social standing, or that law will impose no additional disadvantage on those already disadvantaged by their social standing. This guarantee is as relevant to the question of law's accessibility as it is in other aspects of the relations of citizens and the law.

The next three readings describe the conditions of people on welfare. Each asks us to think about the complex relations of law and citizens under conditions in which the government is the primary source of material subsistence for them. Does, or should, law guarantee to such persons a right to welfare, one which has never been recognized in our constitutional tradition?

How about procedural rights in regard to decisions about eligibility for welfare? Should law recognize and respect such rights? This question implicates the Fourteenth Amendment's due process clause, which says that no citizen shall be "deprived of life, liberty, or property without due process of law." Before the government im-poses a penalty or restriction, it must provide the person being penalized or restricted a chance to contest the government's action. But is welfare a form of "property" the deprivation of which implicates the Fourteenth Amendment? And, are procedural rights useful and productive when people have ongoing relations, such as those between welfare workers and their clients?

In the middle of the twentieth century, there was a "due process revolution" in administrative law. In area after area, rights to notice, hearings, and the opportunity to be heard were recognized. The government, it was argued, created certain "statutory entitlements" when it started public assistance programs and defined eligibility standards for welfare recipients. Goldberg v. Kelly, the next reading, is a landmark in this due process revolution, extending, as it does, due process to persons on welfare. It treats welfare as a kind of property that, once it has been granted, cannot be taken away without a hearing.

As you read the decision, you will encounter several interesting arguments. One is an argument about the proper role of judges in interpreting the Constitution. Like the debate between Justices Rehnquist and Blackmun in the DeShaney case (Chapter 3), here Justice Black accuses Justice Breenan of illegitimate judicial activism, that is, of reading into the Constitutional text things that are just not there. You will also encounter different perceptions of the welfare bureaucracy. Finally, Justice Black, in his dissent, predicts that the result in Goldberg will make it more difficult for people to get on welfare in the first place. His prediction, perhaps not surprisingly, turned out to be wrong. Welfare rolls continued to grow in the 1970s, 1980s, and into the 1990s.

At least in theory, Goldberg guaranteed people on welfare that they would not be treated in an arbitrary manner when it came to the termination of welfare benefits. It made law a vehicle for rationalizing the bureaucracy, which, in the late twentieth century, was more and more important in people's lives.

Mr. Justice Brennan Delivered the Opinion of the Court

The question for decision is whether a State that terminates public assistance payments to a particular recipient without affording him the opportunity for an evidentiary hearing prior to termination denies the recipient procedural due process in violation of the Due Process Clause of the Fourteenth Amendment.

This action was brought in the District Court for the Southern District of New York by residents of New York City receiving financial aid under the federally assisted program of Aid to Families with Dependent Children (AFDC) or under New York State's general Home Relief program.[1] Their complaint alleged that the New York State and New York City officials administering these programs terminated, or were about to terminate, such aid without prior notice and hearing, thereby denying them due process of law.[2] At the time the suits were filed there was no requirement of prior notice or hearing of any kind before termination of financial aid. However, the State and city adopted procedures for notice and hearing after the suits were brought, and the plaintiffs, appellees here, then challenged the constitutional adequacy of those procedures. . . .

I

The constitutional issue to be decided, therefore, is the narrow one whether the Due Process Clause requires that the recipient be afforded an evidentiary hearing before the termination of benefits.[3] . . .

Appellant does not contend that procedural due process is not applicable to the termination of welfare benefits. Such benefits are a matter of statutory entitlement for persons qualified to receive them.[4] Their termination involves state action that adjudicates important rights. The constitutional challenge cannot be answered by an argument that public assistance benefits are "a 'privilege' and not a 'right.'" Shapiro v. Thompson, 394 U.S. 618, 627 n. 6 (1969). . . .

It is true, of course, that some governmental benefits may be administratively terminated without affording the recipient a pre-termination evidentiary hearing.[5] But we agree with the District Court that when welfare is discontinued, only a pre-termination evidentiary hearing provides the recipient with procedural due process. Cf. *Sniadach v. Family Finance Corp.*, 395 U.S. 337 (1969). For qualified recipients, welfare provides the means to obtain essential food, clothing, housing, and medical care. Cf. *Nash v. Florida Industrial Commission*, 389 U.S. 235, 239 (1967). Thus the crucial factor in this context—a factor not present in the case of the blacklisted government contractor, the discharged government employee, the taxpayer denied a tax exemption, or virtually anyone else whose governmental entitlements are ended—is that termination of aid pending resolution of a controversy over eligibility may deprive an eligible recipient of the very means by which to live while he waits. Since he lacks independent resources, his situation becomes immediately desperate. His need to concentrate upon finding the means for daily subsistence, in turn, adversely affects his ability to seek redress from the welfare bureaucracy.[6]

Moreover, important governmental interests are promoted by affording recipients a pre-termination evidentiary hearing. From its founding the Nation's basic commitment has been to foster the dignity and well-being of all persons within its borders. We have come to recognize that forces not within the control of the poor contribute to their poverty.[7] This perception, against the background of our traditions, has significantly influenced the development of the contemporary public assistance system. Welfare, by meeting the basic demands of subsistence, can help bring within the reach of the poor the same opportunities that are available to others to participate meaningfully in the life of the community. At the same time, welfare guards against the societal malaise that may flow from a widespread sense of unjustified frustration and insecurity. Public assistance, then, is not mere charity, but a means to "promote the general Welfare, and secure the Blessings of Liberty to ourselves and our Posterity." The same governmental interests that counsel the provision of welfare, counsel as well its uninterrupted provision to those eligible to receive it; pre-termination evidentiary hearings are indispensable to that end.

Appellant does not challenge the force of these considerations but argues that they are outweighed by countervailing governmental interests in conserving fiscal and administrative resources. These interests, the argument goes, justify the delay of any evidentiary hearing until after discontinuance of the grants. Summary adjudication protects the public fiscal by stopping payments promptly upon discovery of reason to believe that a recipient is no longer eligible. Since most terminations are accepted without challenge, summary adjudication also conserves both the fiscal and administrative time and energy by reducing the number of evidentiary hearings actually held.

We agree with the District Court, however, that these governmental interests are not overriding in the welfare context. The requirement of a prior hearing doubtless involves some greater expense, and the benefits paid to ineligible recipients pending decision at the hearing probably cannot be recouped, since these recipients are likely to be judgment-proof. But the State is not without weapons to minimize these increased costs. Much of the drain on fiscal and administrative resources can be reduced by developing procedures for prompt pre-termination hearings and by skillful use of personnel and facilities. Indeed, the very provision for a post-termination evidentiary hearing in New York's Home Relief program is itself cogent evidence that the State recognizes the primacy of the public interest in correct eligibility determinations and therefore in the provision of procedural safeguards. Thus, the interest of the eligible recipient in uninterrupted receipt of public assistance, coupled with the State's interest that his payments not be erroneously terminated, clearly outweighs the State's competing concern to prevent any increase in its fiscal and administrative burdens. As the District Court correctly concluded, "the stakes are simply too high for the welfare recipient, and the possibility for honest error or irritable misjudgment too great, to allow termination of aid without giving the recipient a chance, if he so desires, to be fully informed of the case against him so that he may contest its basis and produce evidence in rebuttal." 294 F.Supp., at 904–905.

II

We also agree with the District Court, however, that the pre-termination hearing need not take the form of a judicial or quasi-judicial trial. We bear in mind that the statutory "fair hearing" will provide the recipient with a full administrative review.[8] Accordingly, the pre-termination hearing has one function only: to produce an initial determination of the validity of the welfare department's grounds for discontinuance of payments in order to protect a recipient against an erroneous termination of his benefits. Cf. *Sniadach v. Family Finance Corp.*, 395 U.S. 337, 343 (1969) (HARLAN, J., concurring). Thus, a complete record and a comprehensive opinion, which would serve primarily to facilitate judicial review and to guide future decisions, need not be provided at the pre-termination stage. We recognize, too, that both welfare authorities and recipients have an interest in relatively speedy resolution of questions of eligibility, that they are used to dealing with one another informally, and that some welfare departments have very burdensome caseloads. These considerations justify the limitation of the pre-termination hearing to minimum procedural safeguards, adapted to the particular characteristics of welfare recipients, and to the limited nature of the controversies to be resolved. We wish to add that we, no less than the dissenters, recognize the importance of not imposing upon the States or the Federal Government in this developing field of law any procedural requirements beyond those demanded by rudimentary due process.

"The fundamental requisite of due process of law is the opportunity to be heard." *Grannis v. Ordean*, 234 U.S. 385, 394 (1914). The hearing must be "at a meaningful time and in a meaningful manner." *Armstrong v. Manzo*, 380 U.S. 545, 552 (1965). In the present context these principles require that a recipient have timely and adequate notice detailing the reasons for a proposed termination, and an effective opportunity to defend by confronting any adverse witnesses and by presenting his own arguments and evidence orally. These rights are important in cases such as those before us, where recipients have challenged proposed terminations as resting on incorrect or misleading factual premises or on misapplication of rules or policies to the facts of particular cases.[9] . . .

MR. JUSTICE BLACK, DISSENTING

In the last half century the United States, along with many, perhaps most, other nations of the world, has moved far toward becoming a welfare state, that is, a nation that for one reason or another taxes its most affluent people to help support, feed, clothe, and shelter its less fortunate citizens. The result is that today more than nine million men, women, and children in the United States receive some kind of state or federally financed public assistance in the form of allowances or gratuities, generally paid them periodically, usually by the week, month, or quarter.[10] Since these gratuities are paid on the basis of need, the list of recipients is not static, and some people go off the lists and others are added from time to time. These ever-changing lists put a constant administrative burden on government and it certainly could not have reasonably anticipated that this burden would include the ad-

ditional procedural expense imposed by the Court today.

The dilemma of the ever-increasing poor in the midst of constantly growing affluence presses upon us and must inevitably be met within the framework of our democratic constitutional government, if our system is to survive as such. It was largely to escape just such pressing economic problems and attendant government repression that people from Europe, Asia, and other areas settled this country and formed our Nation. Many of those settlers had personally suffered from persecutions of various kinds and wanted to get away from governments that had unrestrained powers to make life miserable for their citizens. It was for this reason, or so I believe, that on reaching these new lands the early settlers undertook to curb their governments by confining their powers within written boundaries, which eventually became written constitutions.[11] They wrote their basic charters as nearly as men's collective wisdom could do so as to proclaim to their people and their officials an emphatic command that: "Thus far and no farther shall you go; and where we neither delegate powers to you, nor prohibit your exercise of them, we the people are left free."[12]

Representatives of the people of the Thirteen Original Colonies spent long, hot months in the summer of 1787 in Philadelphia, Pennsylvania, creating a government of limited powers. They divided it into three departments—Legislative, Judicial, and Executive. The Judicial Department was to have no part whatever in making any laws. In fact proposals looking to vesting some power in the Judiciary to take part in the legislative process and veto laws were offered, considered, and rejected by the Constitutional Convention.[13] In my judgment there is not one word, phrase, or sentence from the beginning to the end of the Constitution from which it can be inferred that judges were granted any such legislative power. True, *Marbury v. Madison*, 1 Cranch 137 (1803), held, and properly, I think, that courts must be the final interpreters of the Constitution, and I recognize that the holding can provide an opportunity to slide imperceptibly into constitutional amendment and law making. But when federal judges use this judicial power for legislative purposes, I think they wander out of their field of vested powers and transgress into the area constitutionally assigned to the Congress and the people. That is precisely what I believe the Court is doing in this case. Hence my dissent. . . .

I would have little, if any, objection to the majority's decision in this case if it were written as the report of the House Committee on Education and Labor, but as an opinion ostensibly resting on the language of the Constitution I find it woefully deficient. Once the verbiage is pared away it is obvious that this Court today adopts the views of the District Court "that to cut off a welfare recipient in the face of . . . 'brutal need' without a prior hearing of some sort is unconscionable," and therefore, says the Court, unconstitutional. The majority reaches this result by a process of weighing "the recipient's interest in avoiding" the termination of welfare benefits against "the governmental interest in summary adjudication." Ante, at 263. Today's balancing act requires a "pre-termination evidentiary hearing," yet there is nothing that indicates what tomorrow's balance will be. Although the majority attempts to bolster its decision with limited quotations from prior cases, it is obvious that today's result does not depend on the language of the Constitution itself or the principles of other decisions, but solely on the collective judgment of the majority as to what would be a fair and humane procedure in this case. . . .

The Court apparently feels that this decision will benefit the poor and needy. In my judgment the eventual result will be just the opposite. While today's decision requires only an administrative, evidentiary hearing, the inevitable logic of the approach taken will lead to constitutionally imposed, time-consuming delays of a full adversary process of administrative and judicial review. In the next case the welfare recipients are bound to argue that cutting off benefits before judicial review of the agency's decision is also a denial of due process. Since, by hypothesis, termination of aid at that point may still "deprive an *eligible* recipient of the very means by which to live while he waits," ante, at 264, I would be surprised if the weighing process did not compel the conclusion that termination without full judicial review would be unconscionable. After all, at each step, as the majority seems to feel, the issue is only one of weighing the government's pocketbook against the actual survival of the recipient, and surely that balance must always tip in favor of the individual. Similarly today's decision requires only the opportunity to have the benefit of counsel at the administrative hearing, but it is difficult to believe that the same reasoning process would not require the appointment of counsel, for otherwise the right to counsel is a meaningless one since these people are too poor to hire their own advocates. Cf. *Gideon v. Wainwright*, 372 U.S. 335, 344 (1963). Thus the end result of today's decision may well be that the government, once it decides to give welfare benefits, cannot reverse that decision until the recipient has had the benefits of full administrative and judicial review, including, of course, the opportunity to present his case to this Court. Since this process will usually entail a delay of several years, the inevitable result of such a constitutionally imposed burden will be that the government will not put a claimant on the rolls initially until it has made an exhaustive investigation to determine his eligibility. While this Court will perhaps have insured that no needy person will be taken off the rolls without a full "due process" proceeding, it will also have insured that many will never get on the rolls, or at least that they will remain destitute during the lengthy proceedings followed to determine initial eligibility.

For the foregoing reasons I dissent from the Court's holding. The operation of a welfare state is a new experiment for our Nation. For this reason, among others, I feel that new experiments in carrying out a welfare program should not be frozen into our constitutional structure. They should be left, as are other legislative determinations, to the Congress and the legislatures that the people elect to make our laws.

Notes

1. AFDC was established by the Social Security Act of 1935, 49 Stat. 627, as amended, 42 U. S. C. §§ 601–610 (1964 ed. and Supp. IV). It is a categorical assistance program supported by federal grants-in-aid but administered by the States according to regulations of the Secretary of Health, Education, and Welfare. See N. Y. Social Welfare Law §§ 343–362 (1966). We considered other aspects of AFDC in *King v. Smith*, 392 U.S. 309 (1968), and in *Shapiro v. Thompson*, 394 U.S. 618 (1969).

   Home Relief is a general assistance program financed and administered solely by New York state and local governments. N. Y. Social Welfare Law §§ 157–165 (1966), since July 1, 1967, Social Services Law §§ 157–166. It assists any person unable to support himself or to secure support from other sources. Id., § 158.

2. Two suits were brought and consolidated in the District Court. The named plaintiffs were 20 in number, including intervenors. Fourteen had been or were about to be cut off from AFDC, and six from Home Relief. During the course of this litigation most, though not all, of the plaintiffs either received a "fair hearing" (see infra, at 259-260) or were restored to the rolls without a hearing. However, even in many of the cases where payments have been resumed, the underlying questions of eligibility that resulted in the bringing of this suit have not been resolved. For example, Mrs. Altagracia Guzman alleged that she was in danger of losing AFDC payments for failure to cooperate with the City Department of Social Services in suing her estranged husband. She contended that the departmental policy requiring such cooperation was inapplicable to the facts of her case. The record shows that payments to Mrs. Guzman have not been terminated, but there is no indication that the basic dispute over her duty to cooperate has been resolved, or that the alleged danger of termination has been removed. Home Relief payments to Juan DeJesus were terminated because he refused to accept counseling and rehabilitation for drug addiction. Mr. DeJesus maintains that he does not use drugs. His payments were restored the day after his complaint was filed. But there is nothing in the record to indicate that the underlying factual dispute in his case has been settled.

3. Appellant does not question the recipient's due process right to evidentiary review *after* termination. For a general discussion of the provision of an evidentiary hearing prior to termination, see Comment, The Constitutional Minimum for the Termination of Welfare Benefits: The Need for and Requirements of a Prior Hearing, 68 Mich. L. Rev. 112 (1969).

4. It may be realistic today to regard welfare entitlements as more like "property" than a "gratuity." Much of the existing wealth in this country takes the form of rights that do not fall within traditional common-law concepts of property. It has been aptly noted that "society today is built around entitlement. The automobile dealer has his franchise, the doctor and lawyer their professional licenses, the worker his union membership, contract, and pension rights, the executive his contract and stock options; all are devices to aid security and independence. Many of the most important of these entitlements now flow from government: subsidies to farmers and businessmen, routes for airlines and channels for television stations; long-term contracts for defense, space, and education; social security pensions for individuals. Such sources of security, whether private or public, are no longer regarded as luxuries or gratuities; to the recipients they are essentials, fully deserved, and in no sense a form of charity. It is only the poor whose entitlements, although recognized by public policy, have not been effectively enforced." Reich, Individual Rights and Social Welfare: The Emerging Legal Issues, 74 Yale L. J. 1245, 1255 (1965). See also Reich, The New Property, 73 Yale L. J. 733 (1964).

5. One Court of Appeals has stated: "In a wide variety of situations, it has long been recognized that where harm to the public is threatened, and the private interest infringed is reasonably deemed to be of less importance, an official body can take summary action pending a later hearing." *R. A. Holman & Co. v. SEC,* 112 U. S. App. D. C. 43, 47, 299 F.2d 127, 131, cert. denied, 370 U.S. 911 (1962) (suspension of exemption from stock registration requirement). See also, for example, *Ewing v. Mytinger & Casselberry, Inc.,* 339 U.S. 594 (1950) (seizure of mislabeled vitamin product); *North American Cold Storage Co. v. Chicago,* 211 U.S. 306 (1908) (seizure of food not fit for human use); *Yakus v. United States,* 321 U.S. 414 (1944) (adoption of wartime price regulations); *Gonzalez v. Freeman,* 118 U. S. App. D. C. 180, 334 F.2d 570 (1964) (disqualification of a contractor to do business with the Government). In *Cafeteria & Restaurant Workers Union v. McElroy,* supra, at 896, summary dismissal of a public employee was upheld because "in [its] proprietary military capacity, the Federal Government . . . has traditionally exercised unfettered control," and because the case involved the Government's "dispatch of its own internal affairs." Cf. *Perkins v. Lukens Steel Co.,* 310 U.S. 113 (1940).

6. His impaired adversary position is particularly telling in light of the welfare bureaucracy's difficulties in reaching correct decisions on eligibility. See Comment, Due Process and the Right to a Prior Hearing in Welfare Cases, 37 Ford. L. Rev. 604, 610–611 (1969).

7. See, e. g., Reich, supra, n. 4, 74 Yale L. J., at 1255.

8. Due process does not, of course, require two hearings. If, for example, a State simply wishes to continue benefits until after a "fair" hearing there will be no need for a preliminary hearing.

9. This case presents no question requiring our determination whether due process requires only an opportunity for written submission, or an opportunity both for written submission and oral argument, where there are no factual issues in dispute or where the application of the rule of law is not intertwined with factual issues. See *FCC v. WJR,* 337 U.S. 265, 275–277 (1949).

10. This figure includes all recipients of Old-Age Assistance, Aid to Families with Dependent Children, Aid to the Blind, Aid to the Permanently and Totally Disabled, and general assistance. In this case appellants are AFDC and general assistance recipients. In New York State alone there are 951,000 AFDC recipients and 108,000 on general assistance. In the Nation as a whole the comparable figures are 6,080,000 and 391,000. U.S. Bureau of the Census, Statistical Abstract of the United States: 1969 (90th ed.), Table 435, p. 297.

11. The goal of a written constitution with fixed limits on governmental power had long been desired. Prior to our colonial constitutions, the closest man had come to realizing this goal was the political movement of the Levellers in England in the 1640's, J. Frank, *The Levellers* (1955). In 1647 the Levellers proposed the adoption of An Agreement of the People which set forth written limitations on the English Government. This proposal contained many of the ideas which later were incorporated in the constitutions of this Nation. *Id.,* at 135–147.

12. This command is expressed in the Tenth Amendment:

> "The powers not delegated to the United States by the Constitution, nor prohibited by it to the States, are reserved to the States respectively, or to the people."

13. It was proposed that members of the judicial branch would sit on a Council of Revision which would consider legislation and have the power to veto it. This proposal was rejected. J. Elliot, 1 Elliot's Debates 160, 164, 214 (Journal of the Federal Convention); 395, 398 (Yates' Minutes); vol. 5, pp. 151, 164–166, 344–349 (Madison's Notes) (Lippincott ed. 1876). It was also suggested that The Chief Justice would serve as a member of the President's executive council, but this proposal was similarly rejected. *Id.,* vol. 5, pp. 442, 445, 446, 462.

NOTES AND QUESTIONS

1. The Fourteenth Amendment protects against deprivations of "life, liberty, or property without due process of law." Should the law equate the statutory entitlement of welfare with the property of an individual? Is welfare a right or a privilege? Is there a case to be made that welfare, as a public benefit, belongs to the public and not to the recipient?

2. According to the majority in *Goldberg*, the government has the right to terminate public benefits without due process in certain cases, but must respect due process in others. What differentiates the two types of public benefits? On what grounds does the Court reason that welfare benefits fit more closely into the latter category?

3. Why does a hearing *after* termination of welfare benefits not fulfill the requirements of due process?

4. In the *Goldberg* decision, is Justice Black right to fault the majority for illegitimate judicial activism? Is the majority legislating or simply interpreting the legal obligations that accompany existing legislation?

5. How compelling is Justice Black's slippery slope argument? In hindsight, we know that the fears he articulated did not materialize, but does this necessarily mean that they were irrational? Why or why not?

6. The majority ruled that the Fourteenth Amendment entitles welfare recipients to the procedural requirements "demanded by rudimentary due process." Is it acceptable for the Court to qualify the degree of due process afforded poor people? If indigents have the "right" to due process in this case, then why are they any less entitled to "robust" due process?

Reprinted from: *Goldberg v. Kelly*, Commissioner of Social Services of the City of New York, 397 U.S. 254 (1970). ✦

Chapter 28

Subordination, Rhetorical Survival Skills, and Sunday Shoes

Notes on the Hearing of Mrs. G.

Lucie E. White

Granting people on welfare a hearing before their benefits can be removed is an important legal right, but it tells us little about how poor people are treated when they exercise that right. As the selection by Merry (Chapter 26) shows, the way people are treated by legal officials is the key to whether they believe that they can turn to, and rely on, law for redress of problems or grievances. This is as true for people on welfare as for victims of domestic violence. How they get treated is a function of prevailing social understandings of what it means to be on welfare.

Lucie E. White analyses what happens when welfare recipients try to take advantage of the legal protections afforded by Goldberg v. Kelly. *White argues that the opportunity to be heard is but one component of what she labels "meaningful participation." She tells the story of Mrs. G., a woman on welfare who contested a decision concerning an alleged overpayment of money, taking advantage of the hearing procedure made possible by* Goldberg. *White argues that "social, economic, and cultural forces" con-*

spired to devalue what Mrs. G. had to say, making access to law a purely formal, rather than substantively meaningful, event.

When White speaks about forces in society, the economy, and culture that limit the accessibility of law for welfare recipients, what does she have in mind? Do you think that the situation of people on welfare in regard to access to law is different from the situation of the working poor? Is White asking too much of law when she demands "meaningful participation"?

> "The profound political intervention of feminism has been . . . to redefine the very nature of what is deemed political. . . . The literary ramifications of this shift involve the discovery of the rhetorical survival skills of the formerly unvoiced. Lies, secrets, silences, and deflections of all sorts are routes taken by voices or messages not granted full legitimacy in order not to be altogether lost."
>
> —B. Johnson, *A World of Difference*

In 1970 the Supreme Court decided *Goldberg v. Kelly*.[1] The case, which held that welfare recipients are entitled to an oral hearing prior to having their benefits reduced or terminated, opened up a far-reaching conversation among legal scholars over the meaning of procedural justice. All voices in this conversation endorse a normative floor that would guarantee all persons the same formal opportunities to be heard in adjudicatory proceedings, regardless of such factors as race, gender, or class identity. Beyond this minimal normative consensus, however, two groups of scholars have very different visions of what procedural justice would entail. One group, seeing procedure as an *instrument* of just government, seeks devices that will most efficiently generate legitimate outcomes in a complex society.[2] Other scholars, however, by taking the perspective of society's marginalized groups, give voice to a very different—I will call it a "humanist"—vision. According to this vision, "procedural justice" is a normative *horizon* rather than a technical problem. This horizon challenges us to realize the promise of formal procedural equality in the real world. But this horizon may beckon us even farther than equality of access to current adjudicatory rituals. It may invite us to create new legal and political institutions that will frame "stronger," more meaningful opportunities for participation[3] than we can imagine within a bureaucratic state.[4] *Goldberg* can be read to pre-figure this humanist vision of procedural justice. The Court's decision to mandate prior oral hearings for welfare recipients suggests "the Nation's basic commitment" to both substantive equality and institutional innovation in participation opportunities, in order to "foster the dignity and well-being of *all* persons within its borders."[5]

I begin this essay by assuming that the meaningful participation by all citizens in the governmental decisions that affect their lives—that is, the humanist vision—reflects a nonnatively compelling and widely shared intuition about procedural justice in our political culture.[6] The essay explores a disjuncture between this vision and the conditions in our society in which procedural rituals are actually played out. Familiar cultural images and long-established legal norms construct the subjectivity and speech of socially subordinated persons as inherently inferior to the speech and personhood of dominant groups. Social subordination itself can lead disfavored groups to deploy verbal strategies that mark their speech as deviant when measured against dominant stylistic norms. These conditions—the web of subterranean speech norms and coerced speech practices that accompany race, gender, and class domination—undermine the capacity of many persons in our society to use the procedural rituals that are formally available to them. Furthermore, bureaucratic institutions disable *all* citizens—especially those from sub-ordinated social groups—from meaningful participation in their own political lives. . . .

VERBAL STRATEGIES: HEDGES AND MIRRORS

Linguists have repeatedly noted significant differences between the speech of dominant and subordinated groups within the same broad language communities. Particularly in the context of gender, such differences, both in language practice and in beliefs about how men and women speak, have been documented across many cultures.[7] In an influential essay published in 1975, linguist Robin Lakoff asked why men and women are often presumed—and observed—to speak differently.[8] In seeking an answer to this question, she suggested that the speech of men and women might be motivated by two contrasting goals, the "transmission of factual knowledge" and "politeness," which correspond to two contrasting verbal styles.

Lakoff links the first of these styles to the typical speech habits of men. In this style, the speaker's primary goal is to inform the listener of new information "by the least circuitous route."[9] The speaker will use succinct, unambiguous, declarative sentences—unqualified factual propositions ordered according to a linear logic. These features convey the speaker's authority. They announce his autonomous power to make truthful statements about the world.

Lakoff claims that a contrasting "polite" style, crafted to sustain *connection* with the listener, typifies the speech of women. Polite speech does not announce the speaker's own authority; rather, it enacts her deference to her listener and gathers "some intuition about his feelings toward [her]."[10] The "polite" speaker gives her listener great linguistic latitude to determine what she, the speaker, means to say. She does so by adding features to declarative sentences that render them ambiguous. These "hedges," as Lakoff calls them, include a rising, questioning intonation, "tag questions,"[11] excessive modals or hyper-polite circumlocutions,[12] and semantically ambiguous adjectives or intensifiers.[13] All of these hedges undercut the claim to authority that is implicit in declarative syntax. They cede to the listener the power to determine what the speaker has to say.

Lakoff's essay has stimulated a vast literature of responses.[14] Some other critics dispute Lakoff's negative evaluation of women's language.[15] These critics seek in women's speech habits a powerful Utopian alternative to male language and male logic.[16] Other critics have begun to document the speech strategies of the economically and racially subordinated women who were excluded from Lakoff's sample.[17] Their work suggests that "women's language" is best understood as the array of speech *strategies* that women—as well as other subordinated speakers—have devised to manage verbal encounters with more powerful Others. The common variable in these encounters is not the speaker's gender identity. Rather, it is the imbalance *between* two speakers in social power.

The work of legal anthropologist William O'Barr lends support to this broad thesis.[18] In observing courtroom testimony, he found that women are more likely than men to use the verbal features that Lakoff labels "women's language."[19] Yet these features correlate more strongly with the speaker's social status than with gender *per se*. Based on this data, O'Barr surmised that women—as well as minority and working class men—tend to use "women's language" not because of any biological or cultural predisposition to speak differently, but rather because these speakers tend to occupy "relatively powerless social positions."

O'Barr has also examined the narrative logic of *pro se* litigants' speech. He has identified two typical storytelling strategies, which he calls "relational" and "rule-oriented."[20] Litigants who use a relational framework do poorly in court because the logic of their stories clashes with the rule-breach-injury logic in which judges have learned to conceptualize legal claims. O'Barr found that socially pow-

erless speakers, already disadvantaged by their verbal style, tend to use this relational logic to structure they testimony. Thus, on the level of story as well as sentence, powerless speakers tend to use speech strategies that increase their disempowerment.

Another O'Barr study casts some empirical light on the feminist debate over the value of "women's language." Using simulated jury trials, O'Barr found that jurors are likely to assess speakers who use "powerless" language as less credible, competent, intelligent, or trustworthy than speakers who use typically "male" speech patterns. W. Lance Bennett and Martha Feldman have drawn similar conclusions from qualitative observations of actual trials. Their work also suggests that jurors from dominant groups will sometimes find subordinate speakers to lack credibility not because of the substance of their testimony, but rather because of the non-dominant linguistic and narrative conventions that they use.[21]

Neither O'Barr nor Bennett and Feldman consider whether "powerless language" should be valued for the implicit critique that it offers of dominant norms of speech. Nor do they ask how juries can be taught greater tolerance for different cultural and linguistic styles, and judges made more aware of the distortions that social inequities bring into the fact-finding process. Rather, their works speak only to the question of how the witness who wants to be taken seriously in the present-day courtroom should learn to speak. On this narrow question, the message of their research is clear. In today's courtrooms, language patterns that correlate with social subordination are not "neutral." Rather, those patterns cue the listener to devalue the speech.

In reflecting on his research, O'Barr has concluded that language practice and social power have a complex, recursive relationship. Socially powerless speakers do not have the luxury of confrontation—or even clarity—when they speak. Avoiding verbal commitment, training one's voice to anticipate the other's pleasure—such moves can defuse the risk of retaliation from a more powerful Other. Yet these strategies offer protection at the cost of confessing, and compounding, the speaker's lack of power.

Sociolinguists and anthropologists have devised methods for mapping conversations across gender, class, and race gaps as complex negotiations of social power.[22] In addition to suggesting social policies to make the courtroom feel fairer, and less dangerous for socially subordinated groups, such mapping exercises can help advocates respond more intelligently to the pressures that clients feel—and the rhetorical strategies that they deploy—in encounters with their own lawyers as well as adversaries and the courts. The second part of this essay is such an exercise.

The Story of Mrs. G.

With one lingering exception,[23] our laws of evidence and procedure now treat the speech of all persons according to the same formal rules, regardless of the speaker's gender, ethnicity, or social class. Indeed, the notion that the law should value speech according to the speaker's gender or caste reads more like a footnote from history than a serious claim; it lies far outside the bounds of current debate over procedural and evidentiary norms. Yet a range of evidence suggests that women and other subordinated groups do not in fact participate in legal proceedings as frequently or as fluently as socially dominant groups. The work of Kristin Bumiller documents how women and minorities injured by discrimination often choose to forego legal remedies, rather than risk the trauma that they expect courtroom exposure to entail.[24] A few case studies look closely at what happens when women dare to bring gender-linked injuries into court. And a growing body of empirical work broadly surveys the experiences of women in court—as judges, experts, attorneys, and jurors as well as claimants and witnesses—and concludes that, in all of these

roles, many women continue to perceive themselves to be an unwelcomed presence in the courtroom.

Some women or minority speakers may not experience these feelings at all: through social advantage and force of personality, they have learned to speak with force and authority. As more women and minorities enter elite social positions, the ranks of such exceptional individuals will increase. They will be more readily accepted by legal audiences as "social males." But for many speakers who are stigmatized by gender, race, or caste—those unwilling or unable to assume the role of a social male—the lived experience of inequality undermines the formal guarantee of an equal opportunity to participate in the rituals of the law. Mrs. G. is one of this majority. Through her story we can trace how the complex realities of social inequality undermine the law's formal promise of procedural justice.

The Story[25]

Mrs. G. is thirty-five years old, Black, and on her own. She has five girls, ranging in age from four to fourteen. She has never told me anything about their fathers; all I know is that she isn't getting formal child support payments from anyone. She lives on an AFDC grant of just over three hundred dollars a month and a small monthly allotment of Food Stamps. She probably gets a little extra money from occasional jobs as a field hand or a maid, but she doesn't share this information with me and I don't ask. She has a very coveted unit of public housing, so she doesn't have to pay rent. She is taking an adult basic education class at the local community action center, which is in the same building as my own office. I often notice her in the classroom as I pass by.

The first thing that struck me about Mrs. G., when she finally came to my office for help one day, was the way she talked. She brought her two oldest daughters with her. She would get very excited when she spoke, breathing hard and waving her hands and straining, like she was searching for the right words to say what was on her mind. Her daughters would circle her, like two young mothers themselves, keeping the air calm as her hands swept through it. I haven't talked with them much, but they strike me as quite self-possessed for their years.

At the time I met Mrs. G., I was a legal aid lawyer working in a small community in south central North Carolina. I had grown up in the state, but had been away for ten years, and felt like an outsider when I started working there. I worked out of two small rooms in the back of the local community action center. The building was run-down, but it was a store front directly across from the Civil War Memorial on the courthouse lawn, so it was easy for poor people to find.

There were two of us in the office, myself and a local woman who had spent a few years in Los Angeles, working as a secretary and feeling free, before coming back to the town to care for her aging parents. Her family had lived in the town for generations. Not too long ago they, and most of the other Black families I worked with, had been the property of our adversaries—the local landowners, businessmen, bureaucrats, and lawyers. Everyone seemed to have a strong sense of family, and of history, in the town.

In the late 1960s, the town had erupted into violence when a local youth who had read some Karl Marx and Malcolm X led some five thousand people down the local highway in an effort to integrate the county swimming pool. He had been charged with kidnapping as a result of the incident and had fled to Cuba, China, and ultimately Detroit. My colleague would talk to me about him in secretive tones. Her father was one of those who sheltered him from justice on the evening of his escape. I think she expected that one day he would come back to take up the project that was abandoned when he fled.

Since World War II, the town had been a real backwater for Black people. People told me that it was a place that was there to be gotten out of, if you could figure out how. Only gradually, in the 1980s, were a few African American families moving back into the area, to take up skilled jobs in chemicals and electronics. But the lives of most Blacks in the county in the early 1980s could be summed up by its two claims to fame. It was the county where the state's arch-conservative senior Senator had grown up. Locals claimed that the Senator's father, the chief of police at one time, was known for the boots he wore and the success he had at keeping Black people in their place. It was also the county where Steven Spielberg filmed *The Color Purple*. By the time Spielberg discovered the county, the dust from the 1960s had long since settled, and the town where I worked had the look of a sleepy Jim Crow village that time had quite entirely passed by.

Mrs. G. and two daughters first appeared at our office one Friday morning at about ten, without an appointment. I was booked for the whole day; the chairs in the tiny waiting room were already filled. But I called her in between two scheduled clients. Mrs. G. looked frightened. She showed me a letter from the welfare office that said she had received an "overpayment" of AFDC benefits. Though she couldn't read very well, she knew that the word "overpayment" meant fraud. Reagan's newly appointed United States attorney, with the enthusiastic backing of Senator Jesse Helms, had just announced plans to prosecute "welfare cheats" to the full extent of the law. Following this lead, a grand jury had indicted several local women on federal charges of welfare fraud. Therefore, Mrs. G. had some reason to believe that "fraud" carried the threat of jail.

The "letter" was actually a standardized notice that I had seen many times before. Whenever the welfare department's computer showed that a client had received an overpayment, it would kick out this form, which stated the amount at issue and advised the client to pay it back. The notice did not say why the agency had concluded that a payment error had been made. Nor did it inform the client that she might contest the county's determination. Rather, the notice assigned the client a time to meet with the county's fraud investigator to sign a repayment contract and warned that if the client chose not to show up at this meeting further action would be taken. Mrs. G.'s meeting with the fraud investigator was set for the following Monday.

At the time, I was negotiating with the county over the routine at these meetings and the wording on the overpayment form. Therefore, I knew what Mrs. G. could expect at the meeting. The fraud worker would scold her and then ask her to sign a statement conceding the overpayment, consenting to a 10 percent reduction of her AFDC benefits until the full amount was paid back, and advising that the government could still press criminal charges against her.

I explained to Mrs. G. that she did not have to go to the meeting on Monday, or to sign any forms. She seemed relieved and asked if I could help her get the overpayment straightened out. I signed her on as a client and, aware of the other people waiting to see me, sped through my canned explanation of how I could help her. Then I called the fraud investigator, canceled Monday's meeting, and told him I was representing her. Thinking that the emergency had been dealt with, I scheduled an appointment for Mrs. G. for the following Tuesday and told her not to sign anything or talk to anyone at the welfare office until I saw her again.

The following Tuesday Mrs. G. arrived at my office looking upset. She said she had gone to her fraud appointment because she had been "afraid not to." She had signed a paper admitting she owed the county about six hundred dollars, and agreeing to have her benefits reduced by thirty dollars a month for the year and a half it would take to repay the amount.

She remembered I had told her not to sign anything; she looked like she was waiting for me to yell at her or tell her to leave. I suddenly saw a woman caught between two bullies, both of us ordering her what to do.

I hadn't spent enough time with Mrs. G. the previous Friday. For me, it had been one more emergency—a quick fix, an appointment, out the door. It suddenly seemed pointless to process so many clients, in such haste, without any time to listen, to challenge, to think together. But what to do, with so many people waiting at the door? I mused on these thoughts for a moment, but what I finally said was simpler. I was furious. Why had she gone to the fraud appointment and signed the repayment contract? Why hadn't she done as *we* had agreed? Now it would be so much harder to contest the county's claim: we would have to attack *both* the repayment contract *and* the underlying overpayment claim. Why hadn't she listened to me?

Mrs. G, just looked at me in silence. She finally stammered that she knew she had been "wrong" to go to the meeting when I had told her not to and she was "sorry."

After we both calmed down I mumbled my own apology and turned to the business at hand. She told me that a few months before she had received a cash settlement for injuries she and her oldest daughter had suffered in a minor car accident. After medical bills had been paid and her lawyer had taken his fees, her award came to $592. Before Mrs. G. cashed the insurance check, she took it to her AEDC worker to report it and ask if it was all right for her to spend it. The system had trained her to tell her worker about every change in her life. With a few exceptions, any "income" she reported would be subtracted, dollar for dollar, from her AFDC stipend.

The worker was not sure how to classify the insurance award. After talking to a supervisor, however, she told Mrs. G. that the check would not affect her AFDC budget and she could spend it however she wanted.

Mrs. G. cashed her check that same afternoon and took her five girls on what she described to me as a "shopping trip." They bought Kotex, which they were always running short on at the end of the month. They also bought shoes, dresses for school, and some frozen food. Then she made two payments on her furniture bill. After a couple of wonderful days, the money was gone.

Two months passed. Mrs. G. received and spent two AFDC checks. Then she got the overpayment notice, asking her to repay to the county an amount equal to her insurance award.

When she got to this point, I could see Mrs. G. getting upset again. She had told her worker everything, but nobody had explained to her what she was supposed to do. She hadn't meant to do anything wrong. I said I thought the welfare office had done something wrong in this case, not Mrs. G. I thought we could get the mess straightened out, but we'd need more information. I asked if she could put together a list of all the things she had bought with the insurance money. If she still had any of the receipts, she should bring them to me. I would look at her case file at the welfare office and see her again in a couple of days.

The file had a note from the caseworker confirming that Mrs. G. had reported the insurance payment when she received it. The note also showed that the worker did not include the amount in calculating her stipend. The "overpayment" got nagged two months later when a supervisor, doing a random "quality control" check on her file, discovered the worker's note. Under AFDC law, the insurance award was considered a "lump sum payment." Aware that the law regarding such payments had recently changed, the supervisor decided to check out the case with the state quality control office.

He learned that the insurance award did count as income for AEDC purposes under the state's regulations; indeed, the county should have cut Mrs. G. off of welfare entirely for almost two months on the theory that her family could live for that time off of the insurance award. The lump sum rule was a Reagan Administration innovation designed to teach poor people the virtues of saving money and planning for the future. Nothing in the new provision required that clients be warned in advance about the rule change, however. Only in limited circumstances was a state free to waive the rule. Without a waiver, Mrs. G. would have to pay back $592 to the welfare office. If the county didn't try to collect the sum from Mrs. G., it would be sanctioned for an administrative error.

I met again with Mrs. G. the following Friday. When I told her what I had pieced together from her file, she insisted that she had asked her worker's permission before spending the insurance money. Then she seemed to get flustered and repeated what had become a familiar refrain. She didn't want to make any trouble. She hadn't meant to do anything wrong. I told her that it looked to me like it was the welfare office, and not her, who had done something wrong. I said I would try to get the county to drop the matter, but I thought we might have to go to a hearing, finally, to win.

Mrs. G. had been in court a few times to get child support and to defend against evictions, but she had never been to a welfare hearing. She knew that it was not a good idea to get involved in hearings, however, and she understood why. Fair hearings were a hassle and an embarrassment to the county. A hearing meant pulling an eligibility worker and several managers out of work for a few hours, which—given the chronic under-staffing of the welfare office—was more than a minor inconvenience. It also meant exposing the county's administrative problems to state-level scrutiny.

Front-line eligibility workers were especially averse to hearings because the county's easiest way to defend against its own blunders was to point to the worker as the source of the problem. As a result, the workers did all they could to persuade clients that they would lose, in the end, if they insisted on hearings. The prophesy was self-fulfilling, given the subtle and diffuse retaliation that would often follow for the occasional client who disregarded this advice.

I could tell that Mrs. G. felt pressure from me to ask for a hearing, but she also seemed angry at the welfare office for asking her to pay for their mistake. I said that it was her decision, and not mine, whether to ask for the hearing, and reassured her that I would do my best to settle the matter, no matter what she decided. I also told her she could drop the hearing request at any time, for any reason, before or even after the event. When she nervously agreed to file the hearing request, I didn't second-guess her decision.

My negotiations failed. The county took the position that the worker should have suspended Mrs. G.'s AFDC as soon as the client had reported the insurance payment. This mistake was "regrettable," but it didn't shift the blame for the overpayment. Mrs. G.—and not the county—had received more welfare money than she was entitled to. End of discussion. I then appealed to state officials. They asked if the county would concede that the worker told Mrs. G. she was free to spend her insurance award as she pleased. When county officials refused, and the details of this conversation did not show up in the client's case file, the state declined to intervene. Mrs. G. then had to drop the matter or gear up for a hearing. After a lot of hesitation, she decided to go forward.

Mrs. G. brought all five of her girls to my office to prepare for the hearing. Our first task was to decide on a strategy for the argument. I told her that I saw two stories we could tell. The first was the story she had told me. It was the "estoppel" story, the

story of the wrong advice she got from her worker about spending the insurance check. The second story was one that I had come up with from reading the law. The state had laid the groundwork for this story when it opted for the "life necessities" waiver permitted by federal regulations. If a client could show that she had spent the sum to avert a crisis situation, then it would be considered "unavailable" as income, and her AFDC benefits would not be suspended. I didn't like this second story very much, and I wasn't sure that Mrs. G. would want to go along with it. How could I ask her to distinguish "life necessities" from mere luxuries, when she was keeping five children alive on three hundred dollars a month, and when she had been given no voice in the calculus that had determined her "needs."

Yet I felt that the necessities story might work at the hearing, while "estoppel" would unite the county and state against us. According to legal aid's welfare specialist in the state capital, state officials didn't like the lump sum rule. It made more paper work for the counties. And, by knocking families off the federally financed AFDC program, the rule increased the pressure on state and county-funded relief programs. But the only way the state could get around the rule without being subject to federal sanctions was through the necessities exception. Behind the scenes, state officials were saying to our welfare specialist that they intended to interpret the exception broadly. In addition to this inside information that state officials would prefer the necessities tale, I knew from experience that they would feel comfortable with the role that story gave to Mrs. G. It would place her on her knees, asking for pity as she described how hard she was struggling to make ends meet.

The estoppel story would be entirely different. In it, Mrs. G. would be pointing a finger, turning the county itself into the object of scrutiny. She would accuse welfare officials of wrong, and claim that they had caused her injury. She would demand that the county bend its own rules, absorb the overpayment out of its own funds, and run the risk of sanction from the state for its error.

As I thought about the choices, I felt myself in a bind. The estoppel story would feel good in the telling, but at the likely cost of losing the hearing, and provoking the county's ire. The hearing officer—though charged to be neutral—would surely identify with the county in this challenge to the government's power to evade the costs of its own mistakes. The necessities story would force Mrs. G. to grovel, but it would give both county and state what they wanted to hear—another "yes sir" welfare recipient.

This bind was familiar to me as a poverty lawyer. I felt it most strongly in disability hearings, when I would counsel clients to describe themselves as totally helpless in order to convince the court that they met the statutory definition of disability. But I had faced it in AFDC work as well, when I taught women to present themselves as abandoned, depleted of resources, and encumbered by children to qualify for relief. I taught them to say yes to the degrading terms of "income security," as it was called—invasions of sexual privacy, disruptions of kin-ties, the forced choice of one sibling's welfare over another's. Lawyers had tried to challenge these conditions, but for the most part the courts had confirmed that the system could take such license with its women. After all, poor women were free to say no to welfare if they weren't pleased with its terms.

As I contemplated my role as an advocate, I felt again the familiar sense that I had been taken. Here I was, asking Mrs. G. to trust me, talking with her about our conspiring together to beat the system and strategizing together to change it. Here I was, thinking that what I was doing was educative and empowering or at least supportive of those agendas, when all my efforts worked, in the end, only to teach her

to submit to the system in all of the complex ways that it demanded.

In the moment it took for these old thoughts to flit through my mind, Mrs. G. and her children sat patiently in front of me, fidgeting, waiting for me to speak. My focus returned to them and the immediate crisis they faced if their AFDC benefits were cut. What story should we tell at the hearing, I wondered out loud. How should we decide? Mechanically at first, I began to describe to her our "options."

When I explained the necessities story, Mrs. G. said she might get confused trying to remember what all she had bought with the money. Why did they need to know those things anyway? I could tell she was getting angry. I wondered if two months of benefits—six hundred dollars—was worth it. Maybe paying it back made more sense. I reminded her that we didn't have to tell this story at the hearing, and in fact, we didn't have to go to the hearing at all. Although I was trying to choose my words carefully, I felt myself saying too much. Why had I even raised the question of which story to tell? It was a tactical decision—not the kind of issue that clients were supposed to decide. Why hadn't I just told her to answer the questions that I chose to ask?

Mrs. G. asked me what to do. I said I wanted to see the welfare office admit their mistake, but I was concerned that if we tried to make them, we would lose. Mrs. G. said she still felt like she'd been treated unfairly but—in the next breath—"I didn't mean to do anything wrong." Why couldn't we tell both stories? With this simple question, I lost all pretense of strategic subtlety or control. I said sure.

I asked for the list she had promised to make of all the things she bought with the insurance money. Kotex, I thought, would speak for itself, but why, I asked, had she needed to get the girls new shoes? She explained that the girls' old shoes were pretty much torn up, so bad that the other kids would make fun of them at school.

Could she bring in the old shoes? She said she could.

We rehearsed her testimony, first about her conversation with her worker regarding the insurance award and then about the Kotex and the shoes. Maybe the hearing wouldn't be too bad for Mrs. G., especially if I could help her see it all as strategy, rather than the kind of talking she could do with people she could trust. She had to distance herself at the hearing. She shouldn't expect them to go away from it understanding why she was angry, or what she needed, or what her life was like. The hearing was their territory. The most she could hope for was to take it over for a moment, leading them to act out her agenda. Conspiracy was the theme she must keep repeating as she dutifully played her role.

We spent the next half hour rehearsing the hearing. By the end, she seemed reasonably comfortable with her part. Then we practiced the cross-examination, the ugly questions that—even though everyone conceded to be irrelevant—still always seemed to get asked . . . questions about her children, their fathers, how long she had been on welfare, why she wasn't working instead. This was the part of these sessions that I disliked the most. We practiced me objecting and her staying quiet and trying to stay composed. By the end of our meeting, the whole thing was holding together, more or less.

The hearing itself was in a small conference room at the welfare office. Mrs. G. arrived with her two oldest daughters and five boxes of shoes. When we got there the state hearing officer and the county AFDC director were already seated at the hearing table in lively conversation. The AFDC director was a youngish man with sandy hair and a beard. He didn't seem like a bureaucrat until he started talking. I knew most of the hearing officers who came to the county, but this one, a pale, greying man who slouched in his chair, was new to me. I started feeling uneasy as I rehearsed

how I would plead this troubling case to a stranger.

We took our seats across the table from the AFDC director. The hearing officer set up a portable tape recorder and got out his bible. Mrs. G.'s AFDC worker, an African American woman about her age, entered through a side door and took a seat next to her boss. The hearing officer turned on the recorder, read his obligatory opening remarks, and asked all the witnesses to rise and repeat before god that they intended to tell the truth. Mrs. G. and her worker complied.

The officer then turned the matter over to me. I gave a brief account of the background events and then began to question Mrs. G. First I asked her about the insurance proceeds. She explained how she had received an insurance check of about six hundred dollars following a car accident in which she and her oldest daughter had been slightly injured. She said that the insurance company had already paid the medical bills and the lawyer, the last six hundred dollars was for her and her daughter to spend however they wanted. I asked her if she had shown the check to her AFDC worker before she cashed it. She stammered. I repeated the question. She said she may have taken the check to the welfare office before she cashed it, but she couldn't remember for sure. She didn't know if she had gotten a chance to talk to anyone about it. Her worker was always real busy.

Armed with the worker's own sketchy notation of the conversation in the case file, I began to cross-examine my client, coaxing her memory about the event we had discussed so many times before. I asked if she remembered her worker telling her anything about how she could spend the money. Mrs. G. seemed to be getting more uncomfortable. It was quite a predicament for her, after all. If she "remembered" what her worker had told her, would her story expose mismanagement in the welfare office, or merely scapegoat another Black woman, who was not too much better off than herself?

When she repeated that she couldn't remember, I decided to leave the estoppel story for the moment. Maybe I could think of a way to return to it later. I moved on to the life necessitates [sic] issue. I asked Mrs. G. to recount, as best she could, exactly how she had spent the insurance money. She showed me the receipts she had kept for the furniture payments and I put them into evidence. She explained that she was buying a couple of big mattresses for the kids and a new kitchen table. She said she had also bought some food—some frozen meat and several boxes of Kotex for all the girls. The others in the room shifted uneasily in their chairs. Then she said she had also bought her daughters some clothes and some shoes. She had the cash register receipt for the purchase.

Choosing my words carefully, I asked why she had needed to buy the new shoes. She looked at me for a moment with an expression that I couldn't read. Then she stated, quite emphatically, that they were Sunday shoes that she had bought with the money. The girls already had everyday shoes to wear to school, but she had wanted them to have nice shoes for church too. She said no more than two or three sentences, but her voice sounded different—stronger, more composed—than I had known from her before. When she finished speaking the room was silent, except for the incessant hum of the tape machine on the table and the fluorescent lights overhead. In that moment, I felt the boundaries of our "conspiracy" shift. Suddenly I was on the outside, with the folks on the other side of the table, the welfare director and the hearing officer. The only person I could not locate in this new alignment was Mrs. G.'s welfare worker.

I didn't ask Mrs. G. to pull out the children's old shoes, as we'd rehearsed. Nor did I make my "life necessities" argument. My lawyer's language couldn't add any-

thing to what she had said. They would have to figure out for themselves why buying Sunday shoes for her children—and saying it—was indeed a "life necessity" for this woman. After the hearing, Mrs. G. seemed elated. She asked me how she had done at the hearing and I told her that I thought she was great. I warned her, though, that we could never be sure, in this game, who was winning, or even what side anyone was on.

We lost the hearing and immediately petitioned for review by the chief hearing officer. I wasn't sure of the theory we'd argue, but I wanted to keep the case open until I figured out what we could do.

Three days after the appeal was filed, the county welfare director called me unexpectedly, to tell me that the county had decided to withdraw its overpayment claim against Mrs. G. He explained that on a careful review of its own records, the county had decided that it wouldn't be "fair" to make Mrs. G. pay the money back. I said I was relieved to hear that they had decided, finally, to come to a sensible result in the case. I was sorry they hadn't done so earlier. I then said something about how confusing the lump sum rule was and how Mrs. G.'s worker had checked with her supervisor before telling Mrs. G. it was all right to spend the insurance money. I said I was sure that the screw up was not anyone's fault. He mumbled a bureaucratic pleasantry and we hung up.

When I told Mrs. G. that she had won, she said she had just wanted to "do, the right thing," and that she hoped they understood that she'd never meant to do anything wrong, I repeated that they were the ones who had made the mistake. Though I wasn't sure exactly what was going on inside the welfare office, at least this crisis was over.

The Terrain

Mrs. G. had a hearing in which all of the rituals of due process were scrupulously observed. Yet she did not find her voice welcomed at that hearing. A complex pattern of social, economic, and cultural forces underwrote the procedural formalities, repressing and devaluing her voice. . . .

THE ROUTE TAKEN: EVASIVE MANEUVERS OR A WOMAN'S VOICE?

If we measure Mrs. G.'s hearing against the norms of procedural formality, it appears to conform. The hearing appears to invite Mrs. G. to speak on equal terms with all other persons. Yet within the local landscape of her hearing, Mrs. G.'s voice is constrained by forces that procedural doctrine will neither acknowledge nor oppose. Each of these forces attaches a specific social cost to her gender and race identity. The caste system implements race and gender ideology in social arrangements. The "fraud issue" revives misogynist and racist stereotypes that had been forced, at least partly, underground by the social movements of the 1960s and 1970s. And the welfare system responds to gender and race-based injustice in the economy by constructing the poor as Woman—as an object of social control. Given the power amassed behind these forces, we might predict that they should win the contest with Mrs. G. for her voice.

Yet to detect these forces, we have read the story through a structuralist lens, which shows only the stark dichotomy of subordination and social control. It is ironic that this lens, which works so well to expose the contours of Mrs. G.'s silence, also leaves her—as a woman actively negotiating the terrain in which she found herself—entirely out of focus. If we re-center our reading on Mrs. G., as a woman shaping events, unpredictably, to realize her own meanings, we can no longer say with certainty what the outcome will be. We cannot tell who prevailed at the hearing, or where the power momentarily came to rest. Rather, what we see is a sequence of surprising moves, a series of questions. Why did Mrs. G. return to the lawyer after meeting with the fraud investigator to sign a settlement agreement? Why did she depart from the script she had rehearsed for the hearing, to remain silent before her own worker, and to speak about Sunday shoes? And why did the county finally abandon its claim to cut her stipend?

Why Did Mrs. G. Return to the Lawyer? The lawyer[26] thought she understood the answer to this question. In her view, Mrs. G.'s life had taught her that to be safe, she must submit to her superiors. Mrs. G. was faced with conflicting commands from the welfare agency and the legal aid office. So, like the archetypical woman, shaped to mold herself to male desire, Mrs. G. said "yes" to everything the Man asked. She said yes when the lawyer asked her to go through with a hearing, yes again when the fraud investigator asked her to drop it, and yes once more when the lawyer demanded her apology. In the lawyer's view, this excess of acquiescence had a sad, but straightforward meaning. It marked Mrs. G.'s lack of social power: this woman could not risk having a point of view of her own.

Yet the lawyer was not situated to see the whole story. Though she aspired to stand beside Mrs. G. as an equal, she also sought to guard her own status—and the modicum of social power that it gave her. She *saw* Mrs. G. as a victim because that was the role she needed her client to occupy to support her own social status. For if Mrs. G. was indeed silenced by the violence around her, she would then be dependent on the lawyer's expertise and protection, and therefore compliant to the lawyer's will. With such clients, the lawyer could feel quite secure of her power, and complacent about the value of her work.

But Mrs. G.'s survival skills were more complex, more subtle, than the lawyer dared to recognize. There might be another meaning to Mrs. G.'s ambivalence about what she wanted to do. Perhaps she was *playing* with the compliance that all of her superiors demanded. By acquiescing to both of the system's opposed orders, she was surely protecting herself from the risks of defiance. But she was also undermining the value—to them—

of her own submission. By refusing to claim any ground as her own, she made it impossible for others to subdue her will.

Self-negation may not have been the *only* meaning that Mrs. G. felt positioned to claim. She finally *came back* to the lawyer, repudiated the settlement, determined to pursue her case. Was this merely one more deft move between two bureaucrats,[27] searching them both for strategic advantage while secretly mocking the rhetoric of both spheres? Or did Mrs. G. finally get fed up at the unfairness of the welfare, and at her own endless submission? When she returned to the lawyer, she was offered a bargain. She might get money, and some limited protection from the welfare, if she went along with the hearing plan. But she might have also heard the lawyer to promise something different from this *quid pro quo*. In her talk of rights and justice, the lawyer offered Mrs. G. not just money, but also vindication. In going forward with the hearing, was Mrs. G. simply making a street-wise calculation to play the game the lawyer offered? Or was she also giving voice to a faint hope—a hope that one day she might really have the legal protections she needed to take part in the shaping of justice?[28]

Why Did Mrs. G. Depart From Her Script?
The lawyer had scripted Mrs. G. as a victim. That was the only strategy for the hearing that the lawyer, within the constraints of her own social position, could imagine for Mrs. G. She had warned her client to play the victim if she wanted to win. Mrs. G. learned her lines. She came to the hearing well-rehearsed in the lawyer's strategy. But in the hearing, she did not play. When she was cued to perform, without any signal to her lawyer she abandoned their script.

The lawyer shared with Mrs. G. the oppression of gender, but was placed above Mrs. G. in the social hierarchies of race and class. The lawyer was paid by the same people who paid for welfare, the federal government. Both programs were part of a social agenda of assisting, but also controlling, the poor.[29] Though the lawyer had worked hard to identify with Mrs. G., she was also sworn, and paid, to defend the basic constitution of the *status quo*. When Mrs. G. "misbehaved" at the hearing, when she failed to talk on cue and then refused to keep quiet, Mrs. G. pointed to the ambiguity of the legal aid lawyer's social role. Through her defiant actions, Mrs. G. told the lawyer that a conspiracy with a double agent is inevitably going to prove an unstable alliance.

The lawyer had tried to "collaborate" with Mrs. G. in devising an advocacy plan. Yet the terms of that "dialogue" excluded Mrs. G.'s voice. Mrs. G. was a better strategist than the lawyer—more daring, more subtle, more fluent—in her own home terrain. She knew the psychology, the culture, and the politics of the white people who controlled her community. She knew how to read, and sometimes control, her masters' motivations; she had to command this knowledge—this intuition—to survive. The lawyer had learned intuition as a woman, but in a much more private sphere. She was an outsider to the county, and to Mrs. G.'s social world. Mrs. G.'s superior sense of the landscape posed a subtle threat to the lawyer's expertise. Sensing this threat, the lawyer steered their strategic "discussion" into the sphere of her own expert knowledge. By limiting the very definition of "strategy" to the manipulation of legal doctrine, she invited Mrs. G. to respond to her questions with silence. And, indeed, Mrs. G. did not talk freely when the lawyer was devising their game-plan. Rather, Mrs. G. waited until the hearing to act out her own intuitions. Although she surely had not plotted those actions in advance, she came up with moves at the hearing which threw everyone else off their guard, and may have proved her the better *legal* strategist of the lawyer-client pair.

The disarming "strategy" that Mrs. G. improvised at the hearing was to appear to *abandon* strategy entirely. For a moment she stepped out of the role of the supplicant. She ignored the doctrinal pigeonholes that would fragment her voice. She put aside all that the lawyer told her the audience wanted to hear. Instead, when asked to point a finger at her caseworker, she was silent. When asked about "life necessities," she explained that she had used her money to meet *her own* needs. She had bought her children Sunday shoes.

Her Silence Before Her Caseworker. When the lawyer asked Mrs. G. about the conversation with her caseworker regarding the insurance payments, Mrs. G. had nothing to say. The lawyer, smarting from her own rejection, felt that Mrs. G. was protecting a vulnerable Black sister with her silence—at her own, and her lawyer's expense. But perhaps something else was going on. Unlike Mrs. G., the caseworker had earned self-respect in the system. Mrs. G. and her like—desperately poor, with no formal schooling, burdened by too many children, "abandoned" by their men—cast a stigma on this woman because of the common color of their skin. Did this woman command a different kind of power over Mrs. G. than the white masters—a power that felt like shame, rather than fear? Perhaps Mrs. G. was not willing to flaunt her own degradation before this woman, as the lawyer demanded. Perhaps she was not willing to grovel—pointing fingers, showing off tattered shoes, listing each of her petty expenses—before this distant, disapproving sister. Perhaps Mrs. G.'s silence before this other Black woman, and her talk about Sunday shoes, expressed a demand—and an affirmation—of her own dignity.

Her Talk About Sunday Shoes. When Mrs. G. talked about Sunday shoes, she was talking about a life necessity. For subordinated communities, physical necessities do not meet the minimum requirements for a human life. Rather, subordinated groups must create cultural practices through which they can elaborate an autonomous, oppositional consciousness. Without shared rituals for sustaining their survival and motivating their resistance, subordinated groups run the risk of total domination—of losing the *will* to use their human powers to subvert their oppressor's control over them. Religion, spirituality, the social institution of the Black Church, has been one such self-affirming cultural practice for the communities of African American slaves, and remains central to the expression of Black identity and group consciousness today. By naming Sunday shoes as a life necessity, Mrs. G. was speaking to the importance of this cultural practice in her life, a truth that the system's categories did not comprehend.

At the same time that Mrs. G.'s statement affirmed the church, it condemned the welfare system. By rejecting the welfare's definition of life necessities, she asserted her need to have a say about *the criteria* for identifying her needs. Her statement was a demand for meaningful participation in the political conversations in which her needs are contested and defined. In the present welfare system, poor women—the objects of welfare—are structurally excluded from those conversations. When Mrs. G. insisted on her need to say for herself what her "life necessities" might be, she expanded, for a moment, the accepted boundaries of those conversations.

Mrs. G.'s statement also spoke to a third dimension of her "life necessity." When Mrs. G. talked about buying Sunday shoes, she defied the rules of legal rhetoric—the rule of relevancy, the rule against "rambling," the unwritten rule that told her to speak like a victim if she wanted to win. Had Mrs. G. spoken the language that was proper for her in the setting, her relevant, logical, submissive, hypercorrect responses to their questions might have been comprehended. But, by dutifully speaking the language of an institution from which subordinated groups have historically been excluded and in which Mrs. G. felt herself to have no stake, her voice would have repeated, and legitimated, the very social and cultural patterns and priorities that had kept her down. Had she been a *respectful* participant in the legal ritual, Mrs. G. would have articulated someone else's need, or pleasure, rather than her own.

Mrs. G. did not boycott the hearing altogether. Rather, in her moment of misbehavior, she may have been standing her ground within it. Although she appeared, at first, to be deferring to the system's categories and rules, when she finally spoke, she animated those categories with her own experience. She stretched the category of "life necessity" to express her own values and turned it around to critique the welfare's systemic disregard of her own point of view. By talking about Sunday shoes, Mrs. G. claimed, for one fragile moment, what was perhaps her most basic "life necessity." She claimed a position of equality in the speech community—an equal power to take part in the *making* of language, the making of shared categories, norms, and institutions—as she spoke through that language about her needs.

When Mrs. G. claimed this power, she affirmed the feminist insight that the dominant languages *do not* construct a closed system, from which there can be no escape. Although dominant groups may control the *social institutions* that regulate these languages, those groups cannot control the *capacity* of subordinated peoples to speak. Thus, women have evaded complete domination through their *practice* of speaking, like Mrs. G. spoke at her hearing, from their own intuitions and their own experience. Feminist writers have drawn three figures—play, archaeology, and poetry—to describe this emancipatory language practice.[30]

When Mrs. G. construed "life necessities" to include Sunday shoes, she turned the hearing into a place where she could talk, on a par with the experts, about her "needs." For a moment she defied the rigid official meaning of necessity, and refused to leave nameless the values and passions that gave sense to her life. Adrienne Rich describes the process:

For many women, the commonest words are having to be sifted through, rejected, laid aside for a long time, or turned to the light for new colors and flashes of meaning: power, love, control, violence, political, personal, private, friendship, community, sexual, work, pain, pleasure, self, integrity. . . . When we become acutely, disturbingly aware of the language we are using and that is using us, we begin to grasp a material resource that women have never before collectively attempted to repossess. . . .

Mrs. G. might want to add "participation" and "need" to the poet's list.

How Was Mrs. G.'s Voice Heard? The third question that the story raises is the ending. The story tells us that the hearing officer ruled against Mrs. G., and then the county welfare department decided to drop the case, restoring her full stipend. But the text does not say how the men across the table experienced the hearing, or why the county eventually gave in. Did Mrs. G.'s paradoxical "strategy" disarm her audience? Did she draw a response from her audience that was different—more compelling—than the pity that her lawyer had wanted to play upon? Did her presentation of herself as an independent, church-going woman, who would exercise her own judgment, and was willing to say what she needed—did these qualities make the men fear her, respect her, regard her for a moment as a person, rather than a case? Did they feel a moment of anger—about the ultimately powerless roles that they were assigned to play in the bureaucracy that regulated all of their lives? Were these men moved, by the hearing, to snatch her case from the computer and subject it to their own human judgment? If this is indeed what happened—and we do not know—would Mrs. G., in retrospect, have wished the story to end that way? Or was this moment of benign discretion a double-edged precedent—more dangerous to her people than the computer's reliable indifference?

We do not know why the county decided to drop Mrs. G.'s case. What we do know, however, is that after the hearing Mrs. G. remained a Black, single mother on welfare—poor, dependent, despised. Mrs. G.'s unruly participation at her hearing was itself political action.

Yet it was an act that did little to change the harsh landscape which constricts Mrs. G. from more sustained and more effective political participation. Substantial change in that landscape will come only as such fragile moments of dignity are supported and validated by the law. . . .

Notes

1. 397 U.S. 254 (1970). *Goldberg* was litigated as part of a broad initiative to increase the power and expand the benefits of welfare recipients. See R. COVER, 0. Fiss & J. RESNIK, PROCEDURE 133 (1988). For more extensive discussion of the National Welfare Rights Organization's political strategy, see F. PIVEN & R. CLOWARD, POOR PEOPLE'S MOVEMENTS: WHY THEY SUCCEED AND HOW THEY FAIL 264–361 (1977); L. BAILIS, BREAD OR JUSTICE: GRASSROOTS ORGANIZING IN THE WELFARE RIGHTS MOVEMENT (1974) and sources cited therein.

2. This position was endorsed by the Supreme Court in *Matthews v. Eldridge,* 424 U.S. 319 (1976) (directing courts to balance accuracy, administrative costs, and other factors to determine the minimal procedures constitutionally required before the slate can infringe a liberty or property interest). Jerry Mashaw has criticized the logic of the *Matthews* decision in *The Supreme Court's Due Process Calculus for Administrative Adjudication in* Matthews v. Eldridge: *Three factors in Search of a Theory of Value,* 44 U. CHL L. REV. 28 (1976). Yet it is Mashaw who has most fully articulated a vision of process as an instrument of just government in a bureaucratic state. See J. MASHAW, DUE PROCESS IN THE ADMINISTRATIVE STATE (1985). See also his pre-Matthews article, *The Management Side of Due Process: Some Theoretical and Litigation Notes on the Assurance of Accuracy, Fairness, and Timeliness in the Adjudication of Social Welfare Claims,* 59 CORNELL L. REV. 772 (1974).

3. See B. BARBER, STRONG DEMOCRACY: PARTICIPATORY POLITICS FOR A NEW AGE (1984).

4. Prominent among the legal scholars engaged in articulating this vision of process are Martha Minow and Frank Michelman. See, e.g., Minow, *Interpreting Rights: an Essay for Robert Cover,* 96 YALE L.J. 1860 (1987); Minow, *The Supreme Court 1987 Term—Foreword: Justice Engendered,* 101 HARV. L. REV. 10 (1987); Michelman, *The Supreme Court 1986 Term—Foreword: Traces of Self-Government,* 100 HARV. L. REV. 4 (1986); Michelman, *Formal and Associational Aims in Procedural Due Process,* in NOMOS, DUE PROCESS 126 (J. Pennock & J. Chapman eds. 1977); Michelman, *The Supreme Court and Litigation Access Fees: The Right to Protect One's Rights,* 1973 DUKE L.J. 1153.

5. Goldberg v. Kelly, *supra* note 1, at 264–265 (emphasis added). It is ironic that the *Goldberg* opinion itself fits best within the instrumentalist conversation about procedural values. Justice Brannan endorses oral pretermination hearings for welfare recipients primarily because he assumes that such hearings will ensure accurate and politically legitimate decisions. Scholars from all political perspectives have raised questions about whether welfare hearings have in fact fulfilled those instrumental objectives, or otherwise increased the power of the poor. See, e.g., Scott, *The Reality of Procedural Due Process—A Study of the Implementation of Fair Hearing Requirements by the Welfare Caseworker,* 13 WM. & MARY L. REV. 725 (1972) (empirical study of the implementation of fair hearings in Virginia welfare offices); Mashaw, *The Management Side of Due Process, supra* note 3 (questioning the efficiency of individualized welfare hearings in every context); Simon, *Legality, Bureaucracy, and Class in the Welfare System,* 92 YALE L.J. 1198 (1983) (statistics show that hearing opportunities are rarely used by unrepresented clients). See also Gabel & Harris, *Building Power and Breaking Images: Critical Legal Theory and the Practice of Law,* 11 N.Y.U. REV. L. & Soc. CHANGE 369 (1982); Rosenblatt, *Legal Entitlements and Welfare Benefits,* in THE POLITICS OF LAW (D. Kairys ed. 1982); J. HANDLER, THE CONDITIONS OF DISCRETION: AUTONOMY, COMMUNITY, BUREAUCRACY (1986); Simon, *Rights and Redistribution in the Welfare*

System, 38 STAN. L. REV. 1431 (1986) (all raising questions about how effective procedural reforms have been in expanding the substantive entitlements or political power of the poor).

6. Studies by social scientist Tom Tyler suggest that one of the major factors that determines the degree of fairness that a litigant *perceives* in a procedure is her opportunity for participation. See Tyler, *What Is Procedural Justice?: Criteria Used by Citizens to Assess the Fairness of Legal Procedures,* 22 LAW & SOC. REV. 103 (1988). See also, Tyler, *The Role of Perceived Injustice in Defendant's Evaluations of Their Courtroom Experience,* 18 LAW & SOC. REV. 51 (1984); J. THIBAUT & L. WALKER, PROCEDURAL JUSTICE: A PSYCHOLOGICAL ANALYSIS (1975). See also O'Neil, *Of Justice Denied: The Welfare Prior Hearing Cases,* 1970 SUP. CR. REV. 161, 187 n. 129 ("(t]he hearing . . .serves a psychological need in the administration of benefit programs that may be even more basic to a civilized system of administration than the function of ascertaining the truth.").

7. Major works of feminist linguistic scholarship from the last two decades include D. CAMERON, FEMINISM AND LINGUISTIC THEORY (1985); LANGUAGE, GENDER, AND SOCIETY (B. Thorne, C. Kramarae & N. Henley eds. 1983); C. KRAMARAE, WOMEN AND MEN SPEAKINO (1981); WOMEN AND LANGUAGE IN LITERATURE AND SOCIETY (S. McConnell-Ginct, R. Borker & N. Funnan eds. 1980); M. KEY, MALE/FEMALE LANGUAGE (1975); and LANGUAGE AND SEX; DIFFERENCE AND DOMINANCE (B. Thorne & N. Henley eds. 1975). For an overview and critique of feminist linguistic investigation, see Elshtain, Feminist Discourse and its Discontents, in FEMINIST THEORY: A CRITIQUE OF IDEOLOGY 127–145 (N. Keohane, M. Rosaldo, & B. Gelpi eds. 1981), and McConnell-Ginet, *Difference and Language: A Linguist's Perspective,* in THE FUTURE Of DIFFERENCE 156–166 (H. Eisenstein & A. Jardine eds., 1987). For a survey of linguistic data about gendered features in non-Western languages, see Bodine, Sex Differentiation in Language, in LANGUAGE AND SEX: DIFFERENCE AND DOMINANCE 130 (B. Thome & N. Henley eds. 1975).

8. R. LAKOFF, LANGUAGE AND WOMAN'S PLACE (1975). Lakoff based her conclusions on introspection and intuition about the speech of white, middle class professional women like herself, rather than on rigorous field studies. *Id.* at 4 ("I have examined my own speech and that of my acquaintances, and have used my own intuitions in analyzing it.").

9. *Id.* at 71.

10. *Id.* at 70.

11. For example, "It's time for dinner, isn't it?"

12. For example, "Wouldn't it be a good idea if you could leave me alone."

13. For example, "That seemed indeed all right."

14. Virtually every linguistic and political claim of Lakoff's has stimulated further research. The technical studies include Brend, *Male-Female Intonation Patterns in American English,* in LANGUAGE AND SEX: DIFFERENCE AND DOMINANCE, and B. PREISLER, LINGUISTIC SEX ROLES IN CONVERSATION: SOCIAL VARIATION IN THE EXPRESSION OF TENTATIVENESS IN ENGLISH (1986). For a broad critique of Lakoff's method and conclusions, see Kramerae, *Women's Speech: Separate but Unequal?* in LANGUAGE AND SEX: DIFFERENCE AND DOMINANCE, at 43–56. For a comprehensive bibliography of the linguistics literature scrutinizing Lakoff's claims, see LANGUAGE, GENDER, AND SOCIETY, (annotated bibliography of linguistic works exploring "Sex Differences and   Similarities in Language Use: Linguistic Components").

15. See, e.g., B. Thorne & N. Henley, *Difference and Dominance: An Overview of Language, Gender, and Society,* in LANGUAGE AND SEX: DIFFERENCE AND DOMINANCE, ("[A]lthough stressing the primacy of social rather than linguistic change, Lakoff seems to argue that equality *should* entail women using the 'stronger' forms now associated with men.") (emphasis in original).

16. These critics argue that women's speech can show us how to use language to negotiate truly human meanings, which are inescapably ambivalent, by attending to the Other, rather

than by imposing an imperial truth on a captive audience. Furthermore, they claim that it is only by revaluing women's language, culture, and life experience that we can talk concretely about what norms and visions should motivate the feminist political project in the long term. See, e.g., Kramerae, *Women's Speech: Separate but Unequal,* at 43–56; Fishman, *Interaction: The Work Women Do,* in LANGUAGE, GENDER, AND SOCIETY.

17. See the essays in LANGUAGE AND POWER (C. Kramarae, M. Schuiz & W. O'Barr eds. 1984). See also Nichols, *Women in their Speech Communities,* in WOMEN AND LANGUAGE IN LITERATURE AND SOCIETY, at 140 (documenting contrasts between women speakers in different speech communities and conversational settings, which the author relates to such variables as social role and activities); Nichols, *Linguistic Options and Choices for Black Women in the Rural South,* in LANGUAGE, GENDER, AND SOCIETY; Scott, *The English Language and Black Womanhood: A Low Blow at Self-esteem,* 1 J. AFRO-AMERICAN ISSUES 218 (1974); Stanback, *Language and Black Woman's Place: Towards a Description of Black Women's Communication* (paper presented at meeting of Speech Communication Association, Louisville, Ky., 1982).

18. See Lind & O'Barr, *The Social Significance of Speech in the Courtroom,* in LANGUAGE AND SOCIAL PSYCHOLOGY (H. Giles. & R. St-Clair eds. 1979); Conley, O'Barr & Lind, *The Power of Language: Presentational Style in the Courtroom,* 1978 DUKE L. J. 1375; Erickson, Lind, Johnson & O'Barr, *Speech Style and Impression Formation in a Court Setting: The Effects of "Powerful" and "Powerless" Speech,* 14 J. EXPERIMENTAL Soc. PSYCH. 266 (1978).

19. O'Barr refers to the linguistic features that Lakoff associates with women—including hedges, hesitation forms, polite forms, question intonation and intensifiers—as "powerless" speech forms. See Conley, O'Barr & Lind, at 1379–1380.

20. Conley & O'Barr, *Rules versus Relationships in Small Claims Disputes,* in CONFLICT TALK (A. Grimshaw ed. 1989) (forthcoming), at 2-3 ("A relational account emphasizes status and relationships, and is organized around the litigant's efforts to introduce these issues into the trial. A *rule-oriented* account emphasizes rules and laws, and is tightly structured around these issues. . . . *Rule-oriented* accounts mesh better with the logic of the law and the courts. They . . . concentrate on the issues that the court is likely to deem relevant to the case. . . . By contrast, relational accounts are filled with background details that are presumably relevant to the litigant, but not necessarily to the court, and emphasize the complex web of relationships between the litigants rather than legal rules or formal contracts") (emphasis in original).

21. See W. BENNETT & M. FELDMAN, RECONSTRUCTING REALITY IN THE COURTROOM: JUSTICE AND JUDGMENT IN AMERICAN CULTURE 171 (1981) ("There are two ways in which systematic biases might result from differences in storytelling practices. First, some people may lack shared cognitive routines for presenting information in story-coded forms. The inability to produce a conventional story would leave individuals vulnerable to having truthful accounts of their actions rejected. Second, even the construction of a coherent story may not guarantee a just outcome if the teller and the audience do not share the norms, experiences, and assumptions necessary to draw connections among story elements. People who have different understandings about society and its norms may disagree about the plausibility of a story. . . . If legal facts are reconstructed as stories whose plausibility depends on understandings drawn from experience, then jurors who come from different social worlds may disagree about the meaning and the plausibility of the same stories.").

22. See, e.g., Jupp, Roberts & Cook-Gumperz, *Language and disadvantage: The hidden process,* in LANGUAGE AND SOCIAL IDENTITY 232 (J. Gumperz ed. 1982) (analyzing verbal interaction between Asian-born workers and welfare functionaries in Britain); Brown & Levinson, Social Structure, Groups and Interaction, in SOCIAL MARKERS IN SPEECH (K. Scherer & H. Giles eds. 1979). A recent example of such work in a legal context analyzes the witnesses' testimony at the Wa-

tergate hearings. See Molotch & Boden, *Talking Social Structure: Discourse, Domination and the Watergate Hearings,* 50 AM. SOC. REV. 273 (June 1985). Investigation has also extended to non-verbal communicative encounters. See, e.g., Henley & Freeman, *The Sexual Politics of Interpersonal Behavior,* in J. Freeman, WOMEN: A FEMINIST PERSPECTIVE 457, 465 (forthcoming) (concluding from such studies that "[i]n any situation in which one group is seen as inferior to another, . . .that group will be more *submissive,* more *readable* (non-verbally expressive), more *sensitive* (accurate in decoding another's non-verbal expressions), and more *accommodating* (adapting to another's non-verbal behaviors). . . . [V]erbal characteristics of persons in inferior status positions [include] the tendencies to hesitate and apologize, often offered as submissive gestures in the face of threats or possible threats. . . . [G]estures of submission [include] falling silent (or not beginning to speak at all) when interrupted or pointed at, and cuddling to the touch." (emphasis in original).

23. This exception is in the area of rape law. Until feminists pressured for reform, the Model Penal Code and the law of many states provided that a person could not be convicted of rape on the uncorroborated testimony of the alleged rape victim, who is generally a woman. See MODEL PENAL CODE § 213.6(5) (1980); Note, *The Rape Corroboration Requirement: Repeal Not Reform,* 81 YALE LJ. 1365, 1366 (1972). One rationale for this corroboration requirement was the widely held belief that rape victims are likely to lie. See, e.g., Note, *Corroborating Charges of Rape,* 67 COLUM. L. REV. 1137, 1138 (1967) ("stories of rape are frequently lies or fantasies"), quoted in S. ESTRICH, REAL RAPE 43 (1987). Although the corroboration requirement has now been eliminated in most jurisdictions, the existence of corroborating evidence is still widely used by prosecutors to determine the disposition of rape claims. See Myers & LaFree, *Sexual Assault and Its Prosecution: a Comparison with Other Crimes,* 73 J. CRIM. L. AND CRIMINOLOGY 1300 (1982); Bienen, *Rape III—National Developments in Rape Reform Legislation,* 6

WOMEN'S RTS. L. REP. 170 (Rutgers Univ., 1980).

24. See, e.g., Bumiller, *Victims in the Shadow of the Law: A Critique of the Model of Legal Protection,* 12 SIGNS 421 (1987); K. BUMILLER, THE CIVIL RIGHTS SOCIETY: THE SOCIAL CONSTRUCTION OF VICTIMS (1988) (describing how victims may blame themselves for their victimization in order to enhance their own assaulted sense of autonomy, and may avoid legal process because they perceive it, and the confrontation with the perpetrator that it requires, as a further assault on their security and equilibrium).

25. This story is based upon my work as a legal aid lawyer in North Carolina from 1982 to 1986. Certain details have been changed to avoid compromising client confidentiality.

26. As I begin this critique of the lawyer's perspective, I must note the ambiguity of my own position in this project. As Mrs. G.'s lawyer, I appeared in her story. Yet I also wrote that story, and I now prepare to read it. The reader should ask what feelings and events I might have left out of the narrative of Mrs. G. because I was not situated to perceive them. Although this reading purports to comment on how the lawyer's viewpoint was limited in the story, my interpretation of the lawyer's limitations is itself shaped by my own present social location and concerns. What questions does this reading pose to the story, and what issues does my reading conceal from view?

27. Legal services lawyers are, after all, functionaries in a government-funded social program. Sociological studies which investigate this thesis include Abel, *Law Without Politics: Legal Aid Under Advanced Capitalism,* 32 U.C.L.A. L. REV. 474 (1985); Menkel-Meadow & Meadow, *Personalized or Bureaucratized Justice in Legal Services: Resolving Sociological Ambivalence in the Delivery of Legal Aid for the Poor,* 9 LAW & HUMAN BEHAVIOR 397 (1985); J. KATZ, POOR PEOPLE'S LAWYERS IN TRANSITION (1982).

28. Cf. Leff, *Law and,* [sic] 87 YALE LJ. 989, 1005 (1978) (in exploring the limits of the game metaphor for legal process, Leff notes "[i]f, however, [adjudication] is not a game, it is not not a game either. It is . . .an amphibian cultural artifact that embodies, simultaneously,

at least two different social mechanisms. . . . [It] reflects simultaneously the causal and metaphoric universes, both integral parts of . . .life but neither dominant over the other").

29. Many works trace the history of this contradiction at the core of our society's conception of welfare. See, e.g., F. PIVEN & R. CLOWARD; Hasenfeld; J. KATZ.

30. The figure of play connotes an exuberant, unruly approach toward conventions of discourse which can disarm an oppressive language-system, reanimating it with women's experiences. Patricia Yaeger elaborates in HONEY-MAD WOMAN, at 18:

> [P]layfulness and word play are very much at issue in the woman writer's reinvention of her culture. . . . [P]lay itself is a form of aesthetic activity in which . . .what has been burdensome becomes—at least momentarily— weightless, transformable, transformative. As women play with old texts, the burden of the tradition is lightened and shifted; it has the potential for being remade.

The figure of archaeology refers to the collective searching of private memories and the shared past to uncover the suppressed meanings that are latent in familiar words. Mary Daly invokes archaeology in GYN/ECOLOGY (1978) at 24 when she describes how, in her writing, she searches for the hidden powers of words:

> Often I unmask deceptive words by dividing them and employing alternate meanings for prefixes. . . . I also unmask their hidden reversals, often by using less known or "obsolete" meanings. . . . Sometimes I simply invite the reader to listen to words in a different way. . . . When I play with words I do this attentively, deeply, paying attention to etymology, to varied dimensions of meaning, to deep Background meanings and subliminal associations.

The third figure that guides this emancipatory language practice is poetry—coaxing the language just beyond its systemic boundaries, toward images and understandings that both expand, and challenge, its rule. Used in this sense, poetry is closely connected to consciousness raising—the feminist method in which women, through their practice of talking together about their own experience, create the common language which makes that talking possible. See T. DE LAURETIS, ALICE DOESN'T: FEMINISM, SEMIOTICS, CINEMA (1984) (defining consciousness raising as "the collective articulation of one's experience of sexuality and gender . . .[which] has produced, and continues to elaborate, a radically new mode of understanding the subject's relation to social-historical reality. Consciousness raising is the original critical instrument that women developed toward such understanding, the analysis of social reality and its critical revision"). Consciousness raising places new demands on the language because, through it, women grope to share feelings that have previously gone unnamed. When those feelings find words, poetry is produced. As Audre Lords expresses the matter in her essay, *Poetry Is Not a Luxury*:

> We can train ourselves to respect our feelings and to transpose them into a language so they can be shared. And where that language does not yet exist, it is our poetry which helps to fashion it.

See A. LORDE, SISTER OUTSIDER 37–38 (1984).

Notes and Questions

1. What does White mean by "meaningful participation"? How do *you* define the term? To what extent is your own participation in the realm of the law "meaningful"?

2. How does White characterize the "humanist vision" of procedural justice? How does this differ from the instrumentalist point of view? Which vision does Justice Brennan's ruling in *Goldberg v. Kelly* reflect?

3. According to linguistic studies, what sort of links exist between human speech patterns and social power structures? How does White relate this association

to law's accessibility and the capacity of subordinate social groups to engage in "meaningful participation" with the law?

4. What is the difference between a "relational" and a "rule-oriented" storytelling strategy? Which is more familiar to lawyers and judges? Why would one strategy tend to sway juries more effectively than the other? What implications does this have for law's supposed neutrality?

5. In your opinion, does Mrs. G. have the opportunity for "meaningful participation" in the legal system? If yes, what is the key evidence that this is so? If no, what social and bureaucratic factors inhibit her capacity to participate in a meaningful way?

6. In the story, Mrs. G. had two choices in pleading her case before the welfare hearing: She could tell her straightforward version and "provoke the county's ire" by pointing a finger of blame at the welfare bureaucracy, or she could plead desperation and grovel her way into a favorable settlement. How do these two options reflect and/or fit into the aforementioned linguistic categories of "relational" and "rule-oriented" storytelling?

7. Can welfare recipients ever afford to have a "rights-defined identity" (Merry, Chapter 26)? According to White, welfare bureaucracies impose arbitrary decisions and dictate policy to welfare recipients, on the grounds that poor people are "free to say no to welfare if they [aren't] pleased with the terms." Do you agree? Do the indigent have the freedom of choice in this case?

8. How did social factors (e.g., race, class, gender, etc.) affect Mrs. G.'s behavior leading up to and during the hearing? Was Mrs. G. afforded due process through the hearing? Does it make any difference that, as White points out, "Within the local landscape of her hearing, Mrs. G.'s voice was constrained by forces that procedural doctrine will neither acknowledge nor oppose"? Hypothetically speaking, could procedural rights ever confront the social forces White is referring to? If so, how? If not, why?

9. Does Mrs. G's case raise questions about the capacity of welfare recipients to benefit from the "rudimentary due process" afforded them by *Goldberg v. Kelly*? Can rudimentary due process be "meaningful" if the subject is poor or not well educated, as was Mrs. G.? What does this suggest about the accessibility of the law to poor citizens? To poor women in particular?

Reprinted from: Lucie E. White, "Subordination, Rhetorical Survival Skills and Sunday Shoes: Notes on the Hearing of Mrs. G. " in *Buffalo Law Review*, 38:1 (1990). Copyright © 1990. ✦

Chapter 29

Dependency by Law

Welfare and Identity in the Lives of Poor Women

Frank Munger

To inquire about the accessibility of law to welfare recipients suggests that they are somehow outside the law. Yet to be on welfare is, for as long as that status lasts, to be already inside the law. As the White reading (Chapter 28) demonstrates, for people on welfare, law is repeatedly encountered in the most ordinary transactions and events of their lives. Legal rules and practices are implicated in determining how recipients will be able to meet some of their most pressing needs. Being on welfare means having a significant part of life organized by a regime of legal rules invoked by officials who claim jurisdiction over choices and decisions, which those who are not on welfare would regard as personal and private.

For welfare recipients, law is not a distant abstraction; it is a web-like enclosure in which they are "caught." It is both a metaphorical trap and a material force. Like the man from the country in Franz Kafka's parable "Before the Law" (Chapter 12), law is an irresistible and inescapable presence. However, it is an already entered space, an enclosure seen from the inside, whose imperative power is clothed in the categories and abstractions of rules. When, like Mrs. G., recipients use the welfare department's hearing procedures, they may be said to be seeking redress from one part of law against another. Moreover, they do so carrying the stigma of dependency and the moral burden of being identified as poor.

The next reading describes how that stigma and burden play out in the lives of women on welfare as well as how they react to and counter both. Law, Frank Munger argues, helps to define the meaning of what it means to be on welfare. Like Merry (Chapter 26), Munger explores the way law helps to shape individual identity. Looking at the reform of welfare in the mid-1990s, Munger suggests that law helps to define what it means to be a rights-bearing subject and a citizen. His essay also explores the intersections of race and poverty, showing yet again the social factors that weave themselves into the fabric of legal life.

As you read this selection, ask yourselves what Munger means when he talks about legal consciousness. Has law failed persons on welfare? How do issues of gender and race affect the experience of being on welfare?

STORIES WE TELL AND LAWS WE CREATE

Enacting a law requires imagining the persons who are to be affected by the law and the circumstances in which the law is to play a part. While imaginative constructions giving meaning to consciousness of law can be subtle and complex, the discursive practices of welfare reformers lie at the opposite extreme. The welfare reforms of the 1990s were created in a public and politicized debate, and the law embodies politically contrived and simplified constructions of the poor and their circumstances.[1]

The stories constructed by politicians and reinforced by the media have had a decisive impact on policies for the poor. The stories link the generosity of the public with the needs of recipients. Because welfare recipients may be inclined toward dependency by past policies that allowed them to remain on welfare beyond the point of real need, the generosity they require is discipline. Recipients are assumed to be weak-willed and self-indulgent because they continue to seek welfare support, and it is assumed they would be better off as self-supporting workers.

Welfare law is designed to force recipients to leave welfare for work and, through work, to become self-sufficient as other Americans are presumed to be.[2] Under the federal reform known as the Temporary Assistance to Needy Families Block Grant, welfare recipients must begin work activity within two years and may not receive welfare for more than a total of five years.[3] Responsibilities for caring for young children or other dependent relatives will not excuse the obligation to work, and opportunities for education beyond high school as an alternative to work are severely restricted. Not only does the law's requirement that all recipients work reflect an assumption that seeking welfare is conclusive evidence of the lack of a work ethic, the law also assumes that recipients can be motivated and morally educated by very small, short-term changes in incentives—much as parental discipline imposes moral lessons on a child through constant supervision and sanctioning. Further, the law assumes that such moral deficits in financial responsibility are closely related to other forms of moral deficit, failure to marry, childbearing out of wedlock, dropping out of school, and a variety of other presumptive requirements for successful self-support. The reformers have required the states to impose behavioral discipline on welfare recipients that will alter each of these deficits. As a consequence of these presumptions about the causes of poverty, the level of moral supervision and control of welfare recipients imposed by welfare law is indisputably very high.

Welfare law is closely related to the public's perceptions of dependency. Receiving welfare benefits has historically been a marker for dependency. Only those who are involuntarily dependent are considered deserving beneficiaries, and many conditions are attached to weed out those who could work and do not

deserve benefits. Receiving welfare, though formally restricted to the "deserving" poor, taints the character of recipients, though deserving and undeserving poor have always been difficult to distinguish.[4] Further, dependency is a problematic category in our society. Historically, dependent persons, such as slaves and women, were denied the full benefits of citizenship.[5] In contemporary society, those who are dependent are often not treated as social equals of those who are perceived as self-sufficient, a distinction that applies to persons with disabilities, the unemployed, and the poor.

Recent welfare reforms reflect widespread revival of an argument about the relationship between welfare and dependency.[6] Reformers have suggested that receiving welfare actually increases dependency. Poor women, they argue, have sought or remained on welfare when they did not truly need it, and they have become less capable of surviving without it. Welfare, it is claimed, is a moral hazard, and poor women lack the moral judgment or will to resist the temptation to receive welfare when they might, through sufficient effort, become independent. Moreover, reformers have argued that receiving welfare has even weakened the identity of poor women as potentially self-sufficient persons. Children of recipients are also said to be affected by a mother's dependence on welfare, and they are, therefore, more likely to choose welfare rather than work.[7] The strict time limits, work requirements, and sanctions related to childbearing and parenting required by the 1996 federal welfare law are justified by these assumptions about the moral character of welfare recipients.

Few groups have been subjected to laws that call for such complete surveillance and control. Yet we know little about the most critical aspects of the involvement of poor women with the new realist welfare policies, namely the way in which their decisions concerning work and family relate to the law. In truth, we know little about whether the welfare law that so powerfully projects an identity for welfare recipients plays any part at all in their everyday lives.

Welfare law may become active in the lives of poor women in at least three ways.[8] First, the meaning that the women themselves give the rights and obligations created by the law will shape the law's most immediate effects on their lives. If the assumptions of legislators about the values and motives of welfare recipients are wrong, then the instrumental effects of the law may be very different from those anticipated. Indeed, life stories show that the law has had few of its intended effects on the trajectories of work and family of some women. While any failure of welfare law to achieve its objectives may be attributed in part to imperfections of administration, far more may be due to a profound misreading of the character of recipients, the dilemmas they face, and a consequent misunderstanding of the support they would most benefit from. Conversely, some of the "success" of the reforms arises because the women have been successful in adapting welfare to goals that better suit the circumstances and needs of their lives. Such adaptations often accommodate complexities not anticipated by the law.

Second, the new welfare law may also become active in the lives of poor women indirectly but no less powerfully by influencing the actions of the organizations with which poor women must interact. Poor women interact with government agencies far more frequently than others who are affluent. Welfare administrators, as well as employers and private social service providers, are directly affected by welfare laws, and, in turn, their actions affect poor women. More subtly, welfare reform has influenced the public's perceptions of welfare recipients and might well influence incidental social interaction between poor women and others.

Third, closely related to the law's influence on the public's perceptions of the poor, welfare reforms may influence a welfare recipient's sense of herself. Law is a powerful cultural presence affecting meaning, actions, and expectations in everyday life. Morally freighted terms such as *workfare, welfare recipient,* and *personal responsibility* become building blocks of everyday awareness. These terms are built on an identity presumed by the law. What role do they play in the self-awareness of welfare recipients?

Welfare laws, like civil rights laws, carry implications about identity and the distinctiveness of rights bearers, and they may, therefore, create a double bind for persons who take advantage of them.[9] Because in the minds of many members of the public the beneficiaries of welfare laws have a particular demographic or social identity, all individuals in that demographic or social group may carry the stigma of welfare. Indeed, the law communicates such strong assumptions about the identity of welfare recipients that one of the law's primary effects may be potentially to reinforce the social fault lines embedded in the reformer's and the public's stereotypes. I will explore the possibility that welfare law, far from being ameliorative, has destructive consequences, isolating welfare recipients from family, community, and other poor women. Among other important factors, race tacitly informs the stereotype of the welfare recipient.[10] I will consider how welfare plays out differently in the lives of women whose identity falls on one side or the other of the fundamental fault line our society has constructed around race.

Exploring the ways in which the law becomes active in the lives of poor women who receive welfare may provide important pieces in a larger puzzle. The life stories of poor women reveal their moral identities as well as the similarities and differences between the identity of the poor who receive welfare and the identity of those who do not receive welfare. In one sense, to interrogate this distinction is to pursue a red herring. Statistical, historical, and ethnographic studies have suggested that women who receive welfare are mostly members of the working poor. Individuals and families move on and off welfare, in and out of work, as well as in and out of poverty. The poverty line itself is arbitrary, and the very meaning of poverty is in part determined by the politics of poverty rather than a comprehensive understanding of the capabilities and opportunities of the poorest members of society.[11] Thus, the law attributes a distinct moral identity to a group that cannot be distinguished from the poor in general, and the distinction maintained by the law has had real effects on the lives of poor women. Life stories illuminate the interplay between the law and women's decisions about work and family that are relevant to the assumed line of demarcation between the moral identities of the deserving and undeserving upon which the institution of means-tested welfare is based. . . .

DEPENDENCY BY LAW

The life stories of poor women suggest that the law's authority is deeply embedded in their lives, but their stories suggest that there is a difference between dependency on welfare and dependency constructed by welfare law. As we have seen, poor women are not weak or without the will to protect their families or to work to support them. Most of the women not only managed child rearing and work, but also dealt with major problems—family needs, neighborhood dangers, personal addiction or hostile caseworkers and other public officials. Welfare provided benefits for these women, but the law also constructed their dependency, by giving arbitrary authority over them to public officials by sanctioning their isolation, and by reinforcing social fault lines that separate poor African-American women from others who share their needs and interests. The women were aware of the law's destructive influence, and their stories displayed their resourcefulness and determination in resisting the construction of their dependency.

Scholars who have considered the place of law and the role of rights in the consciousness of welfare recipients have concluded not unreasonably, that the law is oppressive to the poor. Law subjects few other persons to such close supervision and dependence on the will of administrators as welfare law imposes on welfare recipients. Although it might be argued that recipients voluntarily submit to the terms and supervision required by welfare law, the extreme necessity that must be demonstrated for eligibility suggests recipients have severely constrained choices, and to decline welfare has high costs. Recipients can hardly be said to consent knowingly and freely to the maze of terms and regulations through which benefits trickle or to the nearly unfettered discretion that the complex interplay of conditions grants to administrators. John Gilliom concludes that the welfare recipient lives in a world of "confusion and ignorance about basic regulations" and "fear of the welfare agency and its enforcement of those regulations" that constitutes "an almost totalizing system of laws." The recipient's entrapment is complete, Gilliom notes, because the women are also denied access to the legal system's emancipatory capacity to give voice to those aggrieved by authority.[12] In the world of dependency created by welfare, he concluded, law renders poor women rights-less and without consciousness of rights.[13]

While it cannot be disputed that the power exercised by welfare administrators over poor women is one-sided, the identity and legal consciousness of these women is far from one-dimensional. Welfare mothers' life stories suggest that their understanding of law can be both more complex and, at times, more effective than would follow from the stark picture of naked oppression.[14] The picture of law's oppression of the poor confuses the identity of the welfare recipient constructed by the world of legal and administrative practices with the capabilities of welfare recipients. It confuses dependency as a legal construct with the ability of the poor to use their interactions with welfare administrators in strategic ways. It overlooks the fact that the women's interactions with different institutions of law can be quite different. And it assumes a close relationship between rights and identity, overlooking other sources of identity that provide a different framework for understanding authority and moral behavior (as suggested by Gilliom at other points) and ground legal consciousness in experience outside the welfare system.

Understanding the legal consciousness of poor women and the role of law is made more complex by the women's self-presentation, which often seems to concede that they are incompetent to engage in the discourse of rights required by law. Few of the women spoke of their interactions with welfare administrators in terms of rights. Of course, to expect welfare recipients to speak of welfare in terms of rights seems to be on quite the wrong track because few citizens think of their routine interactions with government bureaucracies in terms of rights. In the welfare setting, however, recipients are often practical and strategic about their relationships with caseworkers and other administrators.[15]

Further, the law's legitimacy in imposing public authority on the irresponsible behavior of the poor seems to be confirmed by widely observed "irrational" behavior of the poor-the welfare recipient buying luxuries with food stamps, the poor family dining out. Similar behavior—including extravagant or self-indulgent purchases—occurs at all income levels. The problem of poverty is that the poor have too little money to live tolerable lives and to be considered rational. Misperception of complex personal histories and the cultural context of poverty also contribute to validation of the supervisory powers created by welfare laws. In our PIC focus group, Cheryl's story about unsuccessful attempts to get a used-car dealer to repair a lemon suggested to other members of the group that she was immature and foolish, as they unself-consciously expected a black welfare mother to be. Her ineptitude following a recent divorce could have created a bond with

the white divorcees if her race and demeanor had counted for less. Such misperceptions and the new realism of welfare reform mutually reinforce each other.

As I noted, at my first listening the Perry Housing focus group seemed to confirm the story of the iconic welfare mother. The slice of each individual biography that was shared in the conversation contained elements that welfare reformers have remarked upon in their efforts to redirect the lives of mothers who rely on public assistance. Each of the participants received some form of public assistance. Each has two or more children. They recounted difficulties with drugs and with live-in boyfriends. Most worked irregularly or were not working.

Yet the picture that is composed from just these elements, like the interpretations embedded in the new law by welfare reformers, is outside of biographical time, outside the life cycle that sequences building social capital, learning about work, making decisions about childbearing, and supporting, in many different ways, other members of a family. The period of time on welfare for most women is far shorter than the public imagines. It is relatively short not because the women eventually acquire the work ethic they lacked, but because childbearing and child rearing constitute only one phase in a life cycle that includes other phases. As a society we allocate these burdens uniquely to women; yet as a society we are unwilling to recognize that women's decisions about work and other desired activities must always take account of that responsibility. Nor are such life cycles constituted in the same way in all parts of our culture.[16] Childbearing, work, marriage, and caring for other members of the family can fall in a very different order in different cultures.[17]

Thus, dependency is often misperceived through the lenses that the law helps to construct. The Perry Housing women often seemed unready to participate in the labor market. How is this to be understood? In general, women in our society are expected to assume responsibilities that are not assigned to men; indeed society pressures women to make child rearing their priority notwithstanding personal aspirations for market labor or a career. In the African-American community of the Perry women, their Christian fundamentalist background and limited family resources combined to make their early childbearing trajectory intelligible. As teenagers, their belief that completing school would have been a waste of time was not unreasonable because so many peers who finished school were unable to make a living wage in the job market. As adults, most have an increased appreciation for their need for education, but the rules of public assistance now bar that alternative. They are undaunted by the risks of working; contrary to the expectations of new realist welfare reformers, all have worked. They have accepted public assistance rather than take other kinds of risks, for example, risks that might affect the well-being of their children. Yet, the law brands them as morally dependent and disrupts an efficient plan for managing both child rearing and education,[18] for example, by imposing a family cap or time limits and requiring work instead of education.

As the PIC women made clear, the public identity of welfare recipients affects the choices of all poor women. The unemployed poor white women in the PIC group made a point of rejecting welfare. Their reasons for doing so may have been influenced in part by the complex interplay between the stigma of welfare and the stigma of a "failed" marriage, or the moral degradation associated even with "deserving" dependency for women. Most of all the white women's rejection of welfare seemed to reflect the racialization of welfare and the stereotype of the welfare mother.[19]

Not only may dependency be misperceived through the lenses that law helps to construct, but poor women have become more dependent through the interplay of law and the conditions of their poverty. The women are often

aware that the law contributes to their dependency. Anita Clark, the strongest voice in the Perry Housing focus group, understood the irony that public supervision leads to loss of autonomy. She observed that public officials undermined the autonomy of parental supervision through welfare conditions that removed parents from the home in order to work or fulfill bureaucratic requirements, through the disorder characteristic of vast, anonymous public housing projects, and through intrusive oversight by Child Protection Services. She was angry that, as a result of undermining parental authority, children grow up requiring greater public supervision on the street, in schools, and ultimately in prisons.

Further, Anita and other group participants understood that the greatest task of a single mother in the projects is policing boundaries between family and the world outside in order to protect her children. She, like the others, has fought to maintain the boundary between her apartment and the unpredictable environment outside, the boundary between her children and the children of neighbors she could not trust, the boundary between the de facto nuclear family (mother and children) and a nonresident father or lover, the boundary between the nuclear family and relatives who have a claim on her emotional, moral, and financial resources. In the complex social and spatial geography that dominated the group's discussion, the public-private boundary became one more border to police.

Welfare law makes poor women dependent by isolating them. For example, the Perry Housing women described ways in which the law's authority has created and reinforced barriers to relationships that might have assisted or sustained them or members of their families. The most pervasive influence in the lives of the Perry Housing women was the Perry Housing project itself. The women emphasized that it was housing of last resort; each of them had lived in better housing and entered the housing project only after misfortune reduced their means of social and financial support. The project is old, poorly maintained, dangerous, but, above all, isolated from public transportation, services, and shopping. The neighborhood is a good example of William Julius Wilson's second-generation ghetto, without members of the working class or middle class to sustain a sense of connection to possibilities for work and a better life. Unless relatives live in the project, the women are unlikely to see them on a regular basis. Sadly, there is a waiting list even for these apartments. The women are not provided opportunities to live elsewhere, and as long as they live in Perry Housing, their chances of reconnecting fully to a better life continue to decline.

Jackie James has another perspective on the interplay between welfare and family separation. Welfare authorities offered to place her teenage son in an apartment of his own during his last years of high school. Their offer seemed an easy way out of her difficulties in parenting the boy. In the project neighborhood, however, teenage boys are at great risk to gang influence and drugs. Jackie's first husband is a member of the police undercover detail that apprehends drug dealers. He is not the boy's father, but his influence over Jackie's son has been extremely important in keeping him from the worst influences on the streets. Those risks were greatly increased, Jackie says, by the welfare department's misplaced generosity. The other strong male presence in her son's life, Jackie's father, will have less frequent contact with him as a result of the change in living arrangements. It is possible to imagine a far better use of the cost of rental housing for the son, for example paying for his enrollment in a private school or doubling Jackie's own rent subsidy and allowing her to move with her children to a better neighborhood closer to her parents.

The cooperation by the Department of Social Services in setting up separate living arrangements for Jackie's son to leave her home is just one example of welfare's micromanagement of household composition. Welfare eligibility rules are far less benign, making it difficult to combine incomes to assure a poverty-level subsistence. Although the days are gone when fathers had to leave a household supported by welfare, new rules for combining sources of income received by others in a household disqualify many individuals living with an extended family with multiple, yet collectively inadequate, sources of income.[20]

Welfare also creates dependency by affecting the way poor women perceive themselves. We know women who receive welfare are not dependent in the way the public thinks because they often work and because their behavior does not support the theory that welfare is a moral hazard. They do not lack determination. Yet, there is a connection between welfare and self-concept.

The moral icon to which welfare is calibrated is the working male. Women are viewed by the new realism of welfare just as the male job market often perceives them, as workers with baggage. After offsetting the distinct cost factors that make female caretakers' job market participation visibly different from males', for example, by providing day care, welfare requires recipients to behave like males. The PIC men's focus group validated this standard by accepting the dominant discourse of the contemporary job market, aptly reflected in the faith expressed by one participant that "there's a job out there for everyone." The implication of this standard is that unemployed men should feel bad about themselves (and they do) and expect no assistance. The self-concept of the women in both focus groups was more complex. The PIC women were sensitive to the imperative imposed on women to care for children. They wanted public resources to help with child rearing and not just resources for minimal day care. Yet, even for them child rearing was not the moral equivalent of work and did not excuse nonwork. Of all the women interviewed in both focus groups, Sarah Cox, the reformed drug addict who had traveled the longest road back to redeem her family and her life, provided a justification for the women's claim to welfare as a universal entitlement based on fair play. Significantly, the foundation for her claim of entitlement to welfare rested on two assumptions, first that everyone will work when they are able to and second that everyone is dependent at some point in life and must give back to the community for the support they receive. Sarah's insightful theory would relieve women of the stigma of welfare, but other women in the focus groups had difficulty separating their experiences and their own values as single parents from the wider cultural significance of their mother-only child rearing.

For the Perry Housing women welfare was often a symbol of a deficiency—unreadiness to become self-sufficient by morally acceptable means, either marriage or work. For the white women in the PIC group, the identity imposed by welfare reinforced preexisting moral fault lines, a failed marriage, the struggle to preserve class and race identity in the descent into poverty. The African-American recipients in the Perry Housing group made a seamless connection between their identities as welfare recipients and the moral degradation they experienced through religious beliefs that identified them as fallen women. The simultaneous moral degradation of their religion and stigmatization by law surely made it harder to resist the public's condemnation. Recipients, including the Perry Housing women, readily criticized other recipients for their abuses of welfare. Their own low self-esteem, evident from the opening moments of their conversation, cannot be very far removed from the public's perceptions of them.

FIGHTING DEPENDENCY IN THE TRENCHES

Although women's stories show that the law's assumptions about the dependency of poor women with children can become a self-

fulfilling prophecy, many of the women struggled to avoid the dependency constructed by welfare law. Some women refused to apply for welfare benefits that might have alleviated their poverty because they found the symbolic costs too high. Other women adopted creative strategies that instrumentalized their relationship to the law in order to benefit themselves or their families in ways that the law did not formally permit. Differences among the women's stories of their resistance to dependency by law remind us that race deeply colors the identity and consciousness of all poor women and their moral judgments about each other.

In the lives of poor women the boundary between public and private always seems to be problematic. Less affluent members of our society have far more contact with government agencies in general,[21] and poor women approach such contacts with far fewer social and cultural resources than most others. The Perry Housing women did not always overtly contest the domain and authority of officials, but they often attempted to manage incursions into their lives. Identity itself may be in the balance for these women. As Tamara commented, self-esteem is affected simply by the power of minor officials to require recipients to come and go, often by making extraordinary efforts to transport and present themselves to satisfy trivial, routine, often apparently meaningless requirements.

Welfare recipients must deal with the enormous discretionary authority of minor functionaries in the welfare bureaucracy. The proliferation of rules under prereform welfare created effectively unlimited discretion.[22] Far from simplifying and clarifying eligibility and other conditions of welfare, reform greatly complicated the task of determining eligibility and coordinating provision of benefits and services. Caseworkers retained their discretionary authority. Many recipients echoed the complaint of Tamara Dent, my collaborator from Project Dandelion, that the power of the system, however it was exercised by caseworkers, was degrading and humiliating. Yet some women described effective strategies for dealing with the discretionary authority of caseworkers. Sometimes, the women found a sympathetic caseworker who used her discretion to the recipient's advantage and occasionally colluded with the recipient in bending rules. For example, one participant found it was possible to extend educational benefits well beyond the permitted maximum time period by judicious cycling on and off welfare and with the help of a sympathetic caseworker. Her goal was a college education and a thirty-thousand-dollar-a-year job, not a minimum wage job. She has postponed marriage until she can, in Carla's words, "bring something to the table."

There are reasons why recipients and caseworkers might be able to establish a sympathetic relationship, although this is by no means universal. Many caseworkers have had experience living on low incomes, and they are themselves closely supervised. Bonds of empathy can be created between recipients and caseworkers, but caseworkers can also respond to their own oppression by becoming hostile to recipients, increasing the frustration and oppression of mothers on welfare. The women in Perry Housing quickly learned how to change caseworkers if necessary by complaining to a supervisor, and a number have asked for fair hearings when dissatisfied with decisions. Few of the Perry women expressed animosity toward or fear of a caseworker, although the women often expressed frustration with the system and the way its rules impeded progress toward independence. The relationship that the women establish with the welfare bureaucracy was instrumental, not rights-oriented, serving specific goals by practical means. In the words of welfare historian Michael Katz, the women have found means of "navigating the welfare state from below."[23]

The women in the Perry Housing group approached other legal authorities with a different consciousness. Their complex relationship with the police reflected their dual perceptions of the role of the police. On one hand, the women believed that the police generally abused their authority in ways that did not occur in other neighborhoods. Anita Clark's claim that the police violated the legal rights of the kids they stopped, threatened, or arrested on the street seems consistent with this perception. On the other, some of the women suggested that Anita Clark's claim that the police violated the rights of kids inappropriately shifted blame away from the kids themselves and their parents. Anita's attempt to place responsibility for her children's troubles on the police by asserting rights was undermined by her own identity as a problematic mother. More generally, the women's responses to Anita revealed their troubled self-perceptions because they blame the police but also blame themselves for the risks their children face.

The women spoke confidently about mobilizing formal legal proceedings when they felt more secure about the legitimacy of a claim to a contested entitlement. For example, a number had requested fair hearings to contest welfare decisions. One mentioned employing an attorney to obtain larger support payments from her former husband.

Perry Housing officials required yet another approach. Because the relationship between the women and housing officials was more frequent and familiar than relations with other officials, it was also more complex. Sometimes the women could go right to the top administrators of the Buffalo Municipal Housing Authority through personal friends. On the other hand, disputes with a housing supervisor were sometimes harder to resolve formally because they could become entangled in mutual personal grievances, involving the women in constant arguing and complaining to obtain services. Thus, the legal consciousness of the Perry Housing women was often pragmatic, depending upon their expectations of results as well as their assessments of the wrongdoing of others and their own deservingness.

We have created a class of dependents by law, but their descriptions of problems they face reflect a double consciousness of dependency and agency. Poor mothers take the moral framework for their public identity seriously, as evidenced by affirmation of the public perception that welfare is widely abused, and at the same time they convey a double consciousness of their moral state. Poor persons, persons of color, and women are often not only conscious of their difference but perceive the world simultaneously in terms of the dominant (male or white) view and in terms centered in their own identity. Some may be more sharply aware of their double consciousness than others, and may believe in the importance of maintaining and developing the difference between meanings and concepts used in the dominant discourse and in their own situated discourse. W. E. B. Du Bois argued that this kind of double consciousness was a necessity among blacks who were destined to live compatibly with whites but never to become assimilated to their culture.[24] Others may simply be ill at ease with the images, rhetoric, or practices that mainstream social relations require. Consciousness is a behavior that responds to context and opportunity and, like identity, grows with the possibilities for new activity. . . .

Notes

1. Lucy Williams, "Race, Rat Bites, and Unfit Mothers: How Media Discourse Informs Welfare Legislation Debate," *Fordham Urban Law Journal* 22 (1995): ii–59; Kost and Munger, "Fooling All the People"; Robert Solow, *Work and Welfare* (Princeton: Princeton University Press, 1998).

2. The assumption of nondependency should be the subject of serious challenge because it is obvious that no one in our society maintains quality of life through individual effort. In the most general sense, society is a collective effort. More specifically, as Martha Fineman argues in "Cracking the Foundational Myths:

Independence, Autonomy, and Self-Sufficiency," *American University Journal of Gender, Social Policy, and the Law* 8 (2000): 13, families are a collective effort, as is the productivity of the "self-sufficient" male breadwinners who have the support of a family. Most particularly, every individual is the product of someone else's effort to parent, nurture, and raise that individual. We tend to perceive little of this effort as productive labor, and, therefore, we are inclined to consider it to be undertaken for personal pleasure and those who perform it as "dependent" on the productive labor of others. These perceptions badly confuse dependence and independence. My research is intended to examine how individuals experience dependence and independence in contrast to our public rhetorical constructions of dependency.

3. Temporary Assistance to Needy Families was enacted as part of the Personal Responsibility and Work Opportunity Reconciliation Act of 1996, 104th Cong., 2d Sess., sec. 910 (1996). It is codified at 42 U.S.C. sec. 601 and includes both work requirements (see, e.g., 42 U.S.C. sec. 602(a)(i)(A)(ii)), and time limits (see, e.g., 42 U.S.C. sec. 607(a)-(d), 608(a)(9)). For a review of the law and its requirements, see Kost and Munger, "Fooling All the People."

4. Joel Handler and Yeheskel Hasenfeld, *Moral Construction of Poverty: Welfare Reform in America* (Newbury Park, Calif.: Sage, 1991).

5. Judith Shklar, *American Citizenship: The Quest for Inclusion* (Cambridge: Harvard University Press, 1991).

6. The argument that welfare encourages improvidence is at least as old as early English welfare but is associated by many with the work of Malthus, who argued that strict work requirements were the only cure for indolence, irresponsible child-bearing, and poverty. See Philip Harvey, "Joblessness and the Law before the New Deal," *Georgetown Journal of Poverty Law and Policy* 6 (1999): 1.

7. The risk that women will choose welfare when they should choose work is said to be a "moral hazard." Many government subsidies create a moral hazard, namely the risk that recipients will change their behavior to make themselves eligible for more of the subsidy. Because subsidies are intended to induce changes in be-

havior, evaluation of the "moral" effects of a subsidy actually depends entirely on judgments about whether the subsidy induces too much or too little reliance. The language of "moral" hazard is misleading since in principle there is no clear threshold above which the motive for seeking an incrementally higher subsidy is corrupt rather than precisely what the law was intended to achieve. Judgments about whether reliance was too great or too little are strongly colored by political preferences; see Martha McCluskey, "The Illusion of Efficiency in Workers' Compensation Reform" *Rutgers Law Review* 50 (1998): 657. A great deal of research already suggests that the costs and benefits of welfare are a great deal more complex and create far less "moral hazard" than the reformers and the public have believed. See Kathryn Edin and Laura Lein, *Making Ends Meet: How Single Mothers Survive Welfare and Low Wage Work* (New York: Russell Sage Foundation, 1997); Karen Seccombe, "So You Think I Drive a Cadillac?" *Welfare Recipients' Perspectives on the System and its Reform* (Boston: Allyn and Bacon, 1999); David Zucchino, Myth of the Welfare Queen: A Pulitzer Prize-Winning Journalist's Portrait of Women on the Line (New York: Scribner, 1997).

8. David Engel and Frank Munger, "Rights, Remembrance, and the Reconciliation of Difference," *Law and Society Review* 30 (1996): 7.

9. Welfare law has some of the features of civil rights law because it provides benefits to a population that is assumed to have a distinct identity and to have fundamentally different needs and abilities from those who do not depend on welfare. But it is in truth an anti-civil rights law because it adds extra burdens to the lives of its target class. Welfare law also has some of the features of the law governing juvenile delinquents because recipients are assumed to be irresponsible and to require special supervision as a condition of receiving benefits. An individual cannot receive benefits under the law without acquiring a public identity as a person in need of help and supervision.

10. Martin Gillens, Why Americans Hate Welfare: Race, Media, and the Politics of Anti-poverty Policy (Chicago: University of Chicago Press, 1999).

11. Christopher Jencks, "Is the American Underclass Growing?" in *Rethinking Social Policy: Race, Poverty, and the Underclass* (Cambridge: Harvard University Press, 1992); Amartya Sen, *Development as Freedom* (New York: Knopf, 1999); Diana Pearce and Jennifer Brooks, *The Self-Sufficiency Standard for New York* (New York: Self-sufficiency Standard Steering Committee, 2000).

12. Austin Sarat, "The Law Is All Over: Power, Resistance, and the Legal Consciousness of the Welfare Poor," *Yale Journal of Law and the Humanities* 2 (1990): 343.

13. John Gilliom, "Welfare Surveillance, Rights, and the Politics of Care: A Case Study of (Non)Legal (Non)Mobilization," paper presented to the Western Political Science Association, Los Angeles, 1998, 4. Gilliom is not alone in making this argument about the law. Patricia Ewick and Susan Silbey similarly suggest that the poor stand disenfranchised before the law; see "Conformity, Contestation, and Resistance: An Account of Legal Consciousness," *New England Law Review* 26 (1993): 731, and The Common Place of Law: Stories from Everyday Life (Chicago: University of Chicago Press, 1998). Gilliom cites Catharine MacKinnon, "Reflections on Law in the Everyday Life of Women," in *Law in Everyday Life*, ed. Austin Sarat and Thomas Kearns (Ann Arbor: University of Michigan Press, 1993) to the same effect.

14. Gilliom proceeds to tell a more hopeful story, although outside the realm of legal consciousness. He describes an alternative consciousness oriented to an ethic of care. I think the women are not so incapable or so unsophisticated as to concede the realm of the legal altogether.

15. Lawyers, who prefer to think of welfare as a cluster of potential entitlements commanding administrators to award benefits, assert not so much the rights that recipients perceive as their own right to speak like lawyers in the administrative setting. See Lucie White's study of Mrs. G's successful self-styled presentation at a fair hearing, in "Subordination, Rhetorical Survival Skills, and Sunday Shoes: Notes on the Hearing of Mrs. G," in *At the*

Boundaries of Law: Feminism and Legal Theory, ed. Martha Fineman (New York: Routledge, 1991). Other discourses are possible in the administrative setting, and they are sometimes successfully employed by welfare recipients, though they often fail.

16. Carol Stack and Linda Burton, "Kinscripts: Reflections on Family, Generation, and Culture," in *Mothering: Ideology, Experience, and Agency,* ed. E. Glenn, G. Chang, and L. Forcey (New York: Routledge, 1994).

17. Even my attempt to describe the life course of the women in the focus group will leave the picture with enormous gaps. One reason for this is that disability, poor health, and limited education place severe restrictions on the ability of a large proportion of the poor to compete in the labor market or to manage daily life without adaptations. We have begun to take account of a limited range of such needs under the Americans with Disabilities Act. Accommodations for differences that limit access to the opportunities needed to have a minimally adequate life, let alone a full life, are now recognized as a civil right. We have not yet made the connection between this understanding of civil rights and the condition of many poor persons who are not identified by any existing understanding of "disability" (Rukmalie Jayakody, Sheldon Danziger, and Harold Pollack, "Welfare Reform, Substance Abuse, and Mental Health," typescript, 1999). A surprising number of the women I interviewed appear to fall into this group, and the incidence of invisible disabilities may be high. Several of the women in the Dandelion group are taking antidepressants. Two of the Perry Project women, Anita Clark and Sarah Cox, have leg injuries that have interfered with their performance of low-paying jobs that require standing for long periods of time or require lifting and carrying. Jackie James has narcolepsy.

18. Donna Franklin, "Early Childbearing Patterns among African Americans: A Socio-historical Perspective," in *Early Parenthood and Coming of Age in the 1900s,* ed. M. Rosenheim and M. Testa (New Brunswick, N.J.: Rutgers University Press, 1992).

19. As I argue below, welfare law reinforces social fault lines, acknowledging the racialization of poverty. The micromanagement of welfare, the moral supervision of recipients, and compulsory work requirements increased dramatically in the 1960s as urban poverty emerged as a "black" problem. These requirements, while not new, historically have received greater or lesser emphasis depending on the public's images of recipients and their beliefs about their moral character (Harvey, "Joblessness and the Law"). Further, because poverty has become racialized, the perception of dependency is a feature of African-American poverty, not just welfare. Katherine Newman's study of low-wage in Harlem, *No Shame in My Game: The Working Poor in the Inner City* (New York: Russell Sage Foundation, 1999), proceeds from an unstated but telling assumptions, namely that we must redeem the *African-American poor* as a class.

20. In her pathbreaking study of poor mothers in the 1970s, *All Our Kin: Strategies for Survival in a Black Community* (New York: Basic Books, 1976), Carol Stack notes the entrapment of poor mothers who cannot survive without assistance but who are forbidden to accumulate sufficient resources to invest in their own future. The present law makes a token effort to change the pattern by permitting personal development accounts, but it continues the same destructive pattern by permitting states to pressure families to isolate their poor and to exhaust all resources before receiving minimal assistance.

21. Leon Mayhew and Albert Reiss, "The Social Organization of Legal Contact," *American Sociological Review* 34 (1969): 9; Felice Levine and E. Preston, "Community Resource Orientation among Low Income Groups," *Wisconsin Law Review* 970 (1970): 80.

22. William Simon, "Legality, Bureaucracy, and Class in the Welfare System," *Yale Law Journal* 92 (1983): 1198.

23. Personal correspondence with the author, August 1997.

24. W. E. B. DuBois, *The Souls of Black Folk* (New York: Bantam, 1989).

NOTES AND QUESTIONS

1. What are the stereotypes assigned to persons on welfare? Where do these images

come from? How do moral judgments and stereotypes impact the structure and execution of public assistance policies for the poor? How did they reform in the mid-1990s?

2. As Merry (Chapter 26) pointed out, women who seek legal protection from a abuse are more likely to win their suit if they fit the description of a "good victim." This concept seems to run parallel to the "deserving beneficiary" on the welfare rolls. What characteristics does the "good victim" have in common with the "deserving beneficiary"?

3. According to Munger, how does welfare shape the identity of its recipients? Is this analogous to the effect of civil rights laws and the construction of racial or ethnic identity? How does the welfare process create a "double bind"?

4. Does the story of Mrs. G. support Munger's theory of the law's identity-shaping power? Is there anything in White's argument that conflicts with or undermines Munger?

5. Munger says that "dependency is often misperceived through the lenses that the law helps to construct." How does he propose to reinterpret the lives of women who are dependent on social assistance?

6. How do the women depicted in the article view their own dependency? What does Munger mean when he calls this a "double consciousness"?

Conclusion to Part III

Kafka's imagining (Chapter 12) of a person seeking admittance to law, but being unable to get it, seems, at first glance, strikingly inappropriate in a society that is as participatory and litigious as ours. When headlines announce that our courts are overwhelmed with lawsuits, such as the McDonald's coffee case (Chapter 18), it hardly seems that our legal system is not accessible enough. Yet the readings in this section complicate this initial response. They do so by raising the "how much" is "too much" question and inviting us to think about the accessibility of law from the bottom up as well as from the top down.

In addition, the readings remind us that the accessibility of law is socially organized in both senses in which that term is used in this book. They highlight the crucial role played by the officials and actors in law's own social organization in encouraging or frustrating access. They also explore biases in legal institutions that differentially affect law's accessibility and responsiveness to men and women, rich and poor people, white people and persons of color.

In addition, the readings point out the implications of the demand for access for the law itself, reminding us that when citizens turn to law they in effect affirm their faith in legal norms and their belief in the relevance of those norms to the social order. When citizens bring their grievances to legal institutions, they express a hope that their status as rights holders will be recognized, that their rights, once recognized, will be realized in practice, and that this realization will, in fact, make a difference in their lives. Moreover, access to justice and citizen participation help to legitimate the legal order by making it appear open, available, and responsive to those with significant grievances and needs. Of course, not all grievances and needs are legally cognizable, but paradoxically, law's legitimacy depends in important ways on maintaining a precarious balance between autonomy and accessible justice, between justice accessible according to rules and justice available on demand. This is a balance that moves and changes over time. Law encourages demands for access by recognizing new rights and yet sometimes responds to social conflict by restricting rights.

The recognition of unequal access threatens legal legitimacy by pointing to gaps and inadequacies in the fulfillment of the self-proclaimed commitment to equal justice under the law. Discovery of systematic inequality in the ability and opportunity to use legal institutions thus undermines faith in their capacity to treat all citizens with dignity and to serve all who merit its service. At the same time, those arguments typically call for reforms in legal rules and practices, or in the provision of legal services, which has the effect of suggesting that law can overcome this defect and that the problems of those without adequate access can be properly addressed through legal change. Finally, access may challenge legitimacy when contact with the legal system disappoints citizens. Citizens—promised majestic, disinterested, impartial judgment—may be disillusioned when they encounter bureaucratic irrationality and political bias. ✦

Suggested Additional Readings for Part III

LINING UP AT THE DOOR OF LAW

Lawrence Friedman, *Total Justice*. New York: Russell Sage Foundation, 1985.

Marc Galanter, "Reading the Landscape of Disputes: What We Know and Don't Know (and Think We Know) About Our Allegedly Contentious and Litigious Society," 31 *UCLA Law Review* (1983), 56.

—— "The Day After the Litigation Explosion," 46 *Maryland Law Review* (1986), 3.

David Jackson, "Litigation Valley," *Time* (November 4, 1996), 72.

Michael McCann and William Halton, *Law's Lore: Tort Reform, Mass Media, and the Social Production of Legal Knowledge*. Chicago: University of Chicago Press, 2004.

Neil Vidmar, "Maps, Gaps, Sociolegal Scholarship, and the Tort Reform Debate," in *Social Science, Social Policy, and the Law*, Patricia Ewick, Robert Kagan, and Austin Sarat, eds. New York: Russell Sage Foundation, 1999.

LAWYERS IN CIVIL CASES

Margaret Cronin Fisk, "Husband-Wife Team Takes On the Tobacco Goliath and Walks Away With a Monster Jury Award," *National Law Journal* (Feb. 19, 2001), at C14.

Hazel Genn, *Hard Bargaining: Out of Court Settlement in Personal Injury Actions*. Oxford: Oxford University Press, 1987.

Herbert Kritzer, "From Litigators of Ordinary Cases to Litigators of Extraordinary Cases: Stratification of the Plaintiffs' Bar in the Twenty-First Century," 51 *DePaul Law Review* (2001), 219.

Austin Sarat and William Felstiner, *Lawyers and Clients in Divorce: Power and Meaning in the Legal Process*. New York: Oxford University Press, 1995.

Jerry Van Hoy, "Markets and Contingency: How Client Markets Influence the Work of Plaintiffs' Personal Injury Lawyers," 6 *International Journal of the Legal Profession* (1999), 345.

WHOSE LAW IS IT ANYWAY?

Christine Carter, ed. *The Other Side of Silence: Women Tell About Their Experiences With Date Rape*. Gilsum, NH: Avocus Publishing, 1995.

James F. Hodgson and Debra S. Kelley, eds., *Sexual Violence: Policies, Practices, and Challenges in the United States and Canada*. Westport, CT: Praeger, 2002.

Kristin Kelly, *Domestic Violence and the Politics of Privacy*. Ithaca, NY: Cornell University Press, 2003.

Catharine MacKinnon, *Sexual Harassment of Working Women: A Case of Sex Discrimination*. New Haven, CT: Yale University Press, 1979.

Jeanne C. Marsh, Alison Geist, and Nathan Caplan, *Rape and the Limits of Law Reform*. Boston: Auburn House Publishing, 1982.

Patricia Searles and Ronald J. Berger, *Rape and Society: Readings on the Problem of Sexual Assault*. Boulder, CO: Westview Press, 1995.

Jennifer Temkin, ed., *Rape and the Criminal Justice System*. Brookfield, VT: Dartmouth, 1995.

WHO SPEAKS AND WHO IS HEARD: THE CONTINUING SIGNIFICANCE OF CLASS

William Forbath, "Caste, Class, and Equal Citizenship," 98 *Michigan Law Review* (1999), 25.

Joel Handler, *The Poverty of Welfare Reform*. New Haven, CT: Yale University Press, 1995.

Sally Merry, *Getting Justice and Getting Even: Legal Consciousness Among Working-Class Americans*. Chicago: University of Chicago Press, 1990.

Austin Sarat, "The Law Is All Over: Power, Resistance, and the Legal Consciousness of the Welfare Poor," 2 *Yale Journal of Law and the Humanities* (1990), 343.

Vicki Schultz, "Labor's Subjects," in *Lives in the Law,* Austin Sarat, Lawrence Douglas, and Martha Umphrey, eds. Ann Arbor: University of Michigan Press, 2002. ✦

Part IV

Severity and Leniency: Administering a System of Discretionary Justice

Part IV takes up the second aspect of law's social organization, the need to balance severity and leniency. Law must be severe enough to deter private violence, yet not so severe as to replicate it. Law must be flexible enough to accommodate and recognize exceptions, to temper justice with mercy. This balancing of severity and leniency is, as the Hay reading (Chapter 13) and the readings in this section show, often played out in the difference between what law says and what law does. Legal systems do not always do what they say they will do, and criminal punishment is one realm in which this gap is manifested.

Balancing severity and leniency, being severe enough to do justice to those who have violated the law and to deter potential rule breakers while being lenient enough to be fair in individual cases, can, if done right, increase the legitimacy of law. Balancing severity and leniency involves the proper deployment of discretionary decision making, in which legal officials decide when, and in which cases, rules should be followed strictly and deals should be made, excuses heeded, and mercy shown. Here we see yet another example of the importance of law's own social organization, in which bureaucrats and other legal officials interpret legal rules and make discretionary decisions. And here we see a place where officials may take notice of the gender, class, or race of the persons with whom they deal and over whom they have discretionary authority.

The next several sections explore the balancing of severity and leniency and the role of discretion in the context of criminal justice in the United States. They take up the practices of plea bargaining and criminal sentencing and the roles of lawyers and jurors in criminal cases.

As you read the following, ask if these practices seem fair. What role do the social characteristics of defendants play in discretionary decisions in the criminal justice system? ✦

Section VIII

From Severity to Leniency: Plea Bargaining and the Possibility of Justice

Chapter 30

American Courts

Process and Policy

Lawrence Baum

A *large proportion of criminal cases are resolved through pleas of guilty. Those pleas are "induced" by reductions in criminal charges or in sentences. In either case, plea bargaining results in the imposition of a lesser punishment than the original crime would have warranted. From one perspective, plea bargaining institutionalizes leniency. Some critics worry that justice is sacrificed for the gains in efficiency that are obtained when criminal defendants waive their right to trial by jury in return for leniency. Others worry that the reductions offered and the atmosphere surrounding plea bargaining are coercive and result in unwarranted sacrifices of rights. The next several readings take up these issues.*

Lawrence Baum describes plea bargaining and provides an account of why people plead guilty. He examines variations in the way criminal cases are handled and argues that plea bargaining affects all aspects of the adjudication of criminal cases, from the decision to charge to the sentence that a judge imposes. He notes that the pervasiveness of plea bargaining is a function of both the need to dispose of a large volume of cases and the sense of fairness that various participants bring to the process.

PLEA BARGAINING

Every criminal defendant must choose whether to plead guilty or not guilty.

Typically, at least in serious cases, the defendant initially pleads innocent; the choice then is whether to change the plea to guilty at some point prior to trial. (Occasionally, a defendant pleads *nolo contendere,* or no contest. This plea, like a guilty plea, waives the right to trial, but it does not constitute an admission of guilt.)

In most courts, the great majority of felony cases carried forward by the prosecutor—typically, more than 85 percent—are resolved through guilty pleas. This means that convictions generally result from guilty pleas rather than trials. In cases that began with felony arrests during one year, 86 percent of the convictions in Portland and 96 percent in San Diego were based on guilty pleas. And guilty pleas are even more dominant in most misdemeanor courts. For example, a study of about 1,600 misdemeanor cases in New Haven, Connecticut, found that "not one case was resolved by trial."

A defendant may plead guilty for a variety of reasons. In minor cases, for instance, the likely penalty may be so light that it would not be worth the expense and trouble of going to trial. But the most common reason is that the defendant expects to receive a more favorable sentence by pleading guilty rather than being convicted at trial.

This expectation may be based on an explicit agreement with the prosecutor or, less often, with the judge. In such an agreement, the defendant is promised benefits related to the sentence in exchange for a guilty plea. Alternatively, there is no explicit agreement, but the defendant still perceives that a guilty plea will produce a more advantageous sentence. This calculation, sometimes called an *implicit bargain,* is especially common in misdemeanor cases.

We can define plea bargaining to include only explicit bargains or to encompass implicit bargains as well. This issue of definition is more than a technical matter, because it affects our judgments about such significant issues as the potential for elimination of plea bargaining. For most purposes, I think it is appropriate to use the broader definition, because a defendant who pleads guilty in the belief that a more favorable sentence will result is in effect making a bargain. And when prosecutors and judges give signals, as they often do, that guilty pleas indeed are rewarded, it is not just the defendant who perceives that a bargain is occurring. In any case, most plea bargains in felony cases are explicit.

The practice of plea bargaining affects every aspect of the adjudication of felony cases. The handling of cases in their early stages is influenced by the expectation of bargaining, and the existence of a bargain constrains judges' sentencing decisions. Even cases that go to trial are influenced by the participants' awareness that the defendant did not plead guilty.

Forms of Plea Bargaining

The implicit bargain represents one form of plea bargaining. Explicit plea bargains take a variety of forms, which can be placed in three categories.

Table 30.1 presents some basic characteristics of each type of plea bargaining. The first is the *charge bargain,* in which the prosecutor reduces the defendant's potential sentence liability by reducing the package of charges. This reduction may be horizontal, with the number of multiple charges for an offense such as burglary being reduced in exchange for a guilty plea to the remaining charges. Or the reduction may be vertical, with the highest charges dropped in exchange for a guilty plea to lesser ones. The latter may be charges already in existence or new ones brought in as substitutes. Reduction of felony charges to a misdemeanor is especially common. Police officers and prosecutors sometimes set the stage for charge bargains by "overcharging" defendants initially—bringing some charges that they have little intention of carrying forward.

Because the defendant's sentence liability is reduced in order to make a guilty plea attractive, the charges to which a defendant pleads guilty may bear little relationship to the original charges or even to the actual offense. Indeed, according to one commentator, "it is no oversimplification to say that courthouse personnel first decide what a defendant's punishment shall be and then hunt around to find a charge that is consistent with their decision." In New York City, shoplifting and assault often are reduced to disorderly conduct, and assault may become harassment. Armed robbery frequently turns into unarmed robbery, a process known as "swallowing the gun." Some years ago a Wisconsin prosecutor who reduced an auto speeding charge to wrong-way driving on a one-way street was embarrassed by the discovery that his town had no one-way streets.

The second category is the *prosecutor's sentence bargain.* Here, the prosecutor gives the

---

Table 30.1
Characteristics of Major Types of Plea Bargaining

Type	Primary Bargainer With Defense	Constraint on Judge's Power?	Certainty of Sentence
Charge bargain	Persecutor	Yes	Low
Prosecutor's sentence bargain	Prosecutor	Yes	Moderate
Judge's sentence bargain	Judge	No	Very high
Implicit bargain	None	No	Very low

Based primarily on John F. Padgett, "The Emergent Organization of Plea Bargaining," *American Journal of Sociology,* 90 (1985), 756–760.

defendant some assurance about the sentence that a judge will hand down. Most commonly, the prosecutor agrees to recommend a particular sentence, with the expectation that the judge will follow that recommendation. Some sentence bargains involve less direct concessions by the prosecutor, such as an agreement to make no sentence recommendation or to schedule a case before a lenient judge.

The final category, almost surely the least common in felony cases is the *judge's sentence bargain.* A judge may indicate the likely sentence that would follow a guilty plea, and the defendant pleads guilty on the assumption that this sentence actually will be imposed.

Multiple forms of bargains sometimes are combined in a particular case; for instance, a prosecutor may reduce the charges against a defendant and offer to recommend a particular sentence in exchange for a guilty plea. Each courthouse community develops its own practices, with different kinds of bargains dominant in different places.

The Bargaining Process

The process of plea bargaining varies as much as its form. Much of that variation, of course, stems from the different forms themselves, which determine whether the defendant and defense attorney negotiate primarily with the prosecutor or with the judge—or, in the case of implicit bargaining, reach a decision to plead guilty without any negotiation. Defense attorneys usually bargain on behalf of their clients, but in cases involving relatively minor misdemeanors, defendants are often unrepresented and negotiate or choose to plead guilty on their own. Plea bargaining usually occurs shortly before the trial is scheduled to begin, but it can come earlier or even later. Indeed, one Virginia murder defendant agreed to a sentence of forty years even while, as it turned out, the jury was in the process of acquitting him.

In each court, routines develop for the initiation and transaction of bargains. In some places, prosecutors "hold court" prior to court sessions in order to negotiate with attorneys who have cases scheduled for trial that day. Some courts use pretrial conferences as a forum for bargaining. The prosecutor and defense attorney may go through a case file together to determine an appropriate bargain.

To a considerable extent, there is also a routine to the *terms* of plea bargains. Although every criminal case might be regarded as unique in some respects, basic patterns recur; members of the courtroom work group become accustomed to the most common forms of offenses, such as burglary and assault. For these "normal crimes," as one scholar has called them, standard terms of bargains— "going rates"—are likely to develop. These standard terms can then be adjusted for special circumstances in cases.

The terms of bargains are likely to be quite standardized in misdemeanor cases, and political scientist Malcolm Feeley has argued that our image of plea bargaining must be adjusted to reflect that reality:

> Discussions of plea bargaining often conjure up images of a Middle Eastern bazaar, in which each transaction appears as a new and distinct encounter unencumbered by precedent or past association. Every interchange involves haggling and haggling anew, in an effort to obtain the best possible deal. The reality of American lower courts is different. They are more akin to modern supermarkets, in which prices for various commodities have been clearly established and labeled in advance. . . . To the extent that there is any negotiation at all, it usually focuses on the nature of the case, and the establishment of relevant "facts." . . .

Although Feeley focused on misdemeanor courts, bargaining in felony courts also follows the supermarket model to a degree.

Both the going rates and the terms of bargains in specific cases reflect multiple factors. One factor is the participants' sense of justice and fairness, as applied to a specific offense and defendant. Perhaps more fundamental is the bargaining power of the participants, which rests largely on their estimates of what would happen if a case went to trial. Thus, in bargaining between prosecutors and defense attorneys, one important consideration is the estimated likelihood of conviction after a trial. Federal prosecutors usually have very strong cases because they carefully screen out the weaker ones; partly for this reason, they need to yield relatively little in exchange for guilty pleas. Similarly, when the sentence will be handed down by a judge who tends to be severe, the prosecutor's position is strengthened. Other considerations also can affect bargaining power. Heavy caseloads, for instance, put prosecutors and judges under pressure to dispose of cases quickly and thus give the defense additional leverage.

Explaining the Prevalence of Plea Bargaining

Why is plea bargaining so common? Perhaps the best explanation lies in the motivations of those who participate in plea bargaining.

Saving Time. One basic motivation for plea bargaining is the desire of lawyers and judges to save time. Of course, time is required to reach bargains and ratify them in court, but trials ordinarily require even more time—especially jury trials in serious cases. This difference is fundamental to plea bargaining. Indeed, historical research suggests that bargaining became popular in part because trials became more time-consuming.

Judges and full-time prosecutors and public defenders gain obvious advantages from reducing the time required to dispose of cases. Plea bargaining allows them to work shorter days, handle more cases in the same work day, or achieve some combination of the two. . . .

Achieving Desirable Results. For its participants, plea bargaining serves purposes that go beyond speed. Most important, plea bargains are a means for both the prosecution and the defense to secure acceptable results in cases, thus eliminating the possibility of highly undesirable outcomes.

In a plea bargain, the prosecutor gains a guaranteed conviction. Any case that goes to court carries at least the risk of an acquittal, and some carry a substantial risk. By eliminating this risk, a plea bargain helps to build high winning percentages for the individual prosecutor and the prosecutor's office. And by reaching bargains and helping to set their terms, prosecutors can also bring about what they see as appropriate outcomes in terms of the kinds of sanctions that defendants receive.

On the other side, the defense attorney and the defendant gain what they perceive as advantages in sentencing. Virtually all the participants in the criminal courts assume that, all else being equal, a defendant who pleads guilty will receive a lighter sentence than one who has been convicted at trial. Indeed, some judges announce such a policy openly; in 1966, for example, a Chicago federal judge proclaimed that he had decided to give four years of imprisonment to draft-law violators who were convicted in bench trials, while those who pleaded guilty would get two years. . . .

The primary rationale for rewarding defendants who plead guilty is that they aid the court in processing cases quickly. As one Chicago judge remarked of a defendant who might go to trial, "He takes some of my time—I take some of his." In Columbus, Ohio, lawyers and judges express the same idea somewhat differently: "Rent is charged for the use of my courtroom." Another rationale is that defendants who plead guilty have taken responsibility for their offenses rather than hoping for a lucky acquittal. The defendant who has cause for going to trial may not be punished, but others can expect to pay for their trials. As one Connecticut judge put it:

There's no penalty for the defendant who goes to trial when he honestly thinks that he shouldn't be found guilty, when he has a good defense to offer. It's a different case, though, when he is just trying to pull some fast one on the court, when the case is obviously so one-sided that no rational person would think he could be acquitted, then he'll get clobbered. . . .

The Impact of the Work Group. As I have already noted, the people who make up the core of the courtroom work group—attorneys and judges—tend to develop close working relationships through their constant interaction and interdependence. Indeed, as one lawyer observed of public defenders and prosecutors, "It's like prison guards and prisoners: They're all locked in together." Plea bargaining is facilitated by these relationships, which foster the development of regular bargaining procedures and tacit understandings about feasible terms under particular circumstances.

The interdependence of work group members also strengthens the pressures for plea bargaining. Not all lawyers and judges like plea bargaining and many come to their jobs expecting to bring most cases to trial. However they generally adapt to a system that is dominated by such bargaining, primarily because they learn its advantages from veteran lawyers and judges.

This adaptation is made more certain by the pressures that other members of the work group can place on a lawyer or judge who is reluctant to bargain. Sometimes this pressure is quite direct, making it clear that a participant will suffer for failing to engage in plea bargaining. Defense attorneys are especially vulnerable to direct pressure, because judges can penalize their clients by giving them unusually heavy sentences if they are convicted after failing to plead guilty.

More often, however, the pressure that people feel is subtle, even unintentional; the reluctant bargainer simply recognizes that other members of the work group depend on bargaining to do their jobs and that it makes sense to go along. One Pennsylvania judge was usually willing to accept plea bargains even when the sentences that were agreed upon struck him as too light. As he explained,

The system is set up so that the prosecutor plea bargains. And he plea bargains because the system demands him to plea bargain. Otherwise the system fails. So I've got to live with that, even though I don't approve of it. . . .

NOTES AND QUESTIONS

1. What is a plea bargain? What is the difference between an implicit plea bargain and an explicit one? What are the three main types of explicit plea bargains outlined by Baum?

2. According to Baum, more than 85 percent of felony cases are convicted on the basis of guilty pleas rather than trials. Is this coercion or efficient justice? What typically leads a defendant to accept a plea bargain?

3. How strong is the connection between the volume of litigation moving through the courts and the prevalence of plea bargaining? What motivations, other than efficiency, drive prosecutors and judges to strike plea bargains?

4. Should all offenses be eligible for plea bargains? Are there any offenses in which plea bargaining should not be allowed? Why or why not?

5. Are there parallels between the institutionalized practice of plea bargaining and the pageantry of "merciful" justice in Hay's account (Chapter 13) of eighteenth-century British jurisprudence? How are the two systems different?

6. Could plea bargaining conceivably contribute to wrongful convictions? How do you weigh this possibility against the knowledge that this practice also certainly secures and expedites the lawful prosecution of many violent criminals?

7. What do you make of such judicial attitudes as "He takes some of my time—I take some of his" and "Rent is charged

for use of my courtroom"? Such comments liken the criminal justice system to a game of high stakes poker in which the accused may either "fold" and cut his losses with a plea bargain, or go "double or nothing" for the chance at a trial. The threat of harder jail time, if they lose, may deter some from going to trial. Is this just? What if the accused is poor?

Suppose he or she is black in a predominantly white jurisdiction? How might the plea bargain gamble work against justice in such cases?

Reprinted from: Lawrence Baum, *American Courts: Process and Policy, Second Edition*; text excerpts from pp. 187–192. Copyright © 1990. Reprinted with the permission of Houghton Mifflin Company. ✦

Chapter 31

Scott v. United States

The plea bargaining system described by Baum (Chapter 30) depends on inducements that prosecutors or other legal officials promise to defendants (e.g., offers to drop charges or impose reduced sentences on those who plead guilty and waive their right to a jury trial). To make inducements work, those who exercise their Sixth Amendment right to trial by jury and are found guilty must receive a more severe sentence than they would have received had they pled guilty. The plea bargaining system seems to depend upon a regular practice of penalizing criminal defendants for the exercise of a right. Yet without sentence discounts, the incentive to plead guilty would be greatly reduced.

In Scott v. United States, *a federal appeals court confronted an unusual situation, namely an open statement by a trial judge that he "might have been more lenient" had a defendant who went to trial pled guilty. The court held that putting a price tag on the exercise of a constitutional right is impermissible and that federal judges should not be involved in plea bargaining. They should not offer inducements to defendants to get them to enter guilty pleas. At the same time, the court found that judges have an obligation to insure that pleas are entered voluntarily and that any plea bargain is fair.*

BAZELON, CHIEF JUSTICE

Vincent Scott was convicted of robbery under 22 D.C. Code § 2901 (1967) and sentenced to prison for five to fifteen years. The proceed-

ings preceding his conviction were, we conclude, free from error.[1] The events surrounding his sentencing, however, present thorny questions concerning what factors the trial judge may properly consider at that stage. We affirm the conviction, but remand for a resentencing in accordance with the principles announced in this opinion. . . .

In many cases, of course, the appellate court does not know whether the sentencing judge has performed his task thoroughly or well. The frequent blankness of the record has led to suggestions that the trial judge should be required to set forth his reasoning in announcing the sentence decided upon.[2] But that problem is not before us. Here the trial judge explained in some detail the reasons for which the sentence was imposed. He stated repeatedly throughout the hearing that he did not believe the exculpatory testimony the appellant had given at trial. And at one point the judge indicated that he was influenced as well by the fact that the appellant had insisted upon a trial in the first place:

> Now the Court didn't believe your story on the stand, the Court believes you deliberately lied in this case. If you had pleaded guilty to this offense, I might have been more lenient with you. . . .

I

The trial judge also stated at the sentencing hearing, "If you had pleaded guilty to this offense, I might have been more lenient with you." The stark import of this comment is that the defendant paid a price for demanding a trial. In view of the prohibitions the Supreme Court has laid down against making the exercise of Fourth,[3] Fifth,[4] and Sixth[5] Amendment rights costly, the pricetag thus placed on the right to a fair trial which these amendments guarantee would, on first impression, seem clearly impermissible.

And yet, despite the startling incongruity, empirical evidence supports the proposition that judges do sentence defendants who have demanded a trial more severely.[6] At least one

Court of Appeals has taken approving "judicial notice of the fact that trial courts quite generally impose a lighter sentence on pleas of guilty than in cases where the accused pleaded not guilty but has been found guilty by a jury."[7] An advisory committee of the American Bar Association has concluded that "it is proper for the court to grant charge and sentence concessions to defendants who enter a plea of guilty when the interest of the public in the effective adminstration of criminal justice would thereby be served."[8]

Much of this adulation for differential sentencing has been rationalized without frank recognition of the fact that whatever its advantages, the practice does exact a price from those who insist upon a trial. But the arguments in favor of differential sentencing cannot be dismissed by a wooden insistence that the exercise of constitutional rights can never be made costly. Some rights may be so vital that no deterrence to their free exercise can be tolerated. The Supreme Court has accorded such preeminent status to the self-incrimination privilege.[9] . . .

Two arguments inevitably appear whenever differential sentencing is discussed. The first is that the defendant's choice of plea shows whether he recognizes and repents his crime. One difficulty with this argument is that no court or commentator has explained why a defendant's insistence upon his self-incrimination privilege is not also evidence of a lack of repentance. Or his insistence that evidence unconstitutionally seized should not be admitted.

Repentance has a role in penology. But the premise of our criminal jurisprudence has always been that the time for repentance comes after trial. The adversary process is a fact-finding engine, not a drama of contrition in which a prejudged defendant is expected to knit up his lacerated bonds to society.

There is a tension between the right of the accused to assert his innocence and the interest of society in his repentance. But we could consider resolving this conflict in favor of the latter interest only if the trial offered an unparalleled opportunity to test the repentance of the accused. It does not. There is other, and better, evidence of such repentance. The sort of information collected in presentence reports provides a far more finely brushed portrait of the man than do a few hours or days at trial. And the offender while on probation or in prison after trial can demonstrate his insight into his problems far better than at trial.

If the defendant were unaware that a proper display of remorse might affect his sentence, his willingness to admit the crime might offer the sentencing judge some guidance. But with the inducement of a lighter sentence dangled before him, the sincerity of any cries of *mea culpa* becomes questionable. Moreover, the refusal of a defendant to plead guilty is not necessarily indicative of a lack of repentance. A man may regret his crime but wish desperately to avoid the stigma of a criminal conviction.[10] . . .

The second argument for differential sentencing is necessity. Most convictions, perhaps as many as 90 percent in some jurisdictions, are the product of guilty pleas.[11] Unless a large proportion of defendants plead guilty, the argument runs, the already crowded dockets in many jurisdictions would collapse into chaos. Since most defendants are indigent, the only price they can be forced to pay for pleading innocent is time in jail. Ergo, differential sentences are justified for those who plead guilty and those who plead innocent.

When approached from this perspective, the problem inevitably becomes entwined with that of plea bargaining. And the difficulties that practice presents are exceeded only by its pervasiveness. In many areas such bargaining dominates the criminal process. Its format may vary. The prosecutor may agree to reduce the charge in exchange for a guilty plea, or he may agree to recommend a lighter sentence. The judge may be aware of the agreement or he may not. If aware that a bargain has been struck, the court may or may not ratify the agreement before a plea is offered and accepted.

When a defendant pleads guilty in exchange for the promise of the prosecutor or court, a subsequent challenge to the voluntariness of his plea raises a recognized constitutional issue. When the accused refuses to plead guilty and subsequently receives a heavier sentence, the invisibility with which the system operates in individual cases too often conceals the constitutional issue. But the problem is the same in both contexts. Whether the defendant surrenders his right to a trial because of a bargain with court or prosecutor, or exercises his right at the cost of a stiffer sentence, a price has been put on the right.

The two sides of this coin are related in a practical sense as well. At least when only a single charge is involved, the effectiveness of plea bargaining depends upon the willingness of the court to impose a lighter sentence when a defendant pleads guilty. If such is the custom within a jurisdiction, the prosecutor enjoys credibility. Indeed, if the custom is sufficiently well known, actual bargaining may be unnecessary: enough defendants will be cowed into guilty pleas simply by the force of their lawyers' warnings that defendants convicted after demanding a trial receive long sentences.[12]

Thus, to the extent that the appellant here received a longer sentence because he pleaded innocent, he was a pawn sacrificed to induce other defendants to plead guilty. Since this is so, to consider the price he paid for the exercise of his right without regard for the process of which it is but one instance would be to ignore reality. . . .

If inducements are to be offered for guilty pleas, there are strong reasons why the court should not be the party to offer them. The trial judge may sacrifice his ability to preside impartially at trial by becoming too involved with pre-trial negotiations. Even if he does not, it may so appear to the defendant. It is important not only that a trial be fair in fact, but also that the defendant believe that justice has been done. The accused may fairly doubt this if he thinks the judge begrudges him the exercise of his right to trial. Moreover, the defendant's uncertainty concerning the expectations or wishes of the judge will prevent his exercise of the best judgment in deciding upon a plea.

Judge Weinfeld has concluded in two careful opinions that whatever the propriety of plea bargaining between prosecutors and defendants, the peculiarly sensitive position of the trial judge renders involuntary any guilty plea induced by a commitment from the bench.[13] His vivid portrayal of the "unequal positions of the judge and the accused, one with the power to commit to prison and the other deeply concerned to avoid prison" presents a compelling brief for demanding that the judge not become a participant in the bargaining process.

In this case the trial judge did not bargain with the defendant. Indeed he did not even point out that he might be more lenient with a defendant who pleaded guilty until after trial. But in so stating at the sentencing hearing he announced to all future defendants the guidelines in his court room. We cannot approve of these guidelines for the same reasons that we could not condone actual plea bargaining by a trial judge. The policy announced by the trial judge may not endanger his actual impartiality at trials as much as his participation in plea bargaining sessions might. And we certainly do not criticize the impartiality displayed by the experienced trial judge in this case. But we cannot ignore the impact of such a policy on the appearance of justice to criminal defendants and their ability to choose wisely between a plea of guilty and an exercise of their right to trial. . . .

II

In announcing the rule that the trial judge should neither participate directly in plea bargaining nor create incentives for guilty pleas by a policy of differential sentences, we must at the same time point out that the trial judge cannot ignore the plea bargaining process. A guilty plea must be not only voluntary, but also knowing and understanding.[14] If the defendant has decided to admit his guilt because of a commitment from the prosecutor, it is essential for the validity of his plea that he have a full and intelligent understanding of the nature and extent of that commitment. To . . . insure that a plea is made only "after proper advice and with full understanding of the consequences,"[15] the trial judge must make certain that the defendant has made a knowing appraisal of the alternatives open to him.[16] . . .

The fact that the trial judge must be aware of any bargain made before accepting a plea of guilty, and perhaps may ratify the agreement in appropriate circumstances, imposes an obligation upon the judge to supervise the fairness of the bargain. Since the trial judge determines the sentence a convicted defendant will receive, he cannot escape this responsibility if plea bargaining takes the form of a promised sentence recommendation. But the functional problem is the same if plea bargaining takes the form of a prosecutorial offer to reduce the charge, as seems to be the practice in the District of Columbia.[17] By deciding what charge or charges to proceed with, the prosecutor can often effectively control the sentence the defendant is likely to receive. To the extent this decision is made independently by the prosecutor before the defendant is called upon to plead, there is no danger that the defendant will be deterred from exercising his right to trial. When, however, the prosecutor makes his decision by offering to reduce the charge in exchange for a plea of guilty, the situation is quite different. If the trial judge is to so supervise the bargain, the law must resolve the troubling issue left in limbo by the Shelton opinion: what inducements to plead guilty are permissible? Since this case does not present that issue, it would be inappropriate to essay a comprehensive answer to the question. Because the problem is so closely entwined with

the policy of differential sentencing, however, several brief comments are in order.

First, the prosecutor clearly cannot have carte blanche to apply whatever tactics he wishes to induce a guilty plea. A policy of deliberately overcharging defendants with no intention of prosecuting on all counts simply in order to have chips at the bargaining table would, for example, constitute improper harassment of the defendant.

Second, there may be circumstances under which the prosecutor may bargain with the defendant without raising the constitutional question of whether the exercise of the right to trial can be made costly. When there is substantial uncertainty concerning the likely outcome of a trial, "each side is interested in limiting these inherent litigation risks."[18] The prosecutor may be willing to accept a plea of guilty on a lesser charge rather than chance an acquittal on the more serious. The accused may be similarly willing to acknowledge his guilt of the lesser charge rather than risk conviction on the more serious, or to accept the promise of a lighter sentence to escape the possibility of conviction after trial and a heavier sentence. . . .

In determining who has or has not "paid a price," it is essential to reason clearly concerning what class of defendants are being compared with what other class of defendants for what purpose and at what point in time. The danger presented by plea bargaining is that defendants deciding upon a plea will be deterred from exercising their right to a trial. The relevant vantage point is thus before trial, and the relevant comparison is between the expectations of those who decide to insist upon a trial and those who decide to eliminate the risk of trial by pleading guilty. If the sentence expectations of those two classes at that time are the same, then there will be no chilling effect upon exercise of the right to trial, and it is accurate to say that no "price" has been placed upon exercise of the right.

To determine the expectations of those defendants who insist upon a trial, we must consider the probability of conviction as well as the sentences received by those who plead innocent and are later convicted. The argument that the defendant who receives a heavier sentence after trial has "paid a price" because he receives a heavier sentence than the defendant who is acquitted (and goes free) or pleads guilty (and receives a shorter sentence on the same or a reduced charge) errs on two counts: (1) the comparison is made at the wrong time—after trial, when the uncertainty of litigation has passed, rather than before trial— and (2) the comparison is made between the wrong categories of defendants—the class of defendants convicted after trial versus the class of defendants who plead guilty or are acquitted rather than the class of defendants who exercise their right to trial versus the class of defendants who do not.

The situation is quite different when the prosecutor engages in bargaining not because he is willing to take a sure half loaf rather than to await the outcome of a trial, but because his limited resources convince him he must deter defendants from demanding a trial.[19] The divide between the two situations may be difficult to locate for even the best-intentioned prosecutor, and even more difficult for a trial judge to review. But the standards which guide prosecutors in the exercise of their discretion are as much a part of the law as the rules applied in court. Indeed, the impact of such standards is more decisive for many defendants than that of any other legal rules. If "it is procedure that spells much of the difference between rule by law and rule by whim or caprice,"[20] the same or more can be said of well-articulated, evenly-applied standards for prosecutorial discretion. If we must as a practical matter rely up on prosecutors to apply these standards in good faith, the responsibility for articulating appropriate standards must belong to the courts, not prosecutors. The nature of the process may well prevent judges from actually reviewing specific instances of prosecutorial discretion in all but the most exceptional cases. But this reality imposes a special duty upon courts to provide what guidance they can for prosecutors entrusted with such discretion. In the area of plea bargaining, the lodestar must be the realization that our law solemnly promises each man accused his day in court. If a prosecutor enters plea and charge negotiations not with the purpose of adjusting the charge to reflect the uncertainties of litigation but with the goal of deterring the defendant from the exercise of his right to a trial, the chasm between promise and reality is no narrower because the trial court affects a righteous air of noninvolvement. Perhaps the promise must be tempered if society is unwilling to pay its price. But that decision should be made in sunlight, and not in the shrouded mist of unguided prosecutorial discretion.

The arguments that the criminal process would collapse unless substantial inducements are offered to elicit guilty pleas have tended to rely upon assumption rather than empirical evidence. In many jurisdictions lacking sophisticated resources for criminal investigations, a large proportion of suspects apprehended are caught virtually redhanded.[21] The argument "But what if everyone did not plead guilty?" has force only to the extent that a sizable proportion of defendants have some motivation to plead innocent. If the defendant does have some hope of acquittal, the right to a trial assumes overarching importance. If he does not, there is some presumption that most men will not indulge in a meaningless act.[22] Moreover, the plea bargaining system itself may actually operate in some instances to burden the docket rather than to lighten it.[23]

If in fact more defendants wish to demand trials than our present system can process, there are two solutions: deter exercise of the right to trial, or commit more resources to the criminal process. This case does not require us to decide whether inadequate resources may constitutionally justify the former course. But we do think it important to phrase the question in the straightforward fashion of whether the cost of honoring a constitutional right can justify making the exercise of that right costly to the individual. The temptation is strong in the area of plea bargaining to assume that defendants convicted after trial receive a "normal" sentence while those who plead guilty and save the Government the cost of a trial receive special "leniency" in exchange. If this analysis were valid, some defendants would win and none would lose. But in reality there are winners and losers. The "normal" sentence is the average sentence for all defendants, those who plead guilty and those who plead innocent.[24] If we are "lenient" toward the former, we are by precisely the same token "more severe" toward the latter.[25]

Notes

1. The appellant claims that the continuation of his trial after his co-defendant changed his plea to guilty at the completion of the Government's case denied him due process of law. In the course of questioning the co-defendant to determine the voluntariness of his changed plea, the trial judge elicited a statement that implicated the appellant. At that time Scott's attorney moved for a mistrial on the ground that the trial judge, having heard the statement, would be prejudiced against the appellant. The motion was denied. On appeal Scott raises a somewhat different claim: that the jury must have realized that the co-defendant had changed his plea, and must have been improperly influenced by this realization in passing upon the appellant's guilt or innocence.

   We can agree with neither step in this reasoning. There is no necessary reason why the jurors should have concluded that because the co-defendant was absent on the second day, he must have changed his plea to guilty. The jury was, in the first place, instructed that they "must not conjecture, speculate, guess or surmise why the other defendant is not before you at this time." Even if we assume that the jurors might have so speculated despite this admonition, there were other possible explanations for his disappearance: he might have jumped bond; he might have been granted a mistrial; the cases might have been severed.

   If the jury did somehow conclude that the

co-defendant had changed his plea, moreover, there is no reason why the appellant should have been prejudiced thereby. The theory of his defense was not that there had been no robbery, nor that he and his co-defendant were not present at the scene. His claim rather was that his co-defendant suggested and executed the crime, while he declined the invitation to participate and resolutely looked the other way. Since the co-defendant was by the appellant's own argument guilty, the jury could hardly have been influenced if they did in fact conclude that the former had changed his plea after the first day of trial. In a similar factual situation, a District Court has recently found no constitutional infirmity in a case where, unlike the appellant's, the change of plea by a co-defendant occurred before the jury. See United States ex rel. Huntt v. Russell, 285 F. Supp. 765 (E.D.Pa., May 23, 1968).

2. See, e.g., Symposium, Appellate Review of Sentencing, 32 F.R.D. 257, 263, 274–275 (1962).

3. See Simmons v. United States, 390 U.S. 377, 389-394, 88 S. Ct. 967, 19 L. Ed. 2d 1247 (1968).

4. See, e.g., Gardner v. Broderick, 392 U.S. 273, 276, 88 S. Ct. 1913, 20 L. Ed. 2d 1082 (1968); Spevack v. Klein, 385 U.S. 511, 515, 87 S. Ct. 625, 17 L. Ed. 2d 574 (1967).

5. See United States v. Jackson, 390 U.S. 570, 581-585, 88 S. Ct. 1209, 20 L. Ed. 2d 138 (1968).

6. See, e.g., Note, The Influence of the Defendant's Plea or Judicial Determination of Sentence, 66 YALE L.J. 204, 206–209 (1956).

7. Dewey v. United States, 268 F.2d 124, 128 (8th Cir. 1959).

8. AMERICAN BAR ASSOCIATION PROJECT ON MINIMUM STANDARDS FOR CRIMINAL JUSTICE, STANDARDS RELATING TO PLEAS OF GUILTY § 1.8(a) (1967) [hereinafter PLEAS OF GUILTY].

9. See, e.g., Gardner v. Broderick, 392 U.S. 273, 276, 88 S. Ct. 1913, 20 L. Ed. 2d 1082 (1968); Spevack v. Klein, 385 U.S. 511, 515, 87 S. Ct. 625, 17 L. Ed. 2d 574 (1967).

10. See The President's Common on Law Enforcement and Administration of Justice, Task Force Report: The Courts 9 (1967) [hereinafter Task Force Report]; D. J. Newman, Conviction: The Determination of Guilt or Innocence Without Trial 3 n. 1 (1966).

11. See The President's Comm'n on Law Enforcement and Administration of Justice, Task Force Report: The Courts 9 (1967) [hereinafter Task Force Report]; D. J. Newman, Conviction: The Determination of Guilt or Innocence Without Trial 3 n. 1 (1966).

12. See Pilot Institute on Sentencing, 26 F.R.D. 231, 289 (1959).

13. United States ex rel. Elksnis v. Gilligan, 256 F. Supp. 244 (S.D.N.Y.1966); United States v. Tateo, 214 F. Supp. 560 (S.D.N.Y.1963); see also Euziere v. United States, 249 F.2d 293 (10th Cir. 1957).

14. Elksnis, 256 F. Supp. at 254.

15. Kercheval v. United States, 274 U.S. 220, 223, 47 S. Ct. 582, 583, 71 L. Ed. 1009 (1927).

16. See Bailey v. MacDougall, 392 F.2d 155 (4th Cir. 1968); United States ex rel. McGrath v. LaVallee, 348 F.2d 373 (2d Cir. 1965), cert. denied, 383 U.S. 952, 86 S. Ct. 1214, 16 L. Ed. 2d 214 (1966).

17. For a partial account of the process in the District of Columbia which nevertheless suggests the complexity of the problem, see H. I. Subin, CRIMINAL JUSTICE IN A METROPOLITAN COURT 15–17, 34–35, 37–38, 42–50 (1966).

18. See TASK FORCE REPORT 10. One commentator well-versed in the realities of plea-bargaining has labeled the problem as one of "variable guilt": "Justice does not flow readily from a computer where the survivor of a fight and witnesses at the taproom relate stories which indicate, in variable quantities, the facts of intoxication, provocation, malice aforethought and self-defense." Specter, Book Review, 76 YALE L.J. 604, 606 (1967). See also Alschuler, The Prosecutor's Role in Plea Bargaining, 36 U.CHI.L.REV. 50, 81 & n. 71 (1968); Weinberg & Babcock, Book Review, 76 YALE L.J. 612, 620–621 (1967).

19. We do not, of course, suggest that a prosecutor can or should ignore resource limitations in deciding which cases to prosecute. Prosecutors cannot pursue every case to a jury verdict. In deciding which cases or charges to drop or reduce, prosecutors must and do consider such factors as the strength of the evidence, aggravating or extenuating circumstances surrounding the offense, and so forth. But it is one thing to use such criteria to tailor docket loads to available resources without consulting the defense, and quite another to combat crowded dockets by confronting individual defendants with the threat that they can demand a trial only at the cost of risking conviction for a more serious charge or, what is of course the same thing, foregoing the "leniency" of a "lighter" charge that would be available in exchange for a guilty plea.

20. Joint Anti-Fascist Refugee Committee v. McGrath, 341 U.S. 123, 179, 71 S. Ct. 624, 652, 95 L. Ed. 817 (1951) (concurring opinion of Douglas, J.).

21. See PRESIDENT'S COMM'N ON LAW ENFORCEMENT AND ADMINISTRATION OF JUSTICE, THE CHALLENGE OF CRIME IN A FREE SOCIETY 96-97 (1967); see also Comment, Interrogations in New Haven: The Impact of Miranda, 76 YALE L.J. 1519, 1588–1589 (1967).

22. The counter argument, of course, is that the defendant has "nothing to lose" by demanding a trial. If this is true, and if enough defendants would demand a useless trial simply out of spite—or perhaps hope of remaining free on bail until trial—that only poses the question of why we should deter defendants from demanding a useless trial by threatening them with additional months or, more commonly, years in jail (whether through longer sentences or conviction on more serious charges). If the trial is truly useless, we should be able to induce guilty pleas with a much smaller stick—perhaps a small bribe for a guilty plea or fine for an innocent plea. But, of course, as the concurring opinion recognizes, a bribe would be an impermissible tactic to induce guilty pleas. And a fine imposed upon defendants who insist upon trial would be no more acceptable. The interesting question is why a literal price-tag upon the right to trial is offensive to our concepts of due process, while the figurative pricetag of time in jail is acceptable. The answer may well be in the tendency to define due process by past process.

23. See Alschuler, The Prosecutor's Role in Plea Bargaining, 36 U.CHI.L.REV. 50, 65 & n. 44, 103, 104 & n. 131 (1968).

24. For a slightly more refined analysis, which does not affect the thrust of the reasoning here, see text supra at p. 23.

25. The all-winners-no-losers analysis succeeds only if we "indulge an operating presumption of the defendant's guilt." Cf. Weinberg & Babcock, Book Review, 76 YALE L.J. 612, 617 (1967). If all defendants were guilty, we would not need to consider the possible chilling effect upon exercise of the right to trial, since upon this assumption there are no innocent defendants for whom the right to trial is important. In this improbable world, if we make the additional assumption that the sentences meted out in the absence of a plea bargaining system would be the same as those meted out after trial in a system characterized by plea bargaining, it might be accurate to say that the defendant who is allowed to "cop" a plea to a less serious charge "wins," while the (by hypothesis guilty) defendant convicted after trial is no worse off than he would be in the absence of a plea bargaining system. The assumption that all defendants are guilty is, of course, ludicrous if made in an absolute sense. But if one believes that as a factual matter a large majority of defendants are guilty, there may be a temptation to conclude that the lighter charges obtained by many guilty defendants in exchange for a plea outweighs by far the cost imposed upon the occasional defendant with a nonfrivolous defense who must risk a heavier sentence by going to trial. Regardless of whether one accepts the sort of calculus implicit in this reasoning, in evaluating the validity of the factual assumption upon which it is premised—that most defendants are guilty—allowance should be made for the likelihood that the operation of a plea bargaining system will reduce the number of defendants actually innocent in fact or law who ever reach trial.

Notes and Questions

1. What is meant by the term "differential sentencing"? What arguments do proponents of differential sentencing usually invoke in its defense? How compelling do you find these arguments?

2. Responding to one argument in support of differential sentencing, Judge Bazelon points out, "There is a tension between the right of the accused to assert his innocence and the interest of society in his repentance." How does the judge propose these two be reconciled?

3. How vital is the right to trial by jury? Bazelon writes, "Some rights may be so vital that no deterrence to their free exercise can be tolerated." He offers, as an example, the Fifth Amendment right against compulsory self-incrimination. Are there any rights that are not vital? Should we ever tolerate anything that deters citizens from exercising their rights?

4. Poor defendants presumably cannot afford to mount the strongest legal defense at trial. They thus assume more risk by exercising their Sixth Amendment right. Ought we to consider such social inequities when answering the questions in number three?

5. What, according to Bazelon and his colleagues, is the difference between a prosecutor's plea bargain and an offer of leniency made by a judge? Is this a practical distinction? What difference does it make in terms of generating voluntary, rather than coerced, guilty pleas?

6. What guidelines do the judges in *Scott* propose for prosecutors to use when soliciting a guilty plea? How useful are those guidelines for ensuring the voluntary nature of guilty pleas? What, if anything, would you change?

7. Are the concurring judges in *Scott* advocating the elimination of plea bargaining all together?

Reprinted from: *Scott v. United States.*, 419 F.2d 264 (1969).✦

Chapter 32

Torture and Plea Bargaining

John H. Langbein

Pleas of guilty are acceptable if they are voluntary. But determining voluntariness is no easy task. When can we say an act is voluntary? Can an act be truly voluntary if incentives and inducements are offered to secure it?

John H. Langbein argues that plea bargaining is never voluntary. It is, in his view, a form of torture. He compares the contemporary practice of plea bargaining with the system of judicial torture that developed in Europe between the thirteenth and eighteenth centuries. He contends that both the system of torture and our system of plea bargaining were developed to cope with the inflexibility of trial systems. In those systems, rules of procedure make it very difficult, if not impossible, to convict factually guilty offenders. Rather than reform those procedures, legal systems develop mechanisms through which the factually guilty can be convicted. In Langbein's view, it would be better to acknowledge the problems with trial procedures and fix them rather than continue to rely on a system that extorts pleas in return for promises of leniency.

What aspects of our trial system are, in Langbein's view, most problematic? Should plea bargaining be abolished?

In this essay I shall set forth some of the case against plea bargaining from a perspective that must appear bizarre, although I hope to show that it is illuminating. I am going to con-trast the modern American system of plea bargaining with the medieval European law of torture. My thesis is that there are remarkable parallels in origin, in function, and even in specific points of doctrine, between the law of torture and the law of plea bargaining. I shall suggest that these parallels expose some important truths about how criminal justice systems respond when their trial procedures fall into deep disorder.

THE LAW OF TORTURE

For about half a millennium, from the middle of the thirteenth century to the middle of the eighteenth, a system of judicial torture lay at the heart of Continental criminal procedure. In our own day the very word "torture" is, gladly enough, a debased term. It has come to mean anything unpleasant, and we hear people speak of a tortured interpretation of a poem, or the torture of a dull dinner party. In discussions of contemporary criminal procedure we hear the word applied to describe illegal police practices or crowded prison conditions. But torture as the medieval European lawyers understood it had nothing to do with official misconduct or with criminal sanctions. Rather, the application of torture was a routine and judicially supervised feature of European criminal procedure. Under certain circumstances the law permitted the criminal courts to employ physical coercion against suspected criminals in order to induce them to confess. The law went to great lengths to limit this technique of extorting confessions to cases in which it was thought that the accused was highly likely to be guilty, and to surround the use of torture with other procedural safeguards that I shall discuss shortly.

This astonishing body of law grew up on the Continent as an adjunct to the law of proof—what we would call the system of trial—in cases of serious crime (for which the sanction was either death or severe physical maiming). The medieval law of proof was designed in the thirteenth century to replace an earlier system of proof, the ordeals, which the Roman Church effectively destroyed in the year 1215. The ordeals purported to achieve absolute certainty in criminal adjudication through the happy expedient of having the Judgments rendered by God, who could not err. The replacement system of the thirteenth century aspired to achieve the same level of safeguard—absolute certainty—for human adjudication.

Although human judges were to replace God in the judgment seat, they would be governed by a law of proof so objective that it would make that dramatic substitution unobjectionable—a law of proof that would *eliminate human discretion* from the determination of guilt or innocence. Accordingly, the Italian Glossators who designed the system developed and entrenched the rule that conviction had to be based upon the testimony of two unimpeachable eyewitnesses to the gravamen of the crime—evidence that was, in the famous phrase, "dear as the noonday sun." Without these two eyewitnesses, a criminal court could not convict an accused who contested the charges against him. Only if the accused *voluntarily* confessed the offense could the court convict him without the eyewitness testimony.

Another way to appreciate the purpose of these rules is to understand their corollary: Conviction could not be based upon circumstantial evidence, because circumstantial evidence depends for its efficacy upon the subjective persuasion of the trier who decides whether to draw the inference of guilt from the evidence of circumstance. Thus, for example, it would not have mattered in this system that the suspect was seen running away from the murdered man's house and that the bloody dagger and the stolen loot were found in his possession. If no eyewitness saw him actually plunge the weapon into the victim, the court could not convict him.

In the history of Western culture no legal system has ever made a more valiant effort to perfect its safeguards and thereby to exclude completely the possibility of mistaken conviction. But the Europeans learned in due course the inevitable lesson. They had set the level of safeguard too high. They had constructed a system of proof that could as a practical matter be effective only in cases involving overt crime or repentant criminals. Because society cannot long tolerate a legal system that lacks the capacity to convict unrepentant persons who commit clandestine crimes, something had to be done to extend the system to those cases. The two-eyewitness rule was hard to compromise or evade, but the confession rule seemed to invite the subterfuge that in fact resulted. To go from accepting a voluntary confession to coercing a confession from someone against whom there was already strong suspicion was a step that began increasingly to be taken. The law of torture grew up to regulate this process of generating confessions.

The spirit of safeguard that had inspired the unworkable formal law of proof also permeated the subterfuge. The largest chapter of the European law of torture concerned the prerequisites for examination under torture. The European jurists devised what Anglo-American lawyers would today call a rule of probable cause, designed to assure that only persons highly likely to be guilty would be examined under torture. Thus, torture was permitted only when a so-called "half proof" had been established against the suspect. That meant either one eyewitness, or circumstantial evidence of sufficient gravity, according to a fairly elaborate tariff. In the example where a suspect was caught with the dagger and the loot, each of those indicia would be a quarter proof. Together they cumulated to a half proof, which was sufficient to permit the authorities to dispatch the suspect for a session in the local torture chamber.

In this way the prohibition against using circumstantial evidence was overcome. The law of torture found a place for circumstantial evidence, but a nominally subsidiary place. Circumstantial evidence was not consulted directly on the ultimate question, guilt or innocence, but on a question of interlocutory procedure—whether or not to examine the accused under torture. Even there the law attempted to limit judicial discretion by promulgating predetermined, ostensibly objective criteria for evaluating the indicia and assigning them numerical values (quarter proofs, half proofs, and the like). Vast legal treatises were compiled on this jurisprudence of torture to guide the examining magistrate in determining whether there was probable cause for torture.

In order to achieve a verbal or technical reconciliation with the requirement of the formal law of proof that the confession be voluntary, the medieval lawyers treated a confession extracted under torture as involuntary, hence ineffective, unless the accused repeated it free from torture at a hearing that was held a day or so later. Often enough the accused who had confessed under torture did recant when asked to confirm his confession. But seldom to avail: The examination under torture could thereupon be repeated. An accused who confessed under torture, recanted, and then found himself tortured anew, learned quickly enough that only a "voluntary" confession at the ratification hearing would save him from further agony in the torture chamber. . . .

THE LAW OF PLEA BARGAINING

I am now going to cross the centuries and cross the Atlantic in order to speak of the rise of plea bargaining in twentieth-century America. The account of the European law of torture that I have just presented . . . should stir among American readers an unpleasant sensation of the familiar, for the parallels between our modern plea bargaining system and the ancient system of judicial torture are many and chilling.

Let us begin by recollecting the rudiments of the American system of plea bargaining in cases of serious crime. Plea bargaining occurs when the prosecutor induces an accused criminal to confess guilt and to waive his right to trial in exchange for a more lenient criminal sanction than would be imposed if the accused were adjudicated guilty following trial. The prosecutor offers leniency either directly, in the form of a charge reduction, or indirectly, through the connivance of the judge, in the form of a recommendation for reduced sentence that the judge will follow. In exchange for procuring this leniency for the accused, the prosecutor is relieved of the need to prove the accused's guilt, and the court is spared having to adjudicate it. The court condemns the accused on the basis of his confession, without independent adjudication.

Plea bargaining is, therefore, a nontrial procedure for convicting and condemning the accused criminal. If you turn to the American Constitution in search of authority for plea bargaining, you will look in vain. Instead, you will find—in no less hallowed a place than the Bill of Rights—an opposite guarantee, a guarantee of trial. The Sixth Amendment provides, "In *all* criminal prosecutions, the accused shall enjoy the right to . . . trial . . . by an impartial jury . . ." (emphasis added).

In our day, jury trial continues to occupy its central place both in the formal law and in the mythology of the law. The Constitution has not changed, the courts pretend to enforce the defendant's right to jury trial, and television transmits a steady flow of dramas in which a courtroom contest for the verdict of the jury leads inexorably to the disclosure of the true culprit. In truth, criminal jury trial has largely disappeared in America. The criminal justice system now disposes of virtually all cases of serious crime through plea bargaining. In the major cities between 95 and 99 percent of felony convictions are by plea. This nontrial procedure has become the ordinary dispositive procedure of American law.

Why has our formal system of proof been set out of force and this nontrial system substituted for the trial procedure envisaged by the Framers? Scholars are only beginning to investigate the history of plea bargaining, but enough is known to permit us to speak with some confidence about the broad outline. In the two centuries from the mid-eighteenth to the mid-twentieth, a vast transformation overcame the Anglo-American institution of criminal jury trial, rendering it absolutely unworkable as an ordinary dispositive procedure and requiring the development of an alternative procedure, which we now recognize to be the plea bargaining system. . . .

PARALLELS TO THE LAW OF TORTURE

Let me now turn to my main theme—the parallels in function and doctrine between the medieval European system of judicial torture and our plea bargaining system. The starting point, which will be obvious from what I have thus far said, is that each of these substitute procedural systems arose in response to the breakdown of the formal system of trial that it subverted. Both the medieval European law of proof and the modern Anglo-American law of jury trial set out to safeguard the accused by circumscribing the discretion of the trier in criminal adjudication. The medieval Europeans were trying to eliminate the discretion of the professional judge by requiring him to adhere to objective criteria of proof. The Anglo-American trial system has been caught up over the last two centuries in an effort to protect the accused against the dangers of the jury system, in which laymen ignorant of the law return a one- or two-word verdict that they do not explain or justify. Each system found itself unable to recant directly on the unrealistic level of safeguard to which it had committed itself, and each then concentrated on inducing the accused to tender a confession that would waive his right to the safeguards.

The European law of torture preserved the medieval law of proof undisturbed for those easy cases in which there were two eyewitnesses or voluntary confession. But in the more difficult cases (where, I might add, safeguard was more important), the law of torture worked an absolutely fundamental change within the system of proof; it largely *eliminated the adjudicative function.* Once probable cause had been determined, the accused was made to concede his guilt rather than his accusers to prove it.

In twentieth-century America we have duplicated the central experience of medieval European criminal procedure. We have moved from an adjudicatory to a concessionary system. We coerce the accused against whom we find probable cause to confess his guilt. To be sure, our means are much more polite; we use no rack, no thumbscrew, no Spanish boot to mash his legs. But like the Europeans of distant centuries who did employ those machines, we make it terribly costly for an accused to claim his right to the constitutional safeguard of trial. We threaten him with a materially increased sanction if he avails himself of his right and is thereafter convicted. This sentencing differential is what makes plea bargaining coercive. There is, of course, a difference between having your limbs crushed if you refuse to confess, or suffering some extra years of imprisonment if you refuse to confess, but the difference is of degree, not kind. Plea bargaining, like torture, is coercive. Like the medieval Europeans, the Americans are now operating a procedural system that engages in condemnation without adjudication. The maxim of the medieval Glossators, no longer applicable to European law, now aptly describes American law, *Confessio est regina probationum,* confession is the queen of proof.

Supporters of plea bargaining typically maintain that a "mere" sentencing differential is not sufficiently coercive to pressure an innocent accused to convict himself. That point can be tested in the abstract simply by imagining a differential so great—for example, death versus a 50-cent fine—that any rational defendant would waive even the strongest defenses. The question of whether significant numbers of innocent people do plead guilty is not, of course, susceptible to empirical testing. It has been established that many of those who plead guilty claim that they are innocent. More important, prosecutors widely admit to bargaining hardest when the case is weakest, which is why the leading article on the subject, by Albert Alschuler ("The Prosecutor's Role in Plea Bargaining," *University of Chicago Law Review,* 1968), concluded that "the greatest pressures to plead guilty are brought to bear on defendants who may be innocent." Alschuler recounted one such case:

> San Francisco defense attorney Benjamin M. Davis recently represented a man charged with kidnapping and forcible rape. The defendant was innocent, Davis says, and after investigating the case Davis was confident of an acquittal. The prosecutor, who seems to have shared the defense attorney's opinion on this point, offered to permit a guilty plea to simple battery. Conviction on this charge would not have led to a greater sentence than 30 days imprisonment, and there was every likelihood that the defendant would be granted probation. When Davis informed his client of this offer, he emphasized that conviction at trial seemed highly improbable. The defendant's reply was simple: "I can't take the chance."

I do not think that great numbers of Americans plead guilty to offenses committed by strangers. (The European law of torture was also not supposed to apply in the easy cases where the accused could forthrightly explain away the evidence that might otherwise have given cause to examine him under torture.) I do believe that plea bargaining is used to coerce the waiver of tenable defenses, as in attorney Davis's example, and in cases where the offense has a complicated conceptual basis, as in tax and other white-collar crimes. Like the medieval law of torture, the sentencing differential in plea bargaining elicits confessions of guilt that would not be freely tendered, and some of the confessions are false. Plea bargaining is therefore coercive in the same sense as torture, although surely not in the same degree. . . .

THE MORAL BLUNDER

Because plea bargaining involves condemnation without adjudication, it undermines a moral postulate of the criminal justice system so basic and elementary that in past centuries Anglo-American writers seldom bothered to express it: Serious criminal sanctions should only be imposed when the trier has examined the relevant evidence and found the accused guilty beyond reasonable doubt. . . .

THE PROSECUTOR

Our law of plea bargaining has not only recapitulated much of the doctrinal folly of the law of torture, complete with the pathetic safeguards of voluntariness and factual basis, but it has also repeated the main institutional blunder of the law of torture. Plea bargaining concentrates effective control of criminal procedure in the hands of a single officer. Our formal law of trial envisages a division of responsibility. We expect the prosecutor to make the charging decision, the Judge and especially the jury to adjudicate, and the judge to set the sentence. Plea bargaining merges these accusatory, determinative, and sanctional phases of the procedure in the hands of the prosecutor. Students of the history of the law of torture are reminded that the great psychological fallacy of the European inquisitorial procedure of that time was that it concentrated in the investigating magistrate the powers of accusation, investigation, torture, and condemnation. The single inquisitor who wielded those powers needed to have what one recent historian has called "superhuman capabilities [in order to] . . . keep himself in his decisional function free from the predisposing influences of his own instigating and investigating activity."

The dominant version of American plea bargaining makes similar demands: It requires the prosecutor to usurp the determinative and sentencing functions, hence to make himself judge in his own cause. There are dangers in this concentration of prosecutorial power. One need not necessarily accept

Jimmy Hoffa's view that Robert Kennedy was conducting a personal and political vendetta against him in order to appreciate the danger that he might have been. The power to prosecute as we know it carries within itself the power to persecute. The modern public prosecutor commands the vast resources of the state for gathering and generating accusing evidence. We allowed him this power in large part because the criminal trial interposed the safeguard of adjudication against the danger that he might bring those resources to bear against an innocent citizen—whether on account of honest error, arbitrariness, or worse. But the plea bargaining system has largely dissolved that safeguard. . . .

THE JURISPRUDENCE OF CONCESSION

Having developed these parallels between torture and plea bargaining, I want to draw some conclusions about what I regard as the lessons of the exercise. The most important is this: A legal system will do almost anything, tolerate almost anything, before it will admit the need for reform in its system of proof and trial. The law of torture endured for half a millennium although its dangers and defects had been understood virtually from the outset; and plea bargaining lives on although its evils are quite familiar to us all. What makes such shoddy subterfuges so tenacious is that they shield their legal systems from having to face up to the fact of breakdown in the formal law of proof and trial.

Why is it so hard for a legal system to reform a decadent system of proof? I think that there are two main reasons, one in a sense practical, the other ideological. From the standpoint of the practical nothing seems quite so embedded in a legal system as the procedures for proof and trial, because most of what a legal system does is to decide matters of proof—what we call "fact finding." (Was the traffic light green or red? Was this accused the man who fired the shot or robbed the bank?) Blackstone emphasized this point in speaking of civil litigation, and it is even more true of criminal litigation. He said: "Experience will abundantly shew, that above a hundred of our lawsuits arise from disputed facts, for one where the law is doubted of." Every institution of the legal system is geared to the system of proof; forthright reconstruction would disturb, at one level or another, virtually every vested interest.

The inertia, the resistance to change that is associated with such deep-seated interests, is inevitably reinforced by the powerful ideological component that underlies a system of proof and trial. Adjudication, especially criminal adjudication, involves a profound intrusion into the lives of affected citizens. Consequently, in any society the adjudicative power must be rested on a theoretical basis that makes it palatable to the populace. Because the theory of proof purports to govern and explain the application of the adjudicative power, it plays a central role in legitimating the entire legal system. The medieval European law of proof assured people that the legal system would achieve certainty. The Anglo-American jury system invoked the inscrutable wisdom of the folk to justify its results. Each of these theories was ultimately untenable—the European theory virtually from its inception, the Anglo-American theory after a centuries-long transformation of jury procedure. Yet the ideological importance of these theories prevented either legal system from recanting them. For example, I have elsewhere pointed out how in the nineteenth century the ideological attachment to the jury retarded experimentation with juryless trial—that is, what we now call bench trial—while the plea bargaining system of juryless nontrial procedure was taking shape out of public sight. Like the medieval European lawyers before us, we have been unable to admit that our theory of proof has resulted in a level of procedural complexity and safeguard that renders our trial procedure unworkable in all but exceptional cases. We have responded to the breakdown of our formal system of proof by taking steps to perpetuate the ideology of the failed system, steps that closely resemble those taken by the architects of the law of torture. *Like the medieval Europeans, we have preserved an unworkable trial procedure in form, we have devised a substitute nontrial procedure to subvert the formal procedure, and we have arranged to place defendants under fierce pressure to "choose" the substitute.*

That this script could have been played out in a pair of legal cultures so remote from each other in time and place invites some suggestions about the adaptive processes of criminal procedural systems. First, there are intrinsic limits to the level of complexity and safeguard that even a civilized people can tolerate. If those limits are exceeded and the repressive capacity of the criminal justice system is thereby endangered, the system will respond by developing subterfuges that overcome the formal law. But subterfuges are intrinsically overbroad, precisely because they are not framed in a careful, explicit, and principled manner directed to achieving a proper balance between repression and safeguard. The upshot is that the criminal justice system is saddled with a lower level of safeguard than it could and would have achieved if it had not pretended to retain the unworkable formal system.

The medieval Europeans insisted on two eyewitnesses and wound up with a law of torture that allowed condemnation with no witnesses at all. American plea bargaining, in like fashion, sacrifices just those values that the unworkable system of adversary jury trial is meant to serve: lay participation in criminal adjudication, the presumption of innocence, the prosecutorial burden of proof beyond reasonable doubt, the right to confront and cross-examine accusers, the privilege against self-incrimination. Especially in its handling of the privilege against self-incrimination does American criminal procedure reach the outer bounds of incoherence. We have exaggerated the privilege to senseless lengths in

formal doctrine, while in the plea bargaining system—which is our routine procedure for processing cases of serious crime—we have eliminated practically every trace of the privilege. . . .

NOTES AND QUESTIONS

1. What was the standard of proof in Medieval European law? How did this contribute to the introduction of torture as a tool for Medieval jurisprudence? How, according to Langbein, does the modern American practice of plea bargaining resemble the Medieval use of torture?

2. How is responsibility formally divided among judges, prosecutors, and juries in the American criminal justice system? How, in Langbein's estimation, does plea bargaining disrupt the intended social organization of criminal justice? Do you agree that it does so?

3. Trial by jury, according to Langbein, is our equivalent to Europe's overzealous standard of proof. Is this comparison fair? Why or why not?

4. Langbein argues that the threat of a sentencing differential, like the physical pain used in the torture chamber, makes it "terribly costly for an accused to claim his right to the constitutional safeguard of a trial." Is this a reasonable comparison? Explain.

5. In *Scott v. United States,* (Chapter 31) to what extent did Judge Bazelon agree with Langbein's view of the relationship between sentencing differentials and the coercive nature of plea bargaining? Does providing plea bargain guidelines for judges and prosecutors address any of Langbein's concerns?

6. While critiquing the American legal system for not reforming "a decadent system of proof," Langbein identifies the practical and ideological factors that re-

tard systemic legal reforms. What are they? In your opinion, are these obstacles surmountable? Does he make any concrete suggestions to resolve this "breakdown in the formal law of proof and trial"?

7. Abolition of trial by jury would certainly eliminate the need for plea bargains by expediting judicial proceedings and al-

lowing every defendant to stand trial before a judge. Would this be an improvement in the judicial system? Would Langbein support such a move? Why or why not?

Reprinted from: John H. Langbein, "Torture and Plea Bargaining" in *The Public Interest*, 46, p.3. Copyright © 1978. Reprinted with the permission of the University of Chicago Law Review. ✦

Section IX

Lawyers in Criminal Cases

Chapter 33

Convictability and Discordant Locales

Reproducing Race, Class, and Gender Ideologies in Prosecutorial Decisionmaking

Lisa Frohmann

The role of lawyers in civil cases and the contributions they make to the resolution of civil cases was previously discussed. This chapter examines lawyers in criminal cases, beginning with prosecutors. Prosecutors exercise the government's power to decide who will be charged with a criminal offense. The prosecutor's charging decisions are almost entirely discretionary. If there is no pattern of discrimination, and as long as charging decisions are not vindictive, who gets charged with what crime is entirely left to prosecutors to decide.

How do prosecutors exercise this power? Here, as elsewhere, we want to know whether and how their decisions are socially organized; we want to know what social factors come into play in prosecutorial decision making. Lisa Frohmann presents a study of the prosecution of sexual assault cases. In those cases, one of the key determinants of prosecutorial action is the prosecutor's assessment of the likelihood that an offender could be convicted if charged. Frohmann argues that in assessing convictability, prosecutors attend to the locations in which crimes happen. They believe that different races and classes have different mores, which means that they understand the world in different ways. By "typifying" the activities, residents, and lifestyles in an area in which a crime occurs, prosecutors make judgments about whether a victim's story will hold up, and whether they could persuade a jury that a sexual assault actually occurred.

What categories do prosecutors use to assess sexual assault cases? What are the ramifications of using case convictability as a decisionmaking standard? How do race, class, and gender become salient in prosecutors' decisions? In this article I attempt to answer these questions by analyzing ethnographic data about prosecutors' work in a sexual assault unit. In the process I show how micro-level processes such as categorization are linked to organizational practices such as the convictability standard and that these contribute to macro-level patterns of race, class, and gender differences.

In the course of everyday work, legal agents categorize places and persons to inform and account for their decisionmaking. Categories describe locations, actors, and actions (Sacks 1972). For example, they may describe a suspect as a "child molester," the location of an incident as "four-corner hustlers' territory," or a defendant's actions as "self-defense." Legal agents' *choice* of descriptions is purposeful activity, selected to accomplish particular tasks, such as establishing the credibility of a defendant or arguing for an out-of-home placement for a juvenile offender. The chosen category implies a set of supplemental features that are typically associated with the category (e.g., "welfare mother" may imply "poor black woman without motivation"). Thus, categorical descriptions are the basis for ascribing other characteristics, activities, and motives to the persons and places under consideration (Sacks 1972; Watson 1978, 1983; Atkinson & Drew 1979; Maynard 1984; Jayyusi 1984; Benson & Hughes 1983).

Categorization work involves the intertwining of description and evaluation (Matoesian 1993; Holstein 1993; Loseke 1992; Miller & Holstein 1991; Jayyusi 1984). Judgments are made through challenge and negotiation over whether descriptions "fit" "normative requirements of categorical incumbency" (Matoesian 1993:26). For example, do this woman's actions leading up to an assault give her the moral authority (i.e., her behavior corresponds with typical features of the cautious woman) to call herself a "victim" (Frohmann 1991; Matoesian 1993)? Or do that woman's behaviors qualify her as a "battered woman" and therefore entitle her to entry into a battered women's shelter (Loseke 1992)? . . .

A little explored dimension of categorization work is the interplay of place and person descriptions. An examination of prosecutors' discourse on case convictability (the likelihood of a guilty verdict at trial) reveals how when deputy district attorneys (DDAs) categorize both victims, defendants, jurors, and their communities and the location of crime incidents, they are constructing *discordant locales.* By ascribing stereotypical characteristics of a neighborhood to victims, defendants, and jurors, prosecutors construct distinct groups with different cultures who live in geographically separate spaces and have different schemes under which they interpret the everyday world. In other words, "discordant locales" refers to a clash of cultures represented by these disparate locations. These descriptions are informed by prosecutors' knowledge of the sociographic landscape, cultural images of race and class, and work-related knowledge. I use "discordant locales" as a shorthand for a discourse practice used by prosecutors to justify case rejection.

Discordant locales create good organizational reasons for case rejection. When jurors, victims, and defendants are from discordant locales, prosecutors anticipate that jurors will misunderstand the victim's actions and misinterpret case facts and this lowers the proba-

bility of guilty verdicts at trial. This is highly problematic for prosecutors because convictability is the organizational standard on which prosecutors file cases. If cases are unconvictable, prosecutors have to bear the consequences.

An analysis of prosecutors' decision-making discourse refines our understanding of the use of moral character by legal agents. In addition to providing an example of how place and person descriptions *work together* in legal settings to construct moral character, prosecutors' construction of places as discordant locales is significant because it acknowledges multiple sets of normative behaviors against which prosecutors can evaluate standards of moral character, as *a* moral or normative standard from which some people deviate. It opens up the possibility of more than one cultural norm. Recognition of more than one normative standard has the potential to decenter dominant social relations, depending on how prosecutors use their knowledge when constructing discordant locales.

For prosecutors, these multiple normative standards are connected to race and class, and the prosecutors routinely focus on gender norms because the cases being considered are sexual assault cases. Thus this study examines how race, class, and gender are *made* salient within the organizational structure and logic of case convictability. I examine how prosecutors' discourse invokes and orients toward race, class, and gender through the categorizations of places and persons. I address the implications of this for a just legal system in the conclusion. . . .

THE CONTEXT OF PROSECUTORIAL CASE FILING DECISIONS

. . .Case filing is the point when prosecutors decide which cases will go on for adjudication by the courts. The standard used by prosecutors for this decision is case convictability—the likelihood that a jury would return a guilty verdict (Miller 1970; Neubauer 1974;

Mather 1979; Stanko 1981–82; Frohmann 1991). Typically, prosecutors assess cases as unconvictable and they are rejected from the system (Frohmann 1991; see Frohmann 1996 for exceptions to this rule).

The concern of district attorneys with convictability is shaped by the organizational policies and procedures of the prosecutor's office and the courts. The decisions are made within the organizational context of the prosecutor's office, the institutional structure of the court system, and the political context of the community. Prosecutors' decisions have implications for promotion possibilities, transfers, their own reputations as well as the reputation of their unit, and the branch office (Neubauer 1974; Frohmann 1992; Martin & Powell 1994).

Concern with convictability creates a "downstream orientation" in prosecutorial decisionmaking—that is, an anticipation and consideration of how others (i.e., jury and defense) will interpret and respond to a case (Emerson & Paley 1992). During complaint filing, prosecutors orient particularly toward "the jury," an ideal type formed from a composite of their previous trial experience, discussions with other prosecutors, and prosecutors' general cultural knowledge about the norms and mores around sexuality, heterosexual relations, and violence. This orientation takes two forms. First, prosecutors anticipate defense arguments to assess whether they can construct a credible account of the incident for the jury. Second, prosecutors invoke anticipated jurors' interpretations of case "facts" as the standard of convictability. Thus, the ability to construct a credible narrative for the jury and the jurors' ability to understand what happened from the victim's viewpoint are pivotal in prosecutors' assessment of case convictability. A prosecutor's anticipated inability to get a guilty verdict from a jury is a legitimate justification for case rejection. Nevertheless, prosecutors grapple with the tension between the organizational criteria for case filing and the implications of rejecting a complaint that is believable but not convictable. . . .

CATEGORIZATION OF CENTER HEIGHTS AND JURORS' COMMUNITIES

Categorization is a process of classifying specific places, persons, and events as general types. The descriptions used in this categorization are drawn from a mixture of prosecutors' experiences with case processing and generic cultural knowledge. These examples provide an overview of the typical categories DDAs use to characterize Center Heights as a location and the victims who live in this community.

In the first excerpt, an investigation into the police mishandling of a call for assistance revealed that the police response was based on the officer's assumption that the girls needing assistance were prostitutes, not victims of sexual assault. In between interviewing the victims and talking to the detective on the case, the DDA commented to me:

> The girls are right. The first cop car responds and says there was no one there. They were right about car 127, it was in the area with two white guys. They didn't believe her so they didn't want to waste their time and left. They see a lot of garbage, but sometimes, 10 percent of the time they are wrong, something really happened. . . . The cops hear a lot of garbage, lots of women lie, like the other case we had. They probably thought they [the girls] were hookers.

A few minutes later, the detective offers the DDA the following explanation for what happened on the street:

> I know what happened out there. They [the patrol officers] probably thought they [the girls] were prostitutes or that these were the girls' boyfriends and they [the boyfriends] took the jacket and [the girls] couldn't get it back. They see so much bullshit out there.

The categories constructed in these comments are prostitutes, "garbage," women who lie, and the area. Through description of what is usual ("garbage," "bullshit"), the DDA and the detective intimate that the majority of women in Center Heights who make accusations are not credible. Both the detective's and the DDA's remarks assume that women on the street at night typically are prostitutes or are playing games with police power for their own gains. Either way, the value and veracity of the women's calls for assistance are not worth much. Even though the DDA admits that in this case "the girls are right," the implication is that in general, the police response would be considered reasonable and acceptable because of how they categorize the women they typically encounter. . . .

The power of the place images can be seen through the extension of the images to those who come into the community from outside. In the next excerpt the woman who was assaulted lives outside of Center Heights. Prosecutors, drawing on their location categories and place images of Center Heights, question the victim's motivation for being in the area. They assume if people come into Center Heights, especially at night, it must be to engage in illegal activity. The victim's presence in Center Heights draws suspicion and challenges her moral character. The DDA is discussing his uncertainty about filing a case with a detective not involved with the case.

The girl is 20 going on 65. She is real skinny and gangly—looks like a cluck head [a person so strung out on drugs they will do anything for a high]—they cut off her hair. They picked her up on the corner of Main and Lincoln. She went to her uncle's house, left her clothes there, drinks some beers and said she was going to visit a friend in Center Heights who she said she met at a drug rehab program. She is not sure where this friend Cadly lives. Why did she go to Center Heights after midnight, God knows? It isn't clear what she was doing between 12 and 4 a.m. Some gang bangers came by and offered

her a ride. I think she was turning a trick, or looking for a rock [crack cocaine], but she wouldn't budge from her story.

In this place description, the DDA implies characteristics about the victim's activities and moral character. These character types are further developed through victim and suspect person descriptions. By interweaving place and person descriptions, the prosecutor constructs an image of the victim as a drug addict who sells her body to support her habit. This image is consistent with prosecutors' typifications of the people and activities in Center Heights.

The question "Why did she go to Center Heights after midnight, God knows?" implies the middle-class white point of view that Center Heights is not a place a reasonable person would choose to go. The prosecutor's suspicion about the victim's motives for being in the area is enhanced by the time of her arrival (after midnight) and her inability to account for her time between midnight and 4:00 a.m., a time when "good" women would be off the streets. This time, together with the space, is used to construct her questionable moral character.

Numerous place descriptions are cited to call her story into question. The "Main and Lincoln" intersection is known by police and prosecutors for its prostitution activity. She came to visit a friend she met in a "drug rehab program." Coming into Center Heights after business hours to visit a friend at an "unknown address" suggests to prosecutors that she is there to engage in illegal activities. Knowledge that she has been in drug treatment and the fact that she goes to her "uncle's house" and has some beers before she goes out bolster the description of her as a drug addict.

The person descriptions used by the prosecutor construct the victim as someone who could reside in Center Heights. That is, she "fits" the place image of Center Heights residents. This nullifies any positive status that could arise from being an outsider. The prosecutor describes her as a "girl 20 going on 65, skinny and gangly, cluckhead," suggesting that the victim is a drug addict who came to Center Heights to trade sex for drugs. This description has moral implications discrediting her as a victim.

Because the victim is not credible, the prosecutor's description of her assailants as "gang bangers" strengthens the prosecutor's position that the victim is a prostitute. The term "gang banger" invokes an image of violent young black men who are involved in activities such as drug dealing and prostitution. Interestingly, if the victim were credible, this description would strengthen the victim's argument that she was raped.

In each of these location categorizations, the moral character of the victims and suspects is discredited, increasing the likelihood that a jury would perceive the case as unconvictable. . . .

CONSTRUCTING DISCORDANT LOCALE CATEGORIZATIONS

Prosecutors presume that we live in a segregated society and that since the occupants of these segregated spaces have distinct cultures, they use different interpretive frames for making sense of and organizing the world. Living in segregated space means people have limited first-hand knowledge of people who are different from themselves. When people have limited contact, they form "place images" of other communities and their residents to make sense of their lives. We acquire these images through television, the news media, film, and music. Place images are

> the various discrete meanings associated with real places or regions regardless of their character in reality. . . . They result from stereotyping . . . or from prejudices. . . . A set of core images forms a widely disseminated and commonly held set of images of a place or space. These form a relatively stable group of ideas in currency, reinforced by their communication value as conventions circulating in a discursive economy. (Shields 1991:60–61)

When prosecutors invoke the different place images of Center Heights and the "other areas" where jurors are depicted as residing, they are constructing discordant locales. Discordant locales are part of the discursive economy of prosecutors.

In the following excerpt, a DDA captures the dilemma prosecutors face constantly in their decisions about case filing and how to try the cases they accept. Convictability, in part, rides on having a jury that understands what life is like for the victim and the defendants. Through contrasting descriptions of actual and ideal jurors, the DDA constructs discordant locales. This comment is made to the detective and myself during a break in voir dire proceedings.

> What I need is a panel of jurors from here [Center Heights] who understand what life is like living here in Peterson Gardens.

By stating the type of jurors she "needs," the DDA is suggesting that the actual members of the jury pool are from outside the community and are uninformed about life in Peterson Gardens. She implies that [cannot read] victims will make it difficult for jurors to make accurate judgments about case facts. Within the context of the larger geographic region, "Peterson Gardens" and "Center Heights" are code words for poor people of color. In much of the prosecutors' talk, race is either taken for granted background knowledge or the "race" and "class" of residents is invoked through place images and descriptions of behavior, communities, and cultural difference. Categories of place are constituting the racial and class identity of the residents (Atkinson & Drew 1979). . . .

VOICE AND THE CONSTRUCTION OF DISCORDANT LOCALE CATEGORIES

In the course of accounting for decisions, prosecutors animate the roles of several court participants (i.e., jurors, detectives, public defenders, and district attorneys) (Goffman 1981). When the DDA enacts a particular social role, s/he is voicing the positions of others (Wortham & Locher 1996; Bakhtin 1981 [1935]). Speaking in multiple voices reveals the various organizational relationships prosecutors orient toward (e.g., the public defender, the jury, the district attorney's office, other agencies, other court events) in the work of case processing (Maynard 1984). These orientations make visible prosecutors' downstream concerns with convictability. They also reveal prosecutors' culpability in the decisions that are made.

Prosecutors voice the positions of others to evaluate actions, actors, events, and locations and as a strategy for producing legitimate, authoritative, and persuasive accounts of case decisions. Through expressing others' positions, the DDA displays the complexity of case processing, giving their accounts a measure of professionalism and authority. They also demonstrate objectivity by taking account of various participants' standpoints (i.e., victims, jurors, and court officials). These multiple positions are a key element in the construction of discordant locales; by shifting between the perspectives of jurors, victims, residents, defense attorneys, and prosecutors, the DDA voices the discordant categorization schemes. . . .

CONCLUSION

Discordant locales are prosecutors' categorizations of places and the people associated with them that they encounter in the work of case prosecution. DDAs' categorizations are informed by their typifications of area activities, residents and their lifestyles, and cultural images and ideologies of specific race/class groups. Mapped onto the place descriptions are sets of attitudes, behaviors values, and norms that are attributed to those who reside in, use, or pass through these areas. Through the interaction of place and person descriptions, prosecutors constitute the moral character of persons and place.

Categorization of places as discordant locales is a justification for case rejection. Prosecutors maintain that different race and class groups create separate cultures, which in turn have distinct categorization schemes for understanding the social world. These differences, according to prosecutors, lead to misinterpretations by jurors of victims that would result in "not guilty" verdicts if the cases were forwarded. The organizational concern with convictability renders discordant locales a legitimate and frequent unofficial justification for case rejection. This would not appear on official, written accounts of case rejection; reasons given there typically would be "victim's unwillingness to cooperate" and "insufficient evidence."

Given the convictability standard, what are the implications of discordant locale categorizations for the legal system? In addition to possible individual miscarriages of justice that occur when prosecutors decide not to pursue cases that they believe to have factual basis, I suggest that the pattern of their decisions has wider sociolegal significance. An intended consequence is the evaluation of cases as convictable or unconvictable, winnowing "weak" cases out of the system. This is seen as organizationally necessary, to relieve the overburdened court system of cases that would use up resources and lead "nowhere." An unintended consequence of prosecutors' decisions is to legitimize specific ideologies of race and class and contribute to the reproduction of social inequality in the criminal justice system. Whether prosecutors are recognizing the force and reality of the moral judgments of middle-class white jurors or adopting these judgments as the basis for their decisions, certain people are more likely to be excluded from justice. As Merry (1990) argues, participation in the justice system is part of a sense of entitlement. Whatever the paradoxes of victims actually using the legal system, when some victims are routinely dismissed because their stories do not fit the hegemonic group's image of a real victim, that widens the division between those who have access to the law and those who do not. Furthermore, prosecutors using this justification reinforce the idea that social arrangements organized around race and class are "natural," which in turn reifies the differences and misunderstandings.

For those working to create a just legal system, these data suggest that changes in organizational policies may be necessary to expand and equalize citizens' access to the law. Reformulating how the convictability standard is used through policy changes would be one possible intervention. For example, allowing prosecutors to file a certain percentage of believable but risky cases without regard to convictability without negative consequences may open the boundaries of what prosecutors conceive as convictable. In addition, giving anticipated jurors' norms and values less weight at the filing process might also bring a greater variety of cases into the system. If prosecutors dealt with actual juries to prosecute more of these cases, they might learn how to win the cases, hence expanding what is perceived as "convictable."

Examining how prosecutors construct discordant locales reveals the depth at which we must look to see how race, class, and gender systems are constituted and maintained through legal decisionmaking. The ideologies that constitute the social order are not just perpetuated by overt or purposeful activity. Micro-level interpretive practices that may not appear to have race-, class-, or gender-biased intentions nevertheless contribute to the institutionalization of these biases. Prosecutorial accounts can unintentionally perpetuate historical social relations by contextualizing prosecution decisions in cultural representations of places and people. We live in a culture that has been built on an unequal distribution of economic and political resources by race, class, and gender. Drawing on these frameworks of interpretation to make sense of case facts and to justify case decisions continues the current social order and its division of resources and influences.

References

Atkinson, J. Maxwell, & Paul Drew (1979) *Order in Court: The Organization of Verbal Interaction in Judicial Settings.* Atlantic Heights, NJ: Humanities Press.

Bakhtin, M. M. (1981 [1935]) "Discourse in the Novel," trans. C. Emerson & M. Holquist, in M. M. Bakhtin, *The Dialogic Imagination: Four Essays,* ed. M. Holquist. Austin: Univ. of Texas Press.

Benson, Douglas, & John A. Hughes (1983) "The Use of Categories and the Display of Culture," in D. Benson & J. A. Hughes, *The Perspective of Ethnomethodology.* New York: Longman.

Emerson, Robert M., & Blair Paley (1992) "Organizational Horizons and Complaint-Filing," in K. Hawkins, ed., *The Uses of Discretion.* New York: Oxford Univ. Press.

Frohmann, Lisa (1991) "Discrediting Victims' Allegations of Sexual Assault: Prosecutorial Accounts of Case Rejection," 38 *Social Problems* 213–226.

———. (1996) "'Hard Cases': Prosecutorial Accounts for Filing Unconvictable Sexual Assault Complaints," in H. Z. Lopata & A. E. Figert, eds., *Current Research on Occupations and Professions,* vol. 9. Greenwich, CT: JAI Press.

Goffman, Erving (1981) *Forms of Talk.* Philadelphia: Univ. of Pennsylvania Press.

Holstein, James A. (1993) *Court-Ordered Insanity: Interpretive Practice and Involuntary Commitment.* New York: Aldine de Gruyter.

Jayyusi, Lena (1984) *Categorization and the Moral Order.* Boston: Routledge Kegan Paul.

Loseke, Donileen R. (1992) *The Battered Woman and the Shelters: The Social Construction of Wife Abuse.* Albany, NY: SUNY Press.

Martin, Patricia Yancy, & R. Marlene Powell (1994) "Accounting for the 'Second Assault': Legal Organizations Framing of Rape Victims," 19 *Law & Social Inquiry* 853–890.

Mather, Lynn M. (1979) *Plea Bargaining or Trial? The Process of Criminal-Case Disposition.* Lexington, MA: Lexington Books.

Matoesian, Gregory M. (1993) *Reproducing Rape: Domination through Talk in the Courtroom.* Chicago: Univ. of Chicago Press.

———. (1995) "Language, Law, and Society: Policy Implications of the Kennedy Smith Rape Trial," 29 *Law & Society Rev.* 669–702.

Maynard, Douglas W. (1984) *Inside Plea Bargaining: The Language of the Negotiator.* New York: Plenum Press.

Merry, Sally Engle (1990) *Getting Justice and Getting Even: Legal Consciousness among Working-Class America.* Chicago: Univ. of Chicago Press.

Miller, Frank W. (1970) *Prosecution: The Decision to Charge a Suspect with a Crime.* Boston: Little, Brown & Co.

Miller, Gale, & James A. Holstein (1991) "Social Problems Work in Street Level Bureaucracies: Rhetoric and Organizational Process," in G. Miller, ed., *Studies in Organizational Sociology: Studies in Honor of Charles K. Warriner.* Greenwich, CT: JAI Press.

Neubauer, David W. (1974) *Criminal Justice in Middle America.* Morristown, NJ: General Learning Press.

Sacks, Harvey (1972) "On the Analyzability of Stories by Children," in J. J. Gumperz & D. H. Hymes, eds., *Directions in Sociolinguistics: The Ethnography of Communication.* New York: Holt, Rinehart & Winston.

Shields, Rob (1991) *Places on the Margin: Alternative Geographies of Modernity.* London: Routledge.

Stanko, Elizabeth Anne (1981–1982) "The Impact of Victim Assessment on Prosecutors' Screening Decisions: The Case of the New York District Attorney's Office," 16 *Law & Society Rev.* 225–239.

Watson, D. R. (1978) "Categorization, Authorization, and Blame-Negotiation in Conversation," 12 *Sociology* 105–113.

———. (1983) "The Presentation of the Victim and Motive in Discourse: The Case of Police Interrogations and Interviews," 8 (1–2) *Victimology* 31–52.

Wortham, Stanton, & Michael Locher (1996) "Voicing on the News: An Analytic Technique for Studying Media Bias," 16 *Text* 557–585.

Notes and Questions

1. What is the "convictability standard" for prosecutors? What is it about the social organization of the district attorney's office and the courts that makes the convictability standard so important? Who benefits from a high convictability standard? A low one?

2. Why are prosecutors concerned with "discordant locales"? How does Frohmann explain this concept? How do assumptions about moral character contribute to the construction of discordant locales? Is this an acceptable part of the criminal justice system? Is it avoidable? What are the implications for equal treatment under law?

3. To assess the convictability of a case, prosecutors must make sweeping assumptions about the attitudes of defense attorneys and potential jurors. According to Frohmann, such "micro-level interpretive practices that may not appear to have race-, class-, or gender-biased intentions nevertheless contribute to the institutionalization of these biases." How so? Do you agree? Are prosecutors solely responsible for the institutionalization of these social biases? What do you think about the interpretive practices of other actors in the social organization of law—police, judges, or legislators, for instance?

4. Suppose the district attorney's office was compelled to prosecute cases strictly upon a *mens rea* standard. How might this change the assessment of convictability? Would it make law more or less accessible overall?

5. By Frohmann's own description, her article examines "how prosecutors' discourse invokes and orients toward race, class, and gender through the categorizations of places and persons." In what ways do Frohmann's case studies reflect White's conception of "law as rhetoric" (Chapter 28)? Do prosecutors have any obligation to use their rhetorical skills to orient cases *away* from race, class,

and gender, or is this an unrealistic expectation? What would White say?

6. How does Frohmann propose to reform the prosecutorial bureaucracy? Is she being realistic? What ideas do you have?

Chapter 34

Understanding Lawyers' Ethics

Monroe H. Freedman
Abbe Smith

We *now turn from prosecutors to criminal defense lawyers. Scholars often stress the roles of defense lawyers as advocates in an adversary system. They emphasize their importance as guardians of the rights of the accused as well as their responsibility to take advantage of legal rules that allocate burdens of proof (the state carries the burden of proving beyond a reasonable doubt the guilt of the accused) and presumptions (the accused is presumed innocent) in criminal cases. They suggest that the ethics of criminal defense work are, and should be, different from the morality that governs ordinary persons.*

The selection from Monroe H. Freedman and Abbe Smith defends zealous advocacy by lawyers in criminal cases. Those lawyers have an obligation to protect their client's rights whether or not they believe the client to be factually guilty. Moreover, in the name of protecting the "dignity" and rights of the accused, defense lawyers should, in Freedman's and Smith's view, be prepared to do undignified things. They illustrate this point by discussing a case in which a lawyer cross examines a witness he knows to be truthful to make her appear to be lying. They defend this practice, even though it frustrates the law's interest in finding the truth and it may harm the truthful witness.

What limits, if any, should there be on a lawyer's obligation to maintain client confidentiality? Should the lawyer's obligation to the client be the same regardless of whether or not he or she believes the client to be guilty?

THE ADVERSARY SYSTEM AND INDIVIDUAL DIGNITY

It is not surprising that in totalitarian societies, there is a sharp contrast in the role of a criminal defense lawyer from that in the American adversary system. As expressed by law professors at the University of Havana, "the first job of a revolutionary lawyer is not to argue that his client is innocent, but rather to determine if his client is guilty and, if so, to seek the sanction which will best rehabilitate him."[1]

Thus, a Bulgarian attorney began his defense in a treason trial by noting that "[i]n a Socialist state there is no division of duty between the judge, prosecutor, and defense counsel.... The defense must assist the prosecution to find the objective truth in a case."[2]...

Under the American adversary system, a trial is not "conflictless," because the lawyer is not the agent or servant of the state. Rather, the lawyer is the client's "champion against a hostile world"[3]—the client's zealous advocate against the government itself.... [T]he American defense lawyer has an obligation to conduct a prompt investigation of the case.[4] All sources of relevant information must be explored, particularly the client.[5] Rather than accepting the government's decision to preserve or destroy evidence, the defense lawyer has a duty to seek out information in the possession of the police and prosecutor.[6] Defense counsel has those duties, moreover, even though the defendant has admitted guilt to the lawyer and has expressed a desire to plead guilty.[7] As explained by the ABA Standards for Criminal Justice, the client may be mistaken about legal culpability or may be able to avoid conviction by persuading the court that inculpatory evidence should be suppressed;

293

also, such an investigation could prove useful in showing mitigating circumstances.[8]

Such rules, reflecting a respect for the rights even of the guilty individual, are a significant expression of the political philosophy that underlies the American system of justice. As Professor Zupancic has observed, "In societies which believe that the individual is the ultimate repository of existential values, his status vis-à-vis the majority will remain uncontested even when he is accused of crime. He will not be an object of purposes and policies, but *an equal partner in a legal dispute.*"[9]

THE ADVERSARY SYSTEM AND INDIVIDUAL RIGHTS

There is also an important systemic purpose served by assuring that even guilty people have rights. Jethro K. Lieberman has made the point by putting forth, and then explaining, a paradox:

> The singular strength of the adversary system is measured by a central fact that is usually deplored: The overwhelming majority of those accused in American courts are guilty. Why is this a strength? Because its opposite, visible in many totalitarian nations within the Chinese and Russian orbits, is this: Without an adversary system, a considerable number of defendants are prosecuted, though palpably innocent. . . . In short, the strength of the adversary system is not so much that it permits the innocent to defend themselves meaningfully, but that in the main it prevents them from having to do so.[10]

Lieberman concludes that "[o]nly because defense lawyers are independent of the state and the ruling political parties and are permitted, even encouraged, to defend fiercely and partisanly do we ensure that the state will be loathe to indict those whom it knows to be innocent." This benefit, however, is largely invisible. "We rarely see who is not indicted, we never see those whom a prosecutor, or even a governor or president, might like to prosecute but cannot."[11]

There is another systemic reason for the zealous representation that characterizes the adversary system. Our purpose as a society is not only to respect the humanity of the guilty defendant and to protect the innocent from the possibility of an unjust conviction. Precious as those objectives are, we also seek through the adversary system "to preserve the integrity of society itself . . .[by] keeping sound and wholesome the procedure by which society visits its condemnation on an erring member."[12] . . .

CROSS-EXAMINING TO DISCREDIT THE TRUTHFUL WITNESS

INTRODUCTION

Is it ever proper for a lawyer to cross-examine an adverse witness who has testified accurately and truthfully in order to make the witness appear to be mistaken or lying?

Our answer is yes.

CROSS-EXAMINING THE RAPE VICTIM

The issue was raised effectively in a symposium on legal ethics through the following hypothetical case, which we have revised in form but not substance.[13]

> The accused works at a gas station. He is charged with rape, an offense that carries a lengthy prison sentence. You are his court-appointed defense counsel. The alleged victim is a twenty-two-year-old graduate student at the divinity school. She is engaged to a young minister. The alleged rape occurred in the early morning hours at a service station where the accused was employed. That is all you know about the case when you have your first interview with your client.
>
> At first the accused will not talk at all. You assure him that you cannot help him unless you know the truth, and that he can

trust you to treat what he says as confidential. He then says that he had sex with the young woman, but that she "told me she really wanted it." He says that he had seen her two or three times before when he was working the day shift at the station, and that she had always started a conversation and, that night, had "come on to me." In fact, he says that after they had talked for a while, she invited him into the car. One thing led to another and, finally, to sex. They were interrupted by the lights of an approaching vehicle which pulled into the station. The accused relates that he got out of the young woman's car to wait on the customer, and the young woman hurriedly drove off.

The accused tells you he was tried for rape in California four years ago and acquitted. He has no previous convictions.

At the grand jury proceedings the complainant testifies that she was returning to her apartment in town from a conference on virtue ethics, where her fiancé presented a paper, when she noticed that her fuel gauge registered empty. She stopped at the first station along the road that was open. The attendant, who seemed to be in sole charge of the station, forced his way into her car, terrified her with threats, and forcibly had sexual intercourse with her. She says he was compelled to stop when an approaching car turned into the station. The alleged victim's fiancé testified as to her timely complaint. No other testimony is presented. The grand jury returns a true bill.

You learn that the complainant has been romantically involved with two men aside from her fiancé. Smith, one of these young men, admits that he and the complainant went together for some time; however, he refuses to say whether he had ever had sex with her or to discuss anything else of an intimate nature, and he says he doesn't think it's any of your business. The other, Jones, apparently a rejected and jealous suitor, tells you right away that he had sex with the complainant early in their relationship, and that he has seen her flirt

with strange men. He once took her to a party, he says, and, having noticed she had been gone for some time, discovered her upstairs with Smith, a friend of his, on a bed with some of her clothes off. He appears eager to testify and says that he doubts that the complainant was raped. You believe Jones, but don't like him much.

In a later interview with the accused, after you have won his confidence, the accused admits to you that his first story was false, and that he forced himself on the woman. However, he refuses to plead guilty to the charge or to any lesser offense. He says he knows that he can get away with his story, because he did once before in California.

Should the defense lawyer use the information supplied by Jones to impeach the young woman—if allowed by the rules of evidence—and if necessary, call Jones as a witness?[14]

The Morality of Absolute and Immutable Rules

One of the panelists who spoke to that question was former Chief Justice (then Judge) Warren Burger. The Chief Justice first discussed the question in terms of "basic and fundamental rules." One of those rules, which he characterized as "clear-cut and unambiguous," is that "a lawyer may never, under any circumstances, knowingly . . . participate in a fraud on the court." That rule, he said, "can never admit of any exception, under any circumstances," and no other consideration "can ever justify a knowing and conscious departure" from it. Moreover, only the "naive and inexperienced" would take a contrary position, which is a "perversion and prostitution of an honorable profession." Indeed, Burger held any other view to be "so utterly absurd and that one wonders why the subject need even be discussed among persons trained in the law."[15]

Despite his powerful rhetoric and assertion of absolute principles, Burger's response to the question of cross-examining the truthful witness was similar to ours. The function of an advocate, he declared, and "particularly the defense advocate in the adversary system," is to use "all legitimate tools available to test the truth of the prosecution's case." Therefore, he concluded, "the testimony of bad repute of the complaining witness, being recent and not remote in point of time, is relevant to her credibility."[16] The Chief Justice was even more explicit in the question period following the panel discussion: he considered it ethical to cast doubt on the young woman's "credibility" by destroying her reputation, even though the lawyer knows that she is telling the truth.

That, of course, is sanction for a deliberate attempt to perpetrate a fraud upon the finder of fact. The lawyer knows that the client is guilty and that the victim is truthful. In cross-examining her, the lawyer has one purpose only: to make it appear, contrary to fact, that the young woman is lying in testifying that she was raped. This, indeed, is what the lawyer will argue to the jury in summation.[17]

There is only one difference in practical effect between presenting the defendant's perjured alibi—which the Chief Justice considered to be clearly improper—and impeaching the truthful victim. In both cases the lawyer participates in an attempt to free a guilty defendant. In both cases the lawyer participates in misleading the finder of fact. In the case of the perjured witness, however, the attorney asks only non-leading questions, while in the case of impeachment, the lawyer takes an active, aggressive role, using his professional training and skill, in a one-on-one attack upon the client's victim.[18] The lawyer thereby personally and directly adds to the suffering of the victim and of those who care for her. In short, under the euphemism of "testing the truth of the prosecution's case," the lawyer communicates a vicious lie to the jury and to the community.

One prominent legal ethics scholar, Professor David Luban, takes a unique view. Luban agrees that defense lawyers generally must attempt to discredit witnesses, even those known to be telling the truth. Nevertheless, he contends that defense lawyers should refrain from cross-examining rape complainants about their sexual history, even when the lawyer believes that the complainant did in fact consent.[19] Luban says that the moral boundaries of zealous criminal defense should be drawn short of allowing cross-examination that "makes the victim look like a whore,"[20] even if she is not telling the truth:[21]

> [T]he cross-examination is morally wrong, even if the victim really did consent to sex with the defendant. Just as the rights of the accused are not diminished when he is guilty, the right of women to invoke the state's aid against rapists without fear of humiliation does not diminish when a [woman] abuses it by making a false accusation. This implies that balancing the defendant's rights against the rape accuser's rights in order to determine the moral bounds of zealous advocacy must be done without considering either the defendant's guilt or the accuser's innocence. What's good for the gander is good for the goose.[22]

Luban acknowledges that the question about the "relative threats posed to the defendant by the state and [those posed] to women by...the male sex" is "a very close call," but one that he ultimately resolves in women's favor. The constitutional protections afforded an accused (including the right to confront adverse witnesses) do not seem to enter into the balance, nor, apparently, does the fact that the complainant is committing perjury to send an innocent man to prison.[23]

We agree that the question of cross-examining witnesses known to be telling the truth is most painful in the rape context. Insofar as Luban's position is an endorsement of rape shield statutes, and insofar as those statutes do no more than prohibit cross-examination on *irrelevant* sexual history or lifestyle of rape complainants, we agree with him. However, we do not share his view that it is better that an innocent man go to jail than that a woman be called a "whore."[24]. . .

Notes

1. J. Kaplan, *Criminal Justice* 264–265 (1973); Berman, *The Cuban Popular Trials,* 60 Colum. L. Rev. 1317, 1341 (1969).

2. *Id.* at 264–265.

3. See ABA, Standards Relating to the Defense Function 145–146 (Approved Draft, 1971).

4. ABA Standards for Criminal Justice 4-4.1 (1979).

5. *Id.,* 4-3.2, 4-4.1.

6. *Id.,* 4-4.1.

7. *Id.,* 4-4.1.

8. *Id.,* Commentary to Standard 4-4.1.

9. Zupancic, *Truth and Impartiality in Criminal Process,* 7 Jour. Contemp. L. 39, 133 (1982) (emphasis added).

10. Lieberman, *Book Review,* 27 N.Y.L. Rev. 695 (1981).

11. *Id.* at 695.

12. Fuller, *The Adversary System,* in Talks on American Law 35 (H. Berman ed., 1960). In more down-to-earth language, John Condon, a Buffalo criminal lawyer, once commented that he is "an expert in quality control."

13. The reference is to Monroe Freedman, *Professional Responsibility of the Criminal Defense Lawyer: The Three Hardest Questions,* 64 Mich. L. Rev. 1469 (1966). The other two questions relate to knowingly presenting perjury, and to giving the client legal advice when there is reason to believe that the client might use it as the basis for creating perjury. These issues are discussed in earlier chapters. At the time the Michigan Law Review article was published, even to raise such issues publicly caused reactions of outrage. These included an effort by former Chief Justice Warren Burger (then a federal appellate judge) and two other federal judges to have Freedman disbarred. The story is related in Monroe H. Freedman, *Lawyers' Ethics in an Adversary System,* Preface (1975).

14. Since the time of the symposium at which this hypothetical was presented, virtually every state in the country has enacted a so-called "rape shield statute." Generally speaking these statutes prohibit cross-examination and the introduction of extrinsic evidence on a rape complainant's sexual history or her reputation for chastity. See generally Joshua Dressler, *Understanding Criminal Law* § 33.07 (3d ed. 2001). However, rape shield statutes have not rendered the hypothetical obsolete:

> [S]ome jurisdictions permit exceptions that can swallow the rule; lawyers can introduce evidence of previous sexual conduct that establishes a pattern of conduct or that judges find more probative than prejudicial. So, for example, in a Glen Ridge, New Jersey, case involving a gang rape of a retarded girl with a baseball bat, defense counsel presented testimony about prior behavior that painted the victim as promiscuous. Even when courts exclude evidence about complainants' sexual background from trial proceedings, inventive lawyers can leak such information through press reports, pretrial records, and indirect questioning. In the rape prosecution of William Kennedy Smith defense counsel placed the complainant on trial and ensured widespread coverage of her Victoria's Secret underwear, out-of-wedlock child, barhopping history, and reputed "wild streak." Similar tactics gained national prominence in a New York City police brutality case. Defense counsel's opening argument suggested that the injuries to a Haitian immigrant could have occurred through a same-sex consensual encounter rather than a police assault.

Deborah Rhode, *In the Interests of Justice* 101 (2000). For a fascinating account of the Glen Ridge rape case, see Bernard Lefkowitz, *Our Guys: The Glen Ridge Rape and the Secret Life of the Perfect Suburb* (1997). For a defense of the tactics in the police brutality case, see Abbe Smith, *Defending Defending,* 28 Hofstra L. Rev. 925 (2000).

15. Warren E. Burger, *Standards of Conduct for Prosecution and Defense Personnel: A Judge's Viewpoint,* 5 AM. Crim. L.Q. 11, 12 (1966).

16. *Id.* at 14–15.

17. "Before the trial starts, the advocate knows what he will say to the jury when it is over . . .[including] the part of it that deals with the credibility of the adversary's witnesses. . . ." Irving Younger, "Cicero on Cross-Examination," in *The Litigation Manual: A Primer for Trial Lawyers* 532, 533–534 (John G. Koeltl, ed., 2d ed. 1989).

18. Trial advocacy manuals consistently recommend that lawyers ask only leading questions in cross-examination so that the lawyer, not the witness, is testifying. The lawyer tells the story, and the properly controlled witness is limited to yes and no responses.

19. See David Luban, *Lawyers and Justice: An Ethical Study* 150–153 (1988).

20. *Id.* at 151.

21. *Id.* at 152.

22. Luban does not usually use either cliches or non-sequiturs, although he does both at once in this last sentence.

23. For example, Luban's view would have prevented Atticus Finch's cross-examination of Mayella Ewell in Finch's much-admired defense of Tom Robinson, who was falsely charged by Ewell with raping her. See Harper Lee, *To Kill a Mockingbird* (1960). See also Steven Lubet, *Reconstructing Atticus Finch*, 97 Mich. L. Rev. 1339, 1348–1353 (1999):

> . . .Atticus tortured Mayella. He held her up as a sexual aggressor at a time when such conduct was absolutely dishonorable and disgraceful. . . .
>
> The "she wanted it" defense was particularly harsh. . . . Atticus Finch . . .designed his defense to exploit a virtual catalog of misconceptions and fallacies about rape, each one calculated to heighten mistrust of the female complainant.
>
> *Fantasy.* . . . According to the defense, Mayella obsessed over Tom for a "slap year," . . .lur[ing] him into an assignation. . . .
>
> *Shame.* . . . Atticus told the jury that Mayella lied "in an effort to get rid of her own guilt. . . ."

> *Sexuality.* . . . Since women can barely control, and sometimes cannot even understand, their desires, they proceed to victimize the men whom they ensnare. As Atticus explained it, "She knew full well the enormity of her offense, but because her desires were stronger than the code she was breaking, she persisted in breaking it. . . . She was white, and she tempted a Negro. . . . No code mattered to her before she broke it, but it came crashing down on her afterwards. . . ."
>
> *Confusion.* Women may be so confused about sex that they do not even understand what they themselves have done. . . . [Finch says to Ewell:] "You're becoming suddenly clear on this point. A while ago you couldn't remember too well, could you? . . .Why don't you tell the truth, child?"

24. See Abbe Smith, *Rosie O'Neill Goes to Law School: The Clinical Education of a Sensitive, New Age Public Defender*, 28 HARV. C.R.-C.L. L. Rev. 1, 42–45 (1993). The authors are lifelong feminists. We believe that most women would agree—especially those wrongly accused of crime—that it is better to be called a name than to be imprisoned for something you didn't do (or even something you did do). See generally Abbe Smith, *Defending the Innocent*, 32 Conn. L. Rev. 486 (2000).

NOTES AND QUESTIONS

1. What is the adversary system? Who does it seek to protect? How is it different from other systems for finding facts?

2. How does the adversary system support individual rights? What other societal values and norms are reflected in the theory of justice based on an adversary system?

3. What purpose does zealous advocacy serve? For instance, how well does the adversary system uphold the right of the accused to be presumed innocent until proven guilty? Why is client trust in the defense counsel so crucial to zealous ad-

vocacy? Can zealous advocacy ever be blamed for hindering justice? At what point does zealous advocacy become *overzealous* advocacy?

4. How does the division of responsibility in the adversary system compromise the defense lawyer's interest in truth? Should a defense attorney be interested in truth, or is that solely the responsibility of judges and jurors?

5. Consider the hypothetical case presented by Freedman and Smith. Is there any difference between impeaching the honesty of the young woman and "knowingly participating in a fraud on the court"?

6. Where does David Luban draw the line between acceptable impeachment of witnesses and unacceptable impeach-

ment? On what grounds do Freedman and Smith contest Luban's logic? With whom do you agree more? Is there any difference between impeaching the credibility of the witness and "putting the victim on trial"?

7. As Freedman and Smith point out, rape-shield laws make the sexual history of the victim inadmissible in sexual assault trials. In your opinion, is sexual history ever relevant in a rape trial? Is it relevant, for instance, if the accuser makes her living as a prostitute?

Chapter 35

Fine Line in Indictment: Defense vs. Complicity

Laura Mansnerus

Conversations between criminal defense lawyers and their clients are generally protected from disclosure by the lawyer-client privilege. This privilege prevents lawyers from being required to divulge what their clients tell them in the course of their representation. It encourages clients to trust their lawyers and allows them to disclose information necessary for an effective defense.

The next reading is a newspaper story about Lynne Stewart, a New York lawyer who represented a convicted terrorist. Ms. Stewart was accused of helping her client direct terrorist activities from prison by passing information from him to other terrorists. She denied the charges and claimed that government agents monitored her conversations with her client and, in so doing, violated lawyer-client confidentiality. Although a judge subsequently dismissed the terrorism charges on the grounds that they were unconstitutionally vague, this reading raises important questions about the need to balance the claims of liberty and of security and about whether the value of zealous advocacy, which Freedman and Smith defend, is outweighed by the government's campaign to prevent terrorism. It revisits issues raised in the readings by Koh (Chapter 6) and Hobbes (Chapter 7).

Defense lawyers always talk about "the line," the one they cannot cross, between zealous advocacy and complicity in crime. But usually the issue is an internal struggle over professional ethics. For Lynne F. Stewart, the issue is her own indictment.

Ms. Stewart, the Manhattan lawyer who represents Sheik Omar Abdel Rahman, who is imprisoned for plotting terrorist attacks in New York City in the early 1990's, was charged on Tuesday with helping him direct further terrorist activities from prison. She pleaded not guilty in Federal District Court in Manhattan. Suddenly, an enraged defense bar is afraid that lawyers will be caught in an expanding net that the Bush administration has cast for potential terrorists.

Many advocates of civil liberties are perturbed by the wider campaign against terrorism as it affects everyone, especially foreign citizens.

But the fact that Ms. Stewart is a lawyer is not incidental. Abbe Smith, a professor at the Georgetown University Law Center, said the danger of knowing or doing too much for a client was inherent in a lawyer's obligation to represent clients "zealously within the bounds of law."

"'Within the bounds of the law'—what does that mean?" Ms. Smith said. "You go right up to that line, and you don't go over it, but you test it."

Ms. Stewart said in an interview yesterday that the legal issues in her case would probably focus on the lawyer-client privilege. Government monitoring of lawyer-client communications has "almost a freezing effect on your ability to defend the person," she said. "And the whole way we operate is to establish a relationship of trust. You want to know everything that happened, and then you decide if the case is defensible or not."

Ms. Stewart was charged, along with three other defendants, with providing material support to a terrorist organization.

The charges stemmed from conversations she had with Mr. Abdel Rahman, a blind Muslim cleric who is believed to have acted from his prison cell to continue directing an organization he led in his native Egypt, the Islamic Group. Ms. Stewart is accused of violating restrictions placed on the sheik's communications with outsiders and serving as a conduit between him and terrorist cells in Egypt.

Prosecutors say the conversations took place in 2000 and in January 2001, well before the U.S.A. PATRIOT Act was enacted last October, greatly expanding the definition of "terrorist activity" and of what constitutes support of terrorism.

There is no question that the government can restrict an inmate's speech, and by extension the information he conveys to outsiders. Legal experts point out that the lawyer's role is not necessarily sacred. The attorney-client privilege does not apply to any conversation not about legal matters, said H. Richard Uviller, a professor of criminal law at the Columbia Law School. "Lawyers can be co-conspirators with their clients."

Stephen Gillers, an expert on legal ethics at the New York University School of Law, said, "If there is reason to believe that a lawyer is helping a client accomplish criminal goals, the government has a right to listen in."

That was certainly the case when William Moran and Michael Abbell, lawyers for drug defendants in Miami, were found to have been a kind of in-house counsel for a Colombian drug cartel. Then, too, some defense lawyers with organized-crime clients have been convicted of money-laundering and similar offenses.

But Ms. Stewart is not charged, as the other defendants were, with soliciting criminal acts. She is accused only of being a conduit for information, a role that may be hard to delineate because she speaks no Arabic. "I can say 'hello' and 'thank you,'" Ms. Stewart said.

Many lawyers said they were mystified by the case because, while they believed Ms. Stewart could only have been duped, the government would probably not press ahead without convincing evidence that she was

not. "The Justice Department must have known there'd be an outcry, so they must have been very careful to proceed on solid ground," Professor Uviller said.

But Ms. Stewart said: "I'm not practicing all these years to suddenly cross that line that I know all too well exists. I'm too long in the tooth to do that." She said agents monitored her conversations under the Foreign Intelligence Surveillance Act, which permits the government to obtain a warrant, with fewer safeguards than an ordinary warrant application. She said neither she nor the other defendants, including her translator, had been notified.

Since Sept. 11, under Attorney General John Ashcroft, the Justice Department has provided for more monitoring of lawyer-client communications, too. A new rule allows the government to notify terrorism suspects and their lawyers that all conversations may be monitored — a change that has alarmed lawyers.

"Under this antiterrorist rule you never have the opportunity for a privileged conversation with your client," said Robert J. Anello, a Manhattan defense lawyer and chairman of the city bar association's committee on professional ethics.

Professor Smith, while calling Ms. Stewart's indictment "a stunning development," said: "I see this as part of a frightening pattern in recent years. Prosecutors have increasingly used strategies to chill zealous defense lawyers—seizing attorney fees, disqualifying counsel and now monitoring."

"It's tough enough to get lawyers to represent social pariahs," she added.

NOTES AND QUESTIONS

1. On what grounds was Ms. Stewart charged with providing material support to a terrorist group? Is "the line" between zealous advocacy and criminal complicity harder to define in the case of suspected terrorism? Why or why not?

2. Do antiterrorist laws undermine the adversary system? Are laws of the kind used against Ms. Stewart warranted or are they a dangerous misuse of government power? Do terrorist suspects have a right to zealous advocacy? How do cultural factors (e.g., racism, xenophobia) affect the post-September 11 debate over liberty versus security?

3. According to Stephen Gillers, "If there is a reason to believe that a lawyer is helping a client accomplish criminal goals, the government has a right to listen in." Thus, the U.S.A. PATRIOT Act greatly expanded the access government has to attorney-client conversations in terrorism cases. Terrorist plotting, like mob activity and drug trafficking, *is* a crime an individual could conceivably continue to commit even while incarcerated, and certain rights afforded defendants in the American criminal justice system *could* facilitate such criminal activities. But does this justify revoking the attorney-client privilege from *all* terrorism suspects, regardless of circumstance? Should there be some standard of probable cause for terrorist suspects before the government may listen-in on "privileged" conversations, or is the threat of terrorism grave enough to merit the broadest governmental prerogative?

4. How can we decide what threats are grave enough to warrant limiting civil liberties? Over 11,000 people are killed by hand guns each year in the United States. That's nearly four times the number of people killed in the terrorist attacks on September 11, 2001. Should those accused of handgun-related violence be denied robust attorney-client privilege on national security grounds? Why or why not?

5. Should terrorist suspects be presumed innocent in criminal trials? Why or why not? Does limitation of the attorney-client privilege effectively presume guilt? What dangers, if any, does the PATRIOT Act pose for terrorism suspects who are wrongly accused? How would Hobbes (Chapter 7) advise us to answer this question of liberty versus security?

Chapter 36

Defending White-Collar Crime

A Portrait of Attorneys at Work

Kenneth Mann

What do lawyers actually do to advance their clients' interests in criminal proceedings? What strategies do they pursue? Do lawyers representing different kinds of clients pursue different strategies? How is criminal defense practice socially organized?

One of the great controversies about the criminal justice system involves the question of whether the guarantee of equal treatment under the law is realized in practice or whether people are able to translate social advantages into legal ones. This controversy is played out in the domain of legal representation. Common sense and scholarly inquiry suggest that the quality of defense lawyers matters in determining the outcomes of criminal cases and that middle- and upper-class individuals who are accused of crime typically are able to secure better legal representation.

Kenneth Mann comes at the question of inequality indirectly by examining the work of lawyers representing defendants accused of white-collar crimes. Those are nonviolent crimes typically involving fraud or deception. Mann reports that lawyers in these cases take on the kind of adversarial roles advocated by Freedman and Smith (Chapter 34), but that their advocacy is focused primarily on the early stages of the criminal process. In particular, they try to prevent their clients from being formally charged or indicted. In this regard, lawyers in white-collar cases concentrate their efforts on information control, namely, preventing the government from obtaining information that would be prejudicial to their client. Mann also describes the work of white-collar crime defense lawyers in other stages of the processes, noting differences between their practices and those of lawyer's defending people accused of street crimes.

The white-collar crime defense attorney, like his counterpart handling street crime, typically assumes that his client is guilty. Certainly that assumption held in every case I describe in this book. But unlike the street-crime defense attorney—and this is a critical difference—the white-collar defense attorney does not assume that the government has the evidence to convict his client. Instead, he starts with the assumption that, though his client is guilty, he may be able to keep the government from knowing this or from concluding that it has a strong enough case to prove it. Though in the end he may have to advise his client to plead guilty and bargain, he often starts his case with the expectation of avoiding compromise.

The white-collar crime defense attorney is zealous in his advocacy of his client's interest, often rejecting government overtures to negotiate and compromise. In contrast to the attorney handling street crime, his time is not a scarce resource, and each case is individually cultivated with great care. In white-collar cases, the defense attorney is usually called in by the client to conduct a defense before the government investigation is completed and in some cases even before it begins. The defense attorney employs his own investigators, who are experts in accounting and finance, as well as a staff of legal researchers. He learns thoroughly the details of the case, usually having a greater ability to do this than the government investigator and prosecutor. This attorney, in distinct contrast to the attorney handling street crime, has a number of opportunities to argue the innocence of his client before the government makes a decision to issue an indictment. A plea agreement may be an important element in the final disposition of the white-collar case, but the compromise that leads to a plea agreement is the result of a carefully managed process of adversary interaction in which cooperation with the government plays little or no part. And in many cases the guilty plea is followed by a second period of intensive advocacy—at the time of sentencing—where compromise and negotiation again remain conspicuously absent. But above all, and this is the central theme of the white-collar crime defense function, the defense attorney works to keep potential evidence out of government reach by controlling access to information.

THE INFORMATION CONTROL DEFENSE AND THE SUBSTANTIVE DEFENSE

The defense attorney's adversaries are the government agents who decide whether a criminal charge should be made—government investigators and, eventually, prosecutors. To prevent issuance of an indictment, the attorney must keep these persons from concluding that the client has done something that warrants criminal prosecution. The central strategy question for the attorney is how to accomplish this end, and this applies in all cases, irrespective of whether the attorney's client has in fact committed a crime, or whether it is a white-collar or a street crime.

This question might seem to lead to a straightforward answer. If an attorney does in the white-collar case what is done in the street-crime case, he takes the evidence presented against his client, and other evidence known to him that is exculpatory of the client, and makes the appropriate legal argument. This evidence, so the attorney argues, fails to show adequately, that is, beyond a reasonable

doubt, that the client committed a crime. The defense attorney's task is to draw on conventional sources of law—statutory and case law—to show his adversary that the client's behavior falls on the "not guilty" side of that line created by the substantive standard of criminal responsibility. This task is conventional legal argument and takes place at all stages of the criminal process. I will call this defense strategy substantive defense.

In making a substantive defense, the defense attorneys studied had a distinctive role because they were handling white-collar cases. Rather than waiting until trial or until the immediate pretrial period when plea negotiations usually take place, these defense attorneys had an opportunity to make a substantive defense before a charge was made. While attorneys in other types of cases also make opportunities for adversary argument before charging, in white-collar cases there is typically a series of institutionalized settings for conducting precharge adversarial proceedings on questions of substantive criminal responsibility. Substantive legal argument before the charge decision is a routinized pattern of defense advocacy in white-collar cases.

The substantive defense is not, however, the initial defense strategy for a competent attorney. The defense attorney's first objective is to prevent the government from obtaining evidence that could be inculpatory of his client and used by the investigator or prosecutor to justify issuance of a formal criminal charge. Instead of preparing legal argument, the defense attorney first devotes himself to keeping evidence out of any prospective adversary forum in which legal argument about the client's criminal responsibility might take place. This action is crucial to prevent issuance of a criminal charge. I call this task information control and the defense strategy built on these actions an information control defense.

Information control entails keeping documents away from and preventing clients and witnesses from talking to government investigators, prosecutors, and judges. It will become evident as I describe defense attorneys handling actual cases of white-collar crime that information control is not the conventional advocacy task of substantive argument in which the defense attorney analyzes a set of facts and argues that a crime is not proved. It occurs before the substantive defense and is in some ways a more important defense. If successful, it keeps the raw material of legal argument out of the hands of the government, it obviates argument about the substantive legal implications of facts about crime, and it keeps the government ignorant of evidence it needs in deciding whether to make a formal charge against a person suspected of committing a crime. And, even if a formal charge is made, it keeps facts about a crime out of the arena of plea negotiations and out of the courtroom if a trial takes place. For these reasons, information control lies at the very heart of the defense function, preventing the imposition of a criminal sanction on an accused person who has committed a crime, as well as on the rare one who has not.

Attorneys act in two different ways to control information. First, they oppose their adversaries in quasi-judicial and court settings. In one situation, the attorney argues to a judge in court or to an investigator in an office that a subpoena for documents is improper because, for instance, it is overburdensome or vague. In another situation, the attorney argues that information already seized by the government should not be admissible evidence because of government misbehavior in making the seizure. The essential feature of these information control arguments is their focus on the behavior of the opposing party, directly by convincing that party not to press the request or indirectly through the sanction of a judge or other decisionmaker. The legal rules used to support these attempts to control information are communicated to the opposing party. For instance, the defense attorney argues that the law of search and seizure prohibits the government from taking the documents. The prosecutor argues that the law permits him to do so. In these contexts, the government has the opportunity to rebut the defense position with its own arguments about what the applicable legal rules require. I will call this adversarial information control.

Second, the defense attorney uses an information control strategy that focuses on the potential source of inculpatory information, rather than on the behavior of the adversary seeking to gain access to the source. The defense attorney's aim is to instruct the client or third party holding inculpatory information how to refrain from disclosing it to the government and, if necessary, to persuade or force him to refrain. The legal justification supporting such information control actions is usually not communicated to the adversary. The setting of this action is typically concealed, behind the attorney-client confidentiality privilege or in private attorney-witness meetings, and concealment is often essential to success of the information control action. When this kind of information control is undertaken, the opposing party has no or little opportunity to rebut it using legal argument. I will call this managerial information control.

When an attorney in a meeting in his office advises a client about to be questioned by a government agent to "avoid answering that question, and if pushed, tell him that you have to examine your books before responding," the target of control is the client and the aim is information control. The attorney has acted on the client and the information in the client's possession, in a setting concealed from the adversary. If the client handles the situation well, he may successfully avoid prosecution or avoid or delay raising of an issue where this result may be important to other defense efforts. Managerial information control focuses on what the attorney does to manage the disposition of information sources.

Information control as a defense strategy is not exclusive to white-collar cases. In many kinds of criminal cases, defense attorneys move to exclude illegally seized evidence, an adversarial control device, and they engage in pretrial coaching of witnesses, a managerial control device. What is distinctive in white-collar cases is the centrality of information control strategies to defense work: they are fundamental modus operandi constituting a basic defense plan, rather than merely tactics in a broader strategy.

While adversarial information control is well recognized—particularly the law of search and seizure—characteristics of managerial information control are not well identified in the literature on law. In the past decade and earlier, attorneys and scholars raised issues bearing on the propriety of information control in the intensely debated question of whether a defense attorney can put a defendant on the witness stand when he suspects that false testimony will be given. But the broader range of information control strategies that will be examined here has not been brought together and considered as a systematic method of action. In large part, this is a result of the difficulty of obtaining research access to the setting in which managerial information control occurs: the attorney-client relationship. But it is also a result of the fact that managerial information control is in the criminal process distinctive to cases of white-collar crime, and white-collar crime has not drawn until recently a substantial research concern.... [T]he opportunities for attorney-assisted information control are more limited in cases of street and violent crime. In cases of white-collar crime, particularly when attorneys are brought into the case early, there are many opportunities for information control, and experienced attorneys have developed special skills for exploiting them.

STAGES OF THE CRIMINAL PROCESS

Defense attorneys handling white-collar cases rarely try cases. Occasionally a trial occupies an attorney for an extended period of time, but this is regarded as an exceptional event in most of the offices I studied. In this important respect, the work of the white-col-lar crime specialist is similar to that of the defense attorney handling street crime. But there are many differences between the practices of these two attorneys. These will emerge in looking at the typical, patterned ways that white-collar and street-crime cases go through the criminal process.

Precharge. In the street-crime practice, defense attorneys are brought into cases by clients after a charge has been made. Before the charging decision, there is little or nothing that the defense attorney can do to control information or argue that the facts available do not prove a crime. This period is therefore generally unimportant for bringing defense resources to bear on the question of the guilt of the client for the crime that is likely to be charged. To the extent that defense attorneys do intervene actively before a charging decision, their work is concentrated on arrest, arraignment and bail processes. Some impact on the fundamental question of guilt may be had here, but substantive argument and information control will rarely reach the high intensity achieved by attorneys in white-collar cases.

The white-collar crime defense attorney more often gets into his case at this stage. Clients typically recruit their attorneys before an official charge is made and are sometimes able to do this simultaneously with or even before the beginning of a long investigative period leading up to the consideration of charges by an investigative agency or prosecutor. It is during the period before the government makes its charging decision that white-collar defense attorneys spend by far the largest portion of their work hours. They discuss their cases with their clients, evaluate documents held by clients, interview third parties, take affidavits from third parties, examine documents held by third parties, meet with investigators to argue their case, and return to clients, third parties, and documents to refine their knowledge of the case and their strategy.

The two main defense strategies—information control and substantive legal argument—are already being used at this period and with more intensity than at any subsequent point in the criminal process. The defense attorney is using all available resources at this stage because his primary objective is to prevent the government from discovering the guilt of the client or from coming to the conclusion that it can prove the guilt of the client. In the white-collar crime defense practice, issuance of a criminal charge is already a significant failure for the defense attorney and is for the client often the most severe sanction that can be meted out, even if at the end of the process a short prison term is given by the sentencing judge.

The centrality of this period to white-collar practice is indicated also by the attoney's desire to enter into plea negotiations at this time if he is forced to give up the preferred strategy of demonstrating the client's innocence. Before charging, the defense's bargaining position is stronger: the government has made less of an institutional commitment to the case, the investigation is at an earlier stage, and the defendant can earn credits for early cooperation. The defense attorney who gets in early wants to take advantage of this potentially better bargaining position. Whether and when to enter into plea negotiations (discussed separately below) is the major strategic choice for a defense attorney during the precharge period of the criminal defense in white-collar cases.

Pretrial. The street-crime defense attorney concentrates his work in the pretrial stage of the criminal process, that is, from the time his client has been charged up to the formal disposition made by guilty plea. In the vast majority of cases processed in lower criminal courts in the United States, this stage is short and the services provided by the attorney to the client are minimal, often negligible. The negotiated deal is the almost exclusive method of disposition. Milton Heumann aptly describes this defense process:

Typically . . . a line forms outside the prosecutor's office the morning before the

court is convened. Defense attorneys shuffle into the prosecutor's office and, in a matter of two or three minutes, dispose of the one or more cases "set down" that day. Generally, only a few words have to be exchanged before agreement is reached. The defense attorney mutters something about the defendant, the prosecutor reads the police report, and concurrence on "what to do" generally, but not always, emerges.

[In court] . . . the defense attorney embellishes the defendant's perfunctory plea of guilty with a brief statement about how repentant the defendant is, and/or how trivial an offense this actually was, and/or what a wonderful person the defendant really is. As the defense attorney drones on, the judge joins the prosecutor in directing his attention to matters other than the words being spoken in the court.

This is a description of defense work in a misdemeanor court; in felony jurisdiction courts, the process may be longer and more formal, but the essence of the defense function remains constant. The defense attorney takes the prosecution's evidence, evaluates it, and makes an agreement about what the case is worth.

Thus, the street-crime defense attorney devotes most of his time to his cases during the pretrial period. That period may be longer or shorter or more or less adversarial depending on the resources of the client and the amount of time available to the attorney. But only in a very small number of cases does the attorney decide to argue that his client is innocent, which means going to trial. In presenting an overall analytic picture of the criminal process, Malcolm Feeley assigns most of what is significant that occurs to a defendant in a lower criminal court into what he calls the pretrial period. Chronologically, some of this—arrest, bail, and arraignment—occurs in what I have called the precharge period, but the processes for determining outcome—plea bargaining, adjudication, and sentencing—

occur after charging and without trial. The pretrial period is the most significant phase in the defense and prosecution of street crime, not at all because a trial is planned for, but because this is where the prosecutor and defense attorney apply whatever resources they have in coming to a resolution about outcome.

The pretrial period may also be important for the white-collar defense attorney, but only where there has been some prior defense failure. This occurs when the defendant fails to recruit an attorney before the government charges or when the attorney fails in an attempt to prevent charging and fails to make a plea bargain before the charge is issued. Though it may seem inappropriate, white-collar defense attorneys tend to regard the case that extends past the precharge stage as a failure. This expresses the defense attorney's perception that a large proportion of guilty clients in white-collar cases are not charged, because they work their way out of the system before the government collects sufficient evidence.

Where the white-collar case moves past the precharge stage into pretrial, strong forces push the defense attorney to have his client plead guilty. But this is not due to the defense attorney's heavy caseload or lack of client resources, factors that make plea bargaining attractive in cases of street crime. It results from the perceived low possibility of winning after indictment, particularly when the defense attorney has already argued his main defense with the investigator or prosecutor in the precharge period.

Trial. The third stage of the criminal process presents very similar problems for the white-collar and street-crime defense attorneys. The defense attorney handling the white-collar case may find it easier to meet his client, and the client may be better at grasping legal principles he needs to know to testify, if he so chooses. But these factors are likely to be insignificant in the overall case. Both attorneys face the well-known problem of keeping witnesses willing to testify and keeping themselves apprised of potential changes in the content of witnesses' testimony. And both attorneys face the problem of picking a jury that will not be biased against either the client's class and place in life or the particular crime he is charged with committing.

One distinguishing feature—so some attorneys contend—is that the white-collar case gives the defense attorney more room to create doubt in the jurors' minds, due to the high level of ambiguity in many white-collar statutes, such as fraud statutes, compared to street-crime statutes, such as assault. These attorneys argue that the average juror has a less well-formed idea of what fraud is than of what assault is, and that this difference makes it easier to raise doubt about the prosecution's case.

This observation about statutes appears true, but a major problem in determining how it affects the trial stage is that white-collar cases are more often subjected to intensive adversarial argument prior to trial. It follows that the case that gets to trial is more likely to be a strong case (from the perspective of the prosecution). The weak cases that get to trial are more likely to be the street-crime cases because investigators and prosecutors are tested by defense attorneys less often and less resolutely. Thus, an alternative view of how ambiguity in statutes affects the criminal process would assert that it creates opportunities for legal argument but that in white-collar crime this effect is vitiated by the time a case gets to trial. Then, the defense attorney has fewer opportunities to create doubt.

It is thus difficult to determine whether there is any difference between white-collar and street-crime cases at trial, other than the amount of resources put into the cases by the defendants. What emerges as persuasive is that there are fewer differences between white-collar and street-crime cases at the trial stage than at other stages of the criminal process.

Sentencing. Much of the sentencing process in cases of street crime takes place in the pretrial stage, during and as a result of plea bargaining. The defendant wants to extricate himself from the criminal process as soon as possible, but not at the cost of a prison sentence or other heavy sanction. The defense attorney aims at getting the client out of the system quickly, a goal that coincides with his own need to handle a large number of cases efficiently, while negotiating to obtain the lowest possible sentence. In most lower criminal courts the range of expected sentences for typical street crimes is familiar to defense attorneys and prosecutors. The bargaining process is then focused on reaching agreement about how to present the case to the judge in order to achieve an agreed-upon sentence. Though the judge is probably not bound by this presentation, the sentence decision is usually predictable within a small margin of error. By the time the formal sentencing stage arrives, the defense attorney expects to have a fairly limited role. The attorney makes a routine plea for leniency and routine recitations of the defendant's good and repentant characteristics. As Heumann states, he "drones on" while the judge and prosecutor direct their attention to other matters.

In the white-collar case, the sentencing hearing is the most important stage in the process, after precharge. The plea bargain reached by the defense attorney at an earlier stage will have been constructed, as in the case of street crime, with the intent of reducing the seriousness of the sanction. But in white-collar cases the role of the defense attorney in setting sentence continues to be important after the completion of the plea bargain. Defense attorneys use the sentencing stage as an opportunity to repeat one of the major tasks of earlier stages: substantive legal argument.

Traditional models of the criminal process place legal argument about substantive responsibility in the stages before sentencing. Distinctive to white-collar cases is the persistence of ambiguity about the true nature of the crime committed and the true extent of the defendant's blameworthiness. The persis-

tence of ambiguity, coupled with the high level of client resources in white-collar cases, extends the salience of substantive legal argument beyond the formal determination of guilt into the formal sentencing stage. The interaction of this factor with the absence of adequate decisional guidelines in a discretionary system of judicial sentencing has given defense attorneys a central role in determining type and length of sentence in white-collar cases. . . .

PLEA BARGAINING AND THE MAJOR STRATEGIC DECISION

Striking a plea bargain for clients is no less important in cases of white-collar crime than it is in street crime. The statutory charges in a charging instrument, the number of counts alleged, the description of the crime, and the sentencing plea made by the government can all be influenced by a plea bargain. Whether the defense attorney enters into serious negotiations before or after charging, what has occurred before those negotiations may determine the nature of the deal that can be struck with the prosecution. There are important differences in the way that plea negotiations are prepared in cases of white-collar crime and street-crime.

In a street-crime case, the defense attorney has limited opportunities to control the facts that reach the government and determine its readiness to make a deal. The defense attorney will have to find substantive weaknesses in the government's case and play on the government's need to resolve cases quickly and efficiently. In addition to making conventional legal arguments about what the available evidence proves, the defense attorney emphasizes the amount of resources that the government will need to take the case to trial.

Because the white-collar crime defense attorney gets into his case earlier, he prepares for plea bargaining by attempting to limit the government's access to facts inculpatory of his client. The strength of his position at the bargaining table vis-à-vis the government is often the result of steps he takes early in an investigation to protect documents from discovery and to influence the content of witnesses' statements. When negotiations are begun, the defense attorney will already have done a substantial amount of fieldwork.

The decision to start plea negotiations is a critical point in white-collar cases. An attorney who starts negotiations is communicating to the government that the client he represents is guilty of something and that the attorney thinks that the government will be able to prove it. When the attorney is conducting an information control defense aimed at preventing the criminal charge, he will not want to communicate this message to the government. The converse is true. The attorney wants to communicate a message of not guilty as long as there remains some possibility of preventing the government from coming to the conclusion that it has a chargeable case. If the defense attorney forgoes negotiations, he increases the possibility of persuading the government not to indict in the marginal case.

The decision not to enter into negotiations in order to maintain the facade of innocence is a difficult one because there are countervailing reasons to negotiate early. If at the end of an investigation the government is likely to decide that it has a strong enough case to charge, the defense attorney has an advantage if he negotiates early. The government will be more ready to grant concessions before it completes its investigation. At an early point in the investigation the government may falsely assume that necessary evidence is inaccessible. If the attorney gets to the investigator or prosecutor when the going is tough, he will be able to obtain a good plea bargain with substantial advantages for his client. The longer the defense attorney waits to start negotiations, the harder it will be to find flexibility in the government's position.

Not only is the government likely to have a stronger case as the investigation advances, but its readiness to compromise in the interest of efficiency becomes progessively weaker. Investigators and prosecutors often work on cases for many months, during which they develop a substantial personal commitment to seeing the results of their investigation bear fruit. When this happens, there is a tendency to be overcommitted to prosecution, rather than, as in the street-crime case, overcommitted to disposing of cases through a plea bargain. Street-crime defense attorneys depend on backlog pressure to facilitate a deal. White-collar defense attorneys lose this advantage, particularly when they wait too long to negotiate.

Because of the importance of the decision to negotiate, one of the main tasks of the defense attorney at the precharge stage is to evaluate the probability of the government's finding enough evidence to charge. To accomplish this goal, the defense attorney must obtain access to the potential pool of information about his client's crime. First, he wants to know, with certain important exceptions that will be explained later, what might be discovered if the government were to be completely successful in its investigation. "What is the objective seriousness of the crime committed by my client?" asks the attorney. "What penalties might the client be exposed to if the government were to discover all the evidence?" Second, and here there is no exception, the attorney wants to know what information has already been found by the government and what information is likely to be found given its present location.

Essential to defense planning is knowing whether the government will be able to prove a crime against the client and, if so, whether it knows the true extent of the crime. Without this information, the attorney cannot properly determine his own position. The defense claim of innocence or limited culpability must be correlated to what the government knows and is likely to learn during the course of its investigation. The attorney conducts his own defense investigation to learn the facts and evaluate what the government knows.

On completion of the defense investigation, the attorney must make the major strategic decision of the precharge stage and what may turn out to be the most important decision in the entire defense: either to go ahead with the information control strategy—essentially a strategy of noncooperation—or to negotiate with the prosecution. As the defense attorney receives new information about what the government is likely to discover, he will have to reconsider this decision throughout the precharge period. . . .

The skill of the attorney in making a plea bargain is first tested by his ability to know when to advise the client to go ahead with a deal—probably destroying the client's professional reputation in the process, even if immunity is obtained. Here again, there is a distinctive element in the white-collar crime defense attorney's preparation for negotiations. This attorney has lead time to influence who cooperates and has more opportunities to test the true strength of the government's legal case. This attorney is continually weighing the advantages in holding out against the advantages in conducting early negotiations. The decision requires that he judge carefully the facts, the law, and what he knows about the customs and policies of the prosecutors and investigator in similar cases. A mistake here can undermine the case completely. . . .

Notes and Questions

1. What distinguishes "substantive defense" from "information control defense"? How do attorneys control information in white-collar cases? Why is an information control defense more challenging to pursue in street crime cases?

2. Mann divides the process of criminal prosecution into four categories: precharge, pretrial, trial, and sentencing. At what stage does the advocacy provided by white-collar crime defense law-

yers tend to be "adversarial," and when is it more "managerial"?

3. How is an information control defense different from obstruction of justice? According to former Chief Justice Warren Burger, "a lawyer may never, under any circumstances, knowingly . . . participate in a fraud on the court." (See Freedman and Smith, Chapter 34.) How can a lawyer actively move to suppress evidence in a case, in which she knows her client to be guilty, without violating Justice Burger's interpretation of the law? Does information control "cross the line" that Mansnerus refers to in Chapter 35?

4. Why do people tend to accept plea bargains in street crime cases? What is the impetus for white-collar defendants to seek a plea bargain postindictment? What makes these two situations different? When considering the guilty pleas of white collar criminals, how compelling is Langbein's depiction (Chapter 32) of the coercive, torturous plea bargain?

5. According to Mann's account, white-collar defendants seem to have few complaints about foregoing their constitutional right to stand trial. What does this suggest about social class and perceptions about "access" to the law?

6. Is it just that certain defendants have access to more zealous forms of advocacy than others? In your estimation, what plays a greater role in determining the type of defense an individual can mount, the nature of the crime or the social status of the defendant? If the latter, can anything be done to remedy this aspect of the social organization of law?

Chapter 37

The Practice of Law as a Confidence Game

Abraham S. Blumberg

In Chapter 36, Kenneth Mann contends that the work of criminal defense lawyers in street cases is substantially different from the work of lawyers in white-collar cases. The former generally begin their work after charges are filed, but much of the work of lawyers in white collar cases occurs before charges are filed. Moreover, the work of ordinary criminal defense lawyers is geared to facilitating the plea bargaining system discussed in Section VIII. In this sense, defense lawyers play a key role in determining how severely or leniently a defendant will be treated in the criminal justice system.

When lawyers help to secure a plea bargain, whose interests are they promoting—those of the client eager for the best deal possible or those of the court eager to avoid the costs in time and money of a full-scale trial? Abraham S. Blumberg's article addresses these questions. It is a classic in the sociology of law, illustrating as it does the gap between the standards and ideals advanced by Freedman and Smith (Chapter 34) and the day-to-day realities of criminal defense work.

Blumberg argues that criminal defense lawyers rarely take a combative, adversarial posture. Instead they play key roles in the social organization of the criminal court, working with prosecutors and judges to convince their clients

to plead guilty. As a result, Blumberg calls these defense lawyers "double agents."

COURT STRUCTURE DEFINES ROLE OF DEFENSE LAWYER

The overwhelming majority of convictions in criminal cases (usually over 90 percent) are not the product of a combative, trial-by-jury process at all, but instead merely involve the sentencing of the individual after a negotiated, bargained-for plea of guilty has been entered.[1] Although more recently the overzealous role of police and prosecutors in producing pretrial confessions and admissions has achieved a good deal of notoriety, scant attention has been paid to the organizational structure and personnel of the criminal court itself. Indeed, the extremely high conviction rate produced without the features of an adversary trial in our courts would tend to suggest that the "trial" becomes a perfunctory reiteration and validation of the pretrial interrogation and investigation.[2]

The institutional setting of the court defines a role for the defense counsel in a criminal case radically different from the one traditionally depicted.[3] Sociologists and others have focused their attention on the deprivations and social disabilities of such variables as race, ethnicity, and social class as being the source of an accused person's defeat in a criminal court. Largely overlooked is the variable of the court organization itself, which possesses a thrust, purpose, and direction of its own. It is grounded in pragmatic values, bureaucratic priorities, and administrative instruments. These exalt maximum production and the particularistic career designs of organizational incumbents, whose occupational and career commitments tend to generate a set of priorities. These priorities exert a higher claim than the stated ideological goals of "due process of law," and are often inconsistent with them.

Organizational goals and discipline impose a set of demands and conditions of practice on the respective professions in the criminal court, to which they respond by abandoning their ideological and professional commitments to the accused client, in the service of these higher claims of the court organization. All court personnel, including the accused's own lawyer, tend to be coopted to become agent-mediators[4] who help the accused redefine his situation and restructure his perceptions concomitant with a plea of guilty.

Of all the occupational roles in the court the only private individual who is officially recognized as having a special status and concomitant obligations is the lawyer. His legal status is that of "an officer of the court" and he is held to a standard of ethical performance and duty to his client as well as to the court. This obligation is thought to be far higher than that expected of ordinary individuals occupying the various occupational statuses in the court community. However, lawyers, whether privately retained or of the legal-aid, public defender variety, have close and continuing relations with the prosecuting office and the court itself through discreet relations with the judges via their law secretaries or "confidential" assistants. Indeed, lines of communication, influence and contact with those offices, as well as with the Office of the Clerk of the court, Probation Division, and with the press, are essential to present and prospective requirements of criminal law practice. Similarly, the subtle involvement of the press and other mass media in the court's organizational network is not readily discernible to the casual observer. Accused persons come and go in the court system schema, but the structure and its occupational incumbents remain to carry on their respective career, occupational and organizational enterprises. The individual stridencies, tensions, and conflicts a given accused person's case may present to all the participants are overcome, because the formal and informal relations of all the groups in the court setting require it. The probability of continued future relations and interaction must be preserved at all costs.

This is particularly true of the "lawyer regulars," i.e., those defense lawyers, who by virtue of their continuous appearances in behalf of defendants, tend to represent the bulk of a criminal court's nonindigent case workload, and those lawyers who are not "regulars," who appear almost casually in behalf of an occasional client. Some of the "lawyer regulars" are highly visible as one moves about the major urban centers of the nation, their offices line the back streets of the courthouses, at times sharing space with bondsmen. Their political "visibility" in terms of local club house ties, reaching into the Judge's chambers and prosecutor's office are also deemed essential to successful practitioners. Previous research has indicated that the "lawyer regulars" make no effort to conceal their dependence upon police, bondsmen, jail personnel. Nor do they conceal the necessity for maintaining intimate relations with all levels of personnel in the court setting as a means of obtaining, maintaining, and building their practice. These informal relations are the *sine qua non* not only of retaining a practice, but also in the negotiation of pleas and sentences.[5]

The client, then, is a secondary figure in the court system as in certain other bureaucratic settings. He becomes a means to other ends of the organization's incumbents. He may present doubts, contingencies, and pressures which challenge existing informal arrangements or disrupt them; but these tend to be resolved in favor of the continuance of the organization and its relations as before. There is a greater community of interest among all the principal organizational structures and their incumbents than exists elsewhere in other settings. The accused's lawyer has far greater professional, economic, intellectual and other ties to the various elements of the court system than he does to his own client. In short, the court is a closed community. . . .

The defense attorneys, therefore, whether of the legal-aid, public defender variety, or privately retained, although operating in terms of pressures specific to their respective role and organizational obligations, ultimately are concerned with strategies which tend to lead to a plea. It is the rational, impersonal elements involving economies of time, labor, expense and a superior commitment of the defense counsel to these rationalistic values of maximum production of court organization that prevail, in his relationship with a client. The lawyer "regulars" are frequently former staff members of the prosecutor's office and utilize the prestige, know-how and contacts of their former affiliation as part of their stock in trade. Close and continuing relations between the lawyer "regular" and his former colleagues in the prosecutor's office generally overshadow the relationship between the regular and his client. The continuing colleagueship of supposedly adversary counsel rests on real professional and organizational needs of a *quid pro quo,* which goes beyond the limits of an accommodation or *modus vivendi* one might ordinarily expect under the circumstances of an otherwise seemingly adversary relationship. Indeed, the adversary features which are manifest are for the most part muted and exist even in their attenuated form largely for external consumption. The principals, lawyer and assistant district attorney, rely upon one another's cooperation for their continued professional existence, and so the bargaining between them tends usually to be "reasonable" rather than fierce. . . .

Defense Lawyer as Double Agent

The lawyer has often been accused of stirring up unnecessary litigation, especially in the field of negligence. He is said to acquire a vested interest in a cause of action or claim which was initially his client's. The strong incentive of possible fee motivates the lawyer to promote litigation which would otherwise never have developed. However, the criminal lawyer develops a vested interest of an entirely different nature in his client's case: to limit its scope and duration rather than do battle. Only in this way can a case be "profitable." Thus, he enlists the aid of relatives not only to assure payment of his fee, but he will also rely on these persons to help him in his agent-mediator role of convincing the accused to plead guilty, and ultimately to help in "cooling out" the accused if necessary.

It is at this point that an accused-defendant may experience his first sense of "betrayal." While he had perhaps perceived the police and prosecutor to be adversaries, or possibly even the judge, the accused is wholly unprepared for his counsel's role performance as an agent-mediator. In the same vein, it is even less likely to occur to an accused that members of his own family or other kin may become agents, albeit at the behest and urging of other agents or mediators, acting on the principle that they are in reality helping an accused negotiate the best possible plea arrangement under the circumstances. Usually, it will be the lawyer who will activate next of kin in this role, his ostensible motive being to arrange for his fee. But soon latent and unstated motives will assert themselves, with entreaties by counsel to the accused's next of kin, to appeal to the accused to "help himself" by pleading. *Gemeinschaft* sentiments are to this extent exploited by a defense lawyer (or even at times by a district attorney) to achieve specific secular ends, that is, of concluding a particular matter with all possible dispatch.

The fee is often collected in stages, each installment usually payable prior to a necessary court appearance required during the course of an accused's career journey. At each stage, in his interviews and communications with the accused, or in addition, with members of his family, if they are helping with the fee payment, the lawyer employs an air of professional confidence and "inside-dopesterism" in order to assuage anxieties on all sides. He makes the necessary bland assurances, and in effect manipulates his client, who is usually willing to do and say the things, true or not, which will help his attorney extricate him. Since the dimensions of what he is essentially selling, organizational influence and expertise, are not technically and precisely measurable, the lawyer can make extravagant claims of influence and secret knowledge with impunity. Thus, lawyers frequently claim to have inside knowledge in connection with information in the hands of the D.A., police, probation officials or to have access to these functionaries. Factually, they often do, and need only to exaggerate the nature of their relationships with them to obtain the desired effective impression upon the client. But, as in the genuine confidence game, the victim who has participated is loathe to do anything which will upset the lesser plea which his lawyer has "conned" him into accepting.[6]

In effect, in his role as double agent, the criminal lawyer performs an extremely vital and delicate mission for the court organization and the accused. Both principals are anxious to terminate the litigation with a minimum of expense and damage to each other. There is no other personage or role incumbent in the total court structure more strategically located, who by training and in terms of his own requirements, is more ideally suited to do so than the lawyer. . . .

Criminal law practice is a unique form of private law practice since it really only appears to be private practice. Actually it is bureaucratic practice, because of the legal practitioner's enmeshment in the authority, discipline, and perspectives of the court organization. Private practice, supposedly, in a professional sense, involves the maintenance of an organized, disciplined body of knowledge and learning; the individual practitioners are imbued with a spirit of autonomy and service, the earning of a livelihood being incidental. In the sense that the lawyer in the criminal court serves as a double agent, serving higher organizational rather than professional ends, he may be deemed to be engaged in bureaucratic rather than private practice. To some extent the lawyer-client "confidence game," in addition to its other functions, serves to conceal this fact. . . .

CONCLUSION

Courts, like many other modern large-scale organizations possess a monstrous appetite for the cooptation of entire professional groups as well as individuals.[7] Almost all who come within the ambit of organizational authority, find that their definitions, perceptions and values have been refurbished, largely in terms favorable to the particular organization and its goals. As a result, recent Supreme Court decisions may have a long range effect which is radically different from that intended or anticipated. The more libertarian rules will tend to produce the rather ironic end result of augmenting the existing organizational arrangements, enriching court organizations with more personnel and elaborate structure, which in turn will maximize organizational goals of "efficiency" and production. Thus, many defendants will find that courts will possess an even more sophisticated apparatus for processing them toward a guilty plea!

Notes

1. F. J. DAVIS et al., SOCIETY AND THE LAW: NEW MEANINGS FOR AN OLD PROFESSION 301 (1962); L. ORFIELD, CRIMINAL PROCEDURE FROM ARREST TO APPEAL 297(1947).

   D. J. Newman, *Pleading Guilty for Considerations: A Study of Bargain Justice*, 46 J. CRIM. L. C. & P.S. 780–790 (1954). Newman's data covered only one year, 1954, in a midwestern community, however, it is in general confirmed by my own data drawn from a far more populous area, and from what is one of the major criminal courts in the country, for a period of fifteen years from 1950 to 1964 inclusive. The English experience tends also to confirm American data, see N. WALKER, CRIME AND PUNISHMENT IN BRITAIN: AN

ANALYSIS OF THE PENAL SYSTEM (1965). See also D. J. NEWMAN, CONVICTION: THE DETERMINATION OF GUILT OR INNOCENCE WITHOUT TRIAL (1966), for a comprehensive legalistic" study of the guilty plea sponsored by the American Bar Foundation. The criminal court as a social system, an analysis of "bargaining" and its functions in the criminal court's organizational structure, are examined in my forthcoming book, THE CRIMINAL COURT: A SOCIOLOGICAL PERSPECTIVE, to be published by Quadrangle Books, Chicago.

2. G. FEIFER, JUSTICE IN MOSCOW (1965). The Soviet trial has been termed "an appeal from the pretrial investigation" and Feifer notes that the Soviet "trial" is simply a recapitulation of the data collected by the pretrial investigator. The notions of a trial being a "tabula rasa" and presumptions of innocence are wholly alien to Soviet notions of justice . . . "the closer the investigation resembles the finished script, the better . . ."Id. at 86.

3. For a concise statement of the constitutional and economic aspects of the right to legal assistance, see M. G. PAULSEN, EQUAL JUSTICE FOR THE POOR MAN (1964); for a brief traditional description of the legal profession see P. A. Freund, *The Legal Profession,* Daedalus 689–700 (1963).

4. I use the concept in the general sense that Erving Goffnum employed it in his ASYLUMS: ESSAYS ON THE SOCIAL SITUATION OF MENTAL PATIENTS AND OTHER INMATES (1961).

5. A. L. Wood, *Informal Relations in the Practice of Criminal Law,* 62 AM. J. SOC. 48–55 (1956); J. E. CARLIN, LAWYERS ON THEIR OWN 105-09 (1962); R. GOLDFARB, RANSOM—A CRITIQUE OF THE AMERICAN BAIL SYSTEM 114-15 (1965). In connection with relatively recent data as to recruitment to the legal profession, and variables involved in the type of practice engaged in, will be found in J. Ladinsky, *Careers of Lawyers, Law Practice, and Legal Institutions,* 28 AM. Soc. REV. 47–54 (1963). See also S. WARKOV & J. ZELAN, LAWYERS IN THE MAKING (1965).

6. The question has never been raised as to whether "bargain justice," "copping a plea," or

justice by negotiation is a constitutional process. Although it has become the most central aspect of the process of criminal law administration, it has received virtually no close scrutiny by the appellate courts. As a consequence, it is relatively free of legal control and supervision. But, apart from any questions of the legality of bargaining, in terms of the pressures and devices that are employed which tend to violate due process of law, there remain ethical and practical questions. The system of bargain-counter justice is like the proverbial iceberg, much of its danger is concealed in secret negotiations and its least alarming feature, the final plea, being the one presented to public view. See A. S. TREBACH, THE RATIONING OF JUSTICE 74–94 (1964); Note, *Guilty Plea Bargaining: Compromises by Prosecutors to Secure Guilty Pleas,* 112 U. PA. L. REV. 865–895 (1964).

7. Some of the resources which have become an integral part of our courts, e.g., psychiatry, social work and probation, were originally intended as part of an ameliorative, therapeutic effort to individualize offenders. However, there is some evidence that a quite different result obtains, than the one originally intended. The ameliorative instruments have been coopted by the court in order to more efficiently deal with a court's caseload, often to the legal disadvantage of an accused person. See F. A. ALLEN, THE BORDERLAND OF CRIMINAL JUSTICE (1964); T. S. SZASZ, LAW, LIBERTY AND PSYCHIATRY (1963) and also Szasz's most recent, PSYCHIATRIC JUSTICE (1965); L. Diana, *The Rights of Juvenile Delinquents: An Appraisal of Juvenile Court Procedures,* 47 J. CRIM. L. C. & P. S. 561–569 (1957).

Notes and Questions

1. Is Blumberg arguing that the adversary system *cannot* work, or is his a description of a repairable, though malfunctioning, system?

2. According to Blumberg, why would a defense lawyer push a client to enter a guilty plea rather than go to trial? What incentive do defense lawyers have to

limit litigation? How does this conflict with "zealous" defense? Does Blumberg offer credible evidence to suggest that defense attorneys tend to act with concerns about the needs of the court in mind?

3. Blumberg argues that bureaucratic priorities and career commitments of officers of the court frequently "exert a higher claim than the stated ideological goals of 'due process of law' and are often inconsistent with them." What parallels can you draw between Blumberg's argument and Frohmann's description (Chapter 33) of the pressures on district attorneys not to prosecute "un-winnable cases"? What aspects of law's social organization influence these decisions?

4. Unlike the class-centered arguments of some who write about plea bargaining, Blumberg's focus shifts from one aspect of law's social organization—race, class, gender—to another—law's bureaucracy. Is one perspective more revealing than the other? How do the two aspects work in tandem (reinforce one another)? Consider, for instance, the effect race and class have on the frequency of an individual's contact with the police,

the selection and deliberation process of a jury, the prosecutorial preoccupation with "disparate locales," or a combination of these.

5. Is it fair of Blumberg to call defense lawyers "double agents"? How compelling is Blumberg's "double agent" theory for white-collar criminal cases? According to Mann (Chapter 36), whose interests are served by a plea bargain? Can plea bargaining actually be the *result* of zealous advocacy? Does this undermine Blumberg's argument? Why or why not?

6. How do the vested interests of criminal lawyers compare with the interests of civil lawyers? In particular, how does consideration for their own income affect each lawyer's attitude toward the length of legal proceedings?

7. Is White's (Chapter 28) characterization of law as a noble profession compatible with Blumberg's depiction of criminal defense lawyers?

Reprinted from: Abraham S. Blumberg, "The Practice of Law as a Confidence Game" in *Law and Society Review*, 2, 1967, pp. 15–39. Copyright © 1967. Reprinted with the permission of the Law and Society Association. ✦

Section X

*Juries in Criminal Cases:
Biased or Conscientious Judgment*

Chapter 38
Trial by Jury

Alexis de Tocqueville

In the criminal justice system, plea bargaining is the norm and trials are the exception. Yet we should not underestimate the significance of trials just because they are infrequent. They can be routine, proceeding in accordance with the rules and procedures laid out to govern the adversary system, or they can be spectacular events that galvanize the attention of the entire nation and provide a kind of national seminar in which crucial cultural and political conflicts are played out. Whether routine or spectacular, criminal trials are occasions for the display and contestation of ideas of blame and responsibility.

Crucial to the social organization of the criminal trial is the jury, a group of citizens empowered to decide questions of fact, and to apply law to facts to determine guilt or innocence. The role and power of citizen jurors as crucial decision makers in criminal trials have been and remain a source of both pride and anxiety for many Americans. We are proud of the jury and regard it as an essential bulwark of our liberties. But we worry about the competence of jurors to decide complex questions and the tendency of juries to disregard their obligation to follow the law. We worry that gender, class, and race may play an illegitimate role in jury decisions.

Alexis de Tocqueville, writing about trial by jury in the early 1800s, captures something of our national pride when he asserts that juries inject a "republican element" into our system of government. Juries are one expression of popular sovereignty. Tocqueville also thought that jury service changes citizens. The jury communicates "the spirit of the judges to the minds of all citizens," and in so doing provides a unique

form of political education. Subsequent readings speak to our national anxiety about the institution of the jury.

As you read Tocqueville, consider if his argument about the importance of the jury is undermined by the pervasiveness of plea bargaining? Is Tocqueville too much of an idealist in his assessment of the consequences of jury service?

Since my subject has led me to speak of the administration of justice in the United States, I will not pass over it without adverting to the institution of the jury. Trial by jury may be considered in two separate points of view; as a judicial, and as a political institution. If it was my purpose to inquire how far trial by jury, especially in civil cases, insures a good administration of justice, I admit that its utility might be contested. As the jury was first established when society was in its infancy, and when courts of justice merely decided simple questions of fact, it is not an easy task to adapt it to the wants of a highly civilized community, when the mutual relations of men are multiplied to a surprising extent, and have assumed an enlightened and intellectual character.

My present purpose is to consider the jury as a political institution; any other course would divert me from my subject. . . .

By the jury, I mean a certain number of citizens chosen by lot, and invested with a temporary right of judging. Trial by jury, as applied to the repression of crime, appears to me an eminently republican element in the government, for the following reasons.

The institution of the jury may be aristocratic or democratic, according to the class from which the jurors are taken; but it always preserves its republican character, in that it places the real direction of society in the hands of the governed, or of a portion of the governed, and not in that of the government. Force is never more than a transient element of success, and after force, comes the notion of right. A government which should be able to reach its enemies only upon a field of battle would soon be destroyed. The true sanction of political laws is to be found in penal legislation; and if that sanction be wanting, the law will sooner or later lose its cogency. He who punishes the criminal is therefore the real master of society. Now, the institution of the jury raises the people itself, or at least a class of citizens, to the bench of judges. The institution of the jury consequently invests the people, or that class of citizens, with the direction of society.

In England, the jury is returned from the aristocratic portion of the nation; the aristocracy makes the laws, applies the laws, and punishes infractions of the laws everything is established upon a consistent footing, and England may with truth be said to constitute an aristocratic republic. In the United States, the same system is applied to the whole people. Every American citizen is qualified to be an elector, a juror, and is eligible to office. The system of the jury, as it is understood in America, appears to me to be as direct and as extreme a consequence of the sovereignty of the people as universal suffrage. . . .

. . . The jury is pre-eminently a political institution; it should be regarded as one form of the sovereignty of the people: when that sovereignty is repudiated, it must be rejected, or it must be adapted to the laws by which that sovereignty is established. The jury is that portion of the nation to which the execution of the laws is intrusted, as the legislature is that part of the nation which makes the laws; and in order that society may be governed in a fixed and uniform manner, the list of citizens qualified to serve on juries must increase and diminish with the list of electors. . . .

. . .The jury . . . serves to communicate the spirit of the judges to the minds of all the citizens; and this spirit, with the habits which attend it, is the soundest preparation for free institutions. It imbues all classes with a respect for the thing judged, and with the notion of right. If these two elements be removed, the love of independence becomes a mere destructive passion. It teaches men to practice equity; every man learns to judge his neighbor as he would himself be judged. And this is especially true of the jury in civil causes; for, whilst the number of persons who have reason to apprehend a criminal prosecution is small, every one is liable to have a lawsuit. The jury teaches every man not to recoil before the responsibility of his own actions, and impresses him with that manly confidence without which no political virtue can exist. It invests each citizen with a kind of magistracy; it makes them all feel the duties which they are bound to discharge towards society, and the part which they take in its government. By obliging men to turn their attention to other affairs than their own, it rubs off that private selfishness which is the rust of society.

The jury contributes powerfully to form the judgment and to increase the natural intelligence of a people; and this, in my opinion, is its greatest advantage. It may be regarded as a gratuitous public school, ever open, in which every juror learns his rights, enters into daily communication with the most learned and enlightened members of the upper classes, and becomes practically acquainted with the laws, which are brought within the reach of his capacity by the efforts of the bar, the advice of the judge, and even by the passions of the parties. I think that the practical intelligence and political good sense of the Americans are mainly attributable to the long use which they have made of the jury in civil causes.

I do not know whether the jury is useful to those who have lawsuits; but I am certain it is highly beneficial to those who judge them; and I look upon it as one of the most efficacious means for the education of the people which society can employ. . . .

Notes and Questions

1. What does Tocqueville mean when he refers to trial by jury as a both a judicial institution and a political institution? Why does Tocqueville assert that the jury

is less useful as a purely judicial institution than it is as a political institution?

2. According to Tocqueville, who is qualified to sit on a jury? What criteria would you use for juror eligibility?

3. No doubt a judge, with years of formal legal training and practice, is more competent than the average juror to interpret the law. To what do you attribute the legitimacy of the jury as a legal institution? What assets does a jury possess, according to Tocqueville, that a judge may lack? Do you agree?

4. Tocqueville writes that the jury "imbues all classes with a respect for the thing judged, and with the notion of right." As such, the jury always "preserves its republican character." To what degree is this true in practice?

5. Though all voting citizens are eligible to sit on juries, some citizens are more likely to be selected during *voir dire* than others. In your opinion, is the jury selection process more likely to render an "aristocratic jury" or a "democratic jury"?

6. Tocqueville writes that the institution of the jury "invests each citizen with a kind of magistracy." What aspects of Hay's account (Chapter 13) of eighteenth-century British jurisprudence does Tocqueville's observation evoke?

7. Tocqueville calls jury duty "the soundest preparation for free institutions." Involving citizens in the judicial process, he argues, is of the utmost importance for healthy civic life. Do you agree with this argument? Beyond his civic concerns, however, he seems uninterested in the ability of juries to make sound legal decisions. "I don't know whether the jury is useful to those who have lawsuits; but I am certain it is highly beneficial to those who judge them." Should he be more concerned with the capacity of juries as a legal institution?

Reprinted from: Francis Bowen, "Trial By Jury in the United States Considered as a Political Institution" in *Democracy in America* by Alexis de Tocqueville, translated by Henry Reeve, pp. 358–367. Copyright ©1876 by John Allyn Publishers. ✦

Chapter 39

Are Twelve Heads Better Than One?

Phoebe C. Ellsworth

Criminal trials can be complicated affairs in part because the adversary system insures that no argument or version of events is left unchallenged. Moreover, legal standards for determining guilt or innocence are not easy to comprehend. For jurors, getting things right may be very difficult. Unlike judges, who have legal training and experience, jurors generally have no formal training for their tasks. What happens when juries deliberate? Do jury deliberations vindicate Tocqueville's arguments? Do the dynamics of jury decision making compensate for possible deficiencies of individual comprehension?

Using "mock juries" composed of adults eligible for jury service, Phoebe C. Ellsworth tries to provide some answers to these questions. Her work renders a divided verdict on the question of jury competence. Ellsworth suggests that juries are better at finding facts than they are at understanding the law and that group deliberations compensate for the factual misunderstandings of individual jurors. However, no such corrective effect occurs in regard to their comprehension of the relevant law. The instructions jurors receive from judges are not effective in educating them about relevant legal standards, and jury deliberation, Ellsworth finds, does not overcome judges' failures to make their instructions clear.

This study highlights the importance of social factors in shaping at least one aspect of jury deliberations. Ellsworth reports that while 65 percent of the mock jurors were female, they selected males to act as forepersons in 16 of 18 cases.

INTRODUCTION

Few advocates of the jury system would argue that the average juror is as competent a tribunal as the average judge. Whatever competence the jury has is a function of two of its attributes: its number and its interaction. The fact that a jury must be composed of at least six people,[1] with different backgrounds, experiences, and perspectives, provides some protection against decisions based on an idiosyncratic view of the facts. Not only must the jury include at least six people, but they must be chosen in a manner that conforms to the ideal of the jury as representative of community opinion.[2] The jury's competence, unlike that of the judge, rests partly on its ability to reflect the perspectives, experiences, and values of the ordinary people in the community—not just the most common or typical community perspective, but the whole range of viewpoints. Representativeness is important not only for ensuring "the essential nature of the jury as a tribunal embodying a broad democratic ideal,"[3] but because it affects the jury's competence directly. Failure to assure that any given group has a fair chance of participation "deprives the jury of a perspective on human events that may have unsuspected importance in any case that may be presented."[4]

A jury decision, however, is more than an average of the verdict preferences of six or twelve citizens who represent a variety of experiences. Ideally, the knowledge, perspectives, and memories of the individual members are compared and combined, and individual errors and biases are discovered and discarded, so that the final verdict is forged from a shared understanding of the case. This understanding is more complete and more accurate than any of the separate versions that contributed to it, or indeed than their average. This transcendent understanding is the putative benefit of the deliberation process.

There is a good deal of evidence that jurors commonly organize the mass of testimony they hear into a story[5] with characters, motives, and plot. Incoming information is assimilated to the basic story framework, and information that does not fit is often forgotten or explained away. It is well known among psychologists that much of what is perceived is a function of the perceiver; it is a particular *construal* of the events perceived, rather than a true reflection.[6] Several different perceivers will come up with several somewhat dissimilar accounts of a sequence of events. Once having arrived at a construal, or a story or explanation of the same sequence of events, most people find it very difficult to imagine a different way of interpreting the same events, and this leads them to underestimate severely their own creative contribution to their "memory."[7] Even though most people recognize in principle that a good deal of perception is really interpretation, they are unable to make adequate inferential adjustments for this process in guiding their own behavior, often behaving exactly as they would if their interpretation were the only possible one.[8]

If it does nothing else, group deliberation (except in extraordinarily one-sided cases) forces people to realize that there are different ways of interpreting the same facts. While this rarely provokes a prompt revision of their own views, it necessarily reminds the jury members that their perceptions are partly conjectural—an obvious truth, but one that is otherwise unlikely to occur to them. A judge does not have this vivid reminder that alternative construals are possible.

A judge, however, has experience on the bench and training in the law. Critics of the jury often focus on the incompetence of people chosen as jurors, compared to that of the judge. At best the venire consists of a representative sample of the community, with a few members having genuine expertise, a large number who are simply average citizens, and a few others who are distinctly below average. In practice, many of the better-educated jurors are excused from service, and others who show knowledge or ability relevant to the particular case at trial may be challenged during the voir dire. Attorneys select jurors for incompetence.[9] Thus, some have argued that the average jury is not only less competent than the average judge, but is also less competent than a random sample of twelve citizens from the community. . . .

The research itself involved the close analysis of the first hour of deliberation of eighteen mock juries.[10] Because of the small sample size, statistical analysis of the data generally would be misguided. The study is most usefully considered as an intensive case study of the process of jury deliberation, although the fact that there are eighteen cases rather than one makes it considerably more useful than the usual case study, because it allows for some assessment of the variability of juries exposed to the same stimulus. A major drawback is that none of the juries reached a verdict in the hour allotted to them.[11] Thus, the study is most useful as an exploration of how juries structure their task, how well they deal with the facts and the law, and what things they discuss. It is very likely that at some point juries move into an "end game" that may differ substantially from the phases preceding it.

METHOD

SUBJECTS AND OVERVIEW

Two hundred and sixteen adults eligible for jury service in Santa Clara or San Mateo County, California, participated in the deliberation study and provided usable data.[12] Thirty-three of them were recruited from the venire lists of the Santa Clara County Superior Court after completion of their terms as jurors. Of the remaining 183 subjects, 156 had responded to a classified advertisement in local newspapers asking for volunteers for a study of "how jurors make decisions." The final twenty-five people were referred by friends who had heard of the study or who were subjects themselves. Each subject was paid ten dollars for participation.

The sample was fairly representative of the suburban upper-middle-class community surrounding Stanford University, except that males and minorities were underrepresented. The sample was 93 percent white and 65.3 percent female. The average age of the subjects was forty-three, and 63 percent of the sample was employed outside the home. Married persons constituted 45 percent of the sample; 26 percent were single, 19 percent divorced, 4 percent separated, and 6 percent widowed. The median educational level was slightly less than a college degree. Democrats made up 46.2 percent of the sample, Republicans 32.4 percent, and Independents 11.6 percent, with the remainder divided among unregistered voters and small parties. In the category of religious affiliation, one-third of the sample listed themselves as Protestant, 15 percent as Catholic, and 9 percent as Jewish; 26 percent listed no affiliation, and 17 percent listed other religions. Finally, 46 percent of the sample had previously performed jury duty, while 37 percent had actually served on juries.

Subjects watched a videotape of a simulated homicide trial that represented all major aspects of an actual criminal trial. After hearing the evidence, arguments, and instructions, the jurors gave an initial verdict. Jurors were then assigned to twelve-person juries and allowed to deliberate for one hour.

THE TRIAL VIDEOTAPE

After viewing simulated trial materials prepared by several other social scientists interested in jury behavior, and after considering creating materials of our own, we chose the videotape prepared by Reid Hastie for use in his research on jury unanimity.[13] This tape is representative of the procedures, setting, style, and issues that commonly occur in actual homicide trials. The case was complex enough to afford several plausible interpretations and verdict preferences. It resembled most real murder trials in that there was no question that the defendant had killed the victim; rather, the evidence centered on the precise sequence of events preceding the killing and on the defendant's state of mind at the time. Finally, the tape was far more vivid and realistic than any others we have encountered. It was highly unlikely that we could have constructed a better tape with our resources.

Hastie's videotape is a reenactment of an actual homicide case based on a complete transcript of the original trial. Each actor portraying a defense or prosecution witness was provided with "a summary of the case highlighting his or her testimony."[14] The judge and the lawyers, portrayed by an actual judge and two experienced criminal attorneys, were given "unabridged copies of the actual judge's instructions, selections of relevant testimony, and the actual attorney's opening and closing arguments as they were originally presented."[15] The attorneys were asked to develop their cases as they would for a real trial. The witnesses were asked to review their materials to get their version of the events firmly in mind. Then, for the actual taping, all actors put aside their materials and engaged in "spontaneous improvisations closely following the original case[16]." . . .

In the trial videotape, the defendant, Frank Johnson, is charged with first-degree murder for the stabbing of Alan Caldwell outside a neighborhood bar. The prosecution brings evidence that the defendant and victim had argued in the bar earlier that day, and that Caldwell had threatened the defendant with a straight razor. Johnson had left after the argument, but had returned with a friend that evening. Johnson was carrying a fishing knife in his pocket. Caldwell later came into the bar, and he and the defendant went outside and began to argue loudly. Two witnesses testify that they saw Johnson stab down into

Caldwell's body. The victim's razor was subsequently found folded in his left rear pocket.

For the defense, Johnson testifies that he had returned to the bar that evening on the invitation of his friend and had entered only after ascertaining that Caldwell was not there. Caldwell had come in later and had asked Johnson to step outside, presumably for the purpose of patching up their quarrel. Once outside, Caldwell had hit him and had come at him with a razor. Johnson had pulled out a fishing knife which he often carried in his pocket and Caldwell had run onto the knife. Johnson's friend corroborates much of this testimony. In cross-examination, the defense attorney casts doubt on the ability of the prosecution's eyewitnesses to see the scuffle, and shows that medical evidence cannot establish whether the defendant stabbed down into the victim or the victim ran onto the knife.

Four verdicts are possible in this case, depending upon the jury's findings of the facts. The defendant may be guilty of first-degree murder, of second-degree murder, of voluntary manslaughter, or he may be not guilty for reason of self-defense or accidental homicide. . . .

CHOOSING A FOREMAN

All juries began by choosing a foreman, not surprisingly, since the experimenter had instructed them to do so. The foreman was always chosen very quickly, with a minimum of discussion. For ten of the eighteen juries, the process of foreman selection can be summed up by the phrase "choose a man who says he has experience." Although 65 percent of the jurors were female, sixteen of the eighteen foremen were male.[17] On the jury composed of eleven women and one man, the man was chosen. . . .

STRUCTURING THE TASK

Once the foreman was selected, the juries took one of two approaches to the task. One-half of the juries began by taking a vote, roughly evenly divided between show-of-hands, secret ballot, and a go-round procedure where each juror states a position and says a little about his or her reasons for taking that position. The other half of the juries began by discussing the facts and issues in the case. The judge's instructions contained a caution to the jurors not to become unduly committed to their position but to remain open-minded. A few jurors interpreted these instructions to mean that they should not begin deliberations with a vote. . . .

Whether or not the jury began with a vote, the general progression of the deliberation moved from an emphasis on facts toward an emphasis on law. In juries that did not begin by voting, the initial discussion resembled a random walk through the facts and issues. A topic would be raised, discussed briefly, and replaced by a totally different topic, with little attempt to organize the discussion and no attempt to resolve the issues. These juries conformed very closely to Kalven and Zeisel's observation that "the talk moves in small bursts of coherence, shifting from topic to topic with remarkable flexibility. It touches an issue, leaves it, and returns again."[18] During the hour of deliberation, the important facts and issues would come up again and again, while trivial issues would be dropped, and new issues added. Typically, as an issue was examined and re-examined, there would be movement toward consensus. . . .

In juries that began with a vote, the discussion tended to be slightly more organized. The average distribution of verdicts prior to deliberation was one for first-degree murder, two for second-degree murder, six for manslaughter, and two for not guilty. Although none of the juries showed exactly this pattern, most of them had a majority of votes in the two middle categories with outliers for not guilty or for both not guilty and first-degree murder. A common tactic was for the middle jurors to begin by asking the outliers to explain their deviant position, typically starting with the proponents of first-degree murder.

Whether or not the jury began with a vote, however, issues were raised and dropped fairly unsystematically, then raised again; slowly, progress was made. Little by little, most juries resolved the issues of fact and spent an increasing proportion of their time on the central issue: the defendant's state of mind.

THE JURY'S ABILITY TO DEAL WITH THE FACTS

Kalven and Zeisel conclude that "the jury does by and large understand the facts and get the case straight."[19] The juries in our study spent more time discussing the facts of the case (47 percent of the units included references to facts brought out in testimony) than anything else. These were rarely purely factual statements. Most of the time facts were raised in connection with a contested issue ("If the officer could clearly identify Frank and saw that he was doing something so that he should say, 'Frank, don't do it,' then that shows that he had very good vision."), a reference to common sense or knowledge ("There's only one way that bone could have been struck and it had to be like that. You couldn't strike down like that and hit right here."), a hypothetical scenario ("Suppose that—that he gets up with the knife, and Caldwell has the razor in this hand, and Caldwell, who is what, 200 pounds, six feet, 200 pounds, lunges toward him."), or a reference to the law ("The razor was in that man's back left pocket . . . so it couldn't have been murder by reason of the man defending himself.").

Most of the juries managed to sort out the factual issues fairly well during the process of deliberation. Conflicting testimony (for example, about the angle of the knife thrust) was recognized as such, so that juries ended up correctly attributing different versions of the story to different witnesses. Questions regarding the distance and angle of vision of the various witnesses were generally resolved correctly, and errors of fact generally were corrected. None of the juries maintained an erroneous perception of an important fact after

the hour of deliberation. Implausible suggestions generally were discussed and rejected, as in the case of someone else putting the razor in the victim's pocket. . . .

THE JURY'S ABILITY TO DEAL WITH THE LAW

Juries worked hard to understand the law. They spent an average of 21 percent of their time discussing the judge's instructions, primarily during the latter half of the hour. Following the hour of deliberation, jurors were given an eighteen-question true-false test on elements of the judge's instructions. On average the jurors answered 11.7 of the questions correctly, a result not significantly different from random guessing. In the larger study of which these deliberation data are a part, there were also seventy-two subjects who saw the videotaped trial, indicated their verdict preference, and filled out the postexpenment questionnaires but did not participate in jury deliberations. The questionnaires revealed no differences between these subjects and those subjects who had deliberated as juries in understanding of the judge's instructions. On a postdeliberation multiple-choice test of factual issues, however, jurors performed quite well, answering correctly an average of 8.8 out of fourteen questions (since there were four response alternatives 3.5 correct answers would be expected by chance). Jurors also performed better than those subjects who did not deliberate. These results suggest that the deliberation process works well in correcting errors of fact but not in correcting errors of law. . . .

During the course of deliberation, jurors generally fought to defend their correct opinions of the facts but not their correct versions of the legal standards. Typically the most forcefully expressed position prevailed, whether or not it was correct. Most of the jurors' discussions of substantive law (that is, the definitions of the verdict categories) conveyed an impression of considerable uncertainty ("Was it . . . I think it was something about passion?"), and jurors who seemed confident about the law were often believed, whether or not their statements corresponded to the judge's instructions. Of the 1752 units across all juries that referred to the law, only seventy-five (4 percent) were error corrections. Only 12 percent of the 609 incorrect and unclear statements were corrected. Examining each jury's last definition of the four verdict choices during the course of the hour, we found that no jury was correct on all four of them. It appears that most jurors failed to absorb a great many of the judge's instructions and that the process of deliberation did not correct this problem. Hastie, Penrod, and Pennington[20] used different judicial instructions for the same case (and their juries deliberated until they reached a verdict); their results were similar to ours.

Further evidence that the jurors learned less than they should have from the judge's instructions come from an examination of the frequency with which various aspects of the law were discussed during deliberation. The instructions most often discussed involved points of law that the jurors were very likely to have heard about before they heard the case; thus, there is a strong possibility that much of their discussion of the law was based not on the instructions they had heard from the judge but on prior knowledge. . . .

CONCLUSION

In summary, the process of deliberation seems to work quite well in bringing out the facts and arriving at a consensus about their sequence. Errors are corrected, and irrelevant facts and implausible scenarios are generally weeded out, at least in deliberations over this relatively simple homicide. The juries also do a good job of gradually narrowing down discussion to the important issues. On the whole, however, the discussion of the facts does not produce changes in votes, since jurors' verdict preferences in the case were rarely a function of a clear mistake on the facts.

Changes in votes are likely to occur after discussion of the law. Unfortunately, the jurors' understanding of the law was substantially inferior to their understanding of the facts and issues. Much of the jurors' discussion of the law revolved around phrases they were likely to have known before they heard the Judge's instructions. The instructions may have been effective in reminding the jurors of terms they had heard before, but the instructions were not very effective in educating them in new areas, or even in focusing their attention on the meaning of the familiar terms.

This failure to apply the law correctly was by no means a failure to take the law seriously. Discussions of the law took up one-fifth of the deliberation time and were carried out with great intensity, frequently with an apparent sense of frustration. The jurors understood that a key aspect of their task was to interpret the evidence in terms of the appropriate legal categories. They struggled to do so, but often failed. . . .

Notes

1. *Ballew v. Georgia,* 435 U.S. 223, 228 (1978) (five-member jury does not satisfy the jury trial guarantee of the sixth amendment).

2. *Strauder v. West Virginia,* 100 U.S. 303 (1880) (equal protection clause guarantees the defendant that the state will not exclude members of his race from the jury venire on account of race); *Thiel v. Southern Pacific Co.,* 328 U.S. 217 (1946) (in an exercise of its supervisory power, the Court granted a new trial where jury had been chosen in a manner which systematically excluded persons who were wage workers); *Taylor v. Louisiana,* 419 U.S. 522 (1975) (fair cross-section requirement of the sixth amendment is violated by the systematic exclusion of women); *Duren v. Missouri,* 439 U.S. 357 (1979) (state statute providing for automatic exemption from jury service for any woman requesting not to serve which produces jury venires averaging less than 15% female violates the sixth amendment's fair cross-section requirement); *Batson v. Kentucky,* 476 U.S. 79 (1986) (prose-

cutor's use of peremptory challenges to exclude blacks from a jury trying a black defendant establishes an equal protection claim of purposeful discrimination). These cases are a small selection of major landmarks in the development of the definition of representativeness as a fundamental characteristic of fair juries.

3. *Ellsworth & Getman, Social Science in Legal Decision Making*, in LAW AND THE SOCIAL SCIENCES 596 (L. Lipson & S. Wheeler eds. 1986).

4. *Peters v. Kiff*, 407 U.S. 493, 503–504 (1972) (plurality opinion of Marshall, J., joined by Douglas and Stewart, JJ.).

5. See W. BENNETT & M. FELDMAN, RECONSTRUCTING REALITY IN THE COURTROOM (1981); Pennington & Hastie, *Evidence Evaluation in Complex Decision Making*, 51 J. PERSONALITY & Soc. PSYCHOLOGY 242 (1986); Pennington & Hastie, *Explanation-Based Decision Making: Effects of Memory Structure on Judgment*, 14 J. EXPERIMENTAL PSYCHOLOGY: LEARNING, MEMORY & COGNITION 521 (1988).

6. See D. SCHNEIDER, A. HASTORF & P. ELLSWORTH, PERSON PERCEPTION (1979); Ross, *The Problem of Construal in Social Inference and Social Psychology*, in A DISTINCTIVE APPROACH TO PSYCHOLOGICAL RESEARCH: THE INFLUENCE OF STANLEY SCHACHTER (N. Grunberg, R. Nisbett & I. Singer eds. 1987).

7. D. Griffin, D. Dunning & L. Ross, The Role of Construal Processes in Overconfident Predictions about the Self and Others (1988) (unpublished manuscript, Stanford University).

8. *Id.*

9. See J. VAN DYKE, JURY SELECTION PROCEDURES (1977); V. HANS & N. VIDMAR, JUDGING THE JURY 63–78 (1986).

10. The deliberation data were collected as part of a study of the relationship between death penalty attitudes and perceptions of guilt. Results relevant to this issue are reported in Cowan, Thompson & Ellsworth, *The Effects of Death Qualification on Jurors' Predisposition to Convict and On the Quality of Deliberation*, 8 LAW & HUM. BEHAV. 53 (1984).

11. Five of the juries had reached 10-2 splits by the end of the hour, as assessed by post-deliberation questionnaires on verdict preferences. The trial used in the research was the same one reported in R. HASTIE, S. PENROD & N. PENNINGTON, INSIDE THE JURY (1983). They found that twelve-person juries operating under a unanimity rule took an average of two hours and 18 minutes to reach a verdict.

12. The study included 20 juries, but two had to be dropped from the analysis, one because of equipment failure in the sound recording, and the other because one of its members was an amateur actor who had recently starred in a production of 12 *Angry Men* (Orion-Nova/UA 1957) and who dominated deliberation using arguments and reasoning drawn from that play.

13. R. HASTIE, S. PENROD & N. PENNINGTON, supra note 11.

14. *Id.*

15. *Id.*

16. *Id.*

17. This gender bias in choice of a foreperson has changed little over the last 40 years See Strodtbeck, James & Hawkins, *Social Status in Jury Deliberations*, 22 AM. Soc. REV 713 (1957) It occurs not only in mock-jury research, but in real trials. See Kerr, Harmon & Graves, *Independence of Multiple Verdicts by Jurors and Juries*, 12 J. APPLIED Soc. PSYCHOLOGY 12, 24–25 (1982); Note, *Gender Dynamics and Jury Deliberations*, 96 YALE L.J. 593 (1987).

18. See H. KALVEN & H. ZEISEL, THE AMERICAN JURY 486 (1966).

19. *Id.* at 149.

20. R. HASTIE, S. PENROD & N. PENNINGTON, supra note 11.

NOTES AND QUESTIONS

1. According to Ellsworth, what gives juries their legitimacy to decide legal questions? How does the individual judgment of a professionally trained judge compare to the group deliberation of a lay jury? What are juries good at? What

are judges good at? What does each struggle with?

2. Prosecutors and defense attorneys get to help choose who is struck from a jury, and who remains; therefore their role in shaping the ultimate verdict is not insignificant. How well does Ellsworth's study of mock juries account for this influence? How might her results have been different if she were able to observe real jury deliberations?

3. Ellsworth's study suggests that consensus will likely develop over the facts of the case, no matter who is involved in the deliberations. However, when it comes to applying law to the perceived facts of the case, jurors disagree. Why? How does the social background of jurors affect how they interpret the law? Does this lend any credence to the prosecutorial concern about "disparate locales" described by Frohmann (Chapter 33)?

4. What does Ellsworth mean when she writes about the failure of the mock jurors "to apply the law correctly"? To what extent is the "correctness" of the jury's legal interpretation in the eye of the beholder? Explain.

5. According to Ellsworth's study, mock jurors understood the judge's instructions no better after an hour of deliberations than did volunteers who engaged in no deliberation at all. On issues of law, "typically the most forceful expressed position prevailed, whether or not it was correct." Why would juries be able to agree over the correct factual information but not over legal interpretation? How do you suppose social factors (e.g., race, class, and gender) affect the influence of certain jurors over others, and how do they influence the direction of jury interpretation?

6. Ellsworth's study offers at least part of an answer to Tocqueville's question (Chapter 38): How competent is a jury at performing its judicial duty? Based on Ellsworth's conclusions, are the shortcomings of the jury as a judicial institution worth the professed benefits of the jury as a political institution? Why or why not?

7. Would it be preferable for a jury to decide the facts of a case and then hand its decision over to a judge to fit the facts with the law? Why or why not?

Reprinted from: Phoebe C. Ellsworth, "Are Twelve Heads Better Than One?" in *Law and Contemporary Problems*, 52:4, 1989, pp. 205–207, 208–210, 211, 213–218, 220, 223. Copyright © 1989. Reprinted with the permission of Duke University School of Law. ✦

Chapter 40
Jury Duty

When History and Life Coincide

Elisabeth Perry

What role do social factors—like gender and race—play in the work of juries? How, if at all, do they influence jury deliberations? In the next selection, Elisabeth Perry describes her experience on a jury in a murder case and reflects on the influence of gender and racial diversity on that jury's deliberations.

Perry begins by noting that, historically, women were exempt and excluded from serving on juries because it was thought that they were not competent—that is, not rational enough to serve and because their role as wives and mothers made it hard for them to be away from home. Today those gender-based exclusions no longer apply. The result of including women on juries, Perry contends, changes the way these juries decide cases.

Perry notes that as her colleagues tried to figure out what happened and how the relevant law should be applied, women and minority jurors interpreted the evidence differently from their white male counterparts. The resulting verdict, she speculates, was different from one that would have been reached by an all white, all male jury. Although she is unable to specify exactly how gender and race shaped the jury's work, she warns that the influence of diversity on a jury "cannot by foretold along stereotypical lines."

Not long ago, I served on a jury for the first time. Most people groan when a jury summons arrives, but I was thrilled. I hadn't received one since 1964, and I had avoided serving then on grounds that I only later realized were discriminatory.

When the first summons came, I was a history graduate student in Southern California, busy teaching sections of "Western Civilization" and preparing for a trip to France for my dissertation research. I panicked. I didn't have time for jury duty! I read the summons through, hoping for a way to escape its imperative. At last I got down to the list of exempted categories. Surely "student" or "teacher" would be on it. No, but "woman" was.

I had no idea why. My graduate-student friends were equally ignorant. One suggested that it was because women menstruate. "You know how they get emotionally unstable every month," he said. I had never suffered from such instability, but getting out of jury duty on any grounds looked good to me. With barely a moment's hesitation, I checked the "woman" box.

Years later, I regretted that act of youthful insouciance. In the mid-1970s, I began to do research in a field new to me, American women's history. I wanted to write a biography of my paternal grandmother, Belle Moskowitz, the social reformer and suffragist who served as New York Gov. Alfred E. Smith's political strategist in the 1920s. After the book came out in 1987, I started a new, still continuing, project that, to myself, I call "From Belle to Bella," on the New York women active in politics from Moskowitz to Bella Abzug, the colorful New York congresswoman of the 1970s.

Early on in the project, I learned why I had been able to get out of jury duty. When women's suffrage was ratified in 1920, more than half the states had not yet legalized woman jurors. Over the next two decades, a number changed their laws to allow women to serve—but only on an elective basis.

In New York, opposition to women on juries rested on two widely held stereotypes. The first was that women were not "fit" to serve: They were incapable of rational judgment and too "delicate" to tolerate the gory details of criminal behavior. The second was that their domestic roles—watching over children and preparing meals—made it hard for them to be away from home. It is interesting that the strongest opposition came from rural women, who argued that jury service would place an extraordinary burden on their already difficult lives.

By 1937, several national and local developments—including the U.S. Department of Justice's approving women as jurors for all federal courts, and a case in which an all-male jury convicted a woman of infanticide—finally persuaded New York legislators to allow women on juries. With a bow to the state's rural women, they made service nonmandatory.

Convinced that women would always be treated as second-class citizens unless they had an equal obligation to civic duties like jury service, a small cadre of New York women persisted in a campaign for mandatory service. Although they made little progress, and gave up their campaign in the 1950s, their cause was making its way through the federal judicial system. In 1975, the U.S. Supreme Court ruled in *Taylor v. Louisiana* that all juries must represent a "fair cross section" of the community. The issue of voluntary versus mandatory service was henceforth moot.

As I reported for jury service, I was thus pleased to have the opportunity. Friends warned me that I might have a long and boring wait before being called. "Take a lunch and a book," they advised. They also predicted that I probably wouldn't make it onto a jury. "Attorneys never pick woman academics," they said. Not true. By that afternoon, I was empaneled on a jury for a murder trial and told to count on being there all week.

In his memoir of jury duty last year, *A Trial by Jury*, [2001] the historian D. Graham Burnett notes that we expect much, but think too

little, about what happens in the jury room. That, I found, is also true about the role gender plays on a jury.

The case before us was complicated. Late one night, two armed men in their 20s, members of the same gang, confronted a third man at the front door of his home. By their own admission, they intended to "get back at him" for an insult. When the man saw their guns, he fled upstairs, out a back porch, and jumped to the alley below. The two would-be assailants followed. A few moments later, the man who fled lay dead in a cellar stairwell. He had seven bullets in his body.

His pursuers had been seen. Knowing that, they threw their shirts into a dumpster and ran. The police found the shirts and picked up one man quickly. He denied having been the shooter, plea-bargained on the lesser charge of burglary (armed breaking and entering), and had begun serving five years. The police did not find his partner for six months. A bruiser of a man, that was our defendant. He had been called in only as "backup," he said, and denied shooting the fatal bullets. Neither man's weapon was ever found.

The testimony was confusingly presented and strikingly incomplete. The prosecutor seemed ill prepared. The public defender was brand-new at her job. The jailed assailant testified, but was so terrified by the presence of the defendant's buddies in the courtroom that he was barely audible. We did, however, grasp his central point: His partner had fired the fatal shots. There was much "expert" testimony about DNA tests on the discarded shirts and the locations of spent shells and bullets; there were photographs of the crime scene and the deceased's body, which we passed among us. We noted that his genitals had been pierced by a bullet. No one flinched, but it was a gruesome sight.

The defendant testified, with his lawyer concentrating more on establishing his good character—despite prior convictions on drug and weapons charges, he was about to be married and to become a father—rather than his innocence, which she could not prove.

The testimony took a day and a half to be heard. None of it illuminated the key question in the case. Someone had fired seven bullets into an unarmed man fleeing for his life. Which assailant had been the shooter?

We, the jury, retired to deliberate. It turned out that we all agreed that the evidence had been poorly presented, but we were nowhere near unanimity. Two jurors favored a finding of first-degree murder. Eight favored second-degree, and two were undecided. We read and reread the judge's instructions about being sure "beyond a reasonable doubt." Endlessly, we rehearsed the definitions of "murder in the first" (planned), "murder in the second" (unplanned), "manslaughter" (recklessly endangering another's life), and "burglary," with which our defendant was also charged. But no matter how many hours we talked and recast our votes, we could reach unanimity only on "burglary." At 5 p.m. on a Friday evening, the judge declared a mistrial on the murder charge. We never found out if the state would try the case again.

Months have passed since my jury service, and I still think about what happened, both in the courtroom and the jury room, to bring about such an unsatisfactory ending. In part, the answer has to do with the way the rules that regulate juries hindered our ability to make well-informed judgments. In our court (although not, I have since learned, in all courts), we were not allowed to take notes. When an elderly juror snoozed, well, that was just too bad. Nor could we question witnesses or lawyers; in our system, the lawyers are in control of presenting the evidence.

Further, our judge refused to let us see the transcript. After the trial was over, she came to the jury room to answer questions. Her tone was consoling. Mistrials are common in murder trials, she said, because the burden of proof is so high. "Why couldn't we consult the transcript?" I asked. Because, she answered, you might focus too closely on one part of the testimony. "We want you to weigh all of the evidence, and we trust that 12 jurors from different walks of life will remember enough correctly to make a sound judgment."

Although probably based on experience, her position disturbed me. Why deny jurors the chance to refresh their memories? Until we had begun to deliberate, we had no idea which part of the testimony was going to be crucial. By the time we knew, it was too late.

More than the limitations on what jurors could see, ask, or hear, however, the gender and racial politics of the jury's deliberations—and the way gender and race overlapped with each other—proved determinative to the trial's outcome. And that is where my scholarship and experience came together for me.

Gender issues were only indirectly at stake in the trial, but it still made a difference that four of us on the jury were women. And it mattered that *only* four of us were. The two jurors who initially wanted first-degree murder were both men. During a break, one of them, a middle-aged white man, made hostile remarks about the judge. She's "me-e-e-an," he drawled. He liked "my women" to be "ladylike," "on a pedestal."

The other man, a retired African-American, had a deep bass voice. When he kept raising its volume to assert his points, I had to ask him to stop shouting. Later, a soft-spoken young African-American woman, who must have found the man intimidating, took me aside and thanked me.

Five of the jurors were white, and seven were African-American, as were all the major players in the trial except the judge and the public defender. Our deliberations reached a climax when, on Friday, the soft-spoken young woman, undecided until then, suddenly blurted out that nothing had convinced her that the bullets in the dead man's body came from a gun our defendant had carried. With intense feeling, she warned that, should we convict the man, we would be "lynching him just because he was a big black nigger."

A shocked silence fell over the room. Her language threw us. What's more, many of us felt guilty. Maybe we had rushed to judgment because our defendant was "big" and "black." By then, the two men who originally voted for a first-degree verdict had already "come down" to second degree. But the young woman remained unconvinced that the evidence was persuasive enough for even that.

We took a short break. When we sat down again, I suggested that, perhaps, we should consider manslaughter. No matter which assailant was lying, I argued, we knew "beyond a reasonable doubt" that our defendant had arrived on the scene armed, and that his "reckless" behavior had endangered the victim's life. At the very least, our defendant was partially responsible for the death.

We took a new vote. This time, everyone, including the young woman, agreed on manslaughter—except for the deep-voiced, African-American man. He had already compromised enough by accepting second-degree murder, he said.

It took us barely a minute to agree on the burglary charge. We all sensed that the defendant, despite his lawyer's efforts to convince us otherwise, was dangerous. On the other charges, we were "hung."

Clearly, the interplay of race and gender here was complex. The young African-American woman's reference to "lynching," and her use of the inflammatory "N" word, was the group's only overt reference to race. Two of the men had originally voted for the harshest sentence; yet one of them, surely the most "sexist" of the men on the jury, had allowed himself to be swayed by a woman's impassioned plea. All but one man had accepted my proposal for manslaughter. Had the one person I failed to convince dug in his heels because I had asked him to compromise? Was he unwilling to accept a suggestion from a woman? Was he just a stubborn person? I'll never know.

Perhaps that's the point. As the historian Linda K. Kerber showed in her 1998 book, *No Constitutional Right to Be Ladies: Women and the Obligations of Citizenship,* until quite recently our laws—because of either ban or exemption—often meant that no women served on juries. And the lack of diversity had an impact, in different ways in different cases.

My experience was undeniably frustrating. I cannot pin down just how race and gender affected each of us on my panel. Indeed, the influence of diversity on a jury cannot be foretold along stereotypical lines—just as it cannot be foretold in the classroom or in society at large. Disqualifying jurors along racial or ethnic or gender grounds is a strategy that cannot have predictable results.

Defending diversity on college campuses, in the work force, or in society, is not a matter of saying that X, or Y, or Z will happen if you include more women, more members of minority or ethnic groups. But my experience showed me that my feminist forebears did make a difference by working so hard to include women on juries. The interplay among factors on a jury will always be complex, messy, and unpredictable. To deny any group participation would skew our system of justice. To allow, indeed to require, women to serve on juries is crucial to creating a true panel of peers. It is crucial to keeping our system of justice as fair and as honest as we can make it.

Notes and Questions

1. In the deliberations Perry describes, what hung the jury? Was it disagreement about facts, irreconcilable interpretations of the law, or some combination of the two? In your opinion, was there enough evidence to convict beyond a reasonable doubt? How do you suppose your race, class, and gender inform your opinion of this case?

2. Why are juries not allowed to see the transcript of a trial? What's wrong with scrutinizing specific parts of testimony? Would seeing transcripts reduce the

number of hung juries? Would this make the criminal justice system more or less just? Why?

3. Beyond the judge's refusal to provide the jury with a transcript, what aspects of courtroom procedure affected the jury's ability to reach a verdict in the case? What purposes do those trial practices serve? Should any of them be reformed? Why or why not?

4. What would compel a juror, eager to convict the defendant of first-degree murder, to accept a mistrial before he would vote for a charge of manslaughter? Considering that the prosecution failed to convince the entire jury of its case, was justice served, or would a manslaughter conviction have been more just?

5. Are Perry's observations of jury deliberations supported by Lucie White's (Chapter 28) ideas about "rule-oriented" versus "relational" storytelling?

6. Does this article paint a positive or a negative picture of the effect of diversity on justice? Perry calls her experience "undeniably frustrating." Is there a case to be made that the diversity on Perry's jury hindered justice? Can diversity open new possibilities for people to engage in "meaningful participation" with the law?

7. How are Tocqueville's civic ideals (Chapter 38) reflected in Perry's experience? What is it about Perry's jury experience that conflicts with Tocqueville's description?

Reprinted from: Elisabeth Perry, "Jury Duty: When History and Life Coincide" originally published in *The Chronicle of Higher Education*, 2002, B15–16. Copyright © 2002. Reprinted with the permission of Elisabeth Perry. ✦

Chapter 41

When Race Trumps Truth in Court

Michael D. Weiss
Karl Zinsmeister

One of the most awesome powers of the jury in criminal cases is the ability to refuse to apply the law, even when it is clearly applicable. This power, called jury nullification, is the ultimate assertion of the kind of sovereignty about which Tocqueville wrote. In their refusal to apply the law, juries make a judgment about the justness of a legal conviction in a particular case. When the consequences of convicting someone seem unduly severe, nullifying jurors "do justice." For some commentators, this kind of jury action is a healthy way of tailoring the result in a criminal trial to the circumstances of a particular case. It is, in their view, a justified discretionary act. For others, jury nullification means jury lawlessness, and it is a distinct problem in the social organization of law.

The 1995 criminal trial and acquittal of O. J. Simpson (on charges that he murdered his wife, Nicole Brown Simpson, and Ronald Goldman), is an example of a spectacular criminal trial in which many thought that jurors engaged in nullification. In addition to its intense media coverage and the fact that it was followed closely by millions of people in the United States and around the world, views of the Simpson verdict were polarized on racial lines. Many white people thought the verdict was incorrect, while African Americans were more supportive of it.

After the trial, commentators speculated that some of the African-American members of the Simpson jury had refused to convict because they saw him as a victim of a racist police force and criminal justice system. Since the Simpson verdict, the question of whether it is appropriate or wise for jurors to engage in jury nullification on racial grounds has escalated dramatically. Unlike the portrait of gender and racial influences that Perry paints (Chapter 40), this article suggests that when jurors nullify on racial grounds, they violate their oaths to make a larger point about biases in the legal system.

The article by Michael D. Weiss and Karl Zinsmeister reports that many legal officials believe that this practice is now widespread. These authors criticize scholars and activists who defend racial nullification as a counterweight to racism in the legal system. They argue that it is harmful to the victims of crime who deserve justice, that it encourages disrespect for law, and that it injures minority communities because African Americans are much more likely to be the victims of violent crime than are whites.

In 1992, a white congressional aide working for Senator Richard Shelby of Alabama was shot to death in his Capitol Hill home. A few weeks later, a young black man named Edward Evans was arrested for the crime. Two of his friends testified that they saw him shoot the young aide; one said that Evans harbored strong anti-white sentiments and had earlier vowed to kill a white man. Although this and the material evidence presented what seemed to be an overwhelming case against Evans, one African American juror refused to convict. A frustrated jury foreman told the judge that Velma McNeil would simply not give any credence to the prosecution's evidence. A hung jury and mistrial resulted. A *Washington Post* photograph showed McNeil emerging from the courtroom hugging a relative of the accused murderer.

In 1994, a Towson State college student who became lost in the Dutch Village section of Baltimore was robbed and murdered by Davon Neverdon. After the student willingly handed over his wallet, Neverdon shot him in the face. Prosecutors presented four eyewitnesses who testified they saw Neverdon kill the man. Two other witnesses reported that Neverdon told them afterwards that he committed the murder. The evidence against Neverdon was so strong he bargained for a forty year sentence in exchange for a guilty plea, an offer which was rejected by the prosecution at the request of the victim's family. Yet a jury comprised of eleven African Americans and one Pakistani acquitted Neverdon because of "witness credibility" problems. Before the verdict, the Pakistani juror reported that "race may be playing some part" in the jury's decision.

In another Baltimore case, a white man was killed when a cinder block was dropped on his head from a third floor balcony of a public housing project. Three witnesses identified the black defendant as the murderer and another testified in court that the defendant had confessed to him. The defendant was acquitted.

After off-duty black police officer Rudy Thomas was murdered in Brooklyn in 1994, defendant Johnny Williams confessed to the crime on videotape, describing his motive and the murder weapon. Williams's fingerprints were found on the slain officer's motorcycle, and bullets from his gun matched those found in the victim. There were also three eyewitnesses to the crime. "We had enough evidence to supply three or four cases," reports the prosecuting attorney. But the defense claimed, with no evidence, that Williams was beaten by the white detective on the case, and a hung jury resulted. A juror who refused to give in to those favoring acquittal reported the deliberations were "blatantly racial."

In 1994, a suburban white woman named Rebecca Gordon was driving through Detroit when she was gunned down by a group of blacks in an adjoining car. Defense counsel played the "race card" at the 1995 trial, and the inner city jury refused to convict defendant Brian Marable of murder, turning in a guilty verdict only on the misdemeanor charge of reckless discharge of a firearm.

Darryl Smith, a black drug dealer in Washington, D.C., tortured eighteen-year-old African American Willie Wilson to death as he begged for mercy in front of witnesses. Despite massive amounts of evidence linking him to the crime, an all-black D.C. jury acquitted Smith in his 1990 murder trial. According to other jurors, forewoman Valerie Blackmon refused to convict because "she didn't want to send any more young black men to jail." After long deliberations, other members of the panel caved in to Blackmon's argument that the "criminal justice system is stacked against blacks" and let Smith off, though most believed that he was guilty. Three weeks after the verdict, a letter from an anonymous juror arrived at D.C. Superior Court expressing regret over the verdict.

On August 19, 1991, after a traffic accident in which a black child was killed by a car carrying a Jewish leader, a black mob rioted down a street in the Crown Heights section of Brooklyn, shouting "Let's go get the Jews." A Jewish scholar visiting New York named Yankel Rosenbaum was stabbed to death when they encountered him on the street. Within minutes police arrived and apprehended Lemrick Nelson, Jr. at the scene with a bloody knife in his pocket. He was taken to the dying Rosenbaum, who identified Nelson as his attacker. Nelson later admitted the crime to two Brooklyn detectives, and signed a written confession. Prosecutors presented this evidence to a predominantly black jury. They refused to convict Nelson. After the acquittal, jurors celebrated with Nelson at a local restaurant. (Nelson later moved to Georgia and was convicted of slashing a schoolmate.)

Clearly, there has been a booming trade in black racism in American courtrooms for some time. Then came the O.J. Simpson verdict. "The jury did not deliberate, it emoted," observed commentator Mona Charen afterwards. "If the prosecution's case was so weak, why did Johnnie Cochran argue in his summation that jurors disregard the evidence? . . . The reaction of so many American blacks to the verdict was unseemly and offensive. . . . One of the jurors, a former member of the Black Panther party, gave the black power salute" to Simpson in court right after the acquittal. "Was the jury fair-minded? Is black America?" asks Charen. "Only a nation of fools would lull itself into believing that this was not a racially motivated and a racist verdict." She warns that even "if Marcia Clark had produced a videotape of the murders in progress, the defense would have argued that the filmmaker was a racist and the jury would have found 'reasonable doubt.'"

Charen's videotape scenario is actually not so far-fetched. Racial legal bias exists not only at the street level among black Americans but also high among today's black leadership. This was clearly illustrated by an article published in December [1995] in the *Yale Law Journal,* and excerpted in the December *Harper's Magazine.* In it, a black George Washington University law professor and former prosecutor in the U.S. Attorney's office in the District of Columbia named Paul Butler describes how "during the trial of Marion Barry, then the second-term mayor of the District of Columbia, Barry was being prosecuted by my office for drug possession and perjury. I learned, to my surprise, that some of my fellow African American prosecutors hoped that the mayor would be acquitted, despite the fact that he was obviously guilty of at least one of the charges—an FBI videotape plainly showed him smoking crack cocaine. These black prosecutors wanted their office to lose its case because they believed that the prosecution of Barry was racist."

In his *Yale Law Journal* and *Harper's Magazine* articles, Butler makes it clear that racialized justice is not only a thriving inner city practice, but also a theory built on determined black intellectual rationalizations. He himself is a case in point. "During a training session for new assistants conducted by experienced prosecutors," he recalls, "we rookies were informed that we would lose many of our cases, despite having persuaded a jury beyond a reasonable doubt that the defendant was guilty. We would lose because some black jurors would refuse to convict black defendants who they knew were guilty . . . some African American jurors vote to acquit black defendants for racial reasons." Though he was then serving as a prosecutor of drug and gun criminals, Butler himself was soon converted to "the juror's desire not to send another black man to jail." Describing America as "a police state," he currently argues that for "pragmatic and political reasons," black jurors have a "moral responsibility . . . to emancipate some guilty black outlaws."

Noting that polls show 66 percent of blacks believe the U.S. criminal justice system is racist, Butler points out that "African American jurors who endorse these critiques are in a unique position to act on their beliefs when they sit in judgment of a black defendant." Today's African Americans "should ask themselves whether the operation of the criminal law system in the United States advances the interests of black people," and if they believe it does not, he urges, they should "opt out," judging defendants by whatever standards they please rather than by the law. This is known as jury nullification.

Butler presents some specific suggestions as to how black juries might take the law into their own hands. He urges that for crimes like drug dealing, gun possession, theft, and perjury, nullification always ought to be considered. He calls for African Americans to exercise double standards as they see fit: "A juror might vote for acquittal, for example, when a poor woman steals from Tiffany's but not when the same woman steals from her next-door neighbor." Specifically conjuring up a case of a black "thief who burglarizes the home of a rich white family," Butler sees "a moral case to be made for nullification."

Certainly big city prosecutors will tell you that they see lots of racialized jury-behavior. Lead prosecutor Marcia Clark told CNN after the Simpson acquittal that "a majority black jury won't bring a conviction in a case like this." She later scurried to retract that "off the record" statement, but other officials are not so shy. Los Angeles County deputy district attorney Bobby Grace states that "growing resentment . . . can affect a jury verdict." Atlanta-area assistant district attorney Leigh Dupre estimates that at least one-fourth of all criminal cases that end in acquittal may involve some form of racial nullification.

Prosecutors agree that urban black jurors have turned extremely skeptical of prosecution witnesses, especially police officers. Brooklyn district attorney Charles Hynes states that "the problem my office faced in court in the Yankel Rosenbaum trial is one that confronts prosecutors in most urban areas today: distrust by inner-city residents of the police officers who are sworn to protect and serve them." Bob Agacinski, deputy chief of the Wayne County prosecutors in Detroit, blames defense counsel for introducing this "racial appeal to juries . . .especially in cases where the witnesses are police officers. Police credibility is easy to attack . . . and juries are buying the argument that the police are looking to lock up any black man. . . . Minor inconsistencies in police testimony become reasonable doubt when the case has racial overtones." Racial pleas are "notoriously overused" by defense counsel, says Agacinski. He estimates that over "50 percent of the cases which go to trial involve some type of racial appeal."

Prosecutors have noted a "more blatant use" of the racial defense since the Simpson trial began. In the summer of 1994, for instance, after an elderly man was beaten to death by a black defendant at a Detroit-area McDonald's, defense attorneys invoked racial sympathies even though the defendant con-fessed the murder to police officers. They claimed the confession was coerced by the white officers, and the predominantly black jury voted to acquit.

Rogue cops really do exist, as the vile Mark Fuhrman recently reminded us. But at present, *every* cop is viewed as a rogue by many inner-city jurors. "Police officers now have to prove that race was *not* an issue in an arrest," reports a former prosecutor in the U.S. attorney's office in Washington D.C. Baltimore assistant state attorney Ahmet Hisim illustrates the problem using a rating scale. In a typical city today, he says, "black jurors will automatically assess at least thirty points out of a hundred against a police officer's credibility, without even hearing any testimony."

Defense counsel are also quick to attack the credibility of non-police prosecution witnesses. A former assistant U.S. attorney in D.C. maintains that "in major metropolitan cities where prosecutors deal with predominantly black juries, defense counsel will put the government on trial because of the kinds of witnesses that the government must use." Often the prosecution has to rely on informants involved in the same kinds of activity as the defendant, and today's suspicious juries leap to discount their testimony. Determined skepticism of this sort can be very difficult to overcome. D.C. Detective Donald Gossage, who worked on the Darryl Smith case, notes that "you don't have your nuns and doctors and lawyers standing on these street corners."

In addition to prosecutors' estimates like the startling ones above from Detroit's Agacinski and Atlanta's Dupre, there are other small and localized indicators of increased racialism in court. More hung juries are one obvious sign. The black teenager who murdered English tourist Gary Colley at a Florida rest stop, for instance, had to be tried three times before he was convicted because his first two trials ended in hung juries. This despite the fact that he and his three teenage accomplices had more than a hundred arrests amongst them at the time of the murder. In California, there are currently between 10,000 and 11,000 hung juries annually—up to 15 percent of all cases tried. That figure represents a lot of foregone justice, and also a huge public expense, given that the average trial costs taxpayers $10,000 a day, according to the California District Attorney's Association.

Hard nationwide figures on acquittals by race of defendant, victim, and jury are hard to come by. Data from the U.S. Bureau of Justice Statistics do show that in the 75 largest counties in the U.S., rates of felony prosecution and conviction are slightly lower for blacks than whites. In a few jurisdictions where clear statistics are available, the patterns are dramatic. Nationwide, the felony acquittal rate for defendants of all races is only 17 percent, but in the Bronx, where more than eight out of ten jurors are black or Hispanic, 48 percent of all black felony defendants are acquitted. In Washington, D.C., where more than 95 percent of defendants and 70 percent of jurors are black, 29 percent of all felony trials ended in acquittal in 1994. In Wayne County, which includes mostly black Detroit, 30 percent of felony defendants are acquitted.

On the day of the O.J. Simpson acquittal, a veteran New York law enforcement official estimated off-handedly to criminologist John DiIulio that "there's 100,000 O.J.s. We've reached the point where the system is rigged to let murderers, and not just rich ones, escape justice."

What are the ultimate effects of this racialized judgment in U.S. courtrooms? Obviously there is tremendous personal hurt in cases where justice is not done, and the number of such cases is rising. There is also more disrespect for the law, and a lot more crime and society-wide damage done by perpetrators who should be locked up instead of roaming the streets.

Former U.S. attorney Joseph DiGenova argues that advocates of jury nullification on racial grounds are "pushing anarchy." The refusal to convict by black juries is "rampant" and getting worse, he warns, and this is feed-ing the inner-city crime cycle. DiGenova also notes that "we fought like hell to get blacks into the system as cops and prosecutors and judges, and now these guys are being fiercely ostracized and pressured, and told in their own community that a black person shouldn't work in such a position. Well who is supposed to respond to black criminals? Or are we just supposed to pretend there aren't any black criminals?"

John DiIulio adds that big city prosecutors today view cases where there is a white victim and a black defendant as "no win situations." Recognizing that it will be difficult to get a conviction, prosecutors pull their punches: avoiding the death penalty like the plague even where it is clearly merited (like the Simpson case), avoiding multiple counts and other moves that might give the appearance of piling on, largely letting defense attorneys pick the juries, and trying desperately to plea bargain everything to avoid going to a jury in the first place. The result, DiIulio says, is that "blacks are being substantially and systematically under-prosecuted today, not only in cases of black-on-white crime, but also in cases of black-on-black."

Baltimore prosecutor Hisim advises that it is dangerous for jurors to attempt to "fix the system by being revolutionary." Recognizing that "black jurors seem to be striking back at society," Hisim suggests that they should be educated about the consequences of racially-based nullification, since ninety percent of crime is committed by people living in a juror's own community. The irony is that by letting clearly guilty individuals go, jurors are only "infecting their own neighborhoods with criminals."

NOTES AND QUESTIONS

1. What is the difference between nullification and reasonable juror skepticism? What objective measure, if any, can the criminal justice system employ to distinguish between the two?

2. Do Weiss and Zinsmeister's examples make a compelling case that juror nullification is as rampant a practice as they claim? Why or why not? How straightforward is their presentation of the facts of each case?

3. Is nullification a recent phenomenon—perhaps a product of more diverse juries—or can you identify parallel historical situations in American jurisprudence?

4. In most of the examples, Weiss and Zinsmeister point to a single juror engaging in jury nullification. Can a unanimous decision ever be called nullification? Why or why not?

5. Is nullification the prerogative of jurors, or do they usurp judicial power when they engage in such discretionary activity?

6. Many argue that jury nullification empowers often disempowered social groups to effectively counterbalance ingrained injustices in American law. Is this a sound argument? According to polls quoted by Weiss and Zinsmeister, 66 percent of black citizens believe the judicial system is racist. Is jury nullification a good answer or just a "band-aid" solution? Does it make the criminal justice system seem more or less racist? To whom?

7. Weiss and Zinsmeister insist that "racial pleas are notoriously overused" by defense attorneys. They argue that this behavior encourages juries to nullify on racial grounds. Do you agree? Can racial tension be excluded from legal proceedings? Should it be?

8. As Weiss and Zinsmeister point out, "police officers now have to prove that race was *not* an issue in an arrest." Should the burden of proving nondiscrimination be placed on the police?

9. Weiss and Zinsmeister conclude that jury nullification has caused "more disrespect for the law, and a lot more crime and society-wide damage done by perpetrators who should be locked up instead of roaming the streets." What, if anything, should be done about jury nullification? Would it generate more respect for the law if unrelenting jurors were removed from trials to ensure convictions? What would the implications of such a campaign be for jury sovereignty and overall judicial legitimacy?

Reprinted from: Michael D. Weiss and Karl Zinsmeister, "When Race Trumps Truth in Court" in the *American Enterprise*, January/February 1996. Copyright © 1996. Reprinted with the permission of *The American Enterprise: a Magazine of Politics, Business, and Culture*. On the web at www.TAEmag.com.✦

Chapter 42

United States v. Thomas

During the 1990s, the U. S. government carried out a "war on drugs," in which police changed their tactics (see Section XII) and punishments for drug-related offenses became much more severe (Section XIII). It is now apparent that the war on drugs has had dramatically different effects in minority communities than it has elsewhere in American society. Although some contend that this war has been effective and was partially responsible for the dramatic drop in the rate of violent crime in the 1990s, others contend that it has been particularly hard on minorities who seem to be disproportionately targeted. This section ends with a court decision on the role of the jury and the responsibilities of jurors in a drug case in which several African Americans were accused of possession and distribution of crack cocaine.

The particular issue in the case is whether a juror can be removed when he or she refuses to apply the law to the facts in such a way as to indicate that nullification is occurring. In its decision, the U. S. Court of Appeals for the Second Circuit reaffirmed that jurors do not have a right to nullify the law but they did acknowledge that "several features of our jury trial system act to protect the jury's power to acquit, regardless of the evidence, when the prosecution's case meets with the jury's moral disapproval." The court also provided a historical overview of both legal doctrine and the practice of jury nullification.

That overview reminds us that in the early years of the American Republic, the right of juries to decide questions of law as well as of fact was widely accepted and that this widespread acceptance lasted until the middle of the nineteenth century. Since then, juries have been regarded as subservient to judges as arbiters of the law. Today, that subservience is well established in both federal and state law.

The Thomas court recognized the right of a trial judge to remove a juror for purposefully disregarding the law but warned that the standard of proof needed for making such a determination is very high. It cautioned trial judges not to confuse nullifying jurors with those who are simply unpersuaded by the government.

We consider here the propriety of the district court's dismissal of a juror allegedly engaged in "nullification"—the intentional disregard of the law as stated by the presiding judge—during the course of deliberations. We address, in turn, (1) whether such alleged misconduct constitutes "just cause" for dismissal of a deliberating juror ... and (2) what evidentiary standard must be met to support a dismissal. . . .

We consider below whether a juror's intent to convict or acquit regardless of the evidence constitutes a basis for the juror's removal during the course of deliberations. . . . We also consider what constitutes sufficient evidence of that intent in light of the limitations on a presiding judge's authority to investigate allegations of nullification required by the need to safeguard the secrecy of jury deliberations. We conclude, inter alia, that—as an obvious violation of a juror's oath and duty—a refusal to apply the law as set forth by the court constitutes grounds for dismissal. . . . We also conclude that the importance of safeguarding the secrecy of the jury deliberation room, coupled with the need to protect against the dismissal of a juror based on his doubts about the guilt of a criminal defendant, require that a juror be dismissed for a refusal to apply the law as instructed only where the record is clear beyond doubt that the juror is not, in fact, simply unpersuaded by the prosecution's case. We hold that the district court erred in dismissing a juror, based largely on its finding that the juror was purposefully disregarding the court's instructions on the law, where the record evidence raised the possibility that the juror's view on the merits of the case was motivated by doubts about the defendants' guilt, rather than by an intent to nullify the law. Accordingly, we vacate the judgments of the district court and remand for a new trial.

I

We have before us the consolidated appeals of ten criminal defendants convicted of related conduct in two trials held in the Northern District of New York. The named defendants in this case, including those whose appeals we consider here, were arrested on May 5, 1994. In an indictment returned on May 13, 1994, they were charged with conspiracy to possess and distribute cocaine and crack cocaine and actual possession and distribution of these substances. A 30-count, superseding indictment was returned on October 14, 1994, which added a series of forfeiture counts against the defendants.

Ceasare Thomas, Myron Thomas, Lamont Joseph, Santo Bolden, and Raymond Eaddy were tried on charges set forth in the superseding indictment beginning on November 22, 1994. After a Government witness apparently made certain prejudicial statements on the stand, a mistrial was declared on November 28, 1994. A second trial of the same defendants began two days later, on November 30, 1994, and the jury returned verdicts of guilty for all defendants but Raymond Eaddy on December 14, 1994. We affirm these convictions in a summary order filed today. See *United States v. Thomas et al.*, 1997 U.S. App. LEXIS 11767, Nos. 95-1337 et al. (2d Cir. May 20, 1997).

The remaining appellants, Grady Thomas, Ramse Thomas, Jason Thomas, Tracey Thomas, and Loray Thomas, along with Terrence Thomas, Shawne Thomas, Carrie Thomas, Stephon Russell, and Robert Gib-

son, were the subject of a separate trial, which began on January 18, 1995. Grady Thomas, Ramse Thomas, Jason Thomas, Tracey Thomas, and Loray Thomas appeal from judgments of conviction entered against them following this trial, and we consider their appeals here. We confine our factual discussion of this trial to the events leading up to and including the ultimate dismissal of one of the jurors. These events provide the basis for the appellants' primary challenge to the proceedings below.

During jury selection, the Government attempted to exercise a peremptory challenge to a juror who would later be empaneled as "Juror No. 5." Because the juror was black—indeed, the only black person remaining as a potential juror in a case in which, as the record indicates, all of the defendants are black—defense counsel objected to the peremptory challenge under *Batson v. Kentucky*, 476 U.S. 79, 90 L. Ed. 2d 69, 106 S. Ct. 1712 (1986), as racially motivated. The Government responded that it wished to exclude the juror based not on his race, but on the fact that he failed to make eye contact with the Government's counsel during the voir dire. Although the district court explicitly found that the Government's peremptory challenge was not motivated by race, the court, in a misapplication of Batson,[1] nevertheless denied the challenge on the ground that the juror's failure to make eye contact was an insufficient basis for his removal. The court would later explain that Juror No. 5's status as the only black juror in a case involving black defendants had motivated its decision to deny the Government's challenge.

Problems regarding Juror No. 5 did not end with his selection for the jury, however. During the course of defense summations on Friday, February 17, 1995, following several weeks of trial, a group of six jurors approached the courtroom clerk to express their concerns about the juror. The six jurors complained that Juror No. 5 was distracting them in court by squeaking his shoe against the floor, rustling cough drop wrappers in his pocket, and showing agreement with points made by defense counsel by slapping his leg and, occasionally during the defense summations, saying "yeah, yes.". . .

The jury deliberated throughout the day on February 22. On February 23, the courtroom clerk reported to the court, and then on the record to all counsel, that she had been approached on two separate occasions earlier in the day by jurors expressing concern over the course of their deliberations. Juror No. 1 reportedly had indicated to the clerk that deliberations were likely to continue beyond February 23 because of a "problem with an unnamed juror." That same morning, Juror No. 12 had also reported to the clerk that "there was a problem . . . in the jury room [with] one of their number, and specifically . . . indicated [that] juror number five, had, at each time a vote was taken, voted not guilty and had indicated verbally that he would not change his mind." The court concluded, after hearing argument from counsel for the parties, that no action was immediately necessary; the court would "give it a little more time to see what develops."

Troubles in the jury room seemed to escalate rapidly, however. On the following morning, February 24, the court received a note from Juror No. 6, apparently written only on his own behalf. The note indicated that, due to Juror No. 5's "predisposed disposition," the jury was unable to reach a verdict. Following an off-the-record conversation with counsel for the parties, the court again conducted *in camera*, on-the-record interviews with each of the jurors outside the presence of counsel. This time, jurors focused their comments more directly on Juror No. 5. Several mentioned the disruptive effect he was having on the deliberations. One juror described him "hollering" at fellow jurors, another said he had called his fellow jurors racists, and two jurors told the court that Juror No. 5 had come close to striking a fellow juror. The judge was also informed by a juror that, at one point, Juror No. 5 pretended to vomit in the bathroom while other jurors were eating lunch outside the bathroom door. The jurors, however, were not unanimous in identifying Juror No. 5 as a source of disruption in the jury room. One juror informed the judge that friction among the jurors had been "pretty well ironed out," and another indicated that the other jurors were in fact "picking on" Juror No. 5.

Although the district court did not specifically inquire into any juror's position on the merits of the case, at least five of the jurors indicated that Juror No. 5 was unyieldingly in favor of acquittal for all of the defendants. The accounts differed, however, regarding the *basis* for Juror No. 5's position. On the one hand, one juror described Juror No. 5 as favoring acquittal because the defendants were his "people," another suggested that it was because Juror No. 5 thought the defendants were good people, two others stated that Juror No. 5 simply believed that drug dealing is commonplace, and another two jurors indicated that Juror No. 5 favored acquittal because he thought that the defendants had engaged in the alleged criminal activity out of economic necessity. On the other hand, several jurors recounted Juror No. 5 couching his position in terms of the evidence—one juror indicated specifically that Juror No. 5 was discussing the evidence, and four recalled him saying that the evidence, including the testimony of the prosecution's witnesses, was insufficient or unreliable. As for Juror No. 5, he said nothing in his interview with the court to suggest that he was not making a good faith effort to apply the law as instructed to the facts of the case. On the contrary, he informed the court that he needed "substantive evidence" establishing guilt "beyond a reasonable doubt" in order to convict.

After interviewing the jurors, the judge met in chambers with counsel for the parties. He had the record of the interviews read aloud and permitted counsel to comment on the appropriate course of action. The Government argued that the jurors' responses indicated that there was "almost a *jury nullification* issue pattern with [Juror No. 5]," and urged the court to order the juror's dismissal, while defense counsel unanimously opposed his removal. Having heard argument from counsel, the judge rendered his decision to remove Juror No. 5. He believed that Juror No. 5 had become a "distraction" and a "focal point" for the jury's attention, and that his removal might "allow [the jury] to deliberate in a full and a fair fashion." The court cited Juror No. 5's failure to live up to his assurances regarding proper conduct, referring in particular to the allegation that he nearly struck another juror and to his feigned vomiting. Most importantly, however, the court found that Juror No. 5 was ignoring the evidence in favor of his own, preconceived ideas about the case:

> I believe after hearing everything that [Juror No. 5's] motives are immoral, that he believes that these folks have a right to deal drugs, because they don't have any money, they are in a disadvantaged situation and probably that's the thing to do. And I don't think he would convict them no matter what the evidence was.

The court found that Juror No. 5 was refusing to convict "because of preconceived, fixed, cultural, economic, [or] social . . . reasons that are totally improper and impermissible."

The court then called Juror No. 5 into chambers to inform him of his dismissal and, that afternoon, announced the dismissal to the remaining jurors. Jurors were instructed that they were "to draw no inferences or conclusions whatsoever" from the removal and told that they were to start over in their deliberations.

On the afternoon of the following Monday, February 27, 1995, the remaining eleven jurors returned a verdict. They found the defendants Grady, Ramse, Tracy, and Terrence Thomas guilty on all counts, Jason Thomas guilty on three of the four counts against him, and Carrie and Loray Thomas each guilty on a conspiracy count. The jury deadlocked on the fourth count against Jason Thomas and acquitted Carrie and Loray Thomas of possession with intent to distribute a controlled substance. Stephon Russell was acquitted of conspiracy to distribute and to possess with intent to distribute, the only count with which he had been charged.

Ramse, Tracey, Loray, Grady, and Jason Thomas here appeal from the judgment of conviction. As their chief argument on appeal, each of these defendants challenges the dismissal of Juror No. 5.

II

The district court dismissed Juror No. 5 pursuant to FED. R. CRIM. P. 23(b), which provides, in pertinent part, that where "the court finds it necessary to excuse a juror for just cause after the jury has retired to consider its verdict, in the discretion of the court a valid verdict may be returned by the remaining 11 jurors." We review the district court's exercise of this authority for abuse of discretion. See, e.g., *United States v. Reese,* 33 F.3d 166, 173 (2d Cir. 1994), *cert. denied,* 513 U.S. 1092, 130 L. Ed. 2d 655, 115 S. Ct. 756 (1995); *United States v. Casamento,* 887 F.2d 1141, 1187 (2d Cir. 1989), *cert. denied,* 493 U.S. 1081, 107 L. Ed. 2d 1043, 110 S. Ct. 1138 (1990).

To determine whether the court erred in dismissing Juror No. 5, we must first decide whether the district court's primary basis for the dismissal—the juror's intention to disregard the applicable criminal laws—constitutes "just cause" for his removal under Rule 23(b). In holding that a presiding judge has a duty to dismiss a juror who purposefully disregards the court's instructions on the law, we briefly review the factors that courts have traditionally considered to be "just cause" for dismissal pursuant to Rule 23(b), and discuss the dangers inherent in so-called "nullification." Having concluded that a deliberating juror's intent to nullify constitutes "just cause" for dismissal, we next consider whether the district court in this case had a sufficient evidentiary basis for concluding that Juror No. 5 was purposefully disregarding the court's instructions on the law.

Dismissal of a Juror During Deliberations: Rule 23(b) and Factors That Traditionally Constitute 'Just Cause'

In evaluating the district court's decision to remove Juror No. 5 pursuant to Rule 23(b), we must first decide whether the reasons that the court cited as grounds for the removal constitute "just cause" as that term is employed in the rule. We consider, in particular, the district court's primary ground for dismissal—that Juror No. 5 refused to apply the law as set out in the court's instructions.[2] Whether a juror's defiance of the court's instructions on the law constitutes "just cause" for that juror's removal under Rule 23(b) is apparently a question of first impression in this Circuit. . . .

Nullification as 'Just Cause' for Dismissal

Here, Chief Judge McAvoy identified a different form of bias as the primary ground for dismissing Juror No. 5—one arising not from an external event or from a relationship between a juror and a party, but rather, from a more general opposition to the application of the criminal narcotics laws to the defendants' conduct. In the court's view, Juror No. 5 believed that the defendants had "a right to deal drugs." Based on what the court described as the juror's "preconceived, fixed, cultural, economic, [or] social . . . reasons that are totally improper and impermissible," the court concluded that Juror No. 5 was unlikely to convict the defendants "no matter what the evidence was." Essentially, the judge found that Juror No. 5 intended to engage in a form of "nullification," a practice whereby a juror votes in purposeful disregard of the evidence, defying the court's instructions on the law.

We take this occasion to restate some basic principles regarding the character of our jury system. Nullification is, by definition, a violation of a juror's oath to apply the law as in-

structed by the court—in the words of the standard oath administered to jurors in the federal courts, to "render a true verdict *according to the law and the evidence*." FEDERAL JUDICIAL CENTER, BENCHBOOK FOR U.S. DISTRICT COURT JUDGES 225 (4th ed. 1996) (emphasis supplied). We categorically reject the idea that, in a society committed to the rule of law, *jury nullification* is desirable or that courts may permit it to occur when it is within their authority to prevent. Accordingly, we conclude that a juror who intends to nullify the applicable law is no less subject to dismissal than is a juror who disregards the court's instructions due to an event or relationship that renders him biased or otherwise unable to render a fair and impartial verdict.

We are mindful that the term "nullification" can cover a number of distinct, though related, phenomena, encompassing in one word conduct that takes place for a variety of different reasons; jurors may nullify, for example, because of the identity of a party, a disapproval of the particular prosecution at issue, or a more general opposition to the applicable criminal law or laws. We recognize, too, that nullification may at times manifest itself as a form of civil disobedience that some may regard as tolerable. The case of John Peter Zenger, the publisher of the *New York Weekly Journal* acquitted of criminal libel in 1735, and the nineteenth-century acquittals in prosecutions under the fugitive slave laws, are perhaps our country's most renowned examples of "benevolent" nullification. See *United States v. Dougherty,* 154 U.S. App. D.C. 76, 473 F.2d 1113, 1130 (D.C. Cir. 1972) (Leventhal, J.); see also SHANNON C. STIMSON, THE AMERICAN REVOLUTION IN THE LAW: ANGLO-AMERICAN JURISPRUDENCE BEFORE JOHN MARSHALL 52–55 (1990) (describing Zenger trial). We are also aware of the long and complicated history of juries acting as judges of the law as well as the evidence, see, e.g., John D. Gordan III, Juries as Judges of the Law: The American Experience, 108

LAW Q. REV. 272 (1992); Mark De Wolfe Howe, Juries as Judges of Criminal Law, 52 HARV. L. REV. 582 (1939), and of the theoretical underpinnings of this practice in the United States, in which legal decisions by juries were sometimes regarded as an expression of faithfulness to the law (regardless of the authority of institutions or officeholders), rather than defiance of the law or "nullification." David Farnham, *Jury Nullification: History Proves It's Not a New Idea*, CRIM. JUST., Winter 1997, at 4, 6–7.

More generally, the very institution of trial by jury in a criminal case, as Judge Learned Hand observed, "introduces a slack into the enforcement of law, tempering its rigor by the mollifying influence of current ethical conventions." U.S. *ex rel. McCann v. Adams*, 126 F.2d 774, 776 (2d Cir.), rev'd on other grounds, 317 U.S. 269, 87 L. Ed. 268, 63 S. Ct. 236 (1942). This is so because, as Judge Hand explained, "the individual can forfeit his liberty—to say nothing of his life—only at the hands of those who, unlike any official, are in no wise accountable, directly or indirectly, for what they do, and who at once separate and melt anonymously in the community from which they came. . . . Since if they acquit their verdict is final, no one is likely to suffer of whose conduct they do not morally disapprove. . . ." Id. 126 F.2d at 775–776.

As courts have long recognized, several features of our jury trial system act to protect the jury's power to acquit, regardless of the evidence, when the prosecution's case meets with the jury's "moral disapproval." Since the emergence of the general verdict in criminal cases and the famous opinion in *Bushell's Case*, 124 Eng. Rep. 1006 (C.P. 1670), freeing a member of the jury arrested for voting to acquit William Penn against the weight of the evidence, nullifying jurors have been protected from being called to account for their verdicts. Moreover, and in addition to the courts' duty to safeguard the secrecy of the jury deliberation room (discussed in greater detail below), the several rules protecting the

unassailability of jury verdicts of acquittal—even where these verdicts are inconsistent with other verdicts rendered by the same jury in the same case, *United States v. Carbone*, 378 F.2d 420, 423 (2d Cir.) (Friendly, J.) (recognizing link between upholding inconsistent verdicts and protecting juries' power of lenity), *cert. denied*, 389 U.S. 914, 19 L. Ed. 2d 262, 88 S. Ct. 242 (1967)—serve to "permit juries to acquit out of compassion or compromise or because of their assumption of a power which they had no right to exercise, but to which they were disposed through lenity." *Standefer v. United States*, 447 U.S. 10, 22, 64 L. Ed. 2d 689, 100 S. Ct. 1999 (1980) (internal quotation marks omitted).

But as the quotation from the Supreme Court's opinion in *Standefer* indicates, in language originally employed by Judge Learned Hand, the power of juries to "nullify" or exercise a power of lenity is just that—a power; it is by no means a right or something that a judge should encourage or permit if it is within his authority to prevent. . . .

. . .[A]lthough the early history of our country includes the occasional Zenger trial or acquittals in fugitive slave cases, more recent history presents numerous and notorious examples of jurors nullifying—cases that reveal the destructive potential of a practice Professor Randall Kennedy of the Harvard Law School has rightly termed a "sabotage of justice." Randall Kennedy, *The Angry Juror*, WALL ST. J., Sept. 30, 1994, at A12. Consider, for example, the two hung juries in the 1964 trials of Byron De La Beckwith in Mississippi for the murder of NAACP field secretary Medgar Evers, or the 1955 acquittal of J.W. Millam and Roy Bryant for the murder of fourteen-year-old Emmett Till, see DAVID HALBERSTAM, THE FIFTIES 431–441 (1993); RANDALL KENNEDY, RACE, CRIME AND THE LAW 60–63, 250 (1997); [after (1993);] JUAN WILLIAMS, EYES ON THE PRIZE: AMERICA'S CIVIL RIGHTS YEARS, 1954–1965, at 38–57, 221–225 (1987)—shameful examples of how "nullification" has been used to sanction murder and lynching.

Inasmuch as no juror has a right to engage in nullification—and, on the contrary, it is a violation of a juror's sworn duty to follow the law as instructed by the court—trial courts have the duty to forestall or prevent such conduct, whether by firm instruction or admonition or, where it does not interfere with guaranteed rights or the need to protect the secrecy of jury deliberations, *see* infra Section II.C, by dismissal of an offending juror from the venire or the jury. If it is true that the jury's "prerogative of lenity," *Dougherty,* 473 F.2d at 1133, introduces "a slack into the enforcement of law, tempering its rigor by the mollifying influence of current ethical conventions," *Adams,* 126 F.2d at 776, then, as part and parcel of the system of checks and balances embedded in the very structure of the American criminal trial, there is a countervailing duty and authority of the judge to assure that jurors follow the law. Although nullification may sometimes succeed—because, among other things, it does not come to the attention of a presiding judge before the completion of a jury's work, and jurors are not answerable for nullification after the verdict has been reached—it would be a dereliction of duty for a judge to remain indifferent to reports that a juror is intent on violating his oath. This is true regardless of the juror's motivation for "nullification," including race, ethnicity or similar considerations. A federal judge, whose own oath of office requires the judge to "faithfully and impartially discharge and perform all the duties incumbent upon [the judge] . . . under the Constitution and laws of the United States," 28 U.S.C. § 453 (1994), may not ignore colorable claims that a juror is acting on the basis of such improper considerations.

Accordingly, every day in courtrooms across the length and breadth of this country, jurors are dismissed from the venire "for cause" precisely because they are unwilling or unable to follow the applicable law. Indeed, one of the principal purposes of voir dire is to ensure that the jurors ultimately selected for service are unbiased and willing and able to apply the law as instructed by the court to the evidence presented by the parties.

So also, a presiding judge possesses both the responsibility and the authority to dismiss a juror whose refusal or unwillingness to follow the applicable law becomes known to the judge during the course of trial. Rule 24(c) of the Federal Rules of Criminal Procedure provides for the substitution of alternates for "jurors who, prior to the time the jury retires to consider its verdict, become or are found to be unable or disqualified to perform their duties." Surely a juror is "unable or disqualified," for purposes of this rule, who is intent on nullifying the applicable law and thereby violating his oath to "render a true verdict *according to the law and the evidence.*"

Similarly, we conclude that a juror who is determined to ignore his duty, who refuses to follow the court's instructions on the law and who thus threatens to "undermine the impartial determination of justice based on law," *Krzyske,* 836 F.2d at 1021, is subject to dismissal during the course of deliberations under Rule 23(b). This conclusion reinforces the court's inherent authority to conduct inquiries in response to reports of improper juror conduct and to determine whether a juror is unwilling to carry out his duties faithfully and impartially. The rule we adopt applies with equal force whether the juror's refusal to follow the court's instructions results from a desire to "nullify" the applicable law or, for example, as in the cases described above, . . .from a perceived physical threat or from a relationship with one of the parties. . . .

Notes

1. Under *Batson,* the Government's burden is to "come forward with a neutral explanation for challenging black jurors." 476 U.S. at 97. The court's finding that the Government's peremptory challenge was not motivated by the race of the challenged juror should have been

sufficient to sustain the Government's request to exercise its peremptory challenge of the juror. Juror No. 5 thus became a member of this jury as a result of the district court's erroneous decision in favor of the defendants.

2. We wish to make clear that nothing in this opinion is intended to suggest that jurors who deliberate under a good faith misinterpretation of the law as instructed by the court are subject to dismissal. In this case we address only the applicability of Rule 23(b) where a juror is alleged to be acting in *purposeful disregard* of the court's instructions.

Notes and Questions

1. How, according to the court in *Thomas*, does nullification violate a juror's oath and duty? When does a judge have "just cause" to remove a juror? On what grounds did the appellate court overrule the lower court's dismissal of Juror No. 5 in *United States v. Thomas*?

2. How do the social characteristics of a dissenting juror cast suspicion or lend credibility to his interpretation of the facts? The trial judge in *Thomas* accused Juror No. 5 of refusing to convict "because of preconceived, fixed, cultural, economic or social reasons that are totally improper and impermissible." Would Juror No. 5's opinion and behavior have been acceptable if he had been an elderly, white woman? Why or why not?

3 In *United States v. Thomas* the court insists that a juror may be dismissed for nullifying only if the record "is clear beyond doubt that the juror is not, in fact, simply unpersuaded by the prosecution's case." Did Juror No. 5's comments cast doubt on his alleged intent to nullify?

4. Witness credibility is often an important factor in criminal trials, yet it is an entirely subjective factor. It was once common practice for defense attorneys to impeach the character of the victim in sexual assault trials, as a means of influencing the jury's factual interpretation of the case. Suppose a juror in another case mistrusts police officers and therefore refuses to believe police testimony. If the prosecution's case is based primarily upon police testimony, can such a juror be accused of nullification, or is it her right to believe whomever she chooses?

5. In the opinion of the trial judge in *Thomas,* Juror No. 5 thought that "these people have a right to deal drugs. I don't think he would convict no matter what the evidence." Clearly the judge favored a guilty verdict and disagreed with Juror No. 5's interpretation of the facts. Whose opinion deserves more credence? Did the judge's disposition in favor of conviction limit his ability to make an impartial decision about nullification?

6. Why is the secrecy of jury deliberations important? If transcripts of jury deliberation were open to judicial review, would this make the decision to remove a nullifying juror easier and less controversial? Would this inhibit jurors from engaging in robust deliberations? How else might such scrutiny impact the judicial process? For better? For worse?

7. How realistic is the concept of the "sovereign jury"? Juries deliver verdicts, yet they must follow judicial guidelines. As we have seen with nullification issues, jurors have freedom to interpret the facts of a case within broad limitations.

Reprinted from: *United States v. Thomas,* 116 F.3d 606 (1997). ✦

Section XI

Sentencing

Chapter 43

Federal Sentencing Guidelines

A View From the Bench

Nancy Gertner

The need to balance severity and leniency is particularly acute in the domain of criminal punishment and sentencing. Here the power of the government is vividly on display. Here society translates its standards of justice into judgments about what particular individuals deserve. Legislatures determine the relation of crime and punishment when they enact criminal law but, as we saw in the Hay reading (Chapter 13), a dramatic gap may exist between what they prescribe and what is actually the sentence of any individual.

In the United States, sentencing was mostly the prerogative of judges until the last decades of the twentieth century. Operating under indeterminate sentencing systems, they were accorded great discretion in crafting a sentence to fit the offense and offender, though the actual amount of time an offender served in prison was often determined later by a parole board. However, during the 1980s this system came under sharp criticism from many sources.

Critics claimed that indeterminate sentencing resulted in radically disparate punishments being given to offenders who committed comparable crimes, that disparity was accompanied by discrimination, that too much power was left to parole boards so it was difficult for the public to know how much punishment offenders actu-

ally were getting, and that judges were often moved by the unique details of an offender's life and were therefore too lenient in sentencing. The result was a series of reforms to end indeterminate sentencing. In state after state, and at the federal level, sentencing guidelines were developed that limited the range of things judges could consider and went far, at least in theory, toward a more predictable and uniform sentencing system.

The article by Nancy Gertner, a federal district judge in Massachusetts, provides a judge's eye view of the federal sentencing guidelines. Although sympathetic to the goals of guideline sentencing (e.g., reducing disparity, eliminating discrimination, proving "truth in sentencing"), Gertner argues that the guidelines are neither just nor effective. The Federal Sentencing Commission, the group who actually writes the guidelines, is more interested in severity and in making sentences more punitive than in justice. In addition, she criticizes the complexity of the guidelines, which makes them difficult to administer. Finally, Gertner contends that discretion in sentencing has not been eliminated; guidelines have instead resulted in a system in which prosecutorial charging decisions (of the kind described by Frohmann in Chapter 33) become crucial. Prosecutors continue to exercise discretion in charging with the result that the guideline sentencing system is not only unduly severe, but it also perpetuates disparity and discrimination.

Sentencing a defendant is—or should be—one of the most important moments in the criminal justice system. After all, it is when state power confronts an individual. With my words of authorization, a citizen's liberty is extinguished, often for extraordinary periods of time.

The sentencing reforms of the 1980s seemed so rational. What could be wrong with giving judges "guidelines" for sentencing, to replace the standardless—some would say lawless—indeterminate sentencing regime of the past one hundred years? What could be wrong with eliminating "unwarranted" disparity in sentencing—where defendants, similarly situated with respect to the offense of conviction—were sentenced to widely different terms? And surely, what could be wrong with eliminating or minimizing racial disparity in sentencing? What could be wrong with an expert sentencing commission, above the political fray, promulgating guidelines after careful study and research? Finally, what could be wrong with "truth in sentencing"—a system that eliminates parole, that ensures that the sentence given by the court is the sentence served by the defendant?

The devil, as they say, was in the details. While sentencing prior to the Sentencing Reform Act of 1984 (SRA), U.S.C. §§ 3551 et seq., was far from perfect, criticism of the federal sentencing guideline regime has come from all corners of the legal profession, including the judiciary and academia. In fact, prior to *Mistretta v. United States*, 488 U.S. 361 (1989), when the U.S. Supreme Court settled the issue, 200 judges declared the guidelines unconstitutional. Significantly, not a single state system that has adopted sentencing guidelines has selected the federal model. Indeed, for a number of state commissions, among the first admonitions made to their commissioners is: Don't copy the federal guidelines if you can avoid it!

Why does the federal model raise these concerns? The problem was not the statute; the SRA, which, although vague and often inconsistent, sounded many of the right themes: Congress called for sentencing reform that would be effective in implementing all of the purposes of sentencing—not just the punitive theories now in vogue, like "just desserts" or incapacitation, but also the old fashioned ones, like rehabilitation and deterrence. It reaffirmed the parsimony principle—that a judge is to impose a sentence only long enough to achieve the purposes of sentencing, but no longer. It recognized that

while uniformity and the elimination of "unwarranted disparity" was important, so too were proportionality and individualized sentencing. Fair sentencing policies must not only avoid "unwarranted disparities: among defendants similarly situated with respect to the offense, but also maintain sufficient flexibility to permit individualized sentences. . . ." 28 U.S.C. § 991(b)(1)(B). And while alarms were sounded about runaway judicial discretion, the legislative history also underscored the importance of "the thoughtful imposition of individualized sentences." Judges were authorized to depart from the guidelines when the individual case required it because of "mitigating or aggravating factors not taken into account in the establishment of general sentencing practices." Finally, the SRA called for the creation of a new agency, the U.S. Sentencing Commission (Commission), an ostensibly neutral, expert body, tasked with carrying out these principles, after careful and dispassionate study.

But the guidelines the Commission invented, in many respects, undermined the lofty ideals of the statute and gave birth to the model from which all state commissions have fled.

SEVERITY OF THE GUIDELINES

The Commission never claimed that the rules they were implementing achieved any of the objectives of sentencing. They merely adopted past sentencing practices—or rather, they *said* they did. In fact, the Commission never studied the actual sentences that judges imposed. They identified a priori the factors they were interested in—for the most part, offense factors, like drug quantity and criminal record—looked for those factors in the presentence reports they studied and correlated them with final sentences. Not surprisingly, the guidelines gave short shrift to issues that had always mattered to judges in deciding how culpable an offender was, like mens rea, a history of addiction, family background, and mental health. Faced with this problem in sentencing a group of defendants, I stated:

> [Although] the Guidelines' emphasis on quantity and criminal history drives these high sentences, sadly, other factors, which I believe bear directly on culpability, hardly count at all: Profound drug addiction, sometimes dating from extremely young ages, the fact that the offender was subject to serious child abuse, or abandoned by one parent or the other, little or no education. Nor may I consider the fact that the disarray so clear in the lives of many of these defendants appears to be repeating itself in the next generation: Many have had children at a young age, and repeat the volatile relationships with their girlfriends that their parents may have had. And I surely cannot evaluate the extent to which lengthy incarceration will exacerbate the problem, separating the defendant from whatever family relationships he may have, or the impact on communities when these young men return.

United States v. Lacy, 99 F. Supp. 2d 108, 111 (D. Mass. 2000).

In dealing with offenses that had mandatory minimum sentences, the Commission set the guideline sentences even higher. In fact, the categories in which the Commission deviated from past practice outnumber all others. In a word, they upped the penalties, without ever explaining why. As a result, the federal incarceration rate skyrocketed. Although before the guidelines nearly 50 percent of federal defendants were sentenced to probation, afterwards it was less than 15 percent. All experimentation with alternatives to incarceration and innovative approaches to sentencing, like restorative justice, was necessarily squelched. While other criminal justice systems—other states, and other countries—ask the eminently reasonable question, what sentences work to effect rehabilitation or deterrence, much less what sentences have an impact on the crime rate, the federal system simply stacked penalties. The only decision

was: Are you going to jail (yes, for most offenders), or are you on the street?

THE LESS THAN TRANSPARENT COMMISSION

And these decisions—fundamental policy decisions—have been made by a Commission that was hardly above politics. The Commission's membership reflected the political divisions of the time. It was, as Justice Scalia described it, a "junior varsity legislature." But unlike their senior varsity counterpart, the Commission's proceedings were less than transparent. The statute exempted the Commission from most of the Administrative Procedure Act; only the "notice and comment" provisions apply. What this means is that rules about snail darters may be challenged in court to see if they are arbitrary and capricious, but guidelines about liberty may not.

Often guidelines are changed without the Commission providing a meaningful justification for the change—in terms of empirical studies or the policies underpinning them. Although the most recent Commission has been much more open, critical decisions are still made with little public visibility or accountability. Guideline amendments become effective within six months unless Congress rejects them. The congressional review process is rarely elaborate. It took only a single day's hearing in the Senate, and six days' hearing in the House, to accept the initial guidelines, all hundreds of pages of it.

THE GRID PROMOTES GRID-LIKE RESPONSES

The sentencing guidelines are extraordinarily complex. The guidelines manual consists of more than 900 pages of technical regulations and amendments. The centerpiece is a 258-box grid called the "Sentencing Table." The horizontal axis of this grid, "Criminal History Category," adjusts severity on the basis of the offender's past conviction record. The vertical axis, "Offense Level," reflects a basic score for the crime committed, adjusted for those characteristics of the defendant's criminal behavior that the Commission has deemed relevant to sentencing. The box at which the two intersect determines the range within which the Judge may sentence the defendant, and a relatively narrow range at that.

Over the past fifteen years, we have seen that the grid invited "grid-like" responses. Even where the case cried out for a departure from the guidelines, judges—many of whom had resoundingly criticized the rigidity of the guidelines—refused to exercise their discretion. Even where the words of the manual were vague—what is an "otherwise extensive organization," a "vulnerable victim," or what do the guidelines mean when they say that family circumstances are not "ordinarily" relevant—judges abdicated all responsibility to create a common law of sentencing. Too often the judge intoned: "I believe the offense is benign but I have no choice but to sentence you to this extraordinarily harsh sentence." Sometimes it is true; often it is not. In a busy court, when any show of leniency risks mention on the evening news, it is far easier and less controversial to just stay within the lines.

Where the judge does depart, he or she is subject to appeal, and confronts a court that likely is enforcing the guidelines with a rigor not contemplated by the drafters, nor required by the text. (Failure to depart is not reviewable; the message is clear.) The SRA provided that trial court departure decisions were to be reviewed by the circuit courts for their reasonableness and their fealty to the underlying purposes of sentencing. As Kevin Reitz has noted, compared to state systems, departure decisions by federal trial judges face a high probability of reversal on appeal. Indeed, courts of appeals have fallen into a technocratic practice of enforcing the four corners of the federal guidelines manual and deferring excessively to the Commission. The result is that they have "left little space for creativity" of the trial bench and have abdicated their own responsibility for common law

rulemaking. Kevin R. Reitz, *Sentencing Guideline Systems and Sentence Appeals: A Comparison of Federal and State Experiences,* 91 NW. U. L REV. 1441, 1450 (1997). . . .

ENDURANCE OF DISPARITY

Nor has "unwarranted" disparity disappeared. There is regional disparity. Different offenses are charged differently by prosecutors, and treated differently by the judge in different parts of the country. Departures are more welcomed in certain circuits than in others. And where judicial departures are discouraged, the prosecutor steps in to exercise his or her discretion, without visibility, often without meaningful review.

Significantly, racial disparities persist. Black and Hispanic defendants are more likely to be charged and convicted pursuant to mandatory minimum drug laws. In 1991, the Commission submitted a report to the Congress that determined that in cases where a mandatory minimum sentence was applicable, whites were sentenced below the applicable mandatory minimum in 25 percent of the cases. Blacks were sentenced in 18 percent and Hispanics, only 11.8 percent. The Commission reported that the statistically significant relationship between race and sentence remained even after considering the nature of the offense and the prior criminal record of the defendant UNITED STATES SENTENCING COMMISSION, THE FEDERAL SENTENCING GUIDELINES: A REPORT ON THE OPERATION OF THE GUIDELINES SYSTEM AND SHORT-TERM IMPACTS ON DISPARITY IN SENTENCING USE OF INCARCERATION, AND PROSECUTORIAL DISCRETION AND PLEA BARGAINING 23 (1991).

In part, the problem is the 100:1 differential in the sentencing between crack cocaine and cocaine powder: White defendants are charged with the distribution of cocaine powder, black defendants with crack. But it goes deeper. The guidelines's emphasis on criminal history enhances whatever inequities were embodied in past sentences. I sentenced a man for the crime of "felon in possession of a firearm," whose criminal record scored high on the guidelines. When I looked closely, I noticed that all the scored offenses were nonviolent, traffic offenses—for instance, driving after his license was suspended. And then 1 wondered: Since no other traffic offense accompanied the license charges, how did the man get stopped? I strongly suspected "Driving While Black." I departed downward, refusing to give literal credit to the record. *United States v. Leviner,* 31 F. Supp. 2d 23 (D. Mass. 1998).

Likewise, I have been concerned about the stereotypes—cultural, racial, gender—that lurk in departures such as those for "extraordinary" family obligations. In *United States v. Thompson,* No. 98-10332 (D. Mass. Feb. 19, 2002), I found that of the forty-eight cases in the District of Massachusetts in which downward departures were given, just over 60 percent were in white collar cases, largely involving defendants with advantaged backgrounds. By contrast, during the comparable period only 27 percent of the sentencings in this district were for white collar offenses. Poor defendants—largely African American—were bound to suffer by comparison with wealthy or even middle-class defendants. So long as the courts apply the guidelines without careful examination, these patterns, and the stereotypes that create them, will not be exposed.

Enhanced Role of Prosecutors

The result of limiting judicial discretion is hydraulic. Discretion passes to other players in the system, and here, to prosecutors. Unless a prosecutor files a motion certifying that the defendant has provided "substantial assistance" in the investigation or prosecution of another person, a federal judge has no authority to impose a sentence below a mandatory minimum. In plea agreements, prosecutors can arrogate to themselves the absolute power to determine whether the defendant

has provided substantial assistance. The decision is often veiled in secrecy. A colleague of mine described it as departures "under the radar screen."

The prosecutor has the ability—just by the way he or she charges a defendant—to bypass the more stringent mechanisms of proof under the Constitution. In *United States v. Astronomo,* 200 WL 1604102 (Nov. 26, 2001), the government sought to prove facts about the criminal conduct of the defendant and his prior criminal history that bore little relation to the allegations of the indictment, the facts to which the defendant pled guilty, or his actual criminal record. The government literally believed Astronomo had gotten away with murder, although it never brought such charges, or even bothered to investigate them. I declined to increase Astronomo's sentence based on outlandish boasts or vague rumors.

It did not have to be this way. Other states have opted for "guidelines," that are really guidelines. They give judges discretion to depart from the guidelines with reason and encourage appellate courts to endorse such decisions. The state commissions take the lead in monitoring important trends in sentencing patterns—racial disparity, prison capacity—and where necessary, suggest reforms. Prosecutors don't sit alone in the driver's seat.

The Result

Consider again the moment when state power confronts the individual. The decision to prosecute is veiled in secrecy. You plead guilty because your chances of success before a jury are minimal. In a sentencing proceeding with few procedural safeguards, hearsay and vague generalizations in police reports pass for proof. The judge tells you that you are at a base offense level of thirty-two and have a criminal history score of VI. The guidelines he or she feels obliged to follow were "passed" by a Commission with a perfunctory explanation, without background materials, legislative history, or data. And they were approved by a Congress without in-depth review. Your background may suggest a host of things that make the likely sentence profoundly unjust, but your circuit discourages departures, however reasonable. The judge announces that your sentence is 151 months. The only explanation the judge gives is how he or she "did the math."

But what the judge has not explained is how that sentence rehabilitates or deters, or even reflects "just desserts." In other words, what the judge cannot explain is how this sentence is just, because far too often—it is not.

NOTES AND QUESTIONS

1. How could a reform program with such good intentions, like guiideline sentencing, produce the disappointing results that Gertner describes? Are the shortcomings of the federal sentencing guidelines a product of poor execution, or do the guidelines aim to resolve intractable problems with too simple a solution?

2. Is the U.S. Sentencing Commission any less fallible than federal judges insofar as class bias, racial prejudice, or both are concerned? Is class or racial bias reflected in the way the guidelines deal with prior offenses and measure the gravity of drug offenses?

3. Although the sentencing guidelines imposed on federal judges in the 1980s purported to do away with racial disparity in sentencing, there remain severe racial disparities between the prison population and the general public. How do you explain this? How does the social organization of law (e.g., contact with police, prosecutorial decisions, access to counsel) contribute to disparities even before an alleged criminal faces a sentencing judge?

4. Do sentencing guidelines have any effect, positive or negative, on the gamble and implicit cost of taking a case to court versus accepting a plea bargain?

5. Until recently, the federal guidelines permitted judges to depart from the strict sentencing framework in the case of mitigating or aggravating factors not taken into account in the establishment of general sentencing practices. According to statistics compiled by the U.S. Sentencing Commission, 35 percent of the sentences handed down in federal court in fiscal year 2001 fell below the range set in the sentencing guidelines. Almost half of those involved plea bargain agreements or other cases of "substantial assistance" to prosecutors, but 18 percent of the "downward departures" were for other reasons. Federal judges imposed sentences that exceeded the guidelines in less than 1 percent of the cases; the Justice Department appealed only 19 of more than 11,000 "downward departure" sentencing decisions. Why do you think that judges used the limited discretion available to them under the guidelines to lessen rather than increase sentence severity?

6. In April, 2003, Congress adopted an amendment to the "Amber alert" legislation on child abductions that curtailed downward departures under the guidelines. It abolished many grounds previously specified as permitting such departures and prohibited federal district judges from downwardly departing on any grounds not set forth in the guidelines themselves. The Feeney Amendment also made it easier for the prosecution to appeal and overturn "downward departures" from the guidelines. Subsequently, Attorney General John D. Ashcroft ordered U. S. Attorneys across the country to become much more aggressive in reporting to the Justice Department cases in which federal judges impose lighter sentences than called for in sentencing guidelines. The more extensive reporting will lay the groundwork for the Justice Department to ap-

peal many more of those sentencing decisions than it has in the past.

7. Some federal judges have spoken out forcefully against what they have portrayed as another assault on their independence. One United States District Judge resigned from a federal court in Manhattan in June, 2003, and accused Congress of attempting "to intimidate judges." "For a judge to be deprived of the ability to consider all of the factors that go into formulating a just sentence is completely at odds with the sentencing philosophy that has been the hallmark of the American system of justice," John S. Martin Jr. wrote in an op-ed page article published in the *New York Times.*

8. Do strict sentencing guidelines bolster deterrence in the criminal justice system? Consider Hay's depiction (Chapter 13) of law's mercy. Is it more important to have clear-cut legal standards with harsh minimum penalties, or leniency via judicial discretion (albeit at the price of inconsistency in sentencing)?

9. Gertner links the inflexibly harsh sentencing guidelines to cycles of violence, poverty, and lawlessness in certain parts of American society. Are faultless individuals (relatives and dependents of criminals) unjustly penalized by the criminal sentencing guidelines?

10. Do you agree with Gertner's unfavorable portrayal of the rehabilitative possibilities under the current federal sentencing guidelines?

11. Suppose you were commissioned by the federal government to reform the federal sentencing guidelines. Where would you begin? What parts would you eliminate, what would you change, and what should be kept the same? Would you try to attain the same goals: reducing disparity, eliminating discrimination, and providing truth in sentencing? Why or why not?

Reprinted from: Nancy Gertner, "Federal Sentencing Guidelines: A View From the Bench" in *Human Rights*, 29:2, 2002. Copyright © 2002. Reprinted with the permission of ABA Publishing. ✦

Chapter 44

Ewing v. California

In addition to sentencing guidelines, other sentencing reforms enacted in the last part of the twentieth century made criminal punishment more severe. One of the most widespread yet controversial of these reforms is "three strikes and you're out." Three strikes for three-time offenders was first implemented in 1993 in Washington State. California soon followed in 1994. By 2000, 24 states and the federal government had some form of three strikes legislation on the books.

One student of three strikes laws recounts the following: "The California law requires that a person convicted of three felonies must serve a mandatory fixed sentence of 25 years to life usually without parole. However, what is considered a 'strike' and what is considered 'out' varies significantly from state to state. For example, in Washington State, all of the strikes must fall under specific violent crimes that are defined by the law. But in California, only the first two crimes must be 'three strike' crimes, but the third can be any felony. In addition, some states have variations on 'three strikes' laws that include 'two-strikes' penalties and 'four-strikes' penalties. For example, Montana requires mandatory life in prison without parole for two violent offenses, such as deliberate homicide or aggravated kidnapping. Not all 24 states require life in prison without parole in their 'three strikes'-type laws."

In the summer of 2003, the United States Supreme Court decided Ewing v. California, which challenged the California three strikes law as a violation of the Eighth Amendment's ban on cruel and unusual punishment. The offense that triggered Ewing's mandatory 25-year-to-life sentence arose from the theft of three golf clubs worth $399 apiece. His previous offenses were three burglaries and a robbery. The Supreme Court found for the State of California, holding that in noncapital cases, the Eighth Amendment forbids only those sentences that are "grossly disproportionate" and that the 25-years-to-life sentence required by the three strikes law reflected a reasonable exercise of legislative judgment.

Justice O'Conner announced the judgment of the Court and delivered an opinion in which The Chief Justice and Justice Kennedy join.

In this case, we decide whether the Eighth Amendment prohibits the State of California from sentencing a repeat felon to a prison term of 25 years to life under the State's "Three Strikes and You're Out" law.

I

A

California's three strikes law reflects a shift in the State's sentencing policies toward incapacitating and deterring repeat offenders who threaten the public safety. The law was designed "to ensure longer prison sentences and greater punishment for those who commit a felony and have been previously convicted of serious and/or violent felony offenses." Cal. Penal Code Ann. § 667(b) (West 1999). On March 3, 1993, California Assemblymen Bill Jones and Jim Costa introduced Assembly Bill 971, the legislative version of what would later become the three strikes law. The Assembly Committee on Public Safety defeated the bill only weeks later. Public outrage over the defeat sparked a voter initiative to add Proposition 184, based loosely on the bill, to the ballot in the November 1994 general election.

On October 1, 1993, while Proposition 184 was circulating, 12-year-old Polly Klaas was kidnapped from her home in Petaluma, California. Her admitted killer, Richard Allen Davis, had a long criminal history that included two prior kidnapping convictions. Davis had served only half of his most recent sentence (16 years for kidnapping, assault, and burglary). Had Davis served his entire sentence, he would still have been in prison on the day that Polly Klaas was kidnapped.

Polly Klaas' murder galvanized support for the three strikes initiative. Within days, Proposition 184 was on its way to becoming the fastest qualifying initiative in California history. On January 3, 1994, the sponsors of Assembly Bill 971 resubmitted an amended version of the bill that conformed to Proposition 184. On January 31, 1994, Assembly Bill 971 passed the Assembly by a 63 to 9 margin. The Senate passed it by a 29 to 7 margin on March 3, 1994. Governor Pete Wilson signed the bill into law on March 7, 1994. California voters approved Proposition 184 by a margin of 72 to 28 percent on November 8, 1994.

California thus became the second state to enact a three strikes law. In November 1993, the voters of Washington State approved their own three strikes law, Initiative 593, by a margin of 3 to 1. U.S. Dept. of Justice, National Institute of Justice, J. Clark, J. Austin, & D. Henry, "Three Strikes and You're Out": A Review of State Legislation 1 (Sept. 1997) (hereinafter Review of State Legislation). Between 1993 and 1995, 24 States and the Federal Government enacted three strikes laws. *Ibid.* Though the three strikes laws vary from State to State, they share a common goal of protecting the public safety by providing lengthy prison terms for habitual felons.

B

California's current three strikes law consists of two virtually identical statutory schemes "designed to increase the prison terms of repeat felons." *People v. Superior Court of San Diego Cty. ex rel. Romero,* 13 Cal. 4th 497, 504, 917 P.2d 628, 630, 53 Cal. Rptr.

2d 789 (1996) (*Romero*). When a defendant is convicted of a felony, and he has previously been convicted of one or more prior felonies defined as "serious" or "violent" in Cal. Penal Code Ann. §§ 667.5 and 1192.7 (West Supp. 2002), sentencing is conducted pursuant to the three strikes law. Prior convictions must be alleged in the charging document, and the defendant has a right to a jury determination that the prosecution has proved the prior convictions beyond a reasonable doubt. § 1025; § 1158 (West 1985).

If the defendant has one prior "serious" or "violent" felony conviction, he must be sentenced to "twice the term otherwise provided as punishment for the current felony conviction." § 667(e)(1) (West 1999); § 1170.12(c)(1) (West Supp. 2002). If the defendant has two or more prior "serious" or "violent" felony convictions, he must receive "an indeterminate term of life imprisonment." § 667(e)(2)(A) (West 1999); § 1170.12(c)(2)(A) (West Supp. 2002). Defendants sentenced to life under the three strikes law become eligible for parole on a date calculated by reference to a "minimum term," which is the greater of (a) three times the term otherwise provided for the current conviction, (b) 25 years, or (c) the term determined by the court pursuant to § 1170 for the underlying conviction, including any enhancements. §§ 667(e)(2)(A)(i-iii) (West 1999); §§ 1170.12(c)(2)(A)(i-iii) (West Supp. 2002).

Under California law, certain offenses may be classified as either felonies or misdemeanors. These crimes are known as "wobblers." Some crimes that would otherwise be misdemeanors become "wobblers" because of the defendant's prior record. For example, petty theft, a misdemeanor, becomes a "wobbler" when the defendant has previously served a prison term for committing specified theft-related crimes. § 490 (West 1999); § 666 (West Supp. 2002). Other crimes, such as grand theft, are "wobblers" regardless of the defendant's prior record. See § 489(b) (West 1999). Both types of "wobblers" are triggering offenses under the three strikes law only when they are treated as felonies. Under California law, a "wobbler" is presumptively a felony and "remains a felony except when the discretion is actually exercised" to make the crime a misdemeanor. *People v. Williams*, 27 Cal.2d 220, 229, 163 P.2d 692, 696 (1945) (emphasis deleted and internal quotation marks omitted).

In California, prosecutors may exercise their discretion to charge a "wobbler" as either a felony or a misdemeanor. Likewise, California trial courts have discretion to reduce a "wobbler" charged as a felony to a misdemeanor either before preliminary examination or at sentencing to avoid imposing a three strikes sentence. Cal. Penal Code Ann. §§ 17(b)(5), 17(b)(1) (West 1999) [*115] ; *People v. Superior Court of Los Angeles Cty. ex rel. Alvarez*, 14 Cal. 4th 968, 978, 928 P.2d 1171, 1177-1178, 60 Cal. Rptr. 2d 93 (1997). In exercising this discretion, the court may consider "those factors that direct similar sentencing decisions," such as "the nature and circumstances of the offense, the defendant's appreciation of and attitude toward the offense, . . . [and] the general objectives of sentencing." *Ibid.* (internal quotation marks and citations omitted).

California trial courts can also vacate allegations of prior "serious" or "violent" felony convictions, either on motion by the prosecution or *sua sponte*. In ruling whether to vacate allegations of prior felony convictions, courts consider whether, "in light of the nature and circumstances of [the defendant's] present felonies and prior serious and/or violent felony convictions, and the particulars of his background, character, and prospects, the defendant may be deemed outside the [three strikes'] scheme's spirit, in whole or in part." *People v. Williams*, 17 Cal. 4th 148, 161, 948 P.2d 429, 437, 69 Cal. Rptr. 2d 917 (1998). Thus, trial courts may avoid imposing a three strikes sentence in two ways: first, by reducing "wobblers" to misdemeanors (which do not qualify as triggering offenses), and second, by

vacating allegations of prior "serious" or "violent" felony convictions.

C

On parole from a 9-year prison term, petitioner Gary Ewing walked into the pro shop of the El Segundo Golf Course in Los Angeles County on March 12, 2000. He walked out with three golf clubs, priced at $399 a piece, concealed in his pants leg. A shop employee, whose suspicions were aroused when he observed Ewing limp out of the pro shop, telephoned the police. The police apprehended Ewing in the parking lot.

Ewing is no stranger to the criminal justice system. In 1984, at the age of 22, he pleaded guilty to theft. The court sentenced him to six months in jail (suspended), three years' probation, and a $300 fine. In 1988, he was convicted of felony grand theft auto and sentenced to one year in jail and three years' probation. After Ewing completed probation, however, the sentencing court reduced the crime to a misdemeanor, permitted Ewing to withdraw his guilty plea, and dismissed the case. In 1990, he was convicted of petty theft with a prior and sentenced to 60 days in the county jail and three years' probation. In 1992, Ewing was convicted of battery and sentenced to 30 days in the county jail and two years' summary probation. One month later, he was convicted of theft and sentenced to 10 days in the county jail and 12 months' probation. In January 1993, Ewing was convicted of burglary and sentenced to 60 days in the county jail and one year's summary probation. In February 1993, he was convicted of possessing drug paraphernalia and sentenced to six months in the county jail and three years' probation. In July 1993, he was convicted of appropriating lost property and sentenced to 10 days in the county jail and two years' summary probation. In September 1993, he was convicted of unlawfully possessing a firearm and trespassing and sentenced to 30 days in the county jail and one year's probation.

In October and November 1993, Ewing committed three burglaries and one robbery at a Long Beach, California, apartment complex over a 5-week period. He awakened one of his victims, asleep on her living room sofa, as he tried to disconnect her video cassette recorder from the television in that room. When she screamed, Ewing ran out the front door. On another occasion, Ewing accosted a victim in the mailroom of the apartment complex. Ewing claimed to have a gun and ordered the victim to hand over his wallet. When the victim resisted, Ewing produced a knife and forced the victim back to the apartment itself. While Ewing rifled through the bedroom, the victim fled the apartment screaming for help. Ewing absconded with the victim's money and credit cards.

On December 9, 1993, Ewing was arrested on the premises of the apartment complex for trespassing and lying to a police officer. The knife used in the robbery and a glass cocaine pipe were later found in the back seat of the patrol car used to transport Ewing to the police station. A jury convicted Ewing of first-degree robbery and three counts of residential burglary. Sentenced to nine years and eight months in prison, Ewing was paroled in 1999.

Only 10 months later, Ewing stole the golf clubs at issue in this case. He was charged with, and ultimately convicted of, one count of felony grand theft of personal property in excess of $400. See Cal. Penal Code Ann., § 484 (West Supp. 2002); § 489 (West 1999). As required by the three strikes law, the prosecutor formally alleged, and the trial court later found, that Ewing had been convicted previously of four serious or violent felonies for the three burglaries and the robbery in the Long Beach apartment complex. See § 667(g) (West 1999); § 1170.12(e) (West Supp. 2002).

At the sentencing hearing, Ewing asked the court to reduce the conviction for grand theft, a "wobbler" under California law, to a misdemeanor so as to avoid a three strikes sentence. See § 17(b) (West 1999); § 667(d)(1); § 1170.12(b)(1) (West Supp. 2002). Ewing also asked the trial court to exercise its discretion to dismiss the allegations of some or all of his prior serious or violent felony convictions, again for purposes of avoiding a three strikes sentence. See *Romero*, 13 Cal. 4th, at 529–531, 917 P. 2d, at 647–648. Before sentencing Ewing, the trial court took note of his entire criminal history, including the fact that he was on parole when he committed his latest offense. The court also heard arguments from defense counsel and a plea from Ewing himself.

In the end, the trial judge determined that the grand theft should remain a felony. The court also ruled that the four prior strikes for the three burglaries and the robbery in Long Beach should stand. As a newly convicted felon with two or more "serious" or "violent" felony convictions in his past, Ewing was sentenced under the three strikes law to 25 years to life.

The California Court of Appeal affirmed in an unpublished opinion. No. B143745 (Apr. 25, 2001). Relying on our decision in *Rummel v. Estelle*, 445 U.S. 263, 63 L. Ed. 2d 382, 100 S. Ct. 1133 (1980), the court rejected Ewing's claim that his sentence was grossly disproportionate under the Eighth Amendment. Enhanced sentences under recidivist statutes like the three strikes law, the court reasoned, serve the "legitimate goal" of deterring and incapacitating repeat offenders. The Supreme Court of California denied Ewing's petition for review, and we granted certiorari, *Ewing v. California*, 535 U.S. 969, 152 L. Ed. 2d 379, 122 S. Ct. 1435 (2002). We now affirm.

II

A

The Eighth Amendment, which forbids cruel and unusual punishments, contains a "narrow proportionality principle" that "applies to noncapital sentences." *Harmelin v. Michigan*, 501 U.S. 957, 996–997, 115 L. Ed. 2d 836, 111 S. Ct. 2680 (1991) (KENNEDY, J., concurring in part and concurring in judgment); cf. *Weems v. United States,* 217 U.S. 349, 371, 54 L. Ed. 793, 30 S. Ct. 544 (1910); *Robinson v. California,* 370 U.S. 660, 667, 8 L. Ed. 2d 758, 82 S. Ct. 1417 (1962) (applying the Eighth Amendment to the States via the Fourteenth Amendment). We have most recently addressed the proportionality principle as applied to terms of years in a series of cases beginning with *Rummel v. Estelle, supra.*

In *Rummel,* we held that it did not violate the Eighth Amendment for a State to sentence a three-time offender to life in prison with the possibility of parole. *Id.,* at 284–285. Like Ewing, Rummel was sentenced to a lengthy prison term under a recidivism statute. Rummel's two prior offenses were a 1964 felony for "fraudulent use of a credit card to obtain $80 worth of goods or services," and a 1969 felony conviction for "passing a forged check in the amount of $28.36." *Id.,* at 265. His triggering offense was a conviction for felony theft—"obtaining $120.75 by false pretenses." *Id.,* at 266.

This Court ruled that "having twice imprisoned him for felonies, Texas was entitled to place upon Rummel the onus of one who is simply unable to bring his conduct within the social norms prescribed by the criminal law of the State." *Id.,* at 284. The recidivism statute "is nothing more than a societal decision that when such a person commits yet another felony, he should be subjected to the admittedly serious penalty of incarceration for life, subject only to the State's judgment as to whether to grant him parole." *Id.,* at 278. We noted that this Court "has on occasion stated that the Eighth Amendment prohibits imposition of a sentence that is grossly disproportionate to the severity of the crime." *Id.,* at 271. But "outside the context of capital punishment, successful challenges to the proportionality of particular sentences have been exceedingly rare." *Id.,* at 272. Although we stated that the proportionality principle "would . . . come into play in the extreme example . . . if a legislature made overtime parking a felony punishable by life imprisonment," *id.,* at 274, n.

11, we held that "the mandatory life sentence imposed upon this petitioner does not constitute cruel and unusual punishment under the Eighth and Fourteenth Amendments" *id.,* at 285. . . .

B

For many years, most States have had laws providing for enhanced sentencing of repeat offenders. See, e.g., U.S. Dept. of Justice, Bureau of Justice Assistance, National Assessment of Structured Sentencing (1996). Yet between 1993 and 1995, three strikes laws effected a sea change in criminal sentencing throughout the Nation. These laws responded to widespread public concerns about crime by targeting the class of offenders who pose the greatest threat to public safety: career criminals. As one of the chief architects of California's three strikes law has explained: "Three Strikes was intended to go beyond simply making sentences tougher. It was intended to be a focused effort to create a sentencing policy that would use the judicial system to reduce serious and violent crime." Ardaiz, California's Three Strikes Law: History, Expectations, Consequences 32 McGeorge L. Rev. 1, 12 (2000) (hereinafter Ardaiz).

Throughout the States, legislatures enacting three strikes laws made a deliberate policy choice that individuals who have repeatedly engaged in serious or violent criminal behavior, and whose conduct has not been deterred by more conventional approaches to punishment, must be isolated from society in order to protect the public safety. Though three strikes laws may be relatively new, our tradition of deferring to state legislatures in making and implementing such important policy decisions is longstanding. *Weems,* 217 U.S., at 379; *Gore v. United States,* 357 U.S. 386, 393, 2 L. Ed. 2d 1405, 78 S. Ct. 1280 (1958); *Payne v. Tennessee,* 501 U.S. 808, 824, 115 L. Ed. 2d 720, 111 S. Ct. 2597 (1991); *Rummel,* U.S., at 274; *Solem,* 463 U.S., at 290; *Harmelin,* 501 U.S., at 998 (KENNEDY, J., concurring in part and concurring in judgment).

Our traditional deference to legislative policy choices finds a corollary in the principle that the Constitution "does not mandate adoption of any one penological theory." *Id.,* at 999 (KENNEDY, J., concurring in part and concurring in judgment). A sentence can have a variety of justifications, such as incapacitation, deterrence, retribution, or rehabilitation. See 1 W. LaFave & A. Scott, Substantive Criminal Law § 1.5, pp. 30–36 (1986) (explaining theories of punishment). Some or all of these justifications may play a role in a State's sentencing scheme. Selecting the sentencing rationales is generally a policy choice to be made by state legislatures, not federal courts.

When the California Legislature enacted the three strikes law, it made a judgment that protecting the public safety requires incapacitating criminals who have already been convicted of at least one serious or violent crime. Nothing in the Eighth Amendment prohibits California from making that choice. To the contrary, our cases establish that "States have a valid interest in deterring and segregating habitual criminals." *Parke v. Raley,* 506 U.S. 20, 27, 121 L. Ed. 2d 391, 113 S. Ct. 517 (1992); Oyler v. Boles, 368 U.S. 448, 451, 7 L. Ed. 2d 446, 82 S. Ct. 501 (1962) ("The constitutionality of the practice of inflicting severer criminal penalties upon habitual offenders is no longer open to serious challenge"). Recidivism has long been recognized as a legitimate basis for increased punishment. See *Almendarez-Torres v. United States,* 523 U.S. 224, 230, 140 L. Ed. 2d 350, 118 S. Ct. 1219 (1998) (recidivism "is as typical a sentencing factor as one might imagine"); *Witte v. United States,* 515 U.S. 389, 399, 132 L. Ed. 2d 351, 115 S. Ct. 2199 (1995) ("In repeatedly upholding such recidivism statutes, we have rejected double jeopardy challenges because the enhanced punishment imposed for the later offense . . .[is] 'a stiffened penalty for the latest crime, which is considered to be an aggravated offense because a repetitive one'" (quot-

ing *Gryger v. Burke,* 334 U.S. 728, 732, 92 L. Ed. 1683, 68 S. Ct. 1256 (1948).

California's justification is no pretext. Recidivism is a serious public safety concern in California and throughout the Nation. According to a recent report, approximately 67 percent of former inmates released from state prisons were charged with at least one "serious" new crime within three years of their release. See U.S. Dept. of Justice, Bureau of Justice Statistics, P. Langan & D. Levin, Special Report: Recidivism of Prisoners Released in 1994, p. 1 (June 2002). In particular, released property offenders like Ewing had higher recidivism rates than those released after committing violent, drug, or public-order offenses. *Id.,* at 8. Approximately 73 percent of the property offenders released in 1994 were arrested again within three years, compared to approximately 61 percent of the violent offenders, 62 percent of the public-order offenders, and 66 percent of the drug offenders. *Ibid.* . . .

To be sure, California's three strikes law has sparked controversy. Critics have doubted the law's wisdom, cost-efficiency, and effectiveness in reaching its goals. See, e.g., Zimring, Hawkins, & Kamin, Punishment and Democracy: Three Strikes and You're Out in California (2001); Vitiello, Three Strikes: Can We Return to Rationality?, 87 J. Crim. L. & C. 395, 423 (1997). This criticism is appropriately directed at the legislature, which has primary responsibility for making the difficult policy choices that underlie any criminal sentencing scheme. We do not sit as a "superlegislature" to second-guess these policy choices. It is enough that the State of California has a reasonable basis for believing that dramatically enhanced sentences for habitual felons "advances the goals of [its] criminal justice system in any substantial way." See *Solem,* 463 U.S., at 297, n. 22.

III

Against this backdrop, we consider Ewing's claim that his three strikes sentence of 25 years to life is unconstitutionally disproportionate to his offense of "shoplifting three golf clubs." Brief for Petitioner 6. We first address the gravity of the offense compared to the harshness of the penalty. At the threshold, we note that Ewing incorrectly frames the issue. The gravity of his offense was not merely "shoplifting three golf clubs." Rather, Ewing was convicted of felony grand theft for stealing nearly $1,200 worth of merchandise after previously having been convicted of at least two "violent" or "serious" felonies. Even standing alone, Ewing's theft should not be taken lightly. His crime was certainly not "one of the most passive felonies a person could commit." *Solem, supra,* at 296 (internal quotation marks omitted). To the contrary, the Supreme Court of California has noted the "seriousness" of grand theft in the context of proportionality review. See *In re Lynch,* 8 Cal.3d 410, 432, n. 20, 503 P.2d 921, 936, n. 20, 105 Cal. Rptr. 217 (1972). Theft of $1,200 in property is a felony under federal law, 18 U.S.C. § 641, and in the vast majority of States. See App. B to Brief for Petitioner 21a. . . .

In weighing the gravity of Ewing's offense, we must place on the scales not only his current felony, but also his long history of felony recidivism. Any other approach would fail to accord proper deference to the policy judgments that find expression in the legislature's choice of sanctions. In imposing a three strikes sentence, the State's interest is not merely punishing the offense of conviction, or the "triggering" offense: "It is in addition the interest . . . in dealing in a harsher manner with those who by repeated criminal acts have shown that they are simply incapable of conforming to the norms of society as established by its criminal law." See *Rummel,* 445 U.S., at 276; *Solem, supra,* at 296. To give full effect to the State's choice of this legitimate penological goal, our proportionality review of Ewing's sentence must take that goal into account.

Ewing's sentence is justified by the State's public-safety interest in incapacitating and deterring recidivist felons, and amply supported by his own long, serious criminal record. Ewing has been convicted of numerous misdemeanor and felony offenses, served nine separate terms of incarceration, and committed most of his crimes while on probation or parole. His prior "strikes" were serious felonies including robbery and three residential burglaries. To be sure, Ewing's sentence is a long one. But it reflects a rational legislative judgment, entitled to deference, that offenders who have committed serious or violent felonies and who continue to commit felonies must be incapacitated. The State of California "was entitled to place upon [Ewing] the onus of one who is simply unable to bring his conduct within the social norms prescribed by the criminal law of the State." *Rummel, supra,* at 284. Ewing's is not "the rare case in which a threshold comparison of the crime committed and the sentence imposed leads to an inference of gross disproportionality." *Harmelin,* 501 U.S., at 1005 (KENNEDY, J., concurring in part and concurring in judgment).

We hold that Ewing's sentence of 25 years to life in prison, imposed for the offense of felony grand theft under the three strikes law, is not grossly disproportionate and therefore does not violate the Eighth Amendment's prohibition on cruel and unusual punishments. The judgment of the California Court of Appeal is affirmed.

It is so ordered. . . .

NOTES AND QUESTIONS

1. What is the legal definition of a serious or violent crime? For the purpose of three strikes laws, what crimes do you think should fall into these categories? For instance, should property crimes be included?

2. Supporters argue that three strikes laws help to deter serious and violent crime

by means of tougher sentencing and more reliable incapacitation of repeat offenders. Do you agree? In serving these purposes, how do three strikes statutes compare with federal sentencing guidelines?

3. What are "wobblers"? How does the three strikes law create "wobblers" out of misdemeanors? How has this contributed to increased prosecutorial discretion under California's three strikes law?

4. What discretion is afforded the courts under three strikes? Is there any reason to believe this discretion will be exercised more frequently than is the case with federal sentencing guidelines? *Should* it be?

5. The defendant in this case, Gary Ewing, is undoubtedly very familiar with incarceration and the criminal justice system.

Despite serving many short sentences on various counts of burglary and theft, Ewing continually failed to reform his behavior. Some would argue that his case illustrates the need for more severe punishment. Others would use it to show the need for rehabilitation. Which interpretation do you find more compelling? Why?

6. How might the mandatory sentencing prescribed by three strikes constitute "cruel and unusual punishment"? On what grounds did the Supreme Court deny Ewing's claim? What is the "proportionality principle"? In your opinion, does Ewing's sentence respect the proportionality principle?

Reprinted from: *Ewing v. California,* 123 S. Ct. 1179; 155 L.2d 108, (2003). ✦

Chapter 45

Thirty Years of Sentencing Reform

The Quest for a Racially Neutral Sentencing Process

Cassia C. Spohn

In addition to her criticism of sentencing guidelines for increasing the severity of punishment without making punishment more just, Judge Gertner (Chapter 43) argued that they had not eliminated either discrimination or disparity in sentencing. The next two articles take up her concerns about discrimination and disparity.

The reading by Cassia C. Spohn asks whether sentencing responds to social difference and then examines whether there is evidence of racial discrimination in sentencing. Spohn notes how difficult it is to answer this question in a rigorous way and that, in the past, researchers often have not been able to document systematic discrimination in sentencing. Reviewing forty studies conducted during the last two decades at both state and federal levels, Spohn presents evidence to suggest that race and ethnicity do play an important role in contemporary sentencing decisions. "Black and Hispanic offenders—particularly those who are young, male, or unemployed—are more likely than their white counterparts to be sentenced to prison." Other categories of racial minorities, those with records of serious prior crimes and those who victimize whites, also appear to get harsher treatment than white offenders with similar crime profiles.

One might wonder whether the findings Spohn describes vindicate the views of those African Americans who believe law to be infected with racism and whether they justify the kind of race-based jury nullification described by Weiss and Zinsmeister in the previous chapter.

Nearly half a century after *Brown v. Board of Education*, the historic Supreme Court decision that outlawed racially segregated public schools, the issue of race relations in the United States continues to evoke controversy and spark debate. On no issue is the debate more spirited or are opinions more polarized than the relationship between race, crime, and justice. Politicians and scholars offer competing explanations for the disproportionate number of blacks arrested, imprisoned, and on death row. Those on one side contend that the war on crime—and particularly the war on drugs—has "caused the ever harsher treatment of blacks by the criminal justice system" (Tonry 1995, 52) and charge that the overrepresentation of blacks in arrest and imprisonment statistics reflects systematic racial discrimination (Mann 1993). Those on the other side assert that these results can be attributed primarily to the disproportionate involvement of blacks in serious criminal activity (Blumstein 1982, 1993) and argue that the idea of systematic discrimination within the criminal justice system is a "myth" (Wilbanks 1987).

Although charges of racial discrimination have been leveled at all stages of the criminal justice process, much of the harshest criticism has focused on judges' sentencing decisions. Critics of the sentencing process contend that crimes by racial minorities are punished more harshly than similar crimes by equally culpable whites. Other scholars challenge this assertion. They contend that the harsher sentences imposed on racial minorities reflect the seriousness of their crimes and prior criminal records as well as other legally relevant factors that judges consider in determining the appropriate sentence.

The findings of more than 40 years of research examining the effect of race on sentencing have not resolved this debate. Some studies have shown that racial/ethnic minorities are sentenced more harshly than whites (Holmes et al. 1996; Kramer and Ulmer 1996; Petersilia 1983; Spohn, Gruhl, and Welch 1981–1982; Zatz 1984), even after crime seriousness, prior criminal record, and other legal variables are taken into account. Other studies have found either no significant racial differences (Klein, Petersilia, and Turner 1990) or that blacks are treated more leniently than whites (Bernstein, Kelly, and Doyle 1977; Gibson 1978; Levin 1972). Still other research has concluded that race influences sentence severity *indirectly* through its effect on variables such as bail status (LaFree 1985b; Lizotte 1978), type of attorney (Spohn, Gruhl, and Welch 1981–1982), or type of disposition (LaFree 1985a; Spohn 1992; Uhlman and Walker 1980), or that race *interacts* with other variables and affects sentence severity only in some types of cases (Barnett 1985; Spohn and Cederblom 1991), in some types of settings (Chiricos and Crawford 1995; Hawkins 1987; Kleck 1981; Myers and Talarico 1986), or for some types of defendants (Chiricos and Bales 1991; LaFree 1989; Nobiling, Spohn, and DeLone 1998; Peterson and Hagan 1984; Spohn 1994; Walsh 1987).

It thus seems clear that, as we enter the 21st century, definitive answers to questions concerning differential sentencing of racial minorities and whites remain elusive. The issue is complicated by the fact that the past three decades have witnessed a virtual revolution in sentencing policies and practices (Tonry 1996).

At both the State and Federal levels, legislators abandoned indeterminate sentencing, replacing it with determinate sentencing, voluntary or presumptive sentencing guidelines, mandatory minimum penalties, and three-strikes laws. Although the goals of those who championed these reforms varied, with liberals arguing that structured sentencing practices would enhance fairness and hold judges accountable for their decisions and conservatives asserting that the reforms would lead to harsher penalties that eventually would deter criminal behavior, reformers on both sides of the political spectrum agreed that the changes were designed to curb discretion and reduce unwarranted disparity. As Tonry (1995, 164) notes, "Amelioration of racial disparities and discrimination was a major objective of proponents of constraints on judicial discretion."

That the reforms were designed to reduce racial disparity and discrimination is clear. What is not clear is whether the reforms have achieved that objective. The U.S. Sentencing Commission's evaluation of the first 4 years' experience with the Federal sentencing guidelines concluded that there had been a substantial reduction in racial disparity (U.S. Sentencing Commission 1991a), but other studies challenged that conclusion (Albonetti 1997; Rhodes 1992; U.S. General Accounting Office 1992; Weisburd 1992). Studies at the State level, most of which focus on the change from indeterminate to determinate sentencing (Petersilia 1983) or on the implementation of guidelines in Minnesota (Dixon 1995; Miethe and Moore 1985; Moore and Miethe 1986; Stolzenberg and D'Alessio 1994) and Pennsylvania (Kramer and Steffensmeier 1993; Kramer and Ulmer 1996; Ulmer and Kramer 1996), have yielded similarly mixed results. These inconsistencies led Tonry (1996, 42) to suggest that "the best conclusion at present is that we do not know whether disparities have increased or decreased."

The task of assessing the effect of race on sentencing is further complicated by the war on drugs, which a number of commentators contend has been fought primarily in minority communities. Tonry (1995, 105), for example, argues that "Urban black Americans have borne the brunt of the War on Drugs." Miller (1996, 80) similarly asserts that "from the first shot fired in the drug war African-Americans were targeted, arrested, and imprisoned in wildly disproportionate numbers." These allegations suggest not only that racial minorities have been arrested for drug offenses at a disproportionately high rate, but also that black and Hispanic drug offenders have been sentenced more harshly than white drug offenders.

There is ample evidence to support the argument that the war on drugs has been fought primarily in minority communities. Since 1976, the number of persons arrested for drug offenses has more than doubled; the number of whites arrested for drug offenses increased by 85 percent, while the number of blacks arrested for these offenses increased fourfold (Tonry 1995). The proportion of all drug arrestees who are black also increased, from 22 percent in 1976 to 39 percent in 1994. These racial differentials in arrest rates are reflected in prison populations, where the trend has been one of decreasing white and increasing black percentages. Between 1986 and 1991, the proportions of blacks and whites in State and Federal prisons reversed, from 53 percent white and 46 percent black to 53 percent black and 46 percent white. Tonry (1995, 113) attributes this reversal to the war on drugs, noting: "At every level of the criminal justice system, empirical analyses demonstrate that an increasing black disproportion has resulted from the War on Drugs—in jail, state and federal prisons, and juvenile institutions.". . .

The . . . purpose of this essay is to inform the debate on race, crime, and justice by critically evaluating recent empirical research investigating the linkages between race and sentence severity and by searching for "clues to the contextual character of possible race effects" (Chiricos and Crawford 1995, 284). As we begin the year 2000, we find increasingly large proportions of young black and Hispanic men in our Nation's jails and prisons. It is critically important to determine whether, and to what extent, this disparity has resulted

from "failed policies and cynical politics" (Tonry 1995, 180) rather than from legitimate and racially neutral efforts to control crime and protect society.

Before turning to an analysis of research on race and sentencing, I define the concepts of disparity and discrimination. I also present a brief overview of the sentencing process and summarize the reforms implemented during the past 30 years.

DISPARITY AND DISCRIMINATION

Critics of the sentencing process contend that unrestrained discretion results in sentence disparities and discrimination. These concepts, while sometimes used interchangeably, are significantly different. *Disparity* refers to a difference in treatment or outcome, but one that does not necessarily involve discrimination. As the Panel on Sentencing Research noted, "*Disparity* exists when 'like cases' with respect to case attributes—regardless of their legitimacy—are sentenced differently" (Blumstein et al. 1983, 72). *Discrimination*, on the other hand, is a difference that results from differential treatment based on illegitimate criteria, such as race, gender, social class, or sexual orientation. With respect to sentencing, discrimination "exists when some case attribute that is objectionable (typically on moral or legal grounds) can be shown to be associated with sentence outcomes after all other relevant variables are adequately controlled" (Blumstein et al. 1983, 72).

There is clear and convincing evidence of racial disparity in sentencing. At the Federal level, for example, 74.3 percent of the white offenders convicted in U.S. district courts during fiscal year 1996 were sentenced to prison. The comparable figures for black offenders and Hispanic offenders were 80.2 percent and 84.9 percent, respectively. The mean prison sentence for black offenders (91.1 months) also was substantially higher than the mean sentences for whites (48.9 months) or Hispanics (48.9 months) (U.S. Department of Justice [DOJ] 1998a). Similar disparities are found at the State level. For example, a study of sentences imposed in State courts nationwide in 1994 found that 55 percent of the blacks and 42 percent of the whites were sentenced to prison; the average prison sentence for blacks also was longer than the average sentence for whites (U.S. DOJ 1998b).

Although these statistics indicate that blacks and Hispanics receive sentences that are more punitive than whites receive, they do not tell us why this occurs. I suggest that there are at least four possible explanations, only three of which reflect racial discrimination. First, the differences in sentence severity could be due to the fact that blacks and Hispanics commit more serious crimes and have more serious prior criminal records than whites. Studies of sentencing decisions consistently have demonstrated the importance of these two legally relevant factors. Offenders who are convicted of more serious offenses, who use a weapon to commit the crime, or who seriously injure the victim receive harsher sentences, as do offenders who have prior felony convictions. The more severe sentences imposed on black and Hispanic offenders, then, might reflect the influence of these legally prescribed factors rather than the effect of racial prejudice on the part of judges.

The differences also could result from economic discrimination. Poor defendants are not as likely as middle- or upper-class defendants to have a private attorney or to be released prior to trial. They also are more likely to be unemployed. All of these factors may be related to sentence severity. Defendants represented by private attorneys or released prior to trial may receive more lenient sentences than those represented by public defenders or in custody prior to trial. Defendants who are unemployed may be sentenced more harshly than those who are employed. Since black and Hispanic defendants are more likely than white defendants to be poor, economic discrimination amounts to *indirect* racial discrimination.

Third, the differences could be due to *direct* racial discrimination on the part of judges. They could be a result of judges taking the race/ethnicity of the offender into account in determining the sentence. This implies that judges who are confronted with black, Hispanic, and white offenders convicted of similar crimes and with similar prior criminal records impose harsher sentences on racial minorities than on whites. It implies that judges, the majority of whom are white, stereotype black and Hispanic offenders as more violent, more dangerous, and less amenable to rehabilitation than white offenders (see Steffensmeier, Ulmer, and Kramer 1998).

Finally, the sentencing disparities could reflect both equal treatment and discrimination, depending on the nature of the crime, the races of the victim and the offender, the type of jurisdiction, the age and gender of the offender, and so on. It is possible, in other words, that racial minorities who commit certain types of crimes (e.g., forgery) are treated no differently than whites who commit these crimes, while those who commit other types of crimes (e.g., sexual assault) are sentenced more harshly than their white counterparts. Similarly, it is possible that racial discrimination in the application of the death penalty is confined to the South or to cases involving black offenders and white victims. This type of discrimination is what Walker, Spohn, and DeLone (1999, 17) refer to as "contextual discrimination." It is discrimination that is found in particular contexts or circumstances.

In summary, there is a significant difference between disparity and discrimination, and discrimination can take different forms. In reviewing the research on race and sentencing, I use the term "direct discrimination" to characterize what researchers refer to as a "main effect." That is, race/ethnicity significantly affects sentence severity after all legally relevant case and offender characteristics are taken into consideration; stated another way, blacks and Hispanics are sentenced more harshly than whites, and these differences cannot be attributed to differences in crime seriousness, prior criminal record, or other legally relevant factors. . . .

RECENT RESEARCH ON RACE AND SENTENCING

The previous reviews of research examining the relationship between race and sentencing typically concluded that race exerted a very modest effect on sentence severity once controls for crime seriousness, prior criminal record, and other legally relevant factors were taken into consideration. Most of the studies included in these reviews, however, used data from the 1970s and earlier. Even the most current of the extant reviews, which examined 38 studies published between 1979 and 1991, included only 6 studies that used post-1980 data (Chiricos and Crawford 1995). This is problematic, given that the past 20 years have witnessed dramatic and widespread changes in sentencing policies and procedures at both the State and Federal levels. The conclusions of these earlier reviews obviously cannot be generalized to the sentencing process in the postreform era.

What follows is a comprehensive and systematic review of recent research examining the effect of race on sentencing. All published research using individual data from the 1980s and 1990s that reports a measure of association between race and sentence outcomes is included. Because previous research has shown that offender race may differentially affect the decision to incarcerate and the decision concerning the length of sentence, I review and assess the findings of research regarding each of these measures of sentence severity. I also include studies that examine alternative indicators of sentence severity: departures from sentencing guidelines; the decision to apply habitual offender provisions; the decision to withhold adjudication; and whether the mandatory minimum sentence was imposed.

As noted earlier, the purpose of this review is not simply to add another voice to the debate concerning the effect of race on sentencing. Rather, the purpose is to highlight the ways in which researchers have responded to calls for theoretical and methodological improvements in sentencing research and to document the extent to which recent research finds evidence of direct *and* subtle racial discrimination in sentencing. I attempt not only to determine whether blacks and Hispanics are sentenced more harshly than whites but also to identify the "structural and contextual conditions that are most likely to result in racial discrimination" (Hagan and Bumiller 1983, 21). In other words, the focus is on determining whether research reveals consistent patterns indicating that offender race/ethnicity operates indirectly through other factors, such as pretrial status or type of disposition, or interacts with other variables (e.g., prior record, type of crime) that are themselves related to sentence severity. I also attempt to determine whether the effect of race/ethnicity varies depending on the formal sentencing structure in the jurisdiction being studied and whether the sentencing reforms enacted during the past three decades have achieved their goal of reducing racial disparity.

RACE AND SENTENCING: EVALUATING THE EVIDENCE

Forty studies examining the relationship between race and sentencing are reviewed here: 32 studies of sentencing decisions in State courts and 8 studies of sentence outcomes at the Federal level. . . .

RACE AND SENTENCE OUTCOMES: A SUMMARY OF MAIN EFFECTS

. . .[T]he 32 studies using State-level data produced 95 estimates of the effect of race on sentence severity and 29 estimates of the effect of ethnicity on sentence severity. Forty-one of the 95 black versus white estimates (43.2 percent) are both positive (i.e., indicative of harsher sentences for blacks) and statistically significant, and 8 of the 29 Hispanic versus white estimates (27.6 percent) are positive (i.e., indicative of harsher sentences for Hispanics) and statistically significant. In contrast, only 6 of the estimates indicate more lenient sentencing for racial minorities (4 of 95 for blacks and 2 of 29 for Hispanics).

. . . [E]ight studies based on Federal-level data . . . produced 22 estimates of the effect of race on sentence severity; more than two-thirds (15 of 22) of the estimates reveal that blacks were sentenced more harshly than whites. The Federal-level studies generated 21 estimates of the relationship between ethnicity and sentence severity; nearly half (10 of 21) of the estimates indicate that Hispanics were sentenced more harshly than whites.

. . . [T]he relationship between race/ethnicity and sentence severity varies by the type of sentence outcome being analyzed. Among defendants sentenced in State courts, both blacks and Hispanics are much more likely to be disadvantaged at the initial decision to incarcerate or not than at the subsequent decision concerning length of the sentence. About half (55.5 percent for blacks and 41.7 percent for Hispanics) of the estimates of the effect of race/ethnicity on the in/out decision are positive and statistically significant. In contrast, just under one-fourth (23.1 percent) of the sentence length estimates indicate longer sentences for blacks and only 1 of the 14 estimates reveals longer sentences for Hispanics. The pattern of results generated by the studies that used Federal sentencing data is somewhat different, especially for blacks. Three of the seven in/out estimates (blacks versus whites) are positive and statistically significant compared with six of the nine sentence length estimates. The results for Hispanics are more similar to those generated by the State-level studies: Three of the seven in/out estimates but only two of the eight sentence length estimates, are positive and significant. . . .

. . .At least at the State level, race and ethnicity have stronger and more consistent direct effects on the decision to incarcerate or not than on the sentence length decision. At the Federal level, race and, to a lesser extent, ethnicity affect both types of sentence outcomes.

In addition to exploring the effect of race/ethnicity on the two traditional measures of sentence severity, a number of the studies included in this review analyzed the relationship between race/ethnicity and other indicators of sentence severity. Several studies examined the likelihood of dispositional or durational departures from sentence guidelines (Kramer and Ulmer 1996; Langan 1996; Moore and Miethe 1986; Maxfield and Kramer 1998; Ulmer 1997; U.S. Sentencing Commission 1995) or the magnitude of durational departures (Maxfield and Kramer 1998). One State-level study examined the decision to withhold adjudication (Spohn, DeLone, and Spears 1998), and another focused on the likelihood of being sentenced as a habitual criminal (Crawford, Chiricos, and Kleck 1998). One study of sentencing under the Federal sentencing guidelines examined the decision to impose the applicable mandatory minimum sentence (U.S. Sentencing Commission 1991b). . . .

. . . [I]t does appear that State and Federal judges take race/ethnicity into account in deciding whether to depart from the guidelines. Studies conducted in Pennsylvania and Minnesota reveal that racial minorities are less likely than whites to receive mitigated dispositional or durational departures. Studies of Federal sentence outcomes similarly reveal that blacks and Hispanics are less likely than whites to benefit from departures for substantial assistance or acceptance of responsibility but are more likely than whites to be sentenced at or above the minimum sentence indicated by applicable mandatory minimum sentencing provisions. There also is evidence that blacks face higher odds than whites of being sentenced as habitual offenders in Florida.

Considered together, the studies reviewed here suggest that race and ethnicity do play an important role in contemporary sentencing decisions. Black and Hispanic offenders sentenced in State and Federal courts face significantly greater odds of incarceration than similarly situated white offenders. In some jurisdictions, they also may receive longer sentences or differential benefits from guideline departures than their white counterparts. The implications of these findings of direct race effects are discussed below.

SENTENCE OUTCOMES: WHEN DOES RACE/ETHNICITY MATTER?

The findings discussed thus far suggest that race does matter in sentencing. Evidence concerning direct racial effects, however, provides few clues to the circumstances under which race matters. Although this evidence reveals that race/ethnicity is a stronger predictor of the decision to incarcerate or not than the decision concerning sentence length, it does not address the possibility of more subtle racial effects. As earlier reviews (Hagan 1974; Zatz 1987) suggested, even the complete absence of direct race effects would not necessarily signal a racially neutral sentencing process.

A number of scholars have argued that the inconsistent findings of pre-1990s research on race and sentencing reflected both specification error and an overly simplistic view of conflict theory. These scholars called for research designed to delineate more precisely the conditions under which defendant race influences judges' sentencing decisions. . . .

Recent research examining the effect of race/ethnicity on sentence severity has responded to these suggestions. A majority of the studies reviewed in this essay attempt not only to determine *whether* race makes a difference but also to identify the contexts in which race matters. . . .

. . . [T]he results of these studies reveal four "themes" or "patterns" of contextual effects. First, the combination of race/ethnicity and other legally irrelevant offender characteristics produces greater sentence disparity than race/ethnicity alone: *gender* (Albonetti 1997; Chiricos and Bales 1991; Nobiling, Spohn, and DeLone 1998; Spohn, DeLone, and Spears 1998; Spohn and Holleran 2000; Steffensmeier, Ulmer, and Kramer 1998; Wooldredge 1998), *age* (Chiricos and Bales 1991; Spohn and Holleran 2000; Steffensmeier, Ulmer, and Kramer 1998), *employment status* (Chiricos and Bales 1991; Nobiling, Spohn, and DeLone 1998; Spohn and DeLone in press; Spohn and Holleran 2000; Spohn and Spears 2000), *income* (Wooldredge 1998), and *education* (Albonetti 1997) all interact with race and ethnicity to produce harsher sentences for more "problematic" black and Hispanic offenders.

Second, a number of process-related factors condition the effect of race/ethnicity on sentence severity. Whereas whites receive a greater sentence discount for providing "substantial assistance" in the prosecution of other Federal offenders (Albonetti 1997) or for hiring a private attorney (Holmes et al. 1996), racial minorities pay a higher penalty for pretrial detention (Chiricos and Bales 1991; Crew 1991) and going to trial rather than pleading guilty (Crew 1991; Ulmer 1997; Ulmer and Kramer 1996; Zatz 1984). There also is evidence that racial minorities are penalized more harshly than whites for having a serious prior criminal record (McDonald and Carlson 1993; Nelson 1994; Spohn and DeLone in press; Spohn, DeLone, and Spears 1998; Spohn and Spears 2000; Wooldredge 1998; Ulmer 1997; Ulmer and Kramer 1996; Zatz 1984).

A third pattern concerns the interaction between the race of the offender and the race of the victim; two studies reveal that substantially harsher sentences are imposed on blacks who sexually assault whites than on blacks who sexually assault other blacks (Spohn and Spears 1996; Walsh 1987). Finally, although the pattern is less obvious, some evidence suggests that racial discrimination is confined to less serious crimes (Crawford, Chiricos, and Kleck 1998; Spohn and DeLone in press). Other evidence points to harsher treatment of racial minorities who are convicted of either drug offenses or more serious drug offenses (Albonetti 1997; Crawford, Chiricos, and Kleck 1998; Klein, Petersilia, and Turner 1990; Myers 1989; Spohn and DeLone in press; Spohn and Spears 2000).

Race/Ethnicity and Other Offender Characteristics. The most important conclusion derived from the findings . . . concerns the interrelationships among race/ethnicity, gender, age, and employment status. A number of studies convincingly demonstrate that *certain types* of racial minorities—males, the young, the unemployed, the less educated—are singled out for harsher treatment at sentencing. Some studies find that each of these offender characteristics, including race/ethnicity, has a direct effect on sentence severity, but that the combination of race/ethnicity and one or more of the other characteristics is a more powerful predictor of sentence severity than any variable individually. Other studies find that the effect of race is confined to racial minorities who are male, young, and/or unemployed; these studies, in other words, find race effects that were masked in the additive analysis. . . .

Further evidence that the effect of race is conditioned by other offender characteristics is found in research exploring the interrelationships among race/ethnicity, gender, age, employment status, and sentence severity. Although some scholars argue that judges will see the unemployed as a threat and that this "belief alone is sufficient to propel them towards stiffening their sentencing practices" (Box and Hale 1985, 209–210), others contend that *certain types* of unemployed offenders will be viewed as particularly threatening and, thus, will be singled out for harsher treatment.

A number of the studies included in this review address this possibility. Chiricos and Bales (1991), for example, found that unemployment had a direct effect on the likelihood of imprisonment; they also found that the effect was strongest if the offender was a young black male. Nobiling and her colleagues

(1998), who analyzed data on offenders convicted of felonies in Chicago and Kansas City, similarly hypothesized that unemployment would primarily affect sentence outcomes for young black and Hispanic males. They found that in Chicago unemployment increased the odds of a prison sentence among young males and young Hispanic males. In this jurisdiction, unemployment also led to a longer prison sentence for males, young males, and black males. In Kansas City, unemployment led to a greater likelihood of incarceration among males and black males but had no effect on sentence length for any of the race/gender/age subgroups examined.

Considered together, these studies provide evidence in support of the notion that certain categories of black and Hispanic offenders are regarded as more problematic than others. They confirm that dangerous or problematic populations are defined "by a mix of economic *and* racial . . . references" (Melossi 1989, 317, emphasis in the original). Black and Hispanic offenders who are also male, young, and unemployed may pay a higher punishment penalty than either white offenders or other types of black and Hispanic offenders.

Race/Ethnicity and Process-Related Factors. A second pattern revealed . . . is that a number of "process-related factors" have differential effects on sentence severity for racial minorities and whites. Some studies reveal that pleading guilty (Ulmer 1997; Ulmer and Kramer 1996) or providing substantial assistance to Federal prosecutors (Albonetti 1997) results in greater sentence discounts for white offenders than for black or Hispanic offenders. Other studies find that race/ethnicity affects sentence severity indirectly through its effect on pretrial status (Chiricos and Bales 1991; Crew 1991), type of attorney (Holmes et al. 1996), or type of disposition (Crew 1991). . . .

The findings of these studies, then, attest to the importance of using a "process-oriented model" (Holmes et al. 1996, 12) that incorporates tests for indirect and/or interaction effects as well as main effects. They suggest that race and ethnicity influence sentence outcomes through their relationships with earlier decisions regarding pretrial detention, pleading guilty, and retention of private counsel. The findings concerning the interaction between race/ethnicity and prior record further suggest that "the major variables affecting justice processing do not operate in the same way for black [and Hispanic] and white offenders."

Race of the Offender and Victim. Two . . . studies . . . provide support for Hawkins' (1987) assertion that theoretical perspectives on race and sentencing must account for the role played by the race of the victim as well as the race of the offender (Spohn and Spears 1996; Walsh 1987). Hawkins (1987) questions social scientists' characterization of findings of leniency toward black offenders as "anomalies." He argues, "These patterns are anomalous only if one adopts an oversimplified version of the conflict perspective as it has been developed within criminology" (p. 740). More to the point, he suggests (pp. 724–725) that "the race of the victim must be seen as a factor that mediates the level of punishment." Thus, blacks who victimize whites will be punished more harshly than blacks who victimize members of their own race. . . .

RACE/ETHNICITY AND CRIME SERIOUSNESS

The importance of "rethinking the conflict perspective on race and criminal punishment" (Chiricos and Bales 1991, 719) is . . . demonstrated by studies examining the effect of race on sentence severity for various types of crimes. Some researchers, building on Kalven and Zeisel's (1966) "liberation hypothesis," assert that blacks will be sentenced more harshly than whites only for less serious crimes. These researchers (cf. Spohn and Cederblom 1991) contend that when the crime is serious, the appropriate sentence (i.e., incarceration) is obvious. In these types

of cases, judges have relatively little discretion and thus few opportunities to consider legally irrelevant factors such as race. In less serious cases, on the other hand, the appropriate sentence is not as clearly indicated by the features of the crime, which may leave judges more disposed to bring extralegal factors, such as race/ethnicity, to bear on the sentencing decision.

Although the findings are somewhat inconsistent, the studies included in this review provide some support of the liberation hypothesis. The strongest evidence is in Crawford, Chiricos, and Kleck's (1998) exploration of the effect of race on the decision to apply habitual offender provisions. The authors used data on 9,690 male offenders who were sentenced to prison in Florida and eligible to be sentenced as habitual offenders. They found that eligible blacks were significantly more likely than eligible whites to be sentenced as habitual offenders; in fact, they concluded that "the strongest odds of being sentenced as a habitual offender are those associated with being black" (p. 496). . . .

Race/Ethnicity and the War on Drugs. As noted in the introduction to this essay, the task of assessing the effect of race on sentence outcomes is complicated by the war on drugs. Social scientists and legal scholars have suggested not only that the war on drugs has been fought primarily in minority communities but also that "the recent blackening of America's prison population is the product of malign neglect of the war's effects on black Americans" (Tonry 1995, 155). Miller (1996, 83), for example, contends: "The racial discrimination endemic to the drug war wound its way through every stage of the processing—arrest, jailing, conviction, and sentencing."

Comments such as these suggest that racial minorities will receive more punitive sentences than whites for drug offenses. This expectation is based in part on recent theoretical discussion of the "moral panic" surrounding drug use and the war on drugs

(Chambliss 1995; Tonry 1995). Moral panic theorists (Jenkins 1994) argue that society is characterized by a variety of commonsense perceptions about crime and drugs that result in community intolerance for such behaviors and increased pressure for punitive action. Many theorists (see Chiricos and DeLone 1992 for a review) argue that this moral panic can become ingrained in the judicial ideology of sentencing judges, resulting in more severe sentences for those—that is, blacks and Hispanics—believed to be responsible for drug use, drug distribution, and drug-related crime. . . .

Considered together, these studies provide evidence in support of assertions that "Urban black Americans have borne the brunt of the War on Drugs" (Tonry 1995, 105). Black and Hispanic drug offenders, and particularly those who engage in drug trafficking, face greater odds of incarceration and longer sentences than their white counterparts.

DISCUSSION

The inconsistent findings of recent studies investigating the relationship between race and sentencing, coupled with competing assertions that racial disparities in sentencing had been reduced by the sentencing reforms of the past three decades but exacerbated by the policies pursued during the war on drugs, suggested that it was time to revisit this important issue. In this essay, I reviewed and critically evaluated 40 studies examining the linkages between race and sentence severity. My purpose was not simply to determine whether recent research provides evidence of direct racial discrimination in sentencing but also to search for clues to the contexts in which blacks and Hispanics are sentenced more harshly than whites. In the following sections, I summarize the major findings of this review and discuss the implications of these findings.

DIRECT RACE EFFECTS

Many of the studies included in this review found evidence of *direct discrimination* against racial minorities. At the State level, 41 of the 95 black versus white estimates and 8 of the 29 Hispanic versus white estimates were indicative of significantly more severe sentences for racial minorities; at the Federal level, two-thirds of the black versus white estimates and one-half of the Hispanic versus white estimates revealed more punitive sentences for racial minorities. Evidence that racial minorities were sentenced more harshly than whites was found primarily, but not exclusively, with respect to the initial decision to incarcerate rather than the subsequent decision regarding sentence length. This pattern was especially obvious at the State level, where about half of the in/out estimates, but fewer than one-fourth of the sentence length estimates, revealed harsher sentences for racial minorities.

These findings call into question earlier conclusions that the evidence concerning the effect of race on sentencing "largely contradicts a hypothesis of overt discrimination against black defendants" (Kleck 1981, 783), or that findings of racial discrimination in sentencing reflect the failure to control for crime seriousness or prior criminal record (Hagan 1974) or are confined primarily to the South. The effects summarized above are all main effects; as such, they provide support for "a hypothesis of overt discrimination." Moreover, although the studies included in this review vary somewhat in quality, they do not suffer from the methodological limitations of the research incorporated in earlier reviews. All of them use appropriate multivariate statistical techniques and control for relevant legal variables, including the offender's prior criminal record (which was the most commonly omitted variable in earlier research). Finally, significant effects are found in non-Southern (California, Illinois, Minnesota, New York, Ohio, and Pennsylvania) as well as Southern (Florida and Georgia) jurisdictions.

Although these findings suggest that race and ethnicity do play a role—a direct role—in contemporary sentencing decisions, it would be misleading to conclude that there is a consistent and widespread pattern of direct discrimination against black and Hispanic offenders in sentencing decisions. Caution is warranted for at least three reasons. First, although each of the 8 studies of Federal sentence outcomes reported significant main effects for race/ethnicity, 6 of the 32 State level studies found no significant main effects for any measure of sentence severity for blacks and/or Hispanics (Crew 1991; Dixon 1995; Simon 1996; Spohn, DeLone, and Spears 1998; Wooldredge 1998; Zatz 1984). Second, 9 of the 25 significant effects for the in/out decision and 6 of the 11 significant effects for sentence length for black offenders are reported in the series of studies conducted in Pennsylvania. This obviously limits the generalizability of findings regarding direct race effects.

A third reason for exercising caution in drawing conclusions is that the effects revealed by many of the studies, while statistically significant, are rather modest. Spohn and DeLone (in press), for example, used the results of their logistic regression analysis to calculate estimated probabilities of incarceration for typical white, black, and Hispanic offenders in each of the three jurisdictions included in their study. They found a difference of 4 percentage points in the likelihood of incarceration between white offenders and black offenders and between white offenders and Hispanic offenders in Chicago; in Miami, there was a difference of 8 percentage points between white offenders and Hispanic offenders. Kramer and Steffensmeier (1993, 367), who noted that tests of statistical significance were not very meaningful given the large number of cases (about 34,000) included in their analysis, reported that "race contributes less than one-half of one percent to explained variation in each of the three in/out classifications." Similarly, Langan's (1996)

analysis of substantial assistance departures under the Federal sentencing guidelines revealed that "race . . . improved the correct prediction rate by less than one-fourth of one percentage point."

These caveats notwithstanding, it is clear that the studies conducted during the fourth wave of research challenge earlier conclusions of racial neutrality in sentencing. These methodologically sophisticated studies demonstrate that while race/ethnicity is not *the* major determinant of sentence severity, it "is *a* determinant of sanctioning, and a potent one at that" (Zatz 1987, 87). This clearly is an important finding. As the Panel on Sentencing Research concluded in 1983, "[E]ven a small amount of racial discrimination is a very serious matter, both on general normative grounds and because small effects in aggregate can imply unacceptable deprivations for large numbers of people" (Blumstein et al. 1983, 13). The fact that a majority of the studies reviewed here found that blacks and Hispanics were more likely than whites to be sentenced to prison, even after taking crime seriousness and prior criminal record into account, suggests that racial discrimination in sentencing is not a thing of the past.

INDIRECT AND INTERACTION EFFECTS

Nearly 30 years ago, Richard Quinney (1970, 142) asserted that "judicial decisions are not made uniformly. Decisions are made according to a host of extralegal factors, including the age of the offender, his race, and social class." The validity of this assertion is confirmed by the studies in this review. There is compelling evidence that offender race and ethnicity affect sentence severity indirectly or in interaction with other legal and extralegal variables. These more subtle effects surfaced in studies that found no direct race effects as well as those that did. In fact, with only two exceptions, each of the State level studies that found no direct race effects found significant contextual effects.

The most intriguing and important pattern of results revealed by the research reviewed here concerns the interaction between offender race/ethnicity and other legally irrelevant offender characteristics. This research convincingly demonstrates that certain types of racial minorities—males, the young, the unemployed, the less educated—are singled out for harsher treatment at sentencing. Some studies find that black and Hispanic offenders generally receive more punitive sentences than white offenders, but that the combination of race/ethnicity and gender, age, and/or employment status results in even larger racial disparities. Other studies find that the effect of race/ethnicity is confined to blacks and Hispanics who are also young, male, and/or unemployed. Both types of studies reveal that young unemployed black and Hispanic males may pay a higher punishment penalty than other categories of offenders. . . .

The studies reviewed here suggest that judges' assessments of dangerousness and culpability, and thus their views of the appropriate punishment, may also rest on other combinations of offender and offense attributes. There is evidence, for example, that the treatment of black men charged with sexual assault depends on the race of the victim: Blacks who victimize whites are punished more harshly than blacks who victimize other blacks. (Studies of the imposition of the death penalty, which are not included in this review, report similar findings.) Although it is not clear whether this reflects the view that black men who cross racial lines to commit sexual assault are more threatening and dangerous than other types of offenders and/or the view that those who sexually assault white women (regardless of their race) deserve harsher punishment than those who assault black women, what is clear is that simply comparing the sentences imposed on black men to those imposed on white men will produce misleading results.

The findings of this review also lend credence to Crawford, Chiricos, and Kleck's (1998, 506) assertion that judges' "punitive impulses" are linked to their perceptions of

"racial threat," which are themselves linked to "urban underclass blacks and drugs." A number of the studies reviewed here conclude that black and Hispanic drug offenders are sentenced more harshly than white drug offenders. Similar to the pattern of results discussed earlier regarding interaction between offender race/ethnicity and other offender characteristics, some studies find that the effect of race/ethnicity is confined to drug offenders, while others find that race/ethnicity has a substantially greater effect on sentencing for drug offenses than for other types of offenses. Still other studies reveal that blacks and Hispanics who engage in the more serious distribution and trafficking offenses face significantly more punitive punishment than other types of drug offenders.

These results suggest that the moral panic surrounding drug use and drug-related crime, coupled with stereotypes linking racial minorities to a drug-involved lifestyle, has resulted in more severe sentences for black and Hispanic drug offenders, and particularly for those convicted of the more serious offenses. It thus appears that judges use race/ethnicity and offense seriousness to define what might be called a "dangerous class" (Adler 1994) of drug offenders. The black or Hispanic drug offender who manufactures or sells large quantities of drugs may be perceived as particularly dangerous or particularly villainous (Peterson and Hagan 1984); as a consequence, he may be sentenced especially harshly.

The indirect and interaction effects revealed by the research included in this review attest to the theoretical and methodological evolutions in research on race and sentencing. Contemporary researchers have moved beyond simply asking whether race makes a difference to attempting to identify the conditions under which and the contexts in which race makes a difference. The studies reviewed here make important contributions to our understanding of the complex interconnections among race/ethnicity, offender and case characteristics, and sentence severity. They provide compelling evidence that black and Hispanic offenders *will not* "receive more severe punishment than whites for all crimes, under all conditions, and at similar levels of disproportion over time" (Hawkins 1987, 724). Rather, certain types of racial minorities—males, the young, the unemployed, those who commit serious drug offenses, those who victimize whites, those who refuse to plead guilty or who are unable to obtain pretrial release—may be perceived as more threatening, more dangerous, and more culpable; as a consequence, they may be punished more harshly than similarly situated whites.

RACE/ETHNICITY IN THE REFORM ERA

The findings of this review suggest that the sentencing reforms implemented during the past 25 years have not achieved their goal of "amelioration of racial disparities and discrimination" (Tonry 1995, 164). In fact, studies of sentences imposed at the Federal level reveal a consistent pattern of disadvantage for black and Hispanic offenders. This pattern is particularly pronounced for the various alternative measures of sentence severity. Although the Federal sentencing guidelines severely constrain judges' discretion in deciding between prison and probation and in determining the length of the sentence, they place only minimal restrictions on the ability of judges (and prosecutors) to reduce sentences for substantial assistance or acceptance of responsibility. Mandatory minimum sentences also can be avoided through charge manipulation. As Albonetti (1997, 790) notes, "these process-related decisions offer potential avenues through which prosecutors [and judges] can circumvent guideline-defined sentence outcomes." The validity of this assertion is confirmed by the fact that each of the six Federal-level studies that examined an alternative measure of sentence severity found evidence of direct discrimination against both blacks and Hispanics. . . .

CONCLUSION

The findings of this review suggest that the disproportionate number of racial minorities confined in our Nation's jails and prisons cannot be attributed solely to racially neutral efforts to control crime and protect society. Although it is irrefutable that the primary determinants of sentencing decisions are the seriousness of the offense and the offender's prior criminal record, race/ethnicity and other legally irrelevant offender characteristics also play a role. Black and Hispanic offenders—and particularly those who are young, male, or unemployed—are more likely than their white counterparts to be sentenced to prison; they also may receive longer sentences than similarly situated white offenders. Other categories of racial minorities—those convicted of drug offenses, those who victimize whites, those who accumulate more serious prior criminal records, or those who refuse to plead guilty or are unable to secure pretrial release—also may be singled out for more punitive treatment. Coupled with the fact that significant race effects were found in Southern and non-Southern jurisdictions, in State and Federal court systems, and in jurisdictions with and without sentencing guidelines, these results suggest that earlier refutations of the discrimination thesis were premature.

References

Adler, Jeffrey S. 1994. The dynamite, wreckage, and scum in our cities: The social construction of deviance in industrial America. *Justice Quarterly* 11:33–49.

Albonetti, Celesta. 1997. Sentencing under the Federal sentencing guidelines: Effects of defendant characteristics, guilty pleas, and departures on sentence outcomes for drug offenses, 1991–1992. *Law & Society Review* 31:789–822.

Barnett, Arnold. 1985. Some distribution patterns for the Georgia death sentence. *U.C. Davis Law Review* 18:1327–1374.

Bernstein, Ilene Nagel, William R. Kelly, and Patricia A. Doyle. 1977. Societal reaction to deviants: The case of criminal defendants. *American Sociological Review* 42:743–795.

Blumstein, Alfred. 1982. On the racial disproportionality of U.S. prison populations. *Journal of Criminal Law and Criminology* 73:1259–1281.

Blumstein, Alfred, Jacqueline Cohen, Susan E. Martin, and Michael H. Tonry, eds. 1983. *Research on sentencing: The search for reform.* Vol. 1. Washington, D.C.: National Academy Press.

Box, Steven, and Chris Hale. 1985. Unemployment, imprisonment, and prison overcrowding. *Contemporary Crises* 9:209–228.

Chambliss, William J. 1995. Crime control and ethnic minorities: Legitimizing racial oppression by creating moral panics. In *Ethnicity, race, and crime,* edited by Darnell Hawkins. Albany: State University of New York Press.

Chiricos, Theodore G., and William D. Bales. 1991. Unemployment and punishment: An empirical assessment. *Criminology* 29:701–724.

Chiricos, Theodore G., and Charles Crawford. 1995. Race and imprisonment: A contextual assessment of the evidence. In *Ethnicity, race, and crime,* edited by Darnell Hawkins. Albany: State University of New York Press.

Chiricos, Theodore G., and Miriam DeLone. 1992. Labor surplus and punishment: A review and assessment of theory and evidence. *Social Problems* 39:421–446.

Crawford, Charles, Ted Chiricos, and Gary Kleck. 1998. Race, racial threat, and sentencing of habitual offenders. *Criminology* 36:481–511.

Crew, Keith. 1991. Race differences in felony charging and sentencing: Toward an integration of decision-making and negotiation models. *Journal of Crime and Justice* 14:99–122.

Dixon, Jo. 1995. The organizational context of criminal sentencing. *American Journal of Sociology* 100:1157–1198.

Gibson, James L. 1978. Race as a determinant of criminal sentences: A methodological critique and a case study. *Law & Society Review* 12:455–478.

Hagan, John. 1974. Extra-legal attributes and criminal sentencing: An assessment of a sociological viewpoint. *Law & Society Review* 8:357–383.

Hagan, John, and Kristin Bumiller. 1983. Making sense of sentencing: A review and critique of sentencing research. In *Research on sentencing: The search for reform,* edited by Alfred Blumstein, Jacqueline Cohen, Susan E. Martin, and Michael H. Tonry. Vol. 2. Washington, D.C.: National Academy Press.

Hawkins, Darnell F. 1987. Beyond anomalies: Rethinking the conflict perspective on race and criminal punishment. *Social Forces* 65:719–745.

Holmes, Malcolm D., Harmon M. Hosch, Howard C. Daudistel, Dolores A. Perez, and Joseph B. Graves. 1996. Ethnicity, legal resources, and felony dispositions in two Southwestern jurisdictions. *Justice Quarterly* 13:11–30.

Jenkins, Phillip. 1994. "The Ice Age": The social construction of a drug panic. *Justice Quarterly* 11:7–31.

Kalven, Harry, Jr., and Hans Zeisel. 1966. *The American jury.* Boston: Little, Brown and Company.

Kleck, Gary. 1981. Racial discrimination in sentencing: A critical evaluation of the evidence with additional evidence on the death penalty. *American Sociological Review* 43:783–805.

Klein, Stephen, Joan Petersilia, and Susan Turner. 1990. Race and imprisonment decisions in California. *Science* 247:812–816.

Kramer, John, and Darrell Steffensmeier. 1993. Race and imprisonment decisions. *Sociological Quarterly* 34:357–376.

Kramer, John H., and Jeffery T. Ulmer. 1996. Sentencing disparity and departures from guidelines. *Justice Quarterly* 13:81–106.

LaFree, Gary D. 1989. *Rape and criminal justice: The social construction of sexual assault.* Belmont, California: Wadsworth Publishing Company.

——. 1985a. Adversarial and nonadversarial justice: A comparison of guilty pleas and trials. *Criminology* 23:289–312.

——. 1985b. Official reactions to Hispanic defendants in the Southwest. *Journal of Research in Crime and Delinquency* 22:213–237.

Langan, Patrick A. 1996. Sentence reductions for drug traffickers for assisting Federal prosecutors. Unpublished manuscript.

Lemelle, Anthony J., Jr. 1995. *Black male deviance.* Westport, Connecticut: Praeger.

Levin, Martin A. 1972. Urban politics and policy outcomes: The criminal courts. In *Criminal justice: Law and politics,* edited by George F. Cole. Belmont, California: Wadsworth Publishing Company.

Lizotte, Alan J. 1978. Extra-legal factors in Chicago's criminal courts: Testing the conflict model of criminal justice. *Social Problems* 25:564–580.

Mann, Coramae Richey. 1993. *Unequal justice: A question of color.* Bloomington, Indiana: University Press.

Maxfield, Linda Drazha, and John H. Kramer. 1998. *Substantial assistance: An empirical yardstick gauging equity in current Federal policy and practice.* Washington, D.C.: U.S. Sentencing Commission.

McDonald, Douglas C., and Kenneth E. Carlson. 1993. *Sentencing in the Federal courts: Does race matter? The transition to sentencing guidelines, 1986–1990.* Research Report, NCJ 145328. Washington, D.C.: U.S. Department of Justice, Bureau of Justice Statistics.

Melossi, Dario. 1989. An introduction: Fifty years later, punishment and social structure in contemporary analysis. *Contemporary Crises* 13:311–326.

Miethe, Terance D., and Charles A. Moore. 1986. Racial differences in criminal processing: The consequences of model selection on conclusions about differential treatment. *Sociological Quarterly* 27:217–237.

Miller, Jerome G. 1996. *Search and destroy: African-American males in the criminal justice system.* New York: Cambridge University Press.

Moore, Charles A., and Terance D. Miethe. 1986. Regulated and unregulated sentencing decisions: An analysis of first-year practices under Minnesota's felony sentencing guidelines. *Law & Society Review* 20:253–277.

Myers, Martha A. 1989. Symbolic policy and the sentencing of drug offenders. *Law & Society Review* 23:295–315.

——. 1987. Economic inequality and discrimination in sentencing. *Social Forces* 65:746–766.

Myers, Martha A., and Susette Talarico. 1987. *The social contexts of criminal sentencing.* New York: Springer-Verlag.

Nelson, James F. 1994. A dollar or a day: Sentencing misdemeanants in New York State. *Journal of Research on Crime and Delinquency* 31:183–201.

Nobiling, Tracy, Cassia Spohn, and Miriam DeLone. 1998. A tale of two counties: Unemployment and sentence severity. *Justice Quarterly* 15:401–427.

Petersilia, Joan. 1983. *Racial disparities in the criminal justice system.* Santa Monica, California: RAND.

Peterson, Ruth, and John Hagan. 1984. Changing conceptions of race: Toward an account of anomalous findings in sentencing research. *American Sociological Review* 49:56–70.

Quinney, Richard. 1970. *The social reality of crime.* Boston: Little, Brown and Company.

Rhodes, William. 1992. Sentence disparity, use of incarceration, and plea bargaining: The post-guideline view from the Commission. *Federal Sentencing Reporter* 5:153–155.

Simon, Lenore M.J. 1996. The effect of the victim-offender relationship on the sentence length of violent offenders. *Journal of Crime and Justice* 19:129–148.

Spohn, Cassia. 1994. Crime and the social control of blacks: The effect of offender/victim race on sentences for violent felonies. In *Inequality, crime, and social control,* edited by George Bridges and Martha Myers. Boulder, Colorado: Westview Press.

——. 1992. An analysis of the "jury trial penalty" and its effect on black and white offenders. *Justice Professional* 7:93–112.

Spohn, Cassia, and Jerry Cederblom. 1991. Race and disparities in sentencing: A test of the liberation hypothesis. *Justice Quarterly* 8:305–327.

Spohn, Cassia, and Miriam DeLone. In press. When does race matter?: An analysis of the conditions under which race affects sentence severity. *Sociology of Crime, Law, and Deviance.*

Spohn, Cassia, Miriam DeLone, and Jeffrey Spears. 1998. Race/ethnicity, gender, and sentence severity in Dade County: An examination of the decision to withhold adjudication. *Journal of Crime and Justice* 21:111–138.

Spohn, Cassia, John Gruhl, and Susan Welch. 1981–1982. The effect of race on sentencing: A re-examination of an unsettled question. *Law & Society Review* 16:72–88.

Spohn, Cassia, and David Holleran. 2000. Research note: The imprisonment penalty paid by young, unemployed black and Hispanic male offenders. *Criminology* 38:501–526.

Spohn, Cassia, and Jeffrey Spears. 2000. Sentencing of drug offenders in three cities: Does race/ethnicity make a difference? In *Crime control and social justice: A delicate balance,* edited by Darnell F. Hawkins, Samuel L. Myers, Jr., and Randolph N. Stone. Westport, Connecticut: Greenwood Publishing Group.

Steffensmeier, Darrell, Jeffery Ulmer, and John Kramer. 1998. The interaction of race, gender, and age in criminal sentencing: The punishment cost of being young, black, and male. *Criminology* 36:763–797.

Stolzenberg, Lisa, and Steward D'Alessio. 1994. Sentencing and unwarranted disparity: An empirical assessment of the long-term impact of sentencing guidelines in Minnesota. *Criminology* 32:301–310.

Tonry, Michael. 1996. *Sentencing matters.* New York: Oxford University Press.

———. 1995. *Malign neglect: Race, crime, and punishment in America.* New York: Oxford University Press.

Uhlman, Thomas M., and N. Darlene Walker. 1980. "He takes some of my time, I take some of his": An analysis of judicial sentencing patterns in jury cases. *Law & Society Review* 14:323–341.

Ulmer, Jeffery T. 1997. *Social worlds of sentencing: Court communities under sentencing guidelines.* Albany: State University of New York Press.

Ulmer, Jeffery T., and John H. Kramer. 1996. Court communities under sentencing guidelines: Dilemmas of formal rationality and sentencing disparity. *Criminology* 34:383–408.

U.S. General Accounting Office. 1992. *Sentencing guidelines: Central questions remain unanswered.* Washington, D.C.

U.S. Sentencing Commission. 1999. *Simplification draft paper: Departures and offender characteristics.* Washington, D.C.

———. 1995. *Substantial assistance departures in the United States courts.* Draft Final Report. Washington, D.C.

———. 1991a. *The Federal sentencing guidelines: A report on the operation of the guidelines system and short-term impacts on disparity in sentencing, use of incarceration, and prosecutorial discretion and plea bargaining.* Washington, D.C.

———. 1991b. *Special report to the Congress: Mandatory minimum penalties in the Federal criminal justice system.* Washington, D.C.

Walker, Samuel, Cassia Spohn, and Miriam DeLone. 1999. *The color of justice: Race, eth-*

nicity, and crime in America. 2d ed. Belmont, California: Wadsworth.

Walsh, Anthony. 1987. The sexual stratification hypothesis and sexual assault in light of the changing conceptions of race. *Criminology* 25:153–173.

Weisburd, David. 1992. Sentencing disparities and the guidelines: Taking a closer look. *Federal Sentencing Reporter* 5:149–152.

Wilbanks, William. 1987. *The myth of a racist criminal justice system.* Monterey, California: Brooks/Cole Publishing Company.

Wooldredge, John. 1998. Analytical rigor in studies of disparities in criminal case processing. *Journal of Quantitative Criminology* 14:155–179.

Zatz, Marjorie S. 1987. The changing forms of racial/ethnic biases in sentencing. *Journal of Research in Crime and Delinquency* 24:69–92.

———. 1984. Race, ethnicity, and determinate sentencing: A new dimension to an old controversy. *Criminology* 22:147–171.

NOTES AND QUESTIONS

1. What evidence does Spohn point to as illustration of what she calls "clear and convincing" racial disparity in sentencing? What four possible explanations does she suggest to explain why this disparity exists? Do you find any of these more plausible than the others? Would you flatly reject any of the explanations? Why or why not?

2. How does Spohn define and use the terms *disparity* and *discrimination?* What is the fundamental difference between the two concepts? Why is this distinction important to Spohn's discussion?

3. What questions does Spohn set out to answer with her analysis? Why is older sentencing data problematic for the purposes of her inquiry?

4. What do Spohn's results suggest about state-level sentencing disparity compared with federal level? How does this support and/or undermine Gertner's

depiction of the problems with federal sentencing guidelines? How likely is a judge to exercise discretion (depart from the guidelines) at the state versus the federal level? Who tends to benefit from such uses of judicial discretion?

5. Analyzing disparity at different stages in the sentencing process, Spohn writes that "Race/ethnicity is a stronger predictor of the decision to incarcerate or not than the decision concerning sentence length." Why might this be the case?

6. Ultimately, how effective have sentencing reforms been with regard to reducing discrimination and disparity? Why does Spohn pay particular attention to the "war on drugs" and its impact on sentencing disparities? How has the drug war detracted from the gains that might have been achieved over the last three decades by sentencing reforms?

7. To what extent does Spohn answer criticisms leveled at previous inquiries into discrimination and disparity in the criminal justice system? What limitations remain in her analysis? What would you question or dispute about her findings?

Chapter 46

Sizing up Sentences

Michael Higgins

Corporate scandals, highly paid executives committing fraud, workers and stockholders losing their life savings—Americans have had several recent reminders of the prevalence and significance of white-collar crimes of the kind discussed by Mann in Chapter 36. Names like Enron, WorldCom, and Arthur Andersen have become symbols of greed and deception. They have raised anew the public's ire about crimes committed with the pen or the computer rather than the gun and have focused attention on sentencing disparities between white collar and street offenses.

Although systematic comparisons are very difficult, it appears that white-collar offenders are less likely to get sentenced to prison or more likely to receive shorter prison terms than are street offenders. The problem in making that comparison is to identify comparable white collar and street offenses. Because the two best predictors of sentencing severity traditionally have been the presence of violence in a crime and whether an offender had a prior criminal record, it is not surprising that white-collar offenders get more lenient treatment.

Nonetheless, attitudes may be changing. As the next reading notes, between 1993 and 1997, 51 percent of white-collar offenders convicted in the nation's federal district courts received some jail time. Yet Michael Higgins points out another kind of disparity that federal sentencing guidelines have not fixed, namely, disparity based on geography. Depending on where in the federal system an offender is prosecuted, the of-fender's sentencing will be more or less severe. For example, in the Western District of Wisconsin, 8 out of 10 white-collar offenders receive prison time; in Arizona, by contrast, fewer than 3 out of 10 go to prison.

Higgins notes several factors in the sentencing guidelines that give prosecutors leeway on how to charge white-collar criminals. Among the most important is the discretion accorded to prosecutors about how to classify the money at issue in a case and to determine whether an offender will be credited with cooperating with the government. Whatever the cause, it seems clear that variations in leniency and severity persist even when the rules governing sentencing are uniform.

In the world of criminal sentencing, the most violent criminals—the killers, rapists and robbers—can be the easiest cases. We all know, or think we know, what should be done with them.

But the sentencing of white-collar crooks—the embezzlers, the scam artists, the contractors who overbill the government—can be a trickier matter. Some suggest saving scarce prison cells for the violent criminals; others balk at the idea of allowing white-collar crooks to "buy their way out" of prison by paying a fine or restitution.

So which view reigns in the federal criminal justice system? The answer appears to be both, judging by disparities in white-collar sentencing throughout 90 federal districts.

For white-collar defendants, the choice between diverging views can mean the difference between prison and freedom. Stephen Hurley, a criminal defense lawyer in Madison, Wis., saw that in the early 1990s when he represented a 58-year-old letter carrier caught in a sting operation.

To test its carriers, the government had put $5 bills in translucent envelopes marked "Green Giant Rebate Offer," Hurley says. One of the envelopes "was placed on his route—to an address that clearly didn't exist and a name that was incorrect," he says. "It's a rebate, so [the carrier says], 'Hell, the company's not expecting it back. I'll just keep it.'"

The carrier was fired and lost his pension. Then, to Hurley's dismay, the government prosecuted, sending his client to jail for several months.

Meanwhile, in the nearby Eastern District of Wisconsin, "Those cases were not even being prosecuted," Hurley says. "I remember just being so sad about the case. . . . I believe there was a great disparity among districts in how these cases were treated."

After that instance, the local U.S. attorney in Madison revised the policy on postal sting cases to be more lenient, Hurley says.

But statistics analyzed by the *ABA Journal* suggest that variations remain in how white-collar criminals are treated throughout the federal system. . . .

GEOGRAPHICAL DIFFERENCES

Nationwide from 1993 to 1997, about one white-collar defendant was sentenced to prison for every two convicted. . . . But prosecutors in some districts were either more willing or more able to put white-collar crooks behind bars.

In the Western District of Wisconsin, more than eight white-collar criminals were sent to prison for every 10 who were convicted. In the Southern District of Florida, the number was more than six for every 10.

Contrast those numbers with figures for the same period in the District of New Jersey, where fewer than three white-collar defendants went to prison for every 10 convicted. In Arizona, the ratio was also fewer than three of 10. . . .

The goal of the federal sentencing guidelines is uniformity—the same conduct yielding the same punishment. Yet, "Everyone knows the guidelines have not achieved that," Hurley argues. "You only have to look at your [white-collar sentencing] statistics to see that."

PROSECUTOR POWER

The sentencing guidelines, put into effect in 1987, attempt to standardize sentences by assigning an offense level, or point value, to every federal crime. Then the guidelines mandate that points be added or subtracted for factors such as a criminal's prior record. Once the point total is determined, judges must sentence the defendant within certain fairly narrow bounds.

But former prosecutors and other experts say that in reality, the process is not that simple. Various factors in the guidelines give prosecutors leeway on how to charge.

For example, prosecutors have more discretion than is sometimes acknowledged to classify the amount of money at issue in a case. Prosecutors also have discretion in deciding which charges to bring. There is also discretion in which cases to bring, and which to leave for state authorities. And there are questions of when a defendant will be credited with substantial assistance for aiding a prosecution, a key to reducing the sentence.

"In practice, the prosecutors have a lot of discretion," says Michael Simons, a former federal prosecutor in the Southern District of New York who is now a law professor at St. John's University in Jamaica, N.Y. He says the reason is partly that "prosecutors control the facts."

How does it work? Unlike, say, a bank robbery, white-collar crimes frequently unfold over a longer period of time. Simons recalls a case in which the defendant had sent small, phony invoices to public companies to try to trick them into paying. The schemer was eventually caught, but bank and phone records didn't clearly reveal how much the scam had netted.

The final plea agreement, like the vast majority of plea agreements, contained a stipulation as to the amount of the loss, Simons says. "It was the subject of some negotiation. It was inexact."

That bargaining can be crucial for the defendant, says T. Mark Flanagan Jr., a former federal prosecutor in the District of Columbia who is now a partner at McKenna & Cuneo in Washington, D.C. "Loss is what drives—more than any other variable—the amount of the prison term," he says.

A basic fraud case, say, in the defense contracting or health care area, might have a base offense level of six, says Flanagan, who cochairs the Sentencing Guidelines Subcommittee of the ABA Criminal Justice Section's White Collar Crime Committee.

Then if the amount at issue was more than $70,000 but less than $120,000, for example, the guidelines add six points for a total of 12 points. That already would qualify the defendant for a 10- to 16-month sentence, although the judge would have some flexibility in regard to how much time the defendant served.

"It doesn't take a lot money...when you're talking about a white-collar fraud case," Flanagan says.

PLAYING THE CHARGE CARD

There's also discretion over how to charge crimes, Flanagan says. Take the case of someone who is lying to cover up a crime. Should prosecutors tack on a charge of making false statements, or the generally more severe obstruction of justice? "Some might go with the false statements; some might go with the obstruction of justice," he says.

Legally, the prosecutor is obligated to bring the charge that most directly applies to the facts of the case, Flanagan says. "Having said that, I'm still saying that there is flexibility," he adds. And, "There is variation among jurisdictions as to how they use that flexibility." ...

Another key decision prosecutors make is when to credit cooperating defendants with "substantial assistance," the key phrase that determines whether a defendant who rolls over for the government has rolled far enough to stay out of prison. If a prosecutor finds a defendant's help to be substantial, the prosecutor can make a motion noting that fact. Without that motion, the judge has no authority to reduce the offender's sentence.

But prosecutors can interpret that key phrase in different ways. Sometimes telling everything you know is good enough. In other cases, that information must be truly new information, not merely confirming what investigators already know. "You must always check with the district you are practicing in to see what the policy is," Poston says.

In some cases, prosecutors demand that the information lead to the conviction of another person, Poston says. In that scenario, "If this person you're cooperating against doesn't plead out, you're stuck with [the result of] a trial," she says.

"That is a huge issue," Shein says. "There are no guidelines as to what . . . constitutes substantial assistance. So you get a very inconsistent application of what happens to someone for their substantial assistance."

So what's going on, for example, in the Western District of Wisconsin, where the most white-collar criminals are going to prison? Nothing but prosecutors following the law, says the U.S. attorney for the district, Peggy Lautenschlager.

Lautenschlager points out that Justice Department policies require lawyers in her office to charge the most serious offenses they believe they can prove. She says her office isn't making a special, conscious effort to send white-collar crooks to prison. (Hurley's postal carrier case happened before Lautenschlager's tenure.)

They are not adding money laundering charges to fraud complaints, a practice Lautenschlager says she doesn't think would account for disparities anyway. And Lautenschlager says the district's white-collar cases have largely involved one defendant acting alone. So substantial assistance has rarely been a consideration.

However, Lautenschlager is quick to acknowledge that when it comes to the dollar amount involved in a fraud, her office is unbending. It's her duty to prove the full extent of a loss, she says, and it's also what the district's judges require. Judges in Madison are more than ready to throw out plea agreements they don't like, and they turn instead to the federal probation office for an assessment of the amount of money involved in a case. . . .

LENIENCY WITHOUT A CAUSE

And what is happening in districts where proportionately fewer white-collar criminals are going to prison?

Officials at the Justice Department referred the *Journal's* questions about variations to the individual districts. In the federal district of New Jersey, spokesman Alan Ables says the office won't comment on any plea bargaining practices or on how judges sentence in the district.

In the federal district of Arizona, officials say they can't tell, based on the numbers available, why Arizona appears to be sending fewer white-collar crooks away.

"I can't think of any reason why it would be Arizona in particular," says Cathy Colbert, spokeswoman for the U.S. attorney's office in Phoenix. "It could be that they're all first-time offenders, but it would be odd that it would fall that way."

It's also possible that the district has been taking lower-dollar-value cases, with $10,000 to $15,000 in losses, that other federal prosecutors might pass on, Colbert says. But she says the office doesn't have statistics to either confirm or disprove that.

In any event, Colbert says the office has taken steps recently that may change the statistical outlook.

For one, the office has changed its approach to bank teller cases, in which a bank employee is caught taking money from the cash drawer. The prosecutors had commonly charged tellers with both a misdemeanor and felony count, then allowed the defendant to plead to the misdemeanor, Colbert says. They're less flexible now, taking only clear felony cases and not bargaining.

And the office recently added a prosecutor who specializes in asset forfeiture and money laundering issues, Colbert says. "You didn't see money laundering in any of our indictments until the last year," she says. "That is something that our office is definitely beefing up, and as that continues to be added to indictments obviously our numbers will change."

What is it that determines whether a district is a good or bad place to be a white-collar crime defendant?

One theory is that smaller, lower-volume districts can afford to be tougher. Hurley of Western Wisconsin says, "In our jurisdiction, where you don't have that many criminal cases, the inducement isn't there" for prosecutors to bargain—or for judges to accept bargains to move cases along.

The more rural districts "are not facing the same pressures they are in the bigger cities," agrees Leonard Cavise, a professor at DePaul law school in Chicago.

But other experts suggest that large, busy districts may be more likely to decline smaller cases, thus leaving themselves mostly prison-worthy cases to prosecute. . . .

Big districts also may have big resources. In the Southern District of Florida, prosecutors have a special health-care fraud task force and other specialized units. Those prosecutors "have a vested interest . . .in that particular genre of cases," Rothman says. "They're going to really stay focused on those particular cases" and not be willing to deal as much.

Officials at the U.S. attorney's office in Miami did not return calls seeking comment.

A clear message from the data is hard to come by. Russell Commbs, a law professor at Rutgers law school in Camden, N.J., calls prosecutors' charging decisions "a big possible source of these variations." But he notes, too, that there are other possibilities, and it's hard to know without delving into the facts in every case. "If you want to know why are there variations, . . .you have to go beyond the data they're giving us," he says.

Tim McGrath, interim staff director of the U.S. Sentencing Commission, makes the same point. The data "doesn't take into consideration the mix of the crimes or the severity of the conduct," he says. "Those issues have to be explored further before you can make any determination whether there is any disparity."

But McGrath also acknowledges that the commission hasn't done any work that would explain variances among districts. Simple demographics don't seem to be the answer; rural districts aren't consistently tougher than urban ones, for example.

So What's the Problem?

To what extent is the variation a problem? Not surprisingly, defense attorneys say the problem is that tough jurisdictions push for prison time in too many cases. And of course, prosecutors and crime victims are more likely to worry about jurisdictions where fraud defendants seem to escape jail too often.

But in any case, should we be worried that the outcome of some cases may depend on geography?

Frank Tuerkheimer, a law professor at the University of Wisconsin in Madison, says some geographic variation is acceptable. Tuerkheimer, U.S. attorney in the Western District of Wisconsin during the Carter administration, says the tough-on-white-collar-crime environment may make sense for the district.

White-collar crime, because it requires planning, "is a wonderful, prototypical example of deterrable conduct," Tuerkheimer reasons. "Somebody goes to jail [in Madison], everybody knows about it. In that way, it's a small town."

Tuerkheimer tells a story from his days as a prosecutor about a judge who was planning on giving a white-collar defendant probation. Then a newspaper reporter walked into the courtroom. The judge promptly sent the defendant to jail for 30 days.

"That judge changed that sentence when he saw it was going to be in the paper, and I can't say that's crazy," Tuerkheimer says. "There is a spirit among the judges here . . .of being concerned with general deterrence. It's part of the ethic of the place."

Hurley calls the idea that Madison is a model for deterrence "hogwash." Maybe tougher sentences make prosecutors feel good, but "I don't think our rate of white-collar crime has dropped," he says. "There just isn't data to support that notion."

Hurley sees it as a simple case of a lack of uniformity. "They're harsh here," he says. "My assumption is [defendants] will always go to prison."

Others see notice as the key factor. Extreme numbers on either side might be troubling, says Edward Ohlbaum, a professor at Temple law school in Philadelphia and the head of the school's clinical program in criminal law. But to the extent a district wants to be tough and has a well-known reputation for that, "I'm not sure there's anything particularly wrong with that. There's a component of notice and fairness in that."

Ohlbaum says he would be more troubled by variation within a district. For example, if a district sent small-time thieves packing but gave probation to more affluent white-collar offenders, that would be unfair.

But Shein suggests there could be a policy regarding how U.S. attorneys make decisions on topics such as when to credit substantial assistance or when to charge money laundering.

"There's got to be some coordination in this," she argues. "Where is their balance? I don't think you're ever going to fix it 100 percent. But you can get better guidance" for U.S. attorneys.

Notes and Questions

1. Is geographic sentencing disparity a serious problem? How does it compare with racial or class-based sentencing disparities?

2. Based on Higgins' account, does prosecutorial discretion have a greater impact on sentencing disparities in white-collar cases than in other types of criminal cases? How should judicial discretion be balanced with the uniform application of

federal sentencing guidelines? To what extent are district-to-district sentencing disparities inevitable?

3. Higgins quotes one legal scholar who calls white-collar crime "a wonderful, prototypical example of deterrable conduct." Do white-collar criminals respond differently than street criminals to displays of severe punishment? What problems does Higgins identify with sentencing disparities in white-collar cases?

4. Federal sentencing guidelines for criminal drug offenses rely partially on quantitative measures of the drug transaction to determine the statutory punishment. According to Higgins, white-collar criminal statutes use monetary loss to determine the severity of punishment. In your opinion, should such loss be considered?

5. Recall Mann's depiction (Chapter 36) of the "information control defense" employed in most white-collar criminal cases. In light of this common tactic, how much do prosecutors depend on "substantial assistance" from the defendant to get a conviction? Is it fair for white-collar defendants to be granted lighter sentences simply because they cooperated with a criminal investigation? Is it avoidable that white-collar offenders are treated more leniently?

Reprinted from: Michael Higgins, "Sizing up Sentences" in *ABA Journal*, November 1999, pp. 42–47. Copyright © 1999. Reprinted with the permission of the *ABA Journal*. ✦

Conclusion to Part IV

Legal rules, legislative enactments, and judicial decisions provide tools with which law seeks to work in the world. But those rules, enactments, and decisions are not self-executing or self-enforcing. They must be interpreted and given meaning by people occupying other roles in the legal system—e.g., trial judges, prosecutors, defense attorneys. Interpretive processes involve attending to the language of the law, assigning meaning to it, and then adapting meanings in particular circumstances. Whether as a prosecutor in plea bargaining, a defense lawyer trying to prevent the indictment of a client, a juror in the criminal trial, or a judge sentencing someone under the Federal Sentencing Guidelines, the processes through which law is given life in the daily operations of institutions are shaped by organizational context, the structure of distinctive roles, the pull of conscience and group loyalty, and views of what *justice* requires in individual cases.

The readings in Part IV take us inside law's own social organization to see these forces at work, but they also draw our attention to the ways the people and processes within the legal bureaucracy respond to the social world beyond its borders. They show us how class, gender, and race affect the processing of criminal cases. Sometimes the effect of these social forces is pretty blunt, as in alleged race-based nullification by African-American jurors; sometimes their effect is more subtle and hard to detect, as in the continuing salience of race in federal sentencing. But whether blunt or subtle, these influences remind us that law is socially organized.

As they interpret, apply, and adapt legal rules, officials may be pulled toward leniency, such as in plea bargaining, because of the demands of the institutions within which they work and to make the punishment fit the offense and the offender. However, they may move toward severity as a response to those who refuse to cooperate with what officials believe to be their legitimate demands (e.g., sentencing more severely criminal defendants who insist on going to trial rather than entering a plea) or because they believe severe punishment is necessary for the protection of innocent citizens. Moreover, what we have seen in the context of criminal justice is replicated every day elsewhere in the legal system, as officials in government agencies regulate business practices in a more or less stringent way, as jurors in civil cases decide whether or not to impose punitive damages, or as judges in divorce cases decide on the amount of child support that a parent must provide for his or her child. Whatever their motives, these officials give life to law as they find the points at which rules, institutional pressures, and personal commitments shape responses to individual cases. ✦

Suggested Additional Readings for Part IV

FROM SEVERITY TO LENIENCY: PLEA BARGAINING AND THE POSSIBILITY OF JUSTICE

Albert Alschuler, "The Prosecutor's Role in Plea Bargaining," 36 *University of Chicago Law Review* (1965), 50.

Milton Heumann, *Plea Bargaining: The Experiences of Prosecutors, Judges, and Defense Attorneys.* Chicago: University of Chicago Press, 1977.

Donald Maynard, *Inside Plea Bargaining.* New York: Plenum, 1984.

Stephen Schulhofer, "Plea Bargaining as Disaster," 101 *Yale Law Journal* (1992), 1979.

Jeffrey Standen, "Plea Bargaining in the Shadow of the Guidelines," 81 *California Law Review* (1993), 1471.

Mary Vogel, "The Social Origins of Plea Bargaining: Conflict and the Law in the Process of State Formation," 33 *Law & Society Review* (1999), 161.

LAWYERS IN CRIMINAL CASES

Albert Alschuler, "The Defense Attorney's Role in Plea Bargaining," 84 *Yale Law Journal* (1975), 1179.

William McDonald, *The Defense Counsel.* Beverly Hills, CA: Sage, 1979.

Austin Sarat, "Between (the Presence of) Violence and (the Possibility of) Justice: Lawyering Against Capital Punishment," in *Cause Lawyering: Political Commitments and Professional Responsibilities,* Austin Sarat and Stuart Scheingold, eds. New York: Oxford University Press (1998), 317.

William Simon, "Moral Pluck: Legal Ethics in Popular Culture," 101 *Columbia Law Review* (2001), 421.

JURIES IN CRIMINAL CASES: BIASED OR CONSCIENTIOUS JUDGMENT

Jeffrey Abramson, *We the Jury: The Jury System and the Ideal of Democracy.* Cambridge, MA: Harvard University Press, 2000.

Alan Alschuler and A. G. Deiss, "A Brief History of the Criminal Jury in the United States," 61 *University of Chicago Law Review* (1994), 867.

David Baldus, George Woodworth, David Zuckerman, Neil Alan Weiner, and Barbara Broffittet, "The Use of Peremptory Challenges in Capital Murder Trials: A Legal and Empirical Analysis," 3 *University of Pennsylvania Journal of Constitutional Law* (2001), 3.

D. Graham Burnett, "Anatomy of a Verdict: The View From the Juror's Chair," *New York Times Magazine* (August 26, 2001), 32.

Hiroshi Fukurai, Edgar W. Butler, and Richard Krooth, *Race and the Jury: Racial Disenfranchisement and the Search for Justice.* New York: Plenum, 1993.

Nancy King, "The American Criminal Jury," 62 *Law and Contemporary Problems* (1999), 41.

Sally Lloyd-Bostock, "The Effects on Juries of Hearing About the Defendant's Previous Criminal Record: A Simulation Study," *Criminal Law Review* (2000), 734.

Alan Scheflin, "Jury Nullification: The Right to Say No," 45 *Southern California Law Review* (1972), 168.

Rita Simon, *The Jury and the Defense of Insanity.* Boston: Little, Brown, 1967.

SENTENCING

Andrew Ashworth, *Sentencing and Criminal Justice,* 3rd edition. London: Butterworth, 2000.

Anthony Bottoms, "The Philosophy and Politics of Punishment and Sentencing," in *The Politics of Sentencing Reform,* Chris Clarkson and Rod Morgan, eds. New York: Oxford University Press, 1994, 17–50.

Shawn Bushway and Anne Morrison Piehl, "Judging Judicial Discretion: Legal Factors and Racial Discrimination in Sentencing," 35 *Law & Society Review* (2001), 733.

Daniel Fried, "Federal Sentencing in the Wake of Guidelines: Unacceptable Limits on the Discretion of Sentencers," 101 *Yale Law Journal* (1992), 1681.

Harmelin v. Michigan, 501 US (1990), 957.

Julian Roberts, "The Role of Criminal Record in the Sentencing Process," in Michael Tonry, ed. *Crime and Justice: A Review of Research* 1997, 22, 303–362.

Cassia Spohn, "The Sentencing Decisions of Black and White Judges: Expected and Unexpected Similarities," 24 *Law & Society Review* (1990), 1197.

Michael Tonry, *Malign Neglect: Race, Crime, and Punishment in America.* New York: Oxford University Press, 1995.

Stanton Wheeler, Kenneth Mann, and Austin Sarat, *Sitting in Judgment: The Sentencing of White-Collar Criminals.* New Haven, CT: Yale University Press, 1988. ✦

Part V

Organizing Law's Violence

Violence of all kinds is done every day with the explicit authorization of legal institutions and officials or with their tacit acquiescence. Law is, by definition, the monopoly of legitimate violence in society. Death is authorized and carried out. People are arrested and find themselves in jail. Property is taken and personal liberty abridged. Some of this violence is done directly by legal officials and some by persons whose violent acts subsequently will be deemed acceptable (e.g., self-defense). The violence done, authorized, or condoned by law's institutions occurs with all the normal abnormality of bureaucratic abstraction in which violence is presented as a routine act of rule following. It is, as a result, sometimes difficult to trace who is responsible for it. Moreover, law's violence has played a small role, and occupied little space, in legal theory and jurisprudence. By failing to confront law's lethal character, legal theory misses much of the moral significance of the social organization of law.

As Robert M. Cover (Chapter 14) noted, the law combines words and violence, language and violent deeds. Its efficacy depends on a distinct division of labor. Those who authorize law's violence, i.e., judges, do not carry it out. Yet judges do violence in both a symbolic and instrumental sense. The violence of legal interpretation is disembodied.

Or rather, the violence that judges authorize is done to people disembodied by law's procedures and its fictions, people stripped of their history and connection to the human community.

Those who deploy law's violence (e.g., police, wardens, jailers, executioners) do so only on the authority of others. If control from above is too tight or rigid, the deployment of law's violence cannot be effective. If, on the other hand, there is too little control from above, law's violence may be applied in a chaotic and even excessive manner and thus come to resemble extra-legal violence. Indeed, it is this distinctive combination of violence and bureaucracy that makes law possible.

The third and last dilemma in the social organization of law involves the ability of legal actors to dispense and, at the same time, control law's violence, to use it in a way that insures it is responsive to common normative standards. This is a problem of bureaucratic control, of the ability to govern violence through rules. In this sense, it provides yet another occasion for the classic law and society interest in determining whether the law on the books controls the law in action. The readings in Part V examine various agents and instances of law's violence in the work of police, jailers, and executioners and raise questions about the salience of social factors, especially race, in explaining how, when, and why law deploys its violence.

As you read the chapters in Part V, you might ask how law's violence differs from violence outside the law. ✦

Section XII

Policing the Police

Chapter 47

Justice Without Trial

Jerome H. Skolnick

The police are among the most visible agents of law's violence. In the United States and many other nations, they are armed and authorized to use force in situations where it would be illegal for ordinary citizens to do so. The police operate in hierarchical organizations and often seek a military style of discipline. Their activities are subject to an elaborate array of legal rules, from constitutional prohibitions against unreasonable searches and seizures to local ordinances and regulations. If law's violence is to be effectively organized and controlled, the rules governing the police must themselves be effective.

In recent years, two debates have been crucial to understanding the contemporary realities of policing. First, police and policing have been the subject of considerable scrutiny as debate has raged over the question of whether different styles of policing make a difference in the battle against crime. Second, police have been involved in several high-profile incidents of questionable conduct. Beatings of suspects, as in the Rodney King incident in Los Angeles in the early 1990s, were recorded on videotape. There have also been several shootings of unarmed citizens, for example the shooting of Amadou Diallo in New York in 1999. These incidents produced intense controversy about the extent to which police act responsibly in deploying law's violence.

In modern society, police are charged with the tasks of maintaining order and enforcing the law. They are authorized to use force to accomplish these tasks. In addition, policing is an inherently dangerous task and one with substantial low-visibility discretion. Most of what the police do, they do in one-on-one encounters with citizens. How they act and how they treat those with whom they interact are enormously important.

The first reading in this chapter highlights the continuing tension between the demands of order maintenance and fidelity to law. Law restrains the exercise of police power, subjecting it to procedure and discipline. This restraint complicates the task of maintaining order. We expect the police to keep us safe, but to do so in a way that respects legal values.

Yet the demands of law do not take into account the working environment of the police, an environment of danger and continuous threats to their authority. To reduce danger and maximize authority, police develop what Skolnick labels "a perceptual shorthand to identify certain kinds of people as symbolic assailants," that is, as people whose dress, language, and behavior suggest a possibility of violence. Reacting to these symbolic assailants is rational from the point of view of the police. However, it also opens up the possibility of racial profiling by the police in which members of minority groups are singled out for intense surveillance and in which race itself becomes one basis for arousing the suspicions of police.

As you read the selection from Skolnick, consider whether the demands that the legal system makes on police should be changed to bring them more into line with the working conditions of the police, or whether new legal regulations are necessary to produce more effective control of the police.

For what social purpose do police exist? What values do the police serve in a democratic society? Are the police to be principally an agency of social control, with their chief value the efficient enforcement of the prohibitive norms of substantive criminal law? Or are the police to be an institution falling under the hegemony of the legal system, with a basic commitment to the rule of law, even if this obligation may result in a reduction of social order? How does this dilemma of democratic society hamper the capacity of the police, institutionally and individually, to respond to legal standards of law enforcement? . . .

The purpose of this study is to show. . .how value conflicts of democratic society create conditions undermining the capacity of police to respond to the rule of law. Its chief conclusion (and orienting hypothesis), elaborated in the closing chapter, may be summarized: *The police in democratic society are required to maintain order and to do so under the rule of law. As functionaries charged with maintaining order, they are part of the bureaucracy. The ideology of democratic bureaucracy emphasizes initiative rather than disciplined adherence to rules and regulations. By contrast, the rule of law emphasizes the rights of individual citizens and constraints upon the initiative of legal officials. This tension between the operational consequences of ideas of order, efficiency, and initiative, on the one hand, and legality, on the other, constitutes the principle problem of police as a democratic legal organization.* . . .

LAW AND ORDER: THE SOURCE OF THE DILEMMA

If the police could maintain order without regard to legality, their short-run difficulties would be considerably diminished. However, they are inevitably concerned with interpreting legality because of their use of *law* as an instrument of order. The criminal law contains a set of rules for the maintenance of social order. This arsenal comprises the *substantive* part of the criminal law, that is, the elements of crime, the principles under which the accused is to be held accountable for alleged crime, the principles justifying the enactment of specific prohibitions, and the crimes themselves. Sociologists usually concentrate here, asking how well this control system operates, analyzing the conditions under which it achieves intended goals, and the circumstances rendering it least efficient.[1]

Another part of the criminal law, however, regulates the conduct of state officials charged with processing citizens who are suspected, accused, or found guilty of crime.[2] Involved here are such matters as the law of search, the law of arrest, the elements and degree of proof, the right to counsel, the nature of a lawful accusation of crime, and the fairness of trial. The procedures of the criminal law, therefore, stress protection of individual liberties *within* a system of social order.[3]

This dichotomy suggests that the common juxtaposition of "law and order" is an oversimplification. Law is not merely an instrument of order, but may frequently be its adversary.[4] There are communities that appear disorderly to some (such as Bohemian communities valuing diversity), but which nevertheless maintain a substantial degree of legality. The contrary may also be found: a situation where order is well maintained, but where the policy and practice of legality is not evident. The totalitarian social system, whether in a nation or an institution, is a situation of order without rule of law. Such a situation is probably best illustrated by martial rule, where military authority may claim and exercise the power of amnesty and detention without warrant. If, in addition, the writ of habeas corpus, the right to inquire into these acts, is suspended, as it typically is under martial rule, the executive can exercise arbitrary powers.[5] Such a system of social control is efficient, but does not conform to generally held notions about the "rule of law."

Although there is no precise definition of the rule of law, or its synonym, the principle of legality, its essential element is the reduction of arbitrariness by officials—for example, constraints on the activities of the police—and of arbitrariness in positive law by the application of "rational principles of civic order."[6] . . .

... [W]hen law is used as the instrument of social order, it necessarily poses a dilemma. The phrase "law and order" is misleading because it draws attention away from the substantial incompatibilities existing between the two ideas. Order under law suggests procedures different from achievement of "social control" through threat of coercion and summary judgment. Order under law is concerned not merely with the achievement of regularized social activity but with the means used to come by peaceable behavior, certainly with procedure, but also with positive law. It would surely be a violation of the rule of law for a legislature to make epilepsy a crime, even though a public "seizure" typically disturbs order in the community. While most law enforcement officials regard drug addicts as menacing to the community, a law making it a crime to *be* an addict has been declared unconstitutional.[7] This example, purposely selected from substantive criminal law, indicates that conceptions of legality apply here as well as in the more traditional realm of criminal procedure. In short, "law" and "order" are frequently found to be in opposition, because law implies rational restraint upon the rules and procedures utilized to achieve order. Order under law, therefore, subordinates the ideal of conformity to the ideal of legality....

THE SECLUSION OF ADMINISTRATION: THE DILEMMA'S SETTING

... Police work constitutes the most secluded part of an already secluded system and therefore offers the greatest opportunity for arbitrary behavior. As invokers of the criminal law, the police frequently act in practice as its chief interpreter. Thus, they are necessarily called upon to test the limits of their legal authority. In so doing, they also define the operative legality of the system of administering criminal law. That is, if the criminal law is especially salient to a population which has more or less recurrent interactions with the police, it is the police who define the system of order to this population. This work of interpretation, this "notice-giving" function of police, is a crucial consideration in assessing the degree to which legality penetrates a system of criminal justice.

Whenever a system of justice takes on an *insular* character, a question is raised as to the degree of justice such a system is capable of generating. Lon L. Fuller, a legal philosopher, has suggested the broadest significance of the seclusion of criminal law administration when he discusses the affinity between legality and justice. He asserts that both share a common quality, since they act by known rule. Fuller discusses the significance of public scrutiny as follows:

> The internal morality of the law demands that there be rules, that they be made known, and that they be observed in practice by those charged with their administration. These demands may seem ethically neutral so far as the external aims of law are concerned. Yet, just as law is a precondition for good law, so acting by known rule is a precondition for any meaningful appraisal of the justice of law. "A lawless unlimited power" expressing itself solely in unpredictable and patternless interventions in human affairs could be said to be unjust only in the sense that it does not act by known rule. *It would be hard to call it unjust in any more specific sense until one discovered what hidden principle, if any, guided its interventions.* It is the virtue of a legal order conscientiously' constructed and administered that it exposes to public scrutiny the rules by which it acts.[8]

The system of justice without trial is not a system of "unpredictable and patternless interventions." Rather, it is one which operates against a background of known rules, but which also, especially in the instance of the police, develops a set of informal norms or "hidden principles" in response to the formal rules. These, in turn, are influential in determining how the formal rules actually operate. . . .

A Sketch of the Policeman's "Working Personality"

A recurrent theme of the sociology of occupations is the effect of a man's work on his outlook on the world.[9] Doctors, janitors, lawyers, and industrial workers develop distinctive ways of perceiving and responding to their environment. Here we shall concentrate on analyzing certain outstanding elements in the police milieu, danger, authority, and efficiency, as they combine to generate distinctive cognitive and behavioral responses in police: a "working personality." Such an analysis does not suggest that all police are alike in "working personality," but that there are distinctive cognitive tendencies in police as an occupational grouping. Some of these may be found in other occupations sharing similar problems. So far as exposure to danger is concerned, the policeman may be likened to the soldier. His problems as an authority bear a certain similarity to those of the schoolteacher, and the pressures he feels to prove himself efficient are not unlike those felt by the industrial worker. The combination of these elements, however, is unique to the policeman. Thus, the police, as a result of combined features of their social situation, tend to develop ways of looking at the world distinctive to themselves, cognitive lenses through which to see situations and events. The strength of the lenses may be weaker or stronger depending on certain conditions, but they are ground on a similar axis.

Analysis of the policeman's cognitive propensities is necessary to understand the practical dilemma faced by police required to maintain order under a democratic rule of law. We have discussed earlier how essential a conception of order is to the resolution of this dilemma. It was suggested that the paramilitary character of police organization naturally leads to a high evaluation of similarity, routine, and predictability. Our intention is to emphasize features of the policeman's environment interacting with the paramilitary police organization to generate a "working personality." Such an intervening concept should aid in explaining how the social environment of police affects their capacity to respond to the rule of law.

We also stated earlier that emphasis would be placed on the division of labor in the police department, that "operational law enforcement" could not be understood outside these special work assignments. It is therefore important to explain how the hypothesis emphasizing the generalizability of the policeman's "working personality" is compatible with the idea that police division of labor is an important analytic dimension for understanding "operational law enforcement." Compatibility is evident when one considers the different levels of analysis at which the hypotheses are being developed. Janowitz states, for example, that the military profession is more than an occupation; it is a "style of life" because the occupational claims over one's daily existence extend well beyond official duties. He is quick to point out that any profession performing a crucial "life and death" task, such as medicine, the ministry, or the police, develops such claims.[10] A conception like "working personality" of police should be understood to suggest an analytic breadth similar to that of "style of life." That is, just as the professional behavior of military officers with similar "styles of life" may differ notably depending upon whether they command an infantry battalion or participate in the work of an intelligence unit, so too does the professional behavior of police officers with similar "working personalities" vary with their assignments.

The policeman's "working personality" is most highly developed in his constabulary role of the man on the beat. For analytical purposes that role is sometimes regarded as an enforcement specialty, but in this general discussion of policemen as they comport themselves while working, the uniformed "cop" is seen as the foundation for the policeman's working personality. There is a sound organizational basis for making this assumption. The police, unlike the military, draw no caste distinction in socialization, even though their order of ranked titles approximates the military's. Thus, one cannot join a local police department as, for instance, a lieutenant, as a West Point graduate joins the army. Every officer of rank must serve an apprenticeship as a patrolman. This feature of police organization means that the constabulary role is the primary one for all police officers, and that whatever the special requirements of roles in enforcement specialties, they are carried out with a common background of constabulary experience. . . .

The element of authority reinforces the element of danger in isolating the policeman. Typically, the policeman is required to enforce laws representing puritanical morality, such as those prohibiting drunkenness, and also laws regulating the flow of public activity, such as traffic laws. In these situations the policeman directs the citizenry, whose typical response denies recognition of his authority, and stresses his obligation to respond to danger. The kind of man who responds well to danger, however, does not normally subscribe to codes of puritanical morality. As a result, the policeman is unusually liable to the charge of hypocrisy. That the whole civilian world is an audience for the policeman further promotes police isolation and, in consequence, solidarity. Finally, danger undermines the judicious use of authority. Where danger, as in Britain, is relatively less, the judicious application of authority is facilitated. Hence, British police may appear to be somewhat more attached to the rule of law, when, in fact, they may appear so because they face less danger, and they are as a rule better skilled than American police in creating the appearance of conformity to procedural regulations.

The Symbolic Assailant and Police Culture

In attempting to understand the policeman's view of the world, it is useful to raise a more general question: What are the conditions under which police, as authorities, may be threatened?[11] To answer this, we must look to the situation of the policeman in the community. One attribute of many characterizing the policeman's role stands out: the policeman is required to respond to assaults against persons and property. When a radio call reports an armed robbery and gives a description of the man involved, every policeman, regardless of assignment, is responsible for the criminal's apprehension. The *raison d'etre* of the policeman and the criminal law, the underlying collectively held moral sentiments which justify penal sanctions, arises ultimately and most clearly from the threat of violence and the possibility of danger to the community. Police who "lobby" for severe narcotics laws, for instance, justify their position on grounds that the addict is a harbinger of danger since, it is maintained, he requires one hundred dollars a day to support his habit, and he must steal to get it. Even though the addict is not typically a violent criminal, criminal penalties for addiction are supported on grounds that he may become one.

The policeman, because his work requires him to be occupied continually with potential violence, develops a perceptual shorthand to identify certain kinds of people as symbolic assailants, that is, as persons who use gesture, language, and attire that the policeman has come to recognize as a prelude to violence. This does not mean that violence by the symbolic assailant is necessarily predictable. On the contrary, the policeman responds to the vague indication of danger suggested by appearance.[12] Like the animals of the experimental psychologist, this policeman finds the threat of random damage more compelling than a predetermined and inevitable punishment. . . .

However complex the motives aroused by the element of danger, its consequences for sustaining police culture are unambiguous. This element requires him, like the combat soldier, the European Jew, the South African (white or black), to live in a world straining toward duality, and suggesting danger when "they" are perceived. Consequently, it is in the nature of the policeman's situation that his conception of order emphasize regularity and predictability. It is, therefore, a conception shaped by persistent *suspicion*. The English "copper," often portrayed as a courteous, easy-going, rather jolly sort of chap, on the one hand, or as a devil-may-care adventurer, on the other, is differently described by Colin MacInnes:

> The true copper's dominant characteristic, if the truth be known, is neither those daring nor vicious qualities that are sometimes attributed to him by friend or enemy, but an ingrained conservatism, and almost desperate love of the conventional. It is untidiness, disorder, the unusual, that a copper disapproves of most of all: far more, even than of crime which is merely a professional matter. Hence his profound dislike of people loitering in streets, dressing extravagantly, speaking with exotic accents, being strange, weak, eccentric, or simply any rare minority—of their doing, in fact, anything that cannot be safely predicted.[13]

Policemen are indeed specifically *trained* to be suspicious, to perceive events or changes in the physical surroundings that indicate the occurrence or probability of disorder. A former student who worked as a patrolman in a suburban New York police department describes this aspect of the policeman's assessment of the unusual:

> The time spent cruising one's sector or walking one's beat is not wasted time, though it can become quite routine. During this time, the most important thing for the officer to do is notice the *normal*. He must come to know the people in his area, their habits, their automobiles and their friends. He must learn what time the various shops close, how much money is kept on hand on different nights, what lights are usually left on, which houses are vacant . . . only then can he decide what persons or cars under what circumstances warrant the appellation "suspicious."[14]

The individual policeman's "suspiciousness" does not hang on whether he has personally undergone an experience that could objectively be described as hazardous. Personal experience of this sort is not the key to the psychological importance of exceptionality. Each, as he routinely carries out his work, will experience situations that threaten to become dangerous. Like the American Jew who contributes to "defense" organizations such as the Anti-Defamation League in response to Nazi brutalities he has never experienced personally, the policeman identifies with his fellow cop who has been beaten, perhaps fatally, by a gang of young thugs. . . .

Police Solidarity

All occupational groups share a measure of inclusiveness and identification. People are brought together simply by doing the same work and having similar career and salary problems. As several writers have noted, however, police show an unusually high degree of occupational solidarity. It is true that the police have a common employer and wear a uniform at work, but so do doctors, milkmen, and bus drivers. Yet it is doubtful that these workers have so close knit an occupation or so similar an outlook on the world as do police. Set apart from the conventional world, the policeman experiences an exceptionally strong tendency to find his social identity within his occupational milieu. . . .

Police Solidarity and Danger

There is still a question, however, as to the process through which danger and authority influence police solidarity. The effect of danger on police solidarity is revealed when we examine a chief complaint of police: lack of public support and public apathy. The complaint may have several referents including police pay, police prestige, and support from the legislature. But the repeatedly voiced broader meaning of the complaint is resentment at being taken for granted. The policeman does not believe that his status as civil servant should relieve the public of responsibility for law enforcement. he feels, however, that payment out of public coffers somehow obscures his humanity and, therefore, his need for help. As one put it:

> Jerry, a cop, can get into a fight with three or four tough kids, and there will be citizens passing by, and maybe they'll look, but they'll never lend a hand. It's their country too, but you'd never know it the way some of them act. They forget that we're made of flesh and blood too. They don't care what happens to the cop so long as they don't get a little dirty.

Although the policeman sees himself as a specialist in dealing with violence, he does not want to fight alone. He does not believe that his specialization relieves the general public of citizenship duties. Indeed, if possible, he would prefer to be the foreman rather than the workingman in the battle against criminals.

The general public, of course, does withdraw from the workaday world of the policeman. The policeman's responsibility for controlling dangerous and sometimes violent persons alienates the average citizen perhaps as much as does his authority over the average citizen. If the policeman's job is to insure that public order is maintained, the citizen's inclination is to shrink from the dangers of maintaining it. The citizen prefers to see the policeman as an automaton, because once the policeman's humanity is recognized, the citizen necessarily becomes implicated in the policeman's work, which is, after all, sometimes dirty and dangerous. What the policeman typically fails to realize is the extent he becomes tainted by the character of the work he

performs. The dangers of their work not only draws policemen together as a group but separates them from the rest of the population. Banton, for instance, comments:

> . . .patrolmen may support their fellows over what they regard as minor infractions in order to demonstrate to them that they will be loyal in situations that make the greatest demands upon their fidelity. . . .

> In the American departments I visited it seemed as if the supervisors shared many of the patrolmen's sentiments about solidarity. They too wanted their colleagues to back them up in an emergency, and they shared similar frustrations with the public.

Thus, the element of danger contains seeds of isolation which may grow in two directions. In one, a stereotyping perceptual shorthand is formed through which the police come to see certain signs as symbols of potential violence. The police probably differ in this respect from the general middle-class white population only in degree. This difference, however, may take on enormous significance in practice. Thus, the policeman works at identifying and possibly apprehending the symbolic assailant; the ordinary citizen does not. As a result, the ordinary citizen does not assume the responsibility to implicate himself in the policeman's required response to danger. The element of danger in the policeman's role alienates him not only from populations with a potential for crime but also from the conventionally respectable (white) citizenry, in short, from that segment of the population from which friends would ordinarily be drawn. As Janowitz has noted in a paragraph suggesting similarities between the police and the military, ". . .any profession which is continually preoccupied with the threat of danger requires a strong sense of solidarity if it is to operate effectively. Detailed regulation of the military style of life is expected to enhance group cohesion, professional loyalty, and maintain the martial spirit."[15]

CONCLUSION

The combination of *danger* and *authority* found in the task of the policeman unavoidably combine to frustrate procedural regularity. If it were possible to structure social roles with specific qualities, it would be wise to propose that these two should never, for the sake of the rule of law, be permitted to coexist. Danger typically yields self-defensive conduct, conduct that must strain to be impulsive because danger arouse fear and anxiety so easily. Authority under such conditions becomes a resource to reduce perceived threats rather than a series of reflective judgments arrived at calmly. The ability to be discreet, in the sense discussed above, is also affected. As a result, procedural requirements take on a "frilly" character, or at least tend to be reduced to a secondary position in the face of circumstances seen as threatening.

If this analysis is correct, it suggests a related explanation drawn from the realm of social environment to account for the apparent paradox that the elements of danger and authority are universally to be found in the policeman's role, yet at the same time fail to yield the same behavior regarding the rule of law. If the element of danger faced by the British policeman is less than that faced by his American counterpart, its ability to undermine the element of authority is proportionately weakened.

Notes

1. See, for example: Harry Elmer Barnes and Negley K. Teeters, *New Horizons in Criminology* (New York: Prentice Hall, 1951); Sheldon Glueck, *Crime and Correction: Selected Papers* (Cambridge: Addison-Wesley Press, 1952); Richard R. Korn and Lloyd W. McCorkle, *Criminology and Penology* (New York: Holt, 1959); Norval Morris, *The Habitual Criminal* (Cambridge: Harvard University Press, 1951); Joseph Slabey Roucek, *Sociology of Crime* (New York: Philosophical Library, 1961); Walter Cade Reckless, *The Crime Problem* (New York: Appleton-Century-Crofts, 1961); and Edwin Hardin Sutherland and Donald R. Cressey, *Principles of Criminology*, 6th ed. (Philadelphia: Lippincott, 1960).

   One exception is the text of Paul W. Tappan, which emphasizes criminal procedure in great detail. Tappan, it should be noted, however, was also trained as a lawyer. See *Crime, Justice and Correction* (New York: McGraw-Hill, 1960).

2. Thus, a current leading casebook in criminal law devotes its final sections to problems in the administration of criminal law. See Monrad G. Paulsen and Sanford H. Kadish, *Criminal Law and Its Processes* (Boston: Little, Brown and Company, 1962).

3. See Sol Rubin, Henry Wiehofen, George Edwards, and Simon Rosenzweig, *The Law of Criminal Correction* (St. Paul: West Publishing Co., 1963); Paul W. Tappan, op. cit.; and Lester B. Orfield, *Criminal Procedure from Arrest to Appeal* (New York: New York University Press, 1947). An excellent discussion of problems of criminal procedure is found in Abraham S. Goldstein, "The State and the Accused: Balance of Advantage in Criminal Procedure," *Yale Law Journal* 69 (June, 1960), 1149–1199.

4. See Alan Barth, *Law Enforcement Versus the Law* (New York: Collier Books, 1963).

5. See Charles Fairman, *The Law of Martial Rule* (Chicago: Callaghan and Company, 1943), especially Chapter 3, "The Nature of Martial Rule," pp. 28–49.

6. Philip Selznick, "Sociology and Natural Law," *Natural Law Forum*, 6 (1961), 95.

7. *United States v. Robinson*, 361 U.S. 220 (1959). Lon Fuller criticizes the grounds of the decision. The court held in this case that the statute violated the Eighth Amendment by imposing a "cruel and unusual punishment" for an "illness." Professor Fuller argues that the statute should have been overturned on grounds that it is both *ex post facto* and vague in *The Morality of Law* (New Haven: Yale University Press, 1964), pp. 105-106. My own position is in between, since I do not conceive of an addict as one who necessarily had the intent of becoming one when he began using drugs. Therefore, I find the *ex post facto* objection less than compelling. On whatever

grounds, however, the case stands as a good example of positive law in violation of the rule of law.

8. Fuller, op. cit., pp. 157–158. (Italics added.)

9. For previous contributions in this area, see the following: Ely Chinoy, *Automobile Workers and the American Dream* (Garden City: Doubleday and Company, Inc., 1955); Charles R. Walker and Robert II. Guest, *The Man on the Assembly Line* (Cambridge: Harvard University Press, 1952); Everett C. Hughes, "Work and The Self," in his Men and Their Work (Glencoe, Illinois: The Free Press, 1958),pp. 42–55; Harold L. Wilensky, Intellectuals in Labor Unions: Organizational Pressures on Professional Holes (Glencoe, Illinois: The Free Press, 1956); Wilensky, "Varieties of Work Experience," in Henry Borow (ed.), Man in a World at Work (Boston: Houghton Mifflin Company, 1964), pp. 125–154; Louis Kriesberg, "The Retail Furrier: Concepts of Security and Success," *American Journal of Sociology*, 57 (March, 1952), 478–485; Waldo Burchard, "Role Conflicts of Military Chaplains," *American Sociological Review,* 19 (October, 1954), 528–535; Howard S. Becker and Blanche Geer, "The Fate of Idealism in Medical School," *American Sociological Review,* 33 (1958), 50–56; and Howard S. Becker and Anselm L. Strauss, "Careers, Personality, and Adult Socialization," *American Journal of Sociology,* 62 (November, 1956), 253–363.

10. Morris Janowitz, *The Professional Soldier: A Social and Political Portrait* (New York: The Free Press of Glencoe, 1964), p. 175.

11. William Westley was the first to raise such questions about the police, when he inquired into the conditions under which police are violent. Whatever merit this analysis has, it owes much to his prior insights, as all subsequent sociological studies of the police must. See his "Violence and the Police," *American Journal of Sociology,* 59 (July, 1953), 34-41; also his unpublished Ph.D. dissertation *The Police: A Sociological Study of Law, Custom, and Morality,* University of Chicago, Department of Sociology, 1951.

12. Something of the flavor of the policeman's attitude toward the symbolic assailant comes across in a recent article by a police expert. In

discussing the problem of selecting subjects for field interrogation, the author writes:

A. Be suspicious. This is a healthy police attitude, but it should be controlled and not too obvious.

B. Look for the unusual. Persons who do not "belong" where they are observed.

13. Colin McInnes, *Mr. Love and Justice* (London: New English Library, 1962), p. 74.

14. Peter J. Connell, "Handling of Complaints by Police," unpublished paper for course in Criminal Procedure, Yale Law School, Fall, 1961.

15. Janowitz, op. cit.

NOTES AND QUESTIONS

1. Law helps to establish social order, and an orderly society facilitates justice through the rule of law. Why, then, does Skolnick call "law and order . . . a misleading term"? What "substantial incompatibilities" exist between law and order? How do different societies resolve this tension?

2. According to Skolnick, the "cognitive lenses through which [police] see situations and events," are heavily tinted by perceptions of danger and threats to authority. In what ways do the danger and need for authority of a policeman's job contribute to his isolation?

3. What does Skolnick mean by the term *working personality?* What factors determine the nature of a police officer's working personality? What significance does this working personality have for the law and order dilemma?

4. What is the interpretive role of the police as agents of the law? What causes the development of "informal norms or hidden principles" in police work? How can these norms further the cause of justice? How can they hinder it?

5. A major component of what Skolnick calls "operational law enforcement" is suspicion of the "symbolic assailant." How do race, class, gender, and other so-

cial factors shape the construction of the symbolic assailant?

6. How does Skolnick account for the unusually high degree of occupational solidarity among police?

Chapter 48

Broken Windows

The Police and Neighborhood Safety

James Q. Wilson
George L. Kelling

The history of policing in the United States has been marked by diverse and divergent theories of how best to deal with the tension between order maintenance and law enforcement. Some of these theories stress professionalism and technology, some the importance of a close connection between the police and the people they serve. Some emphasize the need to direct police resources to the most serious offenses; others describe connections between minor and major crimes and argue that the best way to prevent the latter is to concentrate on the former.

In the last decade of the twentieth century, community policing, as well as what has been called "broken-windows" policing, came back into vogue after a long period of dominance by the professional model. Out of police cars, onto the beat, community policing once again put cops on the streets in ways that made them a visible and important part of the neighborhoods that they served. It came back as part of a crime fighting strategy and as a way to heal a perceived rift between police and citizens in many American cities.

The broken-windows model urged the enforcement of laws prohibiting quality of life offenses, such as graffiti-spraying, aggressive panhandling, and so forth. This model was developed and made popular by James Q. Wil-

son and George L. Kelling, who argued that police should be deployed so as to make their presence visible in the communities they served. Although police dislike foot patrol, it produces greater citizen satisfaction and a greater sense of security, even though there is no evidence that foot patrol directly *reduces* serious crime.

Wilson and Kelling argue that disorder and crime are linked in what they call a "developmental sequence." Broken windows are a signal that no one cares, a sign that a community is out of control. In such places, residents begin to withdraw and, in their withdrawal, leave their neighborhoods vulnerable to serious crime. Foot patrols reduce the fear of being bothered by "disorderly" people—drunks, addicts, street people, and the like. In addition, policing that focuses on minor infractions sends a different signal, one which allegedly discourages crimes of all types and restores a sense of order to the community.

Wilson and Kelling note that in the communities where broken-windows policing occurred, the police were predominantly white and the residents predominantly black. At the same time, they describe a high level of community satisfaction with this style of policing. What is it about this style of policing that allegedly bridges the racial divide between police and community?

I n the mid 1970s The State of New Jersey announced a "Safe and Clean Neighborhoods Program," designed to improve the quality of community life in twenty-eight cities. As part of that program, the state provided money to help cities take police officers out of their patrol cars and assign them to walking beats. The governor and other state officials were enthusiastic about using foot patrol as a way of cutting crime, but many police chiefs were skeptical. Foot patrol, in their eyes, had been pretty much discredited. It reduced the mobility of the police, who thus had difficulty responding to citizen calls for service, and it weakened headquarter's control over patrol officers.

Many police officers also disliked foot patrol, but for different reasons: it was hard work, it kept them outside on cold, rainy nights, and it reduced their chances for making a "good pinch." In some departments, assigning officers to foot patrol had been used as a form of punishment. And academic experts on policing doubted that foot patrol would have any impact on crime rates; it was, in the opinion of most, little more than a sop to public opinion. But since the state was paying for it, the local authorities were willing to go along.

Five years after the program started, the Police Foundation, in Washington, D.C., published an evaluation of the foot-patrol project. Based on its analysis of a carefully controlled experiment carried out chiefly in Newark, the foundation concluded, to the surprise of hardly anyone, that foot patrol had not reduced crime rates. But residents of the foot patrolled neighborhoods seemed to feel more secure than persons in other areas, tended to believe that crime had been reduced, and seemed to take fewer steps to protect themselves from crime (staying at home with the doors locked, for example). Moreover, citizens in the foot-patrol areas had a more favorable opinion of the police than did those living elsewhere. And officers walking beats had higher morale, greater job satisfaction, and a more favorable attitude toward citizens in their neighborhoods than did officers assigned to patrol cars.

These findings may be taken as evidence that the skeptics were right—foot patrol has no effect on crime; it merely fools the citizens into thinking that they are safer. But in our view, and in the view of the authors of the Police Foundation study (of whom Kelling was one), the citizens of Newark were not fooled at all. They knew what the foot-patrol officers were doing, they knew it was different from what motorized officers do, and they knew that having officers walk beats did in fact make their neighborhoods safer.

But how can a neighborhood be "safer" when the crime rate has not gone down—in fact, may have gone up? Finding the answer requires first that we understand what most often frightens people in public places. Many citizens, of course, are primarily frightened by crime, especially crime involving a sudden, violent attack by a stranger. This risk is very real, in Newark as in many large cities. But we tend to overlook another source of fear—the fear of being bothered by disorderly people. Not violent people, nor, necessarily, criminals, but disreputable or obstreperous or unpredictable people: panhandlers, drunks, addicts, rowdy teenagers, prostitutes, loiterers, the mentally disturbed.

What foot-patrol officers did was to elevate, to the extent they could, the level of public order in these neighborhoods. Though the neighborhoods were predominantly black and the foot patrolmen were mostly white, this "order-maintenance" function of the police was performed to the general satisfaction of both parties.

One of us (Kelling) spent many hours walking with Newark foot-patrol officers to see how they defined "order" and what they did to maintain it. One beat was typical: a busy but dilapidated area in the heart of Newark, with many abandoned buildings, marginal shops (several of which prominently displayed knives and straight-edged razors in their windows), one large department store, and, most important, a train station and several major bus stops. Though the area was run-down, its streets were filled with people, because it was a major transportation center. The good order of this area was important not only to those who lived and worked there but also to many others, who had to move through it on their way home, to supermarkets, or to factories.

The people on the street were primarily black; the officer who walked the street was white. The people were made up of "regulars" and "strangers." Regulars included both "decent folk" and some drunks and derelicts who were always there but who "knew their place."

Strangers were, well, strangers, and viewed suspiciously, sometimes apprehensively. The officer—call him Kelly—knew who the regulars were, and they knew him. As he saw his job, he was to keep an eye on strangers, and make certain that the disreputable regulars observed some informal but widely understood rules. Drunks and addicts could sit on the stoops, but could not lie down. People could drink on side streets, but not at the main intersection. Bottles had to be in paper bags. Talking to, bothering, or begging from people waiting at the bus stop was strictly forbidden. If a dispute erupted between a businessman and a customer, the businessman was assumed to be right, especially if the customer was a stranger. If a stranger loitered, Kelly would ask him if he had any means of support and what his business was; if he gave unsatisfactory answers, he was sent on his way. Persons who broke the informal rules, especially those who bothered people waiting at bus stops, were arrested for vagrancy. Noisy teenagers were told to keep quiet.

These rules were defined and enforced in collaboration with the "regulars" on the street. Another neighborhood might have different rules, but these, everybody understood, were the rules for *this* neighborhood. If someone violated them, the regulars not only turned to Kelly for help but also ridiculed the violator. Sometimes what Kelly did could be described as "enforcing the law," but just as often it involved taking informal or extralegal steps to help protect what the neighborhood had decided was the appropriate level of public order. Some of the things he did probably would not withstand a legal challenge.

A determined skeptic might acknowledge that a skilled foot-patrol officer can maintain order but still insist that this sort of "order" has little to do with the real sources of community fear—that is, with violent crime. To a degree, that is true. But two things must be borne in mind. First, outside observers should not assume that they know how much of the anxiety now endemic in many big-city neighborhoods stems from a fear of "real" crime and how much from a sense that the street is disorderly, a source of distasteful, worrisome encounters. The people of Newark, to judge from their behavior and their remarks to interviewers, apparently assign a high value to public order, and feel relieved and reassured when the police help them maintain that order.

Second, at the community level, disorder and crime are usually inextricably linked, in a kind of developmental sequence. Social psychologists and police officers tend to agree that if a window in a building is broken and is left unrepaired, all the rest of the windows will soon be broken. This is as true in nice neighborhoods as in rundown ones. Window-breaking does not necessarily occur on a large scale because some areas are inhabited by determined window-breakers whereas others are populated by window-lovers; rather, one unrepaired broken window is a signal that no one cares, and so breaking more windows costs nothing. (It has always been fun.)

Philip Zimbardo, a Stanford psychologist, reported in 1969 on some experiments testing the broken-window theory. He arranged to have an automobile without license plates parked with its hood up on a street in the Bronx and a comparable automobile on a street in Palo Alto, California. The car in the Bronx was attacked by "vandals" within ten minutes of its "abandonment." The first to arrive were a family—father, mother, and young son—who removed the radiator and battery. Within twenty-four hours, virtually everything of value had been removed. Then random destruction began—windows were smashed, parts torn off, upholstery ripped. Children began to use the car as a playground. Most of the adult "vandals" were well-dressed, apparently clean-cut whites. The car in Palo Alto sat untouched for more than a week. Then Zimbardo smashed part of it with a sledgehammer. Soon, passersby were joining in. Within a few hours, the car had been turned upside down and utterly destroyed.

Again, the "vandals" appeared to be primarily respectable whites.

Untended property becomes fair game for people out for fun or plunder and even for people who ordinarily would not dream of doing such things and who probably consider themselves law-abiding. Because of the nature of community life in the Bronx—its anonymity, the frequency with which cars are abandoned and things are stolen or broken, the past experience of "no one caring"—vandalism begins much more quickly than it does in staid Palo Alto, where people have come to believe that private possessions are cared for, and that mischievous behavior is costly. But vandalism can occur anywhere once communal barriers—the sense of mutual regard and the obligations of civility—are lowered by actions that seem to signal that "no one cares."

We suggest that "untended" behavior also leads to the breakdown of community controls. A stable neighborhood of families who care for their homes, mind each other's children, and confidently frown on unwanted intruders can change, in a few years or even a few months, to an inhospitable and frightening jungle. A piece of property is abandoned, weeds grow up, a window is smashed. Adults stop scolding rowdy children; the children, emboldened, become more rowdy. Families move out, unattached adults move in. Teenagers gather in front of the corner store. The merchant asks them to move; they refuse. Fights occur. Litter accumulates. People start drinking in front of the grocery; in time, an inebriate slumps to the sidewalk and is allowed to sleep it off. Pedestrians are approached by panhandlers.

At this point it is not inevitable that serious crime will flourish or violent attacks on strangers will occur. But many residents will think that crime, especially violent crime, is on the rise, and they will modify their behavior accordingly. They will use the streets less often, and when on the streets will stay apart from their fellows, moving with averted eyes, silent lips, and hurried steps. "Don't get involved." For some residents, this growing atomization will matter little, because the neighborhood is not their "home" but "the place where they live." Their interests are elsewhere; they are cosmopolitans. But it will matter greatly to other people, whose lives derive meaning and satisfaction from local attachments rather than worldly involvement; for them, the neighborhood will cease to exist except for a few reliable friends whom they arrange to meet.

Such an area is vulnerable to criminal invasion. Though it is not inevitable, it is more likely that here, rather than in places where people are confident they can regulate public behavior by informal controls, drugs will change hands, prostitutes will solicit, and cars will be stripped. That the drunks will be robbed by boys who do it as a lark, and the prostitutes' customers will be robbed by men who do it purposefully and perhaps violently. That muggings will occur.

Among those who often find it difficult to move away from this are the elderly. Surveys of citizens suggest that the elderly are much less likely to be the victims of crime than younger persons, and some have inferred from this that the well-known fear of crime voiced by the elderly is an exaggeration: perhaps we ought not to design special programs to protect older persons; perhaps we should even try to talk them out of their mistaken fears. This argument misses the point. The prospect of a confrontation with an obstreperous teenager or a drunken panhandler can be as fear-inducing for defenseless persons as the prospect of meeting an actual robber; indeed, to a defenseless person, the two kinds of confrontation are often indistinguishable. Moreover, the lower rate at which the elderly are victimized is a measure of the steps they have already taken—chiefly, staying behind locked doors—to minimize the risks they face. Young men are more frequently attacked than older women, not because they are easier or more lucrative targets but because they are on the streets more.

Nor is the connection between disorderliness and fear made only by the elderly. Susan Estrich, of the Harvard Law School, has recently gathered together a number of surveys on the sources of public fear. One, done in Portland, Oregon, indicated that three fourths of the adults interviewed cross to the other side of a street when they see a gang of teenagers; another survey, in Baltimore, discovered that nearly half would cross the street to avoid even a single strange youth. When an interviewer asked people in a housing project where the most dangerous spot was, they mentioned a place where young persons gathered to drink and play music, despite the fact that not a single crime had occurred there. In Boston public housing projects, the greatest fear was expressed by persons living in the buildings where disorderliness and incivility, not crime, were the greatest. Knowing this helps one understand the significance of such otherwise harmless displays as subway graffiti. As Nathan Glazer has written, "the proliferation of graffiti, even when not obscene, confronts the subway rider with the inescapable knowledge that the environment he must endure for an hour or more a day is uncontrolled and uncontrollable, and that anyone can invade it to do whatever damage and mischief the mind suggests."

In response to fear people avoid one another, weakening controls. Sometimes they call the police. Patrol cars arrive, an occasional arrest occurs but crime continues and disorder is not abated. Citizens complain to the police chief, but he explains that his department is low on personnel and that the courts do not punish petty or first-time offenders. To the residents, the police who arrive in squad cars are either ineffective or uncaring: to the police, the residents are animals who deserve each other. The citizens may soon stop calling the police, because "they can't do anything."

The process we call urban decay has occurred for centuries in every city. But what is happening today is different in at least two important respects. First, in the period before, say, World War II, city dwellers—because of money costs, transportation difficulties, familial and church connections—could rarely move away from neighborhood problems. When movement did occur, it tended to be along public-transit routes. Now mobility has become exceptionally easy for all but the poorest or those who are blocked by racial prejudice. Earlier crime waves had a kind of built-in self-correcting mechanism: the determination of a neighborhood or community to reassert control over its turf. Areas in Chicago, New York, and Boston would experience crime and gang wars, and then normalcy would return, as the families for whom no alternative residences were possible reclaimed their authority over the streets.

Second, the police in this earlier period assisted in that reassertion of authority by acting, sometimes violently, on behalf of the community. Young toughs were roughed up, people were arrested "on suspicion" or for vagrancy, and prostitutes and petty thieves were routed. "Rights" were something enjoyed by decent folk, and perhaps also by the serious professional criminal, who avoided violence and could afford a lawyer.

This pattern of policing was not an aberration or the result of occasional excess. From the earliest days of the nation, the police function was seen primarily as that of a night watchman: to maintain order against the chief threats to order—fire, wild animals, and disreputable behavior. Solving crimes was viewed not as a police responsibility but as a private one. In the March, 1969, *Atlantic,* one of us (Wilson) wrote a brief account of how the police role had slowly changed from maintaining order to fighting crimes. The change began with the creation of private detectives (often ex-criminals), who worked on a contingency-fee basis for individuals who had suffered losses. In time, the detectives were absorbed in municipal agencies and paid a regular salary simultaneously, the responsibility for prosecuting thieves was shifted from the aggrieved private citizen to the professional prosecutor. This process was not complete in most places until the twentieth century.

In the 1960s, when urban riots were a major problem, social scientists began to explore carefully the order maintenance function of the police, and to suggest ways of improving it—not to make streets safer (its original function) but to reduce the incidence of mass violence. Order maintenance became, to a degree, coterminous with "community relations." But, as the crime wave that began in the early 1960s continued without abatement throughout the decade and into the 1970s, attention shifted to the role of the police as crime-fighters. Studies of police behavior ceased, by and large, to be accounts of the order-maintenance function and became, instead, efforts to propose and test ways whereby the police could solve more crimes, make more arrests, and gather better evidence. If these things could be done, social scientists assumed, citizens would be less fearful.

A great deal was accomplished during this transition, as both police chiefs and outside experts emphasized the crime-fighting function in their plans, in the allocation of resources, and in deployment of personnel. The police may well have become better crime-fighters as a result. And doubtless they remained aware of their responsibility for order. But the link between order-maintenance and crime-prevention, so obvious to earlier generations, was forgotten.

That link is similar to the process whereby one broken window becomes many. The citizen who fears the ill-smelling drunk, the rowdy teenager, or the importuning beggar is not merely expressing his distaste for unseemly behavior; he is also giving voice to a bit of folk wisdom that happens to be a correct generalization—namely, that serious street crime flourishes in areas in which disorderly behavior goes unchecked. The unchecked panhandler is, in effect, the first broken window. Muggers and robbers, whether opportunistic or professional, believe they reduce their chances of being caught or even identified if they operate on streets where potential victims are already intimidated by prevailing conditions. If the neighborhood cannot keep a bothersome panhandler from annoying passersby, the thief may reason, it is even less likely to call the police to identify a potential mugger or to interfere if the mugging actually takes place.

Some police administrators concede that this process occurs, but argue that motorized-patrol officers can deal with it as effectively as foot patrol officers. We are not so sure. In theory, an officer in a squad car can observe as much as an officer on foot; in theory, the former can talk to as many people as the latter. But the reality of police-citizen encounters is powerfully altered by the automobile. An officer on foot cannot separate himself from the street people; if he is approached, only his uniform and his personality can help him manage whatever is about to happen. And he can never be certain what that will be—a request for directions, a plea for help, an angry denunciation, a teasing remark, a confused babble, a threatening gesture.

In a car, an officer is more likely to deal with street people by rolling down the window and looking at them. The door and the window exclude the approaching citizen; they are a barrier. Some officers take advantage of this barrier, perhaps unconsciously, by acting differently if in the car than they would on foot. We have seen this countless times. The police car pulls up to a corner where teenagers are gathered. The window is rolled down. The officer stares at the youths. They stare back. The officer says to one, "C'mere." He saunters over, conveying to his friends by his elaborately casual style the idea that he is not intimidated by authority. "What's your name?" "Chuck." "Chuck who?" "Chuck Jones." "What'ya doing, Chuck?" "Nothin'." "Got a P.O. [parole officer]?" "Nah." "Sure?" "Yeah." "Stay out of trouble, Chuckie." Meanwhile, the other boys laugh and exchange comments among themselves, probably at the officer's expense. The officer stares harder. He cannot be certain what is being said, nor can he join in and, by displaying his own skill at street banter, prove that he cannot be "put down." In the process, the officer has learned almost nothing, and the boys have decided the officer is an alien force who can safely be disregarded, even mocked.

Our experience is that most citizens like to talk to a police officer. Such exchanges give them a sense of importance, provide them with the basis for gossip, and allow them to explain to the authorities what is worrying them (whereby they gain a modest but significant sense of having "done something" about the problem). You approach a person on foot more easily, and talk to him more readily, than you do a person in a car. Moreover, you can more easily retain some anonymity if you draw an officer aside for a private chat. Suppose you want to pass on a tip about who is stealing handbags, or who offered to sell you a stolen TV. In the inner city, the culprit, in all likelihood, lives nearby. To walk up to a marked patrol car and lean in the window is to convey a visible signal that you are a "fink."

The essence of the police role in maintaining order is to reinforce the informal control mechanisms of the community itself. The police cannot, without committing extraordinary resources, provide a substitute for that informal control. On the other hand, to reinforce those natural forces the police must accommodate them. And therein lies the problem.

Should police activity on the street be shaped, in important ways, by the standards of the neighborhood rather than by the rules of the state? Over the past two decades, the shift of police from order-maintenance to law enforcement has brought them increasingly under the influence of legal restrictions, provoked by media complaints and enforced by court decisions and departmental orders. As a consequence, the order maintenance functions of the police are now governed by rules developed to control police relations with suspected criminals. This is, we think, an entirely new development. For centuries, the role of the police as watchmen was judged primarily not in terms of its compliance with appropriate procedures but rather in terms of its attaining a desired objective. The objective was order, an inherently ambiguous term but a condition that people in a given community recognized when they saw it. The means were the same as those the community itself would employ, if its members were sufficiently determined, courageous, and authoritative. Detecting and apprehending criminals, by contrast, was a means to an end, not an end in itself; a judicial determination of guilt or innocence was the hoped-for result of the law-enforcement mode. From the first, the police were expected to follow rules defining that process, though states differed in how stringent the rules should be. The criminal-apprehension process was always understood to involve individual rights, the violation of which was unacceptable because it meant that the violating officer would be acting as a judge and jury—and that was not his job. Guilt or innocence was to be determined by universal standards under special procedures.

Ordinarily, no judge or jury ever sees the persons caught up in a dispute over the appropriate level of neighborhood order. That is true not only because most cases are handled informally on the street but also because no universal standards are available to settle arguments over disorder, and thus a judge may not be any wiser or more effective than a police officer. Until quite recently in many states, and even today in some places, the police made arrests on such charges as "suspicious person" or "vagrancy" or "public drunkenness"—charges with scarcely any legal meaning. These charges exist not because society wants judges to punish vagrants or drunks but because it wants an officer to have the legal tools to remove undesirable persons from a neighborhood when informal efforts to preserve order in the streets have failed.

Once we begin to think of all aspects of police work as involving the application of universal rules under special procedures, we inevitably ask what constitutes an "undesirable person" and why we should "criminalize" vagrancy or drunkenness. A strong and commendable desire to see that people are treated fairly makes us worry about allowing the police to rout persons who are undesirable by some vague or parochial standard. A growing and not-so-commendable utilitarianism leads us to doubt that any behavior that does not "hurt" another person should be made illegal. And thus many of us who watch over the police are reluctant to allow them to perform, in the only way they can, a function that every neighborhood desperately wants them to perform.

This wish to "decriminalize" disreputable behavior that "harms no one"—and thus remove the ultimate sanction the police can employ to maintain neighborhood order—is, we think, a mistake. Arresting a single drunk or a single vagrant who has harmed no identifiable person seems unjust, and in a sense it is. But failing to do anything about a score of drunks or a hundred vagrants may destroy an entire community. A particular rule that seems to make sense in the individual case makes no sense when it is made a universal rule and applied to all cases. It makes no sense because it fails to take into account the connection between one broken window left untended and a thousand broken windows. Of course, agencies other than the police could attend to the problems posed by drunks or the mentally ill, but in most communities—especially where the "deinstitutionalization" movement has been strong—they do not.

The concern about equity is more serious. We might agree that certain behavior makes one person more undesirable than another but how do we ensure that age or skin color or national origin or harmless mannerisms will not also become the basis for distinguishing the undesirable from the desirable? How do we ensure, in short, that the police do not become the agents of neighborhood bigotry?

We can offer no wholly satisfactory answer to this important question. We are not confident that there is a satisfactory answer except to hope that by their selection, training, and supervision, the police will be inculcated with a clear sense of the outer limit of their discretionary authority. That limit, roughly, is this—the police exist to help regulate behavior, not to maintain the racial or ethnic purity of a neighborhood.

Consider the case of the Robert Taylor Homes in Chicago, one of the largest public-housing projects in the country. It is home for nearly 20,000 people, all black, and extends over ninety-two acres along South State Street. It was named after a distinguished black who had been, during the 1940s, chairman of the Chicago Housing Authority. Not long after it opened, in 1962, relations between project residents and the police deteriorated badly. The citizens felt that the police were insensitive or brutal; the police, in turn, complained of unprovoked attacks on them. Some Chicago officers tell of times when they were afraid to enter the Homes. Crime rates soared.

Today, the atmosphere has changed. Police-citizen relations have improved—apparently, both sides learned something from the earlier experience. Recently, a boy stole a purse and ran off. Several young persons who saw the theft voluntarily passed along to the police information on the identity and residence of the thief, and they did this publicly, with friends and neighbors looking on. But problems persist, chief among them the presence of youth gangs that terrorize residents and recruit members in the project. The people expect the police to "do something" about this, and the police are determined to do just that.

But do what? Though the police can obviously make arrests whenever a gang member breaks the law, a gang can form, recruit, and congregate without breaking the law. And only a tiny fraction of gang-related crimes can be solved by an arrest; thus, if an arrest is the only recourse for the police, the residents' fears will go unassuaged. The police will soon feel helpless, and the residents will again believe that the police "do nothing." What the police in fact do is to chase known gang members out of the project. In the words of one officer, "We kick ass." Project residents both know and approve of this. The tacit police-citizen alliance in the project is reinforced by the police view that the cops and the gangs are the two rival sources of power in the area, and that the gangs are not going to win.

None of this is easily reconciled with any conception of due process or fair treatment. Since both residents and gang members are black, race is not a factor. But it could be. Suppose a white project confronted a black gang, or vice versa. We would be apprehensive about the police taking sides. But the substantive problem remains the same: how can the police strengthen the informal social-control mechanisms of natural communities in order to minimize fear in public places? Law enforcement, per se, is no answer: a gang can weaken or destroy a community by standing about in a menacing fashion and speaking rudely to passersby without breaking the law.

We have difficulty thinking about such matters, not simply because the ethical and legal issues are so complex but because we have become accustomed to thinking of the law in essentially individualistic terms. The law defines *my* rights, punishes *his* behavior and is applied by *that* officer because of *this* harm. We assume, in thinking this way, that what is good for the individual will be good for the community and what doesn't matter when it happens to one person won't matter if it happens to many. Ordinarily, those are plausible assumptions. But in cases where behavior that is tolerable to one person is intolerable to many others, the reactions of the others—fear, withdrawal, flight—may ultimately make matters worse for everyone, including the individual who first professed his indifference.

It may be their greater sensitivity to communal as opposed to individual needs that helps explain why the residents of small communities are more satisfied with their police than are the residents of similar neighborhoods in big cities. Elinor Ostrom and her co-workers at Indiana University compared the perception of police services in two poor, all-black Illinois towns—Phoenix and East Chicago Heights with those of three comparable all-black neighborhoods in Chicago. The level of criminal victimization and the quality of police-community relations appeared to be about the same in the towns and the Chicago neighborhoods. But the citizens living in their own villages were much more likely than those living in the Chicago neighborhoods to say that they do not stay at home for fear of crime, to agree that the local police have "the right to take any action necessary" to deal with problems, and to agree that the police "look out for the needs of the average citizen." It is possible that the residents and the police of the small towns saw themselves as engaged in a collaborative effort to maintain a certain standard of communal life, whereas those of the big city felt themselves to be simply requesting and supplying particular services on an individual basis.

If this is true, how should a wise police chief deploy his meager forces? The first answer is that nobody knows for certain, and the most prudent course of action would be to try further variations on the Newark experiment, to see more precisely what works in what kinds of neighborhoods. The second answer is also a hedge—many aspects of order maintenance in neighborhoods can probably best be handled in ways that involve the police minimally if at all. A busy bustling shopping center and a quiet, well-tended suburb may need almost no visible police presence. In both cases, the ratio of respectable to disreputable people is ordinarily so high as to make informal social control effective.

Even in areas that are in jeopardy from disorderly elements, citizen action without substantial police involvement may be sufficient. Meetings between teenagers who like to hang out on a particular corner and adults who want to use that corner might well lead to an amicable agreement on a set of rules about how many people can be allowed to congregate, where, and when.

Where no understanding is possible—or if possible, not observed—citizen patrols may be a sufficient response. There are two traditions of communal involvement in maintaining order: One, that of the "community watchmen," is as old as the first settlement of the New World. Until well into the nineteenth century, volunteer watchmen, not policemen, patrolled their communities to keep order. They did so, by and large, without taking the law into their own hands—without, that is, punishing persons or using force. Their presence deterred disorder or alerted the community to disorder that could not be deterred. There are hundreds of such efforts today in communities all across the nation. Perhaps the best known is that of the Guardian Angels, a group of unarmed young persons in distinctive berets and T-shirts, who first came to public attention when they began patrolling the New York City subways but who claim now to have chapters in more than thirty American cities. Unfortunately, we have little information about the effect of these groups on crime. It is possible, however, that whatever their effect on crime, citizens find their presence reassuring, and that they thus contribute to maintaining a sense of order and civility.

The second tradition is that of the "vigilante." Rarely a feature of the settled communities of the East, it was primarily to be found in those frontier towns that grew up in advance of the reach of government. More than 350 vigilante groups are known to have existed; their distinctive feature was that their members did take the law into their own hands, by acting as judge, jury, and often executioner as well as policeman. Today, the vigilante movement is conspicuous by its rarity, despite the great fear expressed by citizens that the older cities are becoming "urban frontiers." But some community-watchmen groups have skirted the line, and others may cross it in the future. An ambiguous case, reported in the *Wall Street Journal* involved a citizens' patrol in the Silver Lake area of Belleville, New Jersey. A leader told the reporter, "We look for outsiders." If a few teenagers from outside the neighborhood enter it, "we ask them their business," he said. "If they say they're going down the street to see Mrs. Jones, fine, we let them pass. But then we follow them down the block to make sure they're really going to see Mrs. Jones."

Though citizens can do a great deal, the police are plainly the key to order maintenance. For one thing, many communities, such as the Robert Taylor Homes, cannot do the job by themselves. For another, no citizen in a neighborhood, even an organized one, is likely to feel the sense of responsibility that wearing a badge confers. Psychologists have done many studies on why people fail to go to the aid of persons being attacked or seeking help, and they have learned that the cause is not "apathy" or "selfishness" but the absence of some plausible grounds for feeling that one must personally accept responsibility. Ironically, avoiding responsibility is easier when a lot of people are standing about. On streets and in public places, where order is so important, many people are likely to be "around," a fact that reduces the chance of any one person acting as the agent of the community. The police officer's uniform singles him out as a person who must accept responsibility if asked. In addition, officers, more easily than their fellow citizens, can be expected to distinguish between what is necessary to protect the safety of the street and what merely protects its ethnic purity.

But the police forces of America are losing, not gaining, members. Some cities have suffered substantial cuts in the number of officers available for duty. These cuts are not likely to be reversed in the near future. Therefore, each department must assign its existing officers with great care. Some neighborhoods are so demoralized and crime-ridden as to make foot patrol useless; the best the police can do with limited resources is respond to the enormous number of calls for service. Other neighborhoods are so stable and serene as to make foot patrol unnecessary. The key is to identify neighborhoods at the tipping point—where the public order is deteriorating but not unreclaimable, where the streets are used frequently but by apprehensive people, where a window is likely to be broken at any time, and must quickly be fixed if all are not to be shattered.

Most police departments do not have ways of systematically identifying such areas and assigning officers to them. Officers are assigned on the basis of crime rates (meaning that marginally threatened areas are often stripped so that police can investigate crimes in areas where the situation is hopeless) or on the basis of calls for service (despite the fact that most citizens do not call the police when they are merely frightened or annoyed). To allocate patrol wisely, the department must look at the neighborhoods and decide, from first-hand evidence, where an additional officer will make the greatest difference in promoting a sense of safety.

One way to stretch limited police resources is being tried in some public housing projects. Tenant organizations hire off-duty police officers for patrol work in their buildings. The costs are not high (at least not per resident), the officer likes the additional income, and the residents feel safer. Such arrangements are probably more successful than hiring private watchmen, and the Newark experiment helps us understand why. A private security guard may deter crime or misconduct by his presence, and he may go to the aid of persons needing help, but he may well not intervene—that is, control or drive away—someone challenging community standards. Being a sworn

officer—a "real cop"—seems to give one the confidence, the sense of duty, and the aura of authority necessary to perform this difficult task.

Patrol officers might be encouraged to go to and from duty stations on public transportation and, while on the bus or subway car, enforce rules about smoking, drinking, disorderly conduct, and the like. The enforcement need involve nothing more than ejecting the offender (the offense, after all, is not one with which a booking officer or a judge wishes to be bothered). Perhaps the random but relentless maintenance of standards on buses would lead to conditions on buses that approximate the level of civility we now take for granted on airplanes.

But the most important requirement is to think that to maintain order in precarious situations is a vital job. The police know this is one of their functions, and they also believe, correctly, that it cannot be done to the exclusion of criminal investigation and responding to calls. We may have encouraged them to suppose, however, on the basis of our oft-repeated concerns about serious, violent crime, that they will be judged exclusively on their capacity as crime-fighters. To the extent that this is the case, police administrators will continue to concentrate police personnel in the highest-crime areas (though not necessarily in the areas most vulnerable to criminal invasion), emphasize their training in the law and criminal apprehension (and not their training in managing street life), and join too quickly in campaigns to decriminalize "harmless" behavior (though public drunkenness, street prostitution, and pornographic displays can destroy a community more quickly than any team of professional burglars).

Above all, we must return to our long-abandoned view that the police ought to protect communities as well as individuals. Our crime statistics and victimization surveys measure individual losses, but they do not measure communal losses. Just as physicians now recognize the importance of fostering health rather than simply treating illness, so the police—and the rest of us—ought to recognize the importance of maintaining, intact, communities without broken windows.

Notes and Questions

1. According to Wilson and Kelling, citizens "apparently assign a high value to public order, and feel relieved and reassured when the police help them maintain that order." What is the perceived relationship between disorderly conduct and crime for most people? Does this help explain and/or justify the construction of the "symbolic assailant" described by Skolnick in Chapter 47?

2. Describing a foot patrol officer in Newark, New Jersey, Wilson and Kelling observe, "Sometimes what Kelly did could be described as 'enforcing the law,' but just as often it involved taking informal or extralegal steps to help protect what the neighborhood had decided was the appropriate level of public order." Is it problematic that officer Kelly employs law's violence to enforce what would be perceived by an outsider to be arbitrary rules and standards?

3. Wilson and Kelling contend that foot patrols have proved rather effective at breaking down social barriers between police and citizens. What is it about foot patrol that reduces the level of professional isolation described by Skolnick? What impact might we expect foot pa-

trol to have on an officer's working personality? Why?

4. Why do Wilson and Kelling object to the decriminalization of "disreputable behavior"? Do you agree? Why or why not?

5. How does a community policing framework reconceptualize the rights of the individual versus the interests of the community?

6. Is the idea of community policing predicated on the elimination of "broken windows" compatible with equal treatment under law? How can police enforce uniform criminal standards, if, as Wilson and Kelling argue, "the essence of the police role in maintaining order is to reinforce the *informal* control mechanisms of the community itself"?

7. In their conclusion, Wilson and Kelling draw an analogy between a doctor's commitment to health and a police officer's commitment to safety. "Just as physicians now recognize the importance of fostering health rather than simply treating illness, so the police . . . ought to recognize the importance of maintaining, intact, communities without broken windows." Is this a good way of thinking about policing?

Chapter 49

Policing Disorder

Can We Reduce Serious Crime by Punishing Petty Offenses?

Bernard E. Harcourt

T*he next reading is by one of the most severe critics of "broken-windows" policing, law professor Bernard E. Harcourt. Harcourt links the broken-windows theory with another development in the world of crime and punishment, namely, the dramatic growth in the number of people in prison in the United States. Both of these developments, Harcourt contends, reflect a new punitiveness in our society.*

However, in this selection, Harcourt criticizes broken windows not for its punitiveness, but because he does not believe that it works to reduce crime. As he puts it, "The most reliable social scientific evidence suggests that the theory is wrong." In addition, he worries that its collateral consequences, especially increased tensions between police and minority communities, which are the focus of the new style of policing, outweigh any benefits that broken-windows policing produces.

Punishment in these late modern times is marked by two striking developments. The first is a stunning increase in the number of persons incarcerated. Federal and state prison populations nationwide have increased from less than 200,000 in 1970 to more than 1,300,000 in 2000, with another 600,000 per-

sons held in local jails. . . .[1] Today, approximately 2 million men and women are incarcerated in prisons and jails in this country. The intellectual rationale for this increase is provided by "incapacitation theory"—the idea that a hardcore 6 percent of youths and young adults are responsible for the majority of crime and that locking up those persistent offenders will significantly impact crime rates.

A second dramatic development is the popularity of "order-maintenance policing," an approach to policing that emphasizes creating and maintaining orderly public spaces. This policy is driven by the "broken-windows theory"—the idea that tolerating such minor infractions as graffiti spraying, aggressive panhandling, prostitution, public urination, and turnstile jumping encourages serious violent crime by sending a signal that the community is not in control. The broken-windows theory has ignited a virtual "revolution in American policing," also known as the "Blue Revolution.". . .[2] In New York City, where broken-windows policing was introduced under the administration of Mayor Rudolph Giuliani and his first police commissioner, William Bratton, the order-maintenance strategy produced an immediate surge in arrests for misdemeanor offenses. . . .

The broken-windows theory can also be traced to [James Q.] Wilson, who, with his coauthor George L. Kelling, wrote an influential *Atlantic Monthly* article in 1982 called "Broken Windows," a nine-page anecdotal essay that revolutionized policing. Wilson there spelled out and popularized the idea of cracking down on minor disorder as a way to combat serious crime.

Conservative policymakers tend to argue for both incapacitation and broken-windows policing. . . .

What is striking, though, is that among progressives, liberals, and the full spectrum of Democrats, order-maintenance policing has been hailed as the only viable and feasible *alternative* to the three-strikes and mandatory minimum laws that have resulted in massive incarceration. The power and appeal of broken-windows policing for liberals derives precisely from its *opposition* to incapacitation theory. Order maintenance is billed as a milder public-order measure. It represents, according to some progressives, one of the only "politically feasible and morally attractive alternatives to the severe punishments that now dominate America's inner-city crime-fighting prescriptions."[3] This is precisely what makes broken-windows policing "progressive."

As a result, order maintenance is popular today in a way that massive incarceration is not. Whereas the prison boom has received a lot of criticism in the media, among public officials, and in the academy, broken-windows policing has received far less attention and scrutiny. With few notable exceptions, order maintenance continues to receive extremely favorable reviews in policy circles, academia, and the press. . . .

QUESTIONABLE SOCIAL SCIENCE

The result is that today, broken-windows theory seems more popular than ever. And the breadth of its popularity reflects the fact that it is understood as an *alternative* to the incarceration explosion we have witnessed in the latter part of the twentieth century. It has, in effect, captured the liberal imagination.

The difficulty is that there is no good evidence for the theory that disorder causes crime. To the contrary, the most reliable social scientific evidence suggests that the theory is wrong. The popularity of the broken-windows theory, it turns out, is inversely related to the quality of the supporting evidence. . . .

The most comprehensive and thorough study of the broken-windows theory to date is Robert Sampson and Stephen Raudenbush's 1999 study entitled *Systematic Social Observation of Public Spaces: A New Look at Disorder in Urban Neighborhoods*. Their study is based on extremely careful data collection. Using trained observers who drove a sports utility vehicle at five miles per hour down every street in 196 Chicago census tracts, randomly selecting 15,141 streets for analysis, they were able to collect precise data on neighborhood disorder. Sampson and Raudenbush found that disorder and predatory crime are moderately correlated, but that, when antecedent neighborhood characteristics (such as neighborhood trust and poverty) are taken into account, the connection between disorder and crime "vanished in 4 out of 5 tests—including homicide, arguably our best measure of violence." They acknowledge that disorder may have indirect effects on neighborhood crime by influencing "migration patterns, investment by businesses, and overall neighborhood viability." But, on the basis of their extensive research, Sampson and Raudenbush conclude that "[a]ttacking public order through tough police tactics may thus be a politically popular but perhaps analytically weak strategy to reduce crime."[4]

THE NEW YORK STORY

If we look at the criminological evidence, the results are no more helpful to broken-windows proponents. The basic fact is that a number of large U.S. cities—Boston, Houston, Los Angeles, San Diego, and San Francisco, among others—have experienced significant drops in crime since the early 1990s, in some cases proportionally larger than the drop in New York City's crime. But many of these cities have not implemented the type of aggressive order-maintenance policing that New York City did. One recent study found that New York City's drop in homicides, though impressive, is neither unparalleled nor unprecedented. Houston's drop in homicides of 59 percent between 1991 and 1996 outpaced New York City's 51 percent decline over the same period, and both were surpassed by Pittsburgh's 61 percent drop in homicides between 1984 and 1988.[5] Another study looked at the rates of decline in homicides in the seventeen largest U.S. cities from 1976 to 1998 and found that New York City's recent decline, though above average, was the fifth largest, behind San Diego, Washington, D.C., St. Louis, and Houston.[6]

A straight comparison of homicide and robbery rates between 1991 and 1998 reveals that although New York City is again in the top group, with declines in homicide and robbery rates of 70.6 percent and 60.1 percent respectively, San Diego experienced larger declines in homicide and robbery rates (76.4 percent and 62.6 percent respectively), Boston experienced a comparable decline in its homicide rate (69.3 percent), Los Angeles experienced a greater decline in its robbery rate (60.9 percent), and San Antonio experienced a comparable decline in its robbery rate (59.1 percent). Other major cities also experienced impressive declines in their homicide and robbery rates, including Houston (61.3 percent and 48.5 percent respectively) and Dallas (52.4 percent and 50.7 percent respectively).[7]

Many of these cities, however, did not implement New York-style order-maintenance policing. The San Diego police department, for example, implemented a radically different model of policing focused on community-police relations. The police began experimenting with problem-oriented policing in the late 1980s and retrained the police force to better respond to community concerns. They implemented a strategy of sharing responsibility with citizens for identifying and solving crimes. But while recording remarkable drops in crime, San Diego also posted a 15 percent drop in total arrests between 1993 and 1996, and an 8 percent decline in total complaints of police misconduct filed with the police department between 1993 and 1996.[8]

San Francisco also focused on community involvement and experienced decreased arrest and incarceration rates between 1993 and 1998. San Francisco's felony commitments to the California Department of Corrections dropped from 2,136 in 1993 to 703 in 1998, whereas other California counties either maintained or slightly increased their incarcerations. San Francisco also abandoned a youth curfew in the early 1990s and sharply reduced its commitments to the California Youth Authority from 1994 to 1998. Despite this, San Francisco experienced greater drops in its crime rate for rape, robbery, and aggravated assault than did New York City for the period 1995 through 1998. In addition, San Francisco experienced the sharpest decline in total violent crime—sharper than New York City or Boston—between 1992 and 1998.[9]

Other cities, including Los Angeles, Houston, Dallas, and San Antonio, also experienced significant drops in crime without adopting as coherent a policing strategy as New York or San Diego. The fact is, there was a remarkable decline in crime in many major cities in the United States during the 1990s. New York City was certainly a very high performer. But numerous major U.S. cities have achieved substantial declines in crime using a variety of different policing strategies. It would be simplistic to attribute the rate of the decline in New York City solely to the quality-of-life initiative. . . .

The bottom line is that the broken-windows theory—the idea that public disorder sends a message that encourages crime—is probably wrong. As Sampson and Raudenbush observe, "bearing in mind the example of some European and American cities (e.g., Amsterdam, San Francisco) where visible street level activity linked to prostitution, drug use, and panhandling does not necessarily translate into high rates of violence, public disorder may not be so 'criminogenic' after all in certain neighborhood and social contexts."[10]

The title of the new Manhattan Institute report—*Do Police Matter?*—asks a good question, with an obvious answer: Yes. The police are uniquely suited to identifying crime trends and patterns and to implement innovative problem-solving techniques to deal with emerging crime situations. Few other governmental agencies or private companies have the immediate information, know-how, human resources, technology, and skills to perform these tasks. And the Manhattan Institute report offers a few good illustrations of problem-solving policing at its finest in New York City. When Brooklyn's Flatbush precinct experienced a rash of automobile airbag thefts in February and March 2000, for example, the precinct executives implemented numerous strategies—including placing a decoy car in an at-risk area, equipping airbags with tracking devices, readjusting officer deployment, and publicizing these efforts—that resulted in success.

But that question is too easy and is not the right one to ask. The real question is whether an agency like the NYPD needs to implement a policy of making large numbers of arrests for minor misdemeanors and public disorder violations as a primary strategy for combating violent crime. The answer to that question is equally clear: No. The best social scientific and criminological evidence suggests that minor social and physical disorder is not causally related to violent crime.

TROUBLING CONSEQUENCES

But the Manhattan Institute report does, perhaps unwittingly, reveal the true face of broken-windows policing. Since the publication of Wilson and Kelling's *Atlantic Monthly* article, there has always been a lingering question concerning the implementation of a broken-windows approach. After all, if the aim is improved public order, couldn't that be achieved with urban renewal projects, homeless shelters, and social workers, as well as or instead of more police arrests? Now we know, from a reliable source. The only number used in the Manhattan Institute report to measure the extent of broken-windows policing is the number of precinct-level misdemeanor arrests. The authors made a "decision to use arrests for misdemeanors as our measure of 'broken-windows' enforcement."[11] The broken-windows theory, it turns out, is not so much about public order, as it is about arrest-

ing people for misdemeanor and public disorder offenses.

And, of course, that is what we have seen in New York City. Adult misdemeanor arrests in the city have increased throughout the 1990s. According to the New York State Division of Criminal Justice Services, in 1993, the year before Giuliani and Bratton began implementing broken-windows policing, total adult misdemeanor arrests stood at 129,404. By the year 2000, the number was up to 224,663—an increase of almost 75 percent. What is particularly interesting is that the vast majority of those arrests were for misdemeanor drug charges, which are up almost 275 percent from 27,447 in 1993 to 102,712 in 2000. Driving while intoxicated (DWI) arrests were down by almost 40 percent over the period (from 5,621 in 1993 to 3,432 in 2000), while other misdemeanor arrests increased by only a quarter (from 96,336 in 1993 to 118,520 in 2000).[12] At the same time, the NYPD implemented an aggressive stop-and-frisk policy. Between 1997 and 1998, for instance, the Street Crime Unit—with approximately 435 officers at the time—stopped and frisked about 45,000 people.[13]

The trouble is, policing strategies that deliberately emphasize arresting misdemeanor and public order offenders—rather than issuing warnings or implementing alternative problem-solving techniques—have significant racial consequences. The fact is that in New York City, and the United States more generally, adults arrested for misdemeanors are disproportionately African-American in relation to their representation in the community. In 2000, for example, slightly over 50 percent of all adults arrested for misdemeanors in New York City were African-American (113,336 of the total 224,663 adults arrested). Slightly over 50 percent of adults arrested for disorderly conduct (19,563 of the total 38,780) and 45.6 percent of adults arrested for loitering were African-American. For prostitution and drug possession, the proportions are 40.7 percent and 51.7 percent respectively.

(For DWI, interestingly, the proportion is only 22.3 percent).[14] Yet African Americans (in 2000) represented only 24.6 percent of the New York City population.[15] Persons of Hispanic descent represented 31.5 percent of all adult misdemeanor arrests, whereas they constituted only 25.1 percent of the city's population.[16] In contrast, European Americans represented 48.8 percent of the population, and accounted for only 15.5 percent of adults arrested on misdemeanor charges in 2000.

These disparities hold true for large cities across the United States. In 1999, for instance, 43.4 percent of adults arrested for vagrancy in large metropolitan areas were African-American; 34.2 percent, 39 percent, and slightly over 40 percent of those arrested for disorderly conduct, prostitution, and drug abuse charges, respectively, were African-American. (Again, curiously, only 10.7 percent of those arrested for driving under the influence were black). Yet African Americans represent less than 15 percent of the total population of these metropolitan areas.[17]

The point is not that the police are consciously targeting black misdemeanants, but simply that more blacks are arrested for misdemeanors given their proportion in the overall population. In other words, the *decision to arrest misdemeanants*—adopting that policy in preference to other policing strategies—is a choice with significant distributional consequences for African Americans.

Additionally, there is good evidence that New York City's policy of aggressive stop-and-frisks was in fact implemented in a racially discriminatory manner. In 1999, New York State Attorney General Eliot Spitzer, with the assistance of Columbia University's Center for Violence Research and Prevention, analyzed 174,919 stop-and-frisk "UF-250" forms—the forms that NYPD officers are required to fill out in a variety of stop encounters—from the period January 1, 1998 through March 31, 1999. Spitzer found that the raw number of stops was higher for minorities—African Americans and Hispan-

ics—than whites relative to their respective proportion of the population. Spitzer then reanalyzed the raw numbers, this time taking account of the different crime rates and the population composition in different precincts, and found significant disparities across all precincts and crime categories: "in aggregate across all crime categories and precincts citywide, blacks were 'stopped' 23 percent more often (in comparison to the crime rate) than whites. Hispanics were 'stopped' 39 percent more often than whites." Spitzer concluded from the data that "even when crime data are taken into account, minorities are still 'stopped' at a higher rate than would be predicted by both demographics and crime rates."[18]

Broken-windows policing has come with other price tags as well. New York City, for instance, experienced illegal strip searches, mounting financial liability on police misconduct charges, clogged courts, wasted resources, and many traumatic encounters for ordinary citizens. The simple fact is that arrests and prosecutions are expensive: a typical prostitution prosecution—one of the offenses targeted by the quality-of-life initiative—costs upwards of $2,000. That's a lot of money for a single transaction. Moreover, a policy of arrest may have unintended consequences. Someone arrested for turnstile jumping may be fired for missing work; and strained police-civilian relations can create friction between the community and the police force that may be detrimental to solving crimes.

What does this say about order-maintenance as a police technique? First, it is an illusion to think that broken-windows policing operates through increased orderliness. Second, order-maintenance probably contributes to fighting crime through enhanced surveillance. Third, broken-windows policing comes at a significant cost, with negative distributional consequences for African Americans and other minorities. Fourth, there are alternative strategies of problem-solving policing. . . .

A BROKEN THEORY

After all, what exactly is the distinction between eccentricity, nonconformity, unconventionality, difference, disorder, and criminality? What makes distinctive clothes, youthful exuberance, or loitering disorderly? Why does order maintenance focus so heavily on certain types of street disorder and not others? Police brutality is a form of disorder, yet it appears nowhere as a target of broken-windows policing. Everyday tax evasion—paying cash to avoid sales tax, paying nannies under the table, using an out-of-state address—is disorderly. So are public corruption, sham accounting practices, nepotism, insider trading, and fraud. Why does broken windows focus on the dollar-fifty turnstile jump rather than on the hundred-million dollar accounting scam? And what exactly is the meaning of neighborhood disorder? Sure it may signal that a community is not in control of crime. But it may also reflect an alternative subculture, political protest, or artistic creativity. An orderly neighborhood may signal commercial sex, wealthy neighbors with personal bodyguards, foreign diplomats, a strong mafia presence, or a large police force.

The central claim of the broken-windows theory—that disorder causes crime by signaling community breakdown—is flawed. The categories of "disorder" and "the disorderly" lie at the heart of the problem. Those categories do not have well-defined boundaries or settled meanings. When we talk about "disorder," we are really referring to certain minor acts that some of us *come to view* as disorderly mostly because of the punitive strategies that we inflict as a society. We have come to identify certain acts—graffiti spraying, litter, panhandling, turnstile jumping, and prostitution—and not others—police brutality, accounting scams, and tax evasion—as disorderly and connected to broader patterns of serious crime. Hanging out on the front steps of a building or loitering with neighbors only signals that the community is not in control *if* hanging out or loitering is perceived as violating certain rules of conduct. But, of course, that depends on the neighborhood—and in some, in fact, it reflects strong community bonds and informal modes of social control. Graffiti only signals that the neighborhood is indifferent to crime *if* graffiti is viewed as violating the rules of the community. But graffiti is sometimes understood to be political or artistic expression or social commentary.

Order-maintenance policies, ironically, have the effect of reinforcing the idea that disorder causes crime. The "squeegee man," for instance, has become the barometer of crime control in New York City *primarily because of* the quality-of-life campaign. And one might speculate that, as order maintenance has become more and more popular, the categories of the disorderly and law-abider may have become slightly more fixed in meaning. The broken-windows theory has, in this sense, a self-reinforcing logic: it helps shape the perceptions, emotions, and judgments we form about people who are homeless, hustling, or panhandling. Still, the best social scientific evidence suggests that there are mixed signals associated with disorder—disorder does not correlate with crime in most tests. In sum, it is an illusion to believe that the order in order maintenance is necessary to combat crime.

When we peel away disorder from crime, it becomes clear that the model of orderliness offers to contemporary society, first, a classic mode of enhanced surveillance. The criminological evidence suggests that it is not the order, but the surveillance associated with broken-windows policing that has probably contributed to the drop in crime in a city like New York. It is the increased arrests, background checks, fingerprint comparisons, stop-and-frisks, line-ups, and informants. It is, in effect, the increased police-civilian contacts. Are they necessary? The answer is no. Many cities in the United States have experienced remarkable drops in crime during the

1990s without implementing similar order maintenance strategies. The costs are simply too steep, especially to minority communities. And there are alternatives, such as the problem-solving policing discussed, in part, in the new Manhattan Institute report.

Second, order maintenance policing provides a way to enforce an aesthetic preference, under the guise of combating serious crime. Order maintenance is a way to get homeless people, panhandlers, and prostitutes off the street. It is a way to keep the avenues clean of graffiti and litter. Broken-windows policing is a way to repossess red light districts and displace street vendors, panhandlers, and ordinary street life. It is, in effect, a type of "aesthetic policing" that fosters a sterile, Disneyland, consumerist, commercial aesthetic. It reflects a desire to transform New York City into Singapore, or worse, a shopping mall. The truth is, however, that when we lose the dirt, grit, and street life of major American cities, we may also threaten their vitality, creativity, and character.

Notes

1. Kathleen Maguire and Ann L. Pastore, eds., *Sourcebook of Criminal Justice Statistics 2000* (Washington, D.C.: U.S. Government Printing Office, 2001), Table 6.1 and 6.27. Available at: ttp://www.albany.edu/sourcebook [12 March 2002].

2. Christina Nifong, "One Man's Theory Is Cutting Crime in Urban Streets," *The Christian Science Monitor,* 18 February 1997; Michael Massing, "The Blue Revolution," *The New York Review of Books,* 19 November 1998, 32.

3. Dan M. Kahan and Tracey L. Meares, "Law and (Norms of) Order in the Inner City," *Law & Society Review* 32 (1998): 805, 806.

4. Robert J. Sampson and Stephen W. Raudenbush, "Systematic Social Observation of Public Spaces: A New Look at Disorder in Urban Neighborhoods," *American Journal of Sociology* 105 (2000): 637, 638.

5. See Jeffrey Fagan, Franklin Zimring, and June Kim, "Declining Homicide in New York City:

6. See Ana Joanes, "Does the New York City Police Department Deserve Credit for the Decline in New York City's Homicide Rates? A Cross-City Comparison of Policing Strategies and Homicide Rates," *Columbia Journal of Law and Social Problems* 33 (1999): 303–304.

7. See Fox Butterfield, "Cities Reduce Crime and Conflict Without New York-Style Hardball," *The New York Times,* 4 March 2000. Statistics compiled by Alfred Blumstein.

8. Judith A. Greene, "Zero-Tolerance: A Case Study of Police Policies and Practices in New York City," *Crime and Delinquency* 45 (1999): 182–185.

9. Khaled Taqi-Eddin and Dan Macallair, *Shattering 'Broken Windows': An Analysis of San Francisco's Alternative Crime Policies* (San Francisco: Justice Policy Institute, 1999), 4-5, 7, 8, 10, 11. Available at: ttp://www.cjcj.org/jpi/windows.html [12 March 2002].

10. Sampson and Raudenbush, "Public Spaces," 638.

11. Kelling, *Do Police Matter?* 23.

12. New York State Division of Criminal Justice Services, *Criminal Justice Indicators New York City: 1992–2000,* http://criminaljustice.state.ny.us/crimnet/ojsa/areastat/areast.htm [12 March 2002].

13. Jeffrey Rosen, "Excessive Force: Why Patrick Dorismond Didn't Have to Die," *New Republic,* 10 April 2000, 26; Eliot Spitzer, *The New York City Police Department's 'Stop & Frisk' Practices: A Report to the People of the State of New York From The Office Of The Attorney General* (New York: Office of the Attorney General of the State of New York, Civil Rights Bureau, 1999), 56–59. Available at: ttp://www.oag.state.ny.us/press/reports/stop_frisk/stop_frisk.html [15 March 2002].

14. Marge Cohen, New York State Division of Criminal Justice Services, fax to author, 4 January 2002, data from UCR system and Computerized Criminal History system.

15. U.S. Bureau of the Census, *The Black Population: 2000: Census 2000 Brief* (Washington, D.C., 2001).

16. Cohen, New York State Division of Criminal Justice Services, fax to author; U.S. Bureau of

the Census, *2000 Census of Population and Housing: Profiles of General Demographic Characteristics* (Washington, D.C.: U.S. Government Printing Office, 2001), Table DP-1, 345.

17. U.S. Department of Justice, Bureau of Justice Statistics, *Sourcebook of Criminal Justice Statistics 2000* (Washington, D.C.: U.S. Government Printing Office, 2001), Table 4.12, 372; for demographic data, see U.S. Bureau of the Census, *Profiles of General Demographic Characteristics*, Table DP-1, 2. Note that 13.2 percent of the population inside metropolitan areas is African-American.

18. Spitzer, '*Stop & Frisk' Practices*, 89, 123.

Notes and Questions

1. Why, according to Harcourt, do liberals tend to look at broken-windows policing as an alternative rather than a complement to incapacitation theory? What is it about the broken-windows approach that makes it politically feasible and morally palatable?

2. What characteristics do San Diego's and San Francisco's policing strategies share with New York's broken-windows approach? How are they different? Is one superior to the others? Why or why not?

3. How does Harcourt explain the dramatic drop in crime in New York City since the implementation of broken-windows policing? Why is he unimpressed by this achievement?

4. What evidence does Harcourt use to attack broken-windows theory? Overall, whose argument is more compelling,

Harcourt's or Wilson and Kelling's (Chapter 48)?

5. According to Harcourt, how does broken-windows policing heighten racial tension? Can discretionary police policies such as "stop and frisk" ever be successfully implemented without subjecting citizens to undue racial prejudice?

6. Almost by definition, broken-windows policing leads to a sharp increase in misdemeanor arrests. Further, Harcourt identifies "mounting financial liability on police misconduct charges and clogged courts" as costs of such a police strategy. Are the "quality of life" benefits outlined by Wilson and Kelling worth the costs of broken-windows policing? What nonlaw enforcement alternatives does Harcourt suggest might improve public orderliness and quality of life just as well as broken-windows policing?

7. According to Harcourt, the broken-windows theory is flawed first and foremost because the legal concepts of "disorder and the disorderly do not have well-defined boundaries or settled meanings." How do a person's age, race, class, and/or gender determine whether their conduct is likely to be deemed disorderly? Is this just?

Chapter 50

Profiles in Justice?

Police Discretion, Symbolic Assailants, and Stereotyping

Milton Heumann
Lance Cassak

P*rofiling is an important technique of modern policing. It helps prevent crime by identifying potential criminals based on the traits they share with known perpetrators of a particular offense. In the wake of the September 11, 2001, attacks on the World Trade Center, some people argued that efforts to stop terrorism should be focused on those who shared an ethnic identity with the 19 people involved in that attack. For them it made no sense to treat everyone as if they were all equally a threat. However, others objected, saying that to concentrate on a single racial group was to operate on the basis of a damaging stereotype. On the face of it, profiling is simply a rational way to deploy scarce police resources and organize their discretion. It is a way of reading the social world by using certain assumptions about the characteristics of persons and the likelihood of criminal behavior.*

Yet, profiling has become one of the major sources of tension between minority communities and the police, especially when the latter use race as the reason for stopping persons on highways, in airports, and on city streets. In profiling, race becomes an indicator of suspiciousness. In the classic case, a policeman, with nothing else to go on, stops a black person and subjects him to a search on the chance that he may be carrying drugs or weapons. This is sometimes referred to as the offense of "driving while black."

The reading by Heumann and Cassak examines profiling from the perspective of the police as well as the treatment of profiling in courts. The authors suggest that race is frequently a factor in the construction of symbolic assailants and that courts, in the short term, can do little to effectively end this practice. Nonetheless, they argue that courts, especially the U. S. Supreme Court, should be more involved and visible in denouncing profiling on the basis of race.

... **N**ew Jersey State Troopers stop four African-American high school students, who were on their way to basketball tryouts in another state, on the New Jersey Turnpike. In the commotion following the stop, the Troopers shoot the four students.[1]

Police officers stop and check, week after week, the driver's license and registration of an African-American philosophy professor, who must drive every Friday from central New Jersey to western Massachusetts to teach a college course.[2]

Officers of a Special Street Crimes Unit of the New York City Police Department stop an African immigrant in the vestibule of his building. When he reaches for his wallet, which the officers later claim they mistook for a gun, the officers shoot him forty-one times.[3]

INTRODUCTION

The incidents briefly recounted above are among the more famous—or notorious—instances of police action, among many, many more, that have both galvanized and influenced the current debate concerning "profiling," specifically racial profiling.[4] Each month, if not week, seems to present the issue in a new factual setting, and hence in a new light, making it more and more difficult to get a handle on the issues involved.[5] ...

Were an inquiry into profiling simply a reflection of learning more about a current controversy, it would be a matter of great public interest, but might not be one so intriguing to social science and legal scholars. But it is precisely because issues that swirl around "profiling" are at the fascinating intersection of law and social science that we first became intrigued by the practice.[6] The "law" informs what may/could/should/might legally constitute police practice; social science suggests what does/can/might influence police behavior.[7] Behavior certainly does not "trump" legal assertions of "right" and "wrong." But viewing the "law" through the eyes of the police certainly informs our understanding of its wisdom and/or realism.[8] Behavior does not drive doctrine, but just as doctrine might inform behavior, so too it is important to observe how behavior can/might shape doctrine. . . .

PROFILING AS A CONCEPT

. . .Profiling as a separate and distinct law enforcement technique began in the mid-twentieth century and developed along two lines.[9] One path, known as criminal profiling, features the use of behavioral science—most notably psychology—as an aid to investigations in solving certain types of crimes, such as murder, serial murder, arson and rape.[10] That type of profiling is largely reactive, responding to specific known crimes, and is generally the province of a small group of "experts" in self-described "elite" units, such as the Federal Bureau of Investigation's Behavioral Sciences Unit.[11] The second path of profiling that developed has been led mostly by development of the drug courier profile.[12] This type of profiling has some things in common with criminal profiling, but is different in certain important regards. For one thing, it is more proactive, attempting to ferret out criminal activity that has so far gone undetected or that may not yet have begun.[13] This second type of profiling does not use techniques drawn from the behavioral sciences to

look for and analyze unusual or unique behavior, but is concerned with more ordinary types of conduct.[14] It is also not delegated to "elite" units comprised of specially trained scientific experts, but is employed much more broadly by police departments and law enforcement agents.[15] What has come to be called "racial profiling" developed from this second type of profiling.[16]

Profiling may be defined generally as the effort to identify potential perpetrators of crime based on their demonstrating or matching some or all of the traits shared by other known perpetrators of the same offense.[17] Profiles have been developed for a number of offenses.[18] Most ubiquitous or visible is the "drug courier profile,"[19] but others exist. As one student of profiles stated:

> The use of profiles is an increasingly prominent law enforcement tool. Most prominent among the profiles in use today are those used to identify hijackers, and those used to identify persons who smuggle illegal aliens into the country. Less prominent are the drug smuggling vessel profile, the stolen car profile, the stolen truck profile, the alimentary-canal smuggler profile, the battering parent profile, and the poacher profile. In 1983, based on interviews with alleged mass murderer Henry Lee Lucas, the Federal Bureau of Investigation . . .attempted to compile a serial killer profile. To a lesser extent, profiles are developing to help identify serial rapists, child molesters, and arsonists, and the National Center for the Analysis of Violent Crimes plans to expand its operation in an effort to track down these criminals.[20]

The profiles on that list are generally more narrowly drawn and apply to fewer people than the "drug courier profile," which is the most extensively used profile.[21] Profiling as a tool of law enforcement is, depending on your politics, either another of the benefits or another of the wayward policy mistakes of this country's efforts to combat drugs.[22] "Profiling" has been used to describe efforts by agents of the Drug Enforcement Agency and other law enforcement agents to identify possible drug couriers at airports by focusing on odd or unusual behavior.[23] More commonly and more recently, however, profiling has come to focus not on the search for unusual behavior per se, but a search for special characteristics, traits, or conduct that purport to separate the alleged perpetrator from others in the crowd.[24] These traits or conduct, it should be noted, are separate from the acts that are themselves crimes; in fact, profiling often comes to focus on behavior that is perfectly legal and in other contexts (perhaps even in the context at hand) purely innocent.[25]

One issue raised by an effort to define profiling involves the basis for identifying the factors to be used in the profile; as with other related issues, answers to that question vary. Some "profiles" rely on data drawn from past arrests and other historical data to produce commonly recurring but presumably objective, quantifiable factors.[26] Theoretically, at least, reliance on "hard data" should eliminate or reduce many of the objections to the practice.[27] Less precise than arrest-based historical data, but also frequently mentioned as a basis for identification of profiling traits, are inferences or interpretations of facts drawn by the police officer's experience.[28] Finally, at the far end of the spectrum, some practices labeled "profiling" rely on an officer's gut feelings or "hunch."[29] . . .

Finally, we briefly (for now) address the issue of race. Profiling need not consider a suspect's race or ethnicity.[30] Indeed, race was not an issue in the cases in which the United States Supreme Court considered the practice.[31] However, just as profiling does not necessarily consider race, it also does not preclude the use of race or ethnicity.[32] That does not mean that use of race in a profile necessarily means use of racial categories for discrete and insular minorities or racial groups that have been subjected to historic patterns of discrimination, to borrow from related legal concepts.[33] Still, the most recent controversies have indeed featured minority racial categories or ethnicity as at least one of the factors considered by law enforcement.[34] Moreover, race for many has become not just one factor, but the factor or consideration, practically to the exclusion of all other factors.[35] Indeed, for the most vocal and passionate critics of the practice of using a suspect's otherwise innocent conduct or characteristics to trigger police action, the use of race has been blamed for creating a new offense: DWB or "Driving While Black."[36]

Thus, in the current debate, the label of "profiling," especially racial profiling, has been used to describe a wide range of behavior, from a neutral, objective practice based on historical data (at least in theory) to simple unbridled racism.[37] Whether profiling has a role to play in police work should and must depend, at least in part, on how it actually operates in practice. It is to that consideration that we now turn.

Profiling in Practice

When we turn to police practices we quickly get to the heart of the profiling debate. On one hand, as our friend in *Fiddler on the Roof* might note, profiling is about experienced police relying on their observations based on years of working in their role.[38] On the other hand, as some, including some courts (to be discussed below), maintain, profiling based exclusively on the wrong categories (e.g., race) is both illegal (that is, unconstitutional), and morally unacceptable.[39] Indeed, it is negotiating between what experience teaches, and what the law forbids, which is the impetus that propels the inquiry into what one might call permissible and impermissible profiling.[40]

The classic conception of police stereotyping—the conception applauded and endorsed as being a desirable product of police experience—is Skolnick's notion of a "symbolic assailant."[41] Skolnick argues that the context of police work requires that police officers "develop a perceptual shorthand to identify certain kinds of people as symbolic assailants"—persons to watch as potential offenders.[42] Similarly, William Muir Jr. discussed the process by which police "make judgments."

"To make judgments" was to anticipate the future. Judgment referred to the capacity to make accurate predictions of future events. To anticipate what was going to happen, policemen developed a sense for the patterns in human affairs. They formed concepts, or classifications, which helped them to assimilate and distinguish discrete persons and events.[43]

Muir stressed that it was officer's experience that explained the formation of "a series of pigeonholes into which [an officer] slotted similar persons and events."[44] Along the same lines another expert in police behavior, Peter Manning, observed: "the policeman possesses what might be called 'recipes' for the sequences of conduct that he will engage in."[45] They are composed of typications of events, persons, and places that organize his cognitive world and mobilize his potential for action.[46]

The development of a police "shorthand" is a profile, the present negative connotation of profiling notwithstanding.[47] The difficulty arises when "the" or "a" major piece of the profile is a racial or ethnic variable.[48] And the likelihood that this is the case is certainly subtantial. Skolnick, for example, reported that most police officers have "come to identify the black man with danger."[49] Along the same lines, James Q. Wilson, a prominent student of the police, noted that "the line between prejudging . . . [people] purely on the basis of police experience and prejudging them on the basis of personal opinion (showing prejudice) is often very thin.[50] Wilson goes on to note that if a police officer "believes with considerable justification that teenagers, Negroes and lower-income persons commit a disproportionate share of all reported crimes . . . then being in those population categories at all makes one, statistically, more suspect than other persons."[51] Jonathan Rubinstein, in a wonderfully insightful book about police-patrol behavior in local neighborhoods, makes a similar point.[52]

For our first cut at profiling, we are not systematically distinguishing among police profiling practices. Many of the above observations about profiling by experienced police officers turn on street order maintenance practices. Some of these practices have been caught up in the current reconsideration of profiling,[53] though far more attention has been given to turnpike stops of minorities and the putative centrality of profiles to these state police practices. These turnpike stops, in turn, may implicate the same "order maintenance" variables that explain "street level" police practices; alternatively, police stops on highways can be said to be tipping more in the "law enforcement" mode than in the street-level order-maintenance posture.[54] Should "order maintenance" vs. "law enforcement" contribute to the propriety/legality of profiling? Similarly, is profiling at airports or borders—whether for order maintenance or law enforcement purposes somehow "more" justified than is profiling in more conventional settings?[55] Both the order-maintenance/law-enforcement axes, and the distinctions among profiling settings, lead to innumerable additional profiling calculi. Again, for our initial purposes, we choose to set these complexities aside, and deal with the broad-brush issues.

In sum, then, the police officer's experience teaches him or her to put together certain bundles of facts that lead to suspicions about potential offenders. These bundles often—though not necessarily—include racial variables.[56] When the exercise of wise discretion educated by "on-the-job" learning ends, and invidious stereotyping begins, is the question. To simply tackle "profiling" by adopting a facile, dismissive, and pejorative posture to this exercise of police discretion is to unrealistically simplify the complexity of police behavior, and to deem unacceptable some practices which are defensible and which may, indeed, even be laudable.

PROFILING ON THE TURNPIKE: SOME PRELIMINARY DATA

Much of the social science literature on "symbolic assailants" is, as we have noted, derived from observations made during street patrol by police officers.[57] We have used this literature to understand police stereotyping—the use of shortcuts to identify potential criminals. But profiling has received much of its recent attention because of the way it is alleged that state troopers use race in patrolling, not on the streets per se, but major highways in general, and on the Maryland and New Jersey Turnpikes in particular.[58]

Anecdotally, there have been many incidents suggesting this kind of profiling, and these have led to the generalization of widespread profiling practices. Moreover, several court cases in Maryland—cases in which suspects seem to be selected largely for committing the crime of DWB (driving while black)—reinforce perceptions of the prevalence of racially driven profiling.[59] Systematic data about Highway I-95 practices[60] (to which the following discussion will be limited) and more generally about police-patrol practices[61] are less common. But several significant insights emerge from what we already knew and have learned, even if these insights ultimately are dependent on more extensive research. First, in patrolling the turnpikes, police officers clearly have substantial discretion to stop almost every driver for traffic offenses.[62] David Harris, for example, in summarizing the literature on police highway stops, notes that, in addition to standard "moving violations" (speeding, for example), there are a host of other justifications which can "legitimate" a police stop.[63] Some of these are as straightforward as simple "equipment violations"; others are more general standards, which allow almost unbridled discretion (e.g. "unreasonable" driving under particular circumstances).[64] Harris details some of the laws in place in various states that contribute to the conclusion that cops can find justification to stop a driver at almost any time they want.[65] Specifically, in any number of jurisdictions, police can stop drivers not only for driving too fast, but also for driving too slow. In Utah, drivers must signal for at least three seconds before changing lanes. . . . In many states, a driver must signal for at least one hundred feet before turning right. . . . Many states have made it a crime to drive with a malfunctioning taillight, a rear-tag illumination bulb that does not work, or tires without sufficient tread.[66]

The question, of course, is "How is this discretion exercised?" The best evidence on this matter—and, by all accounts, far more data is needed—was collected by Professor John Lamberth, past Chair of the Department of Psychology at Temple University.[67] In published testimony prepared for a Maryland case, Lamberth found that, in fact, race appeared to dramatically affect the exercise of trooper discretion in a particular Maryland corridor of Highway I-95.[68] Lamberth, employing similar techniques to those he used in New Jersey and Virginia, in the context of comparable cases in Maryland, used data that had been collected by the ACLU from January 1995 to September 1996.[69] Lamberth had helped design the ACLU assigned rider project during a twelve-month period.[70] The researchers rode up-and-down I-95, and were given specific guidance to (1) count the overall numbers of cars that passed them; (2) determine the number of potential traffic violators among these cars; (3) classify the race of the driver.[71]

The results of the survey were instructive. Over 5,000 cars were included, and consistent with Harris's contentions about the ease of finding violations, the coders determined that about 93 percent of the drivers were in violation of some traffic law and, thus, could be stopped. Of the drivers, nearly 17 percent were African-Americans, and approximately 74 percent were Caucasians (apparently, in the other cases race could not be confidently determined). During this same study period the Maryland police reported 823 motorist stops in this I-95 stretch.[72] Of these, nearly 73 percent of those stopped were African-American (and another 7 percent were Hispanic or members of other racial minorities). Only about 20 percent of those stopped were Caucasian.[73]

Interestingly, these data was very similar to Lamberth's findings about the southern stretch of the New Jersey Turnpike for *New Jersey v. Soto*.[74] In New Jersey, 98 percent of the drivers committed offenses that could subject them to a stop and 15 percent of the drivers were black.[75] Yet the percentages of trooper stops were remarkably similar to the Maryland stops, with a substantial majority of those stopped being black, and a minority, white.[76]

Before turning to the matter of finding contraband after the stops, two other findings support Lamberth's contention that, with respect to stops, race looms large in this stretch of I-95.[77] First, Lamberth notes that, according to Maryland State Police data, nearly 64 percent of the stops statewide involve whites (in contrast to 20 percent on the selected I-95 strip).[78] Second, stops by race were not randomly distributed among troopers patrolling the studied area.[79] With the exception of one trooper who stopped blacks at close to the percentage of black drivers in the study area, nine of the remaining thirteen troopers who made over ten searches during the study period stopped 75 percent or more blacks.[80] Two of the troopers stopped over 90 percent minorities.[81]

There is one omission in this data—namely data about the efficacy of the stops.[82] Did the stop discover contraband and lead to an arrest? Lamberth reports that about 30 percent of the stops did lead to an arrest of the driver, but this means that in 70 percent of the stops no arrest was made.[83] Intuitively, this strongly suggests that, since blacks are being stopped at dramatically higher rates than the actual proportion of black drivers to white

drivers, many blacks are being subjected to unnecessary police stops because of their race. To support this finding, Lamberth provides state-wide Maryland police data which indicate that "find" rates for black and white drivers are the same (about 28 percent in each group).[84]

But it should be emphasized that, as far as could be determined from Lamberth's testimony, questions remain about the specific data on the stretch of I-95 he examines. First, he does not provide the "find" data for this stretch; it is quite correct to suggest that in light of the general data about the disproportionality of minority stops, and the statewide data, many minorities on this stretch are probably also being subjected to unnecessary stops. Nonetheless, data about the percentage of "finds" for his study group would be valuable. Second, it would be helpful to know more about what is found in the productive stops, and about the specifics (i.e., quantity, type) of what is found. Of course, these matters would not justify racial selection, but they would still assist in assessing how much police "wisdom" should legitimately be weighed in the exercise of police discretion.[85]

Even before the Legal Realists, people had noticed and understood a difference between "law on the books" and "law in action." As we have seen regarding the latter with regard to profiling, there is a fine line between laudable exercise of discretion by experienced police affairs, and the exercise of discretion resting on inappropriate racial or ethnic factors. "Law on the books" regarding profiling, however, presents a somewhat different picture.

Profiling and the Courts

The treatment of profiling in the courts has been significantly different than its treatment by the police and in the larger public debate. In this section we examine not simply what the judiciary has ruled about profiling in general and about racial profiling specifically, but how courts have approached the issues raised, what they have said about the practice and how, or whether, that treatment has influenced or contributed to the larger public debate.

Our focus in this section will be primarily, although not exclusively, on decisions of the United States Supreme Court. It is well settled that, for better or worse, the United States Supreme Court has assumed a dominant position among the judiciary in terms of enunciating fundamental values and articulating general principles in matters that have become the focus of larger public debates, particularly for the types of topics—such as propriety of police tactics and concerns for racial justice—that are at the heart of the debate over racial profiling. That is not to say that what lower courts rule, or the contents of their decisions, are irrelevant, but decisions of the United States Supreme Court necessarily influence and, particularly in the lower federal courts, constrain how those lower courts deal with the issues.

A look at how the courts, and the Supreme Court in particular, have addressed profiling reveals an interesting contrast to how other players have handled the subject. If the tendency in the general public has been to lump a multitude of practices into a general category of "racial profiling," courts usually have gone in the opposite direction—essentially to ignoring profiling as a separate and unique law enforcement technique.[86] At least twice over the past twenty years, the United States Supreme Court has agreed to hear a case in which the constitutionality of profiling as a law enforcement technique has been raised.[87] However, in its rulings, the Court has passed on the opportunity to recognize and consider profiling as a separate and unique law enforcement technique.[88]

Even more striking has been the courts' treatment of the issue of race. If the current public debate has been marked by a near total attention to the issue of race, to the point that the very definition or concept of racial profiling becomes obscure, the approach to the issue of race in the courts, particularly the federal courts led by the Supreme Court, has been to treat it as only a cursory concern.[89]

In short, in federal courts in particular, the courts have generally given short shrift both to the concept of profiling and especially to the issue of race that has driven the debate in other forums. This is interesting in its own right, but it also has a practical effect: largely to write the courts out of the current debate over racial profiling, or at least to greatly reduce any meaningful role for the judiciary in the debate. By itself, this phenomenon would be noteworthy, although courts do not become embroiled in every debate on every matter of significant public concern (it only seems they do). But in this situation, because, as noted above, the issues concerning police practices and racial justice swirling at the heart of the debate about racial profiling are the sort that we have come to expect the courts to address, and perhaps to take the lead on, the courts' hands-off approach has much greater import. . . .

THE COURT'S MISSED OPPORTUNITY

. . . [W]hat is most significant about the Supreme Court's treatment of profiling is the Court's refusal to give it any special attention or consideration as a unique or distinct law enforcement technique. This is particularly so . . . as the appropriateness of profiling, and especially racial profiling, has become such a visible public issue. As *Bush v. Gore* seems to demonstrate, the present United States Supreme Court is not a group that appears shy or reluctant about getting involved in the pressing issues of the day. Therefore, it is somewhat surprising that the Court has not directly and completely addressed the practice of profiling . . . especially as racial profiling has become perhaps the central law enforcement issue of the day.

Not all of the justices have been oblivious to profiling generally or racial profiling in particular. . . . Justice Marshall, joined by Justice Brennan, expressed concern about the practice of profiling and urged the Court (albeit unsuccessfully) to address the practice. . . . And Chief Justice Rehnquist had actually provided a relatively lengthy, and somewhat balanced, discussion of profiling a few years before in his dissenting opinion in *Florida v. Royer,*[90] a case that involved use by law enforcement of a profile that led to an airport stop and search; the central issue in the case, however, did not in the final analysis involve a challenge to the profile.[91]

More recently, mention of profiling—this time to racial profiling—is found in an opinion by Justice Stevens in a case from the October 1999 term, *Illinois v. Wardlow.*[92] In *Wardlow,* the Court ruled that an investigatory stop based essentially on the person's attempting to run away from law enforcement was justified under the Fourth Amendment, relying heavily in its decision on, among other cases, the decision in Sokolow.[93] In a dissenting opinion, Justice Stevens objected,

> Among some citizens, particularly minorities and those residing in high crime areas, there is also the possibility that the fleeing person is entirely innocent, but, with or without justification, believes that contact with the police can itself be dangerous, apart from any criminal activity associated with the officer's sudden presence. For such a person, unprovoked flight is neither "aberrant" nor "abnormal." Moreover, these concerns and fears are known to the police officers themselves, and are validated by law enforcement investigations into their own practices.[94]

In support of that last point, Justice Stevens discussed the New Jersey Attorney General's investigation into racial profiling, as well as an investigation by the Massachusetts Attorney General into police practices in that state.[95]

An even more pointed reference to racial profiling is found in a case from this term, *Atwater v. City of Lago Vista,*[96] again in the dissent. In *Atwater,* the Court ruled that there was no constitutional bar to a custodial arrest for a minor traffic offense, even when the un-

derlying traffic offense could not, by itself, be punished by imprisonment.[97] Dissenting, Justice Sandra Day O'Connor objected to the "unbounded discretion" the Court's decision gave to police officers, and supported her argument with the observation that "as the recent debate over racial profiling demonstrates all too clearly, a relatively minor traffic infraction may often serve as an excuse for stopping and harassing an individual."[98]

What, then, can one conclude. . .about. . .the Court's refusal to take profiling seriously, or at least to discuss it at any length as a separate and legitimate law enforcement technique? Before one rushes to judgment, perhaps the Court has it right. Perhaps the Court considers questions concerning the value of profiling as a unique and legitimate law enforcement technique and whether it should be used, as matters solely for the police and legislature to decide, subject only to whatever constraints are imposed by the Fourth Amendment over the full range of investigation and arrest practices. Perhaps, under this view, the constraints, such as they are. . .actually have a very salutary effect. Profiling as a general policy or unique practice is only a starting point and its use in specific cases will be tested, and hopefully sharpened, by general Fourth Amendment principles and limitations.

. . . The Court never quite explains exactly why it refuses to recognize profiling as a separate and valuable, or inappropriate, law enforcement technique. It could be because the Court does, in fact, consider profiling to be a valuable law enforcement technique, but as noted above, one the use of which is a decision for the police and the legislature alone. Or the Court's hands-off approach to profiling could be based on the premise that profiling really has no intrinsic value at all. Or, perhaps the message one should derive from the Court's decisions is that, while the use of profiles has some value, it is no different—or more valuable—than any other type of law enforcement practice. Or, perhaps the answer is simply that the Court refused to consider the use of profiles as a separate and unique law enforcement technique because, for whatever reason, it did not believe it had to do so to reach the decision required by the governing Fourth Amendment law.

One simply does not know, because the Court does not make clear its thinking on the issue. Of course, courts frequently resort to the principle that, in deciding cases, they should not reach issues not strictly necessary to deciding the case at hand.[99] Moreover, it would be wrong to criticize the Court for failing to assist the current debate by clarifying the concept of profiling and its lawful parameters in two decisions handed down when the issue of profiling was well below the radar screen and not the hot-button issue it is today.

Still, it is at least possible that, had the Court dealt with profiling as a distinct law enforcement practice as it at least twice had the opportunity to do and as Justice Marshall urged . . .the Court may have helped clarify concepts and issues that are currently very much the subject of debate. However, the Court passed on the chance to do so. . . .

Ultimately, though, and perhaps more importantly, one significant result of the Court's hands-off approach to profiling has been to divorce, or at least distance, the Court (and all of the other lower courts that are required to follow the Court's direction on these issues) from the emerging public debate. And that phenomenon is exacerbated by the Court's treatment of what has become the central issue in the larger public debate, the issue of race. We turn to that now.

THE SUPREME COURT AND THE ISSUE OF RACE

RACE AND PROFILING

Race has become a critical, perhaps the critical issue, in the current debate about profiling. The role that consideration of race in criminal justice issues has played and should play has generated a huge literature, particularly with regard to the type of Fourth Amendment issues relevant to the current public debate concerning profiling.[100] It is beyond the scope of this article to delve fully into that literature, but some of the more general themes will be discussed as they relate to profiling and the arguments we surface here.

The Court has not yet dealt with "racial profiling," at least in a case involving a formal law enforcement profile in which race was one factor among many.[101] Neither Reid nor Sokolow, for example, raised the issue of race at all.[102] But that is not to say that the Court's current treatment of race in the context of the Fourth Amendment does not affect the issues surrounding racial profiling.[103] Moreover, just as the Court has refused to treat the use of profiles as a separate law enforcement technique, it has even more directly refused to consider claims of racial bias in assessing Fourth Amendment claims, even as, ironically, the larger public debate has placed the issue of race at the heart of the controversy over profiling. The Court's decisions in this area have served . . .essentially to write the Court out of the current public debate over profiling.[104] . . .

THE COURT STEPS OUT

In assessing this state of affairs, one might argue that perhaps the Court has attempted to reach for the high ground and assume its proper role, as described by the late Alexander M. Bickel in his classic study, *The Least Dangerous Branch.*[105] In defending judicial review against charges that it was counter-majoritarian, Bickel assigned judges the role of rising above the heat and passion of the moment to allow the application of a society's enduring principles to contemporary problems.[106]

The trouble with this analysis as applied to the debate about profiling is that the Supreme Court, and the lower courts that are following its lead, do not appear to be elevating the debate, but rather ducking it. It is difficult to see what higher principle emerges from the Court's opinions on what has become one of the most fiercely debated issue in criminal justice, and how, if at all, the Court has advanced the debate.

Nor is this a case of the Court deferring to the legislative and executive branches on the issue of profiling, a possibility that might even hypothetically be more attractive if the other branches and participants in the debate were doing a better job of defining and considering the relevant issues. Constitutional issues, one might argue, are not always only, or even primarily, for the courts to decide.[107] But that is not what is going on here either and, if it were, abdication by the courts would be even more troubling. Because of the nature of the conduct at issue—law enforcement personnel deciding to stop persons ultimately charged with a crime—the courts must necessarily become involved. And indeed, the Court's refusal to engage in consideration of factors such as the racial motivation of the law enforcement officers making the stops has done nothing to reduce the number of cases coming to the courts involving either profiling strictly defined or, as more generally thought of, such as pre-textual stops. Profiling generally and racial profiling specifically are simply not "political questions." This is particularly so as the debate has raged at a time when the Court has shown itself to be less and less receptive to competing visions of the scope of constitutional rights by other branches of government.[108]

Of course, this observation about the approach of the Court drawn from a series of somewhat disparate decisions over the past decade (or more) is about the role (or, more accurately, the lack of a role) the Court is in effect playing, consciously or not. It is not an assessment of how the Court would or should rule if it does decide to address the practice of racial profiling. Indeed, veteran Supreme Court watchers like to be on the alert for subtle (sometimes not-so-subtle) statements in cases that send a signal that the Court wants or is about to address a given issue.[109] In that regard, perhaps the recent allusions to racial profiling by Justice Stevens in *Wardlow* and

Justice O'Connor in *Atwater* signal that the Court is prepared, perhaps even looking, to address racial profiling head on. Of course, to do so the Court will have to revisit *Whren* and its recent jurisprudential approach to race, either reversing that approach, modifying it, or, in the face of widespread and passionate concern about the interaction of race and profiling, affirming and further cementing the *Whren* approach. And maybe, for those most concerned about racial profiling, the Court's silence or apathy on the issue is not a bad thing. For those who subscribe to this view, perhaps this is not the time (or the Justices) for the Court to jump into the fray.[110]

Still, the Court's hands-off approach is at least curious and ultimately significant, given that the Court has, at least for much of the last half century, been in the forefront on issues related both to police practices and race. Indeed, for a period of time, the two areas were somewhat joined and the Court was arguably the leading voice on issues of racial justice.[111] And while some have come to question whether some of the Court's landmark decisions, such as *Brown v. Board of Education*, were effective[112] or perhaps even counter-productive,[113] few have doubted the central role the Court has played in addressing the key issues. Of course, the current Court is a distant cousin to the Warren Court, as not only *Whren*, but other recent cases in other areas of law make clear.[114] But that makes it no less noteworthy that the Court is not playing a role in the larger public debate.

RESEARCH DIRECTIONS, POLICY CONSIDERATIONS, AND CONCLUSIONS

...On the most basic level it is intriguing to reflect on the evolution of the term "profiling" itself. What began as a laudable, progressive, and wise law enforcement approach to succinctly capturing attributes strongly correlated with illegal behavior—*terrorism*, drug smuggling, etc.—profiling in its latter day incarnation is often synonymous with racism. Public officials compete in their condemnation of profiling. To take just one recent example, in the Democratic debates in the recently concluded Presidential campaign, Bill Bradley attacked Al Gore for not being strong enough in his actions condemning profiling. Gore responded that Bradley is from the very state which gave our nation profiling, and thus should be last to cast stones at others. Similarly, examining the evolution of profiling teaches very important lessons about the separation of powers. Legislative bodies have been quick to jump on the "profiling is racism" bandwagon. Little is to be lost, it appears, by championing this equation, and much is to be gained. The executive branch is more divided, or at least this was the case in New Jersey. On the one hand, once profiling and racism began to be used interchangeably, both the governor and the Attorney General's Office moved toward joining the condemnation of profiling. Prior to the evolution of the "racism equation," these officials were unwilling to concede that race played a role in police decisions, and actively opposed any court challenges arguing the opposite. On the other hand, the police clearly felt, and may still feel, that it was (is) appropriate to use race as one of a number of variables to construct particular profiles. The Federal government was explicitly sending this message, as were their own training materials. This police attitude was well represented in the remarks of the superintendent of the state police who was fired for making the kinds of very popular generalizations about ethnic group involvement in particular crimes that we reviewed earlier. Finally, the judicial branch, particularly on the Federal level, has not appeared to subscribe to the blanket condemnation of racism that has made its way into legislative and some executive voices.

Profiling, it appears, is, or at least may be, both more and less than its treatment by the various branches allows. Profiling—properly understood as the use by law enforcement of a number of factors, drawn from objective data in the historical record, with sufficient probative value of potential criminal activity to warrant law enforcement attention or action—appears to be a much narrower type of specific conduct than it has been labeled by the legislature and has garnered most of the popular reaction.[115] On the other hand, it is also a more unique or distinctive law enforcement technique than courts, or at least the United States Supreme Court, has been willing to recognize so far. Recognition of that fact raises other questions—most notably, as discussed earlier in this article, how effective profiling is at actually detecting criminal activity, but others as well, such as whether the practice is more effective and less subject to abuse in some settings as opposed to others—and, by itself, neither compels nor justifies the use of profiling. But recognition of that fact, it seems to us, should be part of the public debate.

The same is true of the issue of race as it relates to profiling; it also raises additional questions and must be part of the debate. What exactly does it mean to describe "racial profiling" as "singling out" a person for questioning because of the person's race? Does that mean race is the sole factor? Does that cover consideration of a suspect's race as one among many factors? Some may argue that using race as one factor in connection with a carefully devised programming of profiling, properly understood, should eliminate the worst aspects of what is currently being debated: what we have called "hunch policing" and pre-textual stops in which a suspect's race provides all the motivation to stop someone as an opportunity to search for evidence of other crimes for which there is no known evidence at the time of the stop.[116]

But is that enough? Is a suspect's race as part of a carefully devised profile no different from any other neutral fact—such as whether a person has purchased airline tickets with cash to fly to a city associated with the drug trade—that does not otherwise invite controversy? Or will race become the critical factor in the decision to stop a suspect?[117] Moreover, as a practical matter, will race always become the critical factor on which the decision to make a stop is based? Is it possible, as a practical matter, to employ race as a factor in profiling without the practice turning into unchecked targeting of minorities that have historically been discriminated against?[118] Conversely, is it possible, for that matter, to wean police officers off of considerations of race in the performance of their duties? If not, is the best cure to develop an objective "scientific" method of profiling to best control considerations of race and to avoid abusive pre-textual stops?

That last question leads finally to what may be the most challenging questions, the ones most difficult to answer. Even if it is possible to devise an objective method of profiling such that consideration of race as one among many factors adds something reliable to law enforcement's decision whether to detain a suspect, are the psychological and societal costs of such profiling simply too high to justify the practice? We have in the past refused to allow consideration of the impact of race on a practice, even when we were prepared to assume the truth of the facts asserted. For example, when the Civil Rights Act of 1964[119] outlawed discrimination in public accommodations, white hotel or restaurant owners were not allowed an exemption from the law on the grounds that serving African-Americans would drive off the establishment's usual white customers, even if that were true.[120] Indeed, many of those who have written on the subject of racially motivated pre-textual traffic stops have described the humiliating effects of the practice on the persons being stopped and the African-American community in general.[121] On the other hand, there have been settings, albeit limited, in which we have allowed objective considerations of race a role in decision-making; most notably affirmative action, at least until recent judicial decisions appear to be foreclosing that option as well. Is the use of race as one among many factors in profiling a legitimate use of objective, historically-based data or does its use—particularly in the criminal justice setting, in which race has too often played a pernicious and discriminatory role—impose costs too great to bear?

The courts have fairly consistently maintained that race, as one of a number of variables, can be incorporated into a profile of a criminal engaged in a particular kind of crime.[122] It remains to be seen whether the view of the court merely lags the more common current condemnation, or whether the courts retain the view that under certain circumstances consideration of race along with other variables is appropriate. Both the way "profiling" evolved in the popular lexicon, and the ways it has been interpreted differently by the three branches of government, remain matters in need of more careful documentation and examination, for they say much about changing values, changing understanding of appropriate classifications, and about how the different branches of our government process these changes.

We began by suggesting that today's interest in profiling ought not to lead to a facile rejection of police insights. On the other hand, as a society, we must draw lines as to where a police "belief" about probable guilt must stop, no matter the experience the police officer has. The wisdom of experience, together with the moral sanction of the law and a recognition of how each could inform the other, and a recognition that more quantitative and qualitative data are needed to replace anecdotal profiling assertions, are the ways that we should engage the current profiling debates. As we continue to grapple on a doctrinal level with the weights that racial or ethnic variables can have, we ought to undertake a systematic study of the "law in action," of the reasons behind why the police form judgments as they do. An appropriate rush to condemn invidious stereotyping or profiling, ought not also lead us to condemn wise judgments by experienced police officers appropriately weighing factors associated with higher probabilities of offending behavior. To point to this complexity is easy; it will be collecting and assessing the data that will be far more difficult. . . .

Notes

1. John Kifner & David M. Herszenhorn, Racial "Profiling" at Crux of Inquiry Into Shooting by Troopers, *N.Y. Times,* May 8, 1998, at B1.

2. Robert D. McFadden, Four Officers Indicted for Murder in Killing of Diallo, Lawyer Says, *N.Y. Times,* Mar. 26, 1999, at A1.

3. Michael Cooper, Officers in Bronx Fire 41 Shots and an Unarmed Man Is Killed, *N.Y. Times,* Mar. 26, 1999, at A1.

4. See supra notes 1-3 and accompanying text.

5. See *Id.*

6. As one scholar has commented recently, "all parts of the government are crucial to the realization of the promise of the Constitution. Examination of political efforts to construct constitutional meaning reveals that the governing Constitution is a synthesis of legal doctrines, institutional practices, and political norms." Keith E. Whittington, Constitutional Construction: Divided Powers and Constitutional Meaning 3 (1999).

7. For an informative analysis of categorization, schemas, stereotyping, and its effect on police behavior, see Anthony C. Thompson, Stopping the Usual Suspects: Race and the Fourth Amendment, 74 N.Y.U. L. Rev. 956 (1999). For a sample of hypotheses suggesting conditions that shape police behavior, see Dorothy Guyot, Policing as Though People Matter 293–295 (1991) (discussing the invaluable learning experience rookies gain from senior officers); John Kleinig, The Ethics of Policing 39-94 (Douglas MacLean ed., 1996) (discussing the freedom and lack of restraint that envelops law enforcement); Barbara R. Price, Police Professionalism 3–11 (1977) (discussing the social environment within which crime fighting takes place); Jonathan Rubinstein, City Police 32–43 (1973) (discussing the importance of the fraternity of the police squad in teaching the rookie his job).

8. "Lt. Ernest Leatherbury, a spokesman for the Maryland State Police (a department that has been sued twice over race-based traffic stops), explained to the *Washington Post* that stopping an outsized number of blacks was not racism, but rather 'an unfortunate byproduct of sound police policies.'" David A. Harris, The Stories, the Statistics, and the Law: Why "Driving While Black" Matters, 84 Minn. L. Rev. 265, 268 (1999) [hereinafter Harris, The Stories, the Statistics] (quoting Michael A. Fletcher, Driven to Extremes; Black Men Take Steps to Avoid Police Stops, *Wash. Post,* Mar. 29, 1996, at A22).

9. Milton Heumann & Lance Cassak, Good Cop, Bad Cop; Profiling, Race, and Competing Views of Justice (forthcoming 2002) (manuscript on file with authors).

10. Brent E. Turvey, Criminal Profiling: An Introduction to Behavioral Evidence Analysis 1–8 (1999).

11. *Id.*

12. Heumann & Cassak, supra note 9.

13. *Id.*

14. *Id.*

15. *Id.*

16. *Id.*

17. See Randall Kennedy, You Can't Judge a Crook by His Color, The New Republic, Sept. 13, 1999, at 30 reprinted in UTNE Reader, Jan.–Feb. 2000, at 71 [hereinafter Kennedy, You Can't Judge a Crook] (discussing race as a predominant trait of profiling).

18. Charles L. Becton, The Drug Courier Profile: "All Seems Infected That Th' Infected Spy, As All Looks Yellow To the Jaundic'd Eye," 65 N.C. L. Rev. 417, 424–426 (1987).

19. *Id.*

20. *Id.* For a fuller discussion of the evolution of profiling in the late twentieth century, see Heumann & Cassak.

21. Jay M. Zitter, Annotation, Admissibility of Drug Courier Profile Testimony in Criminal Prosecution, 69 A.L.R. 5th 425, 426 (2001) (discussing cases that have considered whether and under what circumstances "drug courier profile" evidence may be admissible in criminal cases).

22. Cf. Michael Tonry, Malign Neglect: Race, Crime and Punishment in America 81–123 (1995) (describing hopes for and unfortunate consequences of the War on Drugs).

23. See, e.g., Peter Verniero & Paul H. Zoubeck, Interim Report of the State Police Review Team Regarding Allegations of Racial Profiling 53 (Apr. 20, 1999).

24. *Id.* at 20.

25. *Id.* at 49. See generally Reid v. Georgia, 448 U.S. 438 (1980) (recognizing that three out of four facts relied on in the stop of defendant at an airport are circumstances that "describe a very large category of presumably innocent travelers"); United States v. Hooper, 935 F.2d 484, 493 (2d Cir. 1991) (indicating that acts innocent in isolation may amount to reasonable suspicion when considered together) (citing United States v. Sokolow, 490 U.S. 1, 9–10 (1989)).

26. See Kennedy, You Can't Judge a Crook, (illustrating the Los Angeles Police Department's predominant use of Colombians as suspects based upon their history of committing a particular crime).

27. But see Verniero & Zoubeck, (arguing that empirical evidence derived from crime trend analysis does not provide objective validity for the use of profiles, but merely reflects the stereotypes of those generating the statistics).

28. *Id.* at 49 ("Police may piece together a series of acts, which by themselves seem innocent, but to a trained officer would reasonably indicate that criminal activity is afoot.") (citing New Jersey v. Patterson, 637 A.2d 593, 597 (N.J. Super. Ct. Law Div. 1993).

29. The practice of relying on a "hunch," however, has been firmly rejected. See Terry v. Ohio, 392 U.S. 1, 27 (1968) (stating that an "inchoate and unparticularized suspicion or 'hunch'" is not to be accorded any weight in determining the reasonableness of an officer's conduct).

30. See, e.g., Sokolow, 490 U.S. at 1; Reid v. Georgia, 448 U.S. 438 (1980) (per curiam).

31. Sokolow, 490 U.S. at 3–11; Reid, 448 U.S. at 439–442 (1980).

32. Some have argued that use of race in profiles, at least the drug courier profile, has become common or routine. See *Id.* See, e.g., Sheri

Lynn Johnson, Race and the Decision to Detain a Suspect, 93 Yale L.J. 214, 234 (1983) [hereinafter Johnson, Race and the Decision to Detain].

33. Perhaps ironically, some less frequently used or publicized profiles, those that have avoided the close scrutiny directed at the drug courier profile and other decisions to stop motorists in the effort to combat drugs, have racial components and that fact has attracted little or no attention. For example, it is part of the standard profile of serial killers that the typical killer is white. See James Alan Fox & Jack Levin, Multiple Homicide: Patterns of Serial and Mass Murder, 23 Crime & Just. 407, 413 (1998).

34. See, e.g., Steven A. Holmes, Clinton Orders Investigation on Possible Racial Profiling, *N.Y. Times*, June 10, 1999, at A22; Kifner & Herszenhorn, supra note 1, at B1.

35. See, e.g., McFadden, supra note 7, at A1; Zitter, see also Neil A. Lewis, Arab-Americans Protest "Profiling" at Airports, *N.Y. Times*, Aug. 10, 1997, at A12.

36. See, e.g., David A. Harris, "Driving While Black" And All Other Traffic Offenses: The Supreme Court and Pretextual Traffic Stops, 87 *J. Crim. L. & Criminology* 544 (1997) [hereinafter Harris, Driving While Black]; Henry Louis Gates, Thirteen Ways of Looking at a Black Man, *New Yorker*, Oct. 23, 1995, at 59 (describing "a moving violation that many African-Americans know as D.W.B.: Driving While Black").

37. See, e.g., Mark Mueller, Papers Show How Profiling Flourished, *Star-Ledger* (Newark, N.J.), Nov. 28, 2000, at 1; Jodi Wilgoren, Police Profiling Debate Hinges on Issue of Experience versus Bias, *N.Y. Times*, Apr. 9, 1999, at B1. On the one side there are charges that profiling "is pure racism and should not stand." Kirk D. Richards, Middle Eastern People Being Booted Off Planes, *Columbus Dispatch*, Sept. 28, 2001, at 01A (quoting Nihan Awad, Director of the Council on American-Islamic Relations in Washington, D.C.). On the other side, there are statements like those made by Bud Hansen, a former chief deputy sheriff in Los Angeles County, who asserts that "street police work is all about profiling . . .it has nothing to do with racial prejudice." Mindy

Cameron, Profiling is an Inherent Part of Police Work, *Seattle Times,* Sept. 30, 2001, at B10.

38. For a discussion of the role experience plays in police behavior and performance, see. . .William K. Muir, Jr., Police: Streetcorner Politicians 47–60 (1977); Roy R. Roberg & Jack Kuykendall, Police and Society 126–155, 159–196 (1993). For more discussion on the role experience plays in discriminatory police practices, see Homer Hawkins & Richard Thomas, White Policing of Black Populations: A History of Race and Social Control in America, in Out of Order: Policing Black People 65–87 (Ellis Cashmore & Eugene McLaughlin eds., 1991); Charles E. Owens & Jimmy Bell, Blacks and Criminal Justice 37–47 (1977); Rubinstein; Katheryn K. Russell, The Color of Crime 26–46 (1998); Jerome H. Skolnick, Justice Without Trial: Law Enforcement in Democratic Society 6, 17, 24, 31, 34, 196 (1967).

39. Some courts have so ruled. See United States v. Avery, 137 F.3d 343, 354 (6th Cir. 1997) (indicating that selective law enforcement based on skin color is forbidden, as investigations based solely on race and other impermissible factors are prohibited under the Fourteenth Amendment); United States v. Laymon, 730 F. Supp. 332, 339 (D. Colo. 1990) (holding that "profile stops may not be predicated on unconstitutional discrimination based on race, ethnicity or state of residence" and granting defendant's motion to suppress evidence based on a finding that a traffic stop was pretextual); New Jersey v. Soto, 734 A.2d 350, 360–361 (N.J. Super. Ct. Law Div. 1996) (granting defendants' motion to suppress where defendants proved a de facto policy by the State Police of targeting blacks which the state failed to rebut); New Jersey v. Kuhn, 517 A.2d 162 (N.J. Super. Ct. App. Div. 1986) (finding an insufficient evidentiary basis for stopping defendant's car and holding that "no rational inference may be drawn from the race of one to be detained that he may be engaged in criminal activities").

40. This stated equilibrium between permissible and impermissible policing assumes that one can "negotiate" between experience and law. However, this also assumes that the law clearly falls either on the side supporting racial profiling or prohibiting racial profiling and as we will review shortly, this is not the case. On the one hand, the Federal Government has evidenced its equivocal approval of racial profiles. See, e.g., David Kocieniewski, New Jersey Argues that the US Wrote the Book on Racial Profiling, *N.Y. Times,* Nov. 29, 2000, at A1; Ron Marisco & Kathy Barrett Carter, State Ties Profiling to Advice on Crime Fighting, Star-Ledger (Newark, N.J.), Nov. 28, 2000, at 26. On the other hand, the courts have sent a much more mixed, and at times muddled, message—to the extent they have sent one at all. While some courts have stated categorically that the decision to stop a suspect cannot be based solely on the suspect's race—more often, courts, including the Supreme Court, have refused to consider the issue or treat it with only passing comment.

The Drug Enforcement Agency ("DEA") stands as the epitome of such a contradictory position. For example, Operation Pipeline, a DEA program, was enacted to aggressively fight the war on drugs and was used by forty-eight states, yet explicitly relied on race as an identifier of crime. See Kocieniewski, at A1; Marsico & Barrett Carter, (discussing "The Cocaine Threat to the United States"). The DEA, a department of the Federal Government, in effect perpetuated the use of profiles. Marsico & Barrett Carter, supra, at 26. Yet, how does one reconcile DEA sponsored approval of profiles of the law with a policy that strictly forbids reliance on race as the determining factor for criminality? Of late, it should be noted, the Federal Government has recognized the difficulty, and during the last five years, the DEA has announced that it has "stopped distributing training videos in which all the drug suspects have Spanish surnames." Kocieniewski, at A1. There is a certain ambiguity in the use of racial variables in training manuals. That ambiguity lies around whether the racial variables are the principle variables, or just one of many variables.

Therefore, not enough detailed information is known to assert that the DEA training manuals advocate racial profiling, simply based on the use of racial variables. For example, last year, the DEA's Newark, New Jersey's office released the "Heroin Trends" report which noted: predominant wholesale traffickers are Colombian, followed by Dominicans, Chinese, West African/Nigerian, Pakistani, Hispanic, and Indian. *Id.* Accordingly, the report leaves it undetermined whether or not it advocates the use of racial variables as the only decisive factor or simply one of many variables to consider.

Nonetheless, while the Federal Government is vocalizing its position against racial profiling and asserting that it is not recognized by the law, the DEA, a part of the Federal Government, is not in total compliance, as it maintains race inclusive training programs and reports. *Id.* Police officers, then, need to reconcile calls to stop racial profiling against instructions to rely on racial variables by the Federal Government. In essence, there may be no equilibrium between permissible and impermissible profiling if the law on profiling remains nebulous. As we shall see shortly, the courts generally conclude that the exclusive use of race as a profile is impermissible; on the other hand the courts also conclude that the use of race as part of a profile may be acceptable. Profiling will remain a questionable police activity, therefore, until the law can agree on whether it is allowed.

41. Skolnick, supra note 38, at 45–46, 217–218.

42. *Id.* at 45.

43. Muir, supra note 38, at 153.

44. *Id.* at 156.

45. Peter Manning, Police Work: The Social Organization of Policing 236 (1979).

46. *Id.*

47. See *Id.*

48. While much of this article concentrates on the use of profiles during highway or street stops, thereby focusing on blacks and Latinos, it would be misleading to ignore that other minorities are affected by profiling. For example, the use of Middle Eastern or Arabian ethnicity is a very common practice at airports when checking bags for explosives and bombs. Beth Krodel, Airport Security Methods Assailed, Detroit Free Press, Sept. 8, 1998, at A1. While this may seem to be a legitimate means to ensure passenger safety, people of Middle Eastern or Arabian origin feel it is equivalent to racial profiling. The manuals used by ground personnel to help determine which passengers are selected for searches explicitly list ethnic associations. Lewis, supra note 63, at A12.

The FAA, after years of fending off complaints, has decided to require the airlines to move towards a computerized profiling system that, officials say, does not allow for discrimination based on ethnic background. Matthew L. Wald, Airlines Criticized for Plans to Flag Suspicious Travelers, *N.Y. Times,* Jan. 1, 1998, at A13. The new system, known as Computerized Assisted Passenger Screening ("CAPS"), would replace the current method of allowing individual security people at the gate to decide who could be a risk based on written manuals by quickly separating passengers into two categories: those who do not require additional security and those who do. White House Commission on Aviation Safety and Security, The Dot Status Report: Improving Security for Travelers (Sept. 19, 1999) 3.19 & 3.24 available at http://www.dot.gov/affairs/whcsec3.htm. This system has been approved by the Department of Justice, which found that CAPS (a) "fully complies with the equal protection guarantee incorporated in the Fifth Amendment to the Constitution"; (b) "does not violate the Fourth Amendment prohibition on unreasonable searches and seizures"; and (c) "does not involve any invasion of passengers personal privacy."*Id.* 3.19 (quoting the Civil Rights Division, Department of Justice Report (Oct. 1, 1997)).

Nonetheless, critics of the CAPS system persist. One common criticism is the blanket assertion that CAPS will lead to discrimination against members of some religious or ethnic groups because the system still works by evaluating a variety of facts about a passenger and comparing them against a profile of a potential terrorist devised by the FAA and security guards. Wald, supra, at A13. Furthermore, the silence of the FAA and airport officials regarding the content of profiles exacerbates any extant criticisms about the discriminatory impact of profiling.

49. Skolnick, supra note 38, at 49; see also Tracey Maclin, Race and the Fourth Amendment, 51 Vand. L. Rev. 333, 387 (1998) [hereinafter Maclin, Race and the Fourth Amendment] (arguing that police seizures disproportionately affect blacks and minorities, for blacks

and minorities, he argues, are singled out even though there may not be empirical evidence that shows blacks are more likely to have contraband).

50. James Wilson, Varieties of Police Behavior 38 (1968) (emphasis added). Another inherent social difficulty facing police officers is having them recognize that their behavior is discriminatory even when it cannot be easily characterized as "biased:" "Some law enforcement agents consciously act on the basis of racial bias, other times discriminatory treatment is the product of unconscious racism." Thompson, supra note 12, at 972.

51. Wilson, supra note 78, at 40.

52. Rubinstein points out that:

> the great majority of suspicion occurs in poor neighborhoods, because that is where street crime is the greatest, where the most drugs are sold in the streets, and where people are the least safe. In some of these neighborhoods policemen stop people for reasons many people might consider reprehensible. For example, when a patrolman sees a white person he does not know in a black neighborhood, he thinks the person is there to buy either drugs or sex. He knows that many people would think him prejudiced or cynical for harboring such thoughts, but he also knows that these people have not seen what he has seen.... This may be an unwholesome perception, but the policeman's experience tells him it is by and large valid. The policeman making the stop is not questioning the person's right to walk there but the infrequency of its occurrence. For the policeman these judgments are rooted in the reality of city life. He is not making a moral judgment (regardless of what his private opinions are) but is responding to what he sees daily on the street.

Rubinstein, supra note 7, at 262–263.

Jesse Jackson has been quoted in a similar vein. Kennedy, You Can't Judge a Crook, supra note 32, at 30. In 1993, he remarked, "there is nothing more painful to me at this stage in my life than to walk down the street

and hear footsteps and start to think robbery and then look around and see somebody white and feel relieved." *Id.*

53. In New York City, for example, questions about police stops in general, and about stops by a special elite unit in particular, have recently been forcefully raised. See Michael Cooper, Street Searches by City's Police Lead to Inquiry, *N.Y. Times,* Mar. 18, 1999, at A1; Benjamin Weiser, Lawsuit Seeks to Curb Street Crime Unit, Alleging Racially Biased Searches, *N.Y. Times,* Mar. 9, 1999, at B3.

54. For more on the reconsideration of order maintenance practices as profiling, see Jeffrey Fagan & Garth Davies, Street Stops and Broken Windows: Terry, Race, and Disorder in New York City, 28 Fordham Urb. L.J. 457, 458–464 (2000), which discusses the difference between the "Broken Windows" theory and the order maintenance theory and the "twist" given recently to it in policing policy in New York City.

Broken window theory, as developed by James Q. Wilson & George L. Kelling, The Police and Neighborhood Safety: Broken Windows, *Atlantic Monthly,* Mar. 1982, at 29, asserts that disorder of a neighborhood communicates or conveys an absence of authority to others who, thereby, interpret the disorder as "tolerance" or an invitation to criminal behavior. The focus of police behavior is on removing or repairing, not just "arresting," physical disorder problems. *Id.* Order Maintenance Policing, as defined by New York City, presents itself as an interpretation of the Broken Window Theory, in which cops attack social disorder [person-focused tactics] rather than physical disorder [place-based police tactics], with an attitude of zero tolerance involving active engagement with and arrest of law violators. *Id.* The focus of police behavior is on "disorder policing." *Id.* Therefore, the so-called "order maintenance" of order maintenance policing is more accurately described as a strain of "law enforcement," where cops seek to maximize their arrests, instead of creating a relationship with the community. *Id.* Order Maintenance Policing has "little to do with fixing broken windows and much more to do with arresting window breakers. . . ." Bernard E. Harcourt,

Reflecting on the Subject: A Critique of the Social Influence Conception of Deterrence, the Broken Windows Theory, and Order-Maintenance Policing New York Style, 97 Mich. L. Rev. 291, 342 (1998).

Fagan and Davies further assert that not only is order maintenance policing in New York City more attuned to law enforcement policing, it is also used in a discriminatory manner. Fagan & Davies, supra, at 458–459. Ceterus paribus [holding race/crime rates constant], the authors of this study found that blacks and Hispanics were stopped more than whites. *Id.* at 477–479. One conclusion for this could be that police make race a motivating factor for stops/frisks, i.e., racial profiling. In fact, The New York City Police Department's "'Stop and Frisk' Practices," shows that race was a factor in the New York Police Department's everyday policing. Civil Rights Bureau, Office of the Attorney General of the State of New York, The New York City Police Department's "Stop and Frisk" Practices (1999) [hereinafter Stop and Frisk Practices]. These results, however, do not unequivocally answer the question of whether police targeted neighborhoods because of the people who lived in certain communities merely because of disorder levels. See generally Stop and Frisk Practices.

To answer this question, the authors put together a rather complex regression analysis to test: (a) for the net effects of race on patterns of policing, after controlling for disorder; and (b) whether the factors or characteristics of neighborhoods that police rely on, factors that are also correlated with race, are significant predictors of stop and frisk patterns after controlling for disorder. Fagan & Davies, supra, at 474, 493–496. The authors hypothesized that crime rates alone would not explain the differences in stops by race or by type of crime and the results confirmed their hypothesis. *Id.* The data revealed that while the arrest rates predicts total and weapons stops, factors other than crime rates also affect stops such as factors attributed to policy or unspoken assumptions about race/neighborhood/criminality. *Id.* For example, policing a certain neighborhood may reflect the economic status of that

neighborhood rather than the physical conditions of its buildings; since impoverished areas in New York City are disproportionately populated by blacks, this policing policy can lead to a singling out of suspects by race. *Id.* The authors conclude that order maintenance policing more closely resembles policing of poor people in poor places than policing disorder. *Id.*

Therefore, asserting that police stops on highways implicate street level order maintenance practices or the law enforcement mode may in fact be stating the same thing. Fagan and Davies would argue that order maintenance policing and law enforcement are becoming increasingly distinguishable. *Id.* at 500–503. Furthermore, the data seem to support the conclusions that both highway stops and the New York City "twist" on order maintenance policing have a disproportionate effect on racial minorities. See *Id.*

55. The use of the drug courier profile at airports parallels the use of the drug courier profile on highways, except perhaps, the fact that some may contend that its use at airports is even more questionable. The airport drug courier profile was the innovation of Special Agent Paul Markonni, a DEA agent who led the battle against narcotic couriers in the late 1970's. . . . Not coincidentally, it was during this time that the drug problem emerged as a mainstream problem. The legacy of Markonni's drug courier profile includes variables such as the "source cities" and "use-cities" and the existence of a "nervous look."

Moreover, statistics reveal that the fluidity of the airport drug courier profile may work disproportionately to the disadvantage of blacks. Holmes, supra note 34, at A22. In 1998, Customs Service conducted 2500 searches on the more than seventy million people who arrived in the United States at legal ports of entry. *Id.* Three out of four strip searches were women, and two out of three of the women were black. Strip Searches May Go Nationwide, (MSNBC television broadcast, July 15, 1998). Another concern should be the effectiveness of such searches. *Id.* In 1997, the records at O'Hare showed 104 total strip searches. *Id.* In twenty cases, inspectors found drugs during the strip search. *Id.* In seven cases, they found drugs in luggage or a pants pocket, which triggered a strip search that found no additional drugs. *Id.* But in seventy-seven cases, the strip searches turned up nothing. *Id.* Furthermore, female passengers were the most likely targets; more than 2/3 (67 percent) of those strip searched last year were women. *Id.* Black women had to undress almost twice as many times as white women. *Id.* But detailed research on stops/searches/seizures in airports, a separate study, is needed to fully understand the situation and to frame policy recommendations.

56. See Kennedy, You Can't Judge a Crook, supra note 17, at 30 (categorizing uses of race in different profiling situations); see also Fagan & Davies, supra note 82, at 478–480 (explaining that the New York Police Department attributes higher percentages of stops of minority groups to higher percentages of such groups which participate in crime, although race is not to be determinative).

57. Skolnik, supra note 38, at 45–48 (describing a police officer's view of "symbolic assailant" as affected by what officer's perception of danger); see Wilson & Kelling, supra note 82, at 33 (arguing that foot-patrol officers are more adept at spotting potential criminals, and that efforts which target these individuals make the community safer).

58. See, e.g., Michael Janofsky, Maryland Troopers Stop Drivers by Race, Suit Says, *N.Y. Times,* June 5, 1998, at A12; Kifner & Herszenhorn, supra note 1, at B1.

59. See, e.g., Derricott v. Maryland, 611 A.2d 592, 598 (Md. 1992); Lawson v. Maryland, 707 A.2d 947, 952–953 (Md. Ct. Spec. App. 1998); Whitehead v. Maryland, 698 A.2d 1115, 1117 (Md. Ct. Spec. App. 1997); First Amended Complaint, N. Div. of Maryland State Conf. of NAACP Branches v. Dep't of Maryland State Police, (D. Md. 1998) (No. CCB-98-1098); see also American Civil Liberties Union Freedom Network, ACLU Fact Sheet: Overview of Race-Based Stops in Litigation In Maryland and Nationwide (June 4, 1998), available at http://aclu.org/news/n060498c.html.

60. American Civil Liberties Union Freedom Network, Report of John Lamberth, Ph.d (1996), available at http://www.aclu.org/court/lamberth.html [hereinafter Lamberth Report] (prepared for Wilkins v. Maryland State Police, No. CCB-93-468 (D. Md. settlement approved Jan. 5, 1995)).

61. See Wilson, supra note 50, at 190–226, for a discussion which links the exercise of police discretion—including weights police assign to the race of suspects—to differences in local community styles or cultures.

62. See Harris, Driving While Black, supra note 36, at 558–559.

63. *Id.* at 545.

64. For example, "the driver making [a] right turn may not slow down 'suddenly' (undefined) without signalling [*sic*]." *Id.* at 558.

65. *Id.* at 558–559.

66. *Id.* If few drivers are aware of the true scope of traffic codes and the limitless opportunities they give police to make pretextual stops, police officers have always understood this point. For example, the statements by police officers that follow come from a book written in 1967:

> You can always get a guy legitimately on a traffic violation if you tail him for a while, and then a search can be made.
>
> You don't have to follow a driver very long before he will move to the other side of the yellow line and then you can arrest and search him for driving on the wrong side of the highway.
>
> In the event that we see a suspicious automobile or occupant and wish to search the person or the car, or both, we will usually follow the vehicle until the driver makes a technical violation of a traffic law. Then we have a means of making a legitimate search.
>
> *Id.* at 559 (citing Lawrence F. Tiffany et. al., Detection of Crime 131 (1967)).

67. See Lamberth Report, supra note 60.

70. *Id.*

71. *Id.*

72 *Id.* ("Between January 1995 and September 1996, the Maryland State Police reported searching 823 motorists on I-95. . . ."). *Id.*

73. *Id.*

74. Kathy Barrett Carter & Michael Raphael, Minority Arrests Spur Probe of Troopers, Star-Ledger (Newark, N.J.), Feb. 11, 1999, at 1; Lamberth Report, supra note 60.

75. See Soto, 734 A.2d at 352 (referring to a 1993 survey whereby 98.1 percent of vehicles that violated traffic laws, 15 percent contained black occupants); Lamberth Report, supra note 60.

76. Barrett Carter & Raphael, supra note 74, at 1.

77. See Lamberth Report, supra note 60 ("Data reported by MSP for motorist searches conducted outside the I-95 corridor is markedly different from that reported by troopers patrolling I-95."). *Id.*

78. *Id.*

79. *Id.* (finding that twelve out of thirteen state troopers "searched blacks and other minority motorists at much higher rates than these motorists travel on the highway"). *Id.*

80. *Id.* tbl.2.

81. *Id.*

82. Indeed, a recent report argues specifically that racial profiling is quite inefficacious: "Racial profiling not only constitutes discrimination against people of color, it is also simply an unsound, inefficient method of policing." Institute on Race & Poverty, University of Minnesota Law School, Report: Components of Racial Profiling Legislation (Mar. 5, 2001) available at http://www1.umn.edu/irp/publications/racialprofiling.html [hereinafter Components of Racial Profiling Legislation].

   The percentage of cars stopped for pretextual reasons that are found to be actually carrying contraband is extremely low. In 1991, the California Patrol Canine Unit stopped and searched 34,000 vehicles as part of "Operation Pipeline." Of the 34,000 vehicles stopped, only 2 percent contained any illegal drugs. Programs such as "Operation Pipeline" have been frequently cited as relying heavily on racial profiling. Components of Racial Profiling Legislation, supra. A comparable argument has been made by Harris:

   > Other statistics on both drug use and drug crime show something surprising in light of the usual beliefs many hold: blacks may not, in fact, be more likely than whites to be involved with drugs. The U.S. Customs Service, which is engaged in drug interdiction efforts at nation's airports, has used various types of invasive searches from pat downs to

body cavity searches against travelers suspected of drug use. The Custom Service's own nationwide figures show that while over 43 percent of those subjected to these searches were either black or Hispanic, "hit rates" for these searches were actually lower for both blacks and Hispanics than for whites.

Harris, The Stories, the Statistics, supra note 8, at 278.

A competing argument suggests the deterrent effect that results from a profiling policy. Jonathan Alter notes that the former New York City Policy Commissioner (William Bratton) opposes profiling, while also calling attention to its deterrent effect. Jonathan Alter, Hillary Raises Her Profile, *Newsweek,* June 25, 2001, at 34. Restating Bratton's position and the views of a number of other prosecutors with whom Alter spoke, Alter notes their view that "in recent years young blacks in Harlem have known the police were stopping them and searching for guns, so they stopped carrying weapons, a major contributor to the reduction in crime." *Id.*

83. Lambert Report, supra note 60.

84. *Id.* It should be noted that a recent paper raises questions about the assertion that cops on Maryland I-95 are participating in racial profiling. See generally John Knowles, et al., Racial Bias in Motor Vehicle Searches: Theory and Evidence (Nat'l Bureau of Econ. Research, Working Paper No. 7449, 1999), available at http://www.nber.org/papers/w7449. The authors contend that the higher search rate of blacks may not be due to race, at least not directly, but rather to other unobservable traits that may be indirectly correlated with race. *Id.* at 3. The authors label this practice "statistical discrimination." *Id.* at 2. In effect, under statistical discrimination, the cost for the police officer of searching white or black motorists is equal [Ta=Tw], but the probability of the two races being searched by a police officer is not equal [y(c,W) does not = y(c,A)] because of the "c" term. *Id.* at 8-13. The variable "c" is probative about possible guilt of defendants, which determines stops and searches; "c" may correlate with race, but under the theory of statistical discrimination, it is the examination of a variable, not race,

which explains stops and searches. *Id.* Therefore, police officers looking to maximize their efficiency and arrest numbers will be particularly keen on motorists with a certain "c," as opposed to those not characterized by "c." *Id.* Consequently, blacks that are stopped and searched, are stopped and searched because they disproportionately display "c," not because of race. *Id.* It should be noted that there is no contention made by the authors that this practice is not discriminatory. Rather, the point the authors are trying to make is that it is economic or statistical discrimination that motivates police behavior, not racial discrimination.

The issue of fairness in this type of policing remains. The data from MD I-95 that Lamberth collected, and were used in this paper, indicate that while the guilty rates of African-Americans and whites are comparable, a much greater number of African-Americans are pulled over than whites. Lamberth Report, *supra* note 60. This incongruity in data leads one to question whether efficiency or the guilt rate would be sacrificed if police officers conducted stops and searches of African-Americans at a number proportional to their population as motorists. . . .

86. See United States v. Sokolow, 490 U.S. 1, 10 (1989) (denying that the Court's "analysis is somehow changed by the [DEA] agents' belief that his behavior was consistent with one of the DEA's drug courier profiles").

87. See, e.g., Sokolow, 490 U.S. at 1; Reid, 448 U.S. at 438. In at least two other cases, the investigative stops at issue involved use of a "profile," but the issue the Court addressed in each case did not turn on the use of the profile. See Florida v. Royer, 460 U.S. 491 (1983); United States v. Mendenhall, 446 U.S. 544 (1980).

88. See Sokolow, 490 U.S. at 10.

89. See Whren v. United States, 517 U.S. 806, 813 (1996). The Supreme Court summarily rejected the argument that alleged racial motivation for a traffic stop violated petitioners' Fourth Amendment rights. *Id.* The Court indicated that a police officer's "subjective intentions play no role in ordinary, probable-cause Fourth Amendment analysis." *Id.*

90. 460 U.S. 491 (1983).

91. In Royer, Justice Rehnquist wrote the following:

As one DEA agent explained: "Basically, it's a number of characteristics which we attribute or which we believe can be used to pick out drug couriers. . . . We began to see a pattern in these characteristics and began using them to pick out individuals we suspected as narcotic couriers without any prior information."

Royer, 460 U.S at 525 n.6 (quoting United States v. McClain, 452 F. Supp. 195, 199 (E.D. Mich. 1977).

In fact, the function of the "profile" has been somewhat overplayed. Certainly, a law enforcement officer can rely on his own experience in detection and prevention of crime. Likewise, in training police officers, instruction focuses on what has been learned through the collective experience of law enforcers. The "drug courier profile" is an example of such instruction. It is not intended to provide a mathematical formula or automatically establish ground rules for a belief that criminal activity is afoot. By the same reasoning, however, simply because those characteristics are accumulated in a "profile," they are not to be given less weight in assessing whether a suspicion is well-founded. While each case will turn on its own facts, sheer logic dictates that where certain characteristics repeatedly are found along drug smugglers, the existence of those characteristics in a particular case is to be considered accordingly in determining whether there are grounds to believe that further investigation is appropriate.

Royer, 460 U.S. at 525 nn.5–6.

92. 528 U.S. 119 (2000).

93. *Id.* at 124.

94. *Id.* at 132-33 (Stevens, J., dissenting) (footnotes omitted).

95. *Id.* at 133 n.10.

96. 532 U.S. 318 (2001).

97. *Id.* at 557.

98. *Id.* at 589 (O'Connor, J., dissenting). It should be noted that the petitioner in the Atwater case was white. Linda Greenhouse, Divided Justices Back Full Arrests on Minor Charges, *N.Y. Times,* Apr. 25, 2001, at A1.

99. On the other hand, one could argue that the Supreme Court, of all the courts, has, over the course of its history, felt less bound by that particular rule than other courts. Indeed, some of the Court's greatest cases, as well as a few more infamous ones—including Marbury v. Madison, 5 U.S. (1 Cranch) 137 (1803), Scott v. Sandford, 60 U.S. (19 How.) 393 (1857), and Brown v. Board of Education, 387 U.S. 483 (1954)—have been hailed or criticized as examples of the Court ambitiously reaching further than it had to in deciding a case of paramount importance on issues affecting far more than the individual parties before it. See, e.g., Cass R. Sunstein, One Case at a Time (1999).

100. See, e.g., David A. Harris, Addressing Racial Profiling in the States: A Case Study of the "New Federalism" in Constitutional Criminal Procedure, 3 U. Pa. J. Const. L. 367 (2001) [hereinafter Harris, Addressing Racial Profiling] (examining whether courts of the "new federalism" era have protected and supported the goal of eliminating racial basis in police practices); Maclin, Race and the Fourth Amendment, supra note 77; David A. Sklansky, Traffic Stops, Minority Motorists, and the Future of the Fourth Amendment, 1997 Sup. Ct. Rev. 271 (1997).

101. See, e.g., Sokolow, 490 U.S. at 1; Reid, 448 U.S. at 438.

102. See Sokolow, 490 U.S. at 1-18; Reid, 448 U.S. at 438–443.

103. Whren, 517 U.S. at 813 (holding that "the constitutional basis for objecting to intentionally discriminatory application of laws is the Equal Protection Clause, not the Fourth Amendment).

104. *Id.*

105. Alexander M. Bickel, The Least Dangerous Branch (1962).

106. *Id.* at 16–17.

107. This view has attracted significant consideration lately, particularly in a provocative book by Mark Tushnet. See generally Mark Tushnet, Taking the Constitution Away Form the Courts (1999).

108. See, e.g., City of Boerne v. Flores, 521 U.S. 507, 536 (1997) (holding that "Congress' discretion is not unlimited . . .and the courts retain the power, as they have since Marbury v. Madison, to determine if Congress has exceeded its authority under the Constitution"). For more on the Court's efforts to act as the sole definer of constitutional norms, see David Cole, The Value of Seeing Things Differently: Boerne v. Flores and Congressional Enforcement of the Bill of Rights, 1997 Sup. Ct. Rev. 31 (1997); Robert C. Post & Reva B. Siegel, Equal Protection By Law: Federal Anti-discrimination Legislation After Morison and Kimel, 110 Yale L.J. 441 (2000) (discussing the Supreme Court's move to limit congressional authority under Section Five of the Fourteenth Amendment).

109. For example, some have claimed that a series of cases in the mid to late 1960s involving issues related to the death penalty, but not directly addressing the practice, sent a signal that the Court was prepared to address a direct challenge to that practice, which it did shortly thereafter in Furman v. Georgia, 408 U.S. 238 (1972). See Michael Meltsner, Cruel and Unusual: The Supreme Court and Capital Punishment 246 (1973).

110. See Harris, Driving While Black, supra note 36, at 544 (arguing that it may be time for those concerned about abuses such as pretextual traffic stops and racial profiling to look to others, besides the courts, for redress).

111. See Sklansky, at 316 ("It is almost commonplace by now that much of the Court's criminal procedure jurisprudence during the middle part of this century was a form of race jurisprudence, prompted largely by the treatment of black suspects and black defendants in the South. The Court's concern with race relations served as the unspoken subtext of many of its significant criminal procedure decisions. . . .").

112. Gerald N. Rosenberg, The Hollow Hope 43 (1991).

113. See, e.g., Michael J. Klarman, Brown, Racial Change, and the Civil Rights Movement, 80 Va. L. Rev. 7 (1994). Even some who support the decision in Brown for the message it sent regarding racial equality have criticized it for its effect on educational opportunities for African-Americans and questioned whether its integrationist ideals did not also send a demeaning message of racial inferiority, even if

unintentionally. See, e.g., Derrick Bell, And We Are Not Saved: The Elusive Quest for Racial Justice 102 (1989); James T. Patterson, Brown v. Board of Education: A Civil Rights Milestone and its Troubled Legacy 200–2001 (2001) .

114. One could cite many cases here, from those involving affirmative action to those dealing with school desegregation orders or other civil rights issues. See, e.g., Adarand Constructors, Inc. v. Pena, 515 U.S. 200 (1995); Freeman v. Pitts, 503 U.S. 467 (1992); Patterson, supra note 287, at 197–201.

115. See generally Katheryn K. Russell, Racial Profiling: A Status Report of the Legal, Legislative, and Empirical Literature, 3 Rutgers Race & L. Rev. 61 (2001) (discussing the prevalence of racial profiling).

116. However, some reported cases may cast doubt on even this modest assessment. In Brown v. City of Oneonta, 221 F.3d 329 (2d Cir. 1999), the Second Circuit upheld the actions of police officers who stopped and questioned every African-American in town after an assault victim was unable to provide any clues to the identity of her assailant other than the assailant's race. *Id.* at 337–339. Brown is not, strictly speaking, a case of racial profiling, in that no profile at all was used and race was not, as in the turnpike cases and some airport searches, a proxy drawn from prior incidents or patterns from which an inference of criminality was drawn. Rather, the assault victim knew the race of her attacker. *Id.*

Unfortunately, that is all she knew about her attacker and that small piece of information was turned into a basis to stop every African-American in town, a practice that was later blessed by the court. See *Id.* at 334, 339. While not an example of racial profiling per se, the actions of the police and the court's approval demonstrate how intractable the issues of race and overbearing law enforcement techniques can be.

117. To put it another way, assume a suspect matches all five factors of a carefully devised profile based on objective data drawn from the historical record. If, in the absence of consideration of race, there is not sufficient grounds to stop the suspect, does knowledge of the suspect's race add enough to justify the stop? If so, does that mean that it has become the critical factor in justifying the stop?

118. There is also the danger that the questionable use of race by police to justify stops and subsequent arrests initially may create a self-fulfilling prophecy, where an initial reliance on race that may not have been justified becomes part of the statistical basis used to justify subsequent stops. Lisa Walter, Eradicating Racial Stereotyping From Terry Stops: The Case For An Equal Protection Exclusionary Rule, 71 U. Colo. L. Rev. 255, 276 (2000). "Racial stereotypes influence police to arrest minorities, thereby creating the arrest statistics to justify the criminal stereotype. Police officers defend their conduct by citing statistics showing higher crime and arrest rates among minorities. This tends to perpetuate the fallacy and generate more unbalanced arrest patterns." *Id.* at 276.

119. Pub. L. No. 88-352, 78 Stat. 241.

120. See, e.g., Heart of Atlanta Motel, Inc. v. United States, 379 U.S. 241, 261 (1964) (holding motel discriminated when renting rooms).

121. The literature on the effects of abusive police tactics on minorities is large and growing. See, e.g., Kennedy, Race, Crime, and the Law, supra note 289; Harris, Driving While Black, supra note 64; Harris, The Stories, the Statistics, supra note 13; Erika L. Johnson, "A Menace To Society:" The Use of Criminal Profiles and Its Effects On Black Males, 38 How. L. J. 629 (1995); Maclin, Race and the Fourth Amendment; Sklansky; Thompson.

122. See Sean P. Trende, Note, Why Modest Proposals Offer the Best Solution for Combating Racial Profiling, 50 Duke L.J. 331, 342 (2000) (stating racial profiling is constitutionally permissible).

NOTES AND QUESTIONS

1. What is profiling? What are the two main types of profiling? What characteristics do they share? How do they differ from one another? When is profiling a useful crime-fighting tool?

2. What are the criteria used to build a profile? Are some types of profiling prac-

tices more subjective and others more objective? When might profiling be objectionable?

3. How have the courts handled the controversy over the legitimacy of different types of profiling for law enforcement? Why, according to Heumann and Cassak, is the Supreme Court's silence on this issue particularly salient? What constitutional questions are raised by the debate over racial profiling?

4. Does the widespread use of profiling as a police tactic afford too much discretion to officers?

5. Are Heumann and Cassak arguing that all types of profiling should be condemned? Would that be a desirable outcome? In your opinion, can the law enforcement benefits of profiling be retained without perpetuating racial stereotypes and institutionalized discrimination?

6. Heumann and Cassak quote Wilson and Kelling's argument that "if a police officer believes with considerable justification that teenagers, Negroes, and lower income persons commit a disproportionate share of the crimes, then being in those population categories at all makes one, statistically, more suspect than other persons." What constitutes "considerable justification"? Who gets to decide this question?

7. Profiling suggests that the question of order-maintenance versus law enforcement spills over into the liberty versus security debate. Consider the example of the philosophy professor stopped every week in his car. Is his liberty being infringed upon? Are the stops justified because the professor's race makes him statistically suspect? Is this equal treatment before the law?

8. How should we weigh the liberty of people in a racially suspect group against the security gained from the successful use of profiling to apprehend a criminal? Does your answer change at all in the context of terrorism? How much curtailment of liberty via racial profiling is permissible in the quest to fend off another act of massive, organized terror on American soil?

Reprinted from: Milton Heumann and Lance Cassak, "Profiles in Justice: Police Discretion, Symbolic Assailants, and Stereotyping" in *Rutgers Law Review* 53:4. Copyright © 2001. Reprinted with the permission of the Rutgers Law Review. ✦

Chapter 51

The Myth of Racial Profiling

Heather MacDonald

Heumann and Cassak end their article (Chapter 50) by calling on students of the law in action to focus on racial profiling. The reading by Heather MacDonald takes up this call. She reviews evidence about racial profiling and concludes that there is no reliable evidence that "hard" profiling (i.e., in which race is the only factor used in assessing criminal suspiciousness) occurs. Moreover, she argues that it ought not to occur. What she calls "soft" profiling, in which race is used as one factor among others, is, in her view, another matter. MacDonald believes that soft profiling is a rational and effective tool of law enforcement.

As MacDonald sees it, the debate about racial profiling seems driven more by politics than by careful assessment of the facts. Reminiscent of the discussion of litigation rates in Chapters 20 and 21, this article criticizes research on profiling for failing to provide "an adequate measure against which to measure if police are pulling over, searching, and arresting 'too many' blacks and Hispanics." She claims that the studies on which people base their claims about racial profiling are incapable of telling us anything meaningful about it. Moreover, she argues that there is nothing illegal about using race as one factor among many in constructing a profile and that police are right to do so. She urges leaders of minority groups to worry less about profiling by the police and more about the high prevalence of crime among members of minority communities. The fuss about racial profiling is, in her view, a damaging distraction.

The anti-"racial profiling" juggernaut must be stopped, before it obliterates the crime-fighting gains of the last decade, especially in inner cities. The anti-profiling crusade thrives on an ignorance of policing and a willful blindness to the demographics of crime. Yet politicians are swarming on board. In February, President George W. Bush joined the rush, declaring portentously: "Racial profiling is wrong, and we will end it in America."

Too bad no one asked President Bush: "What exactly do you mean by 'racial profiling,' and what evidence do you have that it exists?" For the anti-profiling crusaders have created a headlong movement without defining their central term and without providing a shred of credible evidence that "racial profiling" is a widespread police practice.

The ultimate question in the profiling controversy is whether the disproportionate involvement of blacks and Hispanics with law enforcement reflects police racism or the consequences of disproportionate minority crime. Anti-profiling activists hope to make police racism an all but irrebuttable presumption whenever enforcement statistics show high rates of minority stops and arrests. But not so fast.

Two meanings of "racial profiling" intermingle in the activists' rhetoric. What we may call "hard" profiling uses race as the *only* factor in assessing criminal suspiciousness: an officer sees a black person and, without more to go on, pulls him over for a pat-down on the chance that he may be carrying drugs or weapons. "Soft" racial profiling is using race as one factor among others in gauging criminal suspiciousness: the highway police, for example, have intelligence that Jamaican drug posses with a fondness for Nissan Pathfinders are transporting marijuana along the northeast corridor. A New Jersey trooper sees a black motorist speeding in a Pathfinder and pulls him over in the hope of finding drugs.

The racial profiling debate focuses primarily on highway stops. The police are pulling over a disproportionate number of minority drivers for traffic offenses, goes the argument, in order to look for drugs. Sure, the driver committed an infraction, but the reason the trooper chose to stop *him,* rather than the speeder next to him, was his race.

But the profiling critics also fault both the searches that sometimes follow a highway stop and the tactics of urban policing. Any evaluation of the evidence for, and the appropriateness of, the use of race in policing must keep these contexts distinct. Highway stops should almost always be color-blind, I'll argue, but in other policing environments (including highway searches), where an officer has many clues to go on, race may be among them. Ironically, effective urban policing shows that the more additional factors an officer has in his criminal profile, the more valid race becomes—and the less significant, almost to the point of irrelevance.

Before reviewing the evidence that profiling critics offer, recall the demands that the police face every day, far from anti-police agitators and their journalist acolytes.

February 22, 2001, a town-hall meeting at P.S. 153 in Harlem between New York mayor Rudolph Giuliani and Harlem residents: a woman sarcastically asks Giuliani if police officers downtown are paid more than uptown officers, "because we don't have any quality of life in Harlem, none whatsoever. Drug dealers are allowed to stand out in front of our houses every day, to practically invade us, and nothing's done about it." Another woman complains that dealers are back on the street the day after being arrested, and notes that "addicts are so bold that we have to get off the sidewalk and go around *them!*" She calls for the declaration of a state of emergency. A man wonders if cop-basher congressman Charles Rangel, present at the meeting, could "endow the police with more power," and suggests that the NYPD coordinate with the federal Drug Enforcement Administration, the INS, and the IRS to bring order to the streets.

The audience meets Giuliani's assertions that the police have brought crime down

sharply in Harlem with hoots of derision. No one mentions "police brutality.". . .

This is the demand—often angry, sometimes wistful—that urban police forces constantly hear: *get rid of the drugs!* These recent appeals come *after* the most successful war on crime that New York City has ever conducted. A decade and a half ago, when drug-related drive-by shootings became epidemic, inner-city residents nationwide were calling even more frantically for protection from drug violence. When New Jersey, a key state on the drug corridor from Central America to New England, sent its state highway troopers to do foot patrols in Camden and Trenton, residents met them with cheers.

In New York, the mayhem eventually led to the development of the Giuliani administration's assertive policing that strives, quite successfully, to prevent crime from happening. Outside of New York, the widespread pleas to stop drug violence led the Drug Enforcement Administration to enlist state highway police in their anti-drug efforts. The DEA and the Customs Service had been using intelligence about drug routes and the typical itineraries of couriers to interdict drugs at airports; now the interdiction war would expand to the nation's highways, the major artery of the cocaine trade. . . .

According to the racial profiling crowd, the war on drugs immediately became a war on minorities, on the highways and off. Their alleged evidence for racial profiling comes in two varieties: anecdotal, which is of limited value, and statistical, which on examination proves entirely worthless.

The most notorious racial profiling anecdote may have nothing to do with racial profiling at all. On April 23, 1998, two New Jersey state troopers pulled over a van that they say was traveling at 74 miles an hour in a 55-mile-an-hour zone on the New Jersey Turnpike. As they approached on foot, the van backed toward them, knocking one trooper down, hitting the patrol car, and then getting sideswiped as it entered the traffic lane still in reverse. The troopers fired 11 rounds at the van, wounding three of the four passengers, two critically.

Attorneys for the van passengers deny that the van was speeding. The only reason the cops pulled it over, critics say, was that its occupants were black and Hispanic.

If the troopers' version of the incident proves true, it is hard to see how racial profiling enters the picture. The van's alleged speed would have legitimately drawn the attention of the police. As for the shooting: whether justified or not, it surely was prompted by the possibly deadly trajectory of the van, not the race of the occupants. Nevertheless, on talk show after talk show, in every newspaper story denouncing racial profiling, the turnpike shooting has come to symbolize the lethal dangers of "driving while black."

Less notoriously, black motorists today almost routinely claim that the only reason they are pulled over for highway stops is their race. Once they are pulled over, they say, they are subject to harassment, including traumatic searches. Some of these tales are undoubtedly true. Without question, there are obnoxious officers out there, and some officers may ignore their training and target minorities. But since the advent of video cameras in patrol cars, installed in the wake of the racial profiling controversy, most charges of police racism, testified to under oath, have been disproved as lies.

The allegation that police systematically single out minorities for unjustified law enforcement ultimately stands or falls on numbers. In suits against police departments across the country, the ACLU and the Justice Department have waived studies aplenty allegedly demonstrating selective enforcement. None of them holds up to scrutiny.

The typical study purports to show that minority motorists are subject to disproportionate traffic stops. Trouble is, no one yet has devised an adequate benchmark against which to measure if police are pulling over, searching, or arresting "too many" blacks and Hispanics. The question must always be: *too many compared with what?* Even anti-profiling activists generally concede that police pull drivers over for an actual traffic violation, not for no reason whatsoever, so a valid benchmark for stops would be the number of serious traffic violators, not just drivers. If it turns out that minorities tend to drive more recklessly, say, or have more equipment violations, you'd expect them to be subject to more stops. But to benchmark accurately, you'd also need to know the number of miles driven by different racial groups, so that you'd compare stops per man-mile, not just per person. Throw in age demographics as well: if a minority group has more young people—read: immature drivers—than whites do, expect more traffic stops of that group. The final analysis must then compare police deployment patterns with racial driving patterns: if more police are on the road when a higher proportion of blacks are driving—on weekend nights, say—stops of blacks will rise.

No traffic-stop study to date comes near the requisite sophistication. Most simply compare the number of minority stops with some crude population measure, and all contain huge and fatal data gaps. An ACLU analysis of Philadelphia traffic stops, for example, merely used the percentage of blacks in the 1990 census as a benchmark for stops made seven years later. In about half the stops that the ACLU studied, the officer did not record the race of the motorist. The study ignored the rate of traffic violations by race, so its grand conclusion of selective enforcement is meaningless. . . .

But though the numbers to date are incapable of telling us anything about racial profiling, that does not mean that it was not going on in some locations, at some times. Hard racial profiling in car stops—pulling over one speeder among many just because he happens to be black or Hispanic—has surely been rare. But conversations with officers in strong interdiction states such as New Jersey suggest that some troopers probably did practice soft racial profiling—pulling someone over because driver *and* car *and* direction *and* number and type of occupants fit the components of a courier profile.

Over time, officers' experience had corroborated the DEA intelligence reports: minorities were carrying most of the drugs. An example of the patterns they noticed: a group of young blacks with North Carolina plates traveling south out of Manhattan's Lincoln Tunnel into New Jersey? Good chance they're carrying weapons and drugs, having just made a big buy in the city. Catch them northbound? Good chance they're carrying big money and guns. Some officers inevitably started playing the odds—how many, the numbers cannot yet tell us.

Despite the hue and cry, there is nothing illegal about using race as one factor among others in assessing criminal suspiciousness. Nevertheless, the initial decision to pull a car over should be based almost always on seriousness of traffic violation alone—unless, of course, evidence of other law-breaking, such as drug use, is visible. If the result is that drug couriers assiduously observe the speed limit, fine. But compared with most other policing environments, highways are relatively cueless places. In assessing the potential criminality of a driver speeding along with the pack on an eight-lane highway, an officer normally has much less to work with than on a city street or sidewalk. His locational cues—traveling on an interstate pointed toward a drug market, say—are crude, compared with those in a city, where an officer can ask if this particular block is a drug bazaar. His ability to observe the behavior of a suspect over time is limited by the speed of travel. In such an environment, blacks traveling 78 mph should not face a greater chance of getting pulled over than white speeders just because they are black and happen to be driving a car said to be favored by drug mules.

Soft racial profiling was probably not widespread enough to have influenced traffic-stop rates significantly. Nor will eliminating it quickly change the belief among many blacks that any time they get stopped for a traffic violation, it is because of their race. Nevertheless, state police commanders should eliminate any contribution that soft profiling may make to that perception, unless strong evidence emerges (as it has not so far) that soft profiling has had an extremely high success rate in drug interdiction. Far more is at stake here than the use of race in traffic stops. Specious anti-racial profiling analysis threatens to emasculate policing in areas where drug enforcement is on a far stronger basis. . . .

The hue and cry over the alleged New Jersey search rate makes sense only if we assume that drug trafficking is spread evenly across the entire population and that officers are unable to detect the signs of a courier once they have pulled over a car. There are powerful reasons to reject both these assumptions.

Judging by arrest rates, minorities are vastly overrepresented among drug traffickers. Blacks make up over 60 percent of arrests in New Jersey for drugs and weapons, though they are 13.5 percent of the population. Against such a benchmark, the state police search rates look proportionate.

The attorney general's report dismissed this comparison with an argument that has become *de rigueur* among the anti-racial profiling crowd, even in Congress: the "circularity" argument. Arrest and conviction data for drugs and weapons are virtually meaningless, said Verniero. They tell you nothing about the world and everything about the false stereotypes that guide the police. If the police find more contraband on blacks and Hispanics, that is merely because they are looking harder for it, driven by prejudiced assumptions. If the police were to target whites with as much enforcement zeal, goes this reasoning, they would find comparable levels of criminality. David Harris, a University of Toledo law school professor and the leading expert for the anti-profiling forces, makes this preposterous argument. An enforcement effort directed at 40-year-old white law professors, he assures a Senate subcommittee, would yield noticeable busts. The disproportionate minority arrests then reinforce the initial, racist stereotypes, and the vicious cycle begins all over again—too many minorities arrested, too many whites going free.

The circularity argument is an insult to law enforcement and a prime example of the anti-police advocates' willingness to rewrite reality. Though it is hard to prove a negative—in this case, that there is *not* a large cadre of white drug lords operating in the inner cities—circumstantial evidence rebuts the activists' insinuation. Between 1976 and 1994, 64 percent of the homicide victims in drug turf wars were black, according to a Heritage Foundation analysis of FBI data. Sixty-seven percent of known perpetrators were also black. Likewise, some 60 percent of victims and perpetrators in drug-induced fatal brawls are black. These figures match the roughly 60 percent of drug offenders in state prison who are black. Unless you believe that white traffickers are less violent than black traffickers, the arrest, conviction, and imprisonment rate for blacks on drug charges appears consistent with the level of drug activity in the black population. (And were it true that white dealers are less violent, wouldn't we expect police to concentrate their enforcement efforts on the most dangerous parts of the drug trade?)

The notion that there are lots of heavy-duty white dealers sneaking by undetected contradicts the street experience of just about every narcotics cop you will ever talk to—though such anecdotal evidence, of course, would fail to convince the ACLU, convinced as it is of the blinding racism that afflicts most officers. "The hard-core sellers are where the hard-core users are—places like 129th Street in Harlem," observes Patrick Harnett, retired chief of the narcotics division for the NYPD. "It's not white kids from Rockland County who are keeping black sellers in business."

The cops go where the deals are. When white club owners, along with Israelis and Russians, still dominated the Ecstasy trade,

that's whom the cops were arresting. Recently, however, big shipments have been going to minority neighborhoods; subsequent arrests will reflect crime intelligence, not racism.

There's not a single narcotics officer who won't freely admit that there are cocaine buys going down in the men's bathrooms of Wall Street investment firms—though at a small fraction of the amount found on 129th Street. But that is not where community outrage, such as that Mayor Giuliani heard in Harlem, is directing the police, because they don't produce violence and street intimidation.

Ultimately, the circularity argument rests on a massive denial of reality, one that is remarkably vigorous and widespread. In March, 2000, for example, New Jersey senator Robert Torricelli asserted before then-senator John Ashcroft's Judiciary Subcommittee: "Statistically it cannot bear evidence [sic] to those who suggest, as our former superintendent of the state police suggested, that certain ethnic or racial groups disproportionately commit crimes. They do not." Needless to say, Torricelli did not provide any statistics.

The second condition necessary to explain the higher minority search rates on the highway is patrol officers' ability to detect drug trafficking. Unlike the initial decision to pull over a car, the decision to request permission to search rests on a wealth of cues. One of the most frequent is conflicting narratives among passengers and driver. "If a group in a car is carrying drugs, there will always be inconsistencies in their stories," reports Ed Lennon, head of the New Jersey Troopers Union. "It's unbelievable. A lot of times the driver won't know the passengers' first or last names—'I only know him as Bill'—or they'll get the names completely wrong. Sometimes they'll have a preplanned answer regarding their destination, but their purpose in being on the road will vary."

A driver's demeanor may also be a tip-off. "I've stopped white guys in pick-up trucks with a camper compartment on top," recalls Lennon. "Their chest is pounding; they're sweating, though it's the dead of winter. They won't look at you." And they're also hiding drugs.

Once a trooper stops a car, he can see the amount of luggage and its fit with the alleged itinerary, the accumulation of trash that suggests long stretches without stopping, the signs of drug use, the lack of a license and registration, the single key in the ignition and no trunk key, or the signs that the vehicle may have been fitted out with drug and weapon compartments. Some New York narcotics officers recently pulled over an Azusa SUV and noticed welding marks along the rain gutter on top. The occupants had raised the entire roof four inches to create a drug vault. If a car's windows don't roll all the way down, drugs may be concealed in the doors.

The fact that hit rates for contraband tend to be equal across racial groups, even though blacks and Hispanics are searched at higher rates, suggests that the police are successfully targeting dealers, not minorities. Race may play a role in that targeting, or it may not. Most cues of trafficking are race-neutral; it may be that race often correlates with the decision to search rather than causing it. But if race does play a role in the request to search, it is a much diminished one compared with a car stop based on a courier profile. When an officer has many independent indices of suspicion, adding his knowledge of the race of major trafficking groups to the mix is both legitimate and not overly burdensome on law-abiding minorities. . . .

Unfortunately, the flurry of racial profiling analysis is not confined to the highways. It will wreak the most havoc on urban policing. Despite the racket by protesters, it is in city policing that race probably plays its least significant role, because officers have so many other cues from the environment. In assessing whether a pedestrian is behaving suspiciously, for example, they might already know that he is at a drug corner, about which they have received numerous complaints. They know if there has been a string of burglaries in the neighborhood. As they observe him, they can assess with whom he is interacting, and how.

A New York Street Crime Unit sergeant in Queens describes having stopped white pedestrians who had immediately changed directions as soon as they saw his unmarked car or ducked into an alley or a store for eight seconds and then looked for him once they came out. The night I spoke to him, he was patrolling the 102nd Precinct in Woodhaven, a largely white and Hispanic neighborhood. He had earlier questioned a white kid hanging out in front of a factory. "He was breaking his neck looking back at us; we thought he was a burglar." It turns out he was waiting for a friend. Another night in another precinct, the sergeant saw two black kids on bikes. "One guy's arm was hanging straight down, like he was carrying a gun. When they saw us, the other guy took off on his bike and threw a bag away. It was felony-weight drugs." Are you ignoring whites with guns? I asked him. "Of course not; I could see the same thing tonight," he said impatiently. "I don't use race at all. The only question is: are you raising my level of suspicion? Fifteen minutes after a stop, I may not even be able to tell you the color of the guy."

Even car stops on city streets usually have more context than on a highway. "If we pass four or five guys in a car going the opposite direction," explains the Queens sergeant, "and they're all craning their necks to see if we notice them, we may reverse and follow them for a while. We won't pull them over, but our suspicion is up. We'll run their plates. If the plates don't check out, they're done. If they commit a traffic violation, we won't pull everyone out of the car yet; we'll just interview the driver. If he doesn't have paperwork, it may be a stolen car. Now everyone's coming out to be frisked."

Hard as it is to believe, criminals actually do keep turning around to look at officers, though it would seem an obvious give-away. "Thank God they're stupid, or we'd be out of a job," the sergeant laughs.

But urban policing depends on another race-neutral strength: it is data-driven. The greatest recent innovation in policing was New York's Compstat, the computer-generated crime analysis that allows police commanders to pinpoint their enforcement efforts, then allows top brass to hold them accountable for results. If robberies are up in Bushwick, Brooklyn, the precinct commander will strategically deploy his officers to find the perpetrators. Will all the suspects be black? Quite likely, for so is the neighborhood. Does that mean that the officers are racist? Hardly; they are simply going where the crime is. In most high-crime neighborhoods, race is wholly irrelevant to policing, because nearly all the residents are minorities.

Urban police chiefs worry about the data-collection mania as much as highway patrol commanders do. Ed Flynn, chief of police for Virginia's Arlington County, explains why. Last year, the black community in his jurisdiction was demanding heavier drug enforcement. "We had a series of community meetings. The residents said to us: 'Years ago, you had control over the problem. Now the kids are starting to act out again.' They even asked us: 'Where are your jump-out squads [who observe drug deals from their cars, then jump out and nab the participants]?'" So Flynn and his local commander put together an energetic strategy to break up the drug trade. They instituted aggressive motor-vehicle checks throughout the problem neighborhood. Cracked windshield, too-dark windows, expired tags, driving too fast? You're getting stopped and questioned. "We wanted to increase our presence in the area and make it quite unpleasant for the dealers to operate," Flynn says. The Arlington officers also cracked down on quality-of-life offenses like public urination, and used undercover surveillance to take out the dealers.

By the end of the summer, the department had cleaned up the crime hot spots. Community newsletters thanked the cops for breaking up the dealing. But guess what? Says Flynn:

"We had also just generated a lot of data showing 'disproportionate' minority arrests." The irony, in Flynn's view, is acute. "We are responding to heartfelt demands for increased police presence," he says. "But this places police departments in the position of producing data at the community's behest that can be used against them."

The racial profiling analysis profoundly confuses cause and effect. "Police develop tactics in response to the disproportionate victimization of minorities by minorities, and you are calling the *tactics* the problem?" Flynn marvels.

However much the racial profilers try to divert attention away from the facts of crime, those facts remain obdurate. Arlington has a 10 percent black population, but robbery victims identify nearly 70 percent of their assailants as black. In 1998, blacks in New York City were 13 times more likely than whites to commit a violent assault, according to victim reports. As long as those numbers remain unchanged, police statistics will also look disproportionate. This is the crime problem that black leaders should be shouting about. . . .

The Harlem residents who so angrily demanded more drug busts from Mayor Giuliani last February didn't care about the race of the criminals who were destroying their neighborhood. They didn't see "black" or "white." They only saw dealers—and they wanted them out. That is precisely the perspective of most police officers as well; their world is divided into "good people" and "bad people," not into this race or that.

If the racial profiling crusade shatters this commonality between law-abiding inner-city residents and the police, it will be just those law-abiding minorities who will pay the heaviest price.

NOTES AND QUESTIONS

1. What is the difference, according to MacDonald, between hard and soft profiling? Why does she argue that one is

more objectionable than the other? Do you agree? Why or why not?

2. Does MacDonald make a credible case that hard racial profiling does not, in practice, take place? How does she attack the anecdotal and statistical evidence of racial profiling? Do you find Heumann and Cassak's argument any less credible in light of MacDonald's article, or do their statistics hold up to scrutiny?

3. MacDonald refutes claims that minorities are subject to disproportionate traffic stops, arguing "no one yet has devised an adequate benchmark against which to measure if police are pulling over, searching or arresting 'too many' black and Hispanics." If you were to devise a benchmark, what criteria would you use? How would you propose to collect your data?

4. MacDonald asserts that eliminating soft racial profiling will not "quickly change the belief among blacks that any time they get stopped for a traffic violation, it is because of their race." In your opinion, does MacDonald sufficiently explore the reasons *why* African Americans feel this way?

5. To support her argument that racial profiling in drug interdiction is legally and morally justifiable, MacDonald writes, "Judging by arrest rates, minorities are vastly overrepresented among drug traffickers." In a debate over racism and unequal treatment in law enforcement, how fair is it to make assumptions about guilt based on arrest rates?

6. How, according to MacDonald, does criticism of racial profiling analysis harm and "emasculate" law enforcement efforts? Do you agree? If so, does this mean profiling should be afforded freedom from public scrutiny or institutional oversight? Is there a way for officers to effectively respond to the concerns like those expressed in the Harlem neighborhood *without* soft racial profiling?

Chapter 52

Tennessee v. Garner

The order-maintenance policing discussed by Skolnick, Wilson and Kelling, and Harcourt is, in one sense, neither very visible nor very dramatic. When done well, broken-windows policing does not make headlines. At the other extreme are instances in which police do make headlines, instances in which they use lethal force.

Traditionally, police have been authorized to resort to force in situations of self-defense or whenever necessary to prevent the flight of a felon. The threat of force was thought to be effective in deterring flight and in effectuating the arrest of those who commit serious crimes. But, controlling the violence of the police has also been thought of as a mark of professionalism. A professional police force is one that subjects officers to effective discipline and control from above, one in which the use of force is minimized.

In Tennessee v. Garner, the Supreme Court was faced with a challenge to the traditional rule. This case, brought by the father of a felon shot and killed while fleeing the scene of a burglary, alleged that the police who shot Garner violated his Fourth Amendment right against unreasonable search and seizure. The Court agreed, first holding that shooting a fleeing felon constitutes a seizure. To satisfy the reasonableness requirement, force can be used only when it is necessary to prevent an escape and when the officer has "probable cause to believe that the suspect poses a significant threat of death or serious physical injury to the officer or others." In developing this standard, the Court made clear

that it was following a trend of increasing restrictiveness in the laws of different states and in the practices of many police departments rather than imposing an entirely new rule in a completely top-down fashion.

Is the rule concerning the use of lethal force by the police too restrictive or not restrictive enough? In thinking about how you would answer this question, compare the Garner standard with the law governing self-defense (see the selection by George P. Fletcher in Chapter 4).

JUSTICE WHITE DELIVERED THE OPINION OF THE COURT

This case requires us to determine the constitutionality of the use of deadly force to prevent the escape of an apparently unarmed suspected felon. We conclude that such force may not be used unless it is necessary to prevent the escape and the officer has probable cause to believe that the suspect poses a significant threat of death or serious physical injury to the officer or others.

I

At about 10:45 p.m. on October 3, 1974, Memphis Police Officers Elton Hymon and Leslie Wright were dispatched to answer a "prowler inside call." Upon arriving at the scene they saw a woman standing on her porch and gesturing toward the adjacent house.[1] She told them she had heard glass breaking and that "they" or "someone" was breaking in next door. While Wright radioed the dispatcher to say that they were on the scene, Hymon went behind the house. He heard a door slam and saw someone run across the backyard. The fleeing suspect, who was appellee-respondent's decedent, Edward Garner, stopped at a 6-feet-high chain link fence at the edge of the yard. With the aid of a flashlight, Hymon was able to see Garner's face and hands. He saw no sign of a weapon, and, though not certain, was "reasonably sure" and "figured" that Garner was unarmed. App. 41, 56; Record 219. He thought Garner was 17 or 18 years old and about 5'5" or 5'7" tall.[2] While Garner was crouched at the base of the fence, Hymon called out "police, halt" and took a few steps toward him. Garner then began to climb over the fence. Convinced that if Garner made it over the fence he would elude capture,[3] Hymon shot him. The bullet hit Garner in the back of the head. Garner was taken by ambulance to a hospital, where he died on the operating table. Ten dollars and a purse taken from the house were found on his body.[4]

In using deadly force to prevent the escape, Hymon was acting under the authority of a Tennessee statute and pursuant to Police Department policy. The statute provides that "[if], after notice of the intention to arrest the defendant, he either flee or forcibly resist, the officer may use all the necessary means to effect the arrest." Tenn. Code Ann. § 40-7-108 (1982).[5] The Department policy was slightly more restrictive than the statute, but still allowed the use of deadly force in cases of burglary. App. 140–144. The incident was reviewed by the Memphis Police Firearm's Review Board and presented to a grand jury. Neither took any action. *Id.*, at 57.

Garner's father then brought this action in the Federal District Court for the Western District of Tennessee, seeking damages under 42 U. S. C. § 1983 for asserted violations of Garner's constitutional rights. The complaint alleged that the shooting violated the Fourth, Fifth, Sixth, Eighth, and Fourteenth Amendments of the United States Constitution. It named as defendants Officer Hymon, the Police Department, its Director, and the Mayor and city of Memphis. . . .

II

Whenever an officer restrains the freedom of a person to walk away, he has seized that person. *United States v. Brignoni-Ponce,* 422 U.S. 873, 878 (1975). While it is not always clear just when minimal police interference becomes a seizure, see *United States v. Mendenhall,* 446 U.S. 544 (1980), there can be no question that apprehension by the use of deadly force is a seizure subject to the reasonableness requirement of the Fourth Amendment.

A

A police officer may arrest a person if he has probable cause to believe that person committed a crime. *E.g., United States v. Watson,* 423 U.S. 411 (1976). Petitioners and appellant argue that if this requirement is satisfied, the Fourth Amendment has nothing to say about how that seizure is made. This submission ignores the many cases in which this Court, by balancing the extent of the intrusion against the need for it, has examined the reasonableness of the manner in which a search or seizure is conducted. To determine the constitutionality of a seizure "[we] must balance the nature and quality of the intrusion on the individual's Fourth Amendment interests against the importance of the governmental interests alleged to justify the intrusion." *United States v. Place,* 462 U.S. 696, 703 (1983); see *Delaware v. Prouse,* 440 U.S. 648, 654 (1979); *United States v. Martinez-Fuerte,* 428 U.S. 543, 555 (1976). We have described "the balancing of competing interests" as "the key principle of the Fourth Amendment." *Michigan v. Summers,* 452 U.S. 692, 700, n. 12 (1981). See also *Camara v. Municipal Court,* 387 U.S. 523, 536–537 (1967). Because one of the factors is the extent of the intrusion, it is plain that reasonableness depends on not only when a seizure is made, but also how it is carried out. *United States v. Ortiz,* 422 U.S. 891, 895 (1975); *Terry v. Ohio,* 392 U.S. 1, 28–29 (1968). . . .

B

The same balancing process applied in the cases cited above demonstrates that, notwithstanding probable cause to seize a suspect, an officer may not always do so by killing him. The intrusiveness of a seizure by means of deadly force is unmatched. The suspect's fundamental interest in his own life need not be elaborated upon. The use of deadly force also frustrates the interest of the individual, and of society, in judicial determination of guilt and punishment. Against these interests are ranged governmental interests in effective law enforcement.[6] It is argued that overall violence will be reduced by encouraging the peaceful submission of suspects who know that they may be shot if they flee. Effectiveness in making arrests requires the resort to deadly force, or at least the meaningful threat thereof. "Being able to arrest such individuals is a condition precedent to the state's entire system of law enforcement." Brief for Petitioners 14.

Without in any way disparaging the importance of these goals, we are not convinced that the use of deadly force is a sufficiently productive means of accomplishing them to justify the killing of nonviolent suspects. *Cf. Delaware v. Prouse, supra,* at 659. The use of deadly force is a self-defeating way of apprehending a suspect and so setting the criminal justice mechanism in motion. If successful, it guarantees that that mechanism will not be set in motion. And while the meaningful threat of deadly force might be thought to lead to the arrest of more live suspects by discouraging escape attempts,[7] the presently available evidence does not support this thesis.[8] The fact is that a majority of police departments in this country have forbidden the use of deadly force against nonviolent suspects. See infra, at 18–19. If those charged with the enforcement of the criminal law have abjured the use of deadly force in arresting nondangerous felons, there is a substantial basis for doubting that the use of such force is an essential attribute of the arrest power in all felony cases. See *Schumann v. McGinn,* 307 Minn. 446, 472, 240 N. W. 2d 525, 540 (1976) (Rogosheske, J., dissenting in part). Petitioners and appellant have not persuaded us that shooting nondangerous fleeing suspects is so vital as to outweigh the suspect's interest in his own life.

The use of deadly force to prevent the escape of all felony suspects, whatever the circumstances, is constitutionally unreasonable. It is not better that all felony suspects die than that they escape. Where the suspect poses no immediate threat to the officer and no threat to others, the harm resulting from failing to apprehend him does not justify the use of deadly force to do so. It is no doubt unfortunate when a suspect who is in sight escapes, but the fact that the police arrive a little late or are a little slower afoot does not always justify killing the suspect. A police officer may not seize an unarmed, nondangerous suspect by shooting him dead. The Tennessee statute is unconstitutional insofar as it authorizes the use of deadly force against such fleeing suspects.

It is not, however, unconstitutional on its face. Where the officer has probable cause to believe that the suspect poses a threat of serious physical harm, either to the officer or to others, it is not constitutionally unreasonable to prevent escape by using deadly force. Thus, if the suspect threatens the officer with a weapon or there is probable cause to believe that he has committed a crime involving the infliction or threatened infliction of serious physical harm, deadly force may be used if necessary to prevent escape, and if, where feasible, some warning has been given. As applied in such circumstances, the Tennessee statute would pass constitutional muster. . . .

C

In evaluating the reasonableness of police procedures under the Fourth Amendment, we have also looked to prevailing rules in individual jurisdictions. See, e.g., *United States v. Watson,* 423 U.S., at 421–422. The rules in the States are varied. See generally Comment, 18 Ga. L. Rev. 137, 140–144 (1983). Some 19 States have codified the common-law rule,[9] though in two of these the courts have significantly limited the statute.[10] Four States, though without a relevant statute, apparently retain the common-law rule.[11] Two States have adopted the Model Penal Code's provision verbatim.[12] Eighteen others allow, in slightly varying language, the use of deadly force only if the suspect has committed a felony involving the use or threat of physical or deadly force, or is escaping with a deadly weapon, or is likely to endanger life or inflict serious physical injury if not arrested.[13] Louisiana and Vermont, though without statutes or case law on point, do forbid the use of deadly force to prevent any but violent felonies.[14] The remaining States either have no relevant statute or case law, or have positions that are unclear.[15]

It cannot be said that there is a constant or overwhelming trend away from the common-law rule. In recent years, some States have reviewed their laws and expressly rejected abandonment of the common-law rule.[16] Nonetheless, the long-term movement has been away from the rule that deadly force may be used against any fleeing felon, and that remains the rule in less than half the States....

D

Actual departmental policies are important for an additional reason. We would hesitate to declare a police practice of long standing "unreasonable" if doing so would severely hamper effective law enforcement. But the indications are to the contrary. There has been no suggestion that crime has worsened in any way in jurisdictions that have adopted, by legislation or departmental policy, rules similar to that announced today. *Amici* noted that "[after] extensive research and consideration, [they] have concluded that laws permitting police officers to use deadly force to apprehend unarmed, non-violent fleeing felony suspects actually do not protect citizens or law enforcement officers, do not deter crime or alleviate problems caused by crime, and do not improve the crime-fighting ability of law enforcement agencies." *Id.*, at 11. The submission is that the obvious state interests in apprehension are not sufficiently served to warrant the use of lethal weapons against all fleeing felons. See supra, at 10–11, and n. 10.

Nor do we agree with petitioners and appellant that the rule we have adopted requires the police to make impossible, split-second evaluations of unknowable facts. See Brief for Petitioners 25; Brief for Appellant 11. We do not deny the practical difficulties of attempting to assess the suspect's dangerousness. However, similarly difficult judgments must be made by the police in equally uncertain circumstances. See, *e.g., Terry v. Ohio*, 392 U.S., at 20, 27. Nor is there any indication that in States that allow the use of deadly force only against dangerous suspects, see nn. 15, 17–19, supra, the standard has been difficult to apply or has led to a rash of litigation involving inappropriate second-guessing of police officers' split-second decisions. Moreover, the highly technical felony/misdemeanor distinction is equally, if not more, difficult to apply in the field. An officer is in no position to know, for example, the precise value of property stolen, or whether the crime was a first or second offense. Finally, as noted above, this claim must be viewed with suspicion in light of the similar self-imposed limitations of so many police departments....

III

We wish to make clear what our holding means in the context of this case. The complaint has been dismissed as to all the individual defendants. The State is a party only by virtue of 28 U. S. C. § 2403(b) and is not subject to liability. The possible liability of the remaining defendants—the Police Department and the city of Memphis—hinges on *Monell v. New York City Dept. of Social Services*, 436 U.S. 658 (1978), and is left for remand. We hold that the statute is invalid insofar as it purported to give Hymon the authority to act as he did. As for the policy of the Police Department, the absence of any discussion of this issue by the courts below, and the uncertain state of the record, preclude any consideration of its validity.

The judgment of the Court of Appeals is affirmed, and the case is remanded for further proceedings consistent with this opinion.

So ordered. ...

Notes

1. The owner of the house testified that no lights were on in the house, but that a back door light was on. Record 160. Officer Hymon, though uncertain, stated in his deposition that there were lights on in the house. *Id.*, at 209.

2. In fact, Garner, an eighth-grader, was 15. He was 5'4" tall and weighed somewhere around 100 or 110 pounds. App. to Pet. for Cert. A5.

3. When asked at trial why he fired, Hymon stated:

   > Well, first of all it was apparent to me from the little bit that I knew about the area at the time that he was going to get away because, number 1, I couldn't get to him. My partner then couldn't find where he was because, you know, he was late coming around. He didn't know where I was talking about. I couldn't get to him because of the fence here, I couldn't have jumped this fence and come up, consequently jumped this fence and caught him before he got away because he was already up on the fence, just one leap and he was already over the fence, and so there is no way that I could have caught him. App. 52.

   He also stated that the area beyond the fence was dark, that he could not have gotten over the fence easily because he was carrying a lot of equipment and wearing heavy boots, and that Garner, being younger and more energetic, could have outrun him. *Id.*, at 53–54.

4. Garner had rummaged through one room in the house, in which, in the words of the owner, "[all] the stuff was out on the floors, all the drawers was pulled out, and stuff was scattered all over." *Id.*, at 34. The owner testified that his valuables were untouched but that, in addition to the purse and the 10 dollars, one of his wife's rings was missing. The ring was not recovered. *Id.*, at 34–35.

5. Although the statute does not say so explicitly, Tennessee law forbids the use of deadly force in the arrest of a misdemeanant. See *Johnson v. State*, 173 Tenn. 134, 114 S. W. 2d 819 (1938).

6. The dissent emphasizes that subsequent investigation cannot replace immediate apprehension. We recognize that this is so, see n. 13, infra; indeed, that is the reason why there is any dispute. If subsequent arrest were assured, no one would argue that use of deadly force was justified. Thus, we proceed on the assumption that subsequent arrest is not likely. Nonetheless, it should be remembered that failure to apprehend at the scene does not necessarily mean that the suspect will never be caught.

   In lamenting the inadequacy of later investigation, the dissent relies on the report of the President's Commission on Law Enforcement and Administration of Justice. It is worth noting that, notwithstanding its awareness of this problem, the Commission itself proposed a policy for use of deadly force arguably even more stringent than the formulation we adopt today. See President's Commission on Law Enforcement and Administration of Justice, Task Force Report: The Police 189 (1967). The Commission proposed that deadly force be used only to apprehend "perpetrators who, in the course of their crime threatened the use of deadly force, or if the officer believes there is a substantial risk that the person whose arrest is sought will cause death or serious bodily harm if his apprehension is delayed." In addition, the officer would have "to know, as a virtual certainty, that the suspect committed an offense for which the use of deadly force is permissible." Ibid.

7. We note that the usual manner of deterring illegal conduct—through punishment—has been largely ignored in connection with flight from arrest. Arkansas, for example, specifically excepts flight from arrest from the offense of "obstruction of governmental operations." The commentary notes that this "reflects the basic policy judgment that, absent the use of force or violence, a mere attempt to avoid apprehension by a law enforcement officer does not give rise to an independent offense." Ark. Stat. Ann. § 41-2802(3)(a) (1977) and commentary. In the few States that do outlaw flight from an arresting officer, the crime is only a misdemeanor. See, e.g., Ind. Code § 35-44-3-3 (1982). Even forceful resistance, though generally a separate offense, is classified as a misdemeanor. E.g., Ill. Rev. Stat., ch. 38, para. 31-

1 (1984); Mont. Code Ann. § 45-7-301 (1984); N. H. Rev. Stat. Ann. § 642:2 (Supp. 1983); Ore. Rev. Stat. § 162.315 (1983).

This lenient approach does avoid the anomaly of automatically transforming every fleeing misdemeanant into a fleeing felon—subject, under the common-law rule, to apprehension by deadly force—solely by virtue of his flight. However, it is in real tension with the harsh consequences of flight in cases where deadly force is employed. For example, Tennessee does not outlaw fleeing from arrest. The Memphis City Code does, § 22–34.1 (Supp. 17, 1971), subjecting the offender to a maximum fine of $50, § 1–8 (1967). Thus, Garner's attempted escape subjected him to (a) a $50 fine, and (b) being shot.

8. See Sherman, Reducing Police Gun Use, in Control in the Police Organization 98, 120–123 (M. Punch ed. 1983); Fyfe, Observations on Police Deadly Force, 27 Crime & Delinquency 376, 378–381 (1981); W. Geller & K. Karales, Split-Second Decisions 67 (1981); App. 84 (affidavit of William Bracey, Chief of Patrol, New York City Police Department). See generally Brief for Police Foundation et al. as *Amici Curiae.*

9. Ala. Code § 13A-3-27 (1982); Ark. Stat. Ann. § 41-510 (1977); Cal. Penal Code Ann. § 196 (West 1970); Conn. Gen. Stat. § 53a-22 (1972); Fla. Stat. § 776.05 (1983); Idaho Code § 19-610 (1979); Ind. Code § 35-41-3-3 (1982); Kan. Stat. Ann. § 21-3215 (1981); Miss. Code Ann. § 97-3-15(d) (Supp. 1984); Mo. Rev. Stat. § 563.046 (1979); Nev. Rev. Stat. § 200.140 (1983); N. M. Stat. Ann. § 30-2-6 (1984); Okla. Stat., Tit. 21, § 732 (1981); R. I. Gen. Laws § 12-7-9 (1981); S. D. Codified Laws §§ 22-16-32, 22-16-33 (1979); Tenn. Code Ann. § 40-7-108 (1982); Wash. Rev. Code § 9A.16.040(3) (1977). Oregon limits use of deadly force to violent felons, but also allows its use against any felon if "necessary." Ore. Rev. Stat. § 161.239 (1983). Wisconsin's statute is ambiguous, but should probably be added to this list. Wis. Stat. § 939.45(4) (1981–1982) (officer may use force necessary for "a reasonable accomplishment of a lawful arrest"). But see *Clark v. Ziedonis,* 368 F.Supp. 544 (ED Wis. 1973), aff'd on other grounds, 513 F.2d 79 (CA7 1975).

10. In California, the police may use deadly force to arrest only if the crime for which the arrest is sought was "a forcible and atrocious one which threatens death or serious bodily harm," or there is a substantial risk that the person whose arrest is sought will cause death or serious bodily harm if apprehension is delayed. *Kortum v. Alkire,* 69 Cal. App. 3d 325, 333, 138 Cal. Rptr. 26, 30–31 (1977). See also People v. Ceballos, 12 Cal. 3d 470, 476–484, 526 P.2d 241, 245–250 (1974); *Long Beach Police Officers Assn. v. Long Beach,* 61 Cal. App. 3d 364, 373–374, 132 Cal. Rptr. 348, 353–354 (1976). In Indiana, deadly force may be used only to prevent injury, the imminent danger of injury or force, or the threat of force. It is not permitted simply to prevent escape. *Rose v. State,* 431 N. E. 2d 521 (Ind. App. 1982).

11. These are Michigan, Ohio, Virginia, and West Virginia. *Werner v. Hartfelder,* 113 Mich. App. 747, 318 N. W. 2d 825 (1982); *State v. Foster,* 60 Ohio Misc. 46, 59–66, 396 N. E. 2d 246, 255–258 (Com. Pl. 1979) (citing cases); *Berry v. Hamman,* 203 Va. 596, 125 S. E. 2d 851 (1962); *Thompson v. Norfolk & W. R. Co.,* 116 W. Va. 705, 711–712, 182 S. E. 880, 883–884 (1935).

12. Haw. Rev. Stat. § 703–307 (1976); Neb. Rev. Stat. § 28-1412 (1979). Massachusetts probably belongs in this category. Though it once rejected distinctions between felonies, *Uraneck v. Lima,* 359 Mass. 749, 750, 269 N. E. 2d 670, 671 (1971), it has since adopted the Model Penal Code limitations with regard to private citizens, *Commonwealth v. Klein,* 372 Mass. 823, 363 N. E. 2d 1313 (1977), and seems to have extended that decision to police officers, *Julian v. Randazzo,* 380 Mass. 391, 403 N. E. 2d 931 (1980).

13. Alaska Stat. Ann. § 11.81.370(a) (1983); Ariz. Rev. Stat. Ann. § 13-410 (1978); Colo. Rev. Stat. § 18-1-707 (1978); Del. Code Ann., Tit. 11, § 467 (1979) (felony involving physical force and a substantial risk that the suspect will cause death or serious bodily injury or will never be recaptured); Ga. Code § 16-3-21(a) (1984); Ill. Rev. Stat., ch. 38, para. 7-5 (1984); Iowa Code § 804.8 (1983) (suspect has used or threatened deadly force in commission of a felony, or would use deadly force if not caught; Ky. Rev. Stat. § 503.090 (1984) (suspect committed felony involving use or

threat of physical force likely to cause death or serious injury, and is likely to endanger life unless apprehended without delay); Me. Rev. Stat. Ann., Tit. 17-A, § 107 (1983) (commentary notes that deadly force may be used only "where the person to be arrested poses a threat to human life"); Minn. Stat. § 609.066 (1984); N. H. Rev. Stat. Ann. § 627:5(II) (Supp. 1983); N. J. Stat. Ann. § 2C-3-7 (West 1982); N. Y. Penal Law § 35.30 (McKinney Supp. 1984–1985); N. C. Gen. Stat. § 15A-401 (1983); N. D. Cent. Code § 12.1-05-07.2.d (1976); 18 Pa. Cons. Stat. § 508 (1982); Tex. Penal Code Ann. § 9.51(c) (1974); Utah Code Ann. § 76-2-404 (1978).

14. See La. Rev. Stat. Ann. § 14:20(2) (West 1974); Vt. Stat. Ann., Tit. 13, § 2305 (1974 and Supp. 1984). A Federal District Court has interpreted the Louisiana statute to limit the use of deadly force against fleeing suspects to situations where "life itself is endangered or great bodily harm is threatened." *Sauls v. Hutto,* 304 F.Supp. 124, 132 (ED La. 1969).

15. These are Maryland, Montana, South Carolina, and Wyoming. A Maryland appellate court has indicated, however, that deadly force may not be used against a felon who "was in the process of fleeing and, at the time, presented no immediate danger to . . .anyone. . . ." *Giant Food, Inc. v. Scherry,* 51 Md. App. 586, 589, 596, 444 A. 2d 483, 486, 489 (1982).

16. In adopting its current statute in 1979, for example, Alabama expressly chose the common-law rule over more restrictive provisions. Ala. Code § 13A-3-27, Commentary, pp. 67–68 (1982). Missouri likewise considered but rejected a proposal akin to the Model Penal Code rule. See *Mattis v. Schnarr,* 547 F.2d 1007, 1022 (CA8 1976) (Gibson, C. J., dissenting), vacated as moot sub nom. *Ashcroft v. Mattis,* 431 U.S. 171 (1977). Idaho, whose current statute codifies the common-law rule, adopted the Model Penal Code in 1971, but abandoned it in 1972.

NOTES AND QUESTIONS

1. In deciding on the constitutionality of the Tennessee statute, what "competing interests" does the Supreme Court endeavor to balance? Do you agree with the weight assigned each interest in the judgment? Why or why not?

2. Under the *Garner* ruling, police must have "probable cause" to believe that a fleeing criminal "poses a significant threat of death or serious injury to the officer or others" before they may use deadly force. Is this a reasonable requirement for police conduct? Does it afford police sufficient discretion to effectively enforce the law?

3. How do you interpret "probable cause"? What would be sufficient indication that a fleeing criminal poses a serious threat? What criteria can and should be used to decide the threat an individual poses? Is race one of them? Does the court's ruling address these questions?

4. Recall Skolnick's account (Chapter 47) of the police officer's working environment and his "working personality." How do police perceive threats as compared with the average citizen? On this basis, what type of "probable cause" decisions can we expect police officers to make in the heat of a criminal confrontation or pursuit?

5. By restricting some freedom of the police to employ law's violence, the Supreme Court in *Garner* shifted a measure of legal power up the legal hierarchy, away from police. Does *Garner* undermine effective law enforcement by removing a credible threat of force? Why or why not?

6. Though the majority opinion in *Garner* declares policing practices in Tennessee unconstitutional, it claims that its decision is in line with the policies of police departments across the country. To borrow from Heumann and Cassak's discussion (Chapter 50), is this a case of doctrine informing practice or practice influencing doctrine?

Reprinted from: *Tennessee v. Garner,* 105 S. Court 1694 (1985). ✦

Chapter 53

Officers in Bronx Fire 41 Shots, and an Unarmed Man Is Killed

Michael J. Cooper, the New York Times

The Garner *standard requires the police to use judgment and holds them accountable to a probable cause standard. That standard, in turn, is a kind of reasonable police officer rule. It allows for the mistaken use of lethal force, even the shooting of an unarmed man, so long as the mistake is one a reasonable police officer would have made.*

A notorious case of such a mistaken use of lethal force occurred in 1999 in New York City when four police officers shot Amadou Diallo, an unarmed West African immigrant, forty-one times and killed him. The officers were members of the city's Street Crime Unit, a special roving unit of plainclothes officers that allegedly stopped and frisked young black men without cause. Critics called the shooting an indication of pervasive racism in American policing. The Diallo shooting prompted street demonstrations and protests.

Under great pressure from African Americans, the four officers were indicted and charged with murder. About one year later, they were acquitted by a jury, composed of seven white men, one white woman, and four black women, on all

charges arising from the Diallo shooting. After the verdict, thousands of protesters took to the streets in New York City, shouting, "No justice, no peace!" They also chanted, "Forty-one, forty-one, it's a wallet, not a gun," referring to the testimony of the four officers that they thought Diallo had a gun when he reached into his pocket to get his wallet and ID.

Seven of the jurors, speaking on NBC's Today *show, insisted that they had no choice but to acquit, because of the law and evidence presented in court. One juror, Lavette Freeman, said that she understood the anger expressed in the protests, but the prosecution had given her no basis on which to convict. "For me that hurts," said Freeman, who is black.*

The next two readings, both newspaper articles, provide details about the Diallo shooting as well as the reactions of other police officers to the circumstances surrounding it.

Throughout the Diallo case, the question of race loomed large. As in the selections about the Goetz case, the case of Mrs. G, the use of prosecutorial discretion in sexual assault cases, and criminal sentencing, race stood at the center of the social organization of law.

An unarmed West African immigrant with no criminal record was killed early yesterday by four New York City police officers who fired 41 shots at him in the doorway of his Bronx apartment building, the police said.

It was unclear yesterday why the police officers had opened fire on the man at 12:44 A.M. in the vestibule of his building at 1157 Wheeler Avenue in the Soundview section. The man, Amadou Diallo, 22, who came to America more than two years ago from Guinea and worked as a street peddler in Manhattan, died at the scene, the police said.

The Bronx District Attorney's office is investigating the shooting, whose details were still murky last night because there were apparently no civilian witnesses and none of the police officers involved had given statements to investigators. But Inspector Michael Collins, a police spokesman, said that investigators who went to the scene of the shooting did not find a weapon on or near Mr. Diallo.

Relatives and neighbors described Mr. Diallo as a shy, hard-working man with a ready smile, a devout Muslim who did not smoke or drink.

"I am very angry," said his uncle, Mamadou Diallo. "He was a skinny guy. Why would the police shoot somebody of that nature 30 or 40 times? We see the police and we give them all the respect we have."

A friend, Demba Sanyang, 39, said: "We have a very undemocratic society back home, and then we come here. We don't expect to be killed by law enforcement officers."

The four officers involved in the shooting were assigned to the aggressive Street Crimes Unit, which focuses largely on taking illegal guns off the street. All four officers, who were in plainclothes, used their 9-millimeter semiautomatic service pistols, which hold 16 bullets and can discharge all of them in seconds.

Two of the officers, Sean Carroll, 35, and Edward McMellon, 26, emptied their weapons, firing 16 shots each, the police said. Officer Kenneth Boss, 27, fired his gun five times and Officer Richard Murphy, 26, fired four times.

All four have been put on administrative leave, which is standard practice after a police shooting.

Three of the officers—Officers Carroll, McMellon and Boss—have been involved in shootings before, which is unusual in a department where more than 90 percent of all officers never fire their weapons in the line of duty. In those previous incidents, Officers Carroll and McMellon were found to have acted properly, the police said; the case of Officer Boss—he shot and killed a man said to be armed with a shotgun on Oct. 31, 1997, in Brooklyn—is still being reviewed by the Brooklyn District Attorney's office.

Police rules on when officers can fire their guns are explicit: deadly force can be used only when officers fear for their lives or the lives of others. But once they decide to shoot, officers are trained to fire until they "stop" the target from causing harm. They are told not to fire warning shots, and to aim for the center of the body, not arms or legs.

Police officials said it was unclear whether the circumstances of the confrontation between Mr. Diallo and the officers justified such a shooting. What the police say is known is that the four officers were patrolling Mr. Diallo's neighborhood yesterday morning in an unmarked car in the hope that they would make arrests and in the process turn up information about a serial rapist in the area.

At a quarter to one, the officers encountered Mr. Diallo. All four got out of the car and approached him as he stood in the vestibule of his building, the police said.

A police official who spoke on the condition of anonymity said that a neighbor reported after the shooting that he had noticed a man, who the police believe was Mr. Diallo, loitering in the vestibule. The man described him as "acting suspicious," said the official, who did not elaborate.

The officers did not communicate over their radios before they approached Mr. Diallo, the police said, so investigators said they did not know what prompted their initial interest in him.

Nor is it known why the officers began firing. A second police official who spoke on the condition of anonymity said, "We don't know what happened, because we haven't spoken to them, but it looks like one guy may have panicked and the rest followed suit."

After the shooting the officers called in on their radios, the police said, and neighbors telephoned 911. Soon other officers arrived on the scene, followed by detectives and the ranking officers who are required to respond to all police shootings.

An investigation began, and no weapon was found on Mr. Diallo, Inspector Collins said.

A pager and a wallet were found lying next to the body, a police official said, adding that it was unclear whether the officers could have mistaken the pager for a weapon.

Mr. Diallo had lived in New York for two and a half years. A member of the Fulani ethnic group, he came from a village called Lelouma and followed relatives who had moved here. He worked as a street peddler, selling socks, gloves and videos on 14th Street in Manhattan. He sent much of the money he earned to his parents back home, friends said.

Yesterday, Mr. Diallo arrived home from work around midnight, said his roommate, Momodou Kujabi. The two men discussed who was going to pay the Con Edison bill, and then Mr. Diallo turned on the television and Mr. Kujabi went to bed. Another roommate, Mr. Diallo's cousin, Abdou Rahman Diallo, was already asleep.

Mr. Kujabi said he thought Mr. Diallo might have gone out for something to eat, as he often did after coming home from work.

Then came the shots, and a knock on the door, he said. It was the police.

Mr. Kujabi said that the officers brought him down to the vestibule to identify his friend's body. "I said, 'How can this happen?'" Mr. Kujabi recalled telling the officers. "'I left this guy less than 30 minutes ago.'"

An autopsy found that Mr. Diallo died of multiple gunshot wounds to the torso, said Ellen Borakove, a spokeswoman for the Chief Medical Examiner's Office. Further tests are required to learn how many wounds there were and where the bullets entered his body, she said. . . .

. . . Kyle Waters, a lawyer representing Mr. Diallo's family, said he was concerned that the police officers may have overreacted to Mr. Diallo. "There was nothing to indicate that he was a criminal, nothing to indicate that he had a weapon," he said. "For him to be sent back to his homeland in Guinea in a box is a horrible tragedy."

State Assemblyman Ruben Diaz, who represents the area, called the shooting "outrageous," adding that it was clear that excessive force was used. . . .

Chapter 54

To Shoot or Not?

Fellow Officers Say They Fear Facing Same Decision

Katherine E. Finkelstein, the New York Times

The fatal police shooting of Amadou Diallo has provoked many emotions among New York City's officers. Some who spoke yesterday expressed pity for Mr. Diallo and his family. Others said they were surprised by the number of bullets fired and concerned over what the political fallout will be.

But most of all, they said they identified with the four officers who fired 41 shots at Mr. Diallo, a 22-year-old street vendor from Guinea, as he stood in the early hours of Feb. 4 in front of his two-story apartment building in the Bronx with a pager and some keys.

"At night, you see a black shadow coming up, and you might think it's a gun," said Officer Howard Kurz, who was standing outside the Midtown North Precinct station house on West 54th Street yesterday. "I've been a cop for

19 years, worked all over the city, and I'd never arm-chair quarterback what happens at 1 in the morning on a Bronx street."

In interviews with 17 officers in precincts from Harlem to Brooklyn, officers said that they could imagine themselves right there in that vestibule, making a mistake that could cost them their jobs or lead to the death of an innocent civilian.

"I feel sorry for them," said Sgt. Robert Reehil, a plainclothes officer also at Midtown North. "Every day, their names are in the paper. Their addresses are in the paper. Their careers are in the paper." And every day on television, he said, there is file footage of the officers walking out of their lawyer's office.

When he heard the news, Officer Kurz said, he thought: "Those guys are in for a bad ride. They're in the Bronx. They're white cops. Their families are going to be torn up."

The officers who were interviewed yesterday struggled to describe the uncertain world they confront at the beginning of each shift, and the self-doubt that lingers long after the shift ends.

One officer spoke of beginning to squeeze the trigger when he mistook a portable music player for a gun. Another spoke of her fear about whether the commands "freeze" or "don't move" were even comprehensible to many people on the city streets, given the array of languages spoken there.

Then there are the questions that come from officers' spouses, parents and children. Sergeant Reehil said that after the shooting, his wife asked, "How could someone shoot 41 rounds at one guy?" Standing outside the station house yesterday, dressed in khakis and a sweatshirt, he shrugged. "I can't explain it. I wasn't there." But he said his views have been shaped by the fact that his brother, also a police officer, had been shot and wounded in the line of duty.

Yvette Matthews, also an officer at Midtown North, agreed with Sergeant Reehil. "They ask us questions, as though we're supposed to know the answers," he said.

Officers said any of the 30 to 40 calls on a typical shift could explode into catastrophe. Such rapid-fire crises can leave officers stricken by headaches, taut with fear.

"You ever see those kaleidoscopes when you were a kid?" asked Officer Ronald Fagan at the 84th Precinct station house on Tillary Street in Brooklyn. "That's what happens in your brain after a shift and everything you saw and everything you didn't do flashes through your mind."

And then there are the career-ending mistakes.

Some white officers at the 84th Precinct in Brooklyn said they often feel isolated and up against a wall as politicians exploit the racial aspect of such cases and the news media pile on.

"It's more or less like we're political pawns for the public and politicians," said one officer there with 17 years experience, who spoke on the condition of anonymity. "In Nassau and Suffolk, they back you up. Here, you're suspended for 30 days before you even go to trial."

A minority officer at the precinct, who joined the conversation, did not question the role of politicians but rather the number of bullets fired.

Officer Fagan said that he thought the police brass were tough on members of the force. "I don't think that anyone will deny that police officers have a profound lack of due process," he said.

Given the treacherous waters they navigate, some officers said that they feel that vigilance, even fear, can be their closest ally. "Fear is survival," said Officer Matthews of Midtown North.

But it can also lead to rash actions—or no action at all. Officer Kurz recalled the time he was at the Lefrak City apartment complex in Queens and shots were being fired at him. He stood there, terrified, and didn't even take out his gun, he said, because he knew that the shots could have been coming from any one of "10,000 windows."

The reflections of these officers came the day after Mr. Diallo's mother arrived from Guinea to reclaim her son's body and swooned before the house where he was killed. There was little disagreement among officers that the shooting was a tragedy—a life lost, four careers potentially ended and a police force placed under public scrutiny.

"Whether they were right or wrong," Sergeant Reehil said, "they killed an unarmed man and they have to live with that for the rest of their lives.

NOTES AND QUESTIONS

1. Did the police use excessive force in the Diallo shooting? Why or why not? What criteria matter for deciding this question? The time? The location? The especially dangerous nature of the detail to which the four police officers were assigned? Does the number of shots fired make any difference?

2. In light of the police commentary in the second article, does the Diallo shooting fit the *Garner* standard? Was the use of deadly force in this instance a mistake that any reasonable officer might have made?

3. We have read in this section about the suspicion and fear that mark police work. In the second Diallo article, one officer sums up his on-the-job attitude in three words: "Fear is survival." This is no doubt understandable considering the inherent danger in law enforcement, but the *Garner* standard implies that there must be some reasonable limit to the deployment of violence triggered by fear. Because it is fear that prompts officers to use violence, excessive or unchecked discretion could lead to a cha-

otic application of that violence. On the other hand, holding officers to a strictly defined standard may leave them defenseless before dangerous criminals. How can the law facilitate effective enforcement techniques *and* protect officers in the line of duty, without endangering innocent citizens? Assuming the law cannot strike the perfect balance, is it better to err on the side of police discretion or to give citizens the benefit of the doubt?

4. One officer accuses the media and politicians of exploiting the racial aspect of the Diallo case unfairly. Do you agree? How relevant is race to determining the defensibility or injustice of the shooting? Consider, for instance, the role of race in triggering the fear response in the officers. All other factors being the same, what if the victim had been a white woman? Would the officers' fear when she reached for her wallet be considered less reasonable than their fear when a black man reached for his?

5. Referring to the legal procedures afforded police after a high profile shooting, one officer commented, "I don't think anyone would deny that police officers have a profound lack of due process." Do you agree? Are police officers treated unfairly by the law, or is the heightened scrutiny warranted considering the violence they are authorized to inflict in the course of duty?

Chapter 55

Want to Torture? Get a Warrant

Alan M. Dershowitz

Although Dershowitz opposes torture in most instances, he thinks it is permissible it in a ticking bomb situation. These situations involve cases analogous to circumstances where a bomb has been activated and the only person who may have information to prevent the potential damage from an explosion is the suspect, who refuses to disclose this information. The question is whether this suspect should be tortured to force him or her to reveal information that could potentially save many lives. Judicially sanctioned torture, Dershowitz believes, will minimize its use against terrorist suspects. It represents an effort to control the way violence is used by law enforcement officials in extreme situations.

Controlling police and their use of violence is, as the previous readings have shown, difficult under all circumstances. But today's threat of terrorism, and the loss of large numbers of innocent lives that it entails, has led many to revisit the question of whether law enforcement should be allowed to use torture (see Langbein, Chapter 32) on terrorists suspected of having crucial information in "ticking bomb situations." Indeed, in the wake of September 11, 2001, FBI agents suggested that they might resort to torture to compel terrorist suspects to reveal information necessary to prevent a recurrence. A senior FBI official warned, "It could get to that spot where we could go to pressure... where we won't have a choice, and we are probably getting there."

For more than a century, much of the world has condemned the general notion of torture. Yet today, the question of whether it is ever permissible is again on the agenda. Can torture ever be legitimate? Recently, law professor Alan M. Dershowitz stirred considerable controversy by advocating the use of judicially sanctioned, nonlethal torture to force a terrorist suspect to disclose information that would prevent an imminent and massive terrorist attack. Under his proposal, law enforcement officials would be allowed to torture a terrorist suspect after first obtaining a judicial warrant.

If American law enforcement officers were ever to confront the law school hypothetical case of the captured terrorist who knew about an imminent attack but refused to provide the information necessary to prevent it, I have absolutely no doubt that they would try to torture the terrorists into providing the information. Moreover, the vast majority of Americans would expect the officers to engage in that time-tested technique for loosening tongues, notwithstanding our unequivocal treaty obligation never to employ torture, no matter how exigent the circumstances. The real question is not whether torture would be used—it would—but whether it would be used outside of the law or within the law.

Every democracy, including our own, has employed torture outside of the law. Throughout the years, police officers have tortured murder and rape suspects into confessing—sometimes truthfully, sometimes not truthfully. The "third degree" is all too common, not only on TV shows such as *NYPD Blue,* but in the back rooms of real police station houses. No democracy, other than Israel, has ever employed torture within the law. Until quite recently, Israel recognized the power of its security agencies to employ what it euphemistically called "moderate physical pressure" to elicit information from terrorists about continuing threats.

This "pressure" entailed putting the suspect in a dingy cell with a smelly sack over his head and shaking him violently until he disclosed planned terrorist attacks. Israel never allowed the information elicited by these methods to be used in courts of law as confessions. But it did use the information to prevent terrorist acts. Several attacks were prevented by this unpleasant tactic. In a courageous and controversial decision, the president of the Israeli Supreme Court wrote a majority opinion banning the use of this tactic against suspected terrorists.

The Israeli Supreme Court left open the possibility, however, that in an actual "ticking bomb" case—a situation in which a terrorist refused to divulge information necessary to defuse a bomb that was about to kill hundreds of innocent civilians—an agent who employed physical pressure could defend himself against criminal charges by invoking "the law of necessity."

No such case has arisen since this court decision, despite numerous instances of terrorism in that troubled part of the world. Nor has there ever been a ticking bomb case in this country. But inevitably one will arise, and we should be prepared to confront it. It is important that a decision be made in advance of an actual ticking bomb case about how we should deal with this inevitable situation. In my new book, *Shouting Fire: Civil Liberties in a Turbulent Age,* I offer a controversial proposal designed to stimulate debate about this difficult issue. Under my proposal, no torture would be permitted without a "torture warrant" being issued by a judge. An application for a torture warrant would have to be based on the absolute need to obtain immediate information in order to save lives coupled with probable cause that the suspect had such information and is unwilling to reveal it.

The suspect would be given immunity from prosecution based on information elic-ited by the torture. The warrant would limit the torture to nonlethal means, such as sterile needles, being inserted beneath the nails to cause excruciating pain without endangering life.

It may sound absurd for a distinguished judge to be issuing a warrant to do something so awful. But consider the alternatives: Either police would torture below the radar screen of accountability, or the judge who issued the warrant would be accountable. Which would be more consistent with democratic values? Those opposed to the idea of a torture warrant argue—quite reasonably—that establishing such a precedent would legitimize torture and make it easier to extend its permissible use beyond the ticking bomb case.

Those who favor the torture warrant argue that the opposite would be true: By expressly limiting the use of torture only to the ticking bomb case and by requiring a highly visible judge to approve, limit and monitor the torture, it will be far more difficult to justify its extension to other institutions.

The goal of the warrant would be to reduce and limit the amount of torture that would, in fact, be used in an emergency. This is an issue that should be discussed now, before we confront the emergency.

NOTES AND QUESTIONS

1   Would a "torture warrant" legitimize the use of brutal interrogative methods to elicit information from a terrorist suspect? If the government were to authorize the use of torture warrants, what should the standard of proof be to justify torture?

2.   Does torturing a suspect to elicit information undermine the guarantee of "innocent until proven guilty"? Does the collective interest in averting imminent terrorist violence trump the presumption of innocence? Why or why not? What about torturing a convicted ter-

rorist who may have information about a "ticking bomb situation"? Would this be acceptable?

3. In a ticking bomb situation, "the real question," Dershowitz argues, "is not whether torture would be used—it would—but whether it would be used outside the law or within the law." Do you agree? What are the benefits of lowering the bar to match practical behavior? What are the dangers?

4. Any torture, even if it were officially sanctioned by the State, would violate the Geneva conventions. If the U.S. were to adopt an open policy of torture, limited though it might be to judicially reviewed ticking bomb situations, what is to stop other nations from following suit (and perhaps with less oversight)? Is it worth the risk? Is there any meaningful legal or political difference between turning a blind eye to extralegal torture abroad, and officially sanctioning it? In the long run, which is a more useful tool for international security-legalized extreme interrogation methods or idealistic, though imperfect, international legal standards?

5. Some would argue that Dershowitz's "ends justify means" approach to combating terrorism ultimately undermines the very concept of justice. How much weight does this consideration carry in the face of a terrorist threat? Can justice be done justly in this case? In other words, is it possible to battle lawless terrorists within the framework of law? What would Koh (Chapter 6) say?

6. What alternative, legal methods of getting information are there? Are these as effective as the credible threat of torture in a "ticking bomb situation"?

Section XIII

Punishment: Imprisonment

Chapter 56

Persons and Punishment

Herbert Morris

"They acted and looked . . . at us, and around in our house, in a way that had about it the feeling—at least for me—that we were no people. In their eyesight we were just things, that was all."

—Malcolm X

"We have no right to treat a man like a dog."

—Governor Maddox of Georgia

Why do we punish? What are the aims and justifications of punishment? What are the proper limits of punishment? These questions have preoccupied scholars for generations. Although considerable disagreement exists about each of the issues, there is widespread recognition that punishment, whatever its purposes and justifications, always involves the calculated and deliberate use of the coercive force of the law. As the legal theorist H. L. A. Hart notes, punishment "always involves pain or other consequences normally considered unpleasant." It is imposed for the violation of a legal prohibition by "an authority constituted by a legal system against which the offence is committed."

The following reading presents an unusual justification for punishment. People who violate the law, Herbert Morris claims, have a right to be punished. When we use law's violence, we do so to vindicate that right and to discharge a duty that flows from it. The right to be punished derives from the right to be treated as a person, which is fundamental and inalienable. We are treated as persons when our actions are regarded as choices and when those choices are taken seriously by others. When we punish, Morris argues, we treat actions (violations of the law) as choices, and we show that we take those choices seriously.

As you read Morris, ask if there are there different and better justifications for punishment. What are they? What, if anything, does Morris suggest about how we punish?

My aim is to argue for four propositions concerning rights that will certainly strike some as not only false but preposterous: first, that we have a right to punishment; second, that this right derives from a fundamental human right to be treated as a person; third, that this fundamental right is a natural, inalienable, and absolute right; and, fourth, that the denial of this right implies the denial of all moral rights and duties. Showing the truth of one, let alone all, of these large and questionable claims, is a tall order. The attempt or, more properly speaking, the first steps in an attempt follow.

When someone claims that there is a right to be free, we can easily imagine situations in which the right is infringed and easily imagine situations in which there is a point to asserting or claiming the right. With the right to be punished, matters are otherwise. The immediate reaction to the claim that there is such a right is puzzlement. And the reasons for this are apparent. People do not normally value pain and suffering. Punishment is associated with pain and suffering. When we think about punishment we naturally think of the strong desire most persons have to avoid it, to accept, for example, acquittal of a criminal charge with relief and eagerly, if convicted, to hope for pardon or probation. Adding, of course, to the paradoxical character of the claim of such a right is difficulty in imagining circumstances in which it would be denied one. When would one rightly demand punishment and meet with any threat of the claim being denied?

So our first task is to see when the claim of such a right would have a point. I want to approach this task by setting out two complex types of institutions both of which are designed to maintain some degree of social control. In the one a central concept is punishment for wrongdoing and in the other the central concepts are control of dangerous individuals and treatment of disease.

Let us first turn attention to the institutions in which punishment is involved. The institutions I describe will resemble those we ordinarily think of as institutions of punishment; they will have, however, additional features we associate with a system of just punishment.

Let us suppose that men are constituted roughly as they now are, with a rough equivalence in strength and abilities, a capacity to be injured by each other and to make judgments that such injury is undesirable, a limited strength of will, and a capacity to reason and to conform conduct to rules. Applying to the conduct of these men are a group of rules, ones I shall label 'primary,' which closely resemble the core rules of our criminal law, rules that prohibit violence and deception and compliance with which provides benefits for all persons. These benefits consist in noninterference by others with what each person values, such matters as continuance of life and bodily security. The rules define a sphere for each person, then, which is immune from interference by others. Making possible this mutual benefit is the assumption by individuals of a burden. The burden consists in the exercise of self-restraint by individuals over inclinations that would, if satisfied, directly interfere or create a substantial risk of interference with others in proscribed ways. If a person fails to exercise self-restraint even though he might have and gives in to such inclinations, he renounces a burden which others have voluntarily assumed and

thus gains an advantage which others, who have restrained themselves, do not possess. This system then, is one in which the rules establish a mutuality of benefit and burden and in which the benefits of noninterference are conditional upon the assumption of burdens.

Connecting punishment with the violation of these primary rules, and making public the provision for punishment, is both reasonable and just. First, it is only reasonable that those who voluntarily comply with the rules be provided some assurance that they will not be assuming burdens which others are unprepared to assume. Their disposition to comply voluntarily will diminish as they learn that others are with impunity renouncing burdens they are assuming. Second, fairness dictates that a system in which benefits and burdens are equally distributed have a mechanism designed to prevent a maldistribution in the benefits and burdens. Thus, sanctions are attached to noncompliance with the primary rules so as to induce compliance with the primary rules among those who may be disinclined to obey. In this way the likelihood of an unfair distribution is diminished.

Third, it is just to punish those who have violated the rules and caused the unfair distribution of benefits and burdens. A person who violates the rules has something others have—the benefits of the system—but by renouncing what others have assumed, the burdens of self-restraint, he has acquired an unfair advantage. Matters are not even until this advantage is in some way erased. Another way of putting it is that he owes something to others, for he has something that does not rightfully belong to him. Justice—that is, punishing such individuals—restores the equilibrium of benefits and burdens by taking from the individual what he owes, that is, exacting the debt. It is important to see that the equilibrium may be restored in another way. Forgiveness—with its legal analogue of a pardon—while not the righting of an unfair distribution by making one pay his debt is, nevertheless, a restoring of the equilibrium by forgiving the debt. Forgiveness may be viewed, at least in some types of cases, as a gift after the fact, erasing a debt, which had the gift been given before the fact, would not have created a debt. But the practice of pardoning has to proceed sensitively, for it may endanger in a way the practice of justice does not, the maintenance of an equilibrium of benefits and burdens. If all are indiscriminately pardoned less incentive is provided individuals to restrain their inclinations, thus increasing the incidence of persons taking what they do not deserve. . . .

Finally, because the primary rules are designed to benefit all and because the punishments prescribed for their violation are publicized and the defenses respected, there is some plausibility in the exaggerated claim that in choosing to do an act violative of the rules an individual has chosen to be punished. This way of putting matters brings to our attention the extent to which, when the system is as I have described it, the criminal 'has brought the punishment upon himself' in contrast to those cases where it would be misleading to say 'he has brought it upon himself', cases, for example, where one does not know the rules or is punished in the absence of fault.

To summarize, then: first, there is a group of rules guiding the behavior of individuals in the community which establish spheres of interest immune from interference by others; second, provision is made for what is generally regarded as a deprivation of some thing of value if the rules are violated; third, the deprivations visited upon any person are justified by that person's having violated the rules; fourth, the deprivation, in this just system of punishment, is linked to rules that fairly distribute benefits and burdens and to procedures that strike some balance between not punishing the guilty and punishing the innocent, a class defined as those who have not voluntarily done acts violative of the law, in which it is evident that the evil of punishing the innocent is regarded as greater than the nonpunishment of the guilty.

At the core of many actual legal systems one finds, of course, rules and procedures of the kind I have sketched. It is obvious, though, that any ongoing legal system differs in significant respects from what I have presented here, containing 'pockets of injustice.'

I want now to sketch an extreme version of a set of institutions of a fundamentally different kind, institutions proceeding on a conception of man which appears to be basically at odds with that operative within a system of punishment. Rules are promulgated in this system that prohibit certain types of injuries and harms.

In this world we are now to imagine when an individual harms another his conduct is to be regarded as a symptom of some pathological condition in the way a running nose is a symptom of a cold. Actions diverging from some conception of the normal are viewed as manifestations of a disease in the way in which we might today regard the arm and leg movements of an epileptic during a seizure. Actions conforming to what is normal are assimilated to the normal and healthy functioning of bodily organs. What a person does, then, is assimilated, on this conception, to what we believe today, or at least most of us believe today, a person undergoes. We draw a distinction between the operation of the kidney and raising an arm on request. This distinction between mere events or happenings and human actions is erased in our imagined system.[1]

There is, however, bound to be something strange in this erasing of a recognized distinction, for, as with metaphysical suggestions generally, and I take this to be one, the distinction may be reintroduced but given a different description, for example, 'happenings with X type of causes' and 'happenings with Y type of causes.' Responses of different kinds, today legitimated by our distinction between happenings and actions may be legitimated by this new manner of description. And so there may be isomorphism between a system recognizing the distinction and one erasing it. Still, when this distinction is erased certain tendencies of thought and responses might naturally arise that would tend to affect unfavorably values respected by a system of punishment.

I am concerned now, however, with what the implications would be were the world indeed one of therapy and not a disguised world of punishment and therapy, for I want to suggest tendencies of thought that arise when one is immersed in the ideology of disease and therapy.

First, punishment is the imposition upon a person who is believed to be at fault of something commonly believed to be a deprivation where that deprivation is justified by the person's guilty behavior. It is associated with resentment, for the guilty are those who have done what they had no right to do by failing to exercise restraint when they might have and where others have. Therapy is not a response to a person who is at fault. We respond to an individual, not because of what he has done, but because of some condition from which he is suffering. If he is no longer suffering from the condition, treatment no longer has a point. Punishment, then, focuses on the past; therapy on the present. Therapy is normally associated with compassion for what one undergoes, not resentment for what one has illegitimately done.

Second, with therapy, unlike punishment, we do not seek to deprive the person of something acknowledged as a good, but seek rather to help and to benefit the individual who is suffering by ministering to his illness in the hope that the person can be cured. The good we attempt to do is not a reward for desert. The individual suffering has not merited by his disease the good we seek to bestow upon him but has, because he is a creature that has the capacity to feel pain, a claim upon our sympathies and help.

Third, we saw with punishment that its justification was related to maintaining and restoring a fair distribution of benefits and burdens. Infliction of the prescribed punishment carries the implication, then, that one has 'paid one's debt' to society, for the punishment is the taking from the person of something commonly recognized as valuable. It is this conception of 'a debt owed' that may permit, as I suggested earlier, under certain conditions, the nonpunishment of the guilty, for operative within a system of punishment may be a concept analogous to forgiveness, namely pardoning. Who it is that we may pardon and under what conditions—contrition with its elements of self-punishment no doubt plays a role—I shall not go into though it is clearly a matter of the greatest practical and theoretical interest. What is clear is that the conceptions of 'paying a debt' or 'having a debt forgiven' or pardoning have no place in a system of therapy.

Fourth, with punishment there is an attempt at some equivalence between the advantage gained by the wrongdoer—partly based upon the seriousness of the interest invaded, partly on the state of mind with which the wrongful act was performed—and the punishment meted out. Thus, we can understand a prohibition on 'cruel and unusual punishments' so that disproportionate pain and suffering are avoided. With therapy, attempts at proportionality make no sense. It is perfectly plausible giving someone who kills a pill, and treating for a lifetime within an institution one who has broken a dish and manifested accident proneness. We have the concept of 'painful treatment.' We do not have the concept of 'cruel treatment.' Because treatment is regarded as a benefit, though it may involve pain, it is natural that less restraint is exercised in bestowing it than in inflicting punishment. Further, protests with respect to treatment are likely to be assimilated to the complaints of one whose leg must be amputated in order for him to live, and, thus, largely disregarded. To be sure, there is operative in the therapy world some conception of the "cure being worse than the disease," but if the disease is manifested in conduct harmful to others, and if being a normal operating human being is valued highly, there will naturally be considerable pressure to find the cure acceptable.

Fifth, the rules in our system of punishment governing conduct of individuals were rules violation of which involved either direct interference with others or the creation of a substantial risk of such interference. One could imagine adding to this system of primary rules other rules proscribing preparation to do acts violative of the primary rules and even rules proscribing thoughts. Objection to such suggestions would have many sources but a principal one would consist in its involving the infliction of punishment on too great a number of persons who would not, because of a change of mind, have violated the primary rules. Though we are interested in diminishing violations of the primary rules, we are not prepared to punish too many individuals who would never have violated the rules in order to achieve this aim. In a system motivated solely by a preventive and curative ideology there would be less reason to wait until symptoms manifest themselves in socially harmful conduct. It is understandable that we should wish at the earliest possible stage to arrest the development of the disease. In the punishment system, because we are dealing with deprivations, it is understandable that we should forbear from imposing them until we are quite sure of guilt. In the therapy system, dealing as it does with benefits, there is less reason for forbearance from treatment at an early stage.

Sixth, a variety of procedural safeguards we associate with punishment have less significance in a therapy system. To the degree objections to double jeopardy and self-incrimination are based on a wish to decrease the chances of the innocent being convicted and punished, a therapy system, unconcerned with this problem, would disregard such safeguards. When one is out to help people there is also little sense in urging that the burden of

proof be on those providing the help. And there is less point to imposing the burden of proving that the conduct was pathological beyond a reasonable doubt. Further, a jury system which, within a system of justice, serves to make accommodations to the individual situation and to introduce a human element, would play no role or a minor one in a world where expertise is required in making determinations of disease and treatment.

In our system of punishment an attempt was made to maximize each individual's freedom of choice by first of all delimiting by rules certain spheres of conduct immune from interference by others. The punishment associated with these primary rules paid deference to an individual's free choice by connecting punishment to a freely chosen act violative of the rules, thus giving some plausibility to the claim, as we saw, that what a person received by way of punishment he himself had chosen. With the world of disease and therapy all this changes and the individual's free choice ceases to be a determinative factor in how others respond to him. All those principles of our own legal system that minimize the chances of punishment of those who have not chosen to do acts violative of the rules tend to lose their point in the therapy system, for how we respond in a therapy system to a person is not conditioned upon what he has chosen but rather on what symptoms he has manifested or may manifest and what the best therapy for the disease is that is suggested by the symptoms.

Now, it is clear I think, that were we confronted with the alternatives I have sketched, between a system of just punishment and a thoroughgoing system of treatment, a system, that is, that did not reintroduce concepts appropriate to punishment, we could see the point in claiming that a person has a right to be punished, meaning by this that a person had a right to all those institutions and practices linked to punishment. For these would provide him with, among other things, a far greater ability to predict what would happen to him on the occurrence of certain events than the therapy system. There is the inestimable value to each of us of having the responses of others to us determined over a wide range of our lives by what we choose rather than what they choose. A person has a right to institutions that respect his choices. Our punishment system does; our therapy system does not. . . .

The primary reason for preferring the system of punishment as against the system of therapy might have been expressed in terms of the one system treating one as a person and the other not. In invoking the right to be punished, one justifies one's claim by reference to a more fundamental right. I want now to turn attention to this fundamental right and attempt to shed light—it will have to be little, for the topic is immense—on what is meant by 'treating an individual as a person.'

When we talk of not treating a human being as a person or 'showing no respect for one as a person' what we imply by our words is a contrast between the manner in which one acceptably responds to human beings and the manner in which one acceptably responds to animals and inanimate objects. When we treat a human being merely as an animal or some inanimate object our responses to the human being are determined, not by his choices, but ours in disregard of or with indifference to his. And when we 'look upon' a person as less than a person or not a person, we consider the person as incapable of a rational choice. In cases of not treating a human being as a person we interfere with a person in such a way that what is done, even if the person is involved in the doing, is done not by the person but by the user of the person. In extreme cases there may even be an elision of a causal chain so that we might say that X killed Z even though Y's hand was the hand that held the weapon, for Y's hand may have been entirely in X's control. The one agent is in some way treating the other as a mere link in a causal chain. There is, of course, a wide range of cases in which a person is used to accomplish

the aim of another and in which the person used is less than fully free. A person may be grabbed against his will and used as a shield. A person may be drugged or hypnotized and then employed for certain ends. A person may be deceived into doing other than he intends doing. A person may be ordered to do something and threatened with harm if he does not and coerced into doing what he does not want to. There is still another range of cases in which individuals are not used, but in which decisions by others are made that affect them in circumstances where they have the capacity for choice and where they are not being treated as persons.

But it is particularly important to look at coercion, for I have claimed that a just system of punishment treats human beings as persons; and it is not immediately apparent how ordering someone to do something and threatening harm differs essentially from having rules supported by threats of harm in case of noncompliance.

There are affinities between coercion and other cases of not treating someone as a person, for it is not the coerced person's choices but the coercer's that are responsible for what is done. But unlike other indisputable cases of not treating one as a person, for example using someone as a shield, there is some choice involved in coercion. . . .

There is some plausibility in the claim that, in a system of punishment of the kind I have sketched, a person chooses the punishment that is meted out to him. If, then, we can say in such a system that the rules provide none with advantages that others do not have, and further, that what happens to a person is conditioned by that person's choice and not that of others, then we can say that it is a system responding to one as a person.

We treat a human being as a person provided: first, we permit the person to make the choices that will determine what happens to him and second, when our responses to the person are responses respecting the person's choices. When we respond to a person's illness by treating the illness it is neither a case of treating or not treating the individual as a person. When we give a person a gift we are neither treating or not treating him as a person, unless, of course, he does not wish it, chooses not to have it, but we compel him to accept it.

This right to be treated as a person is a fundamental human right belonging to all human beings by virtue of their being human. It is also a natural, inalienable, and absolute right. I want now to defend these claims so reminiscent of an era of philosophical thinking about rights that many consider to have been seriously confused. . . .

In claiming that the right is a right that human beings have by virtue of being human, there are several other features of the right, that should be noted, perhaps better conveyed by labelling them 'natural.' First, it is a right we have apart from any voluntary agreement into which we have entered. Second, it is not a right that derives from some defined position or status. Third, it is equally apparent that one has the right regardless of the society or community of which one is a member. Finally, it is a right linked to certain features of a class of beings. Were we fundamentally different than we now are, we would not have it. But it is more than that, for the right is linked to a feature of human beings which, were that feature absent—the capacity to reason and to choose on the basis of reasons—profound conceptual changes would be involved in the thought about human beings. It is a right, then, connected with a feature of men that sets men apart from other natural phenomena.

The right to be treated as a person is inalienable. To say of a right that it is inalienable draws attention not to limitations placed on what others may do with respect to the possessor of the right but rather to limitations placed on the dispositive capacities of the possessor of the right. Something is to be gained in keeping the issues of alienability and absoluteness separate.

The right is absolute. This claim is bound to raise eyebrows. I have an innocuous point in mind in making this claim.

When I claim, then, that the right to be treated as a person is absolute what I claim is that given that one is a person, one always has the right so to be treated, and that while there may possibly be occasions morally requiring not according a person this right, this fact makes it no less true that the right exists and would be infringed if the person were not accorded it.

Having said something about the nature of this fundamental right I want now, in conclusion, to suggest that the denial of this right entails the denial of all moral rights and duties. This requires bringing out what is surely intuitively clear that any framework of rights and duties presupposes individuals that have the capacity to choose on the basis of reasons presented to them, and that what makes legitimate actions within such a system are the free choices of individuals. . . .

Note

1. "When a man is suffering from an infectious disease, he is a danger to the community, and it is necessary to restrict his liberty of movement. But no one associates any idea of guilt with such a situation. On the contrary, he is an object of commiseration to his friends. Such steps as science recommends are taken to cure him of his disease, and he submits as a rule without reluctance to the curtailment of liberty involved meanwhile. The same method in spirit ought to be shown in the treatment of what is called 'crime.'"

Bertrand Russell, *Roads to Freedom* (London: George Allen and UnwinLtd., 1918), p. 135.

"We do not hold people responsible for their reflexes—for example, for coughing in church. We hold them responsible for their operant behavior—for example, for whispering in church or remaining in church while coughing. But there are variables which are responsible for whispering as well as coughing, and these may be just as inexorable. When we recognize this, we are likely to drop the notion of responsibility altogether and with it the doctrine of free will as an inner causal agent."

B. F. Skinner, *Science and Human Behavior* (1953), pp. 115–116.

"Basically, criminality is but a symptom of insanity, using the term in its widest generic sense to express unacceptable social behavior based on unconscious motivation flowing from a disturbed instinctive and emotional life, whether this appears in frank psychoses, or in less obvious form in neuroses and unrecognized psychoses. . . . If criminals are products of early environmental influences in the same sense that psychotics and neurotics are, then it should be possible to reach them psychotherapeutically."

Benjamin Karpman, "Criminal Psychodynamics," *Journal of Criminal Law and Criminology,* 47 (1956), p. 9.

"We, the agents of society, must move to end the game of tit-for-tat and blow-for-blow in which the offender has foolishly and futilely engaged himself and us. We are not driven, as he is, to wild and impulsive actions. With knowledge comes power, and with power there is no need for the frightened vengeance of the old penology. In its place should go a quiet, dignified, therapeutic program for the rehabilitation of the disorganized one, if possible, the protection of society during the treatment period, and his guided return to useful citizenship, as soon as this can be effected."

Karl Menninger, "Therapy, Not Punishment," *Harper's Magazine* (August 1959), pp. 63–64.

Notes and Questions

1. What does Morris mean by a "right" to be punished? Is this an oxymoron? Generally speaking, rights are considered assets and punishment is a liability. It's easy to see how the general public would desire to punish a criminal, but how, according to Morris, does the criminal benefit?

2. What are the "burdens" and "benefits" for citizens living under the law? What purposes of law are furthered by punishment? How do punishment and "forgiveness" affect the distribution of burdens and benefits?

3. What is "the ideology of disease and therapy"? How, according to Morris, does it affect law? Does he think this is a useful ideology or a hindrance to justice? What do you think? Must justice be pursued in an either-or fashion—either a punishment system or a system of therapy?

4. How accurate is Morris' depiction of freedom of choice in our society? Are the "burdens" and "benefits" of law the same for all citizens? What, if any, "burdens" of social difference does Morris fail to adequately address?

5. According to Morris, how is the "right to be treated as a person" respected when society punishes an individual for a crime? Is this right violated when a criminal is given a lenient sentence? What about in the case of a plea bargain?

6. How does "punishment as a right" inform the severity-leniency debate discussed in Section IV? Does this concept help us to resolve any of the challenging questions raised about prosecutorial discretion, jury deliberations, or sentencing guidelines? If so, how? If not, what is a more useful way to think about how punishment serves justice?

Reprinted from: Herbert Morris, "Persons and Punishment" in *The Monist*, 52:4, 1968. Copyright © 1968. Reprinted with the permission of *The Monist: An International Quarterly Journal of General Philosophical Inquiry*, Peru, Illinois, U.S.A. 61354. ✦

Chapter 57

Punishment, Power, and Justice

Patricia Ewick

The reading by Patricia Ewick notes that much of the available research on punishment focuses on power—power within penal institutions but also the power of punishment and threats of punishment to control behavior in society at large. She tries to shift the focus to ask about the justice, or justness, of punishment. Tracing the history of punishment, Ewick contends that changing uses and understandings of power in punishment have been accompanied by changing conceptions of justice. Most recently, prisons have been governed in accordance with an expanded conception of power and a stunted definition of justice.

As you read Ewick, ask what she means by justice. Is she, like Morris, concerned primarily with the justness of the decision to punish or the justness of the governance of prisons?

INTRODUCTION

The connections between punishment, power, and justice are abundant, obvious, and complex. Whereas in many social institutions, such as schools, families, or hospitals, power lurks, submerged within dominant and often competing discourses of enlightenment, love, or benefaction, within penal institutions the operation of power is rarely dis-

guised or denied by those who deploy it. Despite historical variations in the form, purposes, or rationalities of penal power, it is always conspicuously, publicly, and deliberately exercised. In the acts of surveillance, confiscation, detention, incarceration, reformation, and execution that constitute penality, the state claims for itself the right and obligation to commit acts of violence and transgression that are otherwise forbidden. Whether for expressive (retribution) or instrumental (deterrence or reformation) reasons, in the very act of punishing, penal power announces itself.

In announcing itself, penal power does not, however, present itself as limitless. Systems of penality also define themselves in term of justice. One need only consider the locution "criminal justice system" as an example of such self-definition. Within the official discourse, justice demarcates the limits of penal power by announcing standards against which power can be held accountable. A commitment to distributive justice, for instance, demands that the pain and deprivation that constitute penality be evenly and exacted: like cases will be treated alike. Similarly, standards of justness require that punishments must be reasonable, not cruel, unusual, or excessive. To the extent that it contains and regulates the state's power to punish and afflict pain, justice legitimates that power. By holding itself accountable to standards of justice, the power to punish is made palatable. Wherever penal power is invoked, it is accompanied by some understanding of justice. . . .

. . . The history of penal practices can be read, then, as the dialectic between power and justice.

PENALITY AND POWER

Despite the historically variable meaning of justice and its role in shaping penality, most recent histories of penal practice have focused almost exclusively on power. Power has been accorded a central and determinative role in constituting not only penality but criminality as well. Beginning in the 1960s, theories of social control and crime claimed that social control responses to criminal and deviant behaviors have the perverse effect of exacerbating or even constructing that which they would cure or condemn. Despite a century and a half of penal reform, criminological research, and sociological critique, the project to contain, curb, or cure criminality had, by all accounts, failed. More significantly, the failure seemed unavoidable, leading many social theorists to reevaluate the ostensible goals of the social control project and to conclude that its real objective has never been to eradicate crime or criminals, but rather to construct categories of crime and to produce criminals (Cohen 1985; Foucault 1979; Garland 1985, 1990). According to the various theoretical perspectives subscribing to this view, the delinquent is a result of either the psychological effects of labeling (Lemert 1951; Scheff 1984), the biophysical effects of disciplinary power (Foucault 1979), or the needs of a capitalist economy (Chambliss 1964; Rusche and Kirchheimer 1939). Power, as Foucault would have it, is not deployed negatively to eradicate or suppress criminality but positively to create the delinquent.

The inversion of the relationship between control and deviance has had a number of theoretical and conceptual consequences. First, it shifted the analytic and theoretical focus of criminologists and sociologists away from the criminal actor and systems of criminal behavior and directed it toward the systems and agents of control that have been devised to produce such actors and behaviors. The shift in focus entailed an abandonment of questions regarding etiology and individual depravity, poverty, or powerlessness. In fact, according to Cohen (1989),

> the tendency [within these perspectives] is to see the object of social control (whom or what is being controlled) as a *tabula rasa,* a blank space which is given identity and form only through the operation of social control. Deviance is an artifact of social control, virtually a reflection

of this active and autonomous force which has a life of its own. (1989: 349)

Following from this view, the central questions that have concerned criminologists and sociologists of deviance in the past few decades have been about power and social control with a primary, although not exclusive, focus on the organized power of the state as it has been deployed against crime. The questions that have preoccupied these sociologists concern the different forms and technologies of power that have been used to produce delinquency; the ideological bases of the power to punish or cure; and the ways in which these forms of power and the ideologies that they have produced have been transformed historically.

In addition to making questions of power and its deployment central in the study of penality, the inversion of the relationship between crime and control also led to a radical reconceptualization of power. Once it was noted that the real objective of punishment was not to eradicate crime, a narrative history of penal failure was transformed into a unmitigated success story. Whatever was being done within the courts, prisons, probation offices, and community-based control centers was, appearances notwithstanding, precisely what was *supposed* to be happening. Obviously, this rendition of penal history required a radical reconceptualization of power (in this case the power to control or punish). No longer is power defined as a resource deployed by discrete persons or organizations, operating within particular relationships, animated by identifiable but specific capacities, interests, or motives, the realization of which is historically contingent or problematic (i.e., power might fail, be ineffective, or successfully resisted). Power is instead recast as an ineluctable force that follows a rationale, logic, or a master plan that belies its apparent failures and ineffectiveness and which, in some self-fulfilling process, cannot help but realize its objectives (Cohen 1989; O'Malley 1993). This conceptualization of power has been most clearly and self-consciously articulated by Foucault. However, weaker versions of it predate Foucault: vestiges of it can be found in Durkheim's functional analysis of social control, and a similar, albeit theoretically less elaborated, understanding of power underwrites some of the earliest versions of labeling theory. . . .

Without rewriting the by now familiar history of penal power that has been offered by Foucault and elaborated by many others over the past few decades, I would like to retell it from a slightly different perspective, recasting justice in a more central and pivotal role in the constitution of penal practice. . . .

THE JUSTICE OF TYRANTS: PENALITY AND THE ANCIEN REGIME

The canonical history of penal practice typically begins by describing the period immediately predating the modern period, a period that has been variously labeled the ancien regime or the "classical" period. As a result of Foucault's arresting image, premodern penality is emblemized by the scaffold, a symbol that evokes the public, excessive, corporeal, and ritualistic quality of penal power during this time. Power was directed toward the body of the condemned. It was exacted within the community before an assembled audience. It was excessive and spectacular. And, in proclaiming and avenging the power of the sovereign, it had a face and a name.

But what about justice during this period? By contemporary definitions, justice was conspicuously absent from premodern or classical penality. The secret nature of legal proceedings, the absence of almost all guarantees of due process, the reliance on torture to extract confessions or determine guilt, and the use of hideous forms of execution to punish those convicted of serious offenses all conjure up the image of a system of penality without any operable concept of justice.

Yet, just as we recognize premodern forms of power, we should be prepared to recognize premodern forms of justice. As suggested earlier, justice is not an optional component of penality or power. Justice is a necessary and integral part of power. Given the public, excessive, brutal, and capricious nature of premodern power, demonstrations of justice were as, if not more, important than they would become in subsequent epochs. Because punishment during this period was theatrical, performed before the community to dramatize the power of the sovereign, penality required the belief, support, and legitimacy of the audience assembled to view it. It required, in short, strong and persuasive demonstrations of justice. According to Douglas Hay (1975), the eighteenth-century English gentry "were acutely aware that their security depended on *belief*—belief in the justice of their rule, and in its adamantine strength. The punishment at times had to be waived or mitigated to meet popular ideas of justice, and to prevent popular outrage from going too far and thereby realizing its own strength" (1975: 51).

Acknowledging the necessity and centrality of some form of justice in premodern penal systems is not to suggest that the meaning of justice during this period conformed in any recognizable way to modern notions of justice. For one thing, the distinction that has been so meticulously drawn between procedural and substantive justice was blurred or nonexistent in premodern systems. Second, although contemporary definitions of justice accept punishment and the infliction of some measure of pain as a reasonable and just outcome in cases where there has been a finding of guilt, they do not allow that procedures of investigation and adjudication should produce or inflict pain or deprivation. So committed are we to the value of nonpunitive procedures that social scientists have successfully condemned the legal system with the charge that the "process is the punishment," a phrase intended to evoke a portrait of a system of justice where something has gone terribly wrong. Yet the phrase would stand as nothing more than a bland description, rather than critique, of premodern penal practice.

In the premodern penal system "investigation and punishment had become mixed" (Foucault 1977: 41). During this period, the accused would be routinely subjected to torture during interrogation as a way of extracting a confession. "The body interrogated in torture constituted the point of application of the punishment and the locus of extortion of the truth. And just as presumption was inseparably an element in investigation and a fragment of guilt, the regulated pain involved in judicial torture was a means of *both punishment and investigation*" (1977: 42).

In practice, the distinction between legal procedural and substantive outcomes, and thus the distinction between procedural and substantive *justice* was erased. This blurring of the boundaries between the processes of interrogation and punishment should be seen and understood as a reflection of a premodern, prepositivist epistemology that conceived of truth and methods of its discovery in radically different ways than they are currently understood. Knowledge did not conform to a dualistic system, in which facts or circumstances could be determined to be true or false or defendants to be guilty or not guilty (Foucault 1977). According to this premodern epistemology, there were degrees of truth and gradients of guilt. At each moment in the process of criminal adjudication the evidence revealed more or less guilt, thus warranting more or less punishment. To the degree that the process revealed guilt, it was supposed to be punitive. This premodern epistemology also underwrote the importance placed on confession and legitimated the use of torture in interrogation. Unlike their positivist counterparts in the modern period, investigators placed considerably less reliance on or faith in the physical or material world to reveal guilt or innocence through forensic evidence. The testimony of persons, typically in the form of the confession, re-

flected a commitment to religious practices of receiving truth through revelation and reflection rather than as something gained through scientific methods of observation and deduction. The ideological capacity of confession to legitimate and affirm the power of the sovereign rests in these popular understandings of truth and the means of its discovery.

Modern understandings of the *justness,* or appropriateness, of substantive outcomes are almost invariably based on the calculation of proportion. The belief that the punishment should "fit" the crime, or that the convicted should receive their "just deserts," are typically interpreted in some quantitative way: lesser crimes, or lesser guilt, should receive lesser punishments. In the classical period of penality, however, there was no expectation that there would be a quantitative equivalency between crime and punishment. In fact, the objective of punishment was to produce an excess of pain and suffering on the part of the convicted: not simply to execute but to torture. As Foucault has argued, the principle objective of the scaffold was to demonstrate to the audience assembled the awesome, unrestrained power of the sovereign rather than match the severity of punishment with the seriousness of crime. "The punishment is carried out in such a way as to give a spectacle not of measure, but of imbalance and excess" (Foucault 1977: 49). Rather than a failure of justice, the intended goal of punishment was to achieve a deliberate *dissymmetry* between the crime and its punishment. . . .

While premodern penality was clearly not characterized by the same criteria that appear in contemporary understandings of justice, there were, nonetheless, other criteria of justice to which power was held accountable. For instance, although there was no attempt to achieve a proportionality between the crime and the punishment, some meaningful correspondence between the two was enforced. More specifically, the relationship that was sought between the sanction and crime was mimetic rather than proportional. Punishment was a production designed to be the the-atrical realization of the crime, rather than simply a matching of it in terms of intensity or severity. Executions would occur at the location where the crime was said to have taken place, the specific forms of torture would represent the type of crime (the tongues of blasphemers would be pierced, the hands of murderers cut off), or the condemned would be made to carry the weapon with which he committed the crime. In these ways, the punishment would broadcast its own justification to the audience. . . .

MODERN PENALITY: THE JUSTICE OF INSTITUTIONS

Modern penality, a period that is traced to the early nineteenth century, is distinguished by its relative lack of cruelty, excess, and passion. Penal power appears at this time to be fettered by what are, today, familiar constraints of justice. We see, for instance, the abandonment of torture and other cruel and expressive forms of punishment for measured, rationally administered penalties. We see in place of an inquisitorial model that blurred interrogation and punishment the development of guarantees of due process. And we see the emergence of a new sense of distributive equity that invalidates the particularism, and with it the capriciousness of the classical period.

At one level these changes can and have been understood as the result of the civilizing process. As human societies mature and evolve, the story goes, they adopt more humane (i.e., less primitive or barbaric) forms of penality. We can read in this narrative a teleological, and thus transcendent, view of justice. Systems of penality are seen as maturing as power defers to the values of justice. Rather than a cluster of historically contingent value commitments that collaborates with power to constitute penality, justice is seen in these accounts as that which counters and civilizes raw judicial power.

An alternative reading of this history views changes in the meaning of justice as being of a piece with transformations in penal power, both a result of political and cultural developments that extended beyond the realm of penality.

First, what were understood to be "just" legal procedures reflected an epistemological transformation that redefined the nature of truth and invalidated the earlier ways of discovering and establishing it. Modern definitions of procedural justice are founded on the positivist notion of the truth as an objective fact that must be demonstrated through empirical evidence. The necessity of that demonstration underpins the central commitment of modern procedural justice: the presumed innocence of the defendant until such "proof" is forthcoming. According to Langbein (1976), the abolition of judicial torture, then, was a result of changes in the law of proof in which the judicial evaluation of evidence came to replace the old Roman canon law of statutory proofs.

In fact, most of the specific guarantees and protections that constitute procedural justness work to preserve the objectivity of the methods through which data is obtained and interpretations are made. Recall that the epistemological assumptions that underwrote the use of torture and the extraction of confessions included the belief that "semi-proofs produce semi-truths and semi-guilty persons" (Foucault 1977: 97). Truth, conceived in this way, blurred the line between process and outcome, adjudication and punishment. However, once truth was conceived as existing in the nature of things, that is, apart from its apprehension or the method of its discovery, a separate sphere of legal procedures emerged and with it a radically new understanding of what constituted procedural justice. The truth of guilt or innocence was no longer understood to be a construction or consequence of the judicial process. In the new episteme, the fact of guilt or innocence was recognized to exist prior to and, thus, independently of that process, whose function is now simply to reveal that truth through investigation, observation, and logic. Accessing the truth of the matter, that is, establishing guilt or innocence, necessitated adopting the same standards of objectivity, validity, and logic that defined empirical scientific research.

"With the multiplicity of scientific discourses, a difficult, infinite relation was then forged that penal justice is still unable to control. The master of justice is no longer the master of its truth" (Foucault 1977: 98). The procedural guarantees that characterize modern penality reflected a modern ontology as well as epistemology. As Foucault has argued, beginning in the nineteenth century, the object of punishment shifted away from the body of the condemned to the soul of the prisoner, where the soul represented the knowable, and thus calculable, individual. Perhaps the most salient change in penality in the nineteenth century, the invention of the prison, reflected this shift (Foucault 1977; Rothman 1971). The penitentiary replaced the scaffold as the principal venue and instrument for the operation of penal power. Within the walls of the prison, those subject to penal power were observed, knowledge regarding them was collected, and here they were exposed to the normalizing effects of disciplinary power. Most significantly, however, the modern individual was not merely subjected to this penal discipline, he or she was produced by the operation of these regimes of power. Out of the meticulous and minute regulation of gestures, the spatial deployment, the bodies, and the temporal structuring of days emerged the individual with a soul, that is, a portable, knowable self that was recognized as having an existence outside of the web of hierarchical social relationships. This modern individual could, thus, be invested with capacities and fundamental human rights that transcended the exigencies of time, place, or association. Disciplinary power, in constructing such a subject, also re-

defined the meaning of justice and, thus, the limits of its own legitimate exercise. Against the barbarity of the scaffold and the inhumanity of judicial torture was pitted the humanity of this new being. It was "a 'man-measure'; not of things but of power" (Foucault 1979: 74). Accordingly, what was deemed reasonable, and thus just, punishment was defined at its boundary by this "man-measure." . . .

. . . [K]nowable, calculable individuals, and the categories they would come to constitute, called forth an economy of power that would match taxonomies of crimes and criminals against gradients of punishments, maximizing their effectiveness while minimizing their cost. The result was not simply the abolition of public executions or judicial torture—a civilizing change at the so-called frontiers of punishment—but the creation of an entire schedule of complex and differentiated penalties and professionals designed to deter without excess and punish without anger or enthusiasm (*sine ira ac studio*) (Weber 1958: 214). Justice, lodged in the dehumanized interstices of bureaucratic institutions, appears as power without passion.

POSTMODERN PENALITY: THE ECLIPSE OF POWER AND JUSTICE

While the transition from classical penality to modern penality appears as a clean break, the third moment in this history of penal power and justice lacks such distinctiveness. In the spirit of all that is postmodern, it exists as an amalgam of that which went before: elements of ancien regime penality are juxtaposed with modern techniques and both are overlaid with forms of control that are historically unprecedented. The most distinctive feature of postmodern penality lies, then, in the simultaneous operation of parallel control systems, each system defined, in part, by who and what it excludes.

Modernist disciplinary institutions, such as the prison, survive and expand. Despite the movement toward decarceration and deinstitutionalization, rates of imprisonment have continued to increase in the past few decades, dispelling any notion that discipline as a form of penal control is moribund (Cohen 1985). At the same time, alternative, postdisciplinary forms of social control have also emerged and expanded (O'Malley 1993; Simon 1993). These technologies of control are unusual insofar as they appear as totally non-punitive. In general, the ensemble of postdisciplinary techniques avoid being punitive by managing *opportunities* for behaviors, as opposed to manipulating behaviors themselves.[1]

Postdiscipline control is largely accomplished through the regulation of space, including how it is designed, distributed, and inhabited. Space is made "defensible," for instance, by closing off escape routes or opening up vantage for surveillance (Newman 1972, cited in Simon 1993). Similarly, contemporary office buildings and amusement parks are located and designed to discourage certain types of behaviors or visitors (Shearing and Stenning 1984; Shields 1992). Indeed, if the scaffold is the emblem of power under the ancien regime and the prison of modern penality, the shopping mall has come to symbolize postmodern control.

Of course, the regulation of space has always been an integral component of modern disciplinary (as opposed to postdisciplinary) control. According to Dreyfus and Rabinow (1983),

> Discipline proceeds by the organization of individuals in space, and it therefore requires a specific enclosure of space. In the hospital, the school, or the military field, we find a reliance on an orderly grid. Once established, this grid permits the sure distribution of individuals to be disciplined and supervised; this procedure facilitates the reduction of dangerous multitudes or wandering vagabonds to fixed and docile individuals. (1983: 54–155)

What makes postdisciplinary control distinctive, then, is not the regulation of space per se but the use of particular spatial practices. As the quote from Dreyfus and Rabinow suggests, discipline proceeds through the "enclosure of space" and, once that is achieved, through the containment of individuals within these enclaves. Individuals are located within prisons, schools, or factories, and, once inside, subjected to discipline and surveillance. By contrast, postdisciplinary use of space operates less through containment than through selection and exclusion. The location and architectural design of the modern mall, for example, does not so much contain potentially disruptive populations as it discourages their entry, reserving occupancy for already docile individuals. Along these lines, Jonathan Simon (1993) has observed that postmodern control relies on "channeling" out "those segments of the population that are more likely to pose risks than benefits to the space being controlled" (1993: 7).[2] . . .

Postmodern control is promotive rather than reactive, voluntary rather than coercive, and is based more on choice than on constraint. Within such a market, power seems to have no place. Whereas power in a rationalized bureaucratic context appears passionless, here, eclipsed by the image of individual choice, it seems to disappear altogether. Yet, the orderliness of persons and behaviors within these spaces belies the image of unconstrained individual freedom. . . .

While it is no doubt true, then, that power of some sort is operating within these semiprivate spaces and public markets, it is certainly not a form of penal power. In fact, it is the near total absence of penal power within the regulated hyperspaces that makes its operation elsewhere—in the abandoned spaces of the city: the projects, the dangerous neighborhoods—all the more significant. Only those who can qualify as consumers, those who are on "the inside of freedom" to use Simon's evocative phrase, are eligible for this type of postmodern control. All others, the chronically unemployed, the insane, the socially marginal, are excluded and subjected to the traditional disciplines as practiced by the police and other public officials.

CONCLUSION

I began with the thesis that power and justice mutually define one another within systems of penality. Power is thus made intelligible through justice, just as justice is given meaning through the exercise of power. Relying on a rather conventional history of penal practices, I have attempted to read beyond the typical focus on power to excavate a parallel history of justice. This history indicates that as penal power deploys different technologies of control it activates different conceptions of justice, that is, varying understandings of what are reasonable, appropriate, or fair procedures and distributions. Embedded within these conceptions, moreover, are varying ontological and epistemological commitments. As cultural understandings of knowledge and the possibilities of its apprehension are redefined, power itself is transformed. As the subjects of penal power are differentially constructed, the power that is brought to bear on them is shaped and reshaped.

It follows from this thesis that the bifurcation and stratification of power that has occurred in the postmodern period and, in particular, its submergence within a discourse of choice and freedom, has predictable consequences for the definition of justice. Specifically, as power is effaced within the sanitized, selective spaces of a consumption society, so too is justice. Considerations of just distributions or reasonable and appropriate procedures and interventions become irrelevant once "public" powers to adjudicate and punish disappear or defer to individual choice and "private" regulation. Indeed the ontology that previously underwrote modern definitions of justice, the autonomous individual invested with fundamental unalienable rights, is replaced within a postmodern regime by a new ontology of the individual: that of the consumer.

"Merely to be in attendance at the 'court of commodities' (Benjamin 1973) is to claim one's status as a consumer which under a capitalism which reduces people to their function in an economist equation, is to assert one's *existence* and to be recognized as a person. Being a consumer, with the right to attend these rituals seems to have almost overtaken the importance of being a citizen" (Shields 1989: 159). Given this, it is perhaps not coincidental that, within the United States, both rates of imprisonment and frequency of executions have increased in the past few decades, a time when the postindustrial decay of our inner cities produced an increasing disparity between those who could be regulated via the relays of the market and those who are likely to be perpetually outside of the reach of the "invisible hand." In short, for those denied access to the "court of commodities," the penal power of the state continues to operate, but now with a diminished sense of citizenship and with it a stunted definition of justice.

Notes

1. Recently, for instance, Nynex converted 250 of its public telephones in New York City from pushbutton to rotary dials in an effort to thwart drug dealers from paging customers. This was the latest in an arsenal of tactics used by the company against drug dealing. Previously the company had disabled approximately 8,400 of its public telephones from receiving incoming calls in addition to moving phones away from problem areas and improving lighting (*New York Times,* January 10, 1993, p. 1).

2. In 1993 homicides, while declining, were increasingly concentrated in specific areas of New York City. "Safe" neighborhoods became safer, at the same time other neighborhoods witnessed a rise in the rate of homicide (*New York Times,* January 10, 1993, p. 23).

References

Chambliss, William. 1964. A Sociological Analysis of the Law of Vagrancy. 12 *Social Problems*, 67–77.

Cohen, Stanley. 1985. *Visions of Social Control.* New York: Oxford Univ. Press.

——. 1989. The Critical Discourse on "Social Control": Notes on the Concept as a Hammer. 17 *International Journal of the Sociology of Law*, 347.

Dreyfus, Hubert, and Paul Rabinow. 1983. *Michel Foucault: Beyond Structuralism and Hermeneutics.* Chicago: Univ. of Chicago Press.

Foucault, Michel. 1973. *The Order of Things: An Archaeology of the Human Sciences.* New York: Vintage.

——. 1977. *Discipline and Punish: The Birth of the Prison.* New York: Vintage.

Garland, David. 1985. *Punishment and Welfare.* Brookfield, VT: Gower.

——. 1990. *Punishment and Modern Society.* Chicago: Univ. of Chicago Press.

Hay, Douglas. 1975. Property, Authority and the Criminal Law. In *Albion's Fatal Tree: Crime and Society in Eighteenth-Century England*, ed. Douglas Hay, Peter Linebaugh, John G. Rule, E. P. Thompson, and Cal Winslow, 17–63. New York: Pantheon.

Langbein, John. 1976. *Torture and the Law of Proof.* Chicago: Univ. of Chicago Press.

Lemert, Edwin. 1951. *Social Pathology: A Systematic Approach to the Theory of Sociopathic Behavior.* New York: McGraw-Hill.

O'Malley, Pat. 1993. Containing Our Excitement: Commodity Culture and the Crisis of Discipline. 13 *Research in Law, Politics and Society,* 159.

Rothman, David J. 1971. *The Discovery of the Asylum.* Toronto: Little, Brown.

Rusche, G., and O. Kirchheimer. 1939. *Punishment and Social Structure.* New York: Columbia Univ. Press.

Scheff, Thomas J. 1984. *Being Mentally Ill.* New York: Aldine.

Shearing, Clifford D., and Philip C. Stenning. 1984. From the Panopticon to Disney World: The Development of Discipline. In *Perspectives in Criminal Law,* ed. Anthony N. Doob and Edward L. Greenspan, Q.C. Aurora. Ontario: Canada Law Books, Inc.

Shields, Rob. 1992. *Places on the Margin: Alternative Geographies of Modernity.* New York: Routledge.

Simon, Jonathan. 1993. From Confinement to Waste Management: The Postmodernization of Social Control. 8 *Focus on Law Studies*, 4.

Notes and Questions

1. "Whether for expressive (retribution) or instrumental (deterrence or reformation) reasons, in the very act of punishing, penal power announces itself." Why do we accept penal power in our lives? Where do we draw the line between tyrannous and acceptable uses of penal power?

2. How does Ewick understand the concept of power? What does Ewick mean when she writes that the history of penal practices "can be read as the dialectic between power and justice"? How are power, criminality, and penality linked?

3. How was justice "conspicuously absent from premodern or classical penality"? For what, or for whom, was punishment extracted in premodern law? How is the modern understanding of punishment different?

4. Though proportionality was not a consideration in premodern punishment, how, according to Ewick, was "some meaningful correspondence between the two" enforced? How does our much more literal understanding of proportionality help to justify the exercise of penal power in modern jurisprudence?

5. How does law's bureaucracy and procedure, what Ewick calls "the justice of institutions," help to legitimize law's violence? Does this give justice the appearance of "power without passion"?

6. What is "postmodern penality"? How does it change the way law wields power? What is the "court of commodities"? In the postmodern framework, what deter-

mines an individual's access to law? Do you see postmodern penality in the same way as Ewick in terms of the decay of justice? Why or why not?

Reprinted from: Patricia Ewick, "Punishment, Power, and Justice" in *Justice and Power in Sociolegal Studies*, pp. 36–54. Edited by Bryant Garth and Austin Sarat. Copyright © 1997. Reprinted with the permission of *Northwestern University Press.* ✦

Chapter 58

United States v. Bailey

Punishment can take various forms, from fines and probation to imprisonment and death. Since the middle of the nineteenth century, America has relied on prisons, originally called penitentiaries because they were thought of as places where criminals would do penance and repent for their crimes. Today, the United States is one of the most punitive societies in the world. At the end of 2002, we had more than 2 million people in jails and prisons. We lead the world with a rate of incarceration of 702 per 100,000—a rate five to eight times that of comparable industrialized nations, such as Canada and the countries of Western Europe. Moreover, since 1990 the federal prison population has increased more than 153 percent, with the greatest growth in drug and public-order offenses. Drug offenders now account for 57 percent of the federal inmate population. Finally, prison sentences tend to be longer in the United States than in most other democratic, industrialized nations.

More than 600,000 prisoners a year are being released from state and federal prisons. This is an important fact of our national incarceration boom, and larger numbers of inmates reenter society than ever before. The U. S. Justice Department's Bureau of Justice Statistics reports that 67.5 percent of the prisoners who were released from prison in 1994 were rearrested within three years and that 52 percent were back in prison for committing a new offense or violating the terms of their parole.

Prisons today vary in their severity, with minimum security prisons imposing fewer constraints and restrictions than maximum secu-rity prisons. New supermax prisons are used to house the worst, most dangerous offenders. In such prisons, isolation is not a tool of prison discipline but the standard mode of confinement for all inmates, who sometimes remain alone in a cell 23 hours a day with very limited contact with others.

The conditions of prison are often very bad. Prisons are notoriously dangerous places. Nearly half of the state inmates who have served six or more years say they were injured while in prison. In many maximum-security institutions, the wardens and guards have formal authority but relatively limited power. They must rely on the cooperation of the inmates for the prison to function. As a result, they transfer control to inmates, allowing a "society of captives" to develop with its own informal rules and hierarchy of power.

When guards do exercise power, it is often direct and physical. In the prison, law's violence is harsh if not brutal. Controlling it is difficult. As with the police, there is a "law and order dilemma"; here too, the demand for restraint and respect for the rights of inmates may complicate the task of maintaining an "orderly" prison.

In United States v. Bailey, four inmates who escaped from the District of Columbia jail claimed that their escape was justified by conditions in the D.C. jail, including inadequate medical care, fires set by inmates and guards, and beatings and death threats by guards. However, the U. S. Supreme Court decided that the inmates could introduce no evidence about these conditions to justify their escape because they had a legal obligation to surrender and return to custody as soon as the conditions that had "forced" them to escape no longer threatened them—that is, as soon as they had escaped from jail. Justice Blackmun, in his dissenting opinion, describes in considerable detail the conditions of America's prisons and jails, conditions not unlike those experienced by the inmates in Bailey. He says, "The atrocities and inhuman conditions of prison life in America are almost unbelievable; surely they are nothing less than shocking."

In light of this section's description of the need to dispense yet to organize and control violence, which is the third dilemma of the social organization of law, is it fair to say that the conditions described by Blackmun represent failures of law? Are they the equivalent of the excessive force used by the police in the Diallo case? Do they raise serious questions about law's capacity to organize and control its own violence?

Moreover, does the decision in Bailey *create a "Catch-22" for prisoners? Suppose the case had been decided for the defendants, so that prisoners could use the conditions of their confinement to justify an escape from prison. What would the consequences of such a decision be for our nation's task of maintaining order in prison?*

JUSTICE REHNQUIST DELIVERED THE OPINION OF THE COURT

In the early morning hours of August 26, 1976, respondents Clifford Bailey, James T. Cogdell, Ronald C. Cooley, and Ralph Walker, federal prisoners at the District of Columbia jail, crawled through a window from which a bar had been removed, slid down a knotted bedsheet, and escaped from custody. Federal authorities recaptured them after they had remained at large for a period of time ranging from one month to three and one-half months. Upon their apprehension, they were charged with violating 18 U. S. C. § 751 (a), which governs escape from federal custody.[1] At their trials, each of the respondents adduced or offered to adduce evidence as to various conditions and events at the District of Columbia jail, but each was convicted by the jury. The Court of Appeals for the District of Columbia Circuit reversed the convictions by a divided vote, holding that the District Court had improperly precluded consideration by the respective juries of respondents' tendered evidence. We granted certiorari, 440 U.S. 957, and now reverse the judgments of the Court of Appeals. . . .

I

All respondents requested jury trials and were initially scheduled to be tried jointly. At the last minute, however, respondent Cogdell secured a severance. Because the District Court refused to submit to the jury any instructions on respondents' defense of duress or necessity and did not charge the jury that escape was a continuing offense, we must examine in some detail the evidence brought out at trial.

The prosecution's case in chief against Bailey, Cooley, and Walker was brief. The Government introduced evidence that each of the respondents was in federal custody on August 26, 1976, that they had disappeared, apparently through a cell window, at approximately 5:35 a. m. on that date, and that they had been apprehended individually between September 27 and December 13, 1976.

Respondents' defense of duress or necessity centered on the conditions in the jail during the months of June, July, and August 1976, and on various threats and beatings directed at them during that period. In describing the conditions at the jail, they introduced evidence of frequent fires in "Northeast One," the maximum-security cellblock occupied by respondents prior to their escape. Construed in the light most favorable to them, this evidence demonstrated that the inmates of Northeast One, and on occasion the guards in that unit, set fire to trash, bedding, and other objects thrown from the cells. According to the inmates, the guards simply allowed the fires to burn until they went out. Although the fires apparently were confined to small areas and posed no substantial threat of spreading through the complex, poor ventilation caused smoke to collect and linger in the cellblock.

Respondents Cooley and Bailey also introduced testimony that the guards at the jail had subjected them to beatings and to threats of death. Walker attempted to prove that he was an epileptic and had received inadequate medical attention for his seizures.

Consistently during the trial, the District Court stressed that, to sustain their defenses, respondents would have to introduce some evidence that they attempted to surrender or engaged in equivalent conduct once they had freed themselves from the conditions they described. But the court waited for such evidence in vain. Respondent Cooley, who had eluded the authorities for one month, testified that his "people" had tried to contact the authorities, but "never got in touch with anybody." App. 119. He also suggested that someone had told his sister that the Federal Bureau of Investigation would kill him when he was apprehended.

Respondent Bailey, who was apprehended on November 19, 1976, told a similar story. He stated that he "had the jail officials called several times," but did not turn himself in because "I would still be under the threats of death." Like Cooley, Bailey testified that "the FBI was telling my people that they was going to shoot me." *Id.*, at 169, 175–176.

Only respondent Walker suggested that he had attempted to negotiate a surrender. Like Cooley and Bailey, Walker testified that the FBI had told his "people" that they would kill him when they recaptured him. Nevertheless, according to Walker, he called the FBI three times and spoke with an agent whose name he could not remember. That agent allegedly assured him that the FBI would not harm him, but was unable to promise that Walker would not be returned to the D. C. jail. *Id.*, at 195–200.[2] Walker testified that he last called the FBI in mid-October. He was finally apprehended on December 13, 1976.

At the close of all the evidence, the District Court rejected respondents' proffered instruction on duress as a defense to prison escape.[3] The court ruled that respondents had failed as a matter of law to present evidence sufficient to support such a defense because they had not turned themselves in after they had escaped the allegedly coercive conditions. After receiving instructions to disregard the evidence of the conditions in the jail, the jury

convicted Bailey, Cooley, and Walker of violating § 751 (a)....

By a divided vote, the Court of Appeals reversed each respondent's conviction and remanded for new trials. See 190 U. S. App. D. C. 142, 585 F.2d 1087 (1978); 190 U.S. [*401] App. D. C. 185, 585 F.2d 1130 (1978). The majority concluded that the District Court should have allowed the jury to consider the evidence of coercive conditions in determining whether the respondents had formulated the requisite intent to sustain a conviction under § 751 (a)....

A

Respondents also contend that they are entitled to a new trial because they presented (or, in Cogdell's case, could have presented) sufficient evidence of duress or necessity to submit such a defense to the jury. The majority below did not confront this claim squarely, holding instead that, to the extent that such a defense normally would be barred by a prisoner's failure to return to custody, neither the indictment nor the jury instructions adequately described such a requirement. See 190 U. S. App. D. C., at 155–156, 585 F.2d, at 1100–1101.

Common law historically distinguished between the defenses of duress and necessity. Duress was said to excuse criminal conduct where the actor was under an unlawful threat of imminent death or serious bodily injury, which threat caused the actor to engage in conduct violating the literal terms of the criminal law. While the defense of duress covered the situation where the coercion had its source in the actions of other human beings, the defense of necessity, or choice of evils, traditionally covered the situation where physical forces beyond the actor's control rendered illegal conduct the lesser of two evils. Thus, where A destroyed a dike because B threatened to kill him if he did not, A would argue that he acted under duress, whereas if A destroyed the dike in order to protect more valuable property from flooding, A could claim a defense of necessity. See generally LaFave & Scott 374–384.

Modern cases have tended to blur the distinction between duress and necessity. In the court below, the majority discarded the labels "duress" and "necessity," choosing instead to examine the policies underlying the traditional defenses. See 190 U. S. App. D. C., at 152, 585 F.2d, at 1097. In particular, the majority felt that the defenses were designed to spare a person from punishment if he acted "under threats or conditions that a person of ordinary firmness would have been unable to resist," or if he reasonably believed that criminal action "was necessary to avoid a harm more serious than that sought to be prevented by the statute defining the offense." *Id.*, at 152–153, 585 F.2d, at 1097–1098. The Model Penal Code redefines the defenses along similar lines. See Model Penal Code § 2.09 (duress) and § 3.02 (choice of evils).

We need not speculate now, however, on the precise contours of whatever defenses of duress or necessity are available against charges brought under § 751 (a). Under any definition of these defenses one principle remains constant: if there was a reasonable, legal alternative to violating the law, "a chance both to refuse to do the criminal act and also to avoid the threatened harm," the defenses will fail. LaFave & Scott 379.[4] Clearly, in the context of prison escape, the escapee is not entitled to claim a defense of duress or necessity unless and until he demonstrates that, given the imminence of the threat, violation of § 751 (a) was his only reasonable alternative. See United States v. Boomer, 571 F.2d 543, 545 (CA10), cert. denied sub nom. Heft v. United States, 436 U.S. 911 (1978); People v. Richards, 269 Cal. App. 2d 768, 75 Cal. Rptr. 597 (1969). . . .

We need not decide whether such evidence as that submitted by respondents was sufficient to raise a jury question as to their initial departures. This is because we decline to hold that respondents' failure to return is "just one factor" for the jury to weigh in deciding whether the initial escape could be affirmatively justified. On the contrary, several considerations lead us to conclude that, in order to be entitled to an instruction on duress or necessity as a defense to the crime charged, an escapee must first offer evidence justifying his continued absence from custody as well as his initial departure[5] and that an indispensable element of such an offer is testimony of a bona fide effort to surrender or return to custody as soon as the claimed duress or necessity had lost its coercive force. . . .

We therefore hold that, where a criminal defendant is charged with escape and claims that he is entitled to an instruction on the theory of duress or necessity, he must proffer evidence of a bona fide effort to surrender or return to custody as soon as the claimed duress or necessity had lost its coercive force. We have reviewed the evidence examined elaborately in the majority and dissenting opinions below, and find the case not even close, even under respondents' versions of the facts, as to whether they either surrendered or offered to surrender at their earliest possible opportunity. Since we have determined that this is an indispensable element of the defense of duress or necessity, respondents were not entitled to any instruction on such a theory. Vague and necessarily self-serving statements of defendants or witnesses as to future good intentions or ambiguous conduct simply do not support a finding of this element of the defense.[6]

II

These cases present a good example of the potential for wasting valuable trial resources. In general, trials for violations of § 751 (a) should be simple affairs. The key elements are capable of objective demonstration; the *mens rea,* as discussed above, will usually depend upon reasonable inferences from those objective facts. Here, however, the jury in the trial of Bailey, Cooley, and Walker heard five days of testimony. It was presented with evidence of every unpleasant aspect of prison life from the amount of garbage on the cellblock floor, to the meal schedule, to the number of times the inmates were allowed to shower. Unfortunately, all this evidence was presented in a case where the defense's reach hopelessly exceeded its grasp. Were we to hold, as respondents suggest, that the jury should be subjected to this potpourri even though a critical element of the proffered defenses was concededly absent, we undoubtedly would convert every trial under § 751 (a) into a hearing on the current state of the federal penal system.

Because the juries below were properly instructed on the *mens rea* required by § 751 (a), and because the respondents failed to introduce evidence sufficient to submit their defenses of duress and necessity to the juries, we reverse the judgments of the Court of Appeals.

Reversed. . . .

MR. JUSTICE BLACKMUN, WITH WHOM MR. JUSTICE BRENNAN JOINS, DISSENTING

The Court's opinion, it seems to me, is an impeccable exercise in undisputed general principles and technical legalism: The respondents were properly confined in the District of Columbia jail. They departed from that jail without authority or consent. They failed promptly to turn themselves in when, as the Court would assert by way of justification, *Ante*, at 413, 415, the claimed duress or necessity "had lost its coercive force." Therefore, the Court concludes, there is no defense for a jury to weigh and consider against the respondents' prosecution for escape violative of 18 U. S. C. § 751 (a).

It is with the Court's assertion that the claimed duress or necessity had lost its coercive force that I particularly disagree. The conditions that led to respondents' initial departure from the D. C. jail continue unabated. If departure was justified—and on the record before us that issue, I feel, is for the jury to resolve as a matter of fact in the light of the evidence, and not for this Court to determine as a matter of law—it seems too much to demand that respondents, in order to preserve their le-

gal defenses, return forthwith to the hell that obviously exceeds the normal deprivations of prison life and that compelled their leaving in the first instance. The Court, however, requires that an escapee's action must amount to nothing more than a mere and temporary gesture that, it is to be hoped, just might attract attention in responsive circles. But life and health, even of convicts and accuseds, deserve better than that and are entitled to more than pious pronouncements fit for an ideal world.

The Court, in its carefully structured opinion, does reach a result that might be a proper one were we living in that ideal world, and were our American jails and penitentiaries truly places for humane and rehabilitative treatment of their inmates. Then the statutory crime of escape could not be excused by duress or necessity, by beatings, and by guard-set fires in the jails, for these would not take place, and escapees would be appropriately prosecuted and punished.

But we do not live in an ideal world "even" (to use a self-centered phrase) in America, so far as jail and prison conditions are concerned. The complaints that this Court, and every other American appellate court, receives almost daily from prisoners about conditions of incarceration, about filth, about homosexual rape, and about brutality are not always the mouthings of the purely malcontent. The Court itself acknowledges, *Ante*, at 398, that the conditions these respondents complained about do exist. It is in the light of this stark truth, it seems to me, that these cases are to be evaluated. It must follow, then, that the jail-condition evidence proffered by respondent Cogdell should have been admitted, and that the jury before whom respondents Bailey, Cooley, and Walker were tried should not have been instructed to disregard the jail-condition evidence that did come in. I therefore dissent.

I

The atrocities and inhuman conditions of prison life in America are almost unbelievable; surely they are nothing less than shocking. The dissent in the *Bailey* case in the Court of Appeals acknowledged that "the circumstances of prison life are such that at least a colorable, if not credible, claim of duress or necessity can be raised with respect to virtually every escape." 190 U. S. App. D. C. 142, 167, 585 F.2d 1087, 1112. And the Government concedes: "In light of prison conditions that even now prevail in the United States, it would be the rare inmate who could not convince himself that continued incarceration would be harmful to his health or safety." Brief for United States 27. See Furtado v. Bishop, 604 F.2d 80 (CA1 1979), cert. denied, post, p. 1035. Cf. Bell v. Wolfish, 441 U.S. 520 (1979).

A youthful inmate can expect to be subjected to homosexual gang rape his first night in jail, or, it has been said, even in the van on the way to jail.[7] Weaker inmates become the property of stronger prisoners or gangs, who sell the sexual services of the victim. Prison officials either are disinterested in stopping abuse of prisoners by other prisoners or are incapable of doing so, given the limited resources society allocates to the prison system.[8] Prison officials often are merely indifferent to serious health and safety needs of prisoners as well.[9]

Even more appalling is the fact that guards frequently participate in the brutalization of inmates.[10] The classic example is the beating or other punishment in retaliation for prisoner complaints or court actions.[11]

The evidence submitted by respondents in these cases fits that pattern exactly. . . .

It is society's responsibility to protect the life and health of its prisoners. "[When] a sheriff or a marshall [*sic*] takes a man from the courthouse in a prison van and transports him to confinement for two or three or ten years, *this is our act. We* have tolled the bell for him. And whether we like it or not, we have

made him our collective responsibility. We are free to do something about him; he is not" (emphasis in original). Address by THE CHIEF JUSTICE, 25 Record of the Assn. of the Bar of the City of New York 14, 17 (Mar. 1970 Supp.). . . .

There can be little question that our prisons are badly overcrowded and understaffed and that this in large part is the cause of many of the shortcomings of our penal systems. This, however, does not excuse the failure to provide a place of confinement that meets minimal standards of safety and decency.

Penal systems in other parts of the world demonstrate that vast improvement surely is not beyond our reach. "The contrast between our indifference and the programs in some countries of Europe—Holland and the Scandinavian countries in particular—is not a happy one for us." Address by THE CHIEF JUSTICE, *supra*, at 20. "It has been many years since Swedish prisoners were concerned with such problems as 'adequate food, water, shelter'; 'true religious freedom'; and 'adequate medical treatment.'" Ward, Inmate Rights and Prison Reform in Sweden and Denmark, 63 J. Crim. L., C. & P. S. 240 (1972). See also Profile/Sweden, Corrections Magazine 11 (June 1977). Sweden's prisons are not overcrowded, and most inmates have a private cell. Salomon, Lessons from the Swedish Criminal Justice System: A Reappraisal, 40 Fed. Probation 40, 43 (Sept. 1976). The prisons are small. The largest accommodate 300-500 inmates; most house 50–150. *Id.*, at 43; Profile/Sweden, supra, at 14. "There appears to be a relaxed atmosphere between staff and inmates, and a prevailing attitude that prisoners must be treated with dignity and respect." Siegel, Criminal Justice—Swedish Style: A Humane Search for Answers, 1 Offender Rehabilitation 291, 292 (1977).

II

The real question presented in this case is whether the prisoner should be punished for helping to extricate himself from a situation where society has abdicated completely its basic responsibility for providing an environment free of life-threatening conditions such as beatings, fires, lack of essential medical care, and sexual attacks. To be sure, Congress in so many words has not enacted specific statutory duress or necessity defenses that would excuse or justify commission of an otherwise unlawful act. The concept of such a defense, however, is "anciently woven into the fabric of our culture." J. Hall, General Principles of Criminal Law 416 (2d ed. 1960), quoted in Brief for United States 21. And the Government concedes that "it has always been an accepted part of our criminal justice system that punishment is inappropriate for crimes committed under duress because the defendant in such circumstances cannot fairly be blamed for his wrongful act." *Id.,* at 23.

Although the Court declines to address the issue, it at least implies that it would recognize the common-law defenses of duress and necessity to the federal crime of prison escape, if the appropriate prerequisites for assertion of either defense were met. See *Ante,* at 410–413. Given the universal acceptance of these defenses in the common law, I have no difficulty in concluding that Congress intended the defenses of duress and necessity to be available to persons accused of committing the federal crime of escape.

I agree with most of the Court's comments about the essential elements of the defenses. I, too, conclude that intolerable prison conditions are to be taken into account through affirmative defenses of duress and necessity, rather than by way of the theory of intent espoused by the Court of Appeals. . . .

I, too, conclude that the jury generally should be instructed that, in order to prevail on a necessity or duress defense, the defendant must justify his continued absence from custody, as well as his initial departure. I agree with the Court that the very nature of escape makes it a continuing crime. But I cannot agree that the only way continued absence can

be justified is by evidence "of a bona fide effort to surrender or return to custody." *Ante,* at 413, 415. The Court apparently entertains the view, naive in my estimation, that once the prisoner has escaped from a life- or health-threatening situation, he can turn himself in, secure in the faith that his escape somehow will result in improvement in those intolerable prison conditions. While it may be true in some rare circumstance that an escapee will obtain the aid of a court or of the prison administration once the escape is accomplished, the escapee, realistically, faces a high probability of being returned to the same prison and to exactly the same, or even greater, threats to life and safety.

The rationale of the necessity defense is a balancing of harms. If the harm caused by an escape is less than the harm caused by remaining in a threatening situation, the prisoner's initial departure is justified. The same rationale should apply to hesitancy and failure to return. A situation may well arise where the social balance weighs in favor of the prisoner even though he fails to return to custody. The escapee at least should be permitted to present to the jury the possibility that the harm that would result from a return to custody outweighs the harm to society from continued absence.

Even under the Court's own standard, the defendant in an escape prosecution should be permitted to submit evidence to the jury to demonstrate that surrender would result in his being placed again in a life- or health-threatening situation. The Court requires return to custody once the "claimed duress or necessity had lost its coercive force." *Ante,* at 413, 415. Realistically, however, the escapee who reasonably believes that surrender will result in return to what concededly is an intolerable prison situation remains subject to the same "coercive force" that prompted his escape in the first instance. It is ironic to say that that force is automatically "lost" once the prison wall is passed. . . .

Ruling on a defense as a matter of law and preventing the jury from considering it should be a rare occurrence in criminal cases. "[In] a criminal case the law assigns [the factfinding function] solely to the jury." *Sandstrom v. Montana*, 442 U.S. 510, 523 (1979). The jury is the conscience of society and its role in a criminal prosecution is particularly important. *Duncan v. Louisiana*, 391 U.S. 145, 156 (1968). Yet the Court here appears to place an especially strict burden of proof on defendants attempting to establish an affirmative defense to the charged crime of escape. That action is unwarranted. If respondents' allegations are true, society is grossly at fault for permitting these conditions to persist at the D. C. jail. The findings of researchers and government agencies, as well as the litigated cases, indicate that in a general sense these allegations are credible.[12] The case for recognizing the duress or necessity defenses is even more compelling when it is society, rather than private actors, that creates the coercive conditions. In such a situation it is especially appropriate that the jury be permitted to weigh all the factors and strike the balance between the interests of prisoners and that of society. In an attempt to conserve the jury for cases it considers truly worthy of that body, the Court has ousted the jury from a role it is particularly well suited to serve.

Notes

1. Title 18 U. S. C. § 751 (a) provides:

   " Whoever escapes or attempts to escape from the custody of the Attorney General or his authorized representative, or from any institution or facility in which he is confined by direction of the Attorney General, or from any custody under or by virtue of any process issued under the laws of the United States by any court, judge, or magistrate, or from the custody of an officer or employee of the United States pursuant to lawful arrest, shall, if the custody or confinement is by virtue of an arrest on a charge of felony, or conviction of any offense, be fined not more than $ 5,000 or imprisoned not more than five years, or both; or if the custody or confinement is for extradition or by virtue of an arrest or charge of or for a misdemeanor, and prior to conviction, be fined not more than $ 1,000 or imprisoned not more than one year, or both."

   Respondents were also charged with violating 22 D. C. Code § 2601 (1973), the District of Columbia's statute proscribing escape from prison. The District Court instructed the juries that if they found the respondents guilty of violating 18 U. S. C. § 751 (a) they should not consider the charges under 22 D. C. Code § 2601.

2. On rebuttal, the prosecution called Joel Dean, the FBI agent who had been assigned to investigate Walker's escape in August 1976. He testified that, under standard Bureau practice, he would have been notified of any contact made by Walker with the FBI. According to Dean, he never was informed of any such contact. App. 203–204.

3. Respondents asked the District Court to give the following instruction:

   "Coercion which would excuse the commission of a criminal act must result from:

   "1) Threatening [*sic*] conduct sufficient to create in the mind of a reasonable person the fear of death or serious bodily harm;

   "2) The conduct in fact caused such fear of death or serious bodily harm in the mind of the defendant;

   "3) The fear or duress was operating upon the mind of the defendant at the time of the alleged act; and

   "4) The defendant committed the act to avoid the threatened [*sic*] harm."

4. See also *R. I. Recreation Center, Inc. v. Aetna Casualty & Surety Co.*, 177 F.2d 603, 605 (CA1 1949) (a person acting under a threat of death to his relatives was denied defense of duress where he committed the crime even though he had an opportunity to contact the police); *People v. Richards*, 269 Cal. App. 2d 768, 75 Cal. Rptr. 597 (1969) (prisoner must resort to administrative or judicial channels to remedy coercive prison conditions); Model Penal Code § 2.09 (1) (actor must succumb to a force or threat that "a person of reasonable

firmness in his situation would have been unable to resist"); *Id.,* § 3.02 (1) (actor must believe that commission of crime is "necessary" to avoid a greater harm); Working Papers 277 (duress excuses criminal conduct, "if at all, because given the circumstances other reasonable men must concede that they too would not have been able to act otherwise").

5. We appreciate the fact that neither the prosecution nor the defense in a criminal case may put in all its evidence simultaneously, and to the extent that applicable rules of case law do not otherwise preclude such an approach, a district court is bound to find itself in situations where it admits evidence provisionally, subject to that evidence being later "tied in" or followed up by other evidence that makes the evidence conditionally admitted unconditionally admissible. In a civil action, the question whether a particular affirmative defense is sufficiently supported by testimony to go to the jury may often be resolved on a motion for summary judgment, but of course motions for summary judgment are creatures of civil, not criminal, trials. Thus, when we say that in order to have the theory of duress or necessity as a defense submitted to the jury an escapee must "first" offer evidence justifying his continuing absence from custody, we do not mean to impose a rigid mechanical formula on attorneys and district courts as to the order in which evidence supporting particular elements of a defense must be offered. The convenience of the jurors, the court, and the witnesses may all be best served by receiving the testimony "out of order" in certain circumstances, subject to an avowal by counsel that such testimony will later be "tied in" by testimony supporting the other necessary elements of a particular affirmative defense. Our holding here is a substantive one: an essential element of the defense of duress or necessity is evidence sufficient to support a finding of a bona fide effort to surrender or return to custody as soon as the claimed duress or necessity has lost its coercive force. As a general practice, trial courts will find it saves considerable time to require testimony on this element of the affirmative defense of duress or necessity first, simply because such testimony can be heard in a fairly short time, whereas testimony going to the other necessary elements of duress or necessity may take considerably longer to present. Here, for example, the jury heard five *days* of testimony as to prison conditions, when in fact the trial court concluded, correctly, that testimony as to another essential element of this defense did not even reach a minimum threshold such that if the jury believed it that element of defense could be said to have been made out. But trial judges presiding over indictments based on § 751 (a) are in a far better position than are we to know whether, as a matter of the order of presenting witnesses and evidence, testimony from a particular witness may be allowed "out of order" subject to avowal, proffer, and the various other devices employed to avoid wasting the time of the court and jury with testimony that is irrelevant while at the same time avoiding if possible the necessity for recalling or seriously inconveniencing a witness.

6. Contrary to the implication of MR. JUSTICE BLACKMUN's dissent describing the rationale of the necessity defense as "a balancing of harms," post, at 427, we are construing an Act of Congress, not drafting it. The statute itself, as we have noted, requires no heightened *mens rea* that might be negated by any defense of duress or coercion. We nonetheless recognize that Congress in enacting criminal statutes legislates against a background of Anglo-Saxon common law, see Morissette v. United States, 342 U.S. 246 (1952), and that therefore a defense of duress or coercion may well have been contemplated by Congress when it enacted § 751 (a). But since the express purpose of Congress in enacting that section was to punish escape from penal custody, we think that some duty to return, a duty described more elaborately in the text, must be an essential element of the defense unless the congressional judgment that escape from prison is a crime be rendered wholly nugatory. Our principal difference with the dissent, therefore, is not as to the existence of such a defense but as to the importance of surrender as an element of it. And we remain satisfied that, even if credited by the jury, the testimony set forth at length in MR. JUSTICE BLACKMUN's dissenting opinion could not support a finding that respondents had no alternatives but to

remain at large until recaptured anywhere from one to three and one-half months after their escape. To hold otherwise would indeed quickly reduce the overcrowding in prisons that has been universally condemned by penologists. But that result would be accomplished in a manner quite at odds with the purpose of Congress when it made escape from prison a federal criminal offense.

7. See, e. g., C. Silberman, Criminal Violence, Criminal Justice 389 (1978); Report on Sexual Assaults in a Prison System and Sheriff's Vans, in 3 L. Radzinowicz & M. Wolfgang, eds., Crime and Justice 223–228 (2d ed. 1977).

8. See generally Silberman, supra, at 379–382, 386–392; C. Bartollas, S. Miller, & S. Dinitz, Juvenile Victimization—The Institutional Paradox (1976); C. Weiss & D. Friar, Terror in the Prisons (1974); O. Ballesteros, Behind Jail Bars 26–27 (1979); M. Luttrell, Behind Prison Walls 64–65 (1974).

9. E. g., Weiss & Friar, *supra,* at 183–184 (youth having epileptic seizure sprayed with tear gas, resulting in severe trauma); G. Mueller, Medical Services in Prison: Lessons from Two Surveys, in CIBA Foundation Symposium 16, Medical Care of Prisoners and Detainees 7, 11–16 (1973); J. Mitford, Kind & Usual Punishment 135 (1973); Univ. of Pa. Law School, Health Care and Conditions in Pennsylvania's State Prisons (1972), reprinted in ABA Comm'n on Correctional Facilities and Services, Standards and Materials on Medical and Health Care in Jails, Prisons, and Other Correctional Facilities 71 (1974); Report of the Medical Advisory Committee on State Prisons to Comm'r of Correction and Sec'y of Human Services, Commonwealth of Mass. (1971), reprinted in ABA Standards and Materials 89.

10. See, e. g., Weiss & Friar, supra, at 54–60, 163–164, 176–181, 188, 199–200, 222.

11. See, e. g., Note, Escape From Cruel and Unusual Punishment: A Theory of Constitutional Necessity, 59 B. U. L. Rev. 334, 358–360 (1979); *Landman v. Royster,* 333 F.Supp. 621, 633–634 (ED Va. 1971); *Sostre v. Rockefeller,* 312 F.Supp. 863, 869 (SDNY 1970), rev'd in part, modified in part, aff'd in part sub nom. *Sostre v. McGinnis,* 442 F.2d 178 (CA2 1971) (en banc), cert. denied sub nom. *Sostre v.*

Oswald, 404 U.S. 1049 (1972); Mitford, supra, at 260–262.

12. In addition to the sources cited above, see American Assembly, Prisoners in America (1973); S. Sheehan, A Prison and a Prisoner (1978); V. Williams & M. Fish, Convicts, Codes, and Contraband (1974); Inside—Prison American Style (R. Minton, ed. 1971); T. Murton, The Dilemma of Prison Reform (1976); American Friends Service Committee, Struggle for Justice, A Report on Crime and Punishment in America (1971); Behind Bars: Prisoners in America (R. Kwartler ed. 1977); B. Bagdikian & L. Dash, The Shame of the Prisons (1972); Note, 13 Ga. L. Rev. 300 (1978); Note, Intolerable Conditions as a Defense to Prison Escapes, 26 UCLA L. Rev. 1126 (1979); Comment, 127 U. Pa. L. Rev. 1142 (1979); Note, 54 Chi.-Kent L. Rev. 913 (1978); Comment, 26 Buffalo L. Rev. 413 (1977); Plotkin, Surviving Justice: Prisoners' Rights To Be Free from Physical Assault, 23 Cleve. St. L. Rev. 387 (1974); Note, 45 S. Cal. L. Rev. 1062 (1972); Note, 36 Albany L. Rev. 428 (1972).

Notes and Questions

1. How should the law weigh the rights of prisoners against the imperative to maintain order in prison? Which is more important?

2. How are "duress" and "necessity" defined by law? According to the majority in *Bailey,* if the inmates had "a chance both to refuse to do the criminal act (escaping custody) and also to avoid the threatened harm (brutal prison conditions)," then neither duress nor necessity can be a valid defense. Did the defendants in *Bailey* have such an option? What recourse, if any, do incarcerated individuals have to protect themselves from excessively harsh prison conditions?

3. By focusing on questions of motive and behavior *after* the escape rather than during, the *Bailey* majority sidesteps the question of prison brutality and the con-

ditions of confinement. On what grounds do they refrain from making a judgment on the latter question? Is this a reasonable interpretation of the limits of judicial power or a failure to reign in arbitrary violence?

4. Whether or not the claim of duress "had lost its coercive force" once the defendants escaped federal custody is of vital importance to Justice Blackmun's dissent. At what point should the men have felt secure enough to return themselves to custody? How important is it to their case, as Justice Blackmun argues, that "the conditions that led to respondents' initial departure from the D.C. jail continue unabated"?

5. Justice Blackmun insists that "If the respondents' allegations are true, society is grossly at fault for permitting these conditions to persist at the D.C. jail." Does this situation indicate a breakdown in the hierarchical control of law's violence? If so, what should be the remedy? More governmental oversight of wardens' actions and prison routine? More laws delineating prisoner rights? Should the remedy be a judicial matter or a legislative one?

Reprinted from: *United States v. Bailey,* 444 U.S. 394 (1980). ✦

Chapter 59

Deadly Symbiosis

Rethinking Race and Imprisonment in Twenty-First-Century America

Loïc Wacquant

The impact of the incarceration boom has not been uniform on the citizens of the United States. It has been particularly severe in minority communities. One in eight (12.9 percent) of black males aged 25–29 were in jail or prison by the end of 2002, as were 43 percent of young Hispanic males. The figure was 1.6 percent for white males in the comparable age group. A black male born today has a 29 percent chance of spending time in a state or federal prison in his lifetime. What this means is that our prisons are socially organized with blacks and Hispanics making up almost 70 percent of the nation's inmates.

How can or should we understand the racialization of imprisonment in the United States? Loïc Wacquant offers a distinctive perspective on this development. He presents a macro-sociological account that focuses on the similar social functions of urban ghettoes and prisons. The imprisonment boom occurred coincident with the obsolescence of the ghetto and as a response to the emergence of a form of government that Wacquant labels "neo-liberal." Neo-liberalism gives priority to the accumulation of private wealth and to individualistic conceptions of freedom at the expense of equality and social welfare. It emphasizes empower-

ing individuals and holding them responsible for the choices they make.

The ghettoization of the prison and the "prisonization" of the ghetto work in tandem, Wacquant argues, to manage and control "dispossessed and dishonored" groups. Today, prisons substitute for ghettoes as an apparatus for keeping African Americans in a subordinate position. At the same time, prisons have been ghettoized in several senses, including the racialization of their internal makeup. Finally, mass incarceration of minorities, Wacquant contends, imposes a form of "civic death" on such groups not unlike the "social death" imposed by the institution of slavery.

Consider three brute facts about racial inequality and imprisonment in contemporary America:

1. Since 1989 and for the first time in national history, African Americans make up a majority of those entering prison each year. Indeed, in four short decades, the ethnic composition of the U.S. inmate population has reversed, turning over from 70 percent white at mid-century to nearly 70 percent black and Latino today, although ethnic patterns of criminal activity have not fundamentally changed during that period.

2. The rate of incarceration for African Americans has soared to levels unknown in any other society and is higher now than the total incarceration rate in the Soviet Union at the zenith of the Gulag and in South Africa at the height of the anti-apartheid struggle. As of mid-1999, close to 800,000 black men were in custody in federal penitentiaries, state prisons, and county jails—one male out of every twenty-one, and one out of every nine between twenty and thirty-four.[1] On any given day, upwards of one third of African-American men in their twen-

ties find themselves behind bars, on probation, or on parole. And, at the core of the formerly industrial cities of the North, this proportion often exceeds two thirds.

3. The ratio of black to white imprisonment rates has steadily grown over the past two decades, climbing from about five to one to eight and a half to one. This rising "racial disproportionality" can be traced directly to the War on Drugs launched by Ronald Reagan and expanded under George Bush, Sr. and Bill Clinton. In ten states, African Americans are imprisoned at more than ten times the rate of European Americans. And in the District of Columbia, blacks were thirty-five times more likely than whites to be put behind bars in 1994.[2]

Students of crime and justice know these grim facts but disagree about their explanation. Most analysts account for the sudden "blackening" of the *carceral system*—comprising jails, state prisons, federal prisons, and private detention facilities—in terms of trends in crime and its judicial treatment (arrest, prosecution, sentencing); a few have considered such non-judicial variables as the size of the black population, economic factors (the poverty rate, unemployment, income), the value of welfare payments, support for religious fundamentalism, and the dominant political party. But these factors, taken separately and in conjunction, simply cannot account for the magnitude, rapidity, and timing of the recent racialization of U.S. imprisonment, especially as crime rates have been flat and later declining over the past quarter-century.[3]

Black Hyperincarceration

To understand these phenomena, we first need to break out of the narrow "crime and punishment" paradigm and examine the broader role of the penal system as an *instrument for managing dispossessed and dishon-*

ored groups.[4] And second, we need to take a longer historical view on the shifting forms of ethno-racial domination in the United States. This double move suggests that the astounding upsurge in black incarceration in the past three decades results from the obsolescence of the ghetto as a device for caste control and the correlative need for a substitute apparatus for keeping (unskilled) African Americans in a subordinate and confined position—physically, socially, and symbolically.

In the post-Civil Rights era, the remnants of the dark ghetto and an expanding carceral system have become linked in a single system that entraps large numbers of younger black men, who simply move back and forth between the two institutions. This carceral mesh has emerged from two sets of convergent changes: sweeping economic and political forces have reshaped the mid-century "Black Belt" to *make the ghetto more like a prison*; and the "inmate society" has broken down in ways that *make the prison more like a ghetto*. The resulting symbiosis between ghetto and prison enforces the socioeconomic marginality and symbolic taint of an urban black sub-proletariat. Moreover, by producing a racialized public culture that vilifies criminals, it plays a pivotal role in remaking "race" and redefining the citizenry.

A fuller analysis would reveal that this increasing use of imprisonment to shore up caste division in American society is part of a broader "upsizing" of the state's penal sector, which, together with the drastic "downsizing" of its social welfare sector, aims at enforcing a regime of flexible and casual wage labor as a norm of citizenship for unskilled segments of the postindustrial working class.[5] This emerging *government of poverty* weds the "invisible hand" of a deregulated labor market to the "iron fist" of an omnipresent punitive apparatus. It is anchored not by a "prison industrial complex," as political opponents of the policy of mass incarceration maintain,[6] but by a system of gendered institutions that monitor, train, and neutralize populations recalcitrant or superfluous to the new economic and racial regime: men are handled by its penal wing while (their) women and children are managed by a revamped welfare-workfare system designed to buttress casual employment.

So the hypertrophic growth of imprisonment is one component of a more comprehensive restructuring of the American state to suit the requirements of neoliberalism. But race plays a special role in this emerging system. The United States far outstrips all advanced nations in the international trend towards the penalization of social insecurity. And just as the dismantling of welfare programs was accelerated by a cultural and political conflation of blackness and undeservingness,[7] so, too, the "great confinement" of the rejects of market society—the poor, mentally ill, homeless, jobless, and useless—can be painted as a welcome "crackdown" on *them,* those dark-skinned criminals from a pariah group still considered alien to the national body. The handling of the "underclass" question by the prison system at once reflects, reworks, and reinforces the racial division of American society and plays a key role in the fashioning of a post-Keynesian American state.

FOUR PECULIAR INSTITUTIONS

The task of defining, confining, and controlling African Americans in the United States has been successively shouldered by four "peculiar institutions": slavery, the Jim Crow system, the urban ghetto, and the organizational compound formed by the vestiges of the ghetto and the expanding carceral system. The first three served, each in its own way, both to extract labor from African Americans and to demarcate and ultimately seclude them so that they would not "contaminate" the surrounding white society that viewed them as irrevocably inferior and vile.

These two goals of *labor extraction* and *social seclusion* are in tension: extracting a group's labor requires regular intercourse with its members, which may blur the line separating "us" from "them." Conversely, social isolation can make efficient labor extraction more difficult. When the tension between exploitation and exclusion mounts to the point where it threatens to undermine either of them, the institution is re-stabilized through *physical violence*: the customary use of the lash and ferocious suppression of slave insurrections on the plantation, terroristic vigilantism and mob lynchings in the post-bellum South, and periodic bombings of Negro homes and pogroms against ghetto residents (such as the six-day riot that shook up Chicago in 1919) ensured that blacks kept to their appointed place at each epoch.

But the built-in instabilities of unfree labor and the anomaly of caste partition in a formally democratic and highly individualistic society guaranteed that each of these peculiar institutions would in time be undermined by the weight of its internal tensions as well as by black resistance and external opposition, and be replaced by its successor regime. At each new stage, the apparatus of ethno-racial domination became less total and less capable of encompassing all segments and dimensions of the pariah group's social life. As African Americans differentiated along class lines and acceded to full formal citizenship, the institutional complex charged with keeping them "separate and unequal" grew more differentiated and diffuse, allowing a burgeoning middle and upper class of professionals and salary earners to *partially* compensate for the negative symbolic capital of blackness through their high-status cultural capital and proximity to centers of political power. But lower-class blacks remained burdened by the triple stigma of "race," poverty, and putative immorality.[8] . . .

Analyzing the workings of the ghetto as mechanism of ethno-racial control highlights its *kinship with the prison*. Thus the ghetto is a kind of "ethno-racial prison" in that it encloses a stigmatized population with its own distinctive organizations and culture. And the prison functions as a "judicial ghetto" relegating individuals disgraced by criminal conviction to a secluded space harboring the social relations and cultural norms of a "society of captives."[9] So when the capacity of the ghetto to ensure caste domination was undercut in the 1960s by economic restructuring that made African-American labor expendable and by the mass protest that finally won blacks full voting rights, the carceral system began to function as a substitute apparatus for enforcing the shifting color line and containing segments of the African-American community devoid of economic utility and political pull. As the ghetto became more like a prison (what I call the "hyperghetto") and the prison became more like a ghetto, the two institutions increasingly fused to form the fast-expanding carceral system that constitutes America's fourth "peculiar institution.". . .

'Ghettoization' of the Prison

In the two decades following the climax of the Civil Rights movement, the racial and class backlash that reconfigured the city also ushered in a sweeping transformation in the purpose and social organization of the carceral system. In the past few decades, the explosive growth of the incarcerated population has led to rampant prison overcrowding; the rapid rise in the proportion of inmates serving long sentences, the spread of ethnically-based gangs, and a flood of young convicts and drug offenders deeply rooted in the informal economy and oppositional culture of the street, have combined to undermine the older "inmate society" depicted in the classic prison research of the postwar decades.[10] The "Big House"—with its correctional ideal of melioristic treatment and community reintegration of inmates—gave way to a race-divided and violence-ridden "warehouse" geared solely to the physical sequestering of social rejects.

It is difficult to characterize the changes that have remade the American prison in the image of the ghetto over the past three de-

cades, not only because American prisons are so diverse, but also because we have remarkably little on-the-ground data on social and cultural life inside the contemporary penitentiary. Nonetheless, one can provisionally single out five tendencies that fortify the convergence of ghetto and prison in the large (post)industrial states that have put the United States on the path to mass imprisonment.

The Racial Division of Everything

The world of inmates used to be organized around a relatively stable set of positions and expectations defined primarily in terms of criminal status and prison conduct. In Gresham Sykes's classic account, we have "rats" and "center men" who betray the core value of solidarity among inmates by violating the ban on communication with custodians; "merchants" who peddle goods in the illicit economy of the establishment; "gorillas" who prey on weak inmates to acquire cigarettes, food, clothing, and deference; and "wolfs," "punks," and "fags," who play out sexual scripts adopted behind bars.[11] This older order has now been replaced by a chaotic and conflictual setting wherein "racial division has primacy over all particular identities and influences all aspects of life."[12]

The ethnic provenance or affiliation of the inmates determines their ward, tier, cell, and bunk-bed assignments; their access to food, telephone, television, visitation, and in-house programs; their associations and protections, which in turn determine the probability of being the victim or perpetrator of violence. Elective loyalty to inmates as a generic class, with the possibility of remaining non-aligned, has been superseded by forced and exclusive loyalty to one's "race" defined in rigid, caste-like manner, with no in-between and no position of neutrality—just as it is in the urban ghetto. And the central axis of stratification inside the "pen" has shifted from the vertical cleavage *between prisoners and guards,* (marked by prohibitions against "ratting on a con," "talking to a screw," or exploiting other inmates), to horizontal cleavages between black, Latino, and white prisoners (with Asians most often assimilated to whites and Middle Easterners given a choice of voluntary affiliation).

From 'Convict Code' to 'Street Code'

Along with racial division, the predatory culture of the street, centered on hypermasculine notions of honor, toughness, and coolness has transformed the social structure and culture of jails and prisons. The "convict code," rooted in solidarity among inmates and antagonism towards guards has been swamped by the "code of the street," with its ardent imperative of individual "respect" secured through the militant display and demonstrated readiness to mete out physical violence.[13] According to John Irwin, "the old 'hero' of the prison world—the 'right guy'—has been replaced by outlaws and gang members," who have "raised toughness and mercilessness to the top of prisoners' value systems."[14] Ethnically-based street gangs and "supergangs," such as the Disciples, El Rukn, Vice Lords, and Latin Kings in Illinois, the Mexican Mafia, Black Guerrilla Family, and Aryan Brotherhood in California, and the Netas in New York City, have taken over the illicit prison economy and destabilized the entire social system of inmates, forcing a shift from "doing your own time" to "doing gang time." They have even precipitated a thorough restructuring of the administration of large-scale prison systems, from Illinois to California to Texas.[15]

These changes, together with the rising tide of drugs, have disrupted the old inmate structure of power and produced increased levels of interpersonal and group brutality. As Johnson writes, "what was once a repressive but comparatively safe 'Big House' is now often an unstable and violent social jungle" in which social intercourse is infected with the same disruption, aggression, and unpredictability as in the hyperghetto.[16]

Purging the Undesirables

The Big House of the postwar decades was animated by the idea that punishment should ultimately help resocialize inmates and thus reduce the probability of further offenses once they returned to society. This philosophy of rehabilitation was repudiated in the 1970s, and today's prison aims solely to *neutralize* offenders—individuals thought to be likely to violate the law, such as parolees—both *materially*, by removing them physically into an institutional enclave, and *symbolically*, by drawing a hard and fast line between criminals and law-abiding citizens. The now-dominant "law and order" paradigm jettisons ideas of prevention and proportionality in favor of direct appeals to popular resentment through measures that dramatize the fear and loathing of crime, which is presented as the abhorrent conduct of defective individuals. The mission of today's prison is thus identical to that of the classical ghetto, whose *raison d'être* was precisely to quarantine a polluting group from the urban body.

The Racialization of Judicial Stigma

The contemporary prison can be further likened to the ghetto in that the stigma of penal conviction has been prolonged, diffused, and re-framed in ways that assimilate it to an ethno-racial stigma—something permanently attached to the body of its bearer. In other liberal-democratic societies, the status dishonor and civic disabilities of being a prisoner are temporary and limited: they affect offenders while they are being processed by the criminal justice system and typically wear off shortly after the prisoner's release; to ensure this, laws and administrative rules set strict conditions and limits on the use and diffusion of criminal justice information.

Not so in the United States. Convicts here are subjected to ever-longer and broader post-detention techniques of social control and symbolic branding that durably set them apart from the rest of the population; the criminal files of individual inmates are readily accessible and actively disseminated by the authorities; and a pseudo-scientific discourse couched in genetic terminology and animal-istic imagery pervades public representations of crime in the media, politics, and significant segments of scholarship. . . .

CARCERAL RECRUITMENT AND AUTHORITY

Today's prison further resembles the ghetto for the simple reason that an over-whelming majority of its occupants originate from the racialized core of the country's major cities, and return there upon release—only to be soon caught again in police drag-nets and sent away for ever-longer sojourns behind bars, in a self-perpetuating cycle of es-calating socioeconomic marginality and legal incapacitation. Thus, in the late 1980s, three of every four inmates serving sentences in the entire state of New York came from *seven black and Latino neighborhoods* of New York City, which also happened to be the poorest areas of the city. Every year these segregated and dispossessed districts furnished a fresh contingent of 25,000-odd inmates, while 23,000 ex-convicts were discharged, most of them on parole, right back into these devas-tated areas. A conservative estimate, given a statewide felony recidivism rate of 47 percent, is that within a year, some 15,000 of them found their way back "upstate" and behind bars.[17] The fact that 46 percent of the inmates of New York state prisons issue from neigh-borhoods served by the sixteen worst public schools of the city ensures that their clientele will be duly replenished for years to come.

The contemporary prison system and the ghetto not only display a similarly skewed re-cruitment and composition in terms of class and caste. The prison also duplicates the au-thority structure characteristic of the ghetto in that it places a population of poor blacks under the direct supervision of whites—in this case, lower-class whites. In the communal ghetto of the postwar era, black residents chaffed under the rule of white landlords, white employers, white unions, white social

workers, and white policemen.[18] Likewise, at century's end, the convicts of New York City, Philadelphia, Baltimore, Cleveland, Detroit, and Chicago, who are overwhelmingly Afri-can-American, serve their sentences in estab-lishments staffed by officers who are over-whelmingly white. In Illinois, for instance, two thirds of the state's 41,000 inmates are blacks who live under the watch of an 8,400-member uniformed force that is 84 percent white. In Michigan and Pennsylvania, 55 per-cent of prisoners are black but only 13 and 8 percent of guards, respectively, come from the Afro-American community. In Maryland, the correctional staff is 90 percent white and monitors an inmate population that is 80 per-cent black. With the proliferation of deten-tion facilities in rural areas, the economic stability and social welfare of lower-class whites from the declining hinterland has come to hinge, perversely, on the continued socioeconomic marginality and penal re-straint of ever-larger numbers of lower-class blacks from the urban core.

The convergent changes that have "prison-ized" the ghetto and "ghettoized" the prison in the aftermath of the civil rights revolution sug-gest that the stupendous increasing over-rep-resentation of blacks behind bars does not stem simply from the discriminatory targeting of specific penal policies such as the War on Drugs, (as Michael Tonry suggests) or from the sheer destabilizing effects of the increased pen-etration of ghetto neighborhoods by the penal state, (as Jerome Miller argues).[19] These two factors are clearly at work but they fail to cap-ture the precise nature and full magnitude of the transformations that have interlocked the prison and the (hyper)ghetto into a *single insti-tutional mesh* suited to fulfill anew the mission historically imparted to America's "peculiar institutions."

Thus, consider *the timing of racial transition*: with a lag of about a dozen years, the "blacken-ing" of the carceral population has closely fol-lowed the demise of the Black Belt as a viable instrument of caste containment in the urban-industrial setting. A century earlier, David Oshinsky points out, the sudden penal repression of African Americans had helped to shore up "the walls of white supremacy as the South moved from an era of racial bondage to one of racial caste."[20] The thesis of a structural and functional linkage between ghetto and prison is also verified by the geographic patterning of racial disproportionality: outside of the South—which for obvious historical reasons requires a separate analysis—the black-white gap in incarceration is more pronounced and has increased faster in those states of the Midwest and Northeast that are the historic cradle of the Northern ghetto.[21] The intertwining of the urban Black Belt and the carceral system is further evidenced, and in turn abetted, by the *fusion of ghetto and prison culture,* as vividly expressed in the lyrics of "gangsta rap" singers and hip hop artists, in graffiti and tattooing, and in the dissemination, to the urban core and beyond, of language, dress, and interaction patterns innovated inside of jails and penitentiaries.

Making 'Race,' Shaping Citizens

Slavery, Jim Crow, and the ghetto are each "race making" institutions: they do not simply *process* an independently-existing ethno-racial division; rather, each *produces* (or co-produces) this division (anew) out of inherited demarcations and disparities of group power and inscribes it at every epoch in a distinctive constellation of material and symbolic forms. All three have consistently *racialized* the arbitrary boundary that sets African Americans apart from all others in the United States by actively denying that boundary's cultural origin in history, and ascribing it instead to the fictitious necessity of biology.

The highly particular conception of "race" that America has invented, virtually unique in the world for its rigidity and social consequences, is a direct outcome of the momentous collision between slavery and democracy. The Jim Crow regime reworked the racialized boundary between the free and the enslaved

into a rigid caste separation between "whites" and "Negros" (comprising all persons of known African ancestry, no matter how minimal), that infected every crevice of the postbellum social system in the South. The ghetto, in turn, imprinted this dichotomy onto the spatial and institutional schemas of the industrial metropolis. So much so that, in the wake of the "urban riots" of the sixties, "urban" and "black" became near-synonymous in policy making as well as everyday parlance. And the "crisis" of the city came to stand for the enduring contradiction between the individualistic and competitive tenor of American life, on the one hand, and the continued seclusion of African Americans from it, on the other.[22] Now, a fourth "peculiar institution"—joining the hyperghetto with the carceral system—is remolding the social meaning and significance of "race" in accordance with the dictates of neoliberalism. To be sure, the penal apparatus has long served as accessory to ethnoracial domination. But the role of the carceral institution today is different. For the first time in U.S. history, it is the primary apparatus for the social production of "race."

Perhaps the most important effect of this new system is that it revives and consolidates the centuries-old *association of blackness with criminality* and devious violence. The massively disproportional incarceration of blacks supplies a powerful common-sense warrant for "using color as a proxy for dangerousness," to borrow the words of Randall Kennedy. In recent years, the courts have consistently authorized the police to employ race as "a negative signal of increased risk of criminality" and legal scholars have rushed to endorse it as "a rational adaptation to the demographics of crime," made salient and verified, as it were, by the blackening of the prison population.[23] The conflation of blackness and crime in collective representation and government policy (the other side of this equation being the conflation of blackness and welfare) thus re-activates "race" by giving a legitimate outlet to the expression of anti-black animus in the form of the public vituperation of criminals and prisoners.

A second major effect of the penalization of the "race question" has been to depoliticize it. Reframing problems of ethno-racial division as issues of law enforcement automatically delegitimates any attempt at collective resistance and redress. Established organizations that speak for African Americans cannot directly confront the crisis of hyperincarceration for fear that this might reinforce the very conflation of blackness and crime in public perception that fuels the crisis. Thus the courteous silence of the NAACP, the Urban League, the Black Congressional Caucus, and black churches on the topic. By entombing poor blacks in the concrete walls of the prison, the penal state has effectively smothered and silenced sub-proletarian revolt.

By assuming a central role in the contemporary government of race and poverty—at the crossroads of the deregulated low-wage labor market, a revamped "welfare-workfare" apparatus designed to support casual employment, and the vestiges of the ghetto—the overgrown American carceral system has become a major engine of symbolic production in its own right. Just as bondage imposed "social death" on imported African captives and their descendants,[24] mass incarceration induces civic death for those it ensnares. . . .

Notes

1. An additional 68,000 black women were locked up, a number higher than the *total* carceral population of any one major western European country. Because males compose over 93 percent of the U.S. state and federal prison population and 89 percent of jail inmates, and because the disciplining of women from the lower class and caste continues to operate primarily through welfare and workfare, this article focuses solely on men. But a full-fledged analysis of the distinct causes and consequences of the astonishing growth in the imprisonment of black (and Hispanic) women is urgently needed, in part because the penal confinement of women has immensely deleterious effects on their children.

2. Steven R. Donziger, *The Real War on Crime: The Report of the National Criminal Justice Commission* (New York: Harper Perennial, 1996), 104–105; Marc Mauer, "Racial Disparities in Prison Getting Worse in the 1990s," in *Overcrowded Times* 8 (1997): 8–13.

3. For a more detailed examination, see Loïc Wacquant, "Crime et châtiment en Amérique de Nixon à Clinton," *Archives de politique criminelle* 20 (Spring 1998): 123–138, and Alfred Blumstein, "U.S. Criminal Justice Conundrum: Rising Prison Populations and Stable Crime Rates," *Crime and Delinquency* 44 (1998): 127–135.

4. In this, I follow George Rusche: "Punishment must be understood as a social phenomenon freed from both its juristic concept and its social ends," that is, its official mission of crime control, so that it may be replaced in the complete system of strategies, including social policies, aimed at regulating the poor. But I do *not* follow Rusche in (i) postulating a *direct* link between brute economic forces and penal policy; (ii) reducing economic forces to the sole state of the *labor market*, and still less the supply of labor; (iii) limiting the control function of the prison to lower *classes*, as distinct from other subordinate categories (ethnic or national, for instance); (iv) omitting the ramifying *symbolic* effects that the penal system exercises by drawing, dramatizing, and enforcing group boundaries. Indeed, in the case of black Americans, the symbolic function of the carceral system is paramount. See George Rusche, "Labor Market and Penal Sanction: Thoughts on the Sociology of Punishment," in *Punishment and Penal Discipline*, eds. Tony Platt and Paul Takagi (Berkeley, Calif.: Crime and Social Justice Associates, 1980), 11.

5. See Loïc Wacquant, Les Prisons de la misère (Paris: Editions Raisons d'agir, 1999). Translated as *Prisons of Poverty* (Minneapolis: University of Minnesota Press, forthcoming.)

6. See Avery F. Gordon, "Globalism and the Prison Industrial Complex: An Interview with Angela Davis," *Race and Class* 40 (1999): 145–157.

7. Martin Gilens, *Why Americans Hate Welfare: Race, Media, and the Politics of Anti-Poverty Policy* (Chicago: The University of Chicago Press, 2000).

8. This historical schema should not be read as an ineluctable forward march towards ethno-racial equality. Each new phase of racial domination entailed retrogression as well as progress. And, while it is true that there has been a kind of "civilizing" of racial domination (in Norbert Elias's sense of the term), it remains that each regime has to be evaluated in light of the institutional possibilities it harbors, not simply by contrast to its predecessor(s).

9. A fuller discussion of the homologies between ghetto and prison as institutions of confinement for dishonored groups is in Loïc Wacquant, "The New 'Peculiar Institution': On the Prison as Surrogate Ghetto," *Theoretical Criminology* 4 (2000): 382–385.

10. The essential works on this point are Irwin, *Prisons in Turmoil*; and Irwin, *The Felon*, new edition (Berkeley, Calif.: University of California Press, 1990).

11. Gresham M. Sykes, *The Society of Captives: A Study of a Maximum Security Prison* (Princeton, N.J.: Princeton University Press, 1958).

12. Irwin, *The Felon*, v; see also Leo Carroll, "Race, Ethnicity, and the Social Order of the Prison," in *The Pains of Imprisonment*, eds. Robert Johnson and Hans Toch (Beverly Hills, Calif.: Sage, 1982), 181–201; Robert Johnson, *Hard Time: Understanding and Reforming the Prison*, 2d ed. (Belmont, Calif.: Wadsworth Publishing, 1996); Victor Hassine, *Life Without Parole: Living in Prison Today*, 2d ed. (Los Angeles: Roxbury Publications, 1999), 71–78.

13. On the "inmate code," see Gresham Sykes and Sheldon Messinger, "The Inmate Social System," in *Theoretical Studies in Social Organization of the Prison*, eds. Richard Cloward et al. (New York: Social Science Research Council, 1960), 6–10; on the "street code," see Elijah Anderson, *Code of the Street: Decency, Violence, and the Moral Life of the Inner City* (New York: W.W. Norton & Company, 1998).

14. Irwin, *The Felon*, vii.

15. Jacobs, *Stateville*, 137–174; Irwin, *Prisons in Turmoil*, 186–192; Steve J. Martin and Sheldon Ekland-Olson, *Texas Prisons: The Walls Came Tumbling Down* (Austin, Tex.: Texas Monthly Press, 1987).

16. Johnson, *Hard Time*, 133.

17. Edwin Ellis, *The Non-Traditional Approach to Criminal Justice and Social Justice* (New York: Community Justice Center, 1993).

18. Kenneth B. Clark, *Dark Ghetto: Dilemmas of Social Power* (Middletown, Conn.: Wesleyan University Press, 1965).

19. Michael Tonry, *Malign Neglect: Race, Crime, and Punishment in America* (New York: Oxford University Press, 1995); Miller, *Search and Destroy*.

20. David M. Oshinsky, *"Worse Than Slavery": Parchman Farm and the Ordeal of Jim Crow Justice* (New York: Free Press, 1996), 57.

21. Mauer, "Racial Disparities."

22. Two indicators suffice to spotlight the enduring ostracization of African Americans in U.S. society. They are the only group to be "hypersegregated," with spatial isolation shifting from the macro-level of state and county to the micro-level of municipality and neighborhood so as to minimize contacts with whites throughout the century. See Massey and Denton, *American Apartheid*; also Massey and Zoltan L. Hajnal, "The Changing Geographic Structure of Black-White Segregation in the United States," *Social Science Quarterly* 76 (September 1995), 527–542. African Americans remain barred from exogamy to a degree unknown to any other community, notwithstanding the recent growth of so-called multiracial families, with fewer than 3 percent of black women marrying out compared to a majority of Hispanic and Asian women. See Kim DaCosta, "Remaking the Color Line: Social Bases and Implications of the Multiracial Movement" (Ph.D. diss., University of California, Berkeley, 2000).

23. Randall Kennedy, "Race, Law and Suspicion: Using Color as a Proxy for Dangerousness," *Race, Crime and the Law* (New York: Pantheon, 1997), 136, 143, 146.

24. Patterson, *Slavery and Social Death*.

NOTES AND QUESTIONS

1. What is the "deadly symbiosis" Wacquant refers to in his title? In this context, how

do economic factors shape law? How are race and economics linked?

2. According to Wacquant, the penal system has become little more than "an instrument for managing dispossessed and dishonored groups." Do you agree? Why or why not?

3. Wacquant highlights the way in which the "downsizing" of the social welfare sector in the second half of the twentieth century corresponds to the "upsizing" of the penal sector. How does he link these two? In your opinion, how strong is the correlation? Is there a "penalization of social insecurity" in American society today?

4. What four "peculiar institutions" does Wacquant discuss? According to him, what goals have these institutions served? How are these traditions linked? How have they changed over time?

5. As Wacquant sees it, although the ghetto once served as "a kind of ethno-racial prison," the prison now "functions as a judicial ghetto." What is the social organi-

zation of prison life? Of ghetto life? How have they changed in the last fifty years? How does race become a factor in prison culture?

6. How did the social and political changes of the 1960s contribute to "the ghettoization" of prisons? Can you explain the link between soaring incarceration rates in the black community and the positive achievements of the civil rights movement?

7. What is a "race making" institution? How does it differ from a racially biased institution? On the basis of Wacquant's description, do you think he appropriately characterizes today's prison system? Why or why not?

Reprinted from: Loïc Wacquant, "Deadly Symbiosis: Rethinking Race and Imprisonment in Twenty-First-Century America" in *The Boston Review,* "New Democracy Forum" on Crime and Punishment, 27:2, pp. 23–31. Copyright © 2002. Reprinted with the permission of Loïc Wacquant. ✦

Section XIV

The Death Penalty: Controlling Juries and Preventing Discrimination

Chapter 60

Furman v. Georgia

Death is the ultimate penal sanction, and it is controversial worldwide. Since World War II, moral concerns have led to the death penalty's abolition in many nations, but in 1998 there were still 1,625 official executions in 37 countries, 83 percent of which occurred in the People's Republic of China (1,067), the Democratic Republic of Congo (100), the United States (68), Iran (66), and Egypt (48). By 2003, 111 countries had abolished capital punishment. The European Court of Human Rights banned the death penalty in all nations within the Council of Europe, stating that it violated the European Convention of Human Rights. Other nations, such as the United Kingdom, have refused to extradite prisoners to the United States if they would face possible execution.

Today, proponents of capital punishment defend it by claiming that it is the only just and appropriate response to heinous crimes. Critics respond that it is never right for the state to take the life of one of its citizens and that the risk of executing an innocent person is serious enough that no one should be executed. These debates have occurred against a distinctive legal backdrop. The courts, interpreting the Eighth Amendment's prohibition of cruel and unusual punishment, have outlined the constitutional framework within which the government may, if it chooses, use capital punishment. That framework focuses in particular on two problems of social organization: the role of the jury and the question of whether capital punishment can be administered in a nondiscriminatory fashion.

In Furman v. Georgia, (1972), the U. S. Supreme Court struck down statutes that left to the complete discretion of juries the decision of whether a criminal convicted of a capital crime should be sentenced to death. It found that the death penalty was rarely imposed and that its use was arbitrary, capricious, and discriminatory. Some of the Justices were especially worried that race played an illegitimate role in the decisions that juries made: that juries were using their discretion to punish black offenders more harshly than whites who committed comparable crimes. Chief Justice Burger disagreed. In his view, the fact that capital punishment was rarely imposed was a testament to the scrupulousness of juries in exercising their responsibilities. Moreover, he accused his colleagues of abusing their own power by legislating from the bench.

"Death is different" because it is unusual in its severity and finality, and the Furman majority insisted that this kind of legal violence demands heightened standards of reliability. Unfettered jury discretion does not, in the Court's view, meet that standard.

How would we know if the exercise of jury discretion in capital cases were discriminatory? What does Justice Stewart mean when he says, "Death sentences are cruel and unusual in the same way that being struck by lightning is cruel and unusual"?

Petitioner in No. 69-5003 was convicted of murder in Georgia and was sentenced to death pursuant to Ga. Code Ann. § 26-1005 (Supp. 1971) (effective prior to July 1, 1969). 225 Ga. 253, 167 S. E. 2d 628 (1969). Petitioner in No. 69-5030 was convicted of rape in Georgia and was sentenced to death pursuant to Ga. Code Ann. § 26-1302 (Supp. 1971) (effective prior to July 1, 1969). 225 Ga. 790, 171 S. E. 2d 501 (1969). Petitioner in No. 69-5031 was convicted of rape in Texas and was sentenced to death pursuant to Tex. Penal Code, Art. 1189 (1961). 447 S. W. 2d 932 (Ct. Crim.

App. 1969). Certiorari was granted limited to the following question: "Does the imposition and carrying out of the death penalty in [these cases] constitute cruel and unusual punishment in violation of the Eighth and Fourteenth Amendments?" 403 U.S. 952 (1971). The Court holds that the imposition and carrying out of the death penalty in these cases constitute cruel and unusual punishment in violation of the Eighth and Fourteenth Amendments. The judgment in each case is therefore reversed insofar as it leaves undisturbed the death sentence imposed, and the cases are remanded for further proceedings.

So ordered. . . .

Mr. Justice Douglas, Concurring

In these three cases the death penalty was imposed, one of them for murder, and two for rape. In each the determination of whether the penalty should be death or a lighter punishment was left by the State to the discretion of the judge or of the jury. In each of the three cases the trial was to a jury. They are here on petitions for certiorari which we granted limited to the question whether the imposition and execution of the death penalty constitute "cruel and unusual punishment" within the meaning of the Eighth Amendment as applied to the States by the Fourteenth.[1] I vote to vacate each judgment, believing that the exaction of the death penalty does violate the Eighth and Fourteenth Amendments. . . .

There is increasing recognition of the fact that the basic theme of equal protection is implicit in "cruel and unusual" punishments. "A penalty . . .should be considered 'unusually' imposed if it is administered arbitrarily or discriminatorily."[2] The same authors add that "the extreme rarity with which applicable death penalty provisions are put to use raises a strong inference of arbitrariness."[3] The President's Commission on Law Enforcement and Administration of Justice recently concluded:[4]

"Finally there is evidence that the imposition of the death sentence and the exercise of dispensing power by the courts and the executive follow discriminatory patterns. The death sentence is disproportionately imposed and carried out on the poor, the Negro, and the members of unpopular groups."

A study of capital cases in Texas from 1924 to 1968 reached the following conclusions:[5]

"Application of the death penalty is unequal: most of those executed were poor, young, and ignorant.

"Seventy-five of the 460 cases involved codefendants, who, under Texas law, were given separate trials. In several instances where a white and a Negro were co-defendants, the white was sentenced to life imprisonment or a term of years, and the Negro was given the death penalty.

"Another ethnic disparity is found in the type of sentence imposed for rape. The Negro convicted of rape is far more likely to get the death penalty than a term sentence, whereas whites and Latins are far more likely to get a term sentence than the death penalty."

Warden Lewis E. Lawes of Sing Sing said:[6]

"Not only does capital punishment fail in its justification, but no punishment could be invented with so many inherent defects. It is an unequal punishment in the way it is applied to the rich and to the poor. The defendant of wealth and position never goes to the electric chair or to the gallows. Juries do not intentionally favour the rich, the law is theoretically impartial, but the defendant with ample means is able to have his case presented with every favourable aspect, while the poor defendant often has a lawyer assigned by the court. Sometimes such assignment is considered part of political patronage; usually the lawyer assigned has had no experience whatever in a capital case."

Former Attorney General Ramsey Clark has said, "It is the poor, the sick, the ignorant, the powerless and the hated who are executed."[7] One searches our chronicles in vain for the execution of any member of the affluent strata of this society. The Leopolds and Loebs are given prison terms, not sentenced to death.

Jackson, a black, convicted of the rape of a white woman, was 21 years old. A court-appointed psychiatrist said that Jackson was of average education and average intelligence, that he was not an imbecile, or schizophrenic, or psychotic, that his traits were the product of environmental influences, and that he was competent to stand trial. Jackson had entered the house after the husband left for work. He held scissors against the neck of the wife, demanding money. She could find none and a struggle ensued for the scissors, a battle which she lost; and she was then raped, Jackson keeping the scissors pressed against her neck. While there did not appear to be any long-term traumatic impact on the victim, she was bruised and abrased in the struggle but was not hospitalized. Jackson was a convict who had escaped from a work gang in the area, a result of a three-year sentence for auto theft. He was at large for three days and during that time had committed several other offenses—burglary, auto theft, and assault and battery.

Furman, a black, killed a householder while seeking to enter the home at night. Furman shot the deceased through a closed door. He was 26 years old and had finished the sixth grade in school. Pending trial, he was committed to the Georgia Central State Hospital for a psychiatric examination on his plea of insanity tendered by court-appointed counsel. The superintendent reported that a unanimous staff diagnostic conference had concluded "that this patient should retain his present diagnosis of Mental Deficiency, Mild to Moderate, with Psychotic Episodes associated with Convulsive Disorder." The physi-

cians agreed that "at present the patient is not psychotic, but he is not capable of cooperating with his counsel in the preparation of his defense"; and the staff believed "that he is in need of further psychiatric hospitalization and treatment."

Later, the superintendent reported that the staff diagnosis was Mental Deficiency, Mild to Moderate, with Psychotic Episodes associated with Convulsive Disorder. He concluded, however, that Furman was "not psychotic at present, knows right from wrong and is able to cooperate with his counsel in preparing his defense."

Branch, a black, entered the rural home of a 65-year-old widow, a white, while she slept and raped her, holding his arm against her throat. Thereupon he demanded money and for 30 minutes or more the widow searched for money, finding little. As he left, Jackson said if the widow told anyone what happened, he would return and kill her. The record is barren of any medical or psychiatric evidence showing injury to her as a result of Branch's attack.

He had previously been convicted of felony theft and found to be a borderline mental deficient and well below the average IQ of Texas prison inmates. He had the equivalent of five and a half years of grade school education. He had a "dull intelligence" and was in the lowest fourth percentile of his class.

We cannot say from facts disclosed in these records that these defendants were sentenced to death because they were black. Yet our task is not restricted to an effort to divine what motives impelled these death penalties. Rather, we deal with a system of law and of justice that leaves to the uncontrolled discretion of judges or juries the determination whether defendants committing these crimes should die or be imprisoned. Under these laws no standards govern the selection of the penalty. People live or die, dependent on the whim of one man or of 12. . . .

In a Nation committed to equal protection of the laws there is no permissible "caste" aspect[8] of law enforcement. Yet we know that the discretion of judges and juries in imposing the death penalty enables the penalty to be selectively applied, feeding prejudices against the accused if he is poor and despised, and lacking political clout, or if he is a member of a suspect or unpopular minority, and saving those who by social position may be in a more protected position. In ancient Hindu law a Brahman was exempt from capital punishment,[9] and under that law, "generally, in the law books, punishment increased in severity as social status diminished."[10] We have, I fear, taken in practice the same position, partially as a result of making the death penalty discretionary and partially as a result of the ability of the rich to purchase the services of the most respected and most resourceful legal talent in the Nation.

The high service rendered by the "cruel and unusual" punishment clause of the Eighth Amendment is to require legislatures to write penal laws that are evenhanded, nonselective, and nonarbitrary, and to require judges to see to it that general laws are not applied sparsely, selectively, and spottily to unpopular groups.

A law that stated that anyone making more than $50,000 would be exempt from the death penalty would plainly fall, as would a law that in terms said that blacks, those who never went beyond the fifth grade in school, those who made less than $3,000 a year, or those who were unpopular or unstable should be the only people executed. A law which in the overall view reaches that result in practice[11] has no more sanctity than a law which in terms provides the same.

Thus, these discretionary statutes are unconstitutional in their operation. They are pregnant with discrimination and discrimination is an ingredient not compatible with the idea of equal protection of the laws that is implicit in the ban on "cruel and unusual" punishments.

Any law which is nondiscriminatory on its face may be applied in such a way as to violate the Equal Protection Clause of the Fourteenth Amendment. *Yick Wo v. Hopkins,* 118 U.S. 356. Such conceivably might be the fate of a mandatory death penalty, where equal or lesser sentences were imposed on the elite, a harsher one on the minorities or members of the lower castes. Whether a mandatory death penalty would otherwise be constitutional is a question I do not reach.

I concur in the judgments of the Court....

MR. JUSTICE STEWART, CONCURRING

The penalty of death differs from all other forms of criminal punishment, not in degree but in kind. It is unique in its total irrevocability. It is unique in its rejection of rehabilitation of the convict as a basic purpose of criminal justice. And it is unique, finally, in its absolute renunciation of all that is embodied in our concept of humanity.

For these and other reasons, at least two of my Brothers have concluded that the infliction of the death penalty is constitutionally impermissible in all circumstances under the Eighth and Fourteenth Amendments. Their case is a strong one. But I find it unnecessary to reach the ultimate question they would decide. ...

The opinions of other Justices today have set out in admirable and thorough detail the origins and judicial history of the Eighth Amendment's guarantee against the infliction of cruel and unusual punishments, and the origin and judicial history of capital punishment. There is thus no need for me to review the historical materials here, and what I have to say can, therefore, be briefly stated.

Legislatures—state and federal—have sometimes specified that the penalty of death shall be the mandatory punishment for every person convicted of engaging in certain designated criminal conduct. Congress, for example, has provided that anyone convicted of acting as a spy for the enemy in time of war shall be put to death. The Rhode Island Legislature has ordained the death penalty for a life term prisoner who commits murder. Massachusetts has passed a law imposing the death penalty upon anyone convicted of murder in the commission of a forcible rape. An Ohio law imposes the mandatory penalty of death upon the assassin of the President of the United States or the Governor of a State.

If we were reviewing death sentences imposed under these or similar laws, we would be faced with the need to decide whether capital punishment is unconstitutional for all crimes and under all circumstances. We would need to decide whether a legislature—state or federal—could constitutionally determine that certain criminal conduct is so atrocious that society's interest in deterrence and retribution wholly outweighs any considerations of reform or rehabilitation of the perpetrator, and that, despite the inconclusive empirical evidence,[12] only the automatic penalty of death will provide maximum deterrence.

On that score I would say only that I cannot agree that retribution is a constitutionally impermissible ingredient in the imposition of punishment. The instinct for retribution is part of the nature of man, and channeling that instinct in the administration of criminal justice serves an important purpose in promoting the stability of a society governed by law. When people begin to believe that organized society is unwilling or unable to impose upon criminal offenders the punishment they "deserve," then there are sown the seeds of anarchy—of self-help, vigilante justice, and lynch law.

The constitutionality of capital punishment in the abstract is not, however, before us in these cases. For the Georgia and Texas Legislatures have not provided that the death penalty shall be imposed upon all those who are found guilty of forcible rape.[13] And the Georgia Legislature has not ordained that death shall be the automatic punishment for murder.[14] In a word, neither State has made a legislative determination that forcible rape and murder can be deterred only by imposing the penalty of death upon all who perpetrate those offenses. As MR. JUSTICE WHITE so tellingly puts it, the "legislative will is not frus-

trated if the penalty is never imposed." Post, at 311.

Instead, the death sentences now before us are the product of a legal system that brings them, I believe, within the very core of the Eighth Amendment's guarantee against cruel and unusual punishments, a guarantee applicable against the States through the Fourteenth Amendment. *Robinson v. California*, 370 U.S. 660. In the first place, it is clear that these sentences are "cruel" in the sense that they excessively go beyond, not in degree but in kind, the punishments that the state legislatures have determined to be necessary. *Weems v. United States*, 217 U.S. 349. In the second place, it is equally clear that these sentences are "unusual" in the sense that the penalty of death is infrequently imposed for murder, and that its imposition for rape is extraordinarily rare. But I do not rest my conclusion upon these two propositions alone.

These death sentences are cruel and unusual in the same way that being struck by lightning is cruel and unusual. For, of all the people convicted of rapes and murders in 1967 and 1968,[15] many just as reprehensible as these, the petitioners are among a capriciously selected random handful upon whom the sentence of death has in fact been imposed. My concurring Brothers have demonstrated that, if any basis can be discerned for the selection of these few to be sentenced to die, it is the constitutionally impermissible basis of race. See *McLaughlin v. Florida*, 379 U.S. 184. But racial discrimination has not been proved, and I put it to one side. I simply conclude that the Eighth and Fourteenth Amendments cannot tolerate the infliction of a sentence of death under legal systems that permit this unique penalty to be so wantonly and so freakishly imposed.

For these reasons I concur in the judgments of the Court. . . .

MR. CHIEF JUSTICE BURGER, WITH WHOM MR. JUSTICE BLACKMUN, MR. JUSTICE

POWELL, AND MR. JUSTICE REHNQUIST
JOIN, DISSENTING

If we were possessed of legislative power, I would either join with MR. JUSTICE BRENNAN and MR. JUSTICE MARSHALL or, at the very least, restrict the use of capital punishment to a small category of the most heinous crimes. Our constitutional inquiry, however, must be divorced from personal feelings as to the morality and efficacy of the death penalty, and be confined to the meaning and applicability of the uncertain language of the Eighth Amendment. There is no novelty in being called upon to interpret a constitutional provision that is less than self-defining, but, of all our fundamental guarantees, the ban on "cruel and unusual punishments" is one of the most difficult to translate into judicially manageable terms. The widely divergent views of the Amendment expressed in today's opinions reveal the haze that surrounds this constitutional command. Yet it is essential to our role as a court that we not seize upon the enigmatic character of the guarantee as an invitation to enact our personal predilections into law.

Although the Eighth Amendment literally reads as prohibiting only those punishments that are both "cruel" and "unusual," history compels the conclusion that the Constitution prohibits all punishments of extreme and barbarous cruelty, regardless of how frequently or infrequently imposed. . . .

I do not suggest that the presence of the word "unusual" in the Eighth Amendment is merely vestigial, having no relevance to the constitutionality of any punishment that might be devised. But where, as here, we consider a punishment well known to history, and clearly authorized by legislative enactment, it disregards the history of the Eighth Amendment and all the judicial comment that has followed to rely on the term "unusual" as affecting the outcome of these cases. Instead, I view these cases as turning on the single question whether capital punishment is "cruel" in the constitutional sense. The term

"unusual" cannot be read as limiting the ban on "cruel" punishments or as somehow expanding the meaning of the term "cruel." For this reason I am unpersuaded by the facile argument that since capital punishment has always been cruel in the everyday sense of the word, and has become unusual due to decreased use, it is, therefore, now "cruel and unusual."

II

Counsel for petitioners properly concede that capital punishment was not impermissibly cruel at the time of the adoption of the Eighth Amendment. Not only do the records of the debates indicate that the Founding Fathers were limited in their concern to the prevention of torture, but it is also clear from the language of the Constitution itself that there was no thought whatever of the elimination of capital punishment. The opening sentence of the Fifth Amendment is a guarantee that the death penalty not be imposed "unless on a presentment or indictment of a Grand Jury." The Double Jeopardy Clause of the Fifth Amendment is a prohibition against being "twice put in jeopardy of life" for the same offense. Similarly, the Due Process Clause commands "due process of law" before an accused can be "deprived of life, liberty, or property." Thus, the explicit language of the Constitution affirmatively acknowledges the legal power to impose capital punishment; it does not expressly or by implication acknowledge the legal power to impose any of the various punishments that have been banned as cruel since 1791. Since the Eighth Amendment was adopted on the same day in 1791 as the Fifth Amendment, it hardly needs more to establish that the death penalty was not "cruel" in the constitutional sense at that time.

In the 181 years since the enactment of the Eighth Amendment, not a single decision of this Court has cast the slightest shadow of a doubt on the constitutionality of capital punishment. . . .

The Court's quiescence in this area can be attributed to the fact that in a democratic society legislatures, not courts, are constituted to respond to the will and consequently the moral values of the people. For this reason, early commentators suggested that the "cruel and unusual punishments" clause was an unnecessary constitutional provision.[16] As acknowledged in the principal brief for petitioners, "both in constitutional contemplation and in fact, it is the legislature, not the Court, which responds to public opinion and immediately reflects the society's standards of decency."[17]

Accordingly, punishments such as branding and the cutting off of ears, which were commonplace at the time of the adoption of the Constitution, passed from the penal scene without judicial intervention because they became basically offensive to the people and the legislatures responded to this sentiment.

There are no obvious indications that capital punishment offends the conscience of society to such a degree that our traditional deference to the legislative judgment must be abandoned. It is not a punishment such as burning at the stake that everyone would ineffably find to be repugnant to all civilized standards. Nor is it a punishment so roundly condemned that only a few aberrant legislatures have retained it on the statute books. Capital punishment is authorized by statute in 40 States, the District of Columbia, and in the federal courts for the commission of certain crimes. On four occasions in the last 11 years Congress has added to the list of federal crimes punishable by death. In looking for reliable indicia of contemporary attitude, none more trustworthy has been advanced. . . .

The selectivity of juries in imposing the punishment of death is properly viewed as a refinement on, rather than a repudiation of, the statutory authorization for that penalty. Legislatures prescribe the categories of crimes for which the death penalty should be available, and, acting as "the conscience of the community," juries are entrusted to determine in individual cases that the ultimate punishment is warranted. Juries are undoubtedly influenced in this judgment by myriad factors. The motive or lack of motive of the perpetrator, the degree of injury or suffering of the victim or victims, and the degree of brutality in the commission of the crime would seem to be prominent among these actors. Given the general awareness that death is no longer a routine punishment for the crimes for which it is made available, it is hardly surprising that juries have been increasingly meticulous in their imposition of the penalty. But to assume from the mere fact of relative infrequency that only a random assortment of pariahs are sentenced to death, is to cast grave doubt on the basic integrity of our jury system.

It would, of course, be unrealistic to assume that juries have been perfectly consistent in choosing the cases where the death penalty is to be imposed, for no human institution performs with perfect consistency. There are doubtless prisoners on death row who would not be there had they been tried before a different jury or in a different State. In this sense their fate has been controlled by a fortuitous circumstance. However, this element of fortuity does not stand as an indictment either of the general functioning of juries in capital cases or of the integrity of jury decisions in individual cases. There is no empirical basis for concluding that juries have generally failed to discharge in good faith the responsibility described in *Witherspoon*—that of choosing between life and death in individual cases according to the dictates of community values.[18] . . .

Today the Court has not ruled that capital punishment is *per se* violative of the Eighth Amendment; nor has it ruled that the punishment is barred for any particular class or classes of crimes. The substantially similar concurring opinions of MR. JUSTICE STEWART and MR. JUSTICE WHITE, which are necessary to support the judgment setting aside petitioners' sentences, stop short of reaching the ultimate question. The actual scope of the Court's ruling, which I take to be embodied in these concurring opinions, is not entirely clear. This much, however, seems apparent: if the legislatures are to continue to authorize capital punishment for some crimes, juries and judges can no longer be permitted to make the sentencing determination in the same manner they have in the past.[19] This approach—not urged in oral arguments or briefs—misconceives the nature of the constitutional command against "cruel and unusual punishments," disregards controlling case law, and demands a rigidity in capital cases which, if possible of achievement, cannot be regarded as a welcome change. Indeed the contrary seems to be the case.

As I have earlier stated, the Eighth Amendment forbids the imposition of punishments that are so cruel and inhumane as to violate society's standards of civilized conduct. The Amendment does not prohibit all punishments the States are unable to prove necessary to deter or control crime. The Amendment is not concerned with the process by which a State determines that a particular punishment is to be imposed in a particular case. And the Amendment most assuredly does not speak to the power of legislatures to confer sentencing discretion on juries, rather than to fix all sentences by statute.

The critical factor in the concurring opinions of both MR. JUSTICE STEWART and MR. JUSTICE WHITE is the infrequency with which the penalty is imposed. This factor is taken not as evidence of society's abhorrence of capital punishment—the inference that petitioners would have the Court draw—but as the earmark of a deteriorated system of sentencing. It is concluded that petitioners' sentences must be set aside, not because the punishment is impermissibly cruel, but because juries and judges have failed to exercise their sentencing discretion in acceptable fashion.

To be sure, there is a recitation cast in Eighth Amendment terms: petitioners' sentences are "cruel" because they exceed that which the legislatures have deemed necessary for all cases; petitioners' sentences are "unusual" because they exceed that which is imposed in most cases. This application of the words of the Eighth Amendment suggests that capital punishment can be made to satisfy Eighth Amendment values if its rate of imposition is somehow multiplied; it seemingly follows that the flexible sentencing system created by the legislatures, and carried out by juries and judges, has yielded more mercy than the Eighth Amendment can stand. The implications of this approach are mildly ironical. For example, by this measure of the Eighth Amendment, the elimination of death-qualified juries in *Witherspoon v. Illinois,* 391 U.S. 510 (1968), can only be seen in retrospect as a setback to "the evolving standards of decency that mark the progress of a maturing society." *Trop v. Dulles,* 356 U.S., at 101.

This novel formulation of Eighth Amendment principles—albeit necessary to satisfy the terms of our limited grant of certiorari—does not lie at the heart of these concurring opinions. The decisive grievance of the opinions—not translated into Eighth Amendment terms—is that the present system of discretionary sentencing in capital cases has failed to produce evenhanded justice; the problem is not that too few have been sentenced to die, but that the selection process has followed no rational pattern. This claim of arbitrariness is not only lacking in empirical support, but also it manifestly fails to establish that the death penalty is a "cruel and unusual" punishment. The Eighth Amendment was included in the Bill of Rights to assure that certain types of punishments would never be imposed, not to channelize the sentencing process. The approach of these concurring opinions has no antecedent in the Eighth Amendment cases. It is essentially and exclusively a procedural due process argument.

This ground of decision is plainly foreclosed as well as misplaced. . . .

It seems remarkable to me that with our basic trust in lay jurors as the keystone in our system of criminal justice, it should now be suggested that we take the most sensitive and important of all decisions away from them. I could more easily be persuaded that mandatory sentences of death, without the intervening and ameliorating impact of lay jurors, are so arbitrary and doctrinaire that they violate the Constitution. The very infrequency of death penalties imposed by jurors attests their cautious and discriminating reservation of that penalty for the most extreme cases. I had thought that nothing was clearer in history, as we noted in *McGautha* one year ago, than the American abhorrence of "the common-law rule imposing a mandatory death sentence on all convicted murderers." 402 U.S., at 198. As the concurring opinion of MR. JUSTICE MARSHALL shows, ante, at 339, the 19th century movement away from mandatory death sentences marked an enlightened introduction of flexibility into the sentencing process. It recognized that individual culpability is not always measured by the category of the crime committed. This change in sentencing practice was greeted by the Court as a humanizing development. See *Winston v. United States,* 172 U.S. 303 (1899); *cf. Calton v. Utah,* 130 U.S. 83 (1889). See also *Andres v. United States,* 333 U.S. 740, 753 (1948) (Frankfurter, J., concurring). I do not see how this history can be ignored and how it can be suggested that the Eighth Amendment demands the elimination of the most sensitive feature of the sentencing system.

As a general matter, the evolution of penal concepts in this country has not been marked by great progress, nor have the results up to now been crowned with significant success. If anywhere in the whole spectrum of criminal justice fresh ideas deserve sober analysis, the sentencing and correctional area ranks high on the list. But it has been widely accepted that mandatory sentences for crimes do not best serve the ends of the criminal justice system. Now, after the long process of drawing away from the blind imposition of uniform sentences for every person convicted of a particular offense, we are confronted with an argument perhaps implying that only the legislatures may determine that a sentence of death is appropriate, without the intervening evaluation of jurors or judges. This approach threatens to turn back the progress of penal reform, which has moved until recently at too slow a rate to absorb significant setbacks. . . .

Notes

1. The opinion of the Supreme Court of Georgia affirming Furman's conviction of murder and sentence of death is reported in 225 Ga. 253, 167 S. E. 2d 628, and its opinion affirming Jackson's conviction of rape and sentence of death is reported in 225 Ga. 790, 171 S. E. 2d 501. The conviction of Branch of rape and the sentence of death were affirmed by the Court of Criminal Appeals of Texas and reported in 447 S. W. 2d 932.

2. Goldberg & Dershowitz, Declaring the Death Penalty Unconstitutional, 83 Harv. L. Rev. 1773, 1790.

3. Id., at 1792.

4. The Challenge of Crime in a Free Society 143 (1967).

5. Koeninger, Capital Punishment in Texas, 1924–1968, 15 Crime & Delin. 132, 141 (1969).

6. Life and Death in Sing Sing 155–160 (1928).

7. Crime in America 335 (1970).

8. See Johnson, The Negro and Crime, 217 Annals 93 (1941).

9. See J. Spellman, Political Theory of Ancient India 112 (1964).

10. C. Drekmeier, Kingship and Community in Early India 233 (1962).

11. Cf. B. Prettyman, Jr., Death and The Supreme Court 296–297 (1961).

    The disparity of representation in capital cases raises doubts about capital punishment itself, which has been abolished in only nine states. If a James Avery [345 U.S. 559] can be saved from electrocution because his attorney made timely objection to the selection of a jury by the use of yellow and white tickets, while an Aubry Williams [349 U.S. 375] can be sent to his death by a jury selected in precisely the same manner, we are imposing our most extreme penalty in an uneven fashion.

The problem of proper representation is not a problem of money, as some have claimed, but of a lawyer's ability, and it is not true that only the rich have able lawyers. Both the rich and the poor usually are well represented—the poor because more often than not the best attorneys are appointed to defend them. It is the middle-class defendant, who can afford to hire an attorney but not a very good one, who is at a disadvantage. Certainly William Fikes [352 U.S. 191], despite the anomalous position in which he finds himself today, received as effective and intelligent a defense from his court-appointed attorneys as he would have received from an attorney his family had scraped together enough money to hire.

"And it is not only a matter of ability. An attorney must be found who is prepared to spend precious hours—the basic commodity he has to sell—on a case that seldom fully compensates him and often brings him no fee at all. The public has no conception of the time and effort devoted by attorneys to indigent cases. And in a first-degree case, the added responsibility of having a man's life depend upon the outcome exacts a heavy toll."

12. Many statistical studies—comparing crime rates in jurisdictions with and without capital punishment and in jurisdictions before and after abolition of capital punishment—have indicated that there is little, if any, measurable deterrent effect. See H. Bedau, The Death Penalty in America 258–332 (1967 rev. ed.). There remains uncertainty, however, because of the difficulty of identifying and holding constant all other relevant variables. See Comment, The Death Penalty Cases, 56 Calif. L. Rev. 1268, 1275-1292. See also dissenting opinion of THE CHIEF JUSTICE, post, at 395; concurring opinion of MR. JUSTICE MARSHALL, post, at 346–354.

13. Georgia law, at the time of the conviction and sentencing of the petitioner in No. 69-5030, left the jury a choice between the death penalty, life imprisonment, or "imprisonment and labor in the penitentiary for not less than one year nor more than 20 years." Ga. Code Ann. § 26-1302 (Supp. 1971) (effective prior to July 1, 1969). The current Georgia provision for the punishment of forcible rape continues to leave the same broad sentencing leeway. Ga. Crim. Code § 26-2001 (1971 rev.) (effective July 1, 1969). Texas law, under which the petitioner in No. 69-5031 was sentenced, provides that a "person guilty of rape shall be punished by death or by confinement in the penitentiary for life, or for any term of years not less than five." Texas Penal Code, Art. 1189.

14. Georgia law, under which the petitioner in No. 69-5003, was sentenced, left the jury a choice between the death penalty and life imprisonment. Ga. Code Ann. § 26-1005 (Supp. 1971) (effective prior to July 1, 1969). Current Georgia law provides for similar sentencing leeway. Ga. Crim. Code § 26-1101 (1971 rev.) (effective July 1, 1969).

15. Petitioner Branch was sentenced to death in a Texas court on July 26, 1967. Petitioner Furman was sentenced to death in a Georgia court on September 29, 1968. Petitioner Jackson was sentenced to death in Georgia court on December 10, 1968.

16. See 2 J. Story, On the Constitution § 1903 (5th ed. 1891); 1 T. Cooley, Constitutional Limitations 694 (8th ed. 1927). See also Joseph Story on Capital Punishment (ed. by J. Hogan), 43 Calif. L. Rev. 76 (1955).

17. Brief for Petitioner in *Aikens v. California*, No. 68-5027, p. 19 (cert. dismissed, 406 U.S. 813 (1972)). See post, at 443 n. 38. This, plainly, was the foundation of Mr. Justice Black's strong views on this subject expressed most recently in *McGautha v. California*, 402 U.S. 183, 226 (1971) (separate opinion).

18. Counsel for petitioners make the conclusory statement that "those who are selected to die are the poor and powerless, personally ugly and socially unacceptable." Brief for Petitioner in No. 68-5027, p. 51. However, the sources cited contain no empirical findings to undermine the general premise that juries impose the death penalty in the most extreme cases. One study has discerned a statistically noticeable difference between the rate of imposition on blue collar and white collar defendants; the study otherwise concludes that juries do follow rational patterns in imposing the sentence of death. Note, A Study of the California Penalty Jury in First-Degree-Murder Cases, 21 Stan. L. Rev. 1297 (1969). See also H. Kalven & H. Zeisel, The American Jury 434-449 (1966).

   Statistics are also cited to show that the death penalty has been imposed in a racially discriminatory manner. Such statistics suggest, at least as a historical matter, that Negroes have been sentenced to death with greater frequency than whites in several States, particularly for the crime of interracial rape. See, e. g., Koeninger, Capital Punishment in Texas, 1924–1968, 15 Crime & Delin. 132 (1969); Note, Capital Punishment in Virginia, 58 Va. L. Rev. 97 (1972). If a statute that authorizes the discretionary imposition of a particular penalty for a particular crime is used primarily against defendants of a certain race, and if the pattern of use can be fairly explained only by reference to the race of the defendants, the Equal Protection Clause of the Fourteenth Amendment forbids continued enforcement of that statute in its existing form. Cf. *Yick Wo v. Hopkins,* 118 U.S. 356 (1886); *Gomillion v. Lightfoot,* 364 U.S. 339 (1960).

   To establish that the statutory authorization for a particular penalty is inconsistent with the dictates of the Equal Protection Clause, it is not enough to show how it was applied in the distant past. The statistics that have been referred to us cover periods when Negroes were systematically excluded from jury service and when racial segregation was the official policy in many States. Data of more recent vintage are essential. See *Maxwell v. Bishop,* 398 F.2d 138, 148 (CA8 1968), vacated, 398 U.S. 262 (1970). While no statisti-cal survey could be expected to bring forth absolute and irrefutable proof of a discriminatory pattern of imposition, a strong showing would have to be made, taking all relevant factors into account.

   It must be noted that any equal protection claim is totally distinct from the Eighth Amendment question to which our grant of certiorari was limited in these cases. Evidence of a discriminatory pattern of enforcement does not imply that any use of a particular punishment is so morally repugnant as to violate the Eighth Amendment.

19. Much in the concurring opinion of MR. JUSTICE DOUGLAS similarly suggests that it is the sentencing system rather than the punishment itself that is constitutionally infirm. However, the opinion also indicates that in the wake of the Court's decision in *McGautha v. California,* 402 U.S. 183 (1971), the validity of the sentencing process is no longer open to question.

Notes and Questions

1. How does the court define "cruel and unusual" punishment? What does the Equal Protection Clause have to do with cruel and unusual punishment?

2. According to Justice Douglas, why is jury discretion problematic in death penalty cases?

3. According to Justice Douglas, is the death penalty ever constitutionally permissible? What evidence does he use to support his position?

4. Douglas cites a Texas study that found, "the application of the death penalty is unequal: most of those executed were poor, young, and ignorant." How would MacDonald (Chapter 51) respond to this finding? Does the study offer sound proof that the death penalty constitutes unusual punishment?

5. Why, in the opinion of Justice Stewart, does the death penalty deserve more scrupulous consideration than, say, life

imprisonment? What is unique about capital punishment? Do you agree that the unique nature of capital punishment qualifies it for special Constitutional consideration? Why or why not?

6. Why does Justice Burger accuse his colleagues of legislating from the bench? Do you agree with Burger's accusation? Justice Burger insists in his dissent, "Our constitutional inquiry must be divorced from personal feelings as to the morality and efficacy of the death penalty, and be confined to the meaning and applicability of the uncertain language of the Eighth Amendment." Can the Eighth Amendment be interpreted *without* taking into consideration issues of "morality and efficacy" in the application of punishment?

7. How does Justice Burger approach the question of "cruel and unusual punishment"? What historical arguments does he invoke to support his position? How is the Due Process Clause relevant to *Furman,* according to Justice Burger? Do you agree?

8. What does Justice Burger say about the discretionary power of juries in capital cases? Does he adequately address the race- and class-based discrimination concerns and/or questions of arbitrary application raised by Justices Stewart and Douglas?

9. On the basis of what you have read in other sections, does the ruling in *Furman* actually help to eliminate discriminatory application of the death penalty? Beyond the jury box, where else in the legal system does race become a factor in deciding who gets the death penalty?

Reprinted from: *Furman v. Georgia,* 408 U.S. 238 (1972). ✦

Chapter 61

Gregg v. Georgia

After Furman, *most states quickly reenacted their death penalty statutes to bring them into compliance with the Supreme Court's decision. Some chose to eliminate jury discretion completely, that is, to make the death penalty mandatory for persons convicted of capital crimes. Others tried to find ways to limit and guide jury discretion without eliminating it.*

Four years after Furman, *the Supreme Court reviewed these efforts and revisited the question of the constitutionality of the death penalty. Lest there have been any lingering doubt after* Furman, *the Court stated unequivocally that the death penalty was constitutional. Siding with the proponents of capital punishment, the Court found that the death penalty served important purposes.*

The only question was under what kind of statute death could be administered fairly and in a way that reflected contemporary standards of decency. The Court invalidated statutes that imposed the death penalty in all capital cases, but it upheld a statute limiting and guiding jury discretion by requiring juries to find one or more statutory aggravating factors before it could impose a death sentence. "Guided discretion" was found sufficient to eliminate the arbitrariness and risk of discrimination that had been problematic in Furman. *Since 1976, notable changes have occurred in the Court's capital punishment jurisprudence, yet the framework outlined in* Gregg *still provides the basic structure of legal control over the death penalty.*

As you read Gregg, *consider whether once a jury in a capital case finds a criminal to be death-eligible by virtue of having committed a crime that qualifies for capital punishment under one of the aggravating factors, how is their exercise of discretion different than it would have been under the laws struck down in* Furman?

I

Judgment of the Court, and opinion of Mr. Justice Stewart, Mr. Justice Powell, and Mr. Justice Stevens, announced by Mr. Justice Stewart.

The issue in this case is whether the imposition of the sentence of death for the crime of murder under the law of Georgia violates the Eighth and Fourteenth Amendments.

The petitioner, Troy Gregg, was charged with committing armed robbery and murder. In accordance with Georgia procedure in capital cases, the trial was in two stages, a guilt stage and a sentencing stage. The evidence at the guilt trial established that on November 21, 1973, the petitioner and a traveling companion, Floyd Allen, while hitchhiking north in Florida were picked up by Fred Simmons and Bob Moore. Their car broke down, but they continued north after Simmons purchased another vehicle with some of the cash he was carrying. While still in Florida, they picked up another hitchhiker, Dennis Weaver, who rode with them to Atlanta, where he was let out about 11 p.m. A short time later the four men interrupted their journey for a rest stop along the highway. The next morning the bodies of Simmons and Moore were discovered in a ditch nearby.

On November 23, after reading about the shootings in an Atlanta newspaper, Weaver communicated with the Gwinnett County police and related information concerning the journey with the victims, including a description of the car. The next afternoon, the petitioner and Allen, while in Simmons' car, were arrested in Asheville, N.C. In the search incident to the arrest a .25-caliber pistol, later shown to be that used to kill Simmons and Moore, was found in the petitioner's pocket. After receiving the warnings required by *Miranda v. Arizona,* 384 U.S. 436 (1966), and signing a written waiver of his rights, the petitioner signed a statement in which he admitted shooting, then robbing Simmons and Moore. He justified the slayings on grounds of self-defense. The next day, while being transferred to Lawrenceville, Ga., the petitioner and Allen were taken to the scene of the shootings. Upon arriving there, Allen recounted the events leading to the slayings. His version of these events was as follows: After Simmons and Moore left the car, the petitioner stated that he intended to rob them. The petitioner then took his pistol in hand and positioned himself on the car to improve his aim. As Simmons and Moore came up an embankment toward the car, the petitioner fired three shots and the two men fell near a ditch. The petitioner, at close range, then fired a shot into the head of each. He robbed them of valuables and drove away with Allen.

A medical examiner testified that Simmons died from a bullet wound in the eye and that Moore died from bullet wounds in the cheek and in the back of the head. He further testified that both men had several bruises and abrasions about the face and head which probably were sustained either from the fall into the ditch or from being dragged or pushed along the embankment. Although Allen did not testify, a police detective recounted the substance of Allen's statements about the slayings and indicated that directly after Allen had made these statements the petitioner had admitted that Allen's account was accurate. The petitioner testified in his own defense. He confirmed that Allen had made the statements described by the detective, but denied their truth or ever having admitted to their accuracy. He indicated that he had shot Simmons and Moore because of fear and in self-defense, testifying they had attacked Allen and him, one wielding a pipe and the other a knife.

The trial judge submitted the murder charges to the jury on both felony-murder and nonfelony-murder theories. He also instructed on the issue of self-defense but declined to instruct on manslaughter. He submitted the robbery case to the jury on both an armed-robbery theory and on the lesser included offense of robbery by intimidation. The jury found the petitioner guilty of two counts of armed robbery and two counts of murder.

At the penalty stage, which took place before the same jury, neither the prosecutor nor the petitioner's lawyer offered any additional evidence. Both counsel, however, made lengthy arguments dealing generally with the propriety of capital punishment under the circumstances and with the weight of the evidence of guilt. The trial judge instructed the jury that it could recommend either a death sentence or a life prison sentence on each count. The judge further charged the jury that in determining what sentence was appropriate the jury was free to consider the facts and circumstances, if any, presented by the parties in mitigation or aggravation.

Finally, the judge instructed the jury that it "would not be authorized to consider [imposing] the penalty of death" unless it first found beyond a reasonable doubt one of these aggravating circumstances:

> One—That the offense of murder was committed while the offender was engaged in the commission of two other capital felonies, to-wit the armed robbery of [Simmons and Moore].
>
> Two—That the offender committed the offense of murder for the purpose of receiving money and the automobile described in the indictment.
>
> Three—The offense of murder was outrageously and wantonly vile, horrible and inhuman, in that they [*sic*] involved the depravity of [the] mind of the defendant." Tr. 476–477.

Finding the first and second of these circumstances, the jury returned verdicts of death on each count.

The Supreme Court of Georgia affirmed the convictions and the imposition of the death sentences for murder. . . .

We granted the petitioner's application for a writ of certiorari limited to his challenge to the imposition of the death sentences in this case as "cruel and unusual" punishment in violation of the Eighth and the Fourteenth Amendments. 423 U.S. 1082 (1976).

II

Before considering the issues presented it is necessary to understand the Georgia statutory scheme for the imposition of the death penalty.[1] The Georgia statute, as amended after our decision in *Furman v. Georgia*, 408 U.S. 238 (1972), retains the death penalty for six categories of crime: murder, kidnapping for ransom or where the victim is harmed, armed robbery,[2] rape, treason, and aircraft hijacking.[3] Ga. Code Ann. §§ 26-1101, 26-1311, 26-1902, 26-2001, 26-2201, 26-301 (1972). The capital defendant's guilt or innocence is determined in the traditional manner, either by a trial judge or a jury, in the first stage of a bifurcated trial.

If trial is by jury, the trial judge is required to charge lesser included offenses when they are supported by any view of the evidence. *Sims v. State*, 203 Ga. 668, 47 S.E. 2d 862 (1948). See *Linder v. State*, 132 Ga. App. 624, 625, 208 S.E. 2d 630, 631 (1974). After a verdict, finding, or plea of guilty to a capital crime, a presentence hearing is conducted before whoever made the determination of guilt. The sentencing procedures are essentially the same in both bench and jury trials. At the hearing:

"[T]he judge [or jury] shall hear additional evidence in extenuation, mitigation, and aggravation of punishment, including the record of any prior criminal convictions and pleas of guilty or pleas of

nolo contendere of the defendant, or the absence of any prior conviction and pleas: Provided, however, that only such evidence in aggravation as the State has made known to the defendant prior to his trial shall be admissible. The judge [or jury] shall also hear argument by the defendant or his counsel and the prosecuting attorney . . . regarding the punishment to be imposed." § 27-2503 (Supp. 1975).

The defendant is accorded substantial latitude as to the types of evidence that he may introduce. See *Brown v. State*, 235 Ga. 644, 647–650, 220 S.E. 2d 922, 925–926 (1975).[4] Evidence considered during the guilt stage may be considered during the sentencing stage without being resubmitted. *Eberheart v. State*, 232 Ga. 247, 253, 206 S.E. 2d 12, 17 (1974).[5]

In the assessment of the appropriate sentence to be imposed the judge is also required to consider or to include in his instructions to the jury "any mitigating circumstances or aggravating circumstances otherwise authorized by law and any of [10] statutory aggravating circumstances which may be supported by the evidence. . . ." § 27-2534.1(b) (Supp. 1975). The scope of the nonstatutory aggravating or mitigating circumstances is not delineated in the statute. Before a convicted defendant may be sentenced to death, however, except in cases of treason or aircraft hijacking, the jury, or the trial judge in cases tried without a jury, must find beyond a reasonable doubt one of the 10 aggravating circumstances specified in the statute.[6] The sentence of death may be imposed only if the jury (or judge) finds one of the statutory aggravating circumstances and then elects to impose that sentence. § 26-3102 (Supp. 1975). If the verdict is death, the jury or judge must specify the aggravating circumstance(s) found. § 27-2534.1(c) (Supp. 1975). In jury cases, the trial judge is bound by the jury's recommended sentence. §§ 26-3102, 27-2514 (Supp. 1975).

In addition to the conventional appellate process available in all criminal cases, provision is made for special expedited direct review by the Supreme Court of Georgia of the appropriateness of imposing the sentence of death in the particular case. The court is directed to consider "the punishment as well as any errors enumerated by way of appeal," and to determine:

1. Whether the sentence of death was imposed under the influence of passion, prejudice, or any other arbitrary factor, and

2. Whether, in cases other than treason or aircraft hijacking, the evidence supports the jury's or judge's finding of a statutory aggravating circumstance as enumerated in section 27.2534.1 (b), and

3. Whether the sentence of death is excessive or disproportionate to the penalty imposed in similar cases, considering both the crime and the defendant. § 27-2537 (Supp. 1975).

If the court affirms a death sentence, it is required to include in its decision reference to similar cases that it has taken into consideration. § 27-2537 (e) (Supp. 1975).[7] . . .

III

We address initially the basic contention that the punishment of death for the crime of murder is, under all circumstances, "cruel and unusual" in violation of the Eighth and Fourteenth Amendments of the Constitution. . . .

The Court on a number of occasions has both assumed and asserted the constitutionality of capital punishment. In several cases that assumption provided a necessary foundation for the decision, as the Court was asked to decide whether a particular method of carrying out a capital sentence would be allowed to stand under the Eighth Amendment.[8] But until *Furman v. Georgia,* 408 U.S. 238 (1972), the Court never confronted squarely the fundamental claim that the punishment of death

always, regardless of the enormity of the offense or the procedure followed in imposing the sentence, is cruel and unusual punishment in violation of the Constitution. Although this issue was presented and addressed in *Furman,* it was not resolved by the Court. Four Justices would have held that capital punishment is not unconstitutional *per se;*[9] two Justices would have reached the opposite conclusion;[10] and three Justices, while agreeing that the statutes then before the Court were invalid as applied, left open the question whether such punishment may ever be imposed.[11] We now hold that the punishment of death does not invariably violate the Constitution. . . .

The death penalty is said to serve two principal social purposes: retribution and deterrence of capital crimes by prospective offenders.[12]

In part, capital punishment is an expression of society's moral outrage at particularly offensive conduct.[13] This function may be unappealing to many, but it is essential in an ordered society that asks its citizens to rely on legal processes rather than self-help to vindicate their wrongs.

> "The instinct for retribution is part of the nature of man, and channeling that instinct in the administration of criminal justice serves an important purpose in promoting the stability of a society governed by law. When people begin to believe that organized society is unwilling or unable to impose upon criminal offenders the punishment they 'deserve,' then there are sown the seeds of anarchy—of self-help, vigilante justice, and lynch law." *Furman v. Georgia, supra,* at 308 (STEWART, J., concurring).

"Retribution is no longer the dominant objective of the criminal law," *Williams v. New York,* 337 U.S. 241, 248 (1949), but neither is it a forbidden objective nor one inconsistent with our respect for the dignity of men. *Furman v. Georgia,* 408 U.S., at 394–395 (BURGER, C.J., dissenting); *Id.,* at 452–454

(POWELL, J., dissenting); *Powell v. Texas,* 392 U.S., at 531, 535–536 plurality opinion. Indeed, the decision that capital punishment may be the appropriate sanction in extreme cases is an expression of the community's belief that certain crimes are themselves so grievous an affront to humanity that the only adequate response may be the penalty of death.[14]

Statistical attempts to evaluate the worth of the death penalty as a deterrent to crimes by potential offenders have occasioned a great deal of debate.[15] The results simply have been inconclusive. . . .

Although some of the studies suggest that the death penalty may not function as a significantly greater deterrent than lesser penalties,[16] there is no convincing empirical evidence either supporting or refuting this view. We may nevertheless assume safely that there are murderers, such as those who act in passion, for whom the threat of death has little or no deterrent effect. But for many others, the death penalty undoubtedly is a significant deterrent. There are carefully contemplated murders, such as murder for hire, where the possible penalty of death may well enter into the cold calculus that precedes the decision to act.[17] And there are some categories of murder, such as murder by a life prisoner, where other sanctions may not be adequate.[18]

The value of capital punishment as a deterrent of crime is a complex factual issue the resolution of which properly rests with the legislatures, which can evaluate the results of statistical studies in terms of their own local conditions and with a flexibility of approach that is not available to the courts. *Furman v. Georgia, supra,* at 403–405 (BURGER, C.J., dissenting). Indeed, many of the post-*Furman* statutes reflect just such a responsible effort to define those crimes and those criminals for which capital punishment is most probably an effective deterrent.

In sum, we cannot say that the judgment of the Georgia Legislature that capital punishment may be necessary in some cases is clearly wrong. . . .

IV

We now consider whether Georgia may impose the death penalty on the petitioner in this case.

A

While *Furman* did not hold that the infliction of the death penalty *per se* violates the Constitution's ban on cruel and unusual punishments, it did recognize that the penalty of death is different in kind from any other punishment imposed under our system of criminal justice. Because of the uniqueness of the death penalty, *Furman* held that it could not be imposed under sentencing procedures that created a substantial risk that it would be inflicted in an arbitrary and capricious manner. Mr. Justice White concluded that "the death penalty is exacted with great infrequency even for the most atrocious crimes and . . .there is no meaningful basis for distinguishing the few cases in which it is imposed from the many cases in which it is not." 408 U.S., at 313 (concurring). Indeed, the death sentences examined by the Court in *Furman* were "cruel and unusual in the same way that being struck by lightning is cruel and unusual. For, of all the people convicted of [capital crimes], many just as reprehensible as these, the petitioners [in *Furman* were] among a capriciously selected random handful upon whom the sentence of death has in fact been imposed. . . . [T]he Eighth and Fourteenth Amendments cannot tolerate the infliction of a sentence of death under legal systems that permit this unique penalty to be so wantonly and so freakishly imposed." *Id.,* at 309–310 (Stewart, J., concurring).[19]

Furman mandates that where discretion is afforded a sentencing body on a matter so grave as the determination of whether a human life should be taken or spared, that discretion must be suitably directed and limited so as to minimize the risk of wholly arbitrary and capricious action.

It is certainly not a novel proposition that discretion in the area of sentencing be exercised in an informed manner. We have long recognized that "[f]or the determination of sentences, justice generally requires . . .that there be taken into account the circumstances of the offense together with the character and propensities of the offender.". . .

Jury sentencing has been considered desirable in capital cases in order "to maintain a link between contemporary community values and the penal system—a link without which the determination of punishment could hardly reflect 'the evolving standards of decency that mark the progress of a maturing society.'"[20] But it creates special problems. Much of the information that is relevant to the sentencing decision may have no relevance to the question of guilt, or may even be extremely prejudicial to a fair determination of that question.[21] This problem, however, is scarcely insurmountable. Those who have studied the question suggest that a bifurcated procedure—one in which the question of sentence is not considered until the determination of guilt has been made—is the best answer. . . .

But the provision of relevant information under fair procedural rules is not alone sufficient to guarantee that the information will be properly used in the imposition of punishment, especially if sentencing is performed by a jury. Since the members of a jury will have had little, if any, previous experience in sentencing, they are unlikely to be skilled in dealing with the information they are given. See American Bar Association Project on Standards for Criminal Justice, Sentencing Alternatives and Procedures, § 1.1(b), Commentary, pp. 46–47 (Approved Draft 1968); President's Commission on Law Enforcement and Administration of Justice: The Challenge of Crime in a Free Society, Task Force Report: The Courts 26 (1967). To the extent that this problem is inherent in jury sentencing, it may not be totally correctable. It seems clear, however, that the problem will be alleviated if the jury is given guidance regarding the factors about the crime and the defendant that the State, representing organized society, deems particularly relevant to the sentencing decision.

The idea that a jury should be given guidance in its decisionmaking is also hardly a novel proposition. Juries are invariably given careful instructions on the law and how to apply it before they are authorized to decide the merits of a lawsuit. It would be virtually unthinkable to follow any other course in a legal system that has traditionally operated by following prior precedents and fixed rules of law. See *Gasoline Products Co. v. Champlin Refining Co.*, 283 U.S. 494, 498 (1931); Fed. Rule Civ. Proc. 51. When erroneous instructions are given, retrial is often required. It is quite simply a hallmark of our legal system that juries be carefully and adequately guided in their deliberations.

While some have suggested that standards to guide a capital jury's sentencing deliberations are impossible to formulate,[22] the fact is that such standards have been developed. When the drafters of the Model Penal Code faced this problem, they concluded "that it is within the realm of possibility to point to the main circumstances of aggravation and of mitigation that should be weighed *and weighed against each other* when they are presented in a concrete case." ALI, Model Penal Code § 201.6, Comment 3, p. 71 (Tent. Draft No. 9, 1959) (emphasis in original).[23] While such standards are by necessity somewhat general, they do provide guidance to the sentencing authority and thereby reduce the likelihood that it will impose a sentence that fairly can be called capricious or arbitrary.[24] Where the sentencing authority is required to specify the factors it relied upon in reaching its decision, the further safeguard of meaningful appellate review is available to ensure that death sentences are not imposed capriciously or in a freakish manner.

In summary, the concerns expressed in *Furman* that the penalty of death not be imposed in an arbitrary or capricious manner can be met by a carefully drafted statute that ensures that the sentencing authority is given adequate information and guidance. As a general proposition these concerns are best met by a system that provides for a bifurcated proceeding at which the sentencing authority is apprised of the information relevant to the imposition of sentence and provided with standards to guide its use of the information.

We do not intend to suggest that only the above described procedures would be permissible under *Furman* or that any sentencing system constructed along these general lines would inevitably satisfy the concerns of *Furman*,[25] for each distinct system must be examined on an individual basis. Rather, we have embarked upon this general exposition to make clear that it is possible to construct capital-sentencing systems capable of meeting *Furman's* constitutional concerns.[26]

B

We now turn to consideration of the constitutionality of Georgia's capital-sentencing procedures. In the wake of *Furman,* Georgia amended its capital punishment statute, but chose not to narrow the scope of its murder provisions. See Part II, *supra.* Thus, now as before *Furman,* in Georgia "[a] person commits murder when he unlawfully and with malice aforethought, either express or implied, causes the death of another human being." Ga. Code Ann., § 26-1101(a) (1972). All persons convicted of murder "shall be punished by death or by imprisonment for life." § 26-1101(c) (1972).

Georgia did act, however, to narrow the class of murderers subject to capital punishment by specifying 10 statutory aggravating circumstances, one of which must be found by the jury to exist beyond a reasonable doubt before a death sentence can ever be imposed. In addition, the jury is authorized to consider any other appropriate aggravating or mitigating circumstances. § 27-2534.1 (b) (Supp. 1975). The jury is not required to find any mitigating circumstance in order to make a recommendation of mercy that is binding on the trial court, see § 27-2302 (Supp. 1975), but it must find a

statutory aggravating circumstance before recommending a sentence of death.

These procedures require the jury to consider the circumstances of the crime and the criminal before it recommends sentence. No longer can a Georgia jury do as Furman's jury did: reach a finding of the defendant's guilt and then, without guidance or direction, decide whether he should live or die. Instead, the jury's attention is directed to the specific circumstances of the crime: Was it committed in the course of another capital felony? Was it committed for money? Was it committed upon a peace officer or judicial officer? Was it committed in a particularly heinous way or in a manner that endangered the lives of many persons? In addition, the jury's attention is focused on the characteristics of the person who committed the crime: Does he have a record of prior convictions for capital offenses? Are there any special facts about this defendant that mitigate against imposing capital punishment (e.g., his youth, the extent of his cooperation with the police, his emotional state at the time of the crime). As a result, while some jury discretion still exists, "the discretion to be exercised is controlled by clear and objective standards so as to produce non-discriminatory application." *Coley v. State,* 231 Ga. 829, 834, 204 S.E. 2d 612, 615 (1974).

As an important additional safeguard against arbitrariness and caprice, the Georgia statutory scheme provides for automatic appeal of all death sentences to the State's Supreme Court. That court is required by statute to review each sentence of death and determine whether it was imposed under the influence of passion or prejudice, whether the evidence supports the jury's finding of a statutory aggravating circumstance, and whether the sentence is disproportionate compared to those sentences imposed in similar cases. § 27-2537 (c) (Supp. 1975).

In short, Georgia's new sentencing procedures require as a prerequisite to the imposition of the death penalty, specific jury findings as to the circumstances of the crime or the character of the defendant. Moreover, to guard further against a situation comparable to that presented in *Furman,* the Supreme Court of Georgia compares each death sentence with the sentences imposed on similarly situated defendants to ensure that the sentence of death in a particular case is not disproportionate. On their face these procedures seem to satisfy the concerns of *Furman.* No longer should there be "no meaningful basis for distinguishing the few cases in which [the death penalty] is imposed from the many cases in which it is not." 408 U.S., at 313 (White, J., concurring). . . .

1

Finally, the Georgia statute has an additional provision designed to assure that the death penalty will not be imposed on a capriciously selected group of convicted defendants. The new sentencing procedures require that the State Supreme Court review every death sentence to determine whether it was imposed under the influence of passion, prejudice, or any other arbitrary factor, whether the evidence supports the findings of a statutory aggravating circumstance, and "[w]hether the sentence of death is excessive or disproportionate to the penalty imposed in similar cases, considering both the crime and the defendant." § 27-2537 (c)(3) (Supp. 1975).[27] In performing its sentence-review function, the Georgia court has held that "if the death penalty is only rarely imposed for an act or it is substantially out of line with sentences imposed for other acts it will be set aside as excessive." *Coley v. State,* 231 Ga., at 834, 204 S.E. 2d, at 616. The court on another occasion stated that "we view it to be our duty under the similarity standard to assure that no death sentence is affirmed unless in similar cases throughout the state the death penalty has been imposed generally. . . ." *Moore v. State,* 233 Ga. 861, 864, 213 S.E. 2d 829, 832 (1975). See also *Jarrell v. State, supra,* at 425, 216 S.E. 2d, at 270 (standard is whether "juries generally throughout the state have imposed the death penalty"); *Smith v. State,* 236 Ga. 12, 24, 222 S.E. 2d 308,

318 (1976) (found "a clear pattern" of jury behavior).

It is apparent that the Supreme Court of Georgia has taken its review responsibilities seriously. In *Coley,* it held that "[the] prior cases indicate that the past practice among juries faced with similar factual situations and like aggravating circumstances has been to impose only the sentence of life imprisonment for the offense of rape, rather than death." 231 Ga., at 835, 204 S.E. 2d, at 617. It thereupon reduced Coley's sentence from death to life imprisonment. Similarly, although armed robbery is a capital offense under Georgia law, § 26-1902 (1972), the Georgia court concluded that the death sentences imposed in this case for that crime were "unusual in that they are rarely imposed for [armed robbery]. Thus, under the test provided by statute, . . . they must be considered to be excessive or disproportionate to the penalties imposed in similar cases." 233 Ga., at 127, 210 S.E. 2d, at 667. The court therefore vacated Gregg's death sentences for armed robbery and has followed a similar course in every other armed robbery death penalty case to come before it. See *Floyd v. State,* 233 Ga. 280, 285, 210 S.E. 2d 810, 814 (1974); *Jarrell v. State,* 234 Ga., at 424–425, 216 S.E. 2d, at 270. See *Dorsey v. State,* 236 Ga. 591, 225 S.E. 2d 418 (1976).

The provision for appellate review in the Georgia capital-sentencing system serves as a check against the random or arbitrary imposition of the death penalty. In particular, the proportionality review substantially eliminates the possibility that a person will be sentenced to die by the action of an aberrant jury. If a time comes when juries generally do not impose the death sentence in a certain kind of murder case, the appellate review procedures assure that no defendant convicted under such circumstances will suffer a sentence of death.

V

The basic concern of *Furman* centered on those defendants who were being condemned to death capriciously and arbitrarily. Under the procedures before the Court in that case, sentencing authorities were not directed to give attention to the nature or circumstances of the crime committed or to the character or record of the defendant. Left unguided, juries imposed the death sentence in a way that could only be called freakish. The new Georgia sentencing procedures, by contrast, focus the jury's attention on the particularized nature of the crime and the particularized characteristics of the individual defendant. While the jury is permitted to consider any aggravating or mitigating circumstances, it must find and identify at least one statutory aggravating factor before it may impose a penalty of death. In this way the jury's discretion is channeled. No longer can a jury wantonly and freakishly impose the death sentence; it is always circumscribed by the legislative guidelines. In addition, the review function of the Supreme Court of Georgia affords additional assurance that the concerns that prompted our decision in *Furman* are not present to any significant degree in the Georgia procedure applied here.

For the reasons expressed in this opinion, we hold that the statutory system under which Gregg was sentenced to death does not violate the Constitution. Accordingly, the judgment of the Georgia Supreme Court is affirmed. . . .

Notes

1. Subsequent to the trial in this case limited portions of the Georgia statute were amended. None of these amendments changed significantly the substance of the statutory scheme. All references to the statute in this opinion are to the current version.

2. Section 26-1902 (1972) provides:

   "A person commits armed robbery when, with intent to commit theft, he takes property of another from the person or the immediate presence of another by use of an offensive weapon. The offense robbery by intimidation shall be a lesser included offense in the offense of armed robbery. A person convicted of armed robbery shall be punished by death or imprisonment for life, or by imprisonment for not less than one nor more than 20 years."

3. These capital felonies currently are defined as they were when *Furman* was decided. The 1973 amendments to the Georgia statute, however, narrowed the class of crimes potentially punishable by death by eliminating capital perjury. Compare § 26-2401 (Supp. 1975) with § 26-2401 (1972).

4. It is not clear whether the 1974 amendments to the Georgia statute were intended to broaden the types of evidence admissible at the presentence hearing. Compare § 27-2503(a) (Supp. 1975) with § 27-2534 (1972) (deletion of limitation "subject to the laws of evidence").

5. Essentially the same procedures are followed in the case of a guilty plea. The judge considers the factual basis of the plea, as well as evidence in aggravation and mitigation. See *Mitchell v. State,* 234 Ga. 160, 214 S.E. 2d 900 (1975).

6. The statute provides in part:

   (a) The death penalty may be imposed for the offenses of aircraft hijacking or treason, in any case.

   (b) In all cases of other offenses for which the death penalty may be authorized, the judge shall consider, or he shall include in his instructions to the jury for it to consider, any mitigating circumstances or aggravating circumstances otherwise authorized by law and any of the following statutory aggravating circumstances which may be supported by the evidence:

   (1) The offense of murder, rape, armed robbery, or kidnapping was committed by a person with a prior record of conviction for a capital felony, or the offense of murder was committed by a person who has a substantial history of serious assaultive criminal convictions.

   (2) The offense of murder, rape, armed robbery, or kidnapping was committed while the offender was engaged in the commission of another capital felony, or aggravated battery, or the offense of murder was committed while the offender was engaged in the commission of burglary or arson in the first degree.

(3) The offender by his act of murder, armed robbery, or kidnapping knowingly created a great risk of death to more than one person in a public place by means of a weapon or device which would normally be hazardous to the lives of more than one person.

(4) The offender committed the offense of murder for himself or another, for the purpose of receiving money or any other thing of monetary value.

(5) The murder of a judicial officer, former judicial officer, district attorney or solicitor or former district attorney or solicitor during or because of the exercise of his official duty.

(6) The offender caused or directed another to commit murder or committed murder as an agent or employee of another person.

(7) The offense of murder, rape, armed robbery, or kidnapping was outrageously or wantonly vile, horrible or inhuman in that it involved torture, depravity of mind, or an aggravated battery to the victim.

(8) The offense of murder was committed against any peace officer, corrections employee or fireman while engaged in the performance of his official duties.

(9) The offense of murder was committed by a person in, or who has escaped from, the lawful custody of a peace officer or place of lawful confinement.

(10) The murder was committed for the purpose of avoiding, interfering with, or preventing a lawful arrest or custody in a place of lawful confinement, of himself or another.

(c) The statutory instructions as determined by the trial judge to be warranted by the evidence shall be given in charge and in writing to the jury for its deliberation. The jury, if its verdict be a recommendation of death, shall designate in writing, signed by the foreman of the jury, the aggravating circumstance or circumstances which it found beyond a reasonable doubt. In non-jury cases the judge shall make such designation. Except in cases of treason or aircraft hijacking, unless at least one of the statutory aggravating circumstances enumerated in section 27-2534.1(b) is so found, the death penalty shall not be imposed." § 27-2534.1 (Supp. 1975).

The Supreme Court of Georgia, in *Arnold v. State,* 236 Ga. 534, 540, 224 S.E. 2d 386, 391 (1976), recently held unconstitutional the portion of the first circumstance encompassing persons who have a "substantial history of serious assaultive criminal convictions" because it did not set "sufficiently 'clear and objective standards.'"

7. The statute requires that the Supreme Court of Georgia obtain and preserve the records of all capital felony cases in which the death penalty was imposed after January 1, 1970, or such earlier date that the court considers appropriate. § 27-2537 (f) (Supp. 1975). To aid the court in its disposition of these cases the statute further provides for the appointment of a special assistant and authorizes the employment of additional staff members. §§ 27-2537 (f)-(h) (Supp. 1975).

8. *Louisiana ex rel. Francis v. Resweber,* 329 U.S. 459, 464 (1947); In re *Kemmler,* 136 U.S. 436, 447 (1890); *Wilkerson v. Utah,* 99 U.S. 130, 134–135 (1879). See also *McGautha v. California,* 402 U.S. 183 (1971); *Witherspoon v. Illinois,* 391 U.S. 510 (1968); *Trop v. Dulles,* 356 U.S. 86, 100 (1958) (plurality opinion).

9. 408 U.S., at 375 (BURGER, C.J., dissenting); *Id.,* at 405 (BLACKMUN, J., dissenting); *Id.,* at 414 (POWELL, J., dissenting); *Id.,* at 465 (REHNQUIST, J., dissenting).

10. *Id.,* at 257 (BRENNAN, J., concurring); *Id.,* at 314 (MARSHALL, J., concurring).

11. *Id.,* at 240 (Douglas, J., concurring); *Id.,* at 306 (STEWART, J., concurring); *Id.,* at 310 (WHITE, J., concurring).

Since five Justices wrote separately in support of the judgments in *Furman,* the holding of the Court may be viewed as that position taken by those Members who concurred in the judgments on the narrowest grounds—Mr. Justice Stewart and Mr. Justice White. See n. 36, *infra.*

12. Another purpose that has been discussed is the incapacitation of dangerous criminals and the consequent prevention of crimes that they may otherwise commit in the future. See *People v. Anderson,* 6 Cal. 3d 628, 651, 493 P. 2d 880, 896, cert. denied, 406 U.S. 958 (1972); *Commonwealth v. O'Neal, supra,* at , 339 N.E. 2d, at 685–686.

13. See H. Packer, limits of the Criminal Sanction 43–44 (1968).

14. Lord Justice Denning, Master of the Rolls of the Court of Appeal in England, spoke to this effect before the British Royal Commission on Capital Punishment:

    "Punishment is the way in which society expresses its denunciation of wrong doing: and, in order to maintain respect for law, it is essential that the punishment inflicted for grave crimes should adequately reflect the revulsion felt by the great majority of citizens for them. It is a mistake to consider the objects of punishment as being deterrent or reformative or preventive and nothing else. . . . The truth is that some crimes are so outrageous that society insists on adequate punishment, because the wrong-doer deserves it, irrespective of whether it is a deterrent or not." Royal Commission on Capital Punishment, Minutes of Evidence, Dec. 1, 1949, p. 207 (1950).

    A contemporary writer has noted more recently that opposition to capital punishment "has much more appeal when the discussion is merely academic than when the community is confronted with a crime, or a series of crimes, so gross, so heinous, so cold-blooded that anything short of death seems an inadequate response." Raspberry, Death Sentence, *The Washington Post*, Mar. 12, 1976, p. A27, cols. 5–6.

15. See, e.g., Peck, The Deterrent Effect of Capital Punishment: Ehrlich and His Critics, 85 Yale L.J. 359 (1976); Baldus & Cole, A Comparison of the Work of Thorsten Sellin and Isaac Ehrlich on the Deterrent Effect of Capital Punishment, 85 Yale L.J. 170 (1975); Bowers & Pierce, The Illusion of Deterrence in Isaac Ehrlich's Research on Capital Punishment, 85 Yale L.J. 187 (1975); Ehrlich, The Deterrent Effect of Capital Punishment: A Question of Life and Death, 65 Am Econ. Rev. 397 (June 1975); Hook, The Death Sentence, in The Death Penalty in America 146 (H. Bedau ed. 1967); T. Sellin, The Death Penalty, A Report for the Model Penal Code Project of the American Law Institute (1959).

16. See, e.g., The Death Penalty in America, *supra*, at 258–332; Report of the Royal Commission on Capital Punishment, 1949–1953, Cmd. 8932.

17. Other types of calculated murders, apparently occurring with increasing frequency, include the use of bombs or other means of indiscriminate killings, the extortion murder of hostages or kidnap victims, and the execution-style killing of witnesses to a crime.

18. We have been shown no statistics breaking down the total number of murders into the categories described above. The overall trend in the number of murders committed in the nation, however, has been upward for some time. In 1964, reported murders totaled an estimated 9,250. During the ensuing decade, the number reported increased 123%, until it totaled approximately 20,600 in 1974. In 1972, the year *Furman* was announced, the total estimated was 18,520. Despite a fractional decrease in 1975 as compared with 1974, the number of murders increased in the three years immediately following *Furman* to approximately 20,400, an increase of almost 10%. See FBI, Uniform Crime Reports, for 1964, 1972, 1974, and 1975, Preliminary Annual Release.

19. This view was expressed by other Members of the Court who concurred in the judgments. See 408 U.S., at 255–257 (Douglas, J.); *Id.*, at 291–295 (Brennan, J.). The dissenters viewed this concern as the basis for the *Furman* decision: "The decisive grievance of the opinions . . .is that the present system of discretionary sentencing in capital cases has failed to produce evenhanded justice; . . .that the selection process has followed no rational pattern." *Id.*, at 398–399 (BURGER, C.J., dissenting).

20. *Witherspoon v. Illinois*, 391 U.S., at 519 n. 15, quoting *Trop v. Dulles*, 356 U.S., at 101 (plurality opinion). See also Report of the Royal Commission on Capital Punishment, 1949–1953, Cmd. 8932, § 571.

21. In other situations this Court has concluded that a jury cannot be expected to consider certain evidence before it on one issue, but not another. See, e.g., *Bruton v. United States*, 391 U.S. 123 (1968); *Jackson v. Denna*, 378 U.S. 368 (1964).

22. See *McGautha v. California*, 402 U.S., at 204–207; Report of the Royal Commission on Capital Punishment, 1949–1953, Cmd. 8932, § 595.

23. The Model Penal Code proposes the following standards:

Aggravating Circumstances.

(a) The murder was committed by a convict under sentence of imprisonment.

(b) The defendant was previously convicted of another murder or of a felony involving the use or threat of violence to the person.

(c) At the time the murder was committed the defendant also committed another murder.

(d) The defendant knowingly created a great risk of death to many persons.

(e) The murder was committed while the defendant was engaged or was an accomplice in the commission of, or an attempt to commit, or flight after committing or attempting to commit robbery, rape or deviate sexual intercourse by force or threat of force, arson, burglary or kidnapping.

(f) The murder was committed for the purpose of avoiding or preventing a lawful arrest or effecting an escape from lawful custody.

(g) The murder was committed for pecuniary gain.

(h) The murder was especially heinous, atrocious or cruel, manifesting exceptional depravity.

Mitigating Circumstances.

(a) The defendant has no significant history of prior criminal activity.

(b) The murder was committed while the defendant was under the influence of extreme mental or emotional disturbance.

(c) The victim was a participant in the defendant's homicidal conduct or consented to the homicidal act.

(d) The murder was committed under circumstances which the defendant believed to provide a moral justification or extenuation for his conduct.

(e) The defendant was an accomplice in a murder committed by another person and his participation in the homicidal act was relatively minor.

(f) The defendant acted under duress or under the domination of another person.

(g) At the time of the murder, the capacity of the defendant to appreciate the criminality [wrongfulness] of his conduct or to conform his conduct to the requirements of law was impaired as a result of mental disease or defect or intoxication.

(h) The youth of the defendant at the time of the crime." ALI Model Penal Code § 210.6 (Proposed Official Draft 1962).

24. As Mr. Justice Brennan noted in *McGautha v. California, supra,* at 285–286 (dissenting opinion):

"[E]ven if a State's notion of wise capital sentencing policy is such that the policy cannot be implemented through a formula capable of mechanical application . . .there is no reason that it should not give some guidance to those called upon to render decision."

25. A system could have standards so vague that they would fail adequately to channel the sentencing decision patterns of juries with the result that a pattern of arbitrary and capricious sentencing like that found unconstitutional in *Furman* could occur.

26. In *McGautha v. California, supra,* this Court held that the Due Process Clause of the Fourteenth Amendment did not require that a jury be provided with standards to guide its decision whether to recommend a sentence of life imprisonment or death or that the capital-sentencing proceeding be separated from the guilt-determination process. *McGautha* was not an Eighth Amendment decision, and to the extent it purported to deal with Eighth Amendment concerns, it must be read in light of the opinions in *Furman v. Georgia.* There the Court ruled that death sentences imposed under statutes that left juries with untrammeled discretion to impose or withhold the death penalty violated the Eighth and Fourteenth Amendments. While *Furman* did not overrule *McGautha,* it is clearly in substantial tension with a broad reading of *McGautha's* holding. In view of *Furman, McGautha* can be viewed rationally as a precedent only for the proposition that standardless jury sentencing procedures were not employed in the cases there before the Court so as to violate the Due Process Clause. We note that *McGautha's* assumption that it is not possible to devise standards to guide and regularize jury sentencing in capital cases has been undermined by subsequent experience. In view of that experience and the

considerations set forth in the text, we adhere to *Furman's* determination that where the ultimate punishment of death is at issue a system of standardless jury discretion violates the Eighth and Fourteenth Amendments.

27. The court is required to specify in its opinion the similar cases which it took into consideration. § 27-2537 (e) (Supp. 1975). Special provision is made for staff to enable the court to compile data relevant to its consideration of the sentence's validity. §§ 27-2537 (f)-(h) (Supp. 1975). See generally *supra*, at 166–168.

The petitioner claims that this procedure has resulted in an inadequate basis for measuring the proportionality of sentences. First, he notes that nonappealed capital convictions where a life sentence is imposed and cases involving homicides where a capital conviction is not obtained are not included in the group of cases which the Supreme Court of Georgia uses for comparative purposes. The Georgia court has the authority to consider such cases, see *Ross v. State,* 233 Ga. 361, 365–366, 211 S.E. 2d 356, 359 (1974), and it does consider appealed murder cases where a life sentence has been imposed. We do not think that the petitioner's argument establishes that the Georgia court's review process is ineffective. The petitioner further complains about the Georgia court's current practice of using some pre-*Furman* cases in its comparative examination. This practice was necessary at the inception of the new procedure in the absence of any post-*Furman* capital cases available for comparison. It is not unconstitutional.

NOTES AND QUESTIONS

1. In *Gregg v. Georgia,* the Court ruled that "the punishment of death does not invariably violate the Constitution." According to the majority opinion, what social and legal purposes does capital punishment serve? In your opinion, does the death penalty serve these purposes more effectively than life in prison?

2. What is a "bifurcated procedure"? How does it help juries to make fair decisions?

3. Why, according to the majority opinion, is jury sentencing important in the penalty phase of capital cases? What challenges does jury sentencing pose to the effective delivery of justice?

4. What is meant by "mitigating or aggravating circumstances"? How do they help to eliminate "capricious" or "freakishly imposed" sentences? Under the Georgia statute, what qualifies as an aggravating circumstance? Why do these circumstances make a difference as to the gravity of a crime?

5. As the Court points out, *Furman* (Chapter 60) ruled that "Where discretion is afforded to the sentencing body...[it] must be suitably directed so as to minimize the risks of wholly arbitrary and capricious action." How much discretion was the jury in *Gregg* afforded? Was the direction they received, to sentence according to "mitigating and aggravating circumstances," sufficient to comply with *Furman?*

6. The Court recognizes that even with sentencing guidelines, a jury may enter a sentence of questionable fairness but that, in such a case, "the further safeguard of meaningful appellate review is available to ensure that death sentences are not imposed capriciously or in a freakish manner." Why was appellate review not considered sufficient safeguard against arbitrary jury sentences before *Gregg?* Which statutory changes does the court identify as having made a meaningful difference in the quality of justice delivered post-*Furman?* Do you agree that these changes make a difference?

Reprinted from: Gregg v. Georgia, 428 U.S. 153 (1976). ✦

Chapter 62

McCleskey v. Kemp

The language of discrimination is widely used in America to designate unjustified differential treatment. But how can one prove discrimination? In the context of capital punishment, what does it mean to say that race plays an unacceptable role in decisions about who gets sentenced to death? These questions were not put to rest by Gregg. Indeed, critics of that decision suggested that it had not adequately addressed concerns about discretion and discrimination that had animated Furman's rejection of the death penalty. All Gregg had done, these people suggested, was to narrow the range of cases over which discretion could be exercised, and, in so doing, it had narrowed the range of cases where the risk of discrimination would be present.

There are two different ways to prove discrimination. The first, called disparate treatment, requires a person to prove that an unacceptable consideration played a role in a decision about them. The presence of racist comments or the explicit invocation of race in a context in which it has no bearing are two pieces of evidence that would show disparate treatment. The second way of proving discrimination involves the use of statistical evidence to show that, over a range of cases, apparently neutral criteria had a disparate impact on members of a minority group. With this form of proof, the burden is then shifted to the person or group allegedly guilty of discriminatory treatment, to show a legitimate nondiscriminatory basis for the pattern of disparate outcomes. The latter form of proof is a standard method in employment, housing, and other contexts in which discrimination might occur.

Before Furman, the issue of discrimination was focused on the race of the offender in capital cases. In rape and homicide cases, for example, researchers found that between 1930 and 1967, almost 50 percent of those executed for murder were black. However, this research was unable to disentangle the impact of race from other "legitimate" factors on capital sentencing. Merely showing that the death penalty was more likely to be imposed on black defendants could not, in itself, establish racial discrimination.

In the 1980s, David Baldus and his colleagues undertook research designed to remedy this defect. Using sophisticated multiple regression techniques and a large data set, they set out to isolate the effect of race on capital sentencing in Georgia. First, they found no evidence of discrimination against black defendants in the period after Furman. However, they did find strong effects for the victim's race. Taking over two hundred variables into account, Baldus concluded that someone who killed a white victim was 4.3 times more likely to receive the death penalty than the killer of a black victim. Juries, or so it seemed, even after the efforts of the Supreme Court to prevent arbitrariness or racial discrimination in capital sentencing, still valued white life more highly than the lives of African Americans and were, as a result, sentencing some killers to die on the basis of illegitimate considerations of race.

Subsequently, the Baldus study provided the grounds for a constitutional challenge to the death penalty statutes approved in Gregg. In McCleskey v. Kemp, Warren McCleskey wanted to use it and a disparate impact form of proof to demonstrate that racial discrimination might have impermissibly tainted his death sentence. McCleskey, an African American who murdered a white police officer, claimed that the race-of-the-victim effect documented by Baldus in Georgia's post-Gregg capital sentencing showed the failure of its guided discretion formula to eliminate racial discrimination from the death penalty.

Despite the fact that it accepted the validity of the Baldus study, the U. S. Supreme Court *held that McCleskey had not shown a "constitu-tionally significant" risk of discrimination. Simply put, the Court said that aggregate data, no matter how stark, may not be used to show that any particular case was decided arbitrarily or with bias. The burden of proof is on each de-fendant to show specifically in his case that he was the victim of racial discrimination. This is a very difficult burden to discharge.*

As you read McCleskey, *think about the fol-lowing: What kind of evidence would satisfy the Court that McCleskey had been the subject of racial discrimination? Justice Powell, in his ma-jority opinion in* McCleskey, *said that McCleskey's claim, "taken to its logical conclu-sion, throws into serious question the principles that underlie our entire criminal justice sys-tem." What does he have in mind? What about McCleskey's claim was so threatening?*

JUSTICE POWELL DELIVERED THE OPINION OF THE COURT

This case presents the question whether a complex statistical study that indicates a risk that racial considerations enter into capital sentencing determinations proves that peti-tioner McCleskey's capital sentence is uncon-stitutional under the Eighth or Fourteenth Amendment.

I

McCleskey, a black man, was convicted of two counts of armed robbery and one count of murder in the Superior Court of Fulton County, Georgia, on October 12, 1978. McCleskey's convictions arose out of the rob-bery of a furniture store and the killing of a white police officer during the course of the robbery. The evidence at trial indicated that McCleskey and three accomplices planned and carried out the robbery. All four were armed. McCleskey entered the front of the store while the other three entered the rear. McCleskey secured the front of the store by

rounding up the customers and forcing them to lie face down on the floor. The other three rounded up the employees in the rear and tied them up with tape. The manager was forced at gunpoint to turn over the store receipts, his watch, and $6. During the course of the rob-bery, a police officer, answering a silent alarm, entered the store through the front door. As he was walking down the center aisle of the store, two shots were fired. Both struck the of-ficer. One hit him in the face and killed him.

Several weeks later, McCleskey was ar-rested in connection with an unrelated of-fense. He confessed that he had participated in the furniture store robbery, but denied that he had shot the police officer. At trial, the State introduced evidence that at least one of the bullets that struck the officer was fired from a .38 caliber Rossi revolver. This description matched the description of the gun that McCleskey had carried during the robbery. The State also introduced the testimony of two witnesses who had heard McCleskey ad-mit to the shooting.

The jury convicted McCleskey of murder.[1] At the penalty hearing,[2] the jury heard argu-ments as to the appropriate sentence. Under Georgia law, the jury could not consider im-posing the death penalty unless it found be-yond a reasonable doubt that the murder was accompanied by one of the statutory aggra-vating circumstances. Ga. Code Ann. § 17-10-30(c) (1982).[3]

The jury in this case found two aggravating circumstances to exist beyond a reasonable doubt: the murder was committed during the course of an armed robbery, § 17-10-30(b)(2); and the murder was committed upon a peace officer engaged in the perfor-mance of his duties, § 17-10-30(b)(8). In making its decision whether to impose the death sentence, the jury considered the miti-gating and aggravating circumstances of McCleskey's conduct. § 17-10-2(c). McCleskey offered no mitigating evidence. The jury recommended that he be sentenced to death on the murder charge and to consecutive life sentences on the armed robbery charges. The court followed the jury's recommendation and sentenced McCleskey to death.[4]

On appeal, the Supreme Court of Georgia affirmed the convictions and the sentences. . . .

McCleskey next filed a petition for a writ of habeas corpus in the Federal District Court for the Northern District of Georgia. His petition raised 18 claims, one of which was that the Georgia capital sentencing process is administered in a racially discriminatory manner in violation of the Eighth and Fourteenth Amendments to the United States Constitution. In support of his claim, McCleskey proffered a statistical study performed by Professors David C. Baldus, Charles Pulaski, and George Woodworth (the Baldus study) that purports to show a disparity in the imposition of the death sentence in Georgia based on the race of the murder victim and, to a lesser extent, the race of the defendant. The Baldus study is actually two sophisticated statistical studies that examine over 2,000 murder cases that occurred in Georgia during the 1970's. The raw numbers collected by Professor Baldus indicate that defendants charged with killing white persons received the death penalty in 11 percent of the cases, but defendants charged with killing blacks received the death penalty in only 1 percent of the cases. The raw numbers also indicate a reverse racial disparity according to the race of the defendant: 4 percent of the black defendants received the death penalty, as opposed to 7 percent of the white defendants.

Baldus also divided the cases according to the combination of the race of the defendant and the race of the victim. He found that the death penalty was assessed in 22 percent of the cases involving black defendants and white victims; 8 percent of the cases involving white defendants and white victims; 1 percent of the cases involving black defendants and black victims; and 3 percent of the cases involving white defendants and black victims.

Similarly, Baldus found that prosecutors sought the death penalty in 70 percent of the cases involving black defendants and white victims; 32 percent of the cases involving white defendants and white victims; 15 percent of the cases involving black defendants and black victims; and 19 percent of the cases involving white defendants and black victims.

Baldus subjected his data to an extensive analysis, taking account of 230 variables that could have explained the disparities on nonracial grounds. One of his models concludes that, even after taking account of 39 nonracial variables, defendants charged with killing white victims were 4.3 times as likely to receive a death sentence as defendants charged with killing blacks. According to this model, black defendants were 1.1 times as likely to receive a death sentence as other defendants. Thus, the Baldus study indicates that black defendants, such as McCleskey, who kill white victims have the greatest likelihood of receiving the death penalty.[5] . . .

II

McCleskey's first claim is that the Georgia capital punishment statute violates the Equal Protection Clause of the Fourteenth Amendment.[6] He argues that race has infected the administration of Georgia's statute in two ways: persons who murder whites are more likely to be sentenced to death than persons who murder blacks, and black murderers are more likely to be sentenced to death than white murderers.[7] As a black defendant who killed a white victim, McCleskey claims that the Baldus study demonstrates that he was discriminated against because of his race and because of the race of his victim. In its broadest form, McCleskey's claim of discrimination extends to every actor in the Georgia capital sentencing process, from the prosecutor who sought the death penalty and the jury that imposed the sentence, to the State itself that enacted the capital punishment statute and allows it to remain in effect despite its allegedly discriminatory application. We agree with the

Court of Appeals, and every other court that has considered such a challenge,[8] that this claim must fail.

A

Our analysis begins with the basic principle that a defendant who alleges an equal protection violation has the burden of proving "the existence of purposeful discrimination." *Whitus v. Georgia,* 385 U.S. 545, 550 (1967).[9] A corollary to this principle is that a criminal defendant must prove that the purposeful discrimination "had a discriminatory effect" on him. *Wayte v. United States,* 470 U.S. 598, 608 (1985). Thus, to prevail under the Equal Protection Clause, McCleskey must prove that the decisionmakers in *his* case acted with discriminatory purpose. He offers no evidence specific to his own case that would support an inference that racial considerations played a part in his sentence. Instead, he relies solely on the Baldus study.[10] McCleskey argues that the Baldus study compels an inference that his sentence rests on purposeful discrimination. McCleskey's claim that these statistics are sufficient proof of discrimination, without regard to the facts of a particular case, would extend to all capital cases in Georgia, at least where the victim was white and the defendant is black. . . .

. . .McCleskey's statistical proffer must be viewed in the context of his challenge. McCleskey challenges decisions at the heart of the State's criminal justice system. "One of society's most basic tasks is that of protecting the lives of its citizens and one of the most basic ways in which it achieves the task is through criminal laws against murder." *Gregg v. Georgia,* 428 U.S. 153, 226 (1976) (White, J., concurring). Implementation of these laws necessarily requires discretionary judgments. Because discretion is essential to the criminal justice process, we would demand exceptionally clear proof before we would infer that the discretion has been abused. The unique nature of the decisions at issue in this case also counsels against adopting such an inference from the disparities indicated by the Baldus study. Accordingly, we hold that the Baldus study is clearly insufficient to support an inference that any of the decisionmakers in McCleskey's case acted with discriminatory purpose. . . .

III

McCleskey also argues that the Baldus study demonstrates that the Georgia capital sentencing system violates the Eighth Amendment. . . .

IV

A

In light of our precedents under the Eighth Amendment, McCleskey cannot argue successfully that his sentence is "disproportionate to the crime in the traditional sense." See *Pulley v. Harris,* 465 U.S. 37, 43 (1984). He does not deny that he committed a murder in the course of a planned robbery, a crime for which this Court has determined that the death penalty constitutionally may be imposed. *Gregg v. Georgia,* 428 U.S., at 187. His disproportionality claim "is of a different sort." *Pulley v. Harris, supra,* at 43. McCleskey argues that the sentence in his case is disproportionate to the sentences in other murder cases. . . .

B

Although our decision in *Gregg* as to the facial validity of the Georgia capital punishment statute appears to foreclose McCleskey's disproportionality argument, he further contends that the Georgia capital punishment system is arbitrary and capricious in *application,* and therefore his sentence is excessive, because racial considerations may influence capital sentencing decisions in Georgia. We now address this claim.

To evaluate McCleskey's challenge, we must examine exactly what the Baldus study may show. Even Professor Baldus does not contend that his statistics *prove* that race enters into any capital sentencing decisions or that race was a factor in McCleskey's particular case.[11] Statistics at most may show only a likelihood that a particular factor entered into some decisions. There is, of course, some risk of racial prejudice influencing a jury's decision in a criminal case. There are similar risks that other kinds of prejudice will influence other criminal trials. See *infra,* at 315–318. The question "is at what point that risk becomes constitutionally unacceptable," *Turner v. Murray,* 476 U.S. ___, ___, n. 8, 106 S.Ct. 1683, ___, n. 8, 90 L.Ed.2d 27 (1986). McCleskey asks us to accept the likelihood allegedly shown by the Baldus study as the constitutional measure of an unacceptable risk of racial prejudice influencing capital sentencing decisions. This we decline to do.

Because of the risk that the factor of race may enter the criminal justice process, we have engaged in "unceasing efforts" to eradicate racial prejudice from our criminal justice system. *Batson v. Kentucky,* 476 U.S. ___, ___, 106 S.Ct. 1712, ___, 90 L.Ed.2d 69 (1986).[12] Our efforts have been guided by our recognition that "the inestimable privilege of trial by jury . . .is a vital principle, underlying the whole administration of criminal justice," *Ex parte Milligan,* 4 Wall. 2, 123 (1866). See *Duncan v. Louisiana,* 391 U.S. 145, 155 (1968).[13] Thus, it is the jury that is a criminal defendant's fundamental "protection of life and liberty against race or color prejudice." *Strauder v. West Virginia,* 100 U.S. 303, 309 (1880). Specifically, a capital sentencing jury representative of a criminal defendant's community assures a "'diffused impartiality,'" *Taylor v. Louisiana,* 419 U.S. 522, 530 (1975) (quoting *Thiel v. Southern Pacific Co.,* 328 U.S. 217, 227 (1946) (Frankfurter, J., dissenting)), in the jury's task of "express[ing] the conscience of the community on the ultimate question of life or death," *Witherspoon v. Illinois,* 391 U.S. 510, 519 (1968).[14] Individual jurors bring to their deliberations "qualities of human nature and varieties of human experience, the range of which is unknown and perhaps unknowable." *Peters v.*

Kiff, 407 U.S. 493, 503 (1972) (opinion of Marshall, J.). The capital sentencing decision requires the individual jurors to focus their collective judgment on the unique characteristics of a particular criminal defendant. It is not surprising that such collective judgments often are difficult to explain. But the inherent lack of predictability of jury decisions does not justify their condemnation. On the contrary, it is the jury's function to make the difficult and uniquely human judgments that defy codification and that "buil[d] discretion, equity, and flexibility into a legal system." H. Kalven & H. Zeisel, The American Jury 498 (1966).

McCleskey's argument that the Constitution condemns the discretion allowed decisionmakers in the Georgia capital sentencing system is antithetical to the fundamental role of discretion in our criminal justice system. Discretion in the criminal justice system offers substantial benefits to the criminal defendant. Not only can a jury decline to impose the death sentence, it can decline to convict or choose to convict of a lesser offense. Whereas decisions against a defendant's interest may be reversed by the trial judge or on appeal, these discretionary exercises of leniency are final and unreviewable.[15] Similarly, the capacity of prosecutorial discretion to provide individualized justice is "firmly entrenched in American law." 2 W. LaFave & J. Israel, Criminal Procedure § 13.2(a), p. 160 (1984). As we have noted, a prosecutor can decline to charge, offer a plea bargain,[16] or decline to seek a death sentence in any particular case. Of course, "the power to be lenient [also] is the power to discriminate," K. Davis, Discretionary Justice 170 (1973), but a capital punishment system that did not allow for discretionary acts of leniency "would be totally alien to our notions of criminal justice." *Gregg v. Georgia,* 428 U.S., at 200. . . .

V

Two additional concerns inform our decision in this case. First, McCleskey's claim, taken to its logical conclusion, throws into serious question the principles that underlie our entire criminal justice system. The Eighth Amendment is not limited in application to capital punishment, but applies to all penalties. *Solem v. Helm*, 463 U.S. 277, 289–290 (1983); see *Rummel v. Estelle*, 445 U.S. 263, 293 (1980) (Powell, J., dissenting). Thus, if we accepted McCleskey's claim that racial bias has impermissibly tainted the capital sentencing decision, we could soon be faced with similar claims as to other types of penalty.[17] Moreover, the claim that his sentence rests on the irrelevant factor of race easily could be extended to apply to claims based on unexplained discrepancies that correlate to membership in other minority groups,[18] and even to gender. Similarly, since McCleskey's claim relates to the race of his victim, other claims could apply with equally logical force to statistical disparities that correlate with the race or sex of other actors in the criminal justice system, such as defense attorneys or judges. Also, there is no logical reason that such a claim need be limited to racial or sexual bias. If arbitrary and capricious punishment is the touchstone under the Eighth Amendment, such a claim could—at least in theory—be based upon any arbitrary variable, such as the defendant's facial characteristics, or the physical attractiveness of the defendant or the victim, that some statistical study indicates may be influential in jury decisionmaking. As these examples illustrate, there is no limiting principle to the type of challenge brought by McCleskey. The Constitution does not require that a State eliminate any demonstrable disparity that correlates with a potentially irrelevant factor in order to operate a criminal justice system that includes capital punishment. As we have stated specifically in the context of capital punishment, the Constitution does not "plac[e] totally unrealistic conditions on its use." *Gregg v. Georgia*, 428 U.S., at 199, n. 50.

Second, McCleskey's arguments are best presented to the legislative bodies. It is not the responsibility—or indeed even the right—of this Court to determine the appropriate punishment for particular crimes. It is the legislatures, the elected representatives of the people, that are "constituted to respond to the will and consequently the moral values of the people." *Furman v. Georgia*, 408 U.S., at 383 (Burger, C. J., dissenting). Legislatures also are better qualified to weigh and "evaluate the results of statistical studies in terms of their own local conditions and with a flexibility of approach that is not available to the courts," *Gregg v. Georgia, supra*, at 186. Capital punishment is now the law in more than two-thirds of our States. It is the ultimate duty of courts to determine on a case-by-case basis whether these laws are applied consistently with the Constitution. Despite McCleskey's wide-ranging arguments that basically challenge the validity of capital punishment in our multiracial society, the only question before us is whether in his case, see *supra*, at 283–285, the law of Georgia was properly applied. We agree with the District Court and the Court of Appeals for the Eleventh Circuit that this was carefully and correctly done in this case.

VI

Accordingly, we affirm the judgment of the Court of Appeals for the Eleventh Circuit.

It is so ordered. . . .

Notes

1. The Georgia Code has been revised and renumbered since McCleskey's trial. The changes do not alter the substance of the sections relevant to this case. For convenience, references in this opinion are to the current sections.

   The Georgia Code contains only one degree of murder. A person commits murder "when he unlawfully and with malice aforethought, either express or implied, causes the death of another human being." Ga. Code Ann. § 16-5-1(a) (1984). A person convicted of murder "shall be punished by death or by imprisonment for life." § 16-5-1(d).

2. Georgia Code Ann. § 17-10-2(c) (1982) provides that when a jury convicts a defendant of murder, "the court shall resume the trial and conduct a presentence hearing before the jury." This subsection suggests that a defendant convicted of murder always is subjected to a penalty hearing at which the jury considers imposing a death sentence. But as a matter of practice, penalty hearings seem to be held only if the prosecutor affirmatively seeks the death penalty. If he does not, the defendant receives a sentence of life imprisonment. See Baldus, Pulaski, & Woodworth, Comparative Review of Death Sentences: An Empirical Study of the Georgia Experience, 74 J. Crim. L. & C. 661, 674, n. 56 (1983).

3. A jury cannot sentence a defendant to death for murder unless it finds that one of the following aggravating circumstances exists beyond a reasonable doubt:

"(1) The offense . . .was committed by a person with a prior record of conviction for a capital felony;

"(2) The offense . . .was committed while the offender was engaged in the commission of another capital felony or aggravated battery, or the offense of murder was committed while the offender was engaged in the commission of burglary or arson in the first degree;

"(3) The offender, by his act of murder . . .knowingly created a great risk of death to more than one person in a public place by means of a weapon or device which would normally be hazardous to the lives of more than one person;

"(4) The offender committed the offense . . .for himself or another, for the purpose of receiving money or any other thing of monetary value;

"(5) The murder of a judicial officer, former judicial officer, district attorney or solicitor, or former district attorney or solicitor was committed during or because of the exercise of his official duties;

"(6) The offender caused or directed another to commit murder or committed murder as an agent or employee of another person;

"(7) The offense of murder, rape, armed robbery, or kidnapping was outrageously or wantonly vile, horrible, or inhuman in that it involved torture, depravity of mind, or an aggravated battery to the victim;

"(8) The offense . . .was committed against any peace officer, corrections employee, or fireman while engaged in the performance of his official duties;

"(9) The offense . . .was committed by a person in, or who has escaped from, the lawful custody of a peace officer or place of lawful confinement; or

"(10) The murder was committed for the purpose of avoiding, interfering with, or preventing a lawful arrest or custody in a place of lawful confinement, of himself or another." § 17-10-30(b).

4. Georgia law provides that "where a statutory aggravating circumstance is found and a recommendation of death is made, the court shall sentence the defendant to death." § 17-10-31.

5. Baldus' 230-variable model divided cases into eight different ranges, according to the estimated aggravation level of the offense. Baldus argued in his testimony to the District Court that the effects of racial bias were most striking in the midrange cases. "When the cases become tremendously aggravated so that everybody would agree that if we're going to have a death sentence, these are the cases that should get it, the race effects go away. It's only in the mid-range of cases where the decision-makers have a real choice as to what to do. If there's room for the exercise of discretion, then the [racial] factors begin to play a role." App. 36. Under this model, Baldus found that 14.4 percent of the black-victim midrange cases received the death penalty, and 34.4 percent of the white-victim cases received the death penalty. See Exhibit DB 90, *reprinted in* Supplemental Exhibits 54. According to Baldus, the facts of McCleskey's case placed it within the midrange. App. 45–46.

6. Although the District Court rejected the findings of the Baldus study as flawed, the Court of Appeals assumed that the study is valid and reached the constitutional issues. Accordingly, those issues are before us. As did the Court of Appeals, we assume the study is valid statistically without reviewing the factual findings of the District Court. Our assump-

tion that the Baldus study is statistically valid does not include the assumption that the study shows that racial considerations actually enter into any sentencing decisions in Georgia. Even a sophisticated multiple-regression analysis such as the Baldus study can only demonstrate a risk that the factor of race entered into some capital sentencing decisions and a necessarily lesser risk that race entered into any particular sentencing decision.

7. Although McCleskey has standing to claim that he suffers discrimination because of his own race, the State argues that he has no standing to contend that he was discriminated against on the basis of his victim's race. While it is true that we are reluctant to recognize "standing to assert the rights of third persons," *Arlington Heights v. Metropolitan Housing Dev. Corp.*, 429 U.S. 252, 263 (1977), this does not appear to be the nature of McCleskey's claim. He does not seek to assert some right of his victim, or the rights of black murder victims in general. Rather, McCleskey argues that application of the State's statute has created a classification that is "an irrational exercise of governmental power," Brief for Petitioner 41, because it is not "necessary to the accomplishment of some permissible state objective." *Loving v. Virginia*, 388 U.S. 1, 11 (1967). See *McGowan v. Maryland*, 366 U.S. 420, 425 (1961) (statutory classification cannot be "wholly irrelevant to the achievement of the State's objective"). It would violate the Equal Protection Clause for a State to base enforcement of its criminal laws on "an unjustifiable standard such as race, religion, or other arbitrary classification." *Oyler v. Boles*, 368 U.S. 448, 456 (1962). See *Cleveland Bd. of Ed. v. Lafleur*, 414 U.S. 632, 652-653 (1974) (Powell, J., concurring). Because McCleskey raises such a claim, he has standing.

8. See, e. g., *Shaw v. Martin*, 733 F.2d 304, 311-314 (CA4), cert. denied, 469 U.S. 873 (1984); *Adams v. Wainwright*, 709 F.2d 1443 (CA11 1983) (per curiam), cert. denied, 464 U.S. 1063 (1984); *Smith v. Balkcom*, 660 F.2d 573, 584–585, modified, 671 F.2d 858, 859–860 (CA5 Unit B 1981) (per curiam), cert. denied, 459 U.S. 882 (1982); *Spinkellink v. Wain-*

wright, 578 F.2d 582, 612-616 (CA5 1978), cert. denied, 440 U.S. 976 (1979).

9. See *Arlington Heights v. Metropolitan Housing Dev. Corp.*, *supra*, at 265; *Washington v. Davis*, 426 U.S. 229, 240 (1976).

10. McCleskey's expert testified:

"Models that are developed talk about the effect on the average. They do not depict the experience of a single individual. What they say, for example, [is] that on the average, the race of the victim, if it is white, increases on the average the probability . . .(that) the death sentence would be given.

"Whether in a given case that is the answer, it cannot be determined from statistics." 580 F.Supp., at 372.

11. According to Professor Baldus:

"McCleskey's case falls in [a] grey area where . . .you would find the greatest likelihood that some inappropriate consideration may have come to bear on the decision.

"In an analysis of this type, obviously one cannot say that we can say to a moral certainty what it was that influenced the decision. We can't do that." App. 45–46.

12. This Court has repeatedly stated that prosecutorial discretion cannot be exercised on the basis of race. *Wayte v. United States*, 470 U.S., at 608; *United States v. Batchelder*, 442 U.S. 114 (1979); *Oyler v. Boles*, 368 U.S. 448 (1962). Nor can a prosecutor exercise peremptory challenges on the basis of race. *Batson v. Kentucky*, 476 U.S. 79 (1986); *Swain v. Alabama*, 380 U.S. 202 (1965). More generally, this Court has condemned state efforts to exclude blacks from grand and petit juries. *Vasquez v. Hillery*, 474 U.S. 254 (1986); *Alexander v. Louisiana*, 405 U.S. 625, 628–629 (1972); *Whitus v. Georgia*, 385 U.S., at 549–550; *Norris v. Alabama*, 294 U.S. 587, 589 (1935); *Neal v. Delaware*, 103 U.S. 370, 394 (1881); *Strauder v. West Virginia*, 100 U.S. 303, 308 (1880); *Ex parte Virginia*, 100 U.S. 339 (1880).

Other protections apply to the trial and jury deliberation process. Widespread bias in the community can make a change of venue constitutionally required. *Irvin v. Dowd*, 366 U.S. 717 (1961). The Constitution prohibits racially biased prosecutorial arguments. *Donnelly v. DeChristoforo*, 416 U.S. 637, 643

(1974). If the circumstances of a particular case indicate a significant likelihood that racial bias may influence a jury, the Constitution requires questioning as to such bias. *Ristaino v. Ross,* 424 U.S. 589, 596 (1976). Finally, in a capital sentencing hearing, a defendant convicted of an interracial murder is entitled to such questioning without regard to the circumstances of the particular case. *Turner v. Murray,* 476 U.S. 28 (1986).

13. In advocating the adoption of the Constitution, Alexander Hamilton stated:

"The friends and adversaries of the plan of the convention, if they agree in nothing else, concur at least in the value they set upon the trial by jury; or if there is any difference between them, it consists in this: the former regard it as a valuable safeguard to liberty, the latter represent it as the very palladium of free government." The Federalist No. 83, p. 519 (J. Gideon ed. 1818).

14. In *Witherspoon,* Justice Brennan joined the opinion of the Court written by Justice Stewart. The Court invalidated a statute that permitted a prosecutor to eliminate prospective jurors by challenging all who expressed qualms about the death penalty. The Court expressly recognized that the purpose of the "broad discretion" given to a sentencing jury is "to decide whether or not death is 'the proper penalty' in a given case," noting that "a juror's general views about capital punishment play an inevitable role in any such decision." 391 U.S., at 519 (emphasis omitted). Thus, a sentencing jury must be composed of persons capable of expressing the "conscience of the community on the ultimate question of life or death." Ibid. The Court referred specifically to the plurality opinion of Chief Justice Warren in *Trop v. Dulles,* 356 U.S. 86 (1958), to the effect that it is the jury that must "maintain a link between contemporary community values and the penal system...." 391 U.S., at 519, n. 15.

Justice Brennan's condemnation of the results of the Georgia capital punishment system must be viewed against this background. As to community values and the constitutionality of capital punishment in general, we have previously noted, that the elected representatives of the people in 37 States and the Congress have enacted capital punishment statutes, most of which have been enacted or amended to conform generally to the *Gregg* standards, and that 33 States have imposed death sentences thereunder. In the individual case, a jury sentence reflects the conscience of the community as applied to the circumstances of a particular offender and offense. We reject Justice Brennan's contention that this important standard for assessing the constitutionality of a death penalty should be abandoned.

15. In the guilt phase of a trial, the Double Jeopardy Clause bars reprosecution after an acquittal, even if the acquittal is "based upon an egregiously erroneous foundation." *United States v. DiFrancesco,* 449 U.S. 117, 129 (1980) (quoting *Fong Foo v. United States,* 369 U.S. 141, 143 (1962)). See Powell, Jury Trial of Crimes, 23 Wash. & Lee L. Rev. 1, 7–8 (1966) (Despite the apparent injustice of such an acquittal, "the founding fathers, in light of history, decided that the balance here should be struck in favor of the individual").

In the penalty hearing, Georgia law provides that "unless the jury . . . recommends the death sentence in its verdict, the court shall not sentence the defendant to death." Georgia Code Ann. § 17-10-31 (1982). In *Bullington v. Missouri,* 451 U.S. 430 (1981), this Court held that the Double Jeopardy Clause of the Constitution prohibits a State from asking for a sentence of death at a second trial when the jury at the first trial recommended a lesser sentence.

16. In this case, for example, McCleskey declined to enter a guilty plea. According to his trial attorney: "The Prosecutor was indicating that we might be able to work out a life sentence if he were willing to enter a plea. But we never reached any concrete stage on that because Mr. McCleskey's attitude was that he didn't want to enter a plea. So it never got any further than just talking about it." Tr. in No. 4909, p. 56 (Jan. 30, 1981).

17. Studies already exist that allegedly demonstrate a racial disparity in the length of prison sentences. See, e.g., Spohn, Gruhl & Welch, The Effect of Race on Sentencing: A Reexamination of an Unsettled Question, 16 Law & Soc. Rev. 71 (1981-1982): Unnever, Frazier &

Henretta, Race Differences in Criminal Sentencing, Sociological Q 197 (1980).

18. In *Regents of the University of California v. Bakke,* 438 U.S. 265, 295, 98 S ct. 2733, 2750, 57L.Ed.2d 750 (1978) (opinion of POWELL, J.) we recognized that the national "majority" is composed of various minority groups, most of which can lay claim to a history of prior discrimination at the hands of the State and private individuals. See *id.* at 292, 98 S.Ct. at 2749 (citing *Strauder v. West Virginia)* at 308 (Celtic Irishmen) (dictum); *Yick Wo v. Hopkins* 118 U.S. 356, 6 S.Ct. 1064, 30 L. Ed. 220 (1886) (Chinese); *Truax v. Raich,* 239 U.S. 33, 36, 41-42, 36, S. Ct. L. Ed. 131 (1915) (Austrian resident aliens); *Korematsu v. United States* 323 U.S. 214, 216, 65 S. Ct. 193, 194, 89 L. Ed. 194 (1944) (Japanese); *Hernandex v. Texas,* 347 U.S. 475, 74 S. Ct. 667, 98 L.Ed. 866 (1954) (Mexican-Americans). See also Uniform Guidelines on Employee Selection Procedures (1978) 29 CFR (1986). (employer must keep records as to the following races and ethnic groups: Blacks, American Indians (including Alaskan natives), Asians, Hispanics (including persons of Mexican, Puerto Rican, Cuban, Central or South America, or other Spanish origin or culture regardless of race), and whites.

We also have recognized that the ethnic composition of the Nation is ever-shifting, *Crawford v. Board of Ed.,* 458 U.S. 527, 102 S.Ct. 3211, 73 L.Ed.2d 948 (1982) illustrates demographic facts that we increasingly find in our country, namely; that populations change in composition, and may do so in relatively short time spans. We noted: "In 1968 when the case went to trial, the Los Angeles District was 53.6% white, 22.6% black, 20% Hispanic and 3.8% Asian and other. By October 1980, the demographic composition had altered radically: 23.7% white, 23.3% black, 45.3% Hispanic and 7.7% Asian and other. *Id.,* at 530 n. 1, 102 S.Ct. at 3214 n. 1. Increasingly whites are becoming a minority in many of the larger American cities. There appears to be no reason why a white defendant in such a city could not make a claim similar to McClesky's if racial disparities in sentencing arguably are shown by a statistical study.

Notes and Questions

1. Does McCleskey make a compelling argument as to how he was discriminated against in his criminal proceedings? Considering that jury deliberations are closed and confidential, how could any defendant prove that race was given undue considerations in his death sentence? Who ought to bear the burden of proof that racial prejudice was or was not a factor?

2. The Baldus study, discussed by Justice Powell, shows that a murderer whose victim was white is 4.3 times more likely to receive the law's harshest punishment than a killer whose victim was black. This means that racial factors lead certain defendants to face a higher risk of a death sentence than others. The Court argued that to rule on the racial discrimination charges, the most pertinent question "is at what point that risk becomes constitutionally unacceptable." In your opinion, does a 4.3 risk multiplier qualify as an "arbitrary and capricious" application of capital punishment? Is this an unreasonable violation of equal protection? If not, what level of disparity *would* be constitutionally unacceptable?

3. Recall Georgia's statutory aggravating factors as outlined in *Gregg* (Chapter 61). Are they based on questions of fact or opinion? How much room is there in the post-*Furman* (Chapter 60) aggravating/mitigating framework for a racially prejudiced jury to inflict a harsher punishment on a black defendant than on a white defendant? Could the statutory guidelines do more to root out discriminatory decision making?

4. What is "diffused impartiality?" How does the process of jury deliberation contribute to the fairness of criminal proceedings? Do the benefits of a deci-

sion by a body of average citizens balance out the risk of prejudice?

5. The McCleskey decision focuses primarily on the possible discrimination inherent in jury discretion. How much does prosecutorial discretion (see Frohmann, Chapter 33) contribute to racial disparities in capital punishment? Is this an issue for the judiciary or the legislature to address?

6. Consider Justice Powell's concern that McCleskey's claim, "taken to its logical conclusion, throws into serious question the principles that underlie our entire criminal justice system." Perhaps for the reasons outlined by Powell, the Court declined to address the key question raised by the Baldus study: What should be done about the clearly inconsistent application of law's violence? Is there a way for the law to confront its own arbitrariness and fallibility without undermining the fundamental principles of the criminal justice system?

Reprinted from: *McCleskey v. Kemp,* 107 S. Ct. 1756 (1987). ✦

Chapter 63

Folk Knowledge as Legal Action

Death Penalty Judgments and the Tenet of Early Release in a Culture of Mistrust and Punitiveness

Benjamin D. Steiner
William J. Bowers
Austin Sarat

The Constitution requires that the discretion of jurors in capital cases be limited such that the risk of discrimination is minimized, if not eliminated. One type of social organization, law's hierarchical set of procedures and legal norms, is imposed on juries to insure that their discretion is controlled. From Furman to McCleskey until the present, this image animates the jurisprudence of capital punishment.

But can and do legal norms effectively police jury discretion in capital cases? The Baldus study (Chapter 62) focused on the question of race and the ability of legal norms to eliminate discrimination in capital sentencing, but the next reading examines the governability of death penalty juries in another context—the folk knowledge that citizens bring with them to their jury service. Steiner, Bowers, and Sarat trace the interconnection between such knowledge and legal action. In this case, folk knowledge refers to the assumptions that jurors make about how much time prisoners actually serve if they are given a life sentence. The authors show that specific, and often inaccurate, release estimates play a key role in determining how jurors

vote in capital cases, and they argue that folk knowledge is resistant to legal control. There is little that law can do about the assumptions that jurors bring with them to their jury service. If this is the case, then law cannot effectively control the violence that capital jurors dispense.

Does the inability of law to control those assumptions mean that the death penalty cannot be administered consistently with the heightened standards of reliability required by Furman?

The world of law is a complex and sometimes contradictory compilation of elements—of institutions and their distinctive practices, of orders and decisions, of images and the understandings that citizens carry with them in their daily lives. Law lives as much in folk knowledge as in the pronouncements of appellate courts, in the quotidian as well as the majestic (Sarat & Kearns 1993). It is inseparable from the interests, goals, and understandings that deeply shape or make up social life.[1] It is part of the everyday world, contributing to the apparently stable, taken-for-granted quality of that world.[2] . . .

By "folk knowledge," we mean the everyday, taken-for-granted understandings that shape people's perceptions, thinking, actions, and reactions to events and situations.[3] Attending to folk knowledge as a legal phenomenon involves recognizing "law in society" (Brigham 1996:9) and refusing to privilege one particular source or location of law over another. It involves recognizing that citizens are not merely pushed and pulled by laws that impinge on us from the "outside." We are not merely the inert recipients of law's external pressures. We make law in our daily lives, in our expectations, in our norms, in our knowledges. As a result, state law and legal policy can be, and often are, controversial, seen as out of step with the dictates of ordinary morality or common sense,[4] and in these instances the force of the everyday world, of morality and common sense, of folk knowledge, may stand as a point from which state law is critiqued, resisted, reformulated.[5] As de Certeau (1984:xiii) remarks, citizens often make of "rituals, representations and laws imposed on them something quite different from what their . . . [originators] had in mind."[6] Thus folk knowledge sometimes pushes against, as it pushes into, the domain of state law. It is itself integral to state law, both constitutive and sometimes critical of it. . . .

This article traces interconnections between folk knowledge and legal action. It explores relations between the pictures of law that people carry around with them and the ways they act in the legal world. We seek here to identify the sources of both general and specific folk knowledge, elucidate the construction and concentration of such knowledge, and examine "the consciousness of crime and punishment" as that consciousness comes to bear within the institutional structure of state law.[7] The particular instance on which this study concentrates occurs when citizens are given the responsibility for making legal decisions, in this case the life or death decision made by jurors in capital cases. Folk knowledge about the release of convicted capital murderers not sentenced to death in one state, Georgia, where folk knowledge on this matter is distinctively concentrated and different from other states, is a strategic focus in the analysis. We examine whether jurors in capital cases come to those cases generally believing that convicted murderers get out of prison too soon and how soon they think such offenders usually return to society. After exploring the sources of these beliefs about early release, we show how folk knowledge about crime and punishment influences the exercise of juror discretion in capital sentencing. In conclusion, we consider the implications of our findings for the legal and procedural control of jury decisionmaking in capital cases.

FOLK KNOWLEDGE OF CRIME AND PUNISHMENT

What is true of law in general—its complexity, the interdependence among its constituent parts, its role in everyday life, and the status of folk knowledge as a form of legal action—is equally and especially true where the subject is crime and punishment. These issues have particular visibility and salience within the canon of legal thinking and also in the popular legal imagination (see Gaubatz 1995). "People in general," Friedman (1999: 68–69) contends, "know or think they know far more about the basic contours of criminal justice than about other aspects of the legal system." As a result, crime and punishment are a rich subject for vernacularization and for the development of folk knowledges. "More than most legal phenomena," Garland (1991:192) notes, "the practices of prohibiting and punishing are directed outwards, toward the public . . . and claim to embody the sentiments and moral vision not of lawyers, but of the people. . . . This claim . . . makes penality a particularly apposite site for a culturalist approach." Images, knowledges, and assessments of crime and punishment, says Garland (p. 193; see also Mead 1918), help shape the overarching culture just as "the established frameworks of cultural meaning undoubtedly influence the forms of punishment."

Since the mid-1960s, uneasiness about social disorder generally, and about criminal behavior in particular, has given rise to what Stuart Scheingold (1984) calls the "myth of crime and punishment." This myth stresses punitiveness as the appropriate response to crime, in contrast to seemingly out-of-vogue alternative scenarios he labels the "myth of redemption" and the "myth of rehabilitation."[8] The myth of crime and punishment provides the rationale for scapegoating and stereotyping categories or classes of people as the "criminal element."[9] It calls for harsh and lasting punishment as the appropriate, indeed the only adequate, solution to the frightening scourge of allegedly random, predatory criminal violence.[10]

Mistrust of the criminal justice process is inherent in public advocacy for punitiveness. It is reflected in a cultural common sense that holds that courts do not punish severely or effectively enough, that prisons release incarcerated offenders "far too soon."[11] Underlying these sentiments is the view that the criminal justice system has been, and continues to be, "faulty," especially those agencies responsible for the imposition and administration of criminal punishment.[12] . . .

THE TENET OF EARLY RELEASE: POLITICAL NARRATIVE, MEDIA CONSTRUCTION, AND FOLK KNOWLEDGE

The most visceral confirmation or "proof" of a defective criminal justice system and of the need for more severe punishment is the early release of criminals who return to violent crime. Such cases easily become the focal points for public debate about the "crime problem" and how it should be dealt with. What the public knows or thinks about the release of criminals in general and murderers in particular may well be reinforced and reproduced by the media (Roberts & Doob 1991), politicians (Simon 1997), and others in the "law and order marketplace" with a stake in having the public see the issue in one way or another.[13] The public's apprehension about crime and punishment invites politicians to assume a "get tough" posture in their political campaigns and to tell stories of early release and what they will do about it as a way of garnering support from a public ever wary of crime.[14] Especially when the crime is murder and early release is blamed, emotionally laden media accounts accompanied by allegations of the contributing role of early release will often be the vehicles for presenting the crime problem to the public.[15] . . .

FOLK KNOWLEDGE AS SPECIFIC ESTIMATES: PUBLIC UNDERSTANDINGS OF RELEASE PRACTICE

Citizen surveys about crime and punishment give us a glimpse of the more specific understandings people have about how long offenders actually spend in prison. Surveys in four states—New York, Nebraska, Kansas, and Massachusetts—provide an indication of just how soon people think convicted first degree murderers will usually return to society.[16] Citizens in each of those states were asked, "How many years do you think a convicted first degree murderer will usually spend in prison before being paroled or released back into society?" Their responses to this question together with the mandatory minimum by law for parole eligibility in each state at the time of the survey are shown in Table 63.1.

[M]ost citizens give estimates that fall below the mandatory minimum for parole eligibility for first degree murderers in their states. The median estimates are well below the mandatory minimums in each state. The single most common response in three of the four states is the lowest response option, "less than 10 years." Citizens clearly do not trust the criminal justice system to act predictably in accord with legal requirements, to the extent that they actually know what state law requires. Thus, in none of these states do we see a degree of consensus on the time such offenders would serve of the kind we might expect to find if the media and political rhetoric in a state were focused on a specifically articulated time of release. The relatively low, if not uniform, estimates are, however, consistent with the kind of narrative representation contained in the Horton ads.[17]

CAPITAL JURORS AND THE CONSCIOUSNESS OF CRIME AND PUNISHMENT: FROM CULTURAL CONTEXT TO INSTITUTIONAL PRACTICE

How is commonsense understanding of the state's response to crime, indeed the belief

Table 63.1

Citizens' Estimates of How Long Convicted First Degree Murderers Usually Serve in Prison Before Parole or Release in Four States

	10	10–14	15–19	20–24	25+	Rest of Life	N	Median Estimate	Statutory Minimum
New York[a]	32.2	20.7	17.4	10.1	19.6	N.A.	(397)	12	12 yrs.
Nebraska[b]	23.4	32.0	19.1	14.8	10.7	N.A.	(440)	10–15	LWOP
Kansas	31.7	23.3	21.4	9.8	13.9	N.A.	(360)	10–14	40 yrs.
Massachusetts[c]	38.5	28.4	18.7	7.1	3.7	3.6	(603)	10–14	LWOP

Note: For economy of presentation, the percentages in Table 63.1 are calculated by row, not by column.

[a] An open-ended format was used in the New York survey, which accounts for the greater nonresponse in that sample.

[b] The response options in the Nebraska survey were overlapping ranges (e.g., 10–15, 15–20, 20–25, etc.). The Nebraska response intervals appear in parentheses following the intervals for the other states.

[c] The response option "rest of life in prison" was provided only in the Massachusetts survey. "N.A." entries indicate that the question was not asked in that state.

that first degree murderers will be back on the streets far sooner than the law on the books permits, translated into legal action? To answer that question we turn to the jury. It is in and through jury service that the moral views and commonsense understandings of citizens are given the sanction of the state. Nowhere is this clearer or more consequential than in capital juries. . . .

To assess their folk knowledge about crime and punishment, we asked jurors two questions about the early release of convicted murderers, one intended to tap a general belief that such offenders are out of prison "far too soon" and the other intended to elicit specific estimates of just "how soon" such offenders usually return to society:

Do you agree or disagree [strongly, moderately, or slightly] that persons sentenced to prison for murder in this state are back on the streets far too soon?

How long did you think someone not given the death penalty for a capital murder in this state usually spends in prison?

Jurors' responses to these two questions together with the mandatory minimum sentence convicted capital murderers must serve if not given the death penalty are shown by state in Table 63.2. Specifically, for each state

the table shows the percentage who agree "strongly," "agree somewhat" ("moderately" or "slightly") and do not agree that "murderers in this state get out of prison far too soon" (panel A); the distributions (and medians) of jurors' estimates of how long convicted murderers not given the death penalty in their state usually serve in prison (in five-year intervals except at the extremes) (panel B); and the mandatory minimum sentence that must be served in each state before a capital murderer not given the death penalty becomes eligible for parole (panel C).

The belief that murderers are out on the street far too soon is the accepted wisdom of four out of five jurors (79.3%); indeed, most jurors adhere "strongly" to this proposition (53.4%). In the states, between 67 and 89% of the jurors agree with this statement, and most jurors agree "strongly" with this sentiment in 8 of the 11 states. Hence, a diffuse dissatisfaction about the early release of murderers is widespread in all 11 states, and this sentiment is intensely felt by most jurors in most states.

Like the citizens surveyed in New York, Nebraska, Kansas, and Massachusetts, the jurors in these states consistently believe that murderers not sentenced to death will usually be back on the streets sooner than state law permits.[18] In all 11 states the median estimate of

Table 63.2
Feelings That Murderers Are Out Far Too Soon and Specific Release Estimates for Murderers Not Sentenced to Death Among Capital Jurors in 11 States (%)

	A. Agree That Murderers Are Out Far Too Soon				B. Estimated Years in Prison If Not Given Death Penalty							C. Mandatory \
	Strongly	Somewhat	Not at All	N	0–9	10–14	15–19	20–24	25+	Life	N	Minimum[a]
Alabama	54.4	17.5	28.1	(57)	8.5	18.6	11.9	6.8	10.2	16.9	(59)	LWOP
California	42.1	34.9	23.0	(152)	13.2	13.8	7.9	9.2	2.0	36.2	(152)	LWOP
Florida	54.7	30.8	14.5	(117)	15.4	10.3	12.0	14.5	35.9	5.1	(117)	25
Georgia	62.2	27.0	10.8	(74)	61.0	9.1	5.2	9.1	1.3	2.6	(77)	15
Kentucky	65.4	21.2	13.5	(104)	24.8	19.5	6.2	5.3	8.8	6.2	(113)	12, 25, IND[b]
Missouri	38.2	29.1	32.7	(55)	16.1	12.5	7.1	12.5	30.4	14.3	(56)	LWOP
North Carolina	57.7	17.9	24.4	(78)	10.8	25.3	15.7	30.1	10.8	0.0	(83)	20
Pennsylvania	59.2	22.4	18.4	(49)	28.6	16.3	10.2	20.4	6.1	10.2	(49)	LWOP
South Carolina	46.5	32.5	21.1	(114)	9.6	21.1	14.0	16.7	25.4	0.9	(114)	30
Texas	75.0	12.5	12.5	(48)	16.1	18.0	22.0	8.0	14.0	10.0	(50)	20
Virginia	38.2	29.1	32.7	(44)	10.9	21.7	8.7	17.4	17.4	2.2	(46)	21.75

[a]These are the minimum periods of imprisonment before parole eligibility for capital murders not given the death penalty. (For documentation and additional clarification, see Bowers & Steiner 1999: 646 n. 198.)
[b]"IND" is defined as "indeterminate" to represent the third Kentucky sentencing option.

time usually served is less than the mandatory minimum for parole eligibility, five years less than that minimum in all but one state.[19] Hence, most jurors in every . . .state believe that murderers . . .will usually be back on the streets before completing their sentence.[20]

Across states, jurors seem to have roughly similar ideas about how long such offenders usually spend in prison, quite apart from the wide variation in statutory minimums for parole eligibility in their states. For the five states that have mandatory minimums of 20 to 40 years and the four life-without-parole states, the median estimates of years usually served all fall within the range 15–20 years. At the same time, within most states jurors' estimates are widely divergent. Fewer than a third of the respondents are concentrated in any single response category in five of these states (Alabama, North Carolina, South Carolina, Texas, and Virginia). Even adjacent intervals spanning 10 years do not encompass a majority of the estimates in most of these states.[21] Thus, despite the "strong" agreement among jurors in most states that murderers are back on the streets "far too soon," there is little agreement on the specific timing of release.

There is, however, one glaring exception. Georgia stands in stark contrast to the other states. Most Georgia jurors' estimates (61.0%) fall into the single 0–9 year category. Despite the 15-year mandatory minimum for parole consideration in Class I (capital) murder cases, half (49.3%) of all Georgia jurors, and even more than half (56.0%) of those who volunteered an estimate, agreed on the single specific estimate of release in 7 years. The concentration of estimates in a single category, the substantial agreement on a single estimated value, and the earliness of release it represents are all distinctive to Georgia, unparalleled in any of the other states. . . .

JURORS' ARTICULATION OF FOLK KNOWLEDGE CONCERNING EARLY RELEASE IN GEORGIA

. . . [J]urors in Georgia were extremely vocal in articulating their concern about early release.[22] Their statements provide strong evidence of a cultural common sense focused on "undue solicitude" for defendants' rights and "insufficient severity" in dealing with the most dangerous criminals. Time and again in talking about the cases on which they served, jurors returned to those issues. As one man put it, "The prosecution and the judges. . . . It's the pardons and parole people and the judges that keep interfering with the system that turn them loose." This language is interesting in its separation of particular actors in the criminal justice system from that "system," suggesting that the source of problems is personal rather than institutional. In contrast, another juror's analysis moved from the personal to the systemic as he explained his thinking about crime and punishment: "I feel like our justice system has gotten—now I can get on the soapbox—that our justice system has gone way too much for the criminal instead of the victim. I think they definitely have gotten more."

There are two ways that jurors think that the criminal justice system has gone "too much for the criminal" in capital cases. One is, of course, early release. The other is the phenomenon of prolonged appeals in capital cases. With respect to the former, the specter of early release—of convicted murderers getting out a prison after a very short incarceration—is deeply ingrained in the folk knowledge that jurors bring with them to their jury service. Explaining why she voted to impose a death sentence, one juror said: "I remember thinking that he should never be let out and I remember thinking that if he got life chances were he would end up with parole." A second juror in the same case said: "The fact that we were unsure that he [the defendant] would get a life sentence had a lot to do with the death sentence verdict. Most of the people on the jury were of the opinion that if we didn't give him the death penalty that he would get out in seven years.". . .

. . . The fact that jurors in Georgia come to their service in capital cases with a store of folk knowledge, one crucial tenet of which is early release, seems to drive them toward death as a way of insuring against the future damaging acts of dangerous criminals. But another aspect of their folk knowledge undermines even this confidence that their sentence can protect against future crimes. Jurors also come to court believing that the law grants excessive and undue protections to defendants which result in endless appeals in capital cases.[23] As one juror who sat on a case that resulted in a life sentence said about persons given the death penalty, "They go back and appeal, appeal, appeal so they die of old age." Or as a juror who voted for death in another case explained,

> Just because someone is sentenced to the death penalty doesn't mean he'll ever die. They don't put people to death. For example, [name of defendant] has now been on death row for many years. He's still there. Every time you turn around he's appealing again. . . . I'm very unhappy. I think the man should be put to death.

Still another juror talked about the influence that the allegedly prolonged appeals process had in the deliberations of the jury on which he sat. "There was," he said, "a lot of discussion about the appeals and the money it would cost to keep him trying and in the end he might still get life after years of appeal. . . . So, this came up that there could be appeal after appeal after appeal and in the end you still get life." Finally, another person suggested that for the jury on which he sat the issue of endless appeals was very important. "If this guy gets death," the jury hypothesized, "they are going to appeal the hell out of it on all kinds of grounds because [name of defense lawyer] is that good. . . . If we say he gets the death penalty there is no guarantee that he'll get it. He'll appeal all the way up through the Supreme Court for the next 10 years. And who is to say that through some technicality he won't get off scott free." Thus if a life sentence doesn't necessarily mean life, it is also not clear that a death sentence will mean death. . . .

FOLK KNOWLEDGE AND LEGAL ACTION: JURY SENTENCING IN CAPITAL CASES

The quotations from our interviews with capital jurors in Georgia suggest that folk knowledge about the release of murderers not given the death penalty is very important in their punishment deliberations.[24] Moreover,

Georgia jurors are the most likely of those in any state to agree that murderers are out of prison far too soon and far likelier than those in other states to give an extremely early release estimate. . . . For both these reasons we might expect Georgia jurors to be more likely than those in other states to hand down death sentences. Yet our equal sampling of trials that ended in life and death sentences in the respective states prevents us from making a direct test of this proposition. By examining Georgia jurors separately from those in other states, however, we can at least determine whether folk knowledge about release has the same impact in Georgia as elsewhere, or whether the concentration of specific release estimates about the timing of release is responsible for departures from sentencing patterns in other states. . . .

We . . . examine the effects on decisionmaking of jurors' general belief that murderers get out of prison far too soon and then consider the role of their specific estimates of how soon capital murderers not given death usually return to society.

1. General beliefs that murderers get out of prison far too soon have a modest initial pro-death sentence effect that disappears by the final punishment vote.

After the jury convicts the defendant of capital murder but before the sentencing phase of the trial, there is a modest 10 percentage point difference in the 10-sample states between the pro-death stands of those who strongly agree and those who do not agree that murderers are back on the streets far too soon. This is on a par with the percentage difference at this stage of the trial between jurors who think the alternative punishment is less than 10 years and those who think it is at least 20 years. But the effect of thinking generally that murderers get out far too soon diminishes as the trial proceeds to the point that it becomes wholly negligible as an influence on the final sentencing decision in these states. In Georgia, where we are limited to a

comparison between jurors who strongly agree that murderers are back on the street far too soon and all others, there is also a suggestion in the data that strong concern about early release disposes jurors to take a prodeath stand prior to sentencing deliberations. By the first and final votes on punishment, however, all indications of a pro-death impact are gone.

2. Specific early release estimates have an initially modest pro-death sentence effect that becomes a substantial influence in their decisionmaking during sentencing deliberations.

The shorter time jurors think prison confinement would be if they did not impose the death penalty, the more likely they are to vote for death at the first and especially at the final ballot on the defendant's punishment in the 10-state sample. Comparing jurors who say the alternative is less than 10 years and those who say 20 or more years, the difference in percentage voting for death is 21 points at the first ballot and 25 points at the final ballot. Before the sentencing stage of the trial and before sentencing deliberations, the corresponding differences are 11 and 12 percentage points, respectively. In Georgia, too, jurors who believe release will come sooner are generally more apt to take a pro-death stand and the greatest difference (of 19 percentage points) between the estimates of 7 years or less and more than 10 years comes at the final punishment vote, although the percentage for the latter group is based on relatively few jurors ($N=13$).[25]

Thus, it is having a specific estimate rather than a general impression of the alternative punishment that appears to influence jurors' sentencing decisions both in Georgia and in the 10-state sample. Jurors with the shortest release estimates tend to take a pro-death stand soonest; in the 10-state sample 4 out of 10 (39.2%) take a stand for death during the guilt stage of the trial.[26] Jurors with intermediate estimates of 10–19 years take longer but are, in the end, almost as likely to reach a pro-death stand. At guilt their punishment stands are closer to those of jurors with 20+ year estimates, but by the final punishment vote their stands have gravitated closer to those of the jurors whose estimates are 0–9 years. For jurors with estimates of 0–9 and 10–19 years, the greatest increase in pro-death stands comes during sentencing deliberations, earlier in deliberations for the 0–9 than for the 10–19 group. The corresponding reductions in "undecided" in these two groups suggest that early release estimates are critical in converting those undecided on punishment to pro-death stands during sentencing deliberations (Sandys 1995). By the same token, jurors in the 10-state sample whose release estimates were 20 years or longer experienced the greatest increase in life sentencing stands and the greatest decrease in "undecided" between sentencing instructions and the first vote on punishment. Evidently it is when jurors deliberate specifically about what the punishment should be that their specific release estimates become especially salient. In the context of group decisionmaking, folk knowledge of the timing of release is the currency of negotiation and decisionmaking. Jurors are more apt to be moved by arguments that invoke specific estimates of when offenders will be released rather than by appeals to their more general apprehension that such release will come too soon. In effect, these data suggest that jurors whose folk knowledge leads them to believe that murderers are less likely to be released early if given a life sentence may be more open to mitigating evidence and argument during sentencing deliberations. By contrast, believing that the defendant would soon be released may close jurors' minds to mitigation and, hence, to a sentence less than death. Here we see two ways in which folk knowledge becomes legal action within a state institution. It may do so not only by shaping individual judgments but also by short-circuiting existing legal procedures (in this case the requirement to consider mitigating evidence) (see *Morgan v. Illinois* 1992, drawing on *Woodson v. North Carolina* 1976 and *Lockett v. Ohio* 1978).

Conclusion

Folk knowledge about crime and punishment is widespread, deeply held, and consequential. Crime is neither an esoteric subject nor one far removed from the consciousness of ordinary Americans. It is consistently seen and cited as one of society's most serious problems (Skogan 1995). Social theorists have long pointed out the significance of beliefs about crime and punishment in fostering social solidarity (Durkheim 1984 [1893]; Mead 1918) and bolstering community standards of right and wrong (Malinowski 1926). Embedded in contemporary cultural common sense about crime and punishment is the tenet of early release which holds that state policy is too lenient and so ineffective that murderers not condemned to death will be back in society far too soon, even before they actually become eligible for parole. We have seen that such folk knowledge is an important basis for legal action when citizens are called on to make punishment decisions in capital cases. . . .

Though represented in state law as a strictly regulated and formally guided exercise of reasoned moral judgement, in practice, the capital sentencing decision is often a negotiated social transaction fraught with tactics of persuasion, advocacy, rhetorical claims, intimidation, and the like (see Bowers & Steiner 1999:pt. V). In this context, specific claims about the timing of release become potent tools in negotiations over the right punishment. General beliefs that violent offenders are out of prison too soon are a resource in the sense that they buttress specific release estimates, indeed are the chief determinant of specific release estimates in states except Georgia, where daily media exposure also supports jurors' specific release estimates. But such general sentiments appear to be too vague or slippery to serve as powerful currency in the give and take of jury deliberations. In some instances the apparently confident estimates of one juror may persuade others less certain to reach consensus on the punishment.

Folk knowledge and the cultural common sense which it embodies empower citizens, giving them a conception of how state law does, and should, operate that has a source independent of those whose legal authority derives from formal training or official position. It means that law can, and does, live in society in ways that cannot readily be cabined or controlled by state law.[27] This means that in capital cases, instructing jurors not to think about what the alternative would be when they are deciding guilt and refusing to explain to them what the death penalty alternative would be when they are deciding punishment, while it may make sense within the highly structured ideology of due process,[28] defies cultural common sense and, as such, is regularly resisted.[29] . . .

In the end, our findings illuminate the ability of law in society to resist colonization by state law and/or the way the culture of mistrust and punitiveness preserves a distinctive way of knowing and seeing law. Only by viewing law in this way can we, as Yngvesson (1989:1693) notes, "explain popular consciousness as a force contributing to the production of legal order rather than as simply an anomaly or a pocket of consciousness outside of law, irrelevant to its maintenance and transformation." Thus a public enlisted by the state to impose death will do so, but not in the way required by the constitution as a condition for using death as punishment.

Notes

1. "Law," Geertz (1983:218) explains, "rather than a mere technical add-on to a morally (or immorally) finished society, is, along of course with a whole range of other cultural realities, . . .an active part of it."

2. "[T]he power exerted by a legal regime consists less in the force that it can bring to bear against violators of its rules than in its capacity to persuade people that the world described in its images and categories is the only attainable world in which a sane person would want to live" (Gordon 1984:108; see also Hunt 1980). As Trubek (1984:604) writes:

   > [S]ocial order depends in a nontrivial way on a society's shared "world view." Those world views are basic notions about human and social relations that give meaning to the lives of society's members. Ideals about the law—what it is, what it does, why it exists—are part of the world view of any complex society. . . . Law, like other aspects of belief systems, helps to define the role of an individual in society and the relations with others that make sense. At the same time that law is a system of belief, it is also a basis of organization, a part of the structure in which action is embedded.

3. Folk knowledge lives in daily life and is generally untheorized and always nontechnical, though not always uninformed by technical knowledge (Schutz 1967). Folk knowledge is what Lefebvre (1991:127) calls "the truth in a body and a soul." It is immediate and familiar, the background for projects of reason and science and often the object criticized in those projects. It is "the reality which seems self evident to men. . . . It is the . . .ground of everything given in my experience . . .the taken-for granted frame in which all the problems which I must overcome are placed" (Schutz & Luckmann 1973:3–4). For a different perspective on folk knowledge see Blanchot 1987.

4. As Brigham (1996:20) notes, "Laws sometimes infuse American social life with elements that seem not quite natural. The due process guarantee that the criminal goes free if the constable blunders is one."

5. Jury nullification is such an instance. Citizens not only resist but override state law. Indeed, they substitute "folk law" for state law.

6. Citizens are not merely pushed and pulled by laws that impinge from the "outside." We are

not merely the inert recipients of law's external pressures. We make law in our daily lives, in our expectations, in our norms, in our knowledges, that is, in society (Brigham 1996).

7. Following Ewick and Silbey (1998:224), we believe that "consciousness entails both thinking *and* doing [emphasis added]: telling stories, complaining, lumping grievances, working, playing, marrying, divorcing, suing a neighbor, . . .refusing to call the police."

8. The myth of crime and punishment presents punitiveness as a necessary and sufficient solution to complicated, and otherwise intractable, problems of social order, including but not restricted to crime. Its appeal is greater where people's apprehensions and insecurities are more pronounced, apart from the realities of crime and the risks of victimization (see Connolly 1995:ch. 2). The emphasis on punishment as the solution to crime is rooted in America's cultural themes of "frontier justice" and "individual responsibility," according to Scheingold (1984:64); they are, in his words, "more expressive than instrumental."

9. This image of the incorrigible offender has been reinforced in the public mind through accounts and portrayals of crime in the popular media over the past several decades. John M. Sloop's (1997) analysis of over 40 years of American media portrayal of prisoners and punishment reveals a decisive shift in the characterization of persons convicted of criminal violence. Specifically, his investigation of more than 600 articles in popular periodicals (e.g., *U.S. News & World Report, The Nation, Psychology Today,* and the like) between 1950 and 1993 reveals a distinctive shift in media representations away from the offender capable of redemption to a more irrational, incorrigible, predatory, and dangerous criminal. Although Sloop's analysis reveals important variations in the depiction of criminals by race in previous decades, he finds a convergence in the depiction of the contemporary violent offender as "characteristically represented as animalistic and senseless, arising from warped personalities" (ibid., p. 142). Moreover, contemporary media discourse frames prisons as utterly incapable of reforming prisoners regardless of race: "Violence, simply stated, is constructed as a norm of prison behavior and begins to include inmates of all ethnicities" (ibid., p. 145). Sloop's analysis thus reveals how "the consciousness of crime and punishment" is culturally constructed through popular media discourse.

10. Scheingold (1998:8) notes: "Recent public opinion research reveals increasingly punitive attitudes in the United States." Since the claim that punishment is now too lenient is embedded in cultural understandings rather than experience with crime (Scheingold 1984:226–227), the implication that we are not now imposing enough punishment is a cultural tenet, a value judgment, not subject to empirical refutation.

11. More than three decades of research demonstrates that the public sees courts as too lenient (Roberts 1992). Public attitudes regarding the belief in early release and parole board leniency is less well documented in the United States owing to the absence of questions, not contrary findings. However, one U.S. report found that over 80% of the public who were surveyed in 1993 supported a proposal to make parole more difficult (Maguire & Pastore 1993). In Canada, on the other hand, the belief in early release and parole board leniency has been well documented (Roberts 1988; Canadian Criminal Justice Association 1987).

12. Public mistrust of the criminal justice system is manifest in public opinion surveys asking about confidence in various institutions and agencies. The criminal justice system has ranked lowest, or next to lowest, each year since 1993 when it was added to the Gallup Poll question asking respondents how confident they were in various institutions, including church or organized religion, military, U.S. Supreme Court, banks and banking, public schools, Congress, newspapers, big business, television news, organized labor, police, and the Presidency. Only 15 to 24% of respondents said they had "a great deal" or "quite a lot" of confidence in the criminal justice system over the period 1993–1998 (see Maguire & Pastore 1997:Table 2.14). Moreover, the generalized mistrust of the criminal justice system is due especially to the public's lack of confidence in the two agencies respon-

sible for the imposition and administration of criminal punishment. Local courts and especially state prisons, in contrast to the local police, have the least public confidence (ibid., Tables 2.16, 2.18 , 2.21, and 2.22).

13. "Such distorted or mistaken public perceptions are documented in the cases of fears about escalating crime rates (Sasson 1995), hysteria over stranger child abduction (Best 1990), or the obsession with serial murder (Jenkins 1994).

14. The extent to which issues of crime and punishment are solidly anchored in cultural common sense or are politicized from above is an open question. Beckett (1997) argues that issues of crime and punishment get politicized from above. For a similar view see Friedman (1999:70); as he puts it, "from TV, and from the political pulpit, come messages that somehow play into the public lust for more and tougher punishment."

15. The claims made by the media or politicians "assert the existence of some condition, define it as offensive, harmful, and otherwise undesirable . . .creates a public or political issue over the matter" (Spector & Kitsuse 1987:147). Moreover, as Edelman (1988:12) observes, the way such claims define an issue or social problem come to "constitute people as subjects with particular kinds of aspirations, self-concepts, and fears, and they create beliefs about the relative importance of events and objects."

16. For a discussion of the background and results of the 1991 New York and Nebraska survey data, see Bowers, Vandiver, & Dugan 1994. At the times of these surveys, only Nebraska had the death penalty, though Kansas and New York later enacted capital statutes.

17. We cannot say, of course, to what extent the Horton ads may have fostered the belief in early release in these four states. It is notable that citizens' estimates of the time until release are lowest in Massachusetts, the state where the Horton narrative was supposed to be the reality. But surely the Horton ad's public appeal and political effectiveness in 1988 presidential politics was the result of its resonance with an already prevailing public fear of crime, mistrust of criminal justice policy and practice, and desire for harsh punish-

ment, as embodied in the "myth of crime and punishment" (Scheingold 1984).

18. The release estimates of capital jurors in most states have much in common with those of the citizens examined earlier in Table 1. (1) Specifically, they show greater uniformity than does state law. The median estimates are far less divergent than are the mandatory minimums; all but one fall within 5 years of the 15.2-year average of state medians. (2) The release estimates are largely independent of state law. Having a fixed period before parole or prohibiting it altogether makes relatively little difference; 15.0 years is the average of the median estimates in the six states with an unambiguous mandatory minimum (excluding Kentucky), 16.3 years is the average in the four states that prohibit parole. Nor does the length of the fixed minimum have much effect on jurors' estimates, except for Georgia. Thus, 17.7 years is the average estimate for the three states with mandatory minimums of more than 20 years; 16.0 years is the average for the two states with a 20-year mandatory minimum. (3) There is relatively little consensus within most states on a specific release estimate. Few of the 5-year intervals contain more than a third of the estimates.

19. Only North Carolina with a median estimate three years below the mandatory minimum is the exception. In Kentucky with various sentencing options such a difference is indeterminate.

20. Compared with citizens' estimates (in Table 1), jurors' tend to estimate that murderers serve somewhat more time in jail. Jurors' higher estimates might be expected since they were asked specifically about the narrower class of "death-eligible" capital murderers, instead of "first degree" but not necessarily "death-eligible" murderers. Of course, the jurors, unlike citizens at large, were "death-qualified" (staunch death penalty opponents were eliminated), so differences in their estimates could result from jury selection procedures as well as differences in the questions asked.

21. There is little convergence around the median estimates in most states. Nor is there much convergence around the mandatory minimums for parole eligibility. Among states that

do permit parole, in Florida, and North Carolina, the interval that includes the state's mandatory minimum does attract the most estimates. Yet, only about a third of all responses fall into this interval: 36.0% in Florida and 30.0% in North Carolina. In the other states that permit parole, even fewer occupy the category that embodies the mandatory minimum. Indeed, none of the five-year intervals accounts for as many as 30% of the release estimates in these states.

Among the four states that have life without parole (LWOP), only in California does the "life" response attract more jurors (36.2%) than any other single category. Even so, only half of those who say "life" go on to indicate that there is no parole; hence, fewer than one in five California jurors affirmatively identifies LWOP as the death penalty alternative. In the other three states without parole, the life response is slightly more common than in any of the seven states that permit parole, yet it is the response of only 10.2%, 14.3%, and 16.9% of the jurors in these three states. And even if having LWOP prompted a few more jurors in these states to say that the death penalty alternative is life, there is virtually no indication that it promoted awareness that parole is unavailable. Only three jurors in the three LWOP states qualified his or her life response to indicate that there was no parole.

22. The analysis that follows is based on 77 completed interviews with Georgia capital jurors. The CJP interviews average 3-4 hours and include both structured questions with predetermined response options and open-ended questions crafted to elicit jurors' accounts of their own punishment decisionmaking and that of the jury as a group. See Bowers (1995:1081) for a further discussion of the interviewing strategy.

23. For a discussion of one source of this belief in endless appeals, see Amsterdam 1999.

24. Research on juries in other contexts has reached similar conclusions about the importance of folk knowledge. For examples, see Garfinkel 1967; Manzo 1993, 1994.

25. The concentration of especially low release estimates there suggests that the decision process in Georgia may differ from that in other states. It could be, for example, that this concentration means for most Georgia jurors that early release is taken for granted and that other arguments or considerations come to the fore in deciding on punishment. In other words, for the majority of jurors who agree on release in 7 years, the choice between death and life could be the product of retributive judgments or a reflection of the influence of race, as persuasively demonstrated for Georgia by Baldus and his associates (1990).

Additional evidence from the interviews with jurors points, however, to the central place of concern about the death penalty alternative in punishment deliberation and even during deliberations on guilt among Georgia jurors. . . .

26. Since the difference depends on a small sample of jurors with release estimates of more than 10 years, it must be regarded only as suggesting the role of release-specific estimates in capital decisionmaking among Georgia jurors. A more definitive answer must await additional data on Georgia jurors now being collected.

27. "Legality," Ewick & Silbey (1998:248) observe, "is composed of multiple schemas, and each of the schemas of legal consciousness emplots a particular relationship among ideals and practices, revealing their mutual interdependence. The persistently observed gap is a space not a vacuum; it is one source of law's hegemonic power."

28. One rationale for not telling jurors what the punishment will be is that when parole or good time are possible, the actual sentence that will be served is not something the judge can definitively determine. To properly answer the question means telling jurors what the contingencies are within the law and administrative regulations now in effect or providing them with statistics compiled on the median or mean sentence served by capital murderers not given the death penalty. Here the judge would have to depend on statistics provided by the department of corrections compiled specifically for this purpose by a court administrator.

29. See Bowers, Sandys, & Steiner (1998:pt. IV) for evidence that jurors widely violate instructions not to discuss punishment during

guilt deliberations and Bowers & Steiner (1999:pt. IV) for further evidence of juror frustration about not being informed about the death penalty alternative when making punishment decisions.

References

Amsterdam, Anthony G. (1999) "Selling a Quick Fix for Boot Hill: The Myth of Justice Delayed in Death Cases," in A. Sarat, ed., *The Killing State: Capital Punishment in Law, Politics and Culture.* New York: Oxford Univ. Press.

Baldus, David, C., George Woodworth, & Charles A. Pulaski, Jr. (1990) *Equal Justice and the Death Penalty: A Legal and Empirical Analysis.* Boston: Northeastern Univ. Press.

Beckett, Katherine (1997) *Making Crime Pay: Law and Order in Contemporary American Politics.* New York: Oxford Univ. Press.

Best, Joel (1990) *Threatened Children: Rhetoric and Concern about Child-Victims.* Chicago: Univ. of Chicago Press.

Bowers, William J., & Benjamin D. Steiner (1999) "Death by Default: An Empirical Demonstration of False and Forced Choices in Capital Sentencing," 43 *Texas Law Rev.* 605–717.

Bowers, William J., Margaret Vandiver, & Patricia H. Dugan (1994) "A New Look at Public Opinion on Capital Punishment: What Citizens and Legislators Prefer," 22 *American J. of Criminal Law* 77–115.

Brigham, John (1996) *The Constitution of Interests: Beyond the Politics of Rights.* New York: New York Univ. Press.

Canadian Criminal Justice Association (1987) *Attitudes toward Parole.* Ottawa: Canadian Criminal Justice Association.

Connolly, William E. (1995) *The Ethos of Pluralization.* Minneapolis: Univ. of Minnesota Press.

de Certeau, Michel (1984) *The Practice of Everyday Life,* trans. S. Rendell. Berkeley: Univ. of California Press.

Durkheim, Emile (1984 [1893]) *The Division of Labor in Society,* trans. W. D. Halls. New York: Free Press.

Edelman, Murray (1988) *Constructing the Political Spectacle.* Chicago: Univ. of Chicago Press.

Ewick, Patricia, & Susan Silbey (1998) *The Common Place of Law: Stories from Everyday Life.* Chicago: Univ. of Chicago Press.

Friedman, Lawrence (1999) "On Stage: Some Historical Notes about Criminal Justice," in P. Ewick, R. A. Kagan, & A. Sarat, eds., *Social Science, Social Policy, and the Law.* New York: Russell Sage Foundation.

Garfinkel, Harold (1967) "Some Rules of Correct Decisionmaking that Jurors Respect," in *Studies in Ethnomethodology.* Englewood Cliffs, NJ: Prentice Hall.

Garland, David (1991) "Punishment and Culture: The Symbolic Dimension of Criminal Justice," 11 *Studies in Law, Politics, & Society* 191–224.

Geertz, Clifford (1983) *Local Knowledge: Further Essays in Interpretive Anthropology.* New York: Basic Books.

Gordon, Robert W. (1984) "Critical Legal Histories," 36 *Stanford Law Rev.* 57–125.

Hunt, Alan (1990) "Rights and Social Movements: Counter-Hegemonic Strategies," 17 *J. of Law & Society* 310–333.

Jenkins, Philip (1994) *Using Murder: The Social Construction of Serial Homicide.* New York: Aldine de Gruyter.

Lefebvre, Henri (1991) *Critique of Everyday Life,* trans J. Moore. London: Verso.

Maguire, Kathleen, & Ann L. Pastore, eds. (1993) *Sourcebook of Criminal Justice Statistics.* Washington: U.S. Bureau of Justice Statistics.

Malinowski, Bronislaw (1926) *Crime and Custom in Savage Society.* New York: Harcourt, Brace.

Manzo, John F. (1993) "Jurors' Narratives of Personal Experience in Deliberation Talk," 13 *Text* 267–290.

—— (1994) "'You Wouldn't Take a Seven-Year-Old and Ask Him All These Questions': Jurors' Use of Practical Reasoning in Supporting Their Arguments," 19 *Law & Social Inquiry* 639–663.

Mead, George Herbert (1918) "The Psychology of Punitive Justice," 25 *American J. of Sociology* 577–602.

Roberts, Julian V. (1988) "Early Release from Prison: What Do the Canadian Public Really Think?" 26 *Canadian J. of Criminology* 231–248.

—— (1992) "Public Opinion, Crime, and Criminal Justice" in M. Tonry, ed., *Crime and Justice: A Review of Research.* Chicago: Univ. of Chicago Press.

Roberts, Julian V., & Anthony N. Doob (1991) "News Media Influences on Public Views of Sentencing," 14 *Law & Human Behavior* 451–468.

Sarat, Austin, & Thomas R. Kearns (1993) "Beyond the Great Divide," in A. Sarat & T. R. Kearns, ed., *Law in Everyday Life*. Ann Arbor: Univ. of Michigan Press.

Sasson, Theodore (1995) *Crime Talk*. New York: de Gruyter.

Scheingold, Stuart A. (1984) *The Politics of Law and Order: Street Crime and Public Policy*. New York: Longman.

—— (1998) "Criminology and the Politicization of Crime and Punishment," in G. Mars & D. Nelken, eds., *Politics, Crime Control, and Culture*. Aldershot, Eng.: Dartmouth/Ashgate.

Simon, Jonathan (1997) "Governing through Crime" in L. M. Friedman & G. Fisher, eds., *The Crime Conundrum: Essays in Criminal Justice*. Boulder, CO: Westview Press.

Skogan, Wesley G. (1990) *Disorder and Decline: Crime and the Spiral of Decay in American Neighborhoods*. New York: Free Press.

Sloop, John M. (1996) *The Cultural Prison: Discourse, Prisoners, and Punishment*. Tuscaloosa: Univ. of Alabama Press.

Spector, Malcolm, & John I. Kitsuse (1977) *Constructing Social Problems*. Menlo Park, CA: Cummings.

Trubek, David M. (1984) "Where the Action Is: Critical Legal Studies and Empiricism," 36 *Stanford Law Rev.* 575–622.

Yngvesson, Barbara (1989) "Inventing Law in Local Settings: Rethinking Popular Legal Culture," 98 *Yale Law J.* 1689–1709.

CASES

Locket v. Ohio, 438 U.S. 586 (1978).
Morgan v. Illinois, 504 U.S. 719 (1992).
Woodson v. North Carolina, 428 U.S. 280 (1976).

STATUTE

Georgia Code Annotated, sec. 17-10-31.1 (WESTLAW 1994).

NOTES AND QUESTIONS

1. What constitutes "folk knowledge"? How does it influence law's meaning and application? What do Steiner et al. mean when they write that folk knowledge empowers citizens? Do you agree that it does?

2. According to Steiner et al., what makes crime and punishment a particularly "rich subject for vernacularization and for the development of folk knowledges"?

3. What is Scheingold's "myth of crime and punishment"? Why does he dismiss the ideas of redemption and rehabilitation? How did this theory seep into folk knowledge? What perpetuates it?

4. What is the prevalent folk knowledge about parole for capital crimes? Why is it so out of touch with empirical reality? Is this a problem?

5. Steiner et al. write, "It is in and through jury service that the moral views and commonsense understandings of citizens are given the sanction of the state." Should the state sanction such commonsense understandings? Is the system of guided discretion an effective tool for excluding misinformed folk knowledge from legal proceedings? Why or why not?

6. Anecdotal evidence suggests that juries are delivering harsher sentences than they otherwise might, simply because they mistrust the state's commitment to incapacitate offenders for the full term of their prison sentence. They do not believe that a sentence of life in prison really means that someone will be incarcerated for life. How can the state improve the credibility of life sentences?

7. How does the criminal appeals process contribute to the belief that law is too le-

nient in capital crimes? Is the criminal appeals process biased in favor of convicted criminals? Would it be better if the law denied all appeals beyond a certain point? Who would decide that point? What would be the benefits and the drawbacks?

8. What types of folk knowledge besides assumptions about sentencing severity do you suppose influence juries in criminal trials? Are racial stereotypes a form of folk knowledge?

Reprinted from: Benjamin D. Steiner, William J. Bowers, and Austin Sarat, "Folk Knowledge as Legal Action: Death Penalty Judgments and the Tenet of Early Release in a Culture of Mistrust and Punitiveness" in *Law and Society Review*, 33:1, 1999, pp. 460–505. Copyright © 1999. Reprinted with the permission of the Law and Society Association. ✦

Section XV

The Future of Capital Punishment

Chapter 64

God's Justice and Ours

Antonin Scalia

What is the future of capital punishment, the ultimate form of law's violence? For a long time this question seemed to be pretty settled. From the mid-1970s until very recently, the political and legal climate was very supportive of the death penalty. The Supreme Court moved rather methodically, if not in a linear fashion, to cut off all systemic, "wholesale" challenges (e.g., McCleskey v. Kemp) (Chapter 62) to the constitutionality of capital punishment. Public support for the death penalty rose to unprecedented levels, and the abolition movement seemed virtually invisible. Politicians of every stripe did not want to be caught on the "wrong side" of the death penalty debate. The result was that the population of death row, if not the number of executions, increased dramatically. At the start of 2003, slightly more than 3,600 persons on death row in the United States; 71 were executed in 2002, down from a high of 98 in 1999.

Recently, however, the political climate seems to have altered, if only modestly. A Gallup poll conducted in the summer of 2003 shows that 74 percent of Americans support the death penalty when asked, "Are you in favor of capital punishment for a person convicted of murder?" Yet, this poll reports that Americans are closely divided on the proper sentence for someone convicted of murder, with 53 percent favoring capital punishment, 44 percent life-in-prison without parole, and 3 percent undecided. Moreover, the June 12, 2000, issue of Newsweek reported, "For the first time in a generation, the death

penalty itself is in the dock—on the defensive at home and especially abroad for being too arbitrary and too prone to error." About the same time, the New York Times proclaimed the coming of "the new death penalty politics," saying that "heightened public concern over the fallibility of the criminal justice system [has caused] a dramatic shift in the national debate over capital punishment."

Growing evidence of failures in the criminal justice system, revealed by DNA testing, has been particularly consequential in making this new situation possible. Further, a remarkable moment in this new political climate occurred when, on January 31, 2000, Governor George Ryan of Illinois, a long-time supporter of capital punishment, announced plans to block all executions in that state by granting stays before any scheduled lethal injections were administered. His act effectively imposed a moratorium on the death penalty, the first time this had been done in any state. Ryan said that he was convinced that the death penalty system in Illinois was "fraught with errors" and "broken" and that it should be suspended until thoroughly investigated. In January, 2003, Governor Ryan followed up on the moratorium by pardoning four of Illinois' death row inmates and commuting the sentences of the remaining 167 from death to another punishment.

New and unexpected voices—including such prominent conservatives as the Reverend Pat Robertson and newspaper columnist George Will—have spoken out against what they see as inequality and racial discrimination in the administration of state killing and in are favor of a moratorium. A National Committee to Prevent Wrongful Executions, whose members include death penalty supporters such as William S. Sessions, a former Texas judge and F.B.I. director in the Reagan and Bush administrations, has called for a reexamination of the process that leads to wrongful death sentences.

The final two readings present two different views of the current situation and future of capital punishment in the United States. In the first, U. S. Supreme Court Justice Antonin

Scalia argues that the death penalty continues to be both legally and morally acceptable. Its legality derives from the Constitution; its morality from the conviction that government derives its authority from divine sources. In his view, the death penalty has, and ought to have, a secure future.

Before proceeding to discuss the morality of capital punishment, I want to make clear that my views on the subject have nothing to do with how I vote in capital cases that come before the Supreme Court. That statement would not be true if I subscribed to the conventional fallacy that the Constitution is a "living document"—that is, a text that means from age to age whatever the society (or perhaps the Court) thinks it ought to mean.

In recent years, that philosophy has been particularly well enshrined in our Eighth Amendment jurisprudence, our case law dealing with the prohibition of "cruel and unusual punishments." Several of our opinions have said that what falls within this prohibition is not static, but changes from generation to generation, to comport with "the evolving standards of decency that mark the progress of a maturing society." Applying that principle, the Court came close, in 1972, to abolishing the death penalty entirely. It ultimately did not do so, but it has imposed, under color of the Constitution, procedural and substantive limitations that did not exist when the Eighth Amendment was adopted—and some of which had not even been adopted by a majority of the states at the time they were judicially decreed. For example, the Court has prohibited the death penalty for all crimes except murder, and indeed even for what might be called run-of-the-mill murders, as opposed to those that are somehow characterized by a high degree of brutality or depravity. It has prohibited the mandatory imposition of the death penalty for any crime, insisting that in all cases the jury be permitted to consider all mitigating factors and to impose, if it wishes, a lesser sentence. And it has imposed an age limit at the time of the offense (it is currently seventeen) that is well above what existed at common law.

If I subscribed to the proposition that I am authorized (indeed, I suppose compelled) to intuit and impose our "maturing" society's "evolving standards of decency," this essay would be a preview of my next vote in a death penalty case. As it is, however, the Constitution that I interpret and apply is not living but dead—or, as I prefer to put it, enduring. It means today not what current society (much less the Court) thinks it ought to mean, but what it meant when it was adopted. For me, therefore, the constitutionality of the death penalty is not a difficult, soul-wrenching question. It was clearly permitted when the Eighth Amendment was adopted (not merely for murder, by the way, but for all felonies—including, for example, horse-thieving, as anyone can verify by watching a western movie). And so it is clearly permitted today. There is plenty of room within this system for "evolving standards of decency," but the instrument of evolution (or, if you are more tolerant of the Court's approach, the herald that evolution has occurred) is not the nine lawyers who sit on the Supreme Court of the United States, but the Congress of the United States and the legislatures of the fifty states, who may, within their own jurisdictions, restrict or abolish the death penalty as they wish.

But while my views on the morality of the death penalty have nothing to do with how I vote as a judge, they have a lot to do with whether I can or should be a judge at all. To put the point in the blunt terms employed by Justice Harold Blackmun towards the end of his career on the bench, when he announced that he would henceforth vote (as Justices William Brennan and Thurgood Marshall had previously done) to overturn all death sentences, when I sit on a Court that reviews and affirms capital convictions, I am part of "the machinery of death." My vote, when joined with at least four others, is, in most cases, the last step that permits an execution to proceed. I could not take part in that process if I believed what was being done to be immoral. . . .

I am aware of the ethical principle that one can give "material cooperation" to the immoral act of another when the evil that would attend failure to cooperate is even greater (for example, helping a burglar tie up a householder where the alternative is that the burglar would kill the householder). . . .

. . . I find it hard to see how any appellate judge could find this condition to be met, unless he believes retaining his seat on the bench (rather than resigning) is somehow essential to preservation of the society—which is of course absurd. . . .

It is a matter of great consequence to me, therefore, whether the death penalty is morally acceptable. As a Roman Catholic—and being unable to jump out of my skin—I cannot discuss that issue without reference to Christian tradition and the Church's Magisterium.

The death penalty is undoubtedly wrong unless one accords to the state a scope of moral action that goes beyond what is permitted to the individual. In my view, the major impetus behind modern aversion to the death penalty is the equation of private morality with governmental morality. This is a predictable (though I believe erroneous and regrettable) reaction to modern, democratic self-government.

Few doubted the morality of the death penalty in the age that believed in the divine right of kings. Or even in earlier times. St. Paul had this to say (I am quoting, as you might expect, the King James version):

Let every soul be subject unto the higher powers. For there is no power but of God: the powers that be are ordained of God. Whosoever therefore resisteth the power, resisteth the ordinance of God: and they that resist shall receive to themselves dam-

nation. For rulers are not a terror to good works, but to the evil. Wilt thou then not be afraid of the power? Do that which is good, and thou shalt have praise of the same: for he is the minister of God to thee for good. But if thou do that which is evil, be afraid; for he beareth not the sword in vain: for he is the minister of God, a revenger to execute wrath upon him that doeth evil. Wherefore ye must needs be subject, not only for wrath, but also for conscience sake. (Romans 13:1–5)

This is not the Old Testament, I emphasize, but St. Paul. One can understand his words as referring only to lawfully constituted authority, or even only to lawfully constituted authority that rules justly. But the *core* of his message is that government—however you want to limit that concept—derives its moral authority from God. It is the "minister of God" with powers to "revenge," to "execute wrath," including even wrath by the sword (which is unmistakably a reference to the death penalty). Paul of course did not believe that the *individual* possessed any such powers. Only a few lines before this passage, he wrote, "Dearly beloved, avenge not yourselves, but rather give place unto wrath: for it is written, Vengeance is mine; I will repay, saith the Lord." And in this world the Lord repaid—did justice—through His minister, the state.

These passages from Romans represent the consensus of Western thought until very recent times. Not just of Christian or religious thought, but of secular thought regarding the powers of the state. That consensus has been upset, I think, by the emergence of democracy. It is easy to see the hand of the Almighty behind rulers whose forebears, in the dim mists of history, were supposedly anointed by God, or who at least obtained their thrones in awful and unpredictable battles whose outcome was determined by the Lord of Hosts, that is, the Lord of Armies. It is much more difficult to see the hand of God—or any higher moral authority—behind the fools and rogues (as the losers would have it) whom we ourselves elect to do our own will. How can their power to avenge—to vindicate the "public order"—be any greater than our own?

So it is no accident, I think, that the modern view that the death penalty is immoral is centered in the West. That has little to do with the fact that the West has a Christian tradition, and everything to do with the fact that the West is the home of democracy. Indeed, it seems to me that the more Christian a country is the *less* likely it is to regard the death penalty as immoral. Abolition has taken its firmest hold in post-Christian Europe, and has least support in the church-going United States. I attribute that to the fact that, for the believing Christian, death is no big deal. Intentionally killing an innocent person is a big deal: it is a grave sin, which causes one to lose his soul. But losing this life, in exchange for the next? The Christian attitude is reflected in the words Robert Bolt's play has Thomas More saying to the headsman: "Friend, be not afraid of your office. You send me to God." And when Cranmer asks whether he is sure of that, More replies, "He will not refuse one who is so blithe to go to Him." For the nonbeliever, on the other hand, to deprive a man of his life is to end his existence. What a horrible act!

Besides being *less* likely to regard death as an utterly cataclysmic punishment, the Christian is also *more* likely to regard punishment in general as deserved. The doctrine of free will—the ability of man to resist temptations to evil, which God will not permit beyond man's capacity to resist—is central to the Christian doctrine of salvation and damnation, heaven and hell. The post-Freudian secularist, on the other hand, is more inclined to think that people are what their history and circumstances have made them, and there is little sense in assigning blame.

Of course those who deny the authority of a government to exact vengeance are not entirely logical. Many crimes—for example, domestic murder in the heat of passion—are neither deterred by punishment meted out to others nor likely to be committed a second time by the same offender. Yet opponents of capital punishment do not object to sending such an offender to prison, perhaps for life. Because he deserves punishment. Because it is just.

The mistaken tendency to believe that a democratic government, being nothing more than the composite will of its individual citizens, has no more moral power or authority than they do as individuals has adverse effects in other areas as well. It fosters civil disobedience, for example, which proceeds on the assumption that what the individual citizen considers an unjust law—even if it does not compel *him* to act unjustly—need not be obeyed. St. Paul would not agree. "Ye must needs be subject," he said, "not only for wrath, but also for conscience sake." For conscience sake. The reaction of people of faith to this tendency of democracy to obscure the divine authority behind government should not be resignation to it, but the resolution to combat it as effectively as possible. . . .

It will come as no surprise from what I have said that I do not agree with the encyclical *Evangelium Vitae* and the new Catholic catechism (or the very latest version of the new Catholic catechism), according to which the death penalty can only be imposed to protect rather than avenge, and that since it is (in most modern societies) not necessary for the former purpose, it is wrong. That, by the way, is how I read those documents—and not, as Avery Cardinal Dulles would read them, simply as an affirmation of two millennia of Christian teaching that retribution is a proper purpose (indeed, the principal purpose) of criminal punishment, but merely adding the "prudential judgment" that in modern circumstances condign retribution "rarely if ever" justifies death. (See "Catholicism & Capital Punishment," FT, April 2001.) I cannot square that interpretation with the following passage from the encyclical:

> It is clear that, for these [permissible purposes of penal justice] to be achieved, the

nature and extent of the punishment must be carefully evaluated and decided upon, and ought not go to the extreme of executing the offender except in cases of absolute necessity: *in other words, when it would not be possible otherwise to defend society. Today, however, as a result of steady improvements in the organization of the penal system, such cases are very rare, if not practically nonexistent.* (Emphases deleted and added.)

It is true enough that the paragraph of the encyclical that precedes this passage acknowledges (in accord with traditional Catholic teaching) that "the primary purpose of the punishment which society inflicts is 'to redress the disorder caused by the offense'" by "imposing on the offender an adequate punishment for the crime." But it seems to me quite impossible to interpret the later passage's phrase "when it would not be possible otherwise to defend society" as including "defense" through the redress of disorder achieved by adequate punishment. Not only does the word "defense" not readily lend itself to that strange interpretation, but the immediately following explanation of why, in modern times, "defense" rarely if ever requires capital punishment *has no bearing whatever upon the adequacy of retribution.* In fact, one might say that it has an *inverse* bearing.

How in the world can modernity's "steady improvements in the organization of the penal system" render the death penalty less condign for a particularly heinous crime? One might think that commitment to a really horrible penal system (Devil's Island, for example) might be almost as bad as death. But nice clean cells with television sets, exercise rooms, meals designed by nutritionists, and conjugal visits? That would seem to render the death penalty more, rather than less, necessary. So also would the greatly increased capacity for evil—the greatly increased power to produce moral "disorder"—placed in individual hands by modern technology. Could St. Paul or St. Thomas even have envisioned a crime by an individual (as opposed to one by a ruler, such as Herod's slaughter of the innocents) as enormous as that of Timothy McVeigh or of the men who destroyed three thousand innocents in the World Trade Center? If just retribution is a legitimate purpose (indeed, the principal legitimate purpose) of capital punishment, can one possibly say with a straight face that nowadays death would "rarely if ever" be appropriate?

So I take the encyclical and the latest, hot-off-the-presses version of the catechism (a supposed encapsulation of the "deposit" of faith and the Church's teaching regarding a moral order that does not change) to mean that retribution is not a valid purpose of capital punishment. Unlike such other hard Catholic doctrines as the prohibition of birth control and of abortion, this is not a moral position that the Church has always—or indeed *ever before*—maintained. There have been Christian opponents of the death penalty, just as there have been Christian pacifists, but neither of those positions has ever been that of the Church. The current predominance of opposition to the death penalty is the legacy of Napoleon, Hegel, and Freud rather than St. Paul and St. Augustine. . . .

I am therefore happy to learn from the canonical experts I have consulted that the position set forth in *Evangelium Vitae* and in the latest version of the Catholic catechism does not purport to be binding teaching—that is, it need not be accepted by practicing Catholics, though they must give it thoughtful and respectful consideration. It would be remarkable to think otherwise—that a couple of paragraphs in an encyclical almost entirely devoted not to crime and punishment but to abortion and euthanasia was intended authoritatively to sweep aside (if one could) two thousand years of Christian teaching.

So I have given this new position thoughtful and careful consideration—and I disagree. That is not to say I favor the death penalty (I am judicially and judiciously neutral on that point); it is only to say that I do not find the death penalty immoral. I am happy to have reached that conclusion, because I like my job, and would rather not resign. And I am happy because I do not think it would be a good thing if American Catholics running for legislative office had to oppose the death penalty (most of them would not be elected); if American Catholics running for Governor had to promise commutation of all death sentences (most of them would never reach the Governor's mansion); if American Catholics were ineligible to go on the bench in all jurisdictions imposing the death penalty; or if American Catholics were subject to recusal when called for jury duty in capital cases.

I find it ironic that the Church's new (albeit nonbinding) position on the death penalty—which, if accepted, would have these *disastrous* consequences—is said to rest upon "prudential considerations." Is it prudent, when one is not certain enough about the point to proclaim it in a binding manner (and with good reason, given the long and consistent Christian tradition to the contrary), to effectively urge the retirement of Catholics from public life in a country where the federal government and thirty-eight of the states (comprising about 85 percent of the population) believe the death penalty is sometimes just and appropriate? Is it prudent to imperil acceptance of the Church's hard but traditional teachings on birth control and abortion and euthanasia (teachings that *have been* proclaimed in a binding manner, a distinction that the average Catholic layman is unlikely to grasp) by packaging them—under the wrapper "respect for life"—with another uncongenial doctrine *that everyone knows does not represent the traditional Christian view?* Perhaps, one is invited to conclude, all four of them are recently made-up. We need some new staffers at the Congregation of Prudence in the Vatican. At least the new doctrine should have been urged only upon secular Europe, where it is at home.

NOTES AND QUESTIONS

1. What does it mean to see the Constitution as a "living document"? What does this have to do with how the Supreme Court interprets and applies the provisions of the Eighth Amendment? In the legal system, whose job is it to recognize "the evolving standards of decency that mark the progress of a maturing society"?

2. What does Justice Scalia mean when he writes, "My views on the morality of the death penalty have nothing to do with how I vote as a judge, but they have a lot to do with whether I can or should be a judge at all"?

3. In your opinion, should what Justice Scalia calls "private morality" be held to the same standard as "government morality"? Why or why not? What does Scalia argue? How does this compare with Cover's effort to legitimize law's violence (Chapter 14)?

4. What difference does it make for the morality of the death penalty if one sees state power as derived from the People rather than from God? The historical consensus that government derives its moral authority from God, "has been upset," according to Justice Scalia, "by the emergence of democracy." Is he arguing that a democratic state cannot make sound moral judgments? Explain.

5. How does Justice Scalia illustrate his point that "those who deny the authority of the government to extract vengeance are not entirely logical"? Is incarceration any less vengeful (and thus more morally acceptable) than execution? Why or why not?

6. For those Americans who do believe that the moral authority of the state is derived from the divine, what are the legal ramifications of the Catholic Church's position supporting the death penalty

only "to protect and not to avenge"? Contrary to the position set forth in the *Evangelium Vitae,* how does Justice Scalia set up a defense of vengeance as a legitimate justification for the death penalty?

Reprinted from: Antonin Scalia, "God's Justice and Ours" in *First Things: A Journal of Religion and Public Life,* 2002, 17–21. Copyright © 2002. Reprinted with the permission of First Things 123. ✦

Chapter 65

I Must Act

George H. Ryan

At the time Governor Ryan announced his pardons and commutations, he made a statement explaining his decision. Excerpts are reprinted in the following pages. This statement provides a striking example of what I call "the new abolitionism"—opposition to capital punishment rooted not in concerns about its philosophical justifications, but rather in the fairness of its application.

In the United States, opposition to the death penalty traditionally has been expressed in several guises. Some have opposed the death penalty in the name of the sanctity of life. Even the most heinous criminals, so this argument goes, are entitled to be treated with dignity. In this view, there is nothing that anyone can do to forfeit the "right to have rights." Others have emphasized the moral horror, the "evil," of the state willfully taking the lives of any of its citizens. Still others believe that death as a punishment is always cruel and, as such, is incompatible with the Eighth Amendment that prohibits cruel and unusual punishment.

Each of these arguments has been associated with, and is an expression of, humanist liberalism or political radicalism. Each represents a frontal assault on the simple and appealing retributivist rationale for capital punishment. Each has put the opponents of the death penalty on the side of society's most despised and notorious criminals; to be against the death penalty, one has had to defend the life of the likes of Timothy McVeigh, and of serial killers, cop killers, and child murderers. Thus, it is not surprising that although traditional abolitionist arguments have been raised repeatedly in philosoph-ical commentary, political debate, and legal cases, none of them has ever carried the day in the debate about capital punishment in the United States.

Governor Ryan's decision to empty Illinois' death row found its locus in neither liberal humanism nor radicalism, nor in the defense of the most indefensible among us. It was, instead, firmly rooted in the mainstream legal values of due process and equal protection. Ryan did not reject the death penalty because of its violence, argue against its appropriateness as a response to heinous criminals, or criticize its futility as a tool in the war against crime. Instead, he shifted the rhetorical grounds.

Two things stand out in Ryan's statement. First, he acknowledges his own efforts to purge death sentences of any taint of procedural irregularity and the unwillingness of courts or the state legislature to support those efforts. Second, Ryan presents his decision as a reluctant one, rooted in recognition of the damage that capital punishment does to central legal values and to the legitimacy of the law itself.

Ryan's "I Must Act" echoes former Supreme Court Justice Harry Blackmun, who said, "I feel morally and intellectually obligated simply to concede that the death penalty experiment has failed. It is virtually self-evident to me now that no combination of procedural rules or substantive regulations ever can save the death penalty from its inherent constitutional deficiencies." Ryan and Blackmun have opened an important new avenue for engagement in the political struggle against capital punishment, providing abolitionists a position of political respectability while simultaneously allowing them to change the subject from the legitimacy of execution to the imperatives of due process.

Four years ago I was sworn in as the 39th Governor of Illinois. That was just four short years ago; that's when I was a firm believer in the American System of Justice and the death penalty. I believed that the ultimate penalty for the taking of a life was administrated in a just and fair manner.

Today, 3 days before I end my term as Governor, I stand before you to explain my frustrations and deep concerns about both the administration and the penalty of death. . . .

During my time in public office I have always reserved my right to change my mind if I believed it to be in the best public interest, whether it be about taxes, abortions or the death penalty. But I must confess that the debate with myself has been the toughest concerning the death penalty. I suppose the reason the death penalty has been the toughest is because it is so final, the only public policy that determines who lives and who dies. In addition it is the only issue that attracts most of the legal minds across the country. I have received more advice on this issue than any other policy issue I have dealt with in my 35 years of public service. I have kept an open mind on both sides of the issues of commutation for life or death.

I have read, listened to and discussed the issue with the families of the victims as well as the families of the condemned. I know that any decision I make will not be accepted by one side or the other. I know that my decision will be just that—my decision based on all the facts I could gather over the past 3 years. I may never be comfortable with my final decision, but I will know in my heart, that I did my very best to do the right thing.

Having said that I want to share a story with you:

I grew up in Kankakee which even today is still a small midwestern town, a place where people tend to know each other. Steve Small was a neighbor. I watched him grow up. He would babysit my young children which was not for the faint of heart since Lura Lynn and I had six children, 5 of them under the age of 3. He was a bright young man who helped run the family business. He got married and he and his wife had three children of their own. Lura Lynn was especially close to him and his family. We took comfort in knowing he was there for us and we for him.

One September midnight he received a call at his home. There had been a break-in at the nearby house he was renovating. But as he left his house, he was seized at gunpoint by kidnappers. His captors buried him alive in a shallow hole. He suffocated to death before police could find him.

His killer led investigators to where Steve's body was buried. The killer, Danny Edward was also from my hometown. He now sits on death row. I also know his family. I share this story with you so that you know I do not come to this as a neophyte without having experienced a small bit of the bitter pill the survivors of murder must swallow.

My responsibilities and obligations are more than my neighbors and my family. I represent all the people of Illinois, like it or not. The decision I make about our criminal justice system is felt not only here, but the world over.

The other day, I received a call from former South African President Nelson Mandela who reminded me that the United States sets the example for justice and fairness for the rest of the world. Today the United States is not in league with most of our major allies: Europe, Canada, Mexico, most of South and Central America. These countries rejected the death penalty. We are partners in death with several third world countries. Even Russia has called a moratorium.

The death penalty has been abolished in 12 states. In none of these states has the homicide rate increased. In Illinois last year we had about 1000 murders, only 2 percent of that 1000 were sentenced to death. Where is the fairness and equality in that? The death penalty in Illinois is not imposed fairly or uniformly because of the absence of standards for the 102 Illinois State Attorneys, who must decide whether to request the death sentence. Should geography be a factor in determining who gets the death sentence? I don't think so, but in Illinois it makes a difference. You are 5 times more likely to get a death sentence for first degree murder in the rural area of Illinois than you are in Cook County. Where is the justice and fairness in that, where is the proportionality? . . .

I never intended to be an activist on this issue. I watched in surprise as freed death row inmate Anthony Porter was released from jail. A free man, he ran into the arms of Northwestern University Professor Dave Protess who poured his heart and soul into proving Porter's innocence with his journalism students.

He was 48 hours away from being wheeled into the execution chamber where the state would kill him.

It would all be so antiseptic and most of us would not have even paused, except that Anthony Porter was innocent of the double murder for which he had been condemned to die.

After Mr. Porter's case there was the report by *Chicago Tribune* reporters Steve Mills and Ken Armstrong documenting the systemic failures of our capital punishment system. Half of the nearly 300 capital cases in Illinois had been reversed for a new trial or resentencing.

Nearly Half!

33 of the death row inmates were represented at trial by an attorney who had later been disbarred or at some point suspended from practicing law.

Of the more than 160 death row inmates, 35 were African American defendants who had been convicted or condemned to die by all-white juries.

More than two-thirds of the inmates on death row were African American.

46 inmates were convicted on the basis of testimony from jailhouse informants.

I can recall looking at these cases and the information from the Mills/Armstrong series and asking my staff: How does that happen? How in God's name does that happen? I'm not a lawyer, so somebody explain it to me.

But no one could. Not to this day.

Then over the next few months, there were three more exonerated men, freed because their sentence hinged on a jailhouse informant or new DNA technology proved beyond a shadow of doubt their innocence.

We then had the dubious distinction of exonerating more men than we had executed. 13 men found innocent, 12 executed.

As I reported yesterday, there is not a doubt in my mind that the number of innocent men freed from our Death Row stands at 17, with the pardons of Aaron Patterson, Madison Hobley, Stanley Howard and Leroy Orange.

That is an absolute embarrassment. 17 exonerated death row inmates is nothing short of a catastrophic failure. But the 13, now 17 men, is just the beginning of our sad arithmetic in prosecuting murder cases. During the time we have had capital punishment in Illinois, there were at least 33 other people wrongly convicted on murder charges and exonerated. Since we reinstated the death penalty there are also 93 people where our criminal justice system imposed the most severe sanction and later rescinded the sentence or even released them from custody because they were innocent.

How many more cases of wrongful conviction have to occur before we can all agree that the system is broken? . . .

In the United States, the overwhelming majority of those executed are psychotic, alcoholic, drug addicted or mentally unstable. They frequently are raised in an impoverished and abusive environment.

Seldom are people with money or prestige convicted of capital offenses, even more seldom are they executed. . . .

I started with this issue concerned about innocence. But once I studied, once I pondered what had become of our justice system, I came to care above all about fairness. Fairness is fundamental to the American system of justice and our way of life.

The facts I have seen in reviewing each and every one of these cases raised questions not only about the innocence of people on death row, but about the fairness of the death penalty system as a whole.

If the system was making so many errors in determining whether someone was guilty in the first place, how fairly and accurately was it determining which guilty defendants deserved to live and which deserved to die? What effect was race having? What effect was poverty having?

And in almost every one of the exonerated 17, we not only have breakdowns in the system with police, prosecutors and judges, we have terrible cases of shabby defense lawyers. There is just no way to sugar coat it. There are defense attorneys that did not consult with their clients, did not investigate the case and were completely unqualified to handle complex death penalty cases. They often didn't put much effort into fighting a death sentence. If your life is on the line, your lawyer ought to be fighting for you. As I have said before, there is more than enough blame to go around.

I had more questions.

In Illinois, I have learned, we have 102 decision makers. Each of them are politically elected, each beholden to the demands of their community and, in some cases, to the media or especially vocal victims' families. In cases that have the attention of the media and the public, are decisions to seek the death penalty more likely to occur? What standards are these prosecutors using?

Some people have assailed my power to commute sentences, a power that literally hundreds of legal scholars from across the country have defended. But prosecutors in Illinois have the ultimate commutation power, a power that is exercised every day. They decide who will be subject to the death penalty, who will get a plea deal or even who may get a complete pass on prosecution. By what objective standards do they make these decisions? We do not know, they are not public. There were more than 1000 murders last year in Illinois. There is no doubt that all murders are horrific and cruel. Yet, less than 2 percent of those murder defendants will receive the death penalty. That means more than 98 percent of victims families do not get, and will

not receive whatever satisfaction can be derived from the execution of the murderer. Moreover, if you look at the cases, as I have done both individually and collectively—a killing with the same circumstances might get 40 years in one county and death in another county. I have also seen where co-defendants who are equally or even more culpable get sentenced to a term of years, while another less culpable defendant ends up on death row. . . .

Supreme Court Justice Potter Stewart has said that the imposition of the death penalty on defendants in this country is as freakish and arbitrary as who gets hit by a bolt of lightning. . . .

After the flaws in our system were exposed, the Supreme Court of Illinois took it upon itself to begin to reform its rules and improve the trial of capital cases. It changed the rule to require that States' Attorneys give advance notice to defendants that they plan to seek the death penalty to require notice before trial instead of after conviction. The Supreme Court also enacted new discovery rules designed to prevent trials by ambush and to allow for better investigation of cases from the beginning.

But shouldn't that mean if you were tried or sentenced before the rules changed, you ought to get a new trial or sentencing with the new safeguards of the rules? This issue has divided our Supreme Court, some saying yes, a majority saying no. These justices have a lifetime of experience with the criminal justice system and it concerns me that these great minds so strenuously differ on an issue of such importance, especially where life or death hangs in the balance.

What are we to make of the studies that showed that more than 50 percent of Illinois jurors could not understand the confusing and obscure sentencing instructions that were being used? What effect did that problem have on the trustworthiness of death sentences? A review of the cases shows that often even the lawyers and judges are confused about the instructions—let alone the jurors sitting in judgment. Cases still come before the Supreme Court with arguments about whether the jury instructions were proper.

I spent a good deal of time reviewing these death row cases. My staff, many of whom are lawyers, spent busy days and many sleepless nights answering my questions, providing me with information, giving me advice. It became clear to me that whatever decision I made, I would be criticized. It also became clear to me that it was impossible to make reliable choices about whether our capital punishment system had really done its job.

As I came closer to my decision, I knew that I was going to have to face the question of whether I believed so completely in the choice I wanted to make that I could face the prospect of even commuting the death sentence of Daniel Edwards, the man who had killed a close family friend of mine. I discussed it with my wife, Lura Lynn, who has stood by me all these years. She was angry and disappointed at my decision like many of the families of other victims will be.

I was struck by the anger of the families of murder victims. To a family they talked about closure. They pleaded with me to allow the state to kill an inmate in its name to provide the families with closure. But is that the purpose of capital punishment? Is it to soothe the families? And is that truly what the families experience.

I cannot imagine losing a family member to murder. Nor can I imagine spending every waking day for 20 years with a single minded focus to execute the killer. The system of death in Illinois is so unsure that it is not unusual for cases to take 20 years before they are resolved. And thank God. If it had moved any faster, then Anthony Porter, the Ford Heights Four, Ronald Jones, Madison Hobley and the other innocent men we've exonerated might be dead and buried.

But it is cruel and unusual punishment for family members to go through this pain, this legal limbo for 20 years. Perhaps it would be less cruel if we sentenced the killers . . .to life, and used our resources to better serve victims.

My heart ached when I heard one grandmother who lost children in an arson fire. She said she could not afford proper grave markers for her grandchildren who died. Why can't the state help families provide a proper burial? . . .

President Lincoln often talked of binding up wounds as he sought to preserve the Union. "We are not enemies, but friends. We must not be enemies. Though passion may have strained, it must not break our bonds of affection."

I have had to consider not only the horrible nature of the crimes that put men on death row in the first place, the terrible suffering of the surviving family members of the victims, the despair of the family members of the inmates, but I have also had to watch in frustration as members of the Illinois General Assembly failed to pass even one substantive death penalty reform. Not one. They couldn't even agree on ONE. How much more evidence is needed before the General Assembly will take its responsibility in this area seriously?

The fact is that the failure of the General Assembly to act is merely a symptom of the larger problem. Many people express the desire to have capital punishment. Few, however, seem prepared to address the tough questions that arise when the system fails. It is easier and more comfortable for politicians to be tough on crime and support the death penalty. It wins votes. But when it comes to admitting that we have a problem, most run for cover. Prosecutors across our state continue to deny that our death penalty system is broken or they say if there is a problem, it is really a small one and we can fix it somehow. It is difficult to see how the system can be fixed when not a single one of the reforms proposed by my Capital Punishment Commission has been adopted. Even the reforms the prosecutors agree with haven't been adopted. . . .

As I prepare to leave office, I had to ask myself whether I could really live with the prospect of knowing that I had the opportunity to act, but that I failed to do so because I might be criticized. Could I take the chance that our capital punishment system might be reformed, that wrongful convictions might not occur, that enterprising journalism students might free more men from death row? A system that's so fragile that it depends on young journalism students is seriously flawed.

"There is no honorable way to kill, no gentle way to destroy. There is nothing good in war. Except its ending."

That's what Abraham Lincoln said about the bloody war between the states. It was a war fought to end the sorriest chapter in American history—the institution of slavery. While we are not in a civil war now, we are facing what is shaping up to be one of the great civil rights struggles of our time. Stephen Bright of the Southern Center for Human Rights has taken the position that the death penalty is being sought with increasing frequency in some states against the poor and minorities.

Our own study showed that juries were more likely to sentence to death if the victim were white than if the victim were black—three-and-a-half times more likely to be exact. We are not alone. Just this month Maryland released a study of their death penalty system and racial disparities exist there too. . . .

Another issue that came up in my individual, case-by-case review was the issue of international law. The Vienna Convention protects U.S. citizens abroad and foreign nationals in the United States. It provides that if you arrested, you should be afforded the opportunity to contact your consulate. There are five men on death row who were denied that internationally recognized human right. Mexico's President Vicente Fox contacted me to express his deep concern for the Vienna Convention violations. If we do not uphold international law here, we cannot expect our citizens to be protected outside the United States.

My Commission recommended the Supreme Court conduct a proportionality review of our system in Illinois. While our appellate courts perform a case by case review of the appellate record, they have not done such a big picture study. Instead, we tinker with a case-by-case review as each appeal lands on their docket.

In 1994, near the end of his distinguished career on the Supreme Court of the United States, Justice Harry Blackmun wrote an influential dissent in the body of law on capital punishment. 20 years earlier he was part of the court that issued the landmark *Furman* decision. The Court decided that the death penalty statutes in use throughout the country were fraught with severe flaws that rendered them unconstitutional. Quite frankly, they were the same problems we see here in Illinois. To many, it looked liked the *Furman* decision meant the end of the death penalty in the United States.

This was not the case. Many states responded to *Furman* by developing and enacting new and improved death penalty statutes. In 1976, four years after it had decided *Furman*, Justice Blackmun joined the majority of the United States Supreme Court in deciding to give the States a chance with these new and improved death penalty statutes. There was great optimism in the air.

This was the climate in 1977, when the Illinois legislature was faced with the momentous decision of whether to reinstate the death penalty in Illinois. I was a member of the General Assembly at that time and when I pushed the green button in favor of reinstating the death penalty in this great State, I did so with the belief that whatever problems had plagued the capital punishment system in the past were now being cured. I am sure that most of my colleagues who voted with me that day shared that view.

But 20 years later, after affirming hundreds of death penalty decisions, Justice Blackmun came to the realization, in the twilight of his distinguished career that the death penalty remains fraught with arbitrariness, discrimination, caprice and mistake." He expressed frustration with a 20-year struggle to develop procedural and substantive safeguards. In a now famous dissent he wrote in 1994, "From this day forward, I no longer shall tinker with the machinery of death."

One of the few disappointments of my legislative and executive career is that the General Assembly failed to work with me to reform our deeply flawed system.

I don't know why legislators could not heed the rising voices of reform. I don't know how many more systemic flaws we needed to uncover before they would be spurred to action.

Three times I proposed reforming the system with a package that would restrict the use of jailhouse snitches, create a statewide panel to determine death eligible cases, and reduce the number of crimes eligible for death. These reforms would not have created a perfect system, but they would have dramatically reduced the chance for error in the administration of the ultimate penalty.

The Governor has the constitutional role in our state of acting in the interest of justice and fairness. Our state constitution provides broad power to the Governor to issue reprieves, pardons and commutations. Our Supreme Court has reminded inmates petitioning them that the last resort for relief is the governor.

At times the executive clemency power has perhaps been a crutch for courts to avoid making the kind of major change that I believe our system needs.

Our systemic case-by-case review has found more cases of innocent men wrongfully sentenced to death row. Because our three-year study has found only more questions about the fairness of the sentencing; because of the spectacular failure to reform the system; because we have seen justice delayed for countless death row inmates with potentially meritorious claims; because the Illinois

death penalty system is arbitrary and capricious—and therefore immoral—I no longer shall tinker with the machinery of death.

I cannot say it more eloquently than Justice Blackmun.

The legislature couldn't reform it.

Lawmakers won't repeal it.

But I will not stand for it.

I must act.

Our capital system is haunted by the demon of error, error in determining guilt, and error in determining who among the guilty deserves to die. Because of all of these reasons today I am commuting the sentences of all death row inmates.

This is a blanket commutation. I realize it will draw ridicule, scorn and anger from many who oppose this decision. They will say I am usurping the decisions of judges and juries and state legislators. But as I have said, the people of our state have vested in me to act in the interest of justice. Even if the exercise of my power becomes my burden I will bear it. Our constitution compels it. I sought this office, and even in my final days of holding it I cannot shrink from the obligations to justice and fairness that it demands.

There have been many nights where my staff and I have been deprived of sleep in order to conduct our exhaustive review of the system. But I can tell you this: I will sleep well knowing I made the right decision.

As I said when I declared the moratorium, it is time for a rational discussion on the death penalty. While our experience in Illinois has indeed sparked a debate, we have fallen short of a rational discussion. Yet if I did not take this action, I feared that there would be no comprehensive and thorough inquiry into the guilt of the individuals on death row or of the fairness of the sentences applied.

To say it plainly one more time—the Illinois capital punishment system is broken. It has taken innocent men to a hair's breadth escape from their unjust execution. Legislatures past have refused to fix it. Our new legislature and our new Governor must act to rid our state of the shame of threatening the innocent with execution and the guilty with unfairness.

In the days ahead, I will pray that we can open our hearts and provide something for victims' families other than the hope of revenge. Lincoln once said: " I have always found that mercy bears richer fruits than strict justice." I can only hope that will be so. God bless you. And God bless the people of Illinois.

Notes and Questions

1. Whose arguments from previous chapters do you see reflected in Ryan's contention that "the system is broken"? Which authors would disagree with this conclusion? On what grounds?

2. Does the Baldus study carry more weight in the context of Governor Ryan's arguments than it did in *McCleskey* (chapter 62)? Why or why not?

3. Ryan points out that the absence of standards for Illinois' 102 state prosecutors precludes uniform application of capital punishment. He asks, "Should geography be a factor in determining who gets the death sentence?" Should we be asking this same question for other types of crime and other levels of punishment, as well? Why or why not? If we accept Ryan's argument that the death penalty is acceptable only when administered in a manner compatible with due process and equal protection, why not apply this

standard to incarceration also? What would Justice Powell say about this?

4. By moving the death penalty debate away from the moral judgments that define cruel and unusual punishment, does Ryan undermine Scalia's defense of the death penalty (Chapter 64)? Is it possible to agree with Scalia *and* accept Ryan's argument at the same time?

5. Would a mandatory death sentence for certain crimes lay to rest Governor Ryan's qualms about the unjust application of capital punishment? Explain.

6. Both Justice Scalia's article and Justice Burger's dissent in *Furman* (chapter 60) insist that it is the place of the legislature, not the judiciary, to deal with how the death penalty is applied. Yet, Governor Ryan's frustration is nearly tangible when he recounts how, even in the face of overwhelming evidence of systematic failures of justice, "Members of the Illinois General Assembly failed to pass even one substantive death penalty reform. Not one. They couldn't even agree on ONE." Whose job is it to address the problems with capital punishment? Is it justifiable for one branch of government to step in where another fails to act?

Reprinted from: Former Illinois Governor George H. Ryan, "I Must Act," delivered on January 11, 2003, at Northwestern University School of Law. Reprinted with the permission of former Illinois Governor George H. Ryan. ✦

Conclusion to Part V

Robert M. Cover (Chapter 14) described law as a top-down, hierarchically controlled bureaucracy, with judges sitting at the top making decisions, issuing orders, commanding others to act. Although Cover's image applies to all parts of the legal system, to regulatory agencies for example, it seems most applicable to the criminal justice system, where law seeks to loose violence into the world. Cover believed that law was, and should be, a particular kind of social organization, one in which judges interpret the law and through their interpretations dispense and yet control the violence that is central to law's social life. Law's violence is, for Cover, different than extralegal violence because it is responsive to common normative standards articulated in and through the law. He did not doubt that legal interpretation did violence to other normative systems, but he valued it nonetheless as the only thing that stands between us and a society of revenge, resistance, and reprisal.

The world in and through which law's violence is dispensed seems more complicated than Cover's image of reliable top-down control can capture, however. Police depart-ments and prisons, as we have seen, have their own institutional rhythms and requirements, requirements that sometimes match and other times conflict with the letter of the law. Moreover, the social world in which police act and punishment is dispensed presses in and shapes the way officials interpret and apply legal commands. They develop distinctive ways of knowing that world. Some claim their ways of knowing to be rational, while others label them racist.

Indeed, throughout the readings in this last Part, race has played a key role. As is true for gender, class, and other social differences, the readings show that law is both shaped by and shapes the continuing salience of race in the United States. Sometimes this occurs in highly publicized decisions about affirmative action or hate crimes, and sometimes in the low visibility work of police on the street or jurors in capital trials. In all of these contexts, students of law must come to terms with its success and its failures, its aspirations and its daily routines. Whether law is successful in dispensing and controlling violence in ways that match our aspirations and our values is for each of us to decide. ✦

Suggested Additional Readings for Part V

POLICING AND THE POLICE

Kenneth Adams, "What We Know About Police Use of Force," in *Use of Force by the Police*. Washington, DC: National Institute of Justice, 1999.

Jeannine Bell, *Policing Hatred: Law Enforcement, Civil Rights and Hate Crime*. New York: New York University Press, 2002.

Mark Findlay and Ugliesa Zveki, *Alternate Policing Styles, Cross Cultural Perspectives*. Boston: Kluwer Law and Taxation Publishers, 1993.

Joseph A. Goldstein, "Police Discretion Not to Invoke the Criminal Process: Low-Visibility Decisions in the Administration of Justice." 69 *Yale Law Journal* (1960), 543.

David A. Harris, "The Stories, the Statistics, and the Law: Why 'Driving While Black' Matters," 84 *Minnesota Law Review* (1999), 265.

John Knowles, Nicola Persico, and Petra Todd, "Racial Bias in Motor Vehicle Searches: Theory and Evidence." 109 *Journal of Political Economy* (1999), 203.

Wayne R. LaFave, "The Police and Nonenforcement of the Law—Part II." *Wisconsin Law Review* (1962), 179.

Richard A. Leo, "Inside the Interrogation Room," 86 *The Journal of Criminal Law and Criminology* (1996), 266.

William Lyons, *The Politics of Community Policing: Rearranging the Power to Punish*. Ann Arbor: University of Michigan Press, 1999.

Trish Oberweis and Michael Musheno, "Policing Identities: Cop Decision Making and the Constitution of Citizens," *Law and Social Inquiry* (1999), 897.

Stuart Scheingold, *The Politics of Street Crime*. Philadelphia: Temple University Press, 1991.

Jerome Skolnick and David H. Bayley, *Community Policing: Issues and Practices Around the World*. National Institute of Justice, 1988.

Jerome Skolnick and Abigail Caplovitz, "Guns, Drugs and Profiling: Ways to Target Guns and Minimize Racial Profiling," 43 *Arizona Law Review* (2001), 413.

Jerome Skolnick and James Fyfe, *Above the Law: Police and the Excessive Use of Force*. New York: Free Press, 1993.

Robert Taylor, *Breaking Away from Broken Windows: Baltimore Neighborhoods and the Nationwide Fight Against Crime, Grime, Fear, and Decline*. Boulder, CO: Westview, 2001.

Ronald Weitzer, "Racialized Policing: Residents' Perceptions in Three Neighborhoods," 34 *Law and Society Review* (2000), 129.

PUNISHMENT: IMPRISONMENT

Charles Bright, *The Powers That Punish: Prison and Politics in the Era of the 'Big House,' 1920–1955*. Ann Arbor: University of Michigan Press, 1994.

Richard Cloward, Donald Cressey, George Grosser, Robert McCleery, Lloyd Ohlin, Gresham Sykes, and Sheldon Messinger, *Theoretical Studies in Social Organization of the Prison*. New York: Social Science Research Council, 1960.

John DiIulio, Jr., *Governing Prisons: A Comparative Study of Correctional Management*. New York: Free Press, 1987.

David Greenberg and Fay Stender, "The Prison as a Lawless Agency," 21 *Buffalo Law Review* (1972), 799.

Gordon Hawkins, *The Prison: Policy and Practice*. Chicago: University of Chicago Press, 1976.

John Irwin, *Prisons in Turmoil*. Boston: Little, Brown, 1980.

James Jacobs, *Stateville: The Penitentiary in Mass Society*. Chicago: University of Chicago Press, 1977.

Norval Morris, *The Future of Imprisonment*. Chicago: University of Chicago Press, 1974.

Edward E. Rhine, "The Rule of Law, Disciplinary Practices, and Rahway State Prison: A Case Study in Judicial Intervention and Social Control," in *Courts, Corrections, and the Constitution: The Impact of Judicial Intervention on Prisons and Jails,* John J. DiIulio, Jr., ed. New York: Oxford University Press, 1990.

Jonathan Simon, "Governing Through Crime," in *The Crime Conundrum: Essays in Criminal Justice.* Lawrence M. Friedman and George Fisher, eds. Boulder, CO: Westview, 1997.

Gresham M. Sykes, *The Society of Captives.* Princeton, NJ: Princeton University Press, 1958.

James Whitman, *Harsh Justice: Criminal Punishment and the Widening Divide Between America and Europe.* New York: Oxford University Press, 2003.

Franklin Zimring, *The Scale of Imprisonment.* Chicago: University of Chicago Press, 1991.

The Death Penalty: Controlling Juries/Preventing Discrimination

David Baldus, George Woodworth, and Charles A. Pulaski, Jr., *Equal Justice and the Death Penalty: A Legal and Empirical Analysis.* Boston: Northeastern University Press, 1990.

William Bowers, "The Capital Jury: Is It Tilted Toward Death?" 79 *Judicature* (1996), 220.

Theodore Eisenberg and Martin T. Wells, "Deadly Confusion: Juror Instructions in Capital Cases." 79 *Cornell Law Journal* (1993), 1.

Craig Haney, Lorelei Sontag, and Sally Costanzo, "Deciding to Take a Life." 50 *Journal of Social Issues* (1994), 149.

William Hood, W., "Note: The Meaning of 'Life' for Virginia Jurors and Its Effects on Reliability in Capital Sentencing," 75 *Virginia Law Review* (1989), 1635.

John Manzo, "'You Wouldn't Take a Seven-Year-Old and Ask Him All These Questions': Jurors' Use of Practical Reasoning in Supporting Their Arguments," 19 *Law & Social Inquiry* (1994), 601.

Anthony Paduano and Clive Stafford-Smith, "Deathly Errors: Juror Misperceptions Concerning Parole in the Imposition of the Death Penalty," 18 *Columbia Human Rights Law Review* (1987), 211.

Marla Sandys, "Cross-Overs—Capital Jurors Who Change Their Minds About the Punishment: A Litmus Test for Sentencing Guidelines," 70 *Indiana Law Journal* (1995), 1183.

Austin Sarat, "Doing Death: Violence, Responsibility, and the Role of the Jury in Capital Trials," 70 *Indiana Law Review* (1995), 1103.

The Future of Capital Punishment

Stuart Banner, *The Death Penalty: An American History.* Cambridge, MA: Harvard University Press, 2002.

William Bowers, (1993) "Capital Punishment and Contemporary Values: People's Misgivings and the Court's Misperceptions," 27 *Law & Society Review* (1993), 215.

William Bowers, Margaret Vandiver, and Patricia Dugan, "A New Look at Public Opinion on Capital Punishment: What Citizens and Legislatures Prefer." 22 *American Journal of Criminal Law* (1994), 77.

Phoebe Ellsworth, "Second Thoughts: Americans' Views on the Death Penalty at the Turn of the Century," in *Beyond Repair? America's Death Penalty,* Stephen Garvey, ed. Durham, NC: Duke University Press, 2002.

Phoebe Ellsworth and Samuel R. Gross, "Hardening of the Attitudes: Americans' Views on the Death Penalty," 50 *Journal of Social Issues,* 1994.

James Liebman, Jeffrey Fagan, Valerie West, and Jonathon Lloyd, "Capital Attrition: Error Rates in Capital Cases, 1973–1995," 78 *Texas Law Review* (2000), 1839.

Austin Sarat, *When the State Kills: Capital Punishment and the American Condition.* Princeton: Princeton University Press, 2001.

Franklin Zimring, *The Contradictions of American Capital Punishment.* New York: Oxford University Press, 2003.

Franklin Zimring and Gordon Hawkins, *Capital Punishment and the American Agenda.* New York: Oxford University Press, 1986. ✦

Conclusion to the Book

"Justice," the legal scholar Drucilla Cornell argues, "is precisely what eludes our full knowledge."

We cannot "grasp the Good but only follow it. The Good . . . is a star which beckons us to follow." While justice, what Cornell calls the Good, is, in her account, always present to law, it is never completely realized in law. " . . .[T]he law posits an ideality . . . that it can never realize, and . . . this failure is constitutive of existing law." Law is defined by both its failure to realize the Good and the commitment to its realization. In this failure and commitment, law is two things at once: the arena to which citizens address themselves to pursue justice and the social organization of violence through which state power is exercised in a partisan, biased, and sometimes cruel way.

This book is one resource through which students can explore what law wishes to be and what it is, that is, the aspirations that Cornell argues are constitutive of law as well as the way in which law works in our world. It offers students a journey from the familiar to the strange, from the world of law that they see and know to the more complex world of law that exists just beyond the horizon of their immediate perception. By introducing students to the social organization of law, to its own bureaucratic organization and to the ways it resists and incorporates the social world beyond its boundaries, this book contributes to the continuing effort of scholars to articulate a vision of law as embedded in and arising from social life.

The readings included here examine the social and cultural lives, meanings, and effectivity of law's varied enactments or performances. The language of enactment and performance directs attention to text as well as context, role, and action, without privileging the word over the world or the world over the word, to stated ideals and organizational realities. Studying the social organization of law draws attention to the human actions that go into law's performances. It requires us to think not only about texts and language, but also staging, symbolization, and relation to audience as they are played out in the work of lawyers, judges, police, and prison guards as well as in the everyday world in which citizens live. By stressing the social organization of law, this book connects the mundane and the majestic, in law's performances and the world of violence in which law operates with society's aspirations for a more just and decent world.

Confronting this tension in law is the distinctive work of students and citizens. It requires all of us to face the social realities of law without giving into cynicism, without seeing law's ideals as empty promises, but without also succumbing to the idealist view that law itself is sufficient to the attainment of the justice that it promises. It is our work to give content to the "impossibility" of justice as well as to call law to account when it fails to shift toward that moving horizon. Understanding the social organization of law provides one of the tools through which this work can be done. ✦

Author Index

Subject Index